THE INTERNATIONAL DIRECTORY OF

CIVIL AIRCRAFT

1997/98

by Gerard Frawley

CONTENTS

Published by Aerospace Publications Pty Ltd (ACN: 001 570 458) PO Box 1777, Fyshwick, ACT 2609, Australia. Phone (06) 280 0111 fax (06) 280 0007 – publishers of monthly *Australian Aviation* magazine.

ISBN 1 875671 26 9

Proudly Printed in Australia by Pirie Printers Pty Ltd, 140 Gladstone St, Fyshwick, ACT 2609.
Distributed throughout Australia by Network Distribution Company, 54 Park St, Sydney, 2000. Fax (02) 264 3278
Distributed in North America by Motorbooks International, 729 Prospect Ave, Osceola, Wisconsin, 54020, USA, fax (715) 294 4448. Distributed throughout Europe and the UK by Airlife Publishing Ltd, 101 Longden Rd, Shrewsbury SY3 9EB, Shropshire, UK, fax (743) 232944.

Front cover: (top left) Dassault Falcon 2000; (top right) Cathay Pacific Boeing 777-200; (bottom left) Air Macau Airbus A321; (bottom right) Pilatus PC-6 Turbo Porter. Back cover: (clockwise from top left) A Crossair Saab 2000; McDonnell Douglas Helicopters MD 600N; Technoavia Finist; Avianova Fokker 70; de Havilland Canada DHC-2 Beaver floatplane; Gulf Air Lockheed L-1011 TriStar.

INTRODUCTION

Welcome to the second, thoroughly revised edition of the all colour *International Directory of Civil Aircraft.*

The *Directory* is published every two years and each subsequent edition will include the latest aircraft under development while updating the entries of the more established types. The present pace of aircraft development does not warrant an annual edition and a biennial production is a more economic and cost efficient answer to the problem of providing you with as much data as possible on a wide range of differing types.

A lot of work has gone into updating and improving upon the inaugural *International Directory of Civil Aircraft.* There are over 30 all new aircraft entries in this volume, while almost every single entry carried over from the first edition has had some sort of change made, some have been very significant as important programs evolve and mature (the 777 is a good example). Most of the photos are new, the World Airline Guide listing has been redone completely to reflect the massive changes in this area over the past two years, while some aircraft entries (particularly GA types) have had new technical specs added.

Meanwhile the *International Directory of Military Aircraft* is released during the years that we don't produce the civil edition (the first was released in early 1996). The format and aims are the same with again all operational and under serious development types from helicopters and trainers through to the F-22 listed. Thus no matter whether your specific interest lies with civil or military aviation an updated *Directory* will be ready for your bookshelf each year.

To be eligible for coverage an aircraft must still be in revenue service, in relatively common use in the case of light aircraft or under serious development. Thus while preparing this second civil edition a number of types were retired from service and no longer appear on these pages. An example is the Dassault Mercure. To our surprise a few older types debut with this edition however – namely the Noorduyn Norseman and the Bristol Freighter – as we discovered that they were still in commercial use.

In addition to these this second edition features over two dozen new aircraft types that have been launched since the release of the first, ranging from the Bell Boeing 609 tilt rotor to the Millicer Shrike to the Boeing 777-300. At the big end of town both the Airbus A3XX and Boeing's 747-500X/-600X are detailed despite the fact that neither project had been formally launched at the time of writing. While it's possible that one or both may never be formally launched, their appearance here will at least provide a record of what might have been.

We have included almost all air transport class aircraft, almost all factory General Aviation light aircraft (except for VLAs) and helicopters in addition to the full range of commuter, special use and freighter aircraft that often began life under a different guise.

For ease of reference aircraft are listed under their manufacturer though even this seemingly simple approach is fraught with problems when manufacturers frequently change hands or aircraft types are redesignated. The present day AI(R) Avro RJ series is a perfect example of this, beginning life as the Hawker Siddeley HS.146 project before becoming the British Aerospace 146, then the BAe RJ (Regional Jet) and more latterly the Avro RJ series.

McDonnell Douglas and Douglas have also been treated as a 'before and after' situation with everything prior to the DC-9 being the province of the company originally established so long ago by Donald Douglas. Just to confuse matters further the planned Boeing/McDonnell Douglas merger announced in late 1996 could well see the latest version of what started as the Douglas DC-9, the MD-95, listed under Boeing in the next *Directory of Civil Aircraft.*

GA also is not exempt with various companies such as Grumman, Gulfstream, Aero Commander, Rockwell, American Aviation and many more changing names for aircraft that visually remain similar and are in essence derivatives of each other. The Commander twins and small AA series singles are classic examples of this. Hopefully the *Directory* has made some sense of all this.

Aircraft specifications are detailed in both metric and imperial units (including knots as the latter is far more relevant to aviation than is miles per hour). To ensure that families of aircraft (A320, 747 etc) appear on the same spread of pages as much as possible the otherwise strict alphabetical order aircraft listings have been massaged somewhat. This will make it much easier when cross referencing performance, etc of the various aircraft of the one basic type.

A special vote of thanks must go to all who have once again aided in completing this daunting project to schedule with suggestions and encouragement. In particular votes of appreciation are due to Jim Thorn, Stewart Wilson, Ian Hewitt for his comments and queries, Christine Pratt, Bradley Perrett and Maria Davey. Thanks too to the dozens of photo contributors, particularly Bill Lines, and specially to the manufacturers who have co-operated with us so enthusiastically in helping make this reference book a reality. Our thanks also to the hundreds of airlines which returned our questionnaires confirming their fleet lists, etc. Finally thanks also to Airlife (UK) and Motorbooks (USA) for having the faith in us to order in quantity for their respective markets. To all, sincere thanks.

Gerard Frawley
Canberra, January 1997.

CIVIL AVIATION IN REVIEW

A number of issues have characterised the civil aerospace sector over the past two years – growing passenger numbers, airline profits and aircraft orders, a mini rebirth of light aircraft production, increasingly aggressive competition between Airbus and Boeing and the start of a process of rationalisation among aircraft manufacturers.

Taking the last point first, the biggest aerospace news of 1996 was the announcement of the planned Boeing/McDonnell Douglas merger. If regulatory and shareholder approval is granted the new combined monolith (to be known as Boeing and based in Seattle) could come into existence in mid 1997 and would have predicted sales in 1997 of $US40bn and over 200,000 employees working in 25 US states. Both companies have massive civil and military product lines and their rationalisation will no doubt result in many changes to the next edition of this volume as well as its military companion.

When these words were penned it was unclear exactly what changes would take place to the combined companies' civil airliner programs. In this area as separate companies during 1995/96 their fortunes in the marketplace were at opposite ends of the scale. This period saw Boeing benefit from the upturn in airliner orders more than many other manufacturer, launch two new derivative aircraft programs (the 777-300 and 757-300), begin work on a third (the stretched 767-400ERX), offered for sale to airlines its stretched 747 super jumbos and rollout the latest member of commercial aviation's most successful jetliner program – the 737.

In comparison the sudden leap in new orders had largely passed by McDonnell Douglas' airliner arm, the Douglas Aircraft Company. Most new orders have been placed in the two categories in which Douglas competes – 100 to 200 seat narrowbodies (MD-80/MD-95/MD-90) and 300 seats and over (MD-11), and in both these areas Douglas has an enormous customer base (flying thousands of DC-9s/MD-80s and hundreds of DC-10s) that Airbus would kill for but it just has not been able to capitalise on. At the same time DAC canned its most promising new design, the rewinged and stretched MD-11 development, the MD-XX.

Hopefully the merger into Boeing will not result in the death of another once great airliner builder, but with the possible exception of the 100 seat MD-95 every other member of the Douglas family has a near direct Boeing counterpart which has easily outsold it.

The MD-XX, perhaps the most promising design to be cancelled in the last few years. Will there be more Douglas airliner program cancellations in the wake of the planned Boeing/McDonnell Douglas merger?

At least in the helicopter market the two companies' product lines are complementary. MDC's light helicopters will nicely complement Boeing's heavylift Chinook (which in commercial form may yet return to production in China) and the recently unveiled Bell Boeing 609 nine seat civil tilt rotor.

The consolidation of these two companies should result in considerable cost savings as resources are pooled and administrative overheads are reduced.

No doubt the creation of what would easily be the world's largest aerospace company by a long stretch has raised more than a few eyebrows in Toulouse, home of Airbus Industrie.

Airbus has been *the* success story of commercial aviation of the past two to three decades. From nothing in the late 1960s to a full product line of jet airliners in the late 1990s the European consortium has come a very long way and earned the respect of almost all in the aviation industry, including arch rival Boeing. However there has been a growing realisation, both within and outside Toulouse, that Airbus needs to streamline its operations and evolve from a *Groupement d'Interet Economique* teaming of partner companies to a limited company in its own right.

This would give Airbus direct control of its affairs and allow it to streamline its operations, allocate workshare where it is most efficient and reduce costs to better compete with Boeing. Throughout 1996 Airbus partner BAe has been pushing hard in this direction and its efforts may bear some fruit during the life of this directory.

Sadly 1996 was also characterised by the death of Fokker. Despite a healthy order book for the popular Fokker 70/100 jetliners part owner Deutsche Aerospace pulled the plug in early '96 when it decided it no longer wanted to prop up the debt ridden Dutch company. At the time Fokker appeared doomed unless a third company stepped in to purchase its assets. For a time this seemed possible as first a consortium of Russian interests led by Yakovlev, and then Samsung of South Korea in particular showed strong interest in taking over Fokker's production facilities and substantial order backlog. Sadly Samsung failed to meet crucial timing deadlines to ensure Fokker's survival and in the dying days of 1996 the end appeared near.

One airliner that won't be nearly so missed as the Fokkers is the BAe ATP/Jetstream 61, the only victim of the consolidation of Avro, Jetstream and ATRs' consolidation into the Aero International (Regional), or AI(R), partnership. AI(R) came into being in January 1996 and has since enjoyed a good innings – the Avroliners' fortunes are looking up following Fokker's death, the ATRs continue to sell well and the company was selected as the western partner in the Chinese/Singapore 100-seat jetliner program at Boeing's expense. Through AI(R) Airbus has got on board this program and the AE 100 will have significant commonality with the A320. The 100 seater will no doubt be a debutante in the 1999/2000 *International Directory of Civil Aircraft*.

Another could be the AI(R) 70, a new 70 seat regional jet based on the ATR fuselage but with a new tail and, obviously, engines.

The battle between Boeing and the Europeans to partner the Chinese in building the new Asian 100 seater was hard fought, but nothing like the motions at the big end of town where Airbus and Boeing have been duking it out over who will build the world's first 500 seat plus airliner.

In the red corner Airbus has been working on the A3XX, an all new double decker which would be built in longer range 500 seat and stretched 600 seat versions. In the blue corner Boeing has proposed radically upgrading and stretching the 747 with a new wing, engines and avionics (including fly-by-wire) again in a long range 500 seat and stretched 600 seat variants.

The generally held consensus is that there is room for only one of these giant airliners in what is widely recognised as a relatively small marketplace. Boeing has forecast world demand for 500 plus seaters at about 470 units through to 2014, Airbus estimates 1380. Boeing says it will cost $US6-7bn to develop the 747-500X/600X which will sell for around $US200m. Airbus says its A3XX would need $US8bn to develop and sell for $US198m. Boeing says its design must be cheaper as it is a derivative and production facilities are already in place, whereas Airbus would have to build a new factory to assemble the A3XX. Airbus meanwhile says that as the A3XX would be all new that it would be more efficient and have greater growth potential.

At the bottom end of the scale life has returned to light aircraft manufacture, hopefully time will tell that buyers returned as well. Perhaps the biggest highlight in this area in recent times has been Cessna's return to light aircraft production. Cessna announced that it would restart building light aircraft in 1994. Since that time it has built and commissioned an all new factory in Independence, Kansas, and new build 172 Skyhawks, 182s and T206s are beginning to roll off the lines. Cessna is upbeat about its prospects and plans to build 1000 new 172s in 1997 and 2000 in '98. It will be interesting to see the level of buyer interest light aircraft owners show in

AI(R) is partnering the Chinese and Singaporeans to build the Asian 100 seater, (AI(R)

Workers surround the first Cessna 172R built at the new purpose designed Independence, Kansas plant. Cessna's return to light aircraft manufacture after a decade's absence is big news for the world GA industry. (Cessna)

the new types and if they can be persuaded to trade in their ageing but otherwise honest 172s and 182s on the new aircraft.

Meanwhile Piper has rebounded from near death in 1992 and has an ever growing product line ranging from the Warrior III to the Seneca IV, with others such as the Archer, Saratoga, Malibu and Seminole in between.

In addition to the big names a number of smaller concerns are planning to introduce new light aircraft types into production over the next few years. In the US, Cirrus and Kestrel are among the newcomers offering modern all new four seaters, while in Australia the promising but one-off four seat Victa Aircruiser is being reincarnated for production in 1997 as the Millicer Shrike.

At the top end of GA there has also been plenty of action. The top of the line ultra long range business jets in the form of the Gulfstream V and Canadair/Bombardier Global Express have flown for the first time since the release of the first *Civil Directory*. These two aircraft are in tight competition with each other, sharing similar missions, sizes and engines and are capable of one stop flight between any two points on the globe. Both also face new competition from Boeing/GE's business jet version of the 737-700 which will have a similar range and unit cost but a significantly larger cabin.

Slightly lower down the scale, the Falcon 2000 entered service in early 1995, the Citation X followed suit in mid 1996 and Learjet flew the 45. Raytheon launched development of two all new corporate jets, the entry level Premier I and the 'super midsize' Hawker Horizon.

In the rotary wing world Bell has launched, developed and delivered the already very popular 407, its JetRanger/LongRanger replacement, delivered the 430 and launched the new 427 light twin with Samsung. Meanwhile Sikorsky launched its S-92 Helibus S-61N/L replacement, Eurocopter flew the EC 120 and delivered the EC 135, and McDonnell Douglas revealed and flew the MD 600N and delivered the MD Explorer.

As can be seen there is certainly plenty of activity at all levels of civil aviation in recent times, with hopefully a lot more to come.

AASI Jetcruzer 500

Country of Origin: United States of America

Type: Business and utility transport

Powerplant: 500 – One rear mounted 635kW (850shp) Pratt & Whitney Canada PT6A-42A turboprop driving a three blade constant speed Hartzell propeller.

Performance: 500 – Max operating and max cruising speed 556km/h (300kt). Service ceiling 30,000ft. Max range at economical cruising speed 2920km (1580nm).

Weights: 500 – Empty 1338kg (2950lb), max takeoff 2495kg (5500lb).

Dimensions: 500 – Wing span 12.85m (42ft 2in), length 8.59m (28ft 2in), height 3.17m (10ft 5in). Wing area 17.9m^2 (193.2sq ft).

Capacity: Total seating for six people including pilot in club and standard seating arrangements. Alternative configurations for air ambulance and freight work.

Production: More than 75 provisional sales for the 450 announced by 1996. AASI has predicted annual demand when in production as much as 150. No Jetcruzers had entered service at the time of writing. A second production line may be opened in Taiwan.

History: The Jetcruzer 500 is the first product of Advanced Aerodynamics and Structures Inc (AASI).

AASI (formerly Aerodynamics & Structures Inc) is designing and developing (with plans to manufacture) what it calls new generation light business and utility transports. The Burbank California based manufacturer has a staff of 300 (at the time of writing) and employs a number of designers, engineers and aircraft construction workers formerly from major aircraft manufacturers such as Lockheed Martin, Northrop Grumman and McDonnell Douglas.

Early design work for the innovative Jetcruzer 450 began in 1983. Prototype construction commenced in 1988 and the same year it was displayed at the National Business Aircraft Association (NBAA) exhibition in October. First flight of the Allison 250-C20S powered prototype followed on January 11 1989, while the first production standard aircraft flew on September 13 1992. Type Inspection Authorisation was received in October 1993, prior to being awarded FAA Part 23 certification. Certification was delayed somewhat latter than the planned for date of late 1993, but the Jetcruzer 450 was awarded its type certificate (to FAA Part 23) in mid June 1994.

Notable features of the Jetcruzer are its unconventional pusher engine and canard configuration, resulting in the world's first production aircraft to be certificated as spin resistant. The wing is swept at 20 degrees and has tip mounted fins.

The pressurised Jetcruzer 500 has replaced the 450, and in comparison is stretched by 43cm (17in) in the nose and 25cm (10in) in the fuselage, while leading edge flaps are added to the wing. It is powered by a more powerful 635kW (850shp) PT6A-42. AASI has also proposed two military developments, the ML-2 utility and the ML-1 UAV (Unmanned Aerial Vehicle).

A larger development of the basic Jetcruzer which has been under development is the 10 to 13 seat 691ekW (927ehp) PT6A-135A powered Jetcruzer 650. The company is also developing the Williams-Rolls FJ44 turbofan powered Stratocruzer 1250.

Photo: The Jetcruzer 450 during early flight testing. (AASI)

Aero Boero 95/115/150/180

Country of origin: Argentina

Type: Family of three and four seat light aircraft

Powerplant: AB 95 Standard – One 70kW (95hp) Continental C-90-8F flat four piston engine driving a two blade fixed pitch propeller. AB 115 Trainer – One 85kW (115hp) Textron Lycoming O-235-C2A. AB 180 RVR – One 135kW (180hp) Textron Lycoming O-360-A1A driving a two blade fixed pitch Sensenich or constant speed Hartzell propeller.

Performance: AB 95 – Max speed 204km/h (110kt), cruising speed 170km/h (92kt), long range cruising speed 159km/h (86kt). Range at long range cruising speed 959km (518nm). AB 115 Trainer – Max cruising speed 169km/h (91kt). Initial rate of climb 669ft/min. Range with max fuel 1230km (664nm). AB 180 RVR – Max speed 225km/h (122kt), max cruising speed 201km/h (108kt). Initial rate of climb 1025ft/min. Range with max fuel 1180km (636nm).

Weights: AB 95 – Empty 400kg (882lb), loaded 700kg (1543lb). AB 115 Trainer – Empty 556kg (1226lb), max takeoff 802kg (1768lb). AB 180 RVR – Empty 602kg (1327lb), max takeoff 890kg (1962lb).

Dimensions: AB 95 – Wing span 10.42m (34ft 2in), length 6.91m (22ft 8in), height 2.19m (7ft 2in). AB 115 Trainer & AB 180 RVR – Wing span 10.78m (35ft 5in), length 7.08m (23ft 3in), height 2.05m (6ft 9in). Wing area 17.4m^2 (187.4sq ft).

Capacity: Accommodation for one pilot and two passengers, or three/four passengers in initial AB 180 model. Ag aircraft fitted with ventral tank pod (for approx 270 litres/60Imp gal) and spray bars.

Production: Several hundred of all variants have been built, including over 300 out of a Brazilian Government order for 450 AB 115s for use by aero clubs.

History: Development from the basic AB 95 (which first flew in 1959) has spawned one of the largest families of GA types yet developed in South America.

Versions of the AB 95 include the AB 95 Standard, the AB 95 De Lujo with a 75kW (100hp) Continental O-200-A engine, the AB 95 A Fumigador ag aircraft with the O-200-A engine and fitted for crop dusting or spraying, the AB 115 BS air ambulance fitted with a stretcher, the more powerful AB 95 B, and the AB 95/115 with a more streamlined engine cowling housing a 85kW (115hp) O-235 engine, and main wheel fairings.

From the AB 95/115 Aero Boero developed the AB 115 BS with increased wing span, greater fin sweepback and longer range, and the AB 115 Trainer, of which Brazil ordered 450 in the late 1980s for that country's aero clubs.

The AB 180 first flew in the late 1960s and was offered in three and four seat versions with differing wingspans and a more powerful powerplant than those featured on the earlier AB 95 and AB 115. Developments included the AB 180 RV with greater range, reprofiled fuselage and sweptback fin; the glider tug AB 180 RVR; the high altitude AB 180 Condor with optional engine turbocharger; AB 180 Ag agricultural aircraft and the two seat AB 180 PSA preselection aircraft for student pilot flight grading. A biplane AB 180 SP was also developed. The AB 150 RV and AB 150 Ag have less powerful powerplants than corresponding AB 180 models.

Photo: The two/three seat Aero Boero 115 in flight.

Aeronca 7 Champion & 11 Chief

Country of origin: United States of America

Type: Two seat light aircraft

Powerplant: 7AC – One 50kW (65hp) Continental A65-8 flat four piston engine driving a two blade fixed pitch propeller. 11BC – One 63kW (85hp) Continental C-85-85F.

Performance: 7AC – Max speed 208km/h (112kt), cruising speed 183km/h (99kt). Service ceiling 12,400ft. Range 740km (400nm). 11 – Max speed 169km/h (91kt), cruising speed 153km/h (83kt). Service ceiling 10,800ft. Range 531km (287nm).

Weights: 7AC – Empty 325kg (740lb), max takeoff 533kg (1220lb). 11 – Empty 329kg (725lb), loaded 567kg (1250lb).

Dimensions: 7AC – Wing span 10.73m (35ft 2in), length 6.65m (21ft 6in), height 2.13m (7ft 0in). Wing area 15.8m^2 (170sq ft). 11 – Wing span 11.00m (36ft 1in), length 6.35m (20ft 10in), height 2.08m (6ft 10in). Wing area 16.3m^2 (175.5sq ft).

Capacity: 7 – Pilot and single passenger in tandem. 11 – Accommodation for pilot and passenger side by side.

Production: Exact figures are unclear, although production of the Champion lasted six years with the total number built, including L-16 observation aircraft for the US Army, thought to be around 10,000 units. Approximately 1750 Chiefs were built between 1946 and 1951.

History: The Aeronca Champion was one of a number of popular light aircraft built by the American aircraft industry following WW2 and proved to be a great success.

The Champion was based on the prewar Model K Scout, with which it shares an overall similar configuration, but tandem, instead of side by side seating, and a reduced span but increased chord wing. The first production version of the Champion was the 7AC, with succeeding versions being almost identical except for the powerplant fitted. These versions were the 7BC with a 63kW (85hp) Continental C85-12 or O-190-1; the 7CC with a Continental C90-12F; the 7DC with a Continental C85; and the 7EC with a 67kW (90hp) Continental C90.

Aeronca sold the production rights of the Champion to the Champion Aircraft Corporation in 1954, and this company produced the 7EC and subsequent 7FC tricycle undercarriage Tri-Traveller.

The Aeronca Chief meanwhile was also introduced in 1946, but differed from the Champion from which it was derived in having a wider cabin, side by side seating and different span wing. Versions of the Chief (the initial production version was the 11AC) were the Scout pilot trainer; the 11BC with a dorsal fin and more powerful 63kW (85hp) Continental engine; the 11CC Super Chief with the Continental C85 with improvements to the fuselage giving greater interior space.

Photo: An Aeronca 7AC Champion at rest. The Champion was very popular after the war, particularly in the US. (Bill Lines)

Aero Spacelines Guppy Series

Country of origin: United States of America

Type: Oversize cargo freighter

Powerplants: 201 – Four 3660kW (4912shp) Allison 501-D22C turboprops driving four blade variable pitch propellers.

Performance: 201 – Max cruising speed 463km/h (250kt) at 20,000ft, economical cruising speed 407km/h (220kt) at 20,000ft. Service ceiling 25,000ft. Range with max payload and reserves 815km (440nm).

Weights: Empty 45,360kg (100,000lb), max takeoff 77,110kg (170,000lb).

Dimensions: 201 – Wing span 47.63m (156ft 3in), length 43.84m (143ft 10in), height 14.78m (48ft 6in). Wing area 182.5m^2 (1964.6sq ft).

Capacity: 201 – Flightcrew of three, comprising two pilots and a flight engineer. Cargo hold designed for volume cargo rather than weight, originally designed to transport rocket sections, Airbus aircraft used to transport airframe sections.

Production: Total of seven Guppy conversions performed. Airbus is replacing its 201 Super Guppys, the only aircraft of the series still in service.

History: The distinctive Super Guppy transporter is famous for its crucially important role in transporting oversize airframe constructions between the manufacturing plants and the final assembly lines of the Airbus consortium. Ironically it is based on a Boeing airliner.

The original Guppy conversion was performed by Van Nuys of California to airlift rocket booster stages for the American space program. For its initial conversion Aero Spacelines took a Boeing 377 Stratocruiser, stretched the fuselage by 5.08m (16ft 8in) behind the wing, and added a new distinctive fat rounded upper fuselage that had an internal height 6.02m (19ft 9in). Called the B-377PG Pregnant Guppy, its first flight was on September 19 1962, and it entered service under contract to NASA in July the following year carrying an inert Saturn S-IV stage from Los Angeles to Cape Kennedy.

The Pregnant Guppy was followed by the even larger B-377SG Super Guppy. Based on the Boeing C-97J (the military equivalent of the 377), the B-377SG incorporated 5215kW (7000ehp) Pratt & Whitney T34 turboprops, the hinged nose section, a 9.40m (30ft 10in) fuselage stretch, increased span wing and even greater size fuselage, with an internal diameter of 7.62m (25ft). First flight of the Super Guppy was on August 31 1965, and it could carry the S-IVB third stage of the Saturn V launch vehicle and the Apollo Lunar Module adapter.

The Guppy 201 is based on the B-377SG but is powered by Allison 501 turboprops, and it is this version that is in service with Airbus. Two of the Airbus Super Guppys were built by Aero Spacelines, while UTA Industries converted a further two. The Guppys form a vital link in Airbus' production chain, ferrying oversize constructions, such as wings and fuselage sections, between Airbus's partner companies plants throughout Europe, and the final assembly lines in Hamburg and Toulouse. The Guppys were being replaced by Airbus' own A300-600ST Super Transporters from late 1995.

Photo: An Airbus Skylink Super Guppy. (Airbus)

Aerospatiale/BAe Concorde

Countries of origin: France and United Kingdom

Type: Medium range supersonic airliner

Powerplants: Four 170.2kN (38,050lb) Rolls-Royce SNECMA Olympus 593 Mk 610 afterburning turbojets.

Performance: Max cruising speed at 51,300ft Mach 2.04, or 2179km/h (1176kt), typical supersonic cruise speed Mach 2.02. Range with max payload and reserves at Mach 2.02 cruise and climb speed 6230km (3360nm). Range with max fuel, reserves and 8845kg (19,500lb) payload 6580km (3550nm).

Weights: Operating empty 78,700kg (173,500lb), max takeoff 185,065kg (408,000lb). Max payload 12,700kg (28,000lb).

Dimensions: Wing span 25.56m (83ft 10in), length 62.17m (203ft 9in), height 11.40m (37ft 5in). Wing area 358.3m^2 (3856sq ft).

Capacity: Two pilots and flight engineer on the flightdeck. Accommodation for 128 passengers at four abreast with 86cm (34in) pitch in main cabin. Max seating for 144 at 81cm (32in) pitch.

Production: Two prototypes (001 & 002), two pre production aircraft (01 & 02) and 16 production aircraft. Thirteen remain in use.

History: The Concorde first flew over 25 years ago, and yet it remains the pinnacle of civil aviation development for one reason – speed. The Concorde is the only aircraft in the world operating scheduled passenger flights at supersonic speed.

An engineering masterpiece, the Concorde was the result of highly successful (design wise) and significant collaborative venture between Britain and France. The Concorde dates back to design work for a supersonic airliner carried out by Sud Aviation and Bristol, their respective Super Caravelle and Bristol 233 designs being remarkably similar in configuration to each other. The forecast high costs of any SST program and the similarities in the designs led to a 1962 government agreement between France and Britain which resulted in the British Aircraft Corporation (into which Bristol had been merged) and Sud-Aviation (which became a part of Aerospatiale in 1970) getting together to design and develop the aircraft.

Talks with airlines in the 1960s resulted in a relatively long range aircraft capable of flying trans Atlantic sectors (although for a time Sud offered a short haul version), while design of the airframe was refined to feature a highly complex delta wing with cambering and ogival leading edges with pairs of engines mounted in pods under the wing undersurface. The slender fuselage features a high fineness ratio to keep supersonic drag to a minimum, while the fuel system was designed to trim the aircraft longitudinally by transferring fuel between tanks to combat the change in the centre of pressure as the aircraft accelerates. Another feature is the variable geometry nose which is lowered while taxying, on takeoff and landing to improve the flightcrew's visibility.

A lengthy development program following the Concorde's first flight on March 2 1969 meant that it did not enter into airline service until January 1976, but it has been in continual airline service since. British Airways hopes to maintain Concorde services well into the first decade of the next century.

Photo: A classic inflight portrait of a British Airways Concorde. BA flies seven Concordes, Air France six (five in operation).(British Airways)

Aerospatiale Alouette II & Lama

Country of origin: France

Type: Light utility helicopters

Powerplant: SA 313B Alouette II – One 270kW (360shp) Turboméca Artouste IIC6 turboshaft, driving a three blade main rotor and two blade tail rotor. SA 315B Lama – One 650kW (870shp) Turboméca Artouste IIIB turboshaft, derated to 410kW (550shp).

Performance: SA 313B – Max speed 185km/h (100kt), max cruising speed 165km/h (90kt). Initial rate of climb 825ft/min. Hovering ceiling in ground effect 5400ft. Range with max fuel 300km (162nm), range with max payload 100km (54nm). SA 315B – Max cruising speed 192km/h (103kt). Max initial rate of climb 1080ft/min. Hovering ceiling in ground effect 16,565ft, out of ground effect 15,090ft. Range with max fuel 515km (278nm).

Weights: SA 313B – Empty 895kg (1973lb), max takeoff 1600kg (3527lb). SA 315B – Empty 1020kg (2250lb), max takeoff 1950kg (4300lb), or 2300kg (5070lb) with external sling load.

Dimensions: SA 313B – Main rotor diameter 10.20m (33ft 5in), fuselage length 9.70m (31ft 10in), height 2.75m (9ft 0in). SA 315B – Main rotor diameter 11.02m (36ft 2in), length overall 12.92m (42ft 5in), fuselage length 10.26m (33ft 8in), height overall 3.09m (10ft 2in). Main rotor disc area 95.4m^2 (1026.7sq ft).

Capacity: Typical seating for five. Lama can lift a 1135kg (2500lb) external sling load.

Production: A total of 1303 Alouette IIs, including 360 SA 318Cs, were built for military and commercial customers. Aerospatiale built 407 Lamas, while seven were built in Brazil and more than 240 in India as the HAL Cheetah.

History: Among the very first turbine powered helicopters in the world, the Alouette II and Lama remain in service in fairly large numbers worldwide.

For a time the most successful western European helicopter in terms of numbers built, the Alouette II was based on the original Sud-Est Alouette SA 3120 which flew for the first time on March 12 1955. Two prototypes were built and these were powered by Salmson 9 piston engines. Production deliveries of the turbine powered SE 313B Alouette II occurred from 1957, the first machines bound for the French military. Civil certification was awarded on January 14 1958, although most SA/SE 313B production was for military customers.

The Alouette II was soon followed by a more powerful Turboméca Astazou powered development. This aircraft was designated the SA 318C Alouette II Astazou, and flew for the first time on January 31 1961. Power was supplied by a 395kW (530shp) Astazou IIA derated to 270kW (360shp), which increased the type's maximum speed and max takeoff weight, but otherwise the Alouette II and Alouette II Astazou were similar.

The SA 315B Lama was developed initially as a utility helicopter with excellent hot and high performance for the Indian army. Called Cheetah in Indian service, the Lama mated the Alouette's airframe with the larger Alouette III's dynamic components including the Artouste IIIB engine. The Lama's first flight was on March 17 1969. Aerospatiale built 407 through to 1989, while HAL in India continues licence production.

Photo: A PNG registered Lama in flight.

Aerospatiale Alouette III

Country of origin: France

Type: Light utility helicopter

Powerplant: SA 316B – One 425kW (570shp) Turboméca Artouste IIIB turboshaft, driving a three blade main rotor and three blade tail rotor. SA 319 – One 450kW (600shp) derated Turboméca Astazou XIV turboshaft.

Performance: SA 316B – Max speed 210km/h (113kt), max cruising speed 185km/h (100kt). Max initial rate of climb 885ft/min. Hovering ceiling in ground effect 7380ft/min. Range with max fuel 480km (260nm). SA 319B – Max cruising speed 197km/h (106kt). Initial rate of climb 885ft/min. Hovering ceiling in ground effect 10,170ft, out of ground effect 5575ft. Range with six passengers 605km (327nm).

Weights: SA 316B – Empty 1122kg (2474lb), max takeoff 2200kg (4850lb). SA 319B – Empty 1140kg (2513lb), max takeoff 2250kg (4960lb).

Dimensions: SA 316B/ 319B – Main rotor diameter 11.02m (36ft 2in), length overall 12.54m (42ft 2in), fuselage length 10.03m (32ft 11in), height 3.00, (9ft 10in). Main rotor disc area 95.4m^2 (1026.7sq ft)

Capacity: Typical seating for seven, with two passengers and pilot on front bench seats, and four on rear bench seat. In aerial ambulance configuration accommodates pilot, two medical attendants and two stretcher patients.

Production: Approximately 1500 Alouette IIIs have been built in France, plus production in India (300+), Romania (200) and Switzerland, most for military customers, but some are in civil service.

History: Aerospatiale's most successful helicopter in terms of numbers built until the mid 1980s when surpassed by the Ecureuil, the Alouette III is an enlarged development of the Alouette II series.

Like the Alouette II, the Alouette III traces its development back to the Sud-Est SE 3101 Alouette piston powered prototypes, the first of which flew for the first time on July 31 1951. The largest member of the Alouette series, the III flew as the SE 3160 on February 28 1959. Compared with the Alouette II, the Alouette III is larger and seats seven, but in its initial SA 316A form was also powered by the Turboméca Artouste turboshaft.

This initial SA 316A Alouette III remained in production for almost a decade until 1969, when it was replaced by the improved SA 316B with strengthened transmission and a greater max takeoff weight, but the same Artouste III turboshaft.

Further development led to the SA 319 Alouette III Astazou, which as its name suggests is powered by a 450kW (600shp) Turboméca Astazou XIV turboshaft. The more powerful Astazou engine conferred better hot and high performance and improved fuel economy. The SA 319 entered production in 1968.

The SA 319 and SA 316B remained in production side by side through the 1970s and into the early 1980s. HAL of India continues to licence build Alouette IIIs as the Chetak, mainly for that country's military, but also for government and civil customers. ICA of Brasov in Romania also licence built SA 316Bs as IAR 316Bs.

Like the Alouette II, the III has been used in a wide range of utility roles, and many armed military variants have been built.

Photo: The Alouette III. (Paul Merritt)

Aerospatiale Puma

Country of origin: France

Type: Twin engine medium lift helicopter

Powerplants: SA 330J – Two 1175kW (1575shp) Turboméca Turmo IVC turboshafts driving a four blade main rotor and five blade tail rotor. SA 330G/F – Two 1070kW (1435shp) Turboméca Turmo IIIC4s.

Performance: SA 330J – Max speed 262km/h (141kt), max cruising speed at sea level 257km/h (139kt). Hovering ceiling in ground effect 7315ft. Initial rate of climb 1400ft/min. Max range with standard fuel 550km (297nm).

Weights: Empty 3766kg (8305lb), max takeoff 7500kg (16,535lb) with sling load, standard max takeoff weight 7400kg (16,315lb).

Dimensions: Rotor diameter 15.08m (49ft 6in), length overall 18.15m, fuselage length 14.06m (46ft 2in), height 5.14m (16ft 11in). Main rotor disc area 177.0m^2 (1905sq ft).

Capacity: Crew of one or two pilots on flightdeck, plus jumpseat. Passenger configurations in main cabin range from 8, 10 or 12 seat executive layouts, or for 17 to 20 passengers in an airline arrangement. A 3200kg (7055lb) load can be carried on the external sling.

Production: A total of 696 Pumas of different versions, including military, had been sold, when Aerospatiale production ceased in 1987. Limited production continues in Romania, largely for that country's military. IAR has built over 160 as the IAR-330L.

History: The Aerospatiale Puma is perhaps the most successful European built medium lift helicopter, and while most Pumas have been built for military customers (largely for use as troop transports), a significant number are operated by civilian concerns.

The Puma was first designed to meet a French army requirement for a medium lift helicopter capable of operating in all weather conditions. The first of two SA 330 prototypes flew for the first time on April 15 1965, with the first production aircraft flying in September 1968. A 1967 Royal Air Force decision to order the Puma as its new tactical helicopter transport resulted in substantial Westland participation in design and construction.

Early versions of the Puma were for military customers, including the SA 330B, C, E, and H. The initial civil versions were the Turmo IIIC powered SA 330F passenger and SA 330G freight versions, which became the first helicopters certificated for single pilot IFR operations in A and B conditions. The SA 330J is the definitive civil version, and compared to the earlier F and G, has composite main rotors and an increased maximum takeoff weight. The weather radar equipped J also became the first helicopter certificated for all weather operations including flight in icing conditions in April 1978.

IPTN of Indonesia assembled a small number of SA 330s before switching to the SA 332 Super Puma (described separately under Eurocopter), and after Aerospatiale ceased production in 1987, the sole source for the Puma became IAR of Romania.

Photo: A flotation gear equipped SA 330J Puma of Jayrow Helicopters used for oil rig support missions. (Warwick Henry)

Aerospatiale Gazelle

Country of origin: France

Type: Utility helicopter

Powerplant: SA 342 – One 640kW (858shp) Turboméca Astazou XIV turboshaft driving a three blade main rotor and Fenestron shrouded tail rotor.

Performance: SA 342 – Max continuous speed 270km/h (146kt), cruising speed 238km/h (129kt). Hovering ceiling in ground effect 13,120ft. Range at sea level 785km (424nm), range with a 500kg (1102lb) payload 360km (194nm).

Weights: SA 342 – Empty equipped 975kg (2149lb), max takeoff 1900kg (4190lb).

Dimensions: Main rotor diameter 10.5m (34ft 6in), fuselage length 9.53m (31ft 3in), height 3.18m (10ft 5in). Main rotor disc area 86.5m^2 (931sq ft).

Capacity: Maximum of five people including pilot. Rear seat can be folded down to accommodate freight.

Production: More than 1250 French built Gazelles have been delivered, although the large majority of these were for military service. Further production took place in the UK with Westland, and the former Yugoslavia.

History: The Gazelle will be long remembered for being the first helicopter to introduce Aerospatiale's (and now Eurocopter's) trademark Fenestron shrouded tail rotor system.

The Gazelle is in widespread military service throughout the world, and a large number of military variants have been developed. While civil use is not as widespread, a significant number are in service, largely as personal or corporate transports.

First flight of the original Gazelle SA 340 occurred on April 7 1967. This aircraft was powered by the Astazou III turboshaft, the engine that became the standard powerplant on the subsequent SA 341 production model, which flew for the first time on August 16 1971. Like the larger Puma the Gazelle was the subject of a 1967 agreement that has seen it jointly built by Westland in the UK and Aerospatiale in France.

Civil production Gazelles were designated SA 341G and powered by the Astazou IIIA. The SA 341G was the first helicopter to be certificated to be flown by one pilot under Cat I weather conditions, achieving this in January 1975. This was since upgraded to Cat II operations. Gazelles with their rear fuselage modified to allow an extra 20cm of rear legroom were known as Stretched Gazelles

Further development led to the SA 342 with the more powerful Astazou XIV and refined Fenestron design, giving the civil SA 342J a 100kg (220lb) increase in payload. The SA 342 became available from 1977.

When the helicopter subsidiaries of Deutsche Aerospace and Aerospatiale merged in 1992, low rate production of the Gazelle for military customers continued under the Eurocopter banner.

Photo: The only civil Gazelle on the Australian register. Most Gazelles were built for military customers. (Jim Thorn)

Aerospatiale SA 360 Dauphin

Country of origin: France

Type: Single engine mid size utility helicopter

Powerplant: SA 360 – One 785kW (1050shp) Turboméca Astazou XVIIIA turboshaft driving a four blade main rotor and Fenestron shrouded tail rotor. SA 361 – One 956kW (1282shp) Astazou XX.

Performance: SA 360 – Max cruising speed 278km/h (150kt), economical cruising speed 245km/h (132kt). Initial rate of climb 1770ft/min. Hovering ceiling in ground effect 7380ft. Range with max fuel 650km (351nm). SA 361 – Max cruising speed 282km/h (153kt). Initial rate of climb 1969ft/min. Hovering ceiling in ground effect 13,450ft. Range 685km (370nm).

Weights: SA 360 – Basic operating 1555kg (3428lb), max takeoff 3000kg (6613lb). SA 361 – Empty equipped 1582kg (3487lb), max takeoff 3300kg (6800lb).

Dimensions: Main rotor diameter 11.50m (37ft 9in), fuselage length 10.98m (36ft 0in), height 3.50m (11ft 6in). SA 361 – Same except main rotor diameter 11.68m (38ft 4in).

Capacity: Standard accommodation for 10, including one pilot, in three seat rows, with pilot and two passengers in front row, four passengers in centre row and three passengers in rear row. Max seating for 14. Executive configurations can seat four to six passengers. As an air ambulance accommodates four stretcher patients and a medical attendant. External sling load capacity is 1300kg (2865lb).

Production: Production of the SA 361 and SA 360 ceased in the mid 1980s when it and the twin engine SA 365 were replaced by the AS 365N.

History: Only built in modest numbers, the SA 360 Dauphin was intended as a replacement for the Alouette III. Perhaps its greatest claim to fame is that it forms the basis for the successful twin engined AS 365 and AS 365N Dauphin 2s (described under Eurocopter).

The prototype SA 360 flew for the first time on June 2 1972 and was powered by a 730kW (980shp) Turboméca Astazou XVI turboshaft. The prototype made 180 development flights in this configuration before a more powerful 785kW (1050shp) Astazou XVIIIA was substituted, and weights were fitted to the rotor tips to reduce vibration and to eliminate ground resonance. The first prototype flew for the first time in this new configuration on May 4 1973, earlier a second prototype so configured flew for the first time that January.

These two prototypes now represented production configuration aircraft, while the first production aircraft, designated the SA 360C, flew in April 1975.

The only development of the single engine version to join the SA 360C in production was the SA 361, a more powerful variant optimised for better hot and high performance, with a greater payload capability. Deliveries of the SA 361 took place from the second half of 1978.

A military variant of the SA 361, the SA 361F, was offered fitted with up to eight HOT anti tank missiles.

The SA 360 and SA 361C form the basis for the twin engined SA (later AS) 365 Dauphin 2 (described separately under Eurocopter). The initial SA 365 is basically identical to the SA 360 except for its two Turboméca Arriel turboshafts.

Photo: An SA 360 in flight. (Aerospatiale)

Aerospatiale (Sud) Caravelle

Country of origin: France

Type: Short range airliner

Powerplants: Caravelle 10B – Two 64.4kN (14,500lb) Pratt & Whitney JT8D-9 turbofans. Earlier Caravelle versions (Mk I. IA, III and VI) were powered by two 49.2 to 56.4kN (11,00 to 12,600lb) thrust class Rolls-Royce RA.29 Avon turbojets.

Performance: Caravelle 10B – Max cruising speed 825km/h (445kt). Range with max payload 2650km (1450nm), range with max fuel 3640km (1965nm).

Weights: 10B – Operating empty 30,055kg (66,260lb), max takeoff 56,000kg (123,460lb). Earlier series Avon powered versions max takeoff weights range from 46,000kg (101,413lb) for the Mk III to 50,000kg (110,230lb) for the Mk VI-R.

Dimensions: Caravelle 10B – Wing span 34.30m (112ft 6in), length 33.01m (108ft 3.5in), height 8.72m (28ft 7in). Wing area 146.7m^2 (1579sq ft). Caravelle Mks I, IA, III and VI same except for length 32.01m (105ft 0in). Caravelle 12 featured 3.21m (10ft 7in) fuselage stretch.

Capacity: Caravelle 10 – Flightcrew of two pilots and one flight engineer. Max passengers 100 at five abreast in a high density layout. Typical accommodation for 91 passengers in a mixed class arrangement. Maximum payload 9100kg (20,600lb).

Production: A total of 282 production Caravelles were built between 1958 and 1972. 16 remained in commercial service in late 1996.

History: The twinjet Caravelle was the first jet airliner to enter production in continental Europe.

The Caravelle was designed in response to a French Secretariat General of Commercial and Civil Aviation requirement for a 1600 to 2000km (865 to 1080nm) range airliner (allowing operations between France and its North African dependents) with a 6000 to 7000kg (2725 to 3180lb) payload requirement at a speed of 620km/h (335kt). SNCASE (Societe Nationale de Constructions Aeronautiques de Sud-Est, later Sud Aviation, and then merged into Aerospatiale), responded with a trijet design designated the X120, with three rear mounted SNECMA Atar turbojets. This design then matured to feature two rear mounted Rolls-Royce Avons.

The French government ordered two flying and two static prototypes of the twinjet in 1953, resulting in the type's first flight on May 27 1955. Entry into service of the SE 210 Caravelle I with Air France was on May 12 1959 flying on the Paris/Rome/Istanbul route.

Subsequent to the Caravelle I and similar IA models were the Caravelle III with 51.1kN (11,400lb) RR Avon RA.29 Mk 527s (one Caravelle III was powered by General Electric CJ805-23C turbofans, but production never eventuated); the 54.7kN (12,200lb) Avon RA.2 Mk531 powered Caravelle VI-N; and the VI-R with a modified windscreen and thrust reversers.

The Caravelle 10 introduced more fuel efficient Pratt & Whitney JT8D turbofans, while the 11R was a convertible based on the 10. The ultimate Caravelle model was the 3.2m (10ft 6in) stretched Caravelle 12 or Super Caravelle. Production ceased in 1972.

Photo: A Caravelle 10 in Air Caledonie colours. This aircraft was replaced by a 737-300. (Brian Chidlow)

Aerospatiale Fregate & Mohawk

Country of origin: France

Type: Short range turboprop commuter airliner

Powerplants: 262 Fregate – Two 843kW (1130shp) Turboméca Bastan VIIC turboprops driving three blade variable pitch Ratier-Figeac FH.146 propellers. Mohawk 298 – Two 880kW (1180shp) Pratt & Whitney Canada PT6A-45 turboprops driving five blade variable pitch Hamilton Standard props.

Performance: Fregate – Max level speed 418km/h (225kt) at 20,000ft, economical cruising speed 408km/h (220kt). Max range with full fuel and no reserves 2400km (1295nm), range with 26 pax and reserves 1020km (550nm). Mohawk – Max speed 385km/h (208kt), economical cruising speed 375km/h (203kt). Max range with full fuel and no reserves 2132km (1151nm).

Weights: Fregate – Basic empty 6200kg (13,668lb), max takeoff 10,800kg (23,810lb). Mohawk – Empty 7030kg (15,498lb), max takeoff 10,600kg (23,370lb).

Dimensions: Fregate & Mohawk – Wing span 22.60m (74ft 2in), length 19.28m (63ft 3in), height 6.21m (20ft 4in). Wing area 55.0m^2 (592sq ft).

Capacity: Flightcrew of two and max seating for 29 passengers at three abreast. Standard seating layout for 26 passengers.

Production: A total of 110 of all variants of the 262 (including the 298 and miscellaneous military orders) were built.

History: The original design of the 262 dates back to the Max Holste Super Broussard project, which as the MH 260 flew for the first time on July 29 1960.

This event had been preceded by the first flight of the one-off Pratt & Whitney Wasp piston radial powered but otherwise similar MH 250 prototype on May 20 1959. Nord built just 10 MH 260s (flown by Air Inter and Norway's Wideröe) before undertaking a significant redesign of the type, with the major changes being a redesigned fuselage with a circular cross section, pressurisation and uprated powerplants. Production of the 262 consisted of four major variants, these being the initial production 262A, followed by the 262B, of which only four were built; the 262C Fregate with more powerful engines and greater wing span; and the 262D Fregate. The merger of Nord and Sud during the 262's production life resulted in it becoming a product of Aerospatiale from 1970.

In the late 1970s US commuter airline Allegheny Airlines – through its subsidiary Mohawk Air Services – extensively upgraded its fleet of 262s, resulting in the Mohawk 298 (the designation being derived from the FAA FAR Part 298 airworthiness regulation). The retrofit involved re-engining the 262s with more powerful Pratt & Whitney Canada PT6A-45 turboprops with five blade props, new avionics and a new APU. The first Mohawk 298 flew on January 7 1975, while the last of nine converted was completed in 1978.

Photo: A PT6 powered Mohawk 298 of defunct Australian regional airline Majestic Airlines, pictured in 1994. (Rod Finlayson)

Aerospatiale SN 601 Corvette

Country of origin: France

Type: Light corporate jet

Powerplants: Two 11.1kN (2500lb) Pratt & Whitney Canada JT15D-4 turbofans.

Performance: Max cruising speed 760km/h (410kt), economical cruising speed 566km/h (306kt). Max range with tip tanks and 45 minute reserves at max cruising speed 2390km (1290nm), at economical cruising speed 2555km (1380nm). Range with 12 passengers at max cruising speed 1480km (800nm), at economical cruising speed 1555km (840nm).

Weights: Empty 3510kg (7738lb), max takeoff 6600kg (14,550lb).

Dimensions: Wing span 12.87m (42ft 3in), length 13.83m (45ft 5in), height 4.23m (13ft 11in). Wing area 22.0m^2 (236.8sq ft).

Capacity: Flightcrew of one or two pilots. Main cabin seating for between six and 14 passengers, depending on customer preference. Galley and toilets were available optionally. Alternative configurations for ambulance, freighter, navigation aid calibration and photography missions offered.

Production: One prototype SN 600 built, plus 39 production SN 601s were built, with an estimated 35 remaining in service.

History: Although primarily a small corporate transport, Aerospatiale designed the Corvette to fulfil a variety or roles, including commuter airliner, aerial photography, airline pilot transport trainer, ambulance, air taxi, express freight work and navigation aid calibration.

The Corvette was a commercial failure, and was Aerospatiale's only venture into the executive jet market. The first prototype SN 601 first flew on July 16 1970, but only completed 270 hours of test and development flying before it crashed on March 23 the following year. This aircraft was powered by the less powerful JT15D-1 of 9.8kN (2200lb) thrust.

The subsequent production version, the SN 601, had more powerful JT15D-4 turbofans and a longer fuselage than the prototype. The first SN 601, or Corvette 100, made its maiden flight on December 20 1972. The second SN 601 Corvette (the first to full production standard) flew on March 7 1973, and a third on January 12 1974.

French civil certification for the Corvette was granted on May 28 1974. Customer deliveries, delayed by strikes at engine manufacturer Pratt & Whitney Canada (then UACL) began the following September.

Production of the Corvette continued until 1977. The initial production schedule called for 20 aircraft being delivered in 1974 and production of six a month for 1975 and thereafter. However this proved an overly optimistic assessment of potential sales and only 40 were built (including development aircraft). Plans for a 2.0m (6ft 7in) stretched 18 seat Corvette 200 were also dropped.

Many early Corvette customers were French regional airlines (such as Air Alpes and Air Alsace), with others sold to corporate operators in Europe. Outside Europe however the type generated little sales interest in the face of very strong competition. Many of the Corvettes built remain in service today.

Photo: An SN 601 Corvette at Aerospatiale's Toulouse facility and used by that company as a corporate transport. (Jim Thorn)

Ag-Cat/Schweizer/Grumman Ag-Cat

Country of origin: United States of America

Type: Agricultural biplane

Powerplants: G-164A Super Ag-Cat – One 335kW (450hp) Pratt & Whitney R-985 series nine cylinder radial piston engine, driving a two blade constant speed propeller. G-164B Ag-Cat Super-B Turbine – Choice of 373kW (500shp) Pratt & Whitney Canada PT6A-11AG, or 510kW (680shp) PT6A-15AG, or 560kW (750shp) PT6A-34AG turboprops, driving a three blade constant speed prop.

Performance: G-164A – Max speed 237km/h (128kt), typical working speed range 130 to 160km/h (70 to 86kt). Initial rate of climb 1080ft/min. Super-B Turbine with PT6A-15AG – Working speed 210km/h (113kt). Range with max fuel 318km (172nm).

Weights: G-164A – Empty equipped for spraying 1220kg (2690lb), max certificated takeoff 2040kg (4500lb). Super-B Turbine – Empty equipped for spraying 1429kg (3150lb), max takeoff 3184kg (7020lb).

Dimensions: G-164A – Wing span 10.95m (35ft 11in), length 7.11m (23ft 4in), height 3.27m (10ft 9in). Wing area 20.5m^2 (328sq ft). Super Turbine B – Wing span upper 12.92m (42ft 5in), lower 12.36m (40ft 7in); length 8.41m (27ft 8in), height 3.68m (12ft 1in). Wing area 36.5m^2 (392.7sq ft).

Capacity: Pilot only. Hopper capacity 1514 lt (400US gal/333Imp gal).

Production: Schweizer built 2628 under contract for Grumman between 1959 and 1979, including more than 400 G-164s, 1330 G-164As and 832 G-164Bs. Also built under licence in Ethiopia.

History: The Ag-Cat is one of the most successful purpose designed agricultural aircraft yet built and has been in almost continuous production since 1959.

Grumman developed the G-164 Ag-Cat biplane in the mid 1950s, with the prototype making its maiden flight on May 27 1957. Some 400 initial G-164 Ag-Cats were delivered from 1959, fitted with a variety of radial engines including various Continentals, the 180kW (240hp) Gulf Coast W-670-240, the 185kW (245hp) Jacobs L-4 or 205 to 225kW (275 to 300hp) Jacobs engines.

The G-164A followed and was powered in its basic A/450 form by a 335kW (450hp) Pratt & Whitney R-985, and featured a greater maximum takeoff weight and additional fuel. The A/600 is similar other than its 450kW (600hp) R-1340 engine. The B/450 is based on the A/450 but with increased span wings, while the B/525 is powered by a 390kW (525hp) Continental/Page R-975.

The longer fuselage 450kW (600hp) R-1340 powered C/600 meanwhile forms the basis for the Pratt & Whitney Canada PT6A powered Turbo Ag-Cat D.

Recent models include the 450kW (600hp) R-1340 powered Super-B/600 and the PT6A powered Ag-Cat Super-B Turbine (various PT6A models are offered ranging from 375 to 560kW/680 to 750shp).

Until 1995 Schweizer had built all production Ag-Cats, firstly under contract for Grumman between 1959 and 1979, and again from 1981 when it bought the design and production rights. In 1995 Schweizer sold the Ag-Cat's manufacturing rights to the Ag-Cat Corp of Malden, Missouri. Current Ag-Cat production is of the Ag-Cat Super-B turbine.

Photo: Ag-Cats are often used for joyflights rather than ag-spraying. Pictured is a New Zealand registered example. (Dave Prossor)

Agusta A 109

Country of origin: Italy

Type: Twin engined utility & corporate helicopter

Powerplants: A 109A Mk II – Two Allison 250-C20B turboshafts rated at 300kW (400shp) max continuous operation, or 313kW (4200shp) for takeoff, derated to 260kW (346shp) for twin engine operation. A 109A Plus – Two Allison 250-C20Rs rated at 335kW (450shp).

Performance: A 109A – Max cruising speed 285km/h (154kt), economical cruising speed 233km/h (126kt). Initial rate of climb at sea level 2110ft/min. Range with standard fuel and no reserves 648km (350nm).

Weights: A 109A Mk II – Standard passenger version empty equipped 1418kg (3126lb), max takeoff 2600kg (5732lb). A 109A Plus – Empty equipped weight 1432kg (3157kg).

Dimensions: Main rotor diameter 11.00m (36ft 1in), length with rotors turning 13.05m (42ft 10in), fuselage length 10.71m (35ft 2in), height 3.30m (10ft 10in). Main rotor disc area 95.0m^2 (1022.9sq ft).

Capacity: Total accommodation for eight people including one pilot. In medevac configuration two stretchers and two medical attendants. Can also carry an external under slung load of up to 150kg (331lb).

Production: Approximately 550 A 109s of all variants (civil and military) had been built by 1996.

History: Conceived as a high performance general purpose light to medium helicopter, the A 109 has been one of the most successful and popular helicopters in its class during the course of its quarter century history.

The first of four A 109 prototypes flew on August 4 1971. VFR certification was announced on June 1 1975 and was preceded by series production which began in 1974. First production deliveries took place in late 1976 and certification for single seat IFR operations was granted on January 20 1977.

The base A 109A was superseded by the upgraded A 109A Mk II from September 1981. Improvements incorporated in the Mk II included a greater transmission rating, redesigned tailboom and a new tail rotor driveshaft, improved rotor blade life and modern avionics among others. The Mk II is also available in widebody configuration with increased internal volume courtesy of bulged fuselage side panels and reshaped fuel tanks under the cabin floor. The Mk II Plus has the more powerful 250-C20R-1 engines, as does the A 109C. The 109C also has composite rotor blades.

The A 109K first flew in April 1983 and is powered by two 470kW (640shp) max continuous operation rated Turboméca Arriel 1K1 turboshafts. The latest version of the A 109 to be offered is the PW206C powered A 109 Power, announced in 1995.

The A 109 has been developed into a number of mission specific configurations, aside from executive transport it is used widely in medevac, police and patrol roles worldwide. Previously medevac configured A 109As were based on the standard airframe, but modifications engineered by a US firm has resulted in the A 109 Max, with extended upward opening side doors and fairings giving a greater internal volume. Police versions have been fitted with FLIR and searchlights.

Photo: An EMS configured A 109A. Note the ski undercarriage. (Agusta)

Agusta A 119 Koala

Country of origin: Italy

Type: Light utility helicopter

Powerplants: Prototype – One 595kW (800shp) Turboméca Arriel 1 turboshaft driving a four blade main rotor and two blade tail rotor. Production aircraft – One 747kW (1002shp) takeoff rated Pratt & Whitney Canada PT6B-37 turboshaft.

Performance: Max cruising speed 260km/h (140kt). Service ceiling 17,915ft. Hovering ceiling in ground effect 10,890ft, out of ground effect 8040ft. Max range 653km (352nm). Endurance 3hr 45min.

Weights: Max takeoff with an internal load 1200kg (2645lb), max takeoff with a sling load 2720kg (5997lb).

Dimensions: Main rotor diameter 11.00m (36ft 1in), fuselage length 11.07m (36ft 4in). Main rotor disc area 95.0m^2 (1022.9sq ft).

Capacity: One pilot and passenger on flightdeck. Main cabin seats six in standard configuration. In an EMS configuration can accommodate two stretcher patients.

Production: First deliveries planned for late 1997. Planned annual production rate of 20 to 25 aircraft per year.

History: Agusta's newest helicopter, the widebody A 119 Koala is a relatively large single turbine powered helicopter designed for a range of utility transport missions where it makes economic sense to operate a single when the redundancy of a twin is not required.

Agusta began development work on the Koala in 1994, leading to the first prototype's maiden flight in early 1995. A second prototype flew later in that same year. Agusta was aiming to gain certification for the A 119 in late 1996, with first deliveries of production aircraft planned for late 1997.

The Koala's big selling feature is its large 'widebody' fuselage. Agusta says the cabin is 30% larger than the cabins of any other current production single engine helicopter. A measure of the cabin size is that it can accommodate two stretcher patients in an EMS role, along with two medical attendants. Most other single engine helicopters typically are only equipped for a single stretcher because of a lack of space.

Access to the main cabin is via two large sliding doors, one either side of the fuselage. A baggage compartment in the rear of the fuselage is also accessible in flight.

The first prototype Koala was powered by a Turboméca Arriel 1 turboshaft. Production aircraft meanwhile will have a 747kW (1002shp) takeoff rated Pratt & Whitney Canada PT6B-37. The Koala's composite four blade main rotor features a titanium fully articulated maintenance free hub with elastomeric bearings and composite grips.

Photo: The second A 119 Koala prototype in flight. Agusta claims the Koala's cabin is 30% larger than any other current production single engine helicopter. (Agusta)

AI(R) Avro RJ70 & BAe 146-100

Country of origin: United Kingdom

Type: Short range regional jet airliner

Powerplants: BAe 146-100 – Four 30.0kN (6700lb) Textron Lycoming ALF 502R-3s or four 31.0kN (7000lb) ALF 502R-5 turbofans. RJ70 – Four 27.3kN (6130lb) or 31.0kN (7000lb) Textron Lycoming LF 507 turbofans.

Performance: BAe 146-100 – Cruising speed 767km/h (414kt), long range cruising speed 669km/h (361kt). Range with standard fuel 3000km (1620nm), range with max payload 1630km (880nm). RJ70 – Cruising speed 801km/h (432kt), long range cruising speed 660km/h (356kt). Range with standard fuel 3620km (1952nm), range with max payload 2047km (1104nm).

Weights: 146-100 – Operating empty 23,288kg (51,342lb), max takeoff 38,100kg (84,000lb). RJ70 – Operating empty 23,781kg (52,430lb), max takeoff weight 38,100kg (84,100lb).

Dimensions: Wing span 26.21m (86ft 0in), length 26.20m (85ft 12in), height 8.61m (28ft 3in). Wing area 77.3m^2 (832.0sq ft).

Capacity: Flightcrew of two. Seating for alternatively 70 passengers at 84cm (33in) pitch five abreast, or 82 passengers six abreast in a 84cm (33in) pitch configuration, or up to 94 six abreast at 74cm (29in) pitch. Quiet Trader freighter version of the 146-100 capable of carrying standard size pallets or LD3 containers.

Production: 34 146-100s (including three VIP examples operated by the Royal Air Force) were built before production ceased in 1992. Orders had been placed for 27 RJ70s by late 1996.

History: The BAe 146-100 and Avro RJ70 are the smallest of a three member short range jet airliner family that was first conceived in the early 1970s.

The then Hawker Siddeley Aviation announced it was designing a short range quiet airliner powered by four small turbofans with British Government financial help in August 1973. Under the designation HS.146, large scale development lasted just a few months before a worsening economic recession made the risk of the project seem unjustifiable. Development then continued on a limited scale, but it was not until July 1978 that the project was officially relaunched, by which time Hawker Siddeley had been absorbed into the newly created British Aerospace.

The resulting BAe 146 thus made its first flight on September 3 1981, with certification being granted in early 1983, with first deliveries following shortly afterwards in May 1983.

In 1990 BAe first offered the improved RJ70 and RJ80 both of which are based on the 146-100. Seating 70 and 80 passengers respectively, these designs were optimised as regional jets and have matured into the RJ70 with improved LF 507 engines, and were marketed and manufactured by Avro Aerospace, a separate BAe company. Plans for a partnership with Taiwan Aerospace, which would have seen the RJ series built in Taiwan, fell through and Avro is now part of the AI(R) consortium. First RJ70 deliveries occurred in late 1993.

Photo: A 146-100 in the colours of Indonesian operator National Air. (AI(R)

AI(R) Avro RJ85 & BAe 146-200

Country of origin: United Kingdom

Type: Short range regional airliner

Powerplants: BAe 146-200 – Four 31.1kN (6968lb) Textron Lycoming ALF 502R-5 turbofans. RJ85 – Four 31.1kN (7000lb) Textron Lycoming LF 507 turbofans.

Performance: 146-200 – Cruising speed 767km/h (414kt), long range cruising speed 669km/h (377kt). Range with standard fuel 2910km (1620nm), range with max payload 2095km (1130nm). 146-200QC in freighter configuration – Same except for range with standard fuel 1935km (1045nm). RJ85 – Cruising speed 801km/h (432kt), long range cruising speed 674km/h (364kt). Range with standard fuel 3300km (1782nm), range with max payload 2127km (1148nm).

Weights: 146-200 – Operating empty 23,882kg (52,651lb), max takeoff 42,185kg (93,000lb). RJ85 – Operating empty 24,377kg (53,742lb), max takeoff 42,185kg (93,000lb).

Dimensions: Wing span 26.21m (86ft), length 28.60m (93ft 10in), height 8.59m (28ft 2in). Wing area 77.3m^2 (832sq ft).

Capacity: Flightcrew of two. Max seating in passenger cabin for 112 at six abreast and 74cm (29in) pitch. More typical seating configuration for 85 (hence RJ85 designation) at five abreast and 84cm (33in) pitch. 146-200 & RJ85 QT freighters can accommodate six standard 2.74 x 2.24m (108 x 88in) pallets, or a max of nine standard LD3 containers weighing up to 2720kg (6000lb) each. Max payload of the BAe 146-200QT freighter is 11,827kg (26,075lb), max payload of the BAe 146-200QC is 10,039kg (22,132lb).

Production: Production of the 146-200 ceased in early 1993, after 108 examples had been built. At the time of writing in late 1996 60 RJ85s had been ordered.

History: The BAe 146-200 is a lengthened development of the original short fuselage 146-100, while the AI(R) RJ85 in turn is a modernised version of the 146-200.

The 146-200 is essentially similar to its smaller stablemate, but has a 2.39m (7ft 8in) longer fuselage, is slightly higher, has 35% greater underfloor cargo volume, has slightly different performance figures and heavier weights. The stretch consists of five extra fuselage frame pitches. The first BAe 146-200 made the type's maiden flight on August 1 1982, while the UK CAA awarded the 146-200's type certificate on February 4 the following year.

Versions of the 146-200 include the 'Quiet Trader' freighter, which has been fairly successful because of its low external noise footprint and the 'Quick Change' passenger or freight convertible.

The subsequent RJ85, like the smaller RJ70 and larger RJ100, became a product of the Avro International Aerospace, featuring among improvements new LF 507 engines. First delivery of an RJ85 was in April 1993. Avro is now part of AI(R).

Photo: One of two BAe 146-200QCs operated by French operator Air Jet. (AI(R)

AI(R) Avro RJ100, RJ115 & BAe 146-300

Country of origin: United Kingdom

Type: Short range regional airliner

Powerplants: BAe 146-300 – Four 31.0kN (6970lb) Textron Lycoming ALF 502R-5 turbofans. RJ100 – Four 31.14kN (7000lb) Textron Lycoming LF 507 turbofans.

Performance: 146-300 – Max operating speed Mach 0.73, cruising speed 790km/h (426kt), long range cruising speed 700km/h (377kt). Range with standard fuel 2817km (1520nm), range with max payload 1927km (1040nm). RJ100 – Max operating speed Mach 0.73, cruising speed 800km/h (432kt), long range cruising speed 687km/h (371kt). Range with standard fuel 3098km (1671nm), range with max payload 2159km (1165nm). RJ115 – Same except for range with standard fuel 3325km (1794nm), and range with max payload 2723km (1469nm).

Weights: 146-300 – Operating empty 24,878kg (54,848lb), max takeoff 44,225kg (97,500lb). 146-300QT – Operating empty 23,126kg (50,985lb), max takeoff same. RJ100 – Operating empty 25,362kg (55,915lb), max takeoff 44,225kg (97,500lb). RJ100QT – Operating empty 23,706kg (52,263lb), max takeoff same. RJ115 – Operating empty 26,156kg (57,665lb), max takeoff same.

Dimensions: Wing span 26.21m (86ft 0in), length 30.99m (101ft 8in), height 8.61m (28ft 3in). Wing area 77.3m^2 (832sq ft).

Capacity: Flightcrew of two plus a maximum of 128 passengers at six abreast and 74cm (29in) pitch. Seating arrangements also for 100 at 84cm (33in) pitch and five abreast, and 116 at six abreast. 146-300QT and RJ100QT can accommodate standard 2.74 x 2.24m (108 x 88in) pallets, or LD3 containers. Max payload of 12,490kg (26,075lb).

Production: Production of the 146-300 ceased in early 1993, after 67 examples had been built. At the time of writing in late 1994 33 RJ100s had been ordered while no RJ115s had been ordered.

History: The 146-300 and RJ100 and RJ115 are the longest and largest members of the four engined BAe 146 and Avro/Aero International (Regional) Regional Jet families.

The 146-300 is a further stretched derivative of the original short fuselage BAe 146-100, but unlike the mid size 200 series, was not developed until later in the 1980s. The first 146-300, an aerodynamic prototype based on the original prototype 146-100 airframe, flew for the first time on May 1 1987, with certification granted in September that year.

The RJ100 and RJ115 are improved derivatives of the 146-300, sharing the latter's fuselage length but with new LF 507 engines and other minor improvements. The RJ115 differs from the RJ100 in having mid cabin emergency exits allowing extra high density seating, higher design weights and greater fuel capacity. Like the 146-200 and RJ85, freighter versions of the 146-300 and RJ100 are known as Quiet Traders, or QTs.

Photo: Ansett New Zealand BAe 146-300s on the ground at Christchurch. (Peter Clark)

AI(R) Jetstream 41

Country of origin: United Kingdom

Type: 29 seat commuter airliner

Powerplants: Two 1120kW (1500shp) AlliedSignal TPE331-14GR/HR turboprops driving five blade constant speed McCauley propellers on initial production aircraft, two 1230kW (1650shp) TPE331-14s on current production aircraft.

Performance: Max speed 547km/h (295kt), economical cruising speed 482km/h (260kt). Service ceiling 26,000ft. Range (initial production) with 29 passengers and reserves 1263km (681nm).

Weights: Empty 6350kg (14,000lb), max takeoff initial production 10,433kg (23,100lb), current production max takeoff 10,895kg (24,000lb).

Dimensions: Wing span 18.29m (60ft 0in), length 19.25m (63ft 2in), height 5.74m (18ft 10in). Wing area 32.6m^2 (350.8sq ft).

Capacity: Flightcrew of two. Main cabin seating for up to 29 at three abreast, seating for 27 with galley. Corporate shuttle configured J41s seat 16 at two abreast.

Production: Orders for the Jetstream 41 stood at 101 at late 1996, of which most were in service with airlines in Europe and the USA.

History: The Jetstream 41 is a stretched and modernised development of the 19 seat Jetstream 31, and is designed to compete in the highly competitive 29 seat commuter airliner class alongside such types as the Brasilia, Dornier 328 and Saab 340.

The Jetstream 41 (or J41) is based on the J31, the primary and most obvious difference being the 4.88m (16ft) fuselage stretch, consisting of a 2.51m (8ft 3in) plug forward of the wing, and a 2.36m (7ft 9in) stretch rear. The increased span wing (with reworked ailerons and flaps) is mounted lower on the fuselage so that it does not carry through the fuselage and interrupt the interior cabin aisle, as is the case on the Jetstream 31. Other airframe modifications include a new reprofiled six piece cockpit windscreen and extended wing root fairing with greater baggage capacity. More powerful AlliedSignal TPE331 turboprops, mounted in new nacelles with increased ground clearance, drive advanced five blade McCauley propellers. The flightdeck has modern EFIS cockpit with glass displays.

Development work on the J41 was announced in mid 1989, resulting in the type's first flight on September 25 1991. Three other aircraft were also used in the flight test program, with European JAA certification being awarded on November 23 1992. The first delivery occurred two days later on November 25.

The J41 was initially known as the BAe Jetstream 41, but BAe's establishment of a separate Jetstream Aircraft division in mid 1993 saw the name simplified to just Jetstream 41. From January 1996 the J41 has been part of the Aero International (Regional) stable.

From mid 1994, all aircraft delivered benefited from various payload and range performance improvements, resulting from uprated engines and a higher maximum takeoff weight.

Field Aircraft of the UK and Pilatus of Switzerland are risk sharing partners, while Gulfstream is to build 200 wingsets through to 2000.

Photo: AI(R) hopes to attract many J41 orders from existing J31 operators requiring an increase in capacity.

AI(R) ATR 42

Countries of origin: France and Italy

Type: Turboprop regional airliner

Powerplants: ATR 42-300 – Two flat rated 1340kW (1800shp) Pratt & Whitney Canada PW120s driving four blade constant speed Hamilton Standard propellers. ATR 42-320 – Two flat rated 1950shp (1455kW) PW121s. ATR 42-500 – two PW127Es driving six blade Ratier-Fagiec/ Hamilton Standard props.

Performance: ATR 42-300 – Max cruising speed 490km/h (265kt) economical cruising speed 450km/h (243kt). Range with max fuel and reserves at max cruising speed 4480km (2420nm), or 5040km (2720nm) at economical cruising speed. ATR 42-320 – Same as for ATR 42-300 except max cruising speed 498km/h (269kt). ATR 42-500 cruising speed over 560km/h (300kt).

Weights: ATR 42-300 – Operating empty 10,285kg (22,674lb), max takeoff 16,700kg (36,817lb). ATR 42-320 – Operating empty 10,290kg (22,685lb), max takeoff as per 42-300.

Dimensions: Wing span 24.57m (80ft 8in), length 22.67m (74ft 5in), height 7.59m (24ft 11in). Wing area 54.5m^2 (586.6sq ft).

Capacity: Flightcrew of two. Maximum passenger accommodation for 50, 48 or 46 pax at 76cm (30in) pitch and four abreast. Typical seating arrangement for 42 at 81cm (32in) pitch. ATR 42 Cargo – Nine containers with a 4000kg payload.

Production: As at late 1996 total orders for all versions of the ATR 42 stood at approximately 320, with 295 in service.

History: Aerospatiale and Alenia (then Aeritalia) established Avions de Transport Regional as a *Groupement d'Intéret Economique* (as is Airbus) to develop a family of regional airliners. The ATR 42 was the consortium's first aircraft and was launched in October 1981.

The first of two ATR 42 prototypes flew for the first time on August 16 1984. Italian and French authorities granted certification in September 1985 and the first ATR 42 entered airline service on December 9 1985.

The ATR 42-300 is the initial and standard production version of the ATR 42 family and features greater payload range and a higher takeoff weight than the prototypes. The similar ATR 42-320 differs in having the more powerful PW121 engines for better hot and high performance, while the ATR 42 Cargo is a quick change freight/passenger version of the 42-300.

The ATR 42-500 is the first significantly improved version of the aircraft and features a revised interior, more powerful PW127Es for a substantially increased cruising speed (565km/h/305kt) driving six blade propellers, a 1870km (1010nm) maximum range, the cockpit, elevators and rudders of the stretched ATR 72 (described separately), plus new brakes and landing gear and strengthened wing and fuselage for higher weights. The first ATR 42-500 delivery was first delivered in October 1996.

ATR is now a part of Aero International (Regional), the consortium established in January 1996 and incorporating ATR, Avro and Jetstream. AI(R) handles sales, marketing and support for both the ATRs, plus the Avro RJs and the Jetstream 41.

Photo: An ATR 42 in Royal Air Maroc colours, one of two in service with the airline.

AI(R) ATR 72

Countries of origin: France and Italy

Type: Turboprop regional airliner

Powerplants: ATR 72-200 – Two 1610kW (2160shp) Pratt & Whitney Canada PW124B turboprops driving four blade Hamilton Standard propellers. ATR 72-210 – Two 1850kW (2480shp) P&WC PW127s.

Performance: ATR 72-200 – Max cruising speed at 15,000ft 526km/h (284kt), economical cruising speed 460km/h (248kt). Range with reserves at max optional weight 1195km (645nm), range with 66 pax 2665km (1200nm). ATR 72-210 – Same except for max cruising speed.

Weights: Operating empty 12,500kg (27,558lb), max takeoff 21,500kg (47,400lb).

Dimensions: Wing span 27.05m (88ft 9in), length 21.17m (89ft 2in), height 7.65m (25ft 1in). Wing area 61.0m^2 (656.6sq ft).

Capacity: Flightcrew of two. Max seating for 74 passengers at four abreast and 76cm (30in) pitch. More typical seating for between 64 and 70 passengers, with seat pitch starting from 81cm (32in). With larger forward freight door fitted it can accommodate a payload of 7200kg (15,875lb) in 13 containers. ATR 52C – 7500kg (16,535lb) payload comprising pallets or five LD3 containers.

Production: As at late 1996 approximately 190 ATR 72s had been ordered, of which 175 were in service.

History: The ATR 72 is essentially a stretched larger capacity version of the ATR 42 and was launched in January 1986.

The first of three ATR 72 development aircraft flew for the first time on October 27 1988, followed by the awarding of French and then US certification in late 1989. Entry into service was on October 27 1989.

Significant differences between the ATR 72 and the smaller and older ATR 42 include a 4.50m (14ft 9in) fuselage stretch and reworked wings. The ATR 72's wings are new outboard of the engine nacelles and with 30% of it made up of composite materials, comprising composite spars and skin panels and a carbon fibre wing box.

Aside from the baseline ATR 72-200, two developments have been offered, the ATR 72-210 and the ATR 52C. The ATR 72-210 is optimised for operations in hot and high conditions, and has more powerful PW127 engines for better takeoff performance.

The ATR 52C is an as yet unlaunched derivative with a redesigned tail to incorporate a rear loading ramp. Designed for both military and commercial operators its development depends upon ATR finding risk sharing partners to participate in the development of the revised tail. As with the ATR 42, a military maritime patrol version known as the Petrel 72 has also been offered.

The ATR 72 would have formed the basis for the ATR 82, a 78 seat stretched development. The ATR 82 would have been powered by two Allison AE 2100 turboprops (ATR studied turbofans for a time) and would have a cruising speed as high as 610km/h (330kt). The ATR 82 was suspended when AI(R) was formed in early 1996.

The ATR 42/72 could however form the basis of the AI(R) 58 and AI(R) 70 regional jets which would feature the ATR's fuselage, a new wing and turbofan engines.

Photo: An ATR 72 of New Zealand's Mount Cook. Note fuselage stretch compared with the ATR 42. (AI(R)

Airbus A300B2 & B4

Country of origin: European consortium

Type: Medium range widebody airliner

Powerplants: A300B4 & A300B2 – Two 227kN (51,000lb) General Electric CF6-50Cs or two 236kN (53,000lb) Pratt & Whitney JT9D-9 turbofans.

Performance: Typical high speed cruising speed 917km/h (495kt), typical long range cruising speed 847km/h (457kt). Range with 269 passengers and reserves 5375km (2900nm) for A300B4-200. A300B2-200 range with the same parameters 3430km (1850nm).

Weights: A300B2-200 – Operating empty 85,910kg (189,400lb), max takeoff 142,000kg (313,055lb). A300B4-200 – Operating empty 88,500kg (195,109lb), max takeoff 165,000kg (363,760lb).

Dimensions: Wing span 44.84m (147ft 1in), length 53.62m (175ft 11in), height 16.53m (54ft 2in). Wing area 260.0m^2 (2798.7sq ft).

Capacity: A300B2 & A300B4 – Flightcrew of two pilots and a flight engineer. Seating for between 220 and 336 passengers in main cabin depending on configuration. A300B2 and B4 forward and rear belly hold cargo compartments can carry a total of 20 LD3 containers; or four 2.24 x 3.17m pallets in the forward hold.

Production: Orders for all versions of the A300B2 and B4 stood at 248 when production was completed in 1984. Approximately 244 in service at late 1996.

History: The Airbus A300 is significant not only for being a commercial success in its own right, but for being the first design of Europe's most successful postwar airliner manufacturer.

Aerospatiale of France, CASA of Spain and the forerunners of Germany's Deutsche Aerospace and British Aerospace formed the Airbus Industrie consortium in the late 1960s to specifically develop a twin engined 300 seat widebodied 'air bus' to fill a perceived market gap.

The original 300 seat airliner design matured into a smaller 250 seater, the A300 designation gaining a B to denote the change. Two prototype A300B1s were built, the first of these flying from Toulouse, France on October 28 1972, the second on February 5 the next year. The General Electric CF6 was the powerplant choice for initial A300s. Following the prototype A300B1s was the 2.65m (8ft 8in) longer A300B2, the first production version which first flew in April 1974. The B2 entered service with Air France on May 23, 1974.

Subsequent versions were the B2-200 with Krueger leading edge flaps and different wheels and brakes; the B2-300 with increased weights for greater payload and multi stop capability; the B4-100 a longer range version of the B2 with Krueger flaps; and the increased max takeoff weight B4-200 which featured reinforced wings and fuselage, improved landing gear and optional rear cargo bay fuel tank. A small number of A300C convertibles were also built, these featured a main deck freight door behind the wing on the left hand side.

Production of the A300B4 ceased in May 1984, with manufacture switching to the improved A300-600.

Photo: A GE CF6 powered A300B4 of US carrier Carnival Airlines moments before touchdown. The A300 was the world's first widebody twinjet and laid the foundation for Airbus' commercial success. (Airbus)

Airbus A300-600

Country of origin: European consortium

Type: Medium range widebody airliner

Powerplants: Two 262.4kN (59,000lb) General Electric CF6-80C2A1s, or two 273.6kN (61,500lb) CF6-80C2A5s, or two 249kN (56,000lb) Pratt & Whitney PW4156s or two 258kN (58,000lb) PW4158 turbofans.

Performance: A300-600R – Max cruising speed 897km/h (484kt), long range cruising speed 875km/h (472kt). Range at typical airline operating weight with 267 passengers and baggage and 370km (200nm) reserves and standard fuel 7505km (4050nm) with CF6s, or 7540km (4070nm) with PW4000s. A300-600 – Range at same parameters 6670km (3600nm). A300-600F – Range with max payload, and reserves 4908km (2650nm).

Weights: A300-600 – Operating empty with CF6s 89,670kg (197,686lb), with PW4000s 89,595kg (197,523lb). Max takeoff 170,500kg (375,855lb), or high gross weight option 171,700kg (378,535lb). A300-600R – Operating empty 89,699kg (197,686lb) with CF6s, or 89,595kg (197,523lb) with PW4000s, max takeoff 170,500kg (375,855lb), or optionally 171,700kg (378,535lb). A300-600F – (CF6 powered) Operating empty 78,854kg (173,840lb), max takeoff 170,500kg (375,900lb).

Dimensions: Wing span 44.84m (147ft 1in), length 54.08m (177ft 5in), height 16.62m (54ft 6.5in). Wing area 260.0m^2 (2798.7sq ft).

Capacity: Flightcrew of two. Typical two class arrangement for 26 first class passengers at six abreast and 240 economy class passengers at eight abreast. The A300-600 and -600R can carry a total of 22 LD3 containers in forward and aft belly cargo holds. A300-600F total payload in underfloor and main deck cargo holds 55,017kg (121,290lb).

Production: A total of 224 A300-600s of all variants had been ordered by December 1996, of which 176 were in service.

History: The A300-600 family followed on from the earlier A300B4 and incorporated a number of significant improvements and refinements.

These included a two crew EFIS cockpit, the tail empennage of the A310 which increased freight and passenger payloads, new avionics, small winglets, simplified systems, greater use of composites, Fowler flaps and increased camber on the wings, new brakes and APU, and improved payload/range through an extensive drag reducing airframe clean up.

The A300-600 was further developed into the longer range A300-600R, its extended range courtesy of a fuel trim tank in the tailplane and higher maximum takeoff weights.

Convertible freight and passenger versions of all variants of the A300 have been offered, as has the all freight A300-600F. The first of these new build pure freighter A300s, one of 36 on order for Federal Express, flew in December 1993. Airbus also offers conversion packages of existing passenger A300s into freighters with a left side forward freight door and strengthened floor.

Photo: An Olympic Airways A300-600R, one of eight in service with the Greek flag carrier. (Airbus)

Airbus A310

Country of origin: European consortium

Type: Medium to long range widebody airliner

Powerplants: Initial powerplant choice of either two 213.5kN (48,000lb) Pratt & Whitney JT9D-7R4D1s, or two 222.4kN (50,000lb) General Electric CF6-80A3 turbofans. Current choices of 238kN (53,500lb) CF6-80C2A2s or 262.4kN (59,000lb) CF6-80C2A8 from General Electric, or from Pratt & Whitney either 231.2kN (52,000lb) PW4152s, or 249.1kN (56,000lb) PW4156 turbofans.

Performance: Max cruising speed 897km/h (484kt), long range cruising speed 850km/h (459kt). Range at typical airliner operating weight with 218 passengers and baggage and reserves 6800km (3670nm) for A310-200, 7982km (4310nm) for CF6 powered A310-300, 9580km (5170nm) for high gross weight A310-300 with CF6s.

Weights: A310-200 with CF6-80C2A2s – Operating empty 80,142kg (176,683lb), max takeoff 142,000kg (313,055lb). A310-300 with CF6-80C2A8s – Operating empty 80,329kg (177,095lb), max takeoff 150,000kg (330,695lb) standard, or higher gross weight options through to 164,000kg (361,560lb).

Dimensions: Wing span 43.89m (144ft 0in), length 46.66m (153ft 1in), height 15.80m (51ft 10in). Wing area 219.0m^2 (2357.3sq ft).

Capacity: Flightcrew of two. Max passenger capacity at nine abreast 280. Typical two class arrangement for 20 passengers at six abreast and 192 economy class passenger eight abreast. Cargo capacity in fore and aft underfloor compartments can hold 2.44 x 3.17m (88 x 125in) pallets or a total of up to 15 LD3 containers.

Production: Total orders held for the A310 stood at 258 at December 1996. 222 were in service in late 1996.

History: The A310 first began life as the A300B10, one of a number of projected developments and derivatives of Airbus' original A300B airliner.

While based on the larger A300, the A310 features a number of major differences. The fuselage was shortened by 13 frames compared to the A300B, reducing seating to around 200 to 230 passengers. A new higher aspect ratio wing of smaller span and area was developed. New and smaller horizontal tail surfaces and a two crew flightdeck were new features, while the engine pylons were common to suit both engine options.

The first flight of the A310 occurred on April 3 1982, after the program was launched in July 1978. Service entry was with Lufthansa in April 1983. Early production A310s did not have the small winglets that became a feature of later build A310-200s and the A310-300. The A310-300 is a longer range development of the base A310-200, and has been in production since 1985. This version can carry a further 7000kg (15,430lb) of fuel in the tailplane.

The A310-200F freighter is available new build or as a conversion of existing aircraft (13 A310s were being converted to freighters for Federal Express by Airbus partner Deutsche Aerospace), as is the A310-200C convertible, which first entered service with Dutch operator Martinair in 1984.

Photo: An A310 of France's Air Liberte. Apart from the shorter the fuselage, the A310 can be distinguished from the A300 by the above wing emergency exit. (Airbus)

Airbus A319

Country of origin: European consortium

Type: Short range narrow body airliner

Powerplants: Two 98 to 104kN (22,000 to 23,500lb) class CFM International CFM56-5As turbofans or International Aero Engines IAE V2500-A5s.

Performance: Range at 64 tonne (141,095lb) takeoff weight 3520km (1900nm), range at 68 tonne (149,914lb) takeoff weight 5000km (2700nm).

Weights: Operating empty 39,884kg (87,930lb), max takeoff 64,000 or 68,000kg (141,094 or 149,912lb).

Dimensions: Wing span 33.91m (111ft 3in), length 33.8m (110ft 11in), height (as for A320) 11.80m (38ft 8.5in). Wing area 122.4m^2 (1317.5sq ft).

Capacity: Seating for 124 passengers in a typical two class configuration (eight premium class and 116 economy class). High density single class layout as specified by Air Inter seats 142 passengers.

Production: At late 1996 total orders for the A319 stood at 120.

History: The A319 is the latest and smallest member of Airbus' single aisle airliner family, and is likely to remain the consortium's smallest airliner.

The A319 program was launched at the Paris Airshow in June 1993 on the basis of just six orders placed by ILFC late in 1992 and the predicted better prospects of the commercial airliner market. The first order for the A319 from an airline came from French carrier Air Inter, its order for six was announced in February 1994. Since then Swissair, Air Canada, Lufthansa and United are among the customers that have ordered the A319. Air Canada, Air Inter and United already operate A320s, while Swissair became the first operator of all three Airbus narrowbodies in April 1996, as it also has A320s and A321s on order and in service.

The A319 flew for the first time on August 25 1995 from Hamburg in Germany. European JAA certification and service entry, with Swissair, took place in April 1996.

The A319 is a minimum change, destretched or shortened derivative of the highly successful A320. The major difference between the A320 and A319 is that the latter is shorter by seven fuselage frames, while in almost all other respects the A319 and A320 are identical. A side benefit from the minimum change concept is that the A319 has the same fuel tankage as the A320 but a reduced max takeoff weight, and so has greater range.

Like the A321, A330 and A340, the A319 features Airbus' common two crew glass cockpit with sidestick controllers first introduced on the A320. There are significant crew training cost benefits and operational savings from this arrangement as the A319, A320 and A321 can all be flown by pilots with the same type rating, meaning that the same flightcrew pool can fly any of the three types. Further, the identical cockpit means reduced training times for crews converting to the larger A330 and A340.

Like the A321, the A319's final assembly takes place in Hamburg with Deutsche Aerospace Airbus. Final assembly of all other Airbus airliners, including the A320, takes place at Toulouse.

Photo: An A319 in Swissair livery. This carrier was the first to operate all three members of the A320 family, and the first to place the A319 into service. (Airbus)

Airbus A320

Country of origin: European consortium

Type: Short to medium range narrowbody airliner

Powerplants: Two either 105kN (23,500lb) or 111.2kN (25,000lb) CFM International CFM56-5A1 turbofans or 118kN (26,500lb) CFM56-5A3s or -5B4s or two 111.2kN (25,000lb) International Aero Engines IAE V2500-A1 or V2500-A5 turbofans.

Weights: A320-200 – Operating empty with V2500s 42,069kg (92,746lb); with CFM56s 41,782kg (92,113lb). Standard max takeoff for both versions 73,500kg (162,040lb) or optionally 75,500kg (166,445lb) or 77,000kg (169,755lb).

Performance: A320-200 – Max cruising speed 903km/h (487kt) at 28,000ft, economical cruising speed 840km/h (454kt) at 37,000ft. Range with 150 passengers and reserves with CFM56-5A1s 4905km (2650nm), or 5185km (2800nm) with CFM56-5A3/5B4s, or -5A1s 5278km (2850nm), with V2500s 5000km (2700nm) or optionally 5370km (2900nm) or 5463km (2950nm).

Dimensions: Wing span 33.91m (111ft 3in), length 37.57m (123ft 3in), height 11.80m (38ft 9in). Wing area 122.4m^2 (1317.5sq ft).

Capacity: Flightcrew of two. Main cabin can accommodate a maximum of 179 passengers in a high density layout. Typical two class seating arrangement for 12 passengers at four abreast and 138 at six abreast. A total of seven LD3 derived LD3-46 containers or palletised cargo can be stored in the underbelly forward (four) and rear (three) freight holds.

Production: As of late 1996, firm orders for 778 A320s had been placed, of which 550 were in service around the world.

History: Airbus Industrie's second all new design, slotting into the then vacant 150 seat category, has been a major sales success and incorporates a number of new advanced technologies. The end result was and still is considered the state of the art in airliner design.

A major technological advance with the A320 is its computerised fly-by-wire control system, the first airliner to have this feature. The fly-by-wire system incorporates flight envelope protection features which makes it impossible to exceed certain flight parameters such as G limits and the aircraft's maximum operating speed and angle of attack etc. Central also to the A320 is the advanced electronic cockpit, with six fully integrated EFIS cockpit displays and innovative side stick controllers in place of conventional control columns. The A320 also employs a relatively high percentage of composite materials compared to earlier designs.

The A320's first flight occurred on February 22 1987, while certification was awarded on February 26 1988. Launch customer Air France took delivery of its first A320 in March that year.

The initial production version was the A320-100, which was built in only small numbers before being replaced by the definitive A320-200 (which was certificated in November 1988) with increased max takeoff weight, greater range and winglets. The stretched A321 and shortened A319 are described separately. All three share a common pilot type rating.

Photo: A United Airlines A320. United has ordered 50 A320s and 24 A319s, making it one of the largest confirmed A320 series buyer at the time of writing. (Airbus)

Airbus A321

Country of Origin: European consortium

Type: Short to medium range single aisle airliner

Powerplants: Choice of two 133.4kN (30,000lb) International Aero Engines V2530-A5 or CFM International CFM56-5B1 turbofans. CFM56-5B2s of 139.7kN (31,000lb) available as an option.

Performance: Max cruising speed 903km/h (488kt), economical cruising speed 828km/h (447kt). Range with 186 passengers and reserves 4352km (2350nm) with V2530s, 4260km (2300nm) with CFM56s.

Weights: Operating empty 47,626kg (104,997lb) with V2530s, 47,512kg (104,746lb) with CFM56s. Max takeoff (with either engine option) 83,000kg (182,984lb).

Dimensions: Wing span 34.09m (111ft 10in), length 44.50m (146ft 0in), height 11.80m (38ft 8.5in). Wing area 123.0m^2 (1320sq ft).

Capacity: Flightcrew of two. Maximum passenger accommodation in a high density layout of 220 passengers. Passenger accommodation in a typical two class arrangement consists of 16 passengers at four abreast, and 170 passengers at six abreast. Underfloor forward and rear cargo compartments have 40% greater volume than the A320 and can house LD3 derived LD3-46 containers or palletised cargo. Maximum payload for both engine powered variants is just under 20 tonnes (44,100lb).

Production: Orders for the A321 stood at 199 by late 1996. Total of 60 A321s in service by late 1996.

History: Like the tubby A319, the A321 is a minimum change, in this case stretched, development of the successful A320.

The major change over the A320 is the stretched fuselage, with forward and rear fuselage plugs totalling 6.96m (22ft 10in) (front plug immediately forward of wing 4.27m/14ft, rear plug directly behind the wing 2.67m/8ft 9in). Other changes include strengthening of the undercarriage to cope with the higher weights, more powerful engines, a simplified and refined fuel system and larger tyres for better braking. A slightly modified wing with double slotted flaps and modifications to the flight controls allows the A321's flying characteristics to closely resemble the A320's. The A321 features an identical flightdeck to that on the A319 and A320, and shares the same type rating as the smaller two aircraft.

Close commonality to the A319 and A320 has a number of benefits including reductions in crew training and the common type rating for all three aircraft, common engines and savings on spares. A disadvantage of the minimum change concept with the basic A321-100 though is a reduction in range compared to the A320, as no extra fuel tanks were added to compensate for the extra weight.

To overcome this Airbus launched the longer range, heavier A321-200 development in 1995 which will have a full pax transcontinental US range. This is achieved through higher thrust engines and minor structural strengthening and greater fuel capacity. It first flew in December 1996.

Photo: An Austrian Airlines A321 powered by CFM56s. (Airbus)

Airbus A330

Country of origin: European consortium

Type: Large capacity medium range airliner

Powerplants: A330-300 – Choice of two 300.3kN (67,500lb) General Electric CF6-80E1A2s, 286.7kN (64,000lb) Pratt & Whitney PW4164s, or PW4168s or 304.6kN (68,000lb) Rolls-Royce Trent 768 or Trent 772 turbofans. Long range A330 choice of P&W PW4164s or PW4168s or RR Trent 768s or 772s.

Performance: Max cruising speed 880km/h (475kt) at 33,000ft, economical cruising speed 860km/h (464kt). Range with 335 pax and reserves 8340km (4500nm) with CF6s, or 8430km (4550nm) with P&W engines, or 8600km (4640nm) with Trents; A330 longer range version range 8980km (4850nm) with CF6s or Trents.

Weights: A330-300 – Operating empty 119,745kg (263,993lb) with CF6 engines, 120,311kg (265,240lb) with PW4000s, and 119,472kg (263,391lb) with Trents. Max takeoff 212,000kg (467,380lb). Long range A330 – Empty 120,750kg (266,200lb) with PW4000s or 120,1707kg (264,925lb) with CF6s, max takeoff 217,000kg (478,400lb).

Dimensions: Wing span 60.30m (197ft 10in), length 63.70m (209ft 0in), height 16.83m (55ft 2in). Wing area 363.1m^2 (3908.4sq ft).

Capacity: Flightcrew of two. Passenger seating arrangements for 295 in three classes or 335 in two class (30 first class at 2+3+2 and 305 economy at 2+4+2). Max passengers in high density configuration 440. Front and rear underbelly cargo holds can take 32 LD3 containers or 11 pallets.

Production: Total orders stood at 145 at late 1996, of which 45 were in service.

History: The A330 is the biggest member of Airbus' twinjet family and is closely related to the four engined long range A340 with which it shares near identical systems, airframe, cockpit and wings, the only major difference being the twin engine configuration.

The A340 and A330 were launched simultaneously in June 1987. Although developed in parallel the A330 made its first flight after the A340 on November 2 1992, and it was the first aircraft to achieve simultaneous European Joint Airworthiness Authorities (JAA) and US FAA certification, on October 21 1993. Entry into service took place by the end of that year.

Differences from the A340 aside from the number of engines are slight changes to the wing and internal systems, including fuel tankage. The A330 (like the A340) takes advantage of a number of technologies first pioneered on the A320, including the advanced EFIS cockpit with side stick controllers and fly-by-wire computerised flight control system.

While the standard A330-300 shares the same fuselage length as the A340-300, Airbus has studied various stretched (A330-400) and shortened (A330-100 and -200) versions. The shortened A330-200 was formally launched in 1996 as a long range 767-300ER replacement, but is described separately. One stretched version proposed would have lower deck seating where the forward freight hold currently is.

Photo: This view of a Malaysia Airlines A330 shows to good effect the wing shared by the A330 and A340. (Airbus)

Airbus A330-200

Country of origin: European consortium

Type: Medium to long range widebody airliner

Powerplants: A330-200 – Choice of two 300.3kN (67,500lb) General Electric CF6-80E1A2s, 286.7kN (64,000lb) Pratt & Whitney PW4164s, or PW4168s or 304.6kN (68,000lb) Rolls-Royce Trent 768 or Trent 772 turbofans.

Performance: Max cruising speed 880km/h (475kt) at 33,000ft, economical cruising speed 860km/h (464kt). Range with 256 passengers in three class arrangement and baggage 11,850km (6400nm), range with 293 passengers in a typical two class arrangement 8335km (4500nm).

Weights: A330-200 – Operating empty 120,170kg (264,925lb) with CF6 engines, 120,750kg (266,500lb) with PW4168s, or 120,625kg (265,150lb) with Trents. Max takeoff 230,000kg (507,050lb).

Dimensions: Wing span 60.30m (197ft 10in), length 59.00m (193ft 7in), height 16.83m (55ft 2in). Wing area 363.1m^2 (3908.4sq ft).

Capacity: Flightcrew of two. Passenger seating arrangements for 256 in three classes or 293 in two classes. Front and rear underbelly cargo holds can take 26 LD3 containers or six freight pallets and passenger baggage.

Production: Total A330-200 orders stood at 31 at late 1996, with service entry planned for first half of 1998.

History: The A330-200 is the newest member of Airbus' twinjet family and is a long range, shortened development of the standard A330, developed in part as a replacement for the A300-600R and a competitor to the 767-300ER.

Airbus launched development of the A330-200 in November 1995, followed by the first customer order, for 13 from ILFC, in February 1996. First flight is scheduled for mid 1997, with certification and first customer deliveries planned for the second quarter of 1996.

The A330-200 is closely related to the A330-300 on which it is based, and shares near identical systems, airframe, cockpit and wings, the only major difference being the fuselage length. Compared with the -300 the A330-200 is 10 frames shorter, and so has an overall length of 59.00m (193ft 7in), compared with 63.70m (209ft 0in) for the standard length aircraft. This allows the A330-200 to seat 256 passengers in a three class configuration, or alternatively 293 in two classes.

Because of the decreased length the A330-200 will feature enlarged horizontal and vertical tail services (to compensate in the loss of moment arm with the shorter fuselage). Another important change is the centre fuel tank, which increases the A330-200's fuel capacity over the -300's, and results in the -200's 11,850km (6400nm) range.

Apart from ILFC, A330-200 customers announced at late 1996 were Korean Air (two) and Emirates (16 with seven optioned)

Photo: An A330-200 as it will appear in Emirates livery. Emirates will use the type to replace its fleet of A300s and A310s. (Airbus)

Airbus A340

Country of origin: European consortium

Type: Long to ultra long range widebody airliner

Powerplants: Four 138.8kN (31,200lb) CFM International CFM56-5C or 145kN (32,550lb) CFM56-5C3 turbofans.

Performance: A340-200 – Max cruising speed 914km/h (494kt), economical cruising speed 880km/h (475kt). Range at typical airline operating weight with 263 passengers and reserves 13,805km (7450nm). A340-300 – Speeds same. Range at typical airline operating weight with 295 passengers and reserves 12,415km (6700nm).

Weights: A340-200 – Operating empty 123,085kg (271,350lb), max takeoff 257,000kg (566,590lb). A340-300 – Operating empty 126,873kg (279,700lb), max takeoff 257,000kg (566,590lb) or 260,000kg (573,200lb).

Dimensions: A340-200 – Wing span 60.30m (197ft 0in), length 59.39m (194ft 10in), height 16.74m (54ft 11in). Wing area 363.1m^2 (3908.4sq ft). A340-300 – Same except for length 63.70m (209ft 0in).

Capacity: Flightcrew of two. A340-200 – Typical three class arrangement for 263 pax, or 303 in two classes. A340-300 – Typical three class accommodation for 303, or 335 in two classes. Fore and aft underbelly holds can accommodate LD3 containers or pallets.

Production: A total of 146 A340s had been ordered by late 1996, of which 80 were in airline service.

History: The four engine A340 can currently lay claim to the title of the world's longest range airliner in service.

The combined A330 and A340 program was launched in June 1987, with the A340's first flight occurring four years later on October 25 1991 (an A340-300). The A340 entered service with Lufthansa and Air France in March 1993, following JAA certification being awarded the previous December.

The A340 shares the same cockpit including side stick controllers and EFIS, plus fly-by-wire, basic airframe, systems, fuselage and wing with the A330. The major difference is the four CFM56 powerplants, the four engine configuration being more efficient for long range flights (as twins need more power for engine out on takeoff performance).

Two basic A340 variants on offer are the standard A340-300, which has the same fuselage length as the A330, and the shorter fuselage, longer range A340-200.

The heavier A340-300E is available in 271,000kg (597,450lb) and 275,000kg (606,275lb) max takeoff weights, their typical ranges with 295 passengers are 13,155km (7100nm) and 13,525km (7300nm) respectively. Power for these models is from 152.3kN (34,000lb) CFM56-5C4s (the most powerful CFM56s built). Airbus claims the A340-300E has the greatest cargo capacity of any passenger aircraft with max passengers and bags. The first A340-300Es were delivered to Singapore Airlines in April 1996.

The 275,000kg (606,275lb) max takeoff weight A340-8000 is based on the -200 but has extra fuel in three additional rear cargo hold tanks and offers a 15,000km (8100nm) range with 232 three class passengers (hence the A340-8000 designation). It too is powered by CFM56-5C4s.

All versions are offered with underfloor passenger sleepers.

Photo: One of Singapore Airlines' A340-300Es. (Airbus)

Airbus A340-500 & -600

Country of origin: European consortium

Type: Long range widebody airliners

Powerplants: Four 222 to 267kN (50,000 to 60,000lb) thrust class General Electric turbofans (designation unknown at late 1996).

Performance: Speeds for both variants not published at late 1996, but Airbus says increased design cruise speed over base A340 models. A340-500 – Range with 316 passengers 15,400km (8300nm). A340-600 – Range with 372 passengers 13,710km (7400nm).

Weights: A340-500 – Max takeoff 356,000kg (784,150lb). A340-600 – Max takeoff 356,000kg (784,150lb).

Dimensions: A340-500 – Wing span 63.6m (208.7ft), length 66.8m (205.1ft). A340-600 – Wing span 63.6m (208.7ft), length 74.4m (244.1ft).

Capacity: A340-500 – Flightcrew of two. Typical three class seating for 316 passengers. A340-600 Flightcrew of two. Typical three class seating for 372 passengers.

Production: Launch decision anticipated for early 1997, which would allow an entry into service in 2000. Airbus has forecast a demand for 3600 airliners in the 250 to 400 seat category. Airbus hopes in broadening its product line in this class that it would capture 50% of that market.

History: In late 1996 the Airbus A340-500 and A340-600 seemed very close to launch, which would further broaden the European consortium's product line armoury against the 777-200 and -300.

The A340-600 would be stretched by 10.7m (35ft) compared with the A340-300, which would allow it to seat 372 passengers in a typical three class arrangement. This would give Airbus a true replacement for ageing Boeing 747-100s and -200s and a direct competitor to the stretched 777-300 (albeit one with a 50 tonne higher MTOW and substantially greater range).

The A340-500 meanwhile would be stretched by only 3.2m (10.5ft) compared with the A340-300, and so would seat only 316 in three classes, but it would have a massive range of 15,400km (8300nm), which would make it the longest ranging airliner in the world save for the 747-500X, if the latter is launched.

The two new A340 models would share a common wing. The wing would be based on the A330/A340's but would be 1.6m (5.2ft) longer and have a tapered wingbox insert, increasing wing area and fuel capacity. Both models would feature three fuselage plugs. The other change to the A340 airframe would be the A330-200's larger fin and enlarged horizontal area stabilisers. To cope with the increased weights the centre undercarriage main gear would be a four wheel bogie, rather than a two wheel unit.

Both new A340s would feature Airbus' common two crew flightdeck.

Power would be from four new General Electric turbofans in the 222 to 267kN (50,000 to 60,000lb) thrust class, which would resemble scaled down GE90s, and have a bypass ratio of 9.4. A second possible engine option had not been proposed at the time of writing. Airbus claims the new jets would have 20% better fuel burn and 13% better DOCs per trip compared with the 747-400.

If Airbus launches the new A340s during 1997 (which seemed likely in late 1996) the new derivatives could be in service in 2000.

Photo: An artist's impression of the 375 seat A340-600. (Airbus)

Airbus A300-600ST Super Transporter

Country of origin: European consortium

Type: Oversize cargo freighter

Powerplants: Two 262.4kN (59,000lb) class General Electric CF6-80C2A8 turbofans.

Performance: Max cruising speed 780km/h (421kt). Range with a 40 tonne payload 2400km (1295nm), range with a 30 tonne (66,150lb) payload 4000km (2160nm).

Weights: Max payload 45.5 tonnes (100,310lb), max takeoff 150,000kg (330,675lb).

Dimensions: Wing span 44.84m (147ft 1in), length 56.16m (184ft 4in), height 17.25m (56ft 6in). Wing area 260m^2 (2798.7sq ft). Internal useable length 37.70m (123ft 8in), cross section diameter 7.40m (24ft 3in).

Capacity: The A300-600ST's max payload of 45.5 tonnes (100,300lb) is unlikely to be fully utilised, as the emphasis of the design is on volume rather than payload. The internal main cabin volume is 1400m^3 (49,442cu ft), and can carry a range of oversize components, such as a fully equipped A330 or A340 wing shipset, or two A320/321 wing shipsets, or two A310 fuselage sections (front & rear). Internal volume can also house an Ariane rocket launcher section. It is anticipated that various military and oversize civil freighter roles could be fulfilled.

Production: Airbus is having four A300-600STs constructed for its own use and has an option on a fifth. Delivery of the third and fourth aircraft are planned for April 1997 and June 1998 respectively.

History: The A300-600ST is a $US1 billion program to replace Airbus Industrie's ageing fleet of Boeing Stratocruiser based Super Guppy transports, used by the consortium to ferry oversize components such as wings and fuselage sections between Airbus's partners' plants throughout western Europe.

Development of the A300-600ST, nicknamed Beluga and also Super Flipper, began in August 1991. The A300-600ST's tight development program – for what in many ways is effectively a new aircraft – saw the transport rolled out in June 1994, with its first flight in September. The A300-600ST then entered a 400 flight test program which culminated in mid 1995, with certification awarded that September and with delivery and entry into service with Airbus in January 1996.

The A300-600ST is based on the A300-600 airliner, with which it shares the wing, lower fuselage, main undercarriage and cockpit. The main differences are obvious – a bulged main deck, new forward lower fuselage, and new enlarged tail with winglets and an upwards hinging main cargo door.

Program management of the A300-600ST is the responsibility of the Special Aircraft Transport Company, or SATIC, an economic interest grouping formed on a 50/50 basis by Aerospatiale and Deutsche Aerospace Airbus operating on behalf of Airbus Industrie. While much of the work on the aircraft is performed by the Airbus partners, other European companies are also involved in the program.

Photo: The Beluga performing during an airshow routine. Despite its somewhat unusual proportions, test pilots have described its flying characteristics as docile. (Paul Merritt)

Airbus A3XX

Country of origin: European consortium

Type: Long range high capacity widebody airliner

Powerplants: A3XX-100 – Four 320kN (72,000lb) thrust class Rolls-Royce Trent 900 or General Electric-Pratt & Whitney GP7000 turbofans. A3XX-100R – Four 334kN (75,000lb) class Trent 900s or GP7000s. A3XX-200 – Four 347kN (79,000lb) class Trent 900s or GP7000s.

Performance: A3XX-100 – Design range 13,900km (7500nm). A3XX-100R – Design range 15,750km (8500nm). A3XX-200 – Design range 13,900km (7500nm).

Weights: A3XX-100 – Max takeoff 510,000kg (1,124,550lb). A3XX-100R – Max takeoff 550,000kg (1,212,750lb). A3XX-200 – Max takeoff 550,000kg (1,212,750lb).

Dimensions: A3XX-100 – Wing span 79m (259ft), length 70.8m (232ft).

Capacity: Flightcrew of two. A3XX-100 & -100R – Typical three class seating arrangement for 555. A3XX-200 – Typical three class seating arrangement for 656. In a single class high density arrangement would seat 990, 550 on the main deck and 440 on the upper deck.

Production: Airbus has forecast a market for approx 1380 airliners of 500 seats and above through to 2014 worth $US300bn. A3XX unit cost approx $US198m in 1998. First deliveries could be in 2003.

History: The all new, 500 tonne plus A3XX is without doubt the most ambitious aircraft program currently under serious consideration anywhere in the world and if development go-ahead is given will result in the world's largest civil aircraft.

While Boeing and Airbus Industrie partners BAe, DASA and Aerospatiale studied a Very Large Aircraft in the early 1990s under the VLCT (Very Large Commercial Transport) banner, Airbus began initial concept work on its own VLA should the VLCT not proceed. Not waiting for the VLCT study to be completed Airbus launched engineering development work on its VLA, the A3XX, in June 1994.

Airbus studied numerous design configurations for the A3XX and gave serious consideration to a single deck aircraft which would have seated 12 abreast and have twin vertical tails. However Airbus settled upon a twin deck configuration, mainly because of the significantly lighter structure required.

Other planned design features at late 1996 were the Airbus common two crew cockpit and four 320 to 347kN (72,000 to 78,000lb) class turbofans. Initially Airbus envisaged using the A330 engines but instead has been able to take advantage of the Rolls-Royce Trent 900 and General Electric-Pratt & Whitney GP7000 turbofans now under development.

Key design parameters include the ability to use existing airport gates with little modification, and direct operating costs per seat 15% less than those for the 747-400.

Three A3XX models are envisaged: the baseline 555 seat A3XX-100; the heavier, longer range A3XX-100R and the stretched 656 seat A3XX-200 (with DOCs per seat 20% lower than for the 747-400).

The A3XX is likely to be developed in conjunction with risk sharing partners. Development cost is estimated at $US8bn.

Photo: A late 1996 artist's impression of the A3XX-100. (Airbus)

Airtech CN-235

Countries of Origin: Spain and Indonesia

Type: Utility transport and commuter airliner

Powerplants: Two 1395kW (1870shp) General Electric CT7-9C turboprops, driving four blade constant speed Hamilton Standard propellers.

Performance: CN-235-100 – Max speed 509km/h (275kt), max cruising speed 454km/h (245kt). Initial rate of climb at sea level 1780ft/min. Range with max payload and reserves at 18,000ft 796km (430nm).

Weights: CN-235-100 – Operating empty 9800kg (21,605lb), max takeoff 15,100kg (33,290lb).

Dimensions: Wing span 25.81m (84ft 8in), length 25.81m (70ft 1in), height 8.18m (26ft 10in). Wing area 59.1m^2 (636.17sq ft).

Capacity: Flightcrew of two pilots. Passenger accommodation in airliner version for 45 in four abreast configuration. Quick change convertible passenger/freighters can carry mixtures of passengers and LD2 or LD3 containers. All cargo version can carry four LD3s or five LD2s or palletised freight.

Production: Out of total orders for 215 CN-235s, 60 have been for civil customers. 25 are currently in airline service.

History: The CN-235 was designed and developed as a 50:50 joint venture between CASA of Spain and Indonesia's IPTN.

With development shared equally, one prototype was built in both countries and these were rolled out simultaneously on September 10 1983. First flight was of the Spanish prototype occurring on November 11 1983, with the Indonesian built aircraft flying on December 30 that year. Certification by both Spanish and Indonesian authorities and first deliveries (from the Indonesian line) occurred in December 1986 with entry into commercial service in March 1988.

Two final assembly lines for the CN-235 are in Spain and Indonesia, but all other construction is not duplicated. CASA is responsible for the centre and forward fuselage, wing centre section and inboard flaps, and engine nacelles. IPTN builds outer wings and flaps, ailerons, the rear fuselage and the tail unit.

The initial production CN-235-10 was soon replaced by the CASA built CN-235-100 and IPTN's CN-235-110, incorporating CT7-9C engines in place of CT7-7As, and new composite engine nacelles. Further improvements led to CASA CN-235-200 and similar IPTN CN-235-220 with increased operating weights, better field performance and better range, with structural improvements and improved leading edge flaps and rudder. The CN-235-220 was certificated in March 1992. CASA and IPTN now develop their own CN-235 variants independently.

Other variants on the CN-235 theme are the CN-235 QC quick change capable of carrying passengers or freight or both; IPTN's CN-235 MPA maritime patrol aircraft and CASA's CN-235MP Persuader (which while primarily aimed at military customers, have Customs and boarder patrol applications); and the widely ordered CN-235 M multirole military freighter. IPTN is marketing military CN-235s as the Phoenix.

The CN-235 has succeeded in achieving only a small number of commercial orders, mostly from Indonesian and Spanish operators. In contrast the CN-235's spacious interior and rear loading ramp has helped it win a significant number of military orders.

Photo: A CASA CN-235 civil demonstrator. (CASA)

Air Tractor series

Country of origin: United States of America

Type: Series of piston & turboprop powered agricultural aircraft

Powerplant: AT-301 – One 450kW (600hp) Pratt & Whitney R-1340 radial engine driving two blade Hamilton Standard or Pacific Propeller or three blade Pacific Propeller props. AT-502 – One 507kW (680shp) Pratt & Whitney Canada PT6A series turboprop, optionally a 560kW (750shp) PT6A, driving a three blade constant speed prop. AT-802 – One 1062kW (1424shp) PT6A-67R or -67AF driving a five blade constant speed Hartzell prop.

Performance: AT-301 – Max speed 266km/h (144kt), econ cruising speed 225km/h (122kt). Initial rate of climb 1600ft/min. AT-502 – Max speed at sea level 290kmh (155kt), typical operating speeds 195 to 235km/h (105 to 125kt). Initial rate of climb 1080ft/min. AT-802 – Max speed 338km/h (182kt), max cruising speed 314km/h (170kt). Initial rate of climb 800ft/min. Range with max fuel 805km (434nm).

Weights: AT-301 – Empty 1656kg (3650lb), loaded 3130kg (6900lb). AT-502 – Empty 1870kg (4123lb), max takeoff 4175kg (9200lb). AT-802 – Empty equipped 2860kg (6300lb), max takeoff 7260kg (16,000lb).

Dimensions: AT-301 – Wing span 13.72m (45ft), length 8.23m (27ft), height 2.59m (8ft 6in). Wing area 25.1m^2 (270sq ft). AT-502 – Wing span 15.24m (50ft in), length 9.91m (32ft 6in), height 2.99m (9ft 10in). Wing area 27.9m^2 (300.0sq ft). AT-802 – Wing span 17.68m (58ft 0in) length 11.07m (36ft 4in), height 3.35m (11ft 0in). Wing area 36.3m^2 (391.0sq ft).

Capacity: One pilot and for AT-503A and AT-802 passenger or observer. Various size chemical spray hoppers, ranging in capacity from 1210 litres (AT-301) and 1515 litres (AT-401) upwards.

Production: Over 1400 Air Tractors of all models have been built, including more than 600 AT-301s, 215 AT-401s, 170 AT-402Bs, 330 AT-502s and 35 AT-802s and AT-802As.

History: The Air Tractor was designed by company founder Leyland Snow who earlier designed the Snow S-2 (built by Rockwell and Ayres).

The initial Air Tractor model was the Pratt & Whitney R-1340 radial powered AT-301 which established the Air Tractor series' basic configuration. First flight was in 1974, and 600 were built until replaced by the AT-401. The AT-401 introduced a greater span wing and increased chemical hopper capacity and first flew in 1986. The AT-401 is powered by the R-1340, the AT-401A by a 442kW (592hp) Polish PZL-3S Series 2 radial. The AT-402 is similar other than its 505kW (680shp) PT6A turboprop engine, the AT-402B has increased span wings.

The AT-502A (first flight Feb 1992) is based in the -402B but has a far more powerful 820kW (1100shp) PT6A-45R turbine driving a slow turning five blade prop. Its excess power reserves allow high speed or high altitude operations. The AT-502B has Hoerner wingtips and optional equipment including GPS.

The 5.4 tonne MTOW PT6 powered AT-602 first flew on December 1 1995 and became available for delivery in the second half of 1996.

The larger and heavier two seat AT-802 and single seat AT-802A are the largest purpose designed single engine ag aircraft in production. First flight was in October 1990. The AT 802AF is a single seater.

Photo: The piston powered Air Tractor AT-401. (Bill Lines)

American Champion & Bellanca series

Country or origin: United States of America

Type: Series of two seat utility and aerobatic light aircraft

Powerplant: 7KCAB – One 110kW (150hp) Lycoming AEIO-320-E2B fuel injected flat four driving a two blade fixed pitch propeller. 8GCBC – One 135kW (180hp) Lycoming O-360-C2A driving either a two blade fixed pitch or constant speed prop.

Performance: 7KCAB – Max speed 210km/h (113kt), max cruising speed 208km/h (112kt). Initial rate of climb 1120ft/min. Range 900km (487nm). 8GCBC – Max speed 217km/h (162kt), cruising speed 209km/h (113kt). Initial rate of climb 1110ft/min. Range 725km (390nm).

Weights: 7KCAB – Empty 505kg (1110lb), max takeoff 750kg (1650lb). 8GCBC – Empty 595kg (1315lb), max takeoff 975kg (2150lb).

Dimensions: 7KCAB – Wing span 10.19m (33ft 5in), length 6.91m (22ft 8in), height 2.36m (7ft 9in). Wing area 15.3m^2 (165sq ft). 8GCBC – Wing span 11.02m (36ft 2in), length 6.93m (22ft 9in), height 2.64m (8ft 8in). Wing area 16.7m^2 (180sq ft).

Capacity: Two in tandem. Scout can be fitted for crop spraying.

Production: Over 6000 of all three models built.

History: The Citabria, Bellanca and Scout can trace their lineage back to the Aeronca 7 and 11 models (described separately).

Champion Aircraft Corporation purchased the production rights to the Aeronca 7 in 1951, and from this developed the 7EC Traveller and 7GCB Challenger. The Citabria first flew in May 1964 and incorporated a number of changes over the earlier models. These included more glass area, a squarer tail and stressing for limited (+5g, -2g) aerobatic flight, while other features were the flapless wing and choice of 75kW (100hp) Continental O-200 or 80kW (108hp) Lycoming O-235 engines. Variants on this theme were the 110kW (150hp) O-320 powered 7GCAA and the 7GCBC with a longer span wing fitted with flaps.

Bellanca took over production of the Citabria in September 1970, renaming the 7ECA, which by now was powered by an 85kW (115hp) O-235, as the Citabria; the 7GCAA the Citabria 150 and the 7GCBC the Citabria 150S.

Champion initially developed the 7KCAB model, but Bellanca took this over, resulting in the fully aerobatic 8KCAB Decathlon. The ultimate Decathlon design was the 135kW (180hp) AEIO-360 powered Super Decathlon.

The Scout was designed to perform a number of utility roles, and appeared in 1970, the updated 8GCBC followed in 1974 with a 135kW (180hp) O-360.

Bellanca production ended in 1982, while the Champion Aircraft Company produced the range in limited numbers between 1985 and 1986.

All three models are once again in low rate production, this time with American Champion. American Champion restarted production of the series in 1990, and now builds the baseline 7ECA Citabria Aurora (reintroduced in 1995), the 7GBC Citabria Explorer, 8KCAB Super Decathlon and the 8GCBC Scout (and Scout CS with constant speed propeller). These aircraft are basically similar to their earlier namesakes, save for some minor equipment changes.

Photo: A Bellanca 7ECA Citabria. (Randall Krebbs)

Antonov/PZL Mielec An-2

Countries of origin: Ukraine and Poland

Type: Biplane utility transport

Powerplants: An-2P – One 745kW (1000hp) PZL Kalisz ASz-61IR nine cylinder radial engine driving an AW-2 four blade variable pitch propeller. Y-5B – One 735kW (986hp) PZL Kalisz ASz-61IR-16 or Zhuzhou HS5 nine cylinder radial engine.

Performance: An-2P – Max speed 258km/h (139kt), economical cruising speed 185km/h (100kt). Range with a 500kg (1100lb) cargo 900km (485nm). Y-5B – Max speed 220km/h (120kts), typical cruising speed 160km/h (85kt). Range 845km (455nm).

Weights: An-2P – Empty 3450kg (7605lb), max takeoff 5500kg (12,125lb). Y-5B – Max takeoff 5250kg (11,575lb).

Dimensions: Upper wing span 18.18m (59ft 8in), lower 14.14m (46ft 9in), length (tail down) 12.40m (40ft 8in), height (tail down) 4.01m (12ft 2in). Upper wing area 43.5m^2 (468.7sq ft), lower 28.0m^2 (301.2sq ft).

Capacity: Flightcrew of one or two pilots. Passenger accommodation for 12 at three abreast. Agricultural versions have large chemical hoppers (1400 litres/308Imp gal of liquid chemical or 1200kg/2645lb of dust in the An-2S, or 1960 litres/430Imp gal for the An-2M) with spray bars along the lower wing.

Production: Only approximate production figures are available, but more than 5000 were built in the Ukraine between 1948 and the mid 1960s, before production was transferred to PZL Mielec in Poland, where approximately 12,000 have been built and production continues. Close to 1000 have been built by SAMC in China.

History: The An-2 was originally designed to meet a USSR Ministry of Agriculture and Forestry requirement, resulting in a first flight on August 31 1947.

Entering production and service the following year, Antonov built An-2s were powered by 745kW (1000hp) ASh-62 radials. Soviet production continued through to the mid sixties by which time a number of variants had been developed, including the base model An-2P, An-2S and -2M crop sprayers, An-2VA water bomber, An-2M floatplane and the An-2ZA high altitude meteorological research aircraft.

Production responsibility was transferred to Poland's PZL Mielec in the 1960s, with the first example flying on October 23 1960. Aside from the An-2P, Polish versions include the An-2PK VIP transport, An-2PR for TV relay work, An-2S ambulance, An-2TD paratroop transport, An-2P cargo/passenger version, An-2 Geofiz geophysical survey version, passenger An-2T and An-2TP, and agricultural An-2R.

Chinese production as the Y-5 commenced with Nanchang in 1957, before being transferred to the Shijiazhuang Aircraft Manufacturing Company. The main Chinese version is the standard Y-5N, while the latest development is the Y-5B specialist ag aircraft, which first flew in June 1989.

An Antonov built turboprop powered version, known as the An-3, flew in prototype form but did not enter production.

Photo: The An-2 is noteworthy for being the largest biplane still in operational service. Pictured is a Hungarian registered example. (Bruce Malcolm)

Antonov An-12 & Xian Y-8

Country of origin: Ukraine

Type: Mid sized turboprop freighter

Powerplants: An-12 – Four 2490kW (3495shp) Ivchenko AI-20K turboprops powering AV-68 four blade constant speed propellers. Shaanxi Y-8A – Four 3170kW (4250shp) Zhuzhou WJ6 turboprops driving four blade constant speed propellers.

Performance: An-12 – Max level speed 777km/h (420kt), max cruising speed 670km/h (361kt). Range with max payload 3600km (1940nm), range with full fuel load 5700km (3075nm). Y-8A – Max level speed 660km/h (357kt), economical cruising speed 530km/h (286kt). Range with max fuel load 5615km (3030nm), range with max payload 1275km (690nm).

Weights: An-12 – Empty 28,000kg (61,730lb), max takeoff 61,000kg (135,585lb). Y-8 – Empty equipped 35,490kg (77,237lb), max takeoff 61,000kg (135,585lb).

Dimensions: An-12 – Wing span 38.00m (124ft 8in), length 33.10m (108ft 7in), height 10.53m (34ft 7in). Wing area 121.7m^2 (1310sq ft). Y-8 – Same except for length 34.02m (111ft 8in), height 11.16m (36ft 8in). Wing area 121.9m^2 (1311.7sq ft).

Capacity: Flightcrew consisting of two pilots, a flight engineer, radio operator and navigator housed in the glazed nose. Can be arranged to accommodate 14 passengers plus freight, with military versions carrying up to 90 troops. Max payload 20,000kg (44,090lb).

Production: Production totals for the An-12 are estimated at approximately 900 aircraft, with more than 200 having nominally seen civil service with Aeroflot, plus many other Soviet client state airlines.

History: The An-12 (NATO reporting name 'Cub') was developed to fulfil a Soviet air force requirement for a turboprop freighter, based on the turboprop An-10 developed for Aeroflot service, and is the loose equivalent to the USA's Lockheed Martin Hercules.

The prototype An-12 flew in 1958, powered by Kuznetsov NK-4 turboprops, and was essentially a militarised An-10 with a rear loading cargo ramp. (Approximately 500 An-10s were built, the type seeing service between 1959 and 1973.) Series production of the An-12 in a number of mainly military variants continued until 1973, from which time it was replaced by the Ilyushin Il-76 (described elsewhere).

The An-12BP is the basic transport version of the Cub and it is this model that has been operated by Aeroflot, Cubana, LOT Polish Airlines and Bulair for civil and quasi military work. Other military versions are in use as Elint and ECM platforms.

China's XIAN began redesign work of the An-12 in 1969, and has resulted in a number of Chinese versions, built by the Shaanxi Aircraft Company. Civil variants are the Y-8B and Y-8C, which was developed with co-operation from Lockheed.

Photo: A civil An-12, essentially the old Soviet Bloc's equivalent to the Lockheed Hercules. (Bruce McAllister)

Antonov An-22 Antheus

Country of origin: Ukraine

Type: Long range large capacity turboprop freighter

Powerplants: Four 11,185kW (15,000shp) Kuznetsov (now Kuibyshev) NK-12MA turboprops driving eight blade counter rotating propellers.

Performance: Max level speed 740km/h (400kt). Range with max fuel and 45 tonne (99,200lb) payload 10,950km (5905nm), range with max payload 5000km (2692nm).

Weights: Typical empty equipped 114,000kg (251,325lb), max takeoff 250,000kg (551,160lb).

Dimensions: Wing span 29.2m (95ft 10in), length 25.53m (77ft 3in), height 8.32m (27ft 4in). Wing area 72.5m^2 (780.0sq ft).

Capacity: Flightcrew of up to six, comprising two pilots, navigator, flight engineer and a communications specialist. Up to 29 passengers can be accommodated on the upper deck behind the cockpit. The unpressurised main cabin can house a range of oversize payloads such as main battle tanks in the military role. Total An-22 payload is 80,000kg (176,350lb).

Production: Approximately 70 have been built, of which approximately 50 have been operated in Aeroflot colours. A few dozen remain in Aeroflot and military service.

History: The massive An-22 (NATO reporting name 'Cock') is the largest turboprop powered aircraft yet built, having a maximum takeoff weight similar to that of the Airbus A340, and was designed in response to a largely military requirement for a strategic heavylift freighter.

The An-22 made its first flight on February 27 1965, at that time it was the largest aircraft in the world. Production of the An-22 for the Soviet air force and Aeroflot continued through the 1960s until 1974.

The An-22 set 14 payload to height records in 1967, the pinnacle of which was the carriage of 100 tonnes (220,500lb) of metal blocks to an altitude of 25,748ft (7848m). It also established the record for a maximum payload lifted to a height of 2000m (6562ft), carrying a payload of 104,444kg (221,443lb). A number of speed records were also set in 1972, recording a speed of 608.5km/h (328kt) around a 1000km (540nm) circuit with a 50,000kg (110,250lb) payload. Further speed with payload records were established in 1974 and 1975.

As well as operations into the underdeveloped regions of Russia's northeast, Siberia and Far East, Aeroflot An-22s have commonly been used in military roles, their 'civilian' status allowing much freer access to landing and overflight rights.

Notable aspects of the An-22 include the NK-12 turboprops – which also power the Tu-95/Tu-142 Bear family of bombers and are the most powerful turboprop engines in service – comprehensive navigation and precision drop avionics, and massive undercarriage and tailplane.

Photo: Now largely replaced by the An-124 Ruslan jet transport, the An-22 still proves useful in maintaining an airlift capability into Russia's more remote regions. (Dave Fraser)

Antonov An-24, -30 & -32 & Xian Y7

Country of origin: Ukraine

Type: Regional airliner and freighter

Powerplants: An-24V – Two 1887kW (2530ehp) Ivchenko (Progress) AI-24A turboprops, driving four blade constant speed propellers. An-26 & An-30 – 2103kW (2820ehp) AI-24VT turboprops. Y7-100 – 2080kW (2790shp) Wongan WJ5A I turboprops.

Performance: An-24V – Max cruising speed 500km/h (270kt), long range cruising speed 450km/h (243kt). Range with max payload 550km (296nm). Range with max fuel 2400km (1295nm).

Weights: An-24V – Empty equipped 13,300kg (29,320lb), max takeoff 21,000kg (46,300lb). Y7-100 – Operating empty 14,900kg (32,850lb), max takeoff 21,800kg (48,060lb).

Dimensions: An-24V – Wing span 29.20m (95ft 10in), length 23.53m (77ft 3in), height 8.32m (27ft 4in). Wing area 75.0m^2 (807sq ft). Y7-100 – Wing span 29.64m (97ft 3in), length 23.71m (77ft 10in), height 8.55m (28ft 1in). Wing area 75.0m^2 (807sq ft).

Capacity: Flightcrew of typically two pilots and flight engineer, plus optional accommodation for a radio operator. Seating arrangements for up to 50 passengers at four abreast. Max payload 5500kg (12,125lb).

Production: More than 1100 An-24s were built before production ended. Approximately 850 An-24s remain in service. Chinese production continues.

History: The An-24 is the original aircraft in a prolific and highly successful family of twin turboprop civil and military transports.

The original An-24 first flew in April 1963 with the first production versions entering Aeroflot service in that September. Aeroflot was by far the largest operator of the An-24, although many former Soviet client nations operated the type.

Subsequent production versions of the An-24 were the An-24V and the An-24T freighter. A small turbojet in the right engine nacelle to boost takeoff performance resulted in the An-24RT and An-24RV. The An-24P firebomber was also developed before Ukrainian production ceased in 1978.

The An-24 was also developed into the An-26 'Curl' military tactical transport, which itself evolved into the An-32 with enhancements for better hot and high performance. Over 400 An-26s are in civil service.

The An-30 development has been produced in limited numbers and is used largely for aerial survey and cartography work. This version is identifiable by its extensive nose glazing.

The An-32 first flew in 1976 and features much more powerful 3760kW (5042ehp) Progress engines for improved hot and high performance. The An-32 features above wing mounted engines to give the larger diameter props adequate ground clearance.

China's Xian Aircraft Manufacturing Company is now the sole source for the An-24 as the Y7. The Y7-100 incorporates a number of modifications including a revised passenger interior and flightdeck, and wingtip winglets. It was developed with the technical assistance of HAECO in Hong Kong during the 1980s.

Photo: A civil An-32 on the ramp in Kenya.

Antonov/PZL Mielec An-28 & An-38

Countries of origin: Ukraine and Poland

Type: Commuter airliner and utility transports

Powerplants: An-28 – Two 715kW (960shp) PZL Rzeszów built RKBM/Rybinsk (Glushenkov) TVD-10B turboprops driving three blade props. M-28 – Two 820kW (1100shp) Pratt & Whitney Canada PT6A-65Bs driving five blade props.

Performance: An-28 – Max cruising speed 350km/h (189kt), economical cruising speed 335km/h (181kt). Range with 20 passengers 510km (274nm), range with a full fuel load and 1000kg (455lb) payload 1365km (736nm). M-28 – Economical cruising speed 270km/h (146kt). Initial rate of climb 2657ft/min. Range with max fuel and 1000kg (2205lb) payload 1365km (735nm).

Weights: An-28 – Empty equipped 3900kg (8598lb), max takeoff 6500kg (14,330lb). M-28 – Empty equipped 3917kg (8635lb), max takeoff 7000kg (15,432lb).

Dimensions: Wing span 22.06m (72ft 5in), length 13.10m (42ft 12in), height 4.90m (16ft 1in). Wing area 39.7m^2 (427.5sq ft).

Capacity: Flightcrew of two. Typical passenger accommodation for 17 at three abreast and 72cm (28in) pitch. High density seating for 20 pax. Can also be configured as a mixed freight/passenger combi.

Production: Approximately 200 An-28s have been delivered,.

History: The An-28 was the winner of a competition against the Beriev Be-30 to develop a new light passenger and utility transport for Aeroflot's short haul routes.

The An-28 is substantially derived from the earlier An-14. Commonality with the An-14 includes the high wing layout, twin fins and rudders, but it differs in having a new and far larger fuselage, plus turboprop engines. The original powerplant was the TVD-850, but production versions are powered by the more powerful TVD-10B.

The An-28 made its first flight as the An-14M in September 1969 in the Ukraine. A subsequent preproduction aircraft first flew in April 1975. Production of the An-28 was then transferred to Poland's PZL Mielec in 1978, although it was not until 1984 that the first Polish built production aircraft flew. The An-28's Soviet type certificate was awarded in April 1986.

While of conventional design, one notable feature of the An-28 is that it will not stall, due to its automatic slots. An engine failure that would usually induce the wing to drop 30° is combated by an automatic slot that opens on the opposite wing, restricting wing drop to 12°.

PZL Mielec has been the sole source for production An-28s, and has developed a westernised version powered by 820kW (1100shp) Pratt & Whitney PT6A-65B turboprops with five blade Hartzell propellers, plus some western (Bendix-King) avionics. Designated the An-28PT, first flight was during early 1993 and it is in limited production. Marketed as the M-28 Skytruck, the type received Polish certification equivalent to US FAR Part 23 in March 1996. More than a dozen have been ordered.

The An-28 also forms the basis for the stretched AlliedSignal TPE331 powered Antonov developed An-38. The 26 seat An-38 first flew on June 23 1994. Series production is already underway in Novosibirsk with certification planned for early 1997.

Photo: A TPE331 powered An-38. (Paul Merritt)

Antonov An-124 Ruslan

Country of origin: Ukraine

Type: Heavylift freighter

Powerplants: Four 229.5kN (51,590lb) ZMKB Progress (Lotarev) D-18T turbofans.

Performance: Max cruising speed 865km/h (468kt), typical cruising speeds between 800 and 850km/h (430 to 460kt). Range with max payload 4500km (2430nm), range with full fuel load 16,500km (8900nm).

Weights: Operating empty 175,000kg (385,800lb), max takeoff 405,000kg (892,875lb).

Dimensions: Wing span 73.30m (240ft 6in), length 69.60m (226ft 9in), height 20.78m (68ft 2in). Wing area 628.0m^2 (6760sq ft).

Capacity: Flightcrew of six consisting of two pilots, two flight engineers, navigator and communications operator. Upper deck behind the flightdeck area features a galley, rest room and two relief crew cabins. Upper deck area behind the wing can accommodate up to 88 passengers. Main deck cargo compartment is designed to carry an extremely large range of bulky and oversized cargos including 12 ISO standard containers, heavy machinery, construction equipment, electric generators, oil well equipment and the like. The An-124's total payload in weight is 150 tonnes (330,695lb).

Production: About 60 An-124s had been built by 1996, the main customers being Aeroflot and the CIS military. Some western based freight operators utilise An-124s leased from Antonov for freight charters.

History: The massive An-124 for a time held the mantle of the world's largest aircraft before the arrival of the An-225, a stretched six engine derivative.

Developed primarily as a strategic military freighter (in which role it can carry missile units and main battle tanks), the first prototype An-124 flew on December 26 1982. A second prototype, named Ruslan (after a Russian folk hero), made the type's first western public appearance at the Paris airshow in June 1985, preceding the type's first commercial operations in January 1986. Since that time the An-124 has set a wide range of payload records, a recent achievement being the heaviest single load ever transported by air – a 124 tonne (273,400lb) powerplant generator and its associated weight spreading cradle, a total payload weight of 132.4 tonnes (291,940lb), set in late 1993.

The An-124's configuration is similar to the United States Air Force's Lockheed C-5 Galaxy military transport, which, with a maximum takeoff weight of 380 tonnes, is slightly smaller. Notable features include nose and tail cargo doors, 24 wheel undercarriage allowing operations from semi prepared strips, the ability to kneel to allow easier front loading, and fly-by-wire control system.

One of the largest operators of the An-124, Volga-Dnepr, had approached Rolls-Royce about the possibility of re-engining the transport with RB211-524G turbofans, to extend the type's service life and reduce maintenance. Despite its merits, nothing came of the plan.

Photo: The Ruslan is employed widely by specialist western freight operators and in particular in support of UN operations. Note the complex undercarriage arrangement (Gary Gentle)

Antonov An-225 Myria

Country of origin: Ukraine

Type: Six engine ultra heavy lift transport

Powerplants: Six 229.5kN (51,590lb) ZMKB Progress D-18T turbofans.

Performance: Cruising speed range 800 to 850km/h (430 to 460kt). Range with a 200,000kg (440,900lb) internal payload 4500km (2425nm). Range with a 100,000kg (220,450lb) internal payload 9600km (5180nm). Range with max fuel 15,400km (8310nm).

Weights: Max takeoff 600,000kg (1,322,750lb).

Dimensions: Wing span 88.40m (290ft), length 84.00m (275ft 7in), height 18.20m (59ft 9in). Wing area 905.0m^2 (9741sq ft).

Capacity: Flightcrew of six consisting of two pilots, a navigator, a communications specialist and two flight engineers. Accommodation for a relief crew plus a further 60 to 70 personnel provided in upper deck cabin behind the flightdeck. The maximum payload of 250 tonnes (551,150lb) can be carried internally in the 43m (141ft) long main cargo deck, or externally on two upper fuselage mounting beams.

Production: Thus far only one An-225 has been built, while work on a second was suspended.

History: The truly massive An-225 Myria (or Dream) is easily the world's largest aircraft, and the type holds a raft of international lifting records.

The An-225 was designed to participate in the Soviet space program, with its primary use being the external carriage of the Buran space shuttle orbiter. Design work on the An-225 commenced in mid 1985, culminating in the first flight on December 21 1988. Early into the flight trails program in March 22 1989 the Myria set a total of 106 records on a 3.5 hour flight on which it took off at a weight of 508,200kg (1,120,370lb), with a 156,300kg (344,576lb) payload, flying a 2000km (1080nm) closed circuit at an average speed of 813km/h (439kt), reaching an altitude of 40,485ft. The Myria subsequently made its first flight with the Buran orbiter mounted on its back in May that year.

In simple terms the An-225 is a stretch of the earlier An-124 (itself the world's largest aircraft up until the appearance of the Myria), with a substantially lengthened fuselage, increased span wings, plus six (instead of four) Lotarev turbofans. Other changes include the twin fins, deletion of the rear loading ramp, seven instead of five pairs of main undercarriage wheels on each side, and longitudinal mounting beams and faired attachment points to carry external loads, in particular the Buran orbiter. Like the An-124, the Myria uses fly-by-wire, and the two types share similar avionics suites.

Photo: The only An-225 built thus far taxies into a damp Le Bourget for its startling appearance, complete with Buran orbiter, at the 1989 Paris Salon. It is the only aircraft in the world to have a max takeoff weight over 1,000,000lb. (Peter Ricketts)

Antonov An-72 & An-74

Country of origin: Ukraine

Type: STOL utility and (An-74) polar transport

Powerplants: Two 63.7kN (14,330lb) ZMKB Progress D-36 turbofans.

Performance: An-72A – Max speed 705km/h (380kt), cruising speed range 550 to 600km/h (295 to 325kt). Range with max fuel and reserves 4800km (2590nm), with a 7500kg (16,535lb) payload 2000km (1080nm). An-74 – Speeds similar. Range with reserves and a 10,000kg (22,025lb) payload 1150km (620nm), or with a 1500kg (3310lb) payload 5300km (2860nm).

Weights: Empty 19,050kg, max takeoff (from a 1800m/5900ft runway) 34,500kg (76,060lb). Max takeoff from a 1000m (3280ft) runway 27,500kg (60,625lb).

Dimensions: An-72 – Wing span 31.89m (104ft 8in), length 28.07m (92ft 1in), height 8.65m (28ft 5in). Wing area 98.6m^2 (1062sq ft).

Capacity: Flightcrew of three (two pilots and a flight engineer) for the An-72. An-74 also has provision for a radio operator. Main cabin designed primarily for freight, in which role it can carry a payload of 10 tonnes (22,045lb) including four UAK-2.5 containers, or four 2.5 tonne (5510lb) PAV-2.5 pallets. An-72 can seat 68 on removable seats, while the An-74 when configured for combi passenger/freight tasks can carry eight support crew.

Production: Production totals 150 plus, mostly for military customers.

History: The An-72 was designed as a replacement for the An-26 tactical transport in service with the Soviet air force.

The first of two An-72 prototypes flew for the first time on December 22 1977, although it was not until much later in 1985 that the first of eight extensively revised pre production An-72s flew. Included in this pre series batch were two An-74s, differing from the An-72s in their ability to operate in harsh weather conditions in polar regions. Production of the An-72/74 family continues.

Versions of the An-72/74 family (NATO codename 'Coaler') include the An-72A base model with extended wings and fuselage compared to the prototypes, the An-72 capable of carrying international standard containers, the An-72S VIP transport and An-72P maritime patrol aircraft. Versions of the An-74 include the An-74A, the base An-74 model featuring the enlarged nose radome, the An-74T freighter, the An-74TK, -74TK-100 and -74TK-200 convertible passenger/freighter model, and the An-74P-100 VIP transport.

The most significant design feature of the An-72 and An-74 is the use of the Coanda effect to improve STOL performance, which uses engine exhaust gases blown over the wing's upper surface to boost lift. Other features include multi slotted flaps, rear loading ramp and multi unit landing gear suited to operations from unprepared strips.

Photo: A distinctive feature of the An-72/74 are the two above wing high bypass turbofans. Pictured is an An-74T. (Jim Thorn)

Auster J series

Country of origin: United Kingdom

Type: Two three and four seat general purpose light aircraft

Powerplants: J/1 – One 75kW (100hp) Blackburn Cirrus. J/5B & J/5F – One 97kW (130hp) de Havilland Gipsy Major. J/5G – One 116kW (155hp) Blackburn Cirrus Major 3. All were inline four cylinder piston engines driving two blade fixed pitch propellers.

Performance: J/1 – Max speed 193km/h (104kt), cruising speed 160km/h (86kt). Initial rate of climb 568ft/min. Range with no reserves 515km (278nm). J/5G – Max speed 204km/h (110kt), cruising speed 177km/h (96kt). Initial rate of climb 710ft/min. Range with no reserves 780km (421nm). J/5F – Max speed 212km/h (114kt), cruising speed 180km/h (97kt). Initial rate of climb 705ft/min. Range with no reserves 435km (235nm).

Weights: J/1 – Empty 477kg (1052lb), max takeoff 840kg (1850lb). J/5B – Empty 605kg (1334lb), max takeoff 1090kg (2400lb). J/5G – Empty 620kg (1367lb), max takeoff 1110kg (2450lb). J/5F – Empty 600kg (1323lb), max takeoff 885kg (1950lb).

Dimensions: J/1 – Wing span 10.97m (36ft 0in), length 7.14m (23ft 5in), height 1.98m (6ft 6in). Wing area 17.2m^2 (185sq ft). J/5B – Same except for length 7.11m (23ft 4in), height 2.30m (7ft 6in). J/5G – Same except for length 7.06m (23ft 2in), height 2.30m (7ft 6in). J/5F – Same except for length 7.16m (23ft 6in), height 1.98m (6ft 6in). Wing area 15.2m^2 (164sq ft).

Capacity: Two pilots side by side, plus room for one or two passengers, depending on model type.

Production: Approximate production totals for the series are: J/1 – 420; J/1B – 87; J/1N – 43; J/2 – 44; J/4 – 26; J/5 – 58; J/5B – 92; J/5G – 92; J/5P – 24; J/5F – 56; J/5K, L, R & Q – 40+.

History: The Auster marque traces its lineage back to the Taylorcraft Aeroplanes (England) company, which produced under licence Taylorcraft cabin monoplanes (described separately), and built over 1500 spotter (Air Observation Post) aircraft for the Royal Air Force and British Army.

The first civil Auster (as the company become known in 1946) was the Mk 5 J/1 Autocrat, which was essentially similar to the military Mk 5, but had a Cirrus Minor 2 engine in place of the Mk 5's Lycoming, upholstered seats and a small number of other refinements. The J/1 Autocrat served as the basis for a family of civil aircraft. The next to appear was the two seat J/2 Arrow family, which had a 56kW (75hp) Continental, which was further developed into the J/4 Archer, which replaced the Continental with a Cirrus Minor engine. The J/1N was an attempt to increase sales and overcome the problems associated with fitting the Cirrus Minor engine to the J/1 with less equipment and minor improvements. Most Auster J/5 models were four seaters except for the initial J/5 which was an Autocrat with a more powerful engine, while the J/5B incorporated the enlarged four seat cabin. The J/5F Aiglet trainer was a fully aerobatic two seat trainer.

Photo: Many surviving Austers nowadays sport a period livery reflecting their military past. This particular example is finished in a post WW2 RAAF scheme. (Tex Morton)

Aviat A-1 Husky

Country of origin: United States of America

Type: Two seat utility light aircraft

Powerplant: One 135kW (180hp) Textron Lycoming O-360-C1G flat four piston engine, driving a two blade constant speed Hartzell propeller.

Performance: Cruising speed at 75% power 225km/h (122kt), cruising speed at 55% power 212km/h (115kt). Stalling speed with flaps extended 67km/h (37kt). Initial rate of climb 1500ft/min. Service ceiling 20,000ft. Range with max fuel and reserves at 75% power cruising speed 1020km (550nm).

Weights: Empty 540kg (1190lb), max takeoff 817kg (1800lb).

Dimensions: Wing span 10.73m (35ft 3in), length 6.88m (22ft 7in), height 2.01m (6ft 7in). Wing area 16.7m^2 (180.0sq ft).

Capacity: Typical accommodation for two in tandem.

Production: Approximately 350 Huskies had been delivered by late 1996, many for US Government agencies and police.

History: The Aviat Husky has the distinction of being the only all new light aircraft designed and placed into series production in the United States in the mid to late 1980s.

Similar in configuration, appearance and mission to Piper's venerable Super Cub, the Husky is a much later design, being first conceived in the mid 1980s. The Husky was originally designed by Christen Industries, the company also responsible for the kit built Christen Eagle aerobatic biplane and previous owner of the Pitts Special aerobatic biplane series (described separately, Aviat now owns Pitts and Christen).

Initial design work on the Husky began in late 1985, the aircraft being one of the few in its class designed with the benefit of Computer Aided Design. The prototype Husky flew for the first time in 1986, and the US FAA awarded certification the following year. Production deliveries followed shortly afterwards.

Design features of the Husky include a braced high wing, seating for two in tandem and dual controls. This arrangement was selected for the high wing's good all round visibility, essential for the many observation and patrol roles the Husky is optimised for. Power is supplied by a relatively powerful, for the Husky's weight, 135kW (180hp) Textron Lycoming O-360 flat four turning a constant speed prop. The good power reserves and wing also give good field performance. Unlike most current light aircraft the Husky's structure features steel tube frames and Dacron covering over all but the rear of the fuselage, plus metal leading edges on the wings.

Options include floats, skis and banner and glider hooks.

With more than 300 sold since production began, the Husky has also quietly gone about becoming one of the largest selling GA designs in the late 1980s and early 1990s. Many of the aircraft are used for observation duties, fisheries patrol, pipeline inspection, boarder patrol, glider towing and a range of other utility missions. Notable users include the US Department of the Interior and the US Department of Agriculture. Seven are also in use in Kenya with the Kenya Wildlife Service which flies aerial patrols of elephant herds as part of the fight against illegal ivory poaching.

Photo: Four Huskies await delivery to the Kenya Wildlife Service. Note the large balloon tyres. (Aviat)

Aviat Pitts Special

Country of origin: United States of America

Type: Single and two seat competition aerobatic biplanes

Powerplants: S-1S – One 135kW (180hp) Lycoming IO-360 fuel injected flat four piston engine, driving a two blade fixed pitch propeller. S-2B – One 195kW (260hp) Textron Lycoming AEIO-540-D4A5 flat six, driving a two blade constant speed Hartzell propeller.

Performance: S-1S – Max speed 283km/h (153kt), max cruising speed 227km/h (123kt). Initial rate of climb 2600ft/min. Service ceiling 22,300ft. Max range with no reserves 507km (275nm). S-2B – Max cruising speed 282km/h (152kt). Initial rate of climb 2700ft/min. Service ceiling 21,000ft. Range with max fuel at economical cruising speed 513km (277nm).

Weights: S-1S – Empty 326kg (720lb), max takeoff 520kg (1150lb). S-2B – Empty 520kg (1150lb), max takeoff 737kg (1625lb).

Dimensions: S-1S – Wing span 5.28m (17ft 4in), length 4.71m (15ft 6in), height 1.91m (6ft 3in). Wing area 9.2m^2 (98.5sq ft). S-2B – Wing span (upper) 6.10m (20ft 0in), (lower) 5.79m (19ft 0in), length 5.71m (18ft 9in), height 2.02m (6ft 8in). Wing area 11.6m^2 (125.0sq ft).

Capacity: S-1 series seats pilot only. S-2 series seats two, except for S-2S which seats pilot only.

Production: Current Aviat production is of the S-1T, S-2B and S-2S.

History: The designer of the original Pitts Special aerobatic biplane, Curtiss Pitts, could hardly have appreciated that his design would continue in production for over five decades, and that it would come to be considered by the general public as the definitive aerobatic and display flying aircraft.

The original prototype of the S-1 Special first flew in September 1944. The aircraft was of steel tube construction with fabric covering over wooden spars, while the two wings were braced with wire. Power in early aircraft was supplied by 65 to 95kW (90 to 125hp) four cylinder Continental or Lycomings. Later models were higher powered and of conventional metal construction.

Factory production of the basic single seat S-1 Special included the S-1S with a 135kW (180kW) Lycoming IO-360, driving a fixed pitch prop, and the current S-1T. The S-1T was introduced to production in 1981, and introduced a 150kW (200hp) Lycoming (now Textron Lycoming) AEIO-360 driving a constant speed prop and with symmetrical wings. Homebuilt versions of the S-1 include the S-1D and S-1E (for which plans or kits have been offered), while the S-1S and S-1T are also available in kit form.

The two seat S-2 Special is of the same configuration of the single seat S-1 but is larger overall, and generally regarded as a more capable aerobatic aircraft due to its larger size and heavier weight, more power and aerodynamic changes. For this reason the S-2 is also built in single seat 195kW (260hp) AEIO-540 powered S-2S form, while two seat models are the 150kW (200hp) IO-360 powered S-2A, and current production 195kW (260hp) powered and fully aerobatic with two occupants S-2B.

The Pitts Special is currently marketed and built by Aviat in Wyoming.

Photo: The basic Pitts design revolutionised aerobatic flying and remains popular for recreational aerobatic flying and airshow displays. (Christine Pratt)

Aviation Traders ATL-98 Carvair

Country of origin: United Kingdom

Type: Combined freight and passenger transport aircraft

Powerplants: Four 1080kW (1450hp) Pratt & Whitney R-2000-7M2 Twin Wasp 18 cylinder twin row radial engines driving three blade Hamilton Standard Hydromatic variable pitch propellers.

Performance: Max speed 402km/h (217kt), max cruising speed 342km/h (185kt), economical cruising speed at 10,000ft 334km/h (180kt). Service ceiling at 33,110kg (73,000lb) 18,700ft. Range with max fuel and 4500kg (10,000llb) payload 5560km (3000nm). Range with 8035kg (17,700lb) payload 2745km (1480nm).

Weights: Empty equipped 18,762kg (41,365lb), max takeoff 33,475kg (73,800lb).

Dimensions: Wing span 35.82m (117ft 6in), length 31.27m (102ft 7in), height 9.09m (29ft 10in). Wing area 135.8m^2 (1462sq ft).

Capacity: Flightcrew of three. Maximum seating in a passenger configuration 85 pax five abreast at an 86cm (34in) pitch. When used as a car ferry it was typically outfitted to carry five cars plus 22 passengers in the rear cabin.

Production: Total Carvair conversions number 21, the last of which was completed in 1968. A small number remained in service in 1996.

History: Aviation Traders developed the Carvair in response to Channel Air Bridge's requirement for an air ferry capable of transporting passengers and their cars between the United Kingdom and continental Europe.

Although its external appearance is radically different, the Carvair is a basic conversion of the Douglas DC-4 airliner (or C-54 in military guise), large numbers of which were available after World War 2. The airframe from the wings rearward is that of a standard DC-4, except for a lengthened vertical tail for enhanced controllability. The major modifications performed on the forward fuselage centred on a new lengthened nose section with a hydraulically operated cargo door and an elevated flightdeck (similar in appearance to that which would appear on the Boeing 747 several years later) which allowed nose loading for cars.

First flight of the Carvair conversion was on June 21 1961, the type subsequently entering service with British United Air Ferries (into which Channel Air Bridge had been merged, it later became British Air Ferries and is now known as British World Airways) in March 1962. Deliveries to other operators included three for Aer Lingus of Ireland and two for Aviaco of Spain, with other aircraft delivered to French and Luxembourg carriers. Only a small number of Carvairs now remain in service as pure freighters.

Aviation Traders also proposed a Carvair type conversion of the Douglas DC-6, DC-6B and DC-7, with the option of being re-engined with Rolls-Royce Dart turboprops, although these plans were never carried through.

Photo: One of two Carvairs operated by Hawaii Pacific Air, circa 1992. (Jim Thorn)

Ayres LM 200 Loadmaster

Country of origin: United States of America

Type: Twin engine utility transport

Powerplants: Two LHTEC CTP800 turboshafts together generating 1790kW (2400shp) driving a four blade constant speed propeller through a combining gearbox.

Performance: Performance specifications not released at the time of publication.

Weights: Max takeoff approx 8625kg (19,000lb). Revenue payload approx 3405kg (7500lb).

Dimensions: Provisional – Wing span 18.80m (61ft 8in), length overall 19.15m (62ft 10in), height 6.60m (21ft 8in). Wing area 43.0m^2 (462.5sq ft).

Capacity: Various configurations offered. Can carry 3405kg (7500lb) of freight in four standard size containers, or up to 34 passengers in a high density seating arrangement. Different military versions could seat troops or be configured for surveillance with workstations for operators.

Production: Federal Express signed a memorandum of understanding to buy 50 with an option on a further 200 in November 1996. First deliveries are planned for December 1999, with deliveries of two per month thereafter. Ayres has forecast a market for up to 600 Loadmasters worth $US2bn. Unit cost approx $US3.5m to $US4m.

History: The Loadmaster will be a unique twin engine utility transport, similar in size to some smaller regional airliners, designed for a multitude of roles ranging from the carriage of containerised freight through to passenger transport and firebombing.

Albany, Georgia based Ayres has been developing the Loadmaster for the past few years to meet perceived demand for a larger utility transport than current offerings such as the Cessna Caravan. Unlike any other aircraft close to its size, the Loadmaster is being designed with a pallet freight handling system which will allow the aircraft to interface easily into large package freight operators' networks.

Another important market Ayres sees for the Loadmaster is for use as both a regional airliner and a freighter in developing countries where inadequate surface transportation systems and continued population and economic growth means good air transport links are important. Ayres is also pitching the Loadmaster at potential government users and military operators.

The Loadmaster's attractiveness for package freight was confirmed when in November 1996 Federal Express signed a letter of intent for 50 with options on a further 200. FedEx will take delivery of its first Loadmaster in December 1999, and will use the aircraft to complement its smaller Cessna Caravans and larger Fokker F27s.

Design features of the Loadmaster include its twin LHTEC (Light Helicopter Turbine Engine Company – AlliedSignal/Allison) CTP800 turboprops (a commercial turboprop variant of the military T800) driving a single propeller through a combining gearbox, its raised flightdeck, fixed undercarriage, high mounted wing and square sided fuselage.

Photo: An artist's impression of how the Loadmaster will appear in Federal Express colours, being loaded with four freight containers. (Ayres)

Ayres Thrush & Rockwell Thrush Commander

Country of origin: United States of America

Type: Agricultural aircraft

Powerplant: Thrush Commander-600 – One 450kW (600hp) Pratt & Whitney R-1340 Wasp nine cylinder radial piston engine, driving a two blade constant speed Hamilton Standard propeller. S2R-T34 Turbo-Thrush – One 560kW (750shp) Pratt & Whitney Canada PT6A-34AG, driving a three blade constant speed Hartzell prop.

Performance: 600 – Max speed 225km/h (122kt), max cruising speed at 70% power 200km/h (108kt), typical working speed range 170 to 185km/h (91 to 100kt). Initial rate of climb 900ft/min. Service ceiling 15,000ft. Ferry range with max fuel at 70% power 648km (350nm). S2R-T34 – Max speed with spray equipment 256km/h (138kt), cruising speed at 50% power 240km/h (130kt), working speed range at 30 to 50% power 143 to 240km/h (82 to 130kt). Initial rate of climb 1740ft/min. Service ceiling 25,000ft. Ferry range at 40% power 1230km (665nm).

Weights: 600 – Empty equipped 1678kg (3700lb), max takeoff (agricultural category) 2720kg (6000lb). S2R-T34 – Empty 1633kg (3600lb), max takeoff (ag category) 2720kg (6000lb).

Dimensions: 600 – Wing span 13.51m (44ft 4in), length 8.95m (29ft 5in), height 2.79m (9ft 2in). Wing area 30.3m^2 (326.6sq ft). S2R-T34 – Same except wing span 13.54m (44ft 5in), length 10.06m (33ft 0in).

Capacity: Single pilot only, S2R offered with an optional second seat. Chemical hopper capable of holding 1514 litres or 1487kg of chemicals.

Production: Production includes 1300 built by Rockwell.

History: The original Snow S-2 was designed by Leland Snow, who incorporated his knowledge as an experienced ag pilot into the S-2's design.

The Snow S-2 prototype flew for the first time in 1956 and production deliveries began in 1958. S-2 variants differed in engine options, and included the 165kW (220hp) Continental W-670 powered S-2A, the S-2B and S-2C with a Pratt & Whitney R-985, and the R-1340-AN-1 powered S-2C-600.

Aero Commander acquired the design and production rights to the S-2 series in 1965, and built the improved S-2D Ag Commander. The rights to the S-2 changed hands once more in 1967 when North American Rockwell (later Rockwell) acquired Aero Commander, continuing the series under the Thrush Commander banner. Rockwell models include the Thrush Commander-600 with a 450kW (600hp) R-1340 and the Thrush Commander-800, with a 595kW (800hp) Wright R-1300 Cyclone.

Design and production rights changed hands a final time in 1977 when Ayres (who had previously carried out turboprop conversions to Thrush Commanders) acquired the rights to the Thrush Commander-600. Ayres developments include the S2R-600, which later became the S2R-1340; the Bull Thrush, now just S2R-1820; the Polish PZL-3 powered Pezetel Thrush and the turboprop powered S2R series. The S2R-T11, T15 and T34 are powered by PT6s, the S2R-G6 and S2R-G10 AlliedSignal TPE331s. Special missions developments are the S2R-T65 NEDS Narcotics Eradication Delivery System for the US State Department, and the AlliedSignal powered Vigilante surveillance and close air support version.

Photo: An Ayres S2R-T34 Turbo Thrush. (Bill Lines)

BAe Jetstream 31

Country of origin: United Kingdom

Type: 18 seat commuter airliner

Powerplants: J31 – Two 700kW (940shp) Garret TPE331-10 turboprops, driving four blade constant speed propellers. Super 31 – Two 760kW (1020shp) TPE331-12UARs.

Performance: J31 – Max cruising speed 482km/h (260kt), long range cruising speed 426km/h (230kt). Initial rate of climb 2200ft/min. Range with 19 pax and reserves 1185km (640nm), 1760km (950nm) with 12 pax or 2130km (1150nm) with nine pax. Super 31 – Max cruising speed 490km/h (264kt), long range cruising speed 452km/h (244kt). Initial rate of climb 2240ft/min. Range with 19 pax and reserves 1192km (643nm).

Weights: J31 – Operating empty 4360kg (9613lb), max takeoff 6950kg (15,322lb). Super 31 – Operating empty 4578kg (10,992lb), max takeoff 7350kg (16,204lb).

Dimensions: Wing span 15.85m (52ft 0in), length 14.37m (47ft 2in), height 5.37m (17ft 6in). Wing area 25.1m^2 (270sq ft).

Capacity: Flightcrew of two. Main cabin seating for up to 19 at three abreast and 79cm (31in) pitch, 12 pax in a corporate shuttle configuration, or nine in an executive layout.

Production: Total J31 deliveries of 381, including 161 Super J31s.

History: The successful Jetstream 31 owes its ancestry to the Turboméca Astazou powered Handley Page HP.137 Jetstream 1.

The HP.137 was designed as early ago as 1965, and flew for the first time on August 18 1967. Initial Handley Page production aircraft were powered by 635kW (850hp) Astazou XIVs and named Jetstream 1 (36 built), but deliveries were delayed by excess weight and drag problems. To overcome these problems Handley Page developed the Jetstream 2 with more powerful 800kW (1073shp) Astazou XIVCs. However Handley Page ran into serious financial difficulties in the late 1960s (causing the US Air Force to cancel an order for 10 Garrett TPE331 powered Jetstream C-10As [3Ms] – US law prohibits the military for dealing with companies in liquidation/receivership) and it folded in 1969, bringing to an end development of the more powerful Jetstream 2 and plans to market a civil version of the 3M in the USA.

Development of the Jetstream 2 however resumed under the control of the newly formed Jetstream Aircraft in collaboration with Scottish Aviation as the Jetstream 200 in 1970. Scottish Aviation later assumed overall responsibility for the Jetstream and built a number for Britain's military. Development continued after Scottish Aviation was merged into British Aerospace in 1977, and development on the Jetstream 31 (or J31) began in 1978. The first flight of the Garrett TPE331 powered Jetstream 31 (a converted HP.137) occurred on March 28 1980. The first production aircraft flew in March 1982, and UK certification was granted that June.

Subsequent development led to the Super 31 being certificated in October 1988. The Super 31 features uprated engines, higher weights and better performance.

The last J31 was built in 1993, although all tooling has been kept and the type remains available to order.

Photo: A J31 of Perth based Australian regional airline Skywest. Skywest is part of the Ansett Australia group. (Peter Clark)

BAe ATP & Jetstream 61

Country of origin: United Kingdom

Type: Turboprop powered regional airliners

Powerplants: ATP – Two 1978kW (2653shp) Pratt & Whitney Canada PW126A turboprops driving six blade constant speed BAe/Hamilton Standard propellers. J61 – Two 2050kW (2750shp) PW127Ds.

Performance: ATP – Max cruising speed 493km/h (266kt), economical cruising speed 437km/h (236kt). Range with max payload and reserves 630km (340nm), with 69 passengers and reserves 1480km (800nm). J61 – Max cruising speed 500km/h (270kt). Range with 70 passengers and reserves 1180km (637nm).

Weights: ATP – Operating empty 14,193kg (31,290lb), max takeoff 22,930kg (50,550lb). J61 – Max takeoff 23,678kg (52,200lb).

Dimensions: Wing span 30.63m (100ft 6in), length 26.01m (85ft 4in), height 7.59m (24ft 11in). Wing area 78.3m^2 (842.84sq ft).

Capacity: Flightcrew of two. Typical one class seating for 64 to 68 on ATP or 70 on Jetstream 61 at four abreast and 79cm (31in) pitch. Combi versions can take both passengers and freight.

Production: Total ATP and Jetstream 61 production of 67 (including 4 J61s), of which over 50 were in service.

History: The largest twin turboprop powered western regional airliners currently in service, the ATP and Jetstream 61 trace their development history back to the British Aerospace HS.748.

In simple terms the ATP and J61 are stretched developments of the HS.748, but they incorporate a great number of major and minor detail changes. The 748's fuselage cross section and basic wing structure were retained, but otherwise the ATP and J61 are all new aircraft.

British Aerospace announced it was developing a derivative of the 748 in March 1984. The BAe ATP, or Advanced TurboProp, first flew on August 6 1986, while the first production aircraft flew in February 1988. Certification was granted in March 1988, and the ATP entered airline service that May.

Changes on the ATP include the stretched fuselage taking max seating up to 72 passengers, while Pratt & Whitney Canada PW127 turboprops drive advanced slow turning six blade props. Much of the systems and equipment is new or significantly improved. The flightdeck has EFIS instrumentation, while the cabin interior has been thoroughly revised. The nose was reprofiled, and some sweep back was added to the tail.

The improved Jetstream 61 was marketed and built by the newly created BAe division of Jetstream Aircraft. Apart from the name change it introduced a number of minor technical changes including an interior based on the Jetstream 41 (including the innovative arm rests incorporated into the cabin walls for window seats), more powerful PW127D engines and increased operating weights giving higher speeds and longer range. The Jetstream 61 was available for delivery from 1994, but marketing efforts ceased when the AI(R) consortium was formed so as to not compete with the ATR 72.

Photo: Externally the ATP and J61 are identical. Pictured is a Jetstream 61 demonstrator. (Rob Finlayson)

BAe 748

Country of origin: United Kingdom

Type: Regional airliner

Powerplants: Srs 2A – Two 1700kW (2280ehp) Rolls-Royce Dart RDa.7 Mk 534-2 or Mk 535-2 turboprops, driving four blade propellers. Super 748 – Two 1700kW (2280ehp) Dart Mk 552-2s.

Performance: Srs 2A – Cruising speed 452km/h (244kt). Range with max payload and reserves 1360km (735nm), range with max fuel and reserves 3130km (1690nm). Super 748 – Cruising speed 452km/h (244kt). Max initial rate of climb 1420ft/min. Range with max payload and reserves 1715km (926nm), range with max fuel, 3360kg (7800lb) payload and reserves 2892km (1560nm).

Weights: Srs 2A – Operating empty 12,159kg (26,806lb), max takeoff 21,092kg (46,500lb). Super 748 – Empty 6676kg (14,720lb), max takeoff 12,430kg (27,400lb).

Dimensions: Srs 2A – Wing span 30.02m (98ft 6in), length 20.42m (67ft 0in), height 7.57m (24ft 10in). Wing area 75.4m^2 (810.8sq ft). Super 748 – Same except for wing span 31.23m (102ft 6in). Wing area 77.0m^2 (828.9sq ft).

Capacity: Flightcrew of two. Typical seating for between 48 and 51 passengers, at four abreast and 76cm (30in) pitch.

Production: Production ended in 1988 by which time 382 had been built, including 160 assembled in India, comprising mostly Series 2 models.

History: The rugged HS.748 began life as an Avro design effort to re-enter the civil market in anticipation of a decline in military business.

One of a number of aircraft in this size class to be dogged by the DC-3 replacement tag, the HS.748 has proven to be reasonably successful sales wise, and remains popular in third world nations. Surfacing as the Avro 748 in 1958, Hawker Siddeley took over the 748 design in 1959 (Avro being a part of the Hawker Siddeley Group). The new aircraft made a successful maiden flight on June 24 1960, and four prototype aircraft (two for static testing) were built. The first production Series 1 flew on August 30 1961. Series 1 production aircraft were powered by two 1400kW (1880ehp) Dart RDa.6 Mk 514 turboprops, and the first entered service in December 1961 with Skyways Airways. Only 18 Series 1s were built however, as by that time the improved Series 2 was already flying.

The Series 2, in its 2, 2A and 2C variants, was the most successful of the line, the first flying on November 6 1961. The Series 2 differed from the 1 in having progressively higher weights and more powerful engines. The Series 2B appeared in 1977, offering a range of aerodynamic and other improvements, including an increased wing span.

The most advanced variant of the 748 to appear, the Super 748, made its first flight on July 1984. Incorporating the improvements of the 2B, it also featured an advanced flightdeck, improved efficiency and hushkitted Dart engines, and new galley and internal fittings.

Photo: This Air Marshall Islands BAe 748-2B was withdrawn from service in February 1996 following its replacement with a Saab 2000. (Richard Kuluz)

BAe (BAC) One-Eleven

Country of origin: United Kingdom

Type: Short haul airliner

Powerplants: Srs 200 – Two 46.3kN (10,330lb) Rolls-Royce Spey Mk 506 turbofans. Srs 400 – Two 51.1kN (11,400lb) Spey Mk 511s. Srs 500 – Two 56.0kN (12,500lb) Spey Mk 512-14DWs.

Performance: Max cruising speed 870km/h (470kt), economical cruising speed 742km/h (400kt). Series 200 – Range with typical payload and reserves 1410km (760nm). Srs 400 – Range with typical payload and reserves 2300km (1240nm). Srs 500 – Range with typical payload and reserves 2745km (1480nm).

Weights: Srs 200 – Empty 21,049kg (79,000lb), max takeoff 35,833kg (79,000lb). Srs 400 – Empty 22,493kg (49,857lb), max takeoff 40,153kg (88,500lb). Srs 500 – Operating empty 24,758kg (54,582lb), max takeoff 47,400kg (104,500lb).

Dimensions: Srs 200, 300, 400 – Wing span 26.97m (88ft 6in), length 26.97m (93ft 6in), height 7.47m (24ft 6in). Wing area 93.2m² (1003sq ft). Srs 500 – Same as Srs 475 except for length 32.61m (107ft).

Capacity: Flightcrew of two. Srs 200, 300, 400 & 475 – Single class seating for up to 89 passengers. Srs 500 – Seating for up to 119.

Production: UK total 232, comprising 56 Srs 200s, nine Srs 300s, 70 Srs 400s, 89 Srs 500s and nine production 475s. Production transferred to Romania, where nine have been built. Over 100 One-Elevens remained in service in late 1996.

History: The BAe One-Eleven can trace its origins back to the proposed Hunting H.107 jet airliner project of 1956.

Protracted development followed, but by 1961, when Hunting had been absorbed into British Aircraft Corporation (BAC), a larger Rolls-Royce Spey turbofan powered design was settled upon.

British United Airways placed a launch order for 10 of the new aircraft, then known as the BAC.111, in May 1961. The new aircraft took to the skies for the first time on August 20 1963, while the first production Series 200 first flew on December 19 1963. Certification was eventually awarded on April 6 1965, following a troubled flight test program, during which one prototype crashed with the loss of its crew, the cause attributed to deep stall from the engine and the T tail layout. With the deep stall problem solved, the BAC.111 entered service on April 6 1965.

Development of the basic Series 200 led to the higher weight Series 300, followed by the Series 400 designed for American requirements with a higher US equipment content. The Series 500 introduced a stretched fuselage and lengthened wings and a larger seating capacity, while the Series 475 was optimised for hot and high operations, combining the Series 500's more powerful engines with the earlier shorter length fuselage.

The last UK built One-Eleven (by this time a BAe product) flew in 1982, by which time production was progressively being transferred to Romaero in Romania where a small number were built.

Romaero is now building a Rolls-Royce Tay 650 powered development called the Airstar 2500. The 47.4 tonne MTOW, 95 to 115 passenger Airstar was due to fly in late 1996. US airline Kiwi International Airlines had 11 on order (with five options) but this carrier collapsed in October 1996.

Photo: An Air Bristol BAC-111-500 at London Gatwick. (Dave Fraser)

Beagle B.121 Pup

Country of origin: United Kingdom

Type: Two, three and four place trainer

Powerplant: 100 – One 75kW (100hp) Rolls-Royce Continental O-200-A flat four piston engine, driving a two blade fixed pitch propeller. 150 – One 110kW (150hp) Lycoming O-320-A2B flat four. 160 – One 120kW (160hp) Lycoming IO-320.

Performance: 100 – Max speed 204km/h (110kt), max cruising speed 190km/h (103kt), economical cruising speed 153km/h (83kt). Initial rate of climb 575tft/min. Range with no reserves 916km (495nm). 150 – Max speed 222km/h (120kt), max cruising speed 211km/h (114kt), economical cruising speed 175km/h (95kt). Initial rate of climb 800ft/min. Range with no reserves 708km (382nm). Range with optional additional fuel and no reserves 1019km (550nm).

Weights: 100 – Empty 482kg (1063lb), max takeoff 725kg (1600lb). 150 – Empty 522kg (1151lb), max takeoff 873kg (1925lb).

Dimensions: 100 – Wing span 9.45m (31ft 0in), length 6.99m (22ft 11in), height 2.29m (7ft 6in). Wing area 11.2m² (120sq ft). 150 – Same except length 7.06m (23ft 2in).

Capacity: 100 – Two side by side, plus two children behind. 150 – Three adults and one child.

Production: Production total for the Pup was 173, consisting of 66 Pup 100s; 98 Pup 150s; and 9 Pup 160s.

History: The Pup was one of two new designs to be produced by the British Executive and General Aviation Ltd or Beagle company, which was formed in October 1960 following the merger of Auster and Miles.

The Pup originates from the Miles M.117 project, which was to have made extensive use of plastics. A range of Pups was planned, from a 75kW (100hp) two seat trainer through to retractable undercarriage four seaters, a light twin and a fully aerobatic 155kW (210hp) military trainer, the Bull Pup. All of these would have featured metal construction.

The Pup made its first flight on April 8 1967. Deliveries of the initial Pup 100 began a year later in April 1968.

In the meantime Beagle had flown the first of the more powerful Pup 150s in October 1967. The 150 featured a 110kW (150hp) engine, as the designation suggested, and seating for an extra adult.

Another more powerful variant originally designed in response to an Iranian Civil Air Training Organisation requirement was the Pup 160. The Pup 160 featured a 120kW (160hp) IO-320 Lycoming, but only a nine were built.

Continuing financial difficulties finally forced Beagle to close its doors in January 1970, after building 152 Pups, and despite holding orders for an additional 276. As a result plans for the extended Pup based family came to nought. A further 21 were subsequently completed.

The military variant was built as the Bulldog and first flew in May 1969. Scottish Aviation built 328 Bulldogs for a number of air forces, including Britain's Royal Air Force. These aircraft are powered by a 150kW (200hp) Lycoming IO-360 and would no doubt prove very popular with civil pilots if they are disposed off. Scottish Aviation was one of the companies merged to form British Aerospace in the late 1970s.

Photo: The Pup is one of the few light aircraft to feature control sticks and not control columns. Pictured is a Pup 150. (Ben Sampson)

Beagle B.206

Country of origin: United Kingdom

Type: Six/eight place cabin twin

Powerplants: B.206C – Two 230kW (310hp) Continental GIO-470-A geared, fuel injected flat six piston engines, driving three blade constant speed propellers. B.206-S – Two 255kW (340hp) Continental GTSIO-520-C geared, turbocharged and fuel injected engines.

Performance: B.206C – Max speed 354km/h (191kt), max cruising speed 333km/h (180kt), economical cruising speed 298km/h (160kt). Initial rate of climb 1170ft/min. Range with no reserves 2905km (1570nm). B.206-S – Max speed 415km/h (224kt), max cruising speed 380km/h (205kt), econ cruising speed 301km/h (163kt). Initial rate of climb 1340ft/min. Range with no reserves 2462km (1330nm).

Weights: B.206C – Empty equipped 2381kg (5250lb), max takeoff 3401kg (7499lb). B.206-S – Empty equipped 2450kg (5400lb), max takeoff 3401kg (7499lb).

Dimensions: Wing span 13.96m (45ft 10in), length 10.26m (33ft 8in), height 3.43m (11ft 4in). Wing area 19.9m^2 (214sq ft).

Capacity: Eight comprising one or two pilots plus six passengers behind them.

Production: A total production run of 79 aircraft included one 206X; one 206Y; two 206Z; 20 206R Bassets for the Royal Air Force; 43 206-S; and one Series 3.

History: The Beagle B.206's origins lie in a late 1950s Bristol project for a four seat twin.

Although not built, the Bristol 220 evolved into one of Beagle's first and few designs to reach production. The prototype of the new twin engine design, known as the B.206X, made its first flight on August 15 1961. This was a smaller five/six seater powered by two 195kW (260hp) Continental IO-470 engines. Considered too small by its creators, the design grew into the B.206Y with 230kW (310hp) Continental GIO-470 engines, greater wing span, a larger cabin with increased seating capacity, greater fuel capacity and increased weights.

This allowed it to fulfil a Royal Air Force requirement for a communications aircraft capable of transporting a V-bomber support crew. Twenty were ordered for this role in place of the originally mooted 80, in preference to the DH Dove. In RAF service the B.206 was designated the CC.1 Basset. Basset deliveries began in May 1965.

From the B.206Y came two evaluation B.206Z aircraft, followed by the initial civil production version, the Series 1 B.206C. Poor hot and high performance was in part responsible for sluggish sales at best. In response, Beagle designed the Series 2 B.206-S with more powerful turbocharged GTSIO-520 engines. The B.206-S also introduced a slightly revised cabin to seat eight and the entry door repositioned from above the wing to the rear port side fuselage.

A commuter airliner development was also built in prototype form, the 10 seat Series 3 which had a further enlarged cabin. However, nothing became of this as Beagle entered liquidation early in 1970.

Photo: A Beagle 206-S, which features turbocharged engines. (Stewart Wilson)

Beechcraft Model 18

Country of origin: United States of America

Type: Light utility transport

Powerplants: Super H18 – Two 335kW (450hp) Pratt & Whitney R-985AN-14B Wasp Junior nine cylinder radial piston engines, driving two blade constant speed propeller. Turboliner – Two 525ekW (705ehp) AiResearch (Garrett) TPE331-1-101B turboprops, driving three blade constant speed Hartzell propellers.

Performance: Super H18 – Max cruising speed 354km/h (191kt), economical cruising speed 298km/h (160kt). Initial rate of climb 1400ft/min. Service ceiling 21,400ft. Range with max fuel 2460km (1330nm). Turboliner – Max speed 450km/h (243kt), economical cruising speed 412km/h (222kt). Initial rate of climb 1520ft/min. Service ceiling 24,000ft. Range with max fuel and reserves 3340km (1800nm), range with max payload and reserves 555km (300nm).

Weights: Super H18 – Empty equipped 2650kg (5845lb), max takeoff 4490kg (9900lb). Turboliner – Empty (airliner) 2993kg (6600lb), max takeoff 5215kg (11,500lb).

Dimensions: Super H18 – Wing span 15.14m (49ft 8in), length 10.70m (35ft 3in), height 2.84m (9ft 4in). Wing area 33.5m^2 (360.7sq ft). Turboliner – Wing span 14.02m (46ft 0in), length 13.47m (44ft 3in), height 2.92m (9ft 7in). Wing area 34.8m^2 (374sq ft).

Capacity: Most Beech 18s seat two crew and seven to nine passengers in main cabin. Volpar Turboliner conversion seats up to 15.

Production: Over 9000 Beech 18s of all models built between 1937 and 1969, of which 2000 were built postwar. Wartime military production accounts for majority of Beech 18s built (approx 5000).

History: Beech's most successful airliner, more than 9000 Beech 18s were built over an uninterrupted three decade long production run, and while many of those were built against wartime military contracts, vast numbers went on to see civil service.

The prototype Beech 18 was flown for the first time on January 15 1937. The design followed conventional design wisdom at the time, including twin radial engines, metal construction and taildragger undercarriage, while less common were the twin tail fins. Early production aircraft were either powered by two 225kW (300hp) Jacobs L-6s or 260kW (350hp) Wright R-760Es, although the Pratt & Whitney Wasp Junior became the definitive engine from the prewar C18S onwards.

The arrival of World War 2 significantly boosted the already successful Beech 18's fortunes, with 5000 built as C-45s and used as transports and pilot trainers.

Postwar, large numbers of C-45s entered civil service, although Beech resumed production of the C18S. Progressive development resulted in the D18S of 1946, the Continental powered D18C of 1947, the E18S of 1954, the G18S from 1959 and the H18 with optional tricycle undercarriage from 1962. Beech production ceased in 1969.

The Beech 18 has also been the subject of numerous conversions. Volpar has offered simple tricycle undercarriage conversions, conversions with TPE331 turboprops and stretched and TPE331 powered conversions (described above). Hamilton meanwhile converted Beech 18s as Westwinds with Pratt & Whitney Canada PT6 turboprops and also offered stretches.

Photo: A tricycle undercarriage H18. (Bill Lines)

Beechcraft 35 Bonanza

Country of origin: United States of America

Type: Four & six seat high performance light aircraft

Powerplant: D35 – One 153kW (205hp) Continental E-185-11 flat six piston engine, driving a two blade constant speed propeller. P35 – One 195kW (260hp) fuel injected Continental IO-470-N. V35TC – One 210kW (285hp) turbocharged and fuel injected Continental TSIO-520-D.

Performance: D35 – Max speed 306km/h (165kt), cruising speed 281km/h (152kt). Initial rate of climb 1100ft/min. Range with no reserves 1247km (673nm). P35 – Max speed 330km/h (178kt), cruising speed 306km/h (165kt). Initial rate of climb 1150ft/min. Range with optional fuel and no reserves 1955km (1056nm). V35TC – Max speed 386km/h (208kt), max cruising speed 360km/h (194kt), long range cruising speed 262km/h (141kt). Initial rate of climb 1225ft/min. Range with standard fuel and reserves 917km (495nm), with opt fuel 1770km (955nm).

Weights: D35 – Empty 760kg (1675lb), max takeoff 1236kg (2725lb). P35 – Empty 841kg (1855lb), max takeoff 1418kg (3125lb). V35TC – Empty 907kg (2000lb), max takeoff 1542kg (3400lb).

Dimensions: D35 – Wing span 10.00m (32ft 10in), length 7.67m (25ft 2in). Wing area 16.5m^2 (177.6sq ft). P35 – Wing span 10.20m (33ft 6in), length 7.65m (25ft 1in). Wing area 16.8m^2 (181sq ft). V35TC – Wing span 10.20m (33ft 6in), length 8.04m (26ft 5in), height 2.31m (7ft 7in). Wing area 16.8m^2 (181sq ft).

Capacity: Models 35 through to J35 four people, K35 optional fifth passenger, later models from S35 onwards six people.

Production: Approximately 10,400 Model 35 Bonanzas of all variants were built between 1945 and 1982.

History: The distinctive Model 35 Bonanza is one of general aviation's most famous and prolific types, and enjoyed a production life spanning four decades.

The original 35 Bonanza flew on December 22 1945, heralding a new class of high performance GA aircraft, as it featured metal construction, retractable undercarriage and high performance. The design also incorporated the distinctive V-tail, a feature designed for aerodynamic efficiency and reduced weight. Deliveries of production aircraft began in 1947.

Subsequent development led to a massive family of subtypes. Briefly these are the A35 of 1949, with a greater max takeoff weight; the B35 with a 146kW (196hp) E-185-8 engine; the 153kW (205hp) E-185-11 powered C, D & E models through to 1954; the F & G35 with third cabin window and 170kW (225hp) E-225-8 of the mid fifties; the 180kW (240hp) Continental O-470-G powered H35 of 1957; the fuel injected 187kW (250hp) powered J35; 1960's M35 with larger rear windows; the N35 & P35 with a 195kW (260hp) IO-470-N and greater max takeoff weight; the redeveloped S35 of 1964 with six seats and redesigned rear cabin, optional three blade prop, 215kW (285hp) IO-520-B engine and yet greater weights; the heavier V35 of 1966; and turbocharged V35TC; the more raked windscreen V35 & V35A-TC of 1968; and the V35B and V35B-TC (just seven built) from 1970. The V35B remained in production until 1982 and underwent a number of detail changes in that time.

Photo: The S35 Bonanza was introduced in 1964 and was the first six seater Bonanza. (Bill Lines)

Beechcraft Debonair & Bonanza

Country of origin: United States of America

Type: Four to six seat high performance light aircraft

Powerplant: C33 – One 170kW (225hp) Continental fuel injected IO-470-K flat six driving a two blade constant speed propeller. A36 – One 225kW (300hp) Teledyne Continental IO-550-B engine driving a three blade constant speed McCauley propeller. B36TC – One 225kW (300hp) turbocharged Teledyne Continental TIO-520-UB engine.

Performance: C33 – Max speed 312km/h (168kt), max cruising speed 298km/h (161kt), long range cruising speed 248km/h (134kt). Initial rate of climb 930ft/min. Range with standard fuel and no reserves 957km (515nm), with optional tanks 1818km (980nm). A36 – Max speed 340km/h (184kt), max cruising speed 326km/h (176kt). Initial rate of climb 1208ft/min. Range with 45 minute reserves 1694km (914nm). B36TC – Max speed 394km/h (213kt), high speed cruise 370km/h (200kt). Initial rate of climb 1053ft/min. Range with 45 minute reserves 2022km (1092nm).

Weights: C33 – Empty 807kg (1780lb), max takeoff 1383kg (3050lb). A36 – Empty 1040kg (2295lb), max takeoff 1665kg (3650lb). B36TC – Empty 1104kg (2433lb), max takeoff 1746kg (3850lb).

Dimensions: C33 – Wing span 10.00m (32ft 10in), length 7.77m (25ft 6in), height 2.51m (8ft 3in). Wing area 16.5m^2 (177.6sq ft). A36 – Wing span 8.38m (27ft 6in), length 8.13m (26ft 8in), height 2.62m (8ft 7in). Wing area 16.8m^2 (181sq ft). B36TC – Same as for A36.

Capacity: All Model 33s seat one pilot and three passengers with some models having an optional fifth seat, all Model 36s seat one pilot and five passengers.

Production: More than 3350 Model 33s and 3500 Model 36s in all their variants have been built with production continuing.

History: First conceived in the late 1950s as a lower cost derivative of the V-tail Bonanza with a conventional tail, the Debonair and Bonanza family remains in production today.

The very first model 33 Debonair was little changed in configuration from the equivalent Model 35, except for the conventional three surface tail, a less powerful engine and a more austere interior fit. It first flew on September 14 1959 and was included in Beech's model range the following year.

The subsequent A33 and B33 Debonairs offered a small number of changes, while the C33 introduced a third cabin window and restyled interior. The Debonair was dropped from the range in 1967, by which time the C33A had been released, an aircraft very similar in performance and trim level to the V-tail Bonanzas, and the name Bonanza was adopted for this model range as well. Development of the 33 continued with the E33 and 155kW (285hp) E33A, the aerobatic E33C, the economy G33 and the F33, available in 155kW (285hp) A and aerobatic C models. The F33A remains in production.

The larger six seat Model 36 was first released in 1968, featuring a stretched cabin, 155kW (285hp) engine and greater takeoff weights. This aircraft remains in production today as the A36. The turbocharged 225kW (300hp) A36TC first appeared in 1979, production switched to the current B36TC in 1981.

Photo: An A36, which along with the F33 and B36TC are the only Bonanzas currently in production. (Raytheon)

Beech Musketeer, Sierra & Sundowner

Country of origin: United States of America

Type: Four seat light aircraft

Powerplant: A23A – One 125kW (165hp) Lycoming IO-346-A fuel injected flat four piston engine driving a two blade fixed pitch propeller. B19 – One 112kW (150hp) Lycoming O-320-E2D. C23 – One 135kW (180hp) Lycoming O-360-A4K. C23R – One 150kW (200hp) fuel injected Lycoming IO-360-A1B6 driving a variable pitch propeller.

Performance: A23A – Max speed 235km/h (127kt), long range cruising speed 188km/h (102kt). Initial rate of climb 728ft/min. Range with reserves 1252km (676nm). B19 – Max speed 225km/h (169kt), long range cruising speed 182km/h (98kt). Initial rate of climb 700ft/min. Range with reserves 1420km (1064nm). C23 – Max speed 228km/h (123kt), long range cruising speed 182km/h (98kt). Initial rate of climb 700ft/min. Range with reserves 1168km (631nm). C23R – Max speed 262km/h (141kt), long range cruising speed 213km/h (115kt). Initial rate of climb 927ft/min. Range with reserves 1271km (686nm).

Weights: A23A – Empty 624kg (1375lb), max takeoff 1089kg (2400lb). B19 – Empty 630kg (1390lb), max takeoff 1020kg (2250lb). C23 – Empty 681kg (1502lb), max takeoff 1111kg (2450lb). C24R – Empty 777kg (1713lb), max takeoff 1250kg (2750lb).

Dimensions: Wing span all versions 10.00m (32ft 9in), height all versions 2.51m (8ft 3in). Wing area all versions 13.6m^2 (146sq ft). Length: A23A – 7.62m (25ft 0in); B19, C23 & C23R – 7.84m (25ft 9in).

Capacity: All versions seat four, including pilot. Additional seating for two children in Musketeer Super III

Production: Total of 4455 built, including 2390 Musketeers, I/II/III/Custom & Sundowners; 904 Sports; 793 Super R/Sierras; and 369 Supers.

History: Beechcraft developed the Musketeer family as a lower cost, lower performance four seater below its Bonanza, and in competition with the Cessna 172 and Piper Cherokee.

The prototype Musketeer flew in October 1961, Beech adding the type to its sales range in 1962. What followed was a series of continual product updating resulting in the aircraft in its final Sierra form being very different to the original Musketeer. The first improved model was the A23 Musketeer II with a 125kW (165hp) Continental IO-346 engine (later replaced with a Lycoming O-360 as the B23).

The A23 was further developed into a three aircraft family (dubbed the Three Musketeers by Beech marketing), these being the A23A Musketeer Custom III with greater max takeoff weight, the reduced MTOW A23-19 Musketeer Sport III trainer with a 110kW (150hp) Lycoming O-320, and 150kW (200hp) IO-360 powered and increased MTOW Musketeer Super III. From 1970 these three introduced a more rounded fuselage and were renamed the Musketeer B19 Sport, C23 Custom and A24 Super respectively.

A retractable undercarriage variant of the Super is the A24R Super R. The Musketeer name was dropped in 1971, with the Custom renamed the Sundowner, and Super R the Sierra, with the Musketeer Sport becoming simply the Sport. The Sierra underwent significant changes to evolve into the 1974 model with a new cowling, quieter engine and more efficient prop. Further aerodynamic clean ups were made in 1977. Series production ended in 1983.

Photo: A 19A Musketeer Sport III. (Bill Lines)

Beechcraft 77 Skipper

Country of origin: United States of America

Type: Two seat pilot training aircraft

Powerplant: One 85kW (115hp) Lycoming O-235-L2C flat four piston engine, driving a two blade fixed pitch propeller.

Performance: Max speed 196km/h (106kt), max cruising speed 195km/h (105kt), long range cruising speed 158km/h (85kt). Initial rate of climb 720ft/min. Range with reserves 764km (413nm).

Weights: Empty 500kg (1103lb), max takeoff 760kg (1675lb).

Dimensions: Wing span 9.14m (30ft 0in), length 7.32m (24ft 0in), height 2.41m (7ft 11in). Wing area 12.1m^2 (129.8sq ft).

Capacity: Two people (typically trainee and instructor) seated side by side.

Production: Production of the Skipper ceased in 1981 after 312 had been built.

History: Beech developed the Skipper as a low expense two seat trainer in response to the growing costs (mainly fuel) of pilot training in the mid 1970s.

Starting life as Beech's PD (Preliminary Design) 285, the new Skipper was intended to be a simple and cost effective new generation pilot training aircraft combining low purchasing and operating costs, and lightweight but sturdy construction. A PD285 prototype flew on February 6 1975, but this differed from production aircraft in that it was powered by a 75kW (100hp) Continental O-200 engine, and featured a conventional low set tailplane.

Protracted development meant that the first of the definitive Model 77 Skippers did not fly until September 1978, by which time the 85kW (115hp) Lycoming O-235 engine and T-tail had been settled upon.

US FAA certification was awarded in April 1979, and the first production aircraft were delivered in May 1979 to Beechcraft's own Beech Aero Centre pilot training centres. Production lasted just three years until 1981 during which time little more than 300 had been built. Unsold Skipper stocks kept the type available for a further year.

The Skipper was in direct competition with Piper's very successful PA-40 Tomahawk and Cessna's 152. The Tomahawk was developed in a very similar time scale to the Skipper (entering service in early 1978) and both aircraft share a T-tail, low wing and canopy style canopy configuration (with 360° all round vision and a door on each side), and the Lycoming O-235 powerplant.

Other features of the Skipper design are a NASA developed GA(W)-1 high lift wing (the result of joint NASA and Beech research into high lift, supercritical aerofoils) bonded metal construction, tubular spars, and flap and aileron actuation by torque tubes in place of the more conventional cable and pulley system. New construction techniques meanwhile were intended to reduce manufacturing costs.

Photo: Of the three definitive primary trainers of the late 1970s and early 1980s, the Skipper was the least successful. Piper's Tomahawk and Cessna's 152 easily outsold the Beech product. (Bill Lines)

Beechcraft 76 Duchess

Country of origin: United States of America

Type: Four place light twin and twin engined trainer

Powerplants: Two 135kW (180hp) Lycoming O-360-A1G6D flat four piston engines driving two blade constant speed propellers.

Performance: Max speed 317km/h (171kt), max cruising speed 307km/h (165kt), long range cruising speed 280km/h (151kt). Initial rate of climb 1248ft/min. Max range with reserves 1445km (780nm).

Weights: Empty 1110kg (2446lb), max takeoff 1780kg (3900lb).

Dimensions: Wing span 11.58m (38ft 0in), length 8.85m (29ft 1in), height 2.89m (9ft 6in). Wing area 16.8m² (181.1sq ft).

Capacity: Seats for four, usually including one pilot. Pilot and student pilot seated side by side for twin engine flying training missions.

Production: A total of 437 Duchesses were built between 1978 and 1982.

History: The Model 76 Duchess represented a new class of light four place twins developed in the mid 1970s.

The prototype of the Duchess, designated the PD289, made its first flight in September. However a further 30 months of development work passed before the first production Model 76 took to the air in May 1977. Certification was granted in early 1978, with first deliveries commencing in that May, slotting between the Bonanza and the Baron in the Beechcraft model range.

Aside from the prototype PD289, no variations of the Duchess 76 were built before production ended in 1982. All Duchesses therefore feature two Lycoming O-360 engines, a T-tail (incorporated to reduce control forces and improve elevator response), entry doors on either side of the cabin and electric trim and flap controls (the prototype PD289 featured manually operated flaps).

Like many Beechcrafts, the Duchess has a bonded honeycomb structure wing, and a four place cabin. The fuselage was based on the Sierra's, and the two types share common structural components.

Like its contemporaries the Grumman/Gulfstream American Cougar and Piper Seminole, the Duchess's success was hampered through unfortunate timing. Ever increasing advances in engine efficiency, safety and reliability led to a rise in popularity for big high performance singles such as Beech's own Bonanza series, which lacked the maintenance overheads of two engines, but had comparable performance. To a greater extent than the Seminole and Cougar though, the Duchess enjoyed some success as a twin engine pilot trainer, a role in which it continues to serve in.

Beech developed the Duchess for low cost, high volume production, but the falling popularity of light twins, an economic recession and crippling product liability laws in the USA all contributed to a relatively short production run.

Photo: Many Duchesses are employed in the twin engine training role. The Duchess was one of a number of GA aircraft designed in the 1970s to feature a T-tail. (Lance Higgerson)

Beechcraft 55, 56 & 58 Baron

Country of origin: United States of America

Type: Four or six place business twin

Powerplants: B55 – Two 140kW (260hp) Continental IO-470-L fuel injected horizontally opposed flat six piston engines, driving two blade constant speed propellers. 58 – Two 225kW (300hp) Teledyne Continental IO-550-C engines driving three blade constant speed McCauley propellers.

Performance: B55 – Max speed 373km/h (201kt), max cruising speed 348km/h (188kt), long range cruising speed 320km/h (173kt). Initial rate of climb 1693ft/min. Range with reserves 1836km (990nm). 58 – Max speed 386km/h (208kt), cruising speed 367km/h (198kt). Initial rate of climb 1735ft/min. Range with reserves 2920km (1575nm).

Weights: B55 – Empty 1468kg (3236lb), max takeoff 2313kg (5100lb). 58 – Empty 1619kg (3570lb), max takeoff 2495kg (5500lb).

Dimensions: B55 – Wing span 11.53m (37ft 10in), length 8.53m (28ft 0in), height 2.92m (9ft 7in). Wing area 18.5m² (199.2sq ft). 58 – Wing span 11.53m (37ft 10in), length 9.09m (29ft 10in), height 2.97m (9ft 9in). Wing area 18.5m² (199.2sq ft).

Capacity: Models 55 and 56 had standard seating for four, with some models offering an optional fifth seat. Model 58 has optional fifth and sixth seats.

Production: Production of the Model 58 Baron continues, with more than 2410 of all variants built by late 1996.

History: The successful and long running Baron line is widely regarded as the most successful of its class, comfortably outlasting its main rivals from Piper and Cessna in production.

Development of the Baron began in the late 1950s, the first to fly, the Model 95-55 on February 29 1960, essentially being a re-engined development of the Model 95 Travel Air. As a result the Baron can lay claim to Bonanza and T-34 Mentor lineage, as the Travel Air combined the fuselage of the former with the tail of the latter, plus twin engines, a new wing and other new features.

The first Barons were delivered during early 1961, although these early production examples were soon followed off the line in 1962 by the improved A55. The subsequent B55 of 1965 is a definitive Baron model and remained in production until 1982, during which time it was continually refined. During the B55's model life other variants entered production, these included the more powerful C55, D55 and E55. In the meantime the turbocharged Baron 56TC appeared in 1967 and the A56TC in 1970, although these were produced only in limited numbers.

The Model 58 is a stretched version of the 55, and first entered production in 1970. It remains in production today, having evolved somewhat in production during that time. Versions include the pressurised 58P and the turbocharged 58TC. Both are powered by 240kW (325hp) Continental TSIO-520s.

Photo: Today the popular Baron is the benchmark that other twins are measured by. Pictured is a Baron 58. (Raytheon)

Beechcraft Queen Air

Country of origin: United States of America

Type: Utility, light executive transport and commuter airliner

Powerplants: 65 – Two 255kW (340hp) IGSO-480-A1E6 Lycoming fuel injected supercharged flat six piston engines, driving three blade constant speed propellers. B80 – Two 285kW (380hp) Lycoming IGSO-540-A1D piston engines.

Performance: 65 – Max speed 385km/h (208kt), max cruising speed 344km/h (186kt), long range cruising speed 267km/h (144kt). Range with reserves and standard fuel 1682km (908nm), with optional fuel 2670km (1442nm). B80 – Max speed 400km/h (215kt), max cruising speed 362km/h (195kt), typical cruising speed 335km/h (181kt). Range with reserves 1950km (1053nm).

Weights: 65 – Empty 2324kg (5123lb), max takeoff 3719kg (8200lb). B80 – Empty 2394kg (5277lb), max takeoff 3992kg (8800lb).

Dimensions: Wing span 15.32m (50ft 3in), length 10.82m (35ft 6in), height 4.33m (14ft 3in). Wing area 27.3m^2 (294sq ft).

Capacity: One or two pilots and up to nine passengers in commuter configuration, or six passengers in executive transport role.

Production: 1001 Queen Airs of all models built (404 Model 65s & A65s, 42 Model 70s, 510 Model 80s and 45 Model 88s), including U-8F Seminoles for the US Army.

History: When it first appeared in the late 1950s, the versatile Queen Air was the largest Beech built since the WW2 era radial engine powered Beech 18.

Beech's prototype Model 65 made its first flight on August 28 1958, with deliveries of production aircraft in late 1960 marking the beginning of a production lifespan that would last almost two decades. This first model combined the wings, undercarriage, Lycoming engines and tail surfaces of the Model E50 Twin Bonanza with a new and substantially larger fuselage. A Queen Air 65 established a new class altitude record of 34,882ft in 1960.

Subsequent variants to follow were many, and included the 3630kg (8000lb) max takeoff weight Model 80 with more powerful 285kW (380hp) engines and swept fin and rudder. This model evolved into the A80, the first to be offered as a commuter airliner. Introduced in 1964, the A80 had a redesigned nose and interior, increased wing span and a 227kg (500lb) greater takeoff weight. The pressurised 88 had round windows and the longer wingspan of the A80 and a 3992kg (8800lb) MTOW.

The Model B80 was the last major production model and appeared in 1966. It featured the longer span wing and the 88's MTOW. The model A65 was essentially a Model 65 with the swept fin and rudder of the Model 80, and entered production in 1967. The Model 70 entered production in 1969, it featured the longer span wings, 3720kg (8200lb) MTOW and 255kW (340hp) engines. Production of the Queen Air ceased in 1977.

Photo: Successful in its own right, the Queen Air was also the precursor to the very popular turboprop King Air. Pictured is a model B80, the last major Queen Air production variant. (Lance Higgerson)

Beechcraft King Air 90 & 100

Country of origin: United States of America

Type: Twin turboprop corporate and utility transport

Powerplants: 90 – Two 373kW (500shp) United Aircraft of Canada, (now Pratt & Whitney Canada) PT6A-6 turboprops driving three blade Hartzell constant speed propellers. F90 – Two 560kW (750shp) P&WC PT6A-135s driving four blade props. B100 – Two 533kW (715shp) Garrett TPE331-6-252Bs driving three blade props.

Performance: 90 – Max speed 450km/h (243kt), max cruising speed 435km/h (235kt). Initial rate of climb 1900ft/min. Range with reserves 2520km (1360nm). F90 – Max cruising speed 494km/h (267kt). Initial rate of climb 2455ft/min. Range 2920km (1576nm). B100 – Max speed 491km/h (265kt). Initial rate of climb 2140ft/min. Range at max cruising speed 2343km (1264nm), at economical cruising speed 2455km (1325nm).

Weights: 90 – Empty equipped 2412kg (5318lb), max takeoff 4218kg (9300lb). F90 – Empty 2971kg (6549lb), max takeoff 4967kg (10,950lb). B100 – Empty equipped 3212kg (7092lb), max takeoff 5352kg (11,800lb).

Dimensions: 90 – Wing span 13.98m (45ft 11in), length 10.82m (35ft 6in), height 4.47m (14ft 8in). Wing area 25.9m^2 (279.7sq ft). F90 – Wing span 14.00m (45ft 11in), length 12.13m (39ft 10in), height 4.60m (15ft 1in). Wing area 26.0m^2 (279.7sq ft). B100 – Wing span 14.00m (45ft 11in), length 12.17m (39ft 11in), height 4.70m (15ft 5in). Wing area 26.0m^2 (279.7sq ft).

Capacity: 90 – One or two pilots side by side on the flightdeck, plus seating for four in an executive layout. Maximum seating for eight. 100 – Six to eight passengers in corporate configuration, or max seating for 13 passengers.

Production: Approximately 1500 of all variants of the King Air model 90 family built since 1963 (including 250 military orders). Approximately 350 King Air 100s were built.

History: The Model 90 King Air family is the basis for the largest and most successful family of corporate turboprop twins yet built.

Beechcraft announced that it was designing a new Queen Air based twin turboprop powered aircraft in August 1963, with the subsequent prototype, known as the 65-90, taking to the air for the first time on January 20 1964. Certification was granted in May that year, with production deliveries occurring by year's end. In simple terms these first aircraft were turboprop powered and pressurised Queen Airs. A prolific family of subtypes followed.

Variants on the Model 90 theme include the A90 and B90 with PT6A-20 engines; the C90 with PT6A-21s; the E90 with more powerful PT6A-34Bs; and the F90 with the T-tail of the 200 (described separately), four blade props and other mods. The less expensive 90SE Special Edition was released during 1994, and remains in production alongside the C90B, which was introduced in 1991.

Beech announced it was developing the King Air 100 series in May 1969. Compared with the 90 series it was 1.27m (4ft 2in) longer, allowing greater seating capacity, and featured a reduced wing span and larger rudder. The A100 is a military version, while the B100 is powered by 535kW (715shp) Garrett TFE331s. Production of the 100 ceased in 1984.

Photo: A King Air C90B. (Beech)

Beechcraft Super King Air 200

Country of origin: United States of America

Type: Twin turboprop corporate, passenger & utility transport

Powerplants: 200 – Two 635kW (850shp) Pratt & Whitney Canada PT6A-41 turboprops driving three blade constant speed propellers. B200 – Two 635kW (850shp) P&WC PT6A-42s.

Performance: 200 – Max speed 536km/h (289kt), max cruising speed 515km/h (278kt). Initial rate of climb 2450ft/min. Range with reserves at max cruising speed 3254km (1757nm), at economical cruising speed 3495km (1887nm). B200 – Max speed 536km/h (289kt), economical cruising speed 523km/h (282kt). Initial rate of climb 2450ft/min. Range with max fuel and reserves 3658km (1974nm) at 31,000ft and economical cruising speed.

Weights: 200 – Empty 3318kg (7315lb), max takeoff 5670kg (12,500lb). B200 – Empty 3675kg (8102lb), max takeoff 5670kg (12,500lb).

Dimensions: Wing span 16.61m (54ft 6in), length 13.34m (43ft 9in), height 4.57m (15ft 0in). Wing area 28.2m^2 (303.0sq ft).

Capacity: Flightcrew of one or two. Accommodation for a maximum of 13 passengers in main cabin, plus a further passenger beside the pilot on flightdeck. Typical corporate seating layout for six in main cabin.

Production: Over 1600 Super King Air 200s have been delivered to civil and commercial customers, while over 380 have been delivered to military forces.

History: The Super King Air 200 is a continuation of the King Air line, with new features including the distinctive T-tail, more powerful engines, greater wing area and span, increased cabin pressurisation, greater fuel capacity and higher operating weights compared to the King Air 100.

Beech began design work on the Super King Air 200 in October 1970, resulting in the type's first flight on October 27 1972. Certificated in mid December 1973, the King Air 200 went on to be the most successful aircraft in its class, eclipsing such rivals as the Cessna Conquest and Piper Cheyenne. Today the Super King Air is the only one of the three in production.

The improved B200 entered production in May 1980, this version features more efficient PT6A-42 engines, increased zero fuel max weight and increased cabin pressurisation. Sub variants include the B200C with a 1.32m x 1.32m (4ft 4in x 4ft 4in) cargo door, the B200T with removable tip tanks, and the B200CT with tip tanks and cargo door. The Special Edition B200SE was certificated in October 1995 and features EFIS avionics as standard.

Various special mission King Air 200s and B200s have been built, including for navaid calibration, maritime patrol and resource exploration. In addition several hundred Super King Airs have been built for the US military under the designation C-12. C-12s perform a range of missions from electronic surveillance to VIP transport.

Photo: A regional airliner configured Super King Air 200 in colours of the now defunct Lord Howe Island Airlines. Note the T-tail and stretched fuselage compared with the King Air 90 series.

Beechcraft Super King Air 300 & 350

Country of origin: United States of America

Type: Turboprop powered corporate and utility aircraft

Powerplants: Two 783kW (1050shp) Pratt & Whitney Canada PT6A-60A turboprops, driving four blade constant speed Hartzell propellers.

Performance: 300 – Max cruising speed 583km/h (315kt), economical cruising speed 568km/h (307kt). Initial rate of climb 2844ft/min. Range with max fuel and reserves 3630km (1960nm). 300LW – Same except for max initial rate of climb 3277ft/min. 350 – Max speed 584km/h (315kt), max cruising speed 576km/h (311kt), typical cruising speed 558km/h (301kt). Initial rate of climb 775ft/min. Range with four passengers and reserves 3763km (2031nm).

Weights: 300 – Empty 3850kg (8490lb), max takeoff 6350kg (14,000lb). 300LW – Empty same, max takeoff 5670kg (12,500lb). 350 – Empty 4096kg (9030lb), max takeoff 6805kg (15,000lb).

Dimensions: 300 & 300LW – Wing span 16.61m (54ft 6in), length 13.36m (43ft 10in), height 4.37m (14ft 4in). Wing area 28.2m^2 (303sq ft). 350 – Wing span 17.65m (57ft 11in), length 14.22m (46ft 8in), height 4.37m (14ft 4in). Wing area 28.8m^2 (310.0sq ft).

Capacity: 300 – One or two pilots on flightdeck, with standard layout for six passengers in main cabin. Alternative high density seating for 15 (including pilot). 350 – Typical passenger seating for eight in main cabin, optional seating for an extra two, plus one in toilet compartment and one on flightdeck next to the pilot, making a total of 13.

Production: 219 Super King Air 300s were built when production ended in 1991. Production of the 300LW ceased in 1994 after 35 had been built. Over 150 Super King Air 350s delivered.

History: The Super King Air 300 is an updated version of the successful B200 series, and it itself was replaced by the further improved Super King Air 350, the latest model in this long running and successful line of corporate and utility transports.

Design of an improved model of the successful Super King Air B200 series commenced in August 1981, the 14 month design effort culminating in the first flight of the modernised 300 model in October the following year. Improvements to the B200 were many, with the main change being the installation of more powerful PT6A-60A turboprops in place of the -42s of the earlier model. Other mods include reprofiled and more aerodynamically clean engine cowls and exhausts, extended wing leading edges plus minor internal changes. Both empty and max takeoff weights are also increased.

The max weight was reduced for the 300LW or 'Light Weight', this move was primarily intended to minimise the effects of airways user fees particularly in Europe. The 300AT was an airline pilot trainer.

The Super King Air 350 replaced the 300, its major improvements being a lengthened fuselage and the addition of winglets. The latest member of the King Air family, it had its first flight in 1988, and has been in production since late 1989. The Super King Air 350C features a built-in airstair and a 132 x 132cm (52 x 52in) freight door. The 350 is also available in a range of special missions and military variants.

Photo: A Super King Air 350. Note the fuselage stretch compared with the 200 series. A 350 delivered in June 1996 was the 5000th King Air (of all models) built. (Raytheon)

Beechcraft 99 Commuter & Airliner

Country of origin: United States of America

Type: Commuter airliner

Powerplants: B99 – Two 505kW (680shp) Pratt & Whitney Canada PT6A-28s turboprops driving three blade constant speed Hartzell propellers. C99 – Two 535kW (715shp) PT6A-36s.

Performance: B99 – Max cruising speed 460km/h (247kt). Initial rate of climb 2090ft/min. Range at max cruising speed 1665km (900nm), range at cruising speed 1887km (1019nm). C99 – Max speed 496km/h (268kt) at 8000ft, cruising speed at 8000ft 461km/h (249kt). Range with max fuel and reserves 1686km (910nm).

Weights: B99 – Empty equipped 2620kg (5777lb), max takeoff 4944kg (10,900lb). C99 – Operating empty 3040kg (6700lb), max takeoff 5125kg (11,300lb).

Dimensions: B99 – Wing span 14.00m (45ft 11in), length 13.58m (44ft 7in), height 4.38m (14ft 4in). C99 – Same except for wing span 13.98m (45ft 11in). Wing area 26.0m^2 (279.7sq ft).

Capacity: Flightcrew of one or two. Typical passenger accommodation for 15 at two abreast. Baggage stowed in nose compartment and underbelly cargo pod.

Production: Total Model 99 production of 239. This includes 164 99s, A99s, A99-As and B99s between 1967 and 1975 and production of 75 C99s between 1980 and 1986, when production ceased.

History: The Beech 99 is an evolution of the successful Queen Air/King Air series, and shares the King Air's basic powerplant and layout, but essentially is an all new design, with a significantly lengthened cabin with greater seating capacity.

Design of the 99 began in the late 1960s in part as a replacement for the venerable Beech 18. In December 1965 a stretched fuselage Queen Air was flown for the first time, while the Pratt & Whitney Canada PT6 powered prototype model 99 made its first flight in July 1966. The first customer aircraft was delivered in May 1968, the series then known as the Commuter 99. Subsequent models were the A99, A99-A and B99, with differing powerplants and weights. The B99 was available in two variants, the B99 Airliner and the B99 Executive, a corporate transport version with seating for between eight and 17 passengers.

Production of early models was halted in 1975, and it was not until 1979 that the improved C99 Commuter (plus the larger 1900, described separately) was announced as part of Beech's return to the commuter airliner market. A converted B99 fitted with P&WC PT6A-34 engines served as the C99 prototype, and flew in this form for the first time in June 1980. Production aircraft featured the PT6A-36 engines, and deliveries recommenced following certification in July 1981. Shortly afterwards it became known as the C99 Airliner. Production of the C99 then ceased in 1986.

Photo: A C99 Airliner fitted with the optional underbelly external cargo pod. (Andrew Eyre)

Beechcraft 1900

Country of origin: United States of America

Type: Regional airliner and corporate transport

Powerplants: 1900C – Two 820kW (1100shp) Pratt & Whitney Canada PT6A-65B turboprops, driving four blade constant speed Hartzell propellers. 1900D – Two 955kW (1280shp) P&WC PT6A-67D turboprops.

Performance: 1900C – Max cruising speed 495km/h (267kt). Range with 10 pax at long range cruise speed with reserves 2907km (1570nm). 1900D – Max cruising speed 533km/h (288kt). Range with 10 pax and reserves at long range cruising speed 2776km (1498nm).

Weights: 1900C – Empty 4327kg (9540lb), max takeoff 7530kg (16,600lb). 1900D – Operating empty 4670kg (10,360lb), max takeoff 7688kg (16,950lb).

Dimensions: 1900C – Wing span 16.60m (54ft 6in), length 17.63m (57ft 10in), height 4.54m (14ft 11in). Wing area 28.2m^2 (303sq ft). 1900D – Wing span (over winglets) 17.65m (57ft 11in), length 17.60m (57ft 11in), height 4.60m (14ft 11in). Wing area 28.2m^2 (303sq ft).

Capacity: Flightcrew of two. Standard passenger accommodation for 19 at two abreast. Exec-Liner configurations range for between 10 to 18, depending on customer requirements.

Production: 207 civil Beech 1900Cs were built when production ended. More than 200 1900Ds had been ordered at the time of writing.

History: The Beech 1900 19 seat commuter was chosen along with the smaller 1300, both developments of the King Air 200, and the C99 as Beech's re-entry into the regional airliner market.

The most obvious change from the King Air 200 to the 1900C is the substantially lengthened fuselage (17.63m/57ft 10in compared to 13.34m/43ft 9in). Other changes include more powerful engines, a modified tail with tailets, and stabilons on the lower rear fuselage.

Development of the 1900 commenced in 1979, with first flight occurring on September 3 1982. US FAA certification was awarded in November 1983, prior to the 1900C's entry into service in February the following year. The first Exec-Liner corporate transport version was delivered in mid 1985.

During the course of 1900C production a wet wing was introduced increasing fuel capacity by 927 litres (204Imp gal/245US gal), while military transport, maritime patrol and electronic surveillance versions were offered.

Production switched to the 1900D in 1991, with certification awarded in March 1991. The main change was the substantially deeper fuselage with stand-up headroom, plus larger passenger and freight doors and windows. This model has sold particularly well. For example the 1900D's biggest customer is Mesa Airlines, a United Airlines feeder, which has placed total firm orders for 118.

Photo: This Beech 1900C is in the colours of Alta Airlines. Although out of production, Raytheon Beech continues to market second hand 1900Cs alongside new build 1900Ds. (Raytheon)

Beechcraft 60 Duke

Country of origin: United States of America

Type: Four or six place light business twin

Powerplants: B60 – Two 285kW (380hp) Avco Lycoming TIO-541-E1C4 turbocharged fuel injected flat six piston engines, driving three blade constant speed propellers.

Performance: 60 – Max speed 460km/h (248kt), cruising speed 395km/h (214kt). Range with optional fuel and 45 minute reserves 1890km (1020nm). B60 – Max level speed 455km/h (246kt) at 23,000ft, max cruising speed 443km/h (239kt) at 25,000ft, cruising speed 431km/h (233kt) at 25,000ft.

Weights: 60 – Empty equipped 1860kg (4100lb), max takeoff 3050kg (6725lb). B60 – Empty equipped 1987kg (4380lb), max takeoff 3073kg (6775lb).

Dimensions: Wing span 11.96m (39ft 3in), length 10.31m (33ft 10in), height 3.76m (12ft 4in). Wing area 19.8m^2 (212.9sq ft).

Capacity: Standard seating for four with optional fifth and sixth seats and toilet.

Production: Beechcraft built 584 Dukes between 1968 and 1982, including 113 60s, 121 A60s and 350 B60s.

History: Slotting in between the Beech Baron and Queen Air in size, performance and general capabilities, the Duke was a pioneer in the pressurised high performance light business twin class.

Beechcraft began design work on its new Model 60 in early 1965, with the resulting first flight of the prototype occurring the following year on December 29. Design features of the sleekly styled Duke included turbocharged TIO-541 engines driving three blade propellers and a 0.32 bars (4.6psi) cabin pressure differential.

The airframe was based loosely on the Baron's wing and undercarriage, plus a new fuselage employing bonded honeycomb construction. Optional fuel tanks in the wings were offered, increasing range.

Deliveries of the initial 60 model began in July 1968. Further development led to the improved A60, features of which included an enhanced pressurisation system and longer life yet lighter turbochargers which increased the maximum altitude at which the engine could deliver maximum power, thus improving performance.

The definitive model of the Duke family is the B60. New interior arrangements and more improvements to the turbochargers were the main changes to this model, which first appeared in 1970. Production ceased in 1982.

Since its introduction into service the Duke has been regarded as something of a hot ship, with its high performance in a relatively small package the main attractions. However, this image did not translate into anything other than modest sales because of the Duke's relatively complex systems and high operating costs.

Photo: The Duke B60 accounted for about two thirds of all Duke production, although the B60's production total of 350 is relatively modest for a US GA type of its era. This example is modified with after market winglets.

Beechcraft 2000 Starship

Country of origin: United States of America

Type: Advanced technology corporate transport

Powerplants: Two 895kW (1200shp) Pratt & Whitney Canada PT6A-67As, driving five blade constant speed McCauley propellers.

Performance: 2000 – Max cruising speed 622km/h (335kt), economical cruising speed 546km/h (295kt). Initial rate of climb 3225ft/min. Max range 2630km (1634nm). 2000A – Max cruising speed 621km/h (335kt), economical cruising speed 570kt (307kt). Initial rate of climb 2748ft/min. Range with max usable fuel and reserves 2920km (1576nm).

Weights: 2000 – Empty equipped 4484kg (9887lb, max takeoff 6531kg (14,400lb). 2000A – Empty equipped 4574kg (10,085lb), max takeoff 6758kg (14,900lb).

Dimensions: Wing span 16.60m (54ft 5in), length 14.05m (46ft 1in), height 3.94m (12ft 11in). Wing area 26.1m^2 (280.9sq ft).

Capacity: Flightcrew of one or two pilots. Standard passenger layout for eight in 2000 or six in 2000A.

Production: Production ceased in early 1995 after three prototypes, 18 Starship 2000s and 32 Starship 2000As had been built

History: Despite its extensive use of modern technologies and innovative design the Starship was a commercial failure.

Conceived as a new generation light corporate transport in the King Air class, the Starship traces back to the 85% scale proof of concept demonstrator built by Scaled Composites, which first flew in August 1983. The prototype Starship 2000 proper made its first flight on February 26 1986, provisionally powered by PT6A-65 turboprops. A second prototype equipped with Collins avionics entered the flight test program in June 1986, while a third development aircraft took flight in January 1987. Initial US FAA certification was awarded on June 14 1988, while the first production example was flown on April 25 1989.

The unconventional Starship design incorporates many innovations. Foremost of these is its rear mounted laminar flow wing and variable geometry canards or foreplanes. The foreplanes sweep forward with flap extension for pitch trim compensation, designed to make it impossible for the Starship to stall on takeoff or landing.

The wing itself is constructed almost entirely of composites (something which attracted much criticism because of the associated difficulties of inspecting it thoroughly), and has tip mounted tails. The rear mounted engines are in a tractor arrangement, being behind the cabin noise is reduced, while their close proximity to each other also improves single engine handling. The EFIS flightdeck has Collins avionics with early generation colour and monochrome CRTs.

The improved Starship 2000A was certificated in April 1992. Changes include seating for six instead of eight, a slightly higher max takeoff weight, and increased range.

A lack of customer interest forced Beech to stop Starship production in early 1995 after just 53 had been built (including three prototypes), a somewhat inglorious end to a technologically innovative and promising design.

Photo: A Starship 2000A. (Raytheon)

Bell 47

Country of origin: United States of America

Type: Two or three seat light utility helicopter

Powerplant: 47G – Various Lycoming flat six piston engines ranging in output from 150kW (200hp) to 210kW (280hp), including the 47G-3B-2A's 210kW (280hp) Lycoming TVO-435-F1A, driving two blade main and tail rotors. 47J Ranger – One 230kW (305hp) Lycoming VO-540-B1B flat six.

Performance: 47G-3B-2A – Max speed 169km/h (91kt), cruising speed 135km/h (73kt) at 5000ft. Initial rate of climb 880ft/min. Range 397km (214nm) at 6000ft. 47J Ranger – Max speed 169km/h (91kt), cruising speed 130km/h (70kt). Initial rate of climb 800ft/min. Range with max fuel and no reserves 413km (223nm).

Weights: 47G-3B-2A – Empty 858kg (1893lb), max takeoff 1340kg (2950lb). 47J Ranger – 785kg (1730lb), max takeoff 1340kg (2950lb).

Dimensions: 47G-3B-2A – Rotor diameter 11.32m (37ft 2in), fuselage length 9.63m (31ft 7in), height 2.83m (9ft 4in). Main rotor disc area 100.8m^2 (1085sq ft). 47J Ranger – Same except for fuselage length 9.90m (32ft 5in).

Capacity: 47G – Pilot and two passengers on a single bench seat. 47J Ranger – One pilot and three passengers.

Production: Bell built more than 4000 47s between the late 1940s and 1974. Agusta-Bell of Italy licence built over 1200; Kawasaki of Japan 239; and Westland of the UK 239.

History: The familiar and distinctive Bell 47 is an especially significant aircraft as it was one of the world's first practical helicopters.

The ubiquitous Bell 47 dates back to Bell's Model 30 of 1943, an experimental helicopter evaluated by the US Army, 10 of which were ordered for that service. The first subsequent prototype Bell Model 47 (with a car type cabin with two seats) first took to the skies on December 8 1945, with this model becoming the first helicopter to be certificated, in May 1946.

The first civil variants to be produced however were the largely similar Model 47B, and the 47B-3 with an open cockpit. The 47D followed and was the first model to feature the famous 'goldfish bowl' canopy and the distinctive uncovered tail boom. The Model 47E was similar but powered by a 150kW (200hp) Franklin engine.

The definitive Model 47G followed the 47E into production in 1953, and it was this variant, in a number of successively more powerful versions, that remained in production until 1974, a testament to the utility and success of Bell's basic design. The 47G had optional metal rotor blades and was powered by a range of Lycoming engines outputting 150 to 210kW (200 to 280hp).

The Model 47H is based on the 47G, but with a fully enclosed fuselage and conventional cabin, and formed the basis for the 47J Ranger. The Ranger had a further enlarged cabin for four, and entered production in 1956. The 47J-2 Ranger introduced powered controls and metal blades as standard, and was powered by a 195kW (260hp) VO-540.

Photo: The world's first practical mass produced helicopter, the 47 remains in strong demand for the very same reason that initially made it successful – simplicity and reliability. Pictured is a Kawasaki Bell KH-4. The Kawasaki developed, 200kW (270hp) TVO-435 powered KH-4 seats four and is based on the 47G-3B. (Bill Lines)

Bell 206 JetRanger

Country of origin: United States of America

Type: Light utility helicopter

Powerplant: 206B JetRanger II – One 300kW (400shp) Allison 250-C20 turboshaft driving a two blade main rotor and two blade tail rotor. 206B-3 JetRanger III – One 315kW (420shp) Allison 250-C20J.

Performance: 206B – Max cruising speed 219km/h (118kt). Initial rate of climb 1540ft/min. Range 702km (379nm). 206B-3 – Max speed 225km/h (122kt), max cruising speed 214km/h (115kt). Initial rate of climb 1280ft/min. Range with max fuel and no reserves 732km (385nm).

Weights: 206B – Empty 660kg (1455lb), max takeoff 1360kg (3000lb). 206B-3 – Empty 737kg (1635lb), max takeoff with external load 1521kg (3350lb), with internal load 1451kg (1500lb).

Dimensions: Main rotor diameter 10.16m (33ft 4in), fuselage length 9.50m (31ft 2in), height 2.91m (9ft 7in). Main rotor disc area 81.1m^2 (872.7sq ft).

Capacity: Total accommodation for five, including one pilot and one passenger in the front, and three behind them on the rear bench seat. Max internal payload (Model 206B) 635kg (1400lb), max external sling load 680kg (1500lb).

Production: Over 7700 military and civil versions of the JetRanger have been built by Bell in the USA and Canada, Agusta-Bell in Italy and other licensees. More than 4200 built for civilian customers.

History: The ubiquitous JetRanger series has been the definitive turbine powered light utility and corporate helicopter for three decades.

The JetRanger can trace its lineage back to an unsuccessful contender for a US Army competition for a light observation helicopter, which was won by the Hughes (now McDonnell Douglas) 500. This first Model 206 made its first flight on December 8 1962, while the following civil 206A, powered by a 235kW (317shp) Allison C18A, followed on January 10 1966. Deliveries of the first production JetRangers began late in that same year.

In the early 1970s production switched to the Model 206B JetRanger II with a 300kW (400shp) 250-C20 turboshaft, while conversion kits to upgrade earlier As to the new standard were made available. The third major variant of the JetRanger is the 315kW (420shp) 250-C20B powered JetRanger III, with first deliveries commencing in late 1977. Once again Bell offered a conversion kit to update earlier helos to the new standard. Other features of the JetRanger III were a larger and improved tail rotor and minor modifications.

JetRanger production was switched to Mirabel in Canada in 1986, and the current production model is the 206B-3.

The JetRanger was also accepted by the US Army as an observation helicopter as the OH-58 Kiowa, and variants of the Kiowa remain in production in the USA. Military 206Bs were also built in Australia for the Australian Army, and plans were held to build further civilian 206Bs for the Australian market, but these fell through.

Photo: The Bell 206 JetRanger is without doubt the most popular light turbine helicopter in the world. Although still in production, its replacement, the LongRanger based Bell 407, is now also in production. Pictured is a JetRanger III. (Martin Grimm)

Bell 206L LongRanger

Country of origin: United States of America

Type: Light utility helicopter

Powerplant: 206L LongRanger I – One 315kW (420shp) Allison 250-C20B turboshaft driving a two blade main rotor and two blade tail rotor. 206L-1 LongRanger II – One 375kW (500shp) Allison 250-C28B. 206L-3 LongRanger III & 206L-4 LongRanger IV – One 485kW (650shp) Allison 250-C30P.

Performance: 206L – Max speed 232km/h (125kt), cruising speed 229km/h (124kt). Hovering ceiling in ground effect 8200ft. Range 628km (339nm). 206L-1 – Same except for range 692km (374nm). 206L-3 – Max speed 241km/h (130kt), max cruising speed 203km/h (110kt). Range with no reserves 666km (360nm) at 5000ft. 206L-4 – Same except for range 661km (357nm) at 5000ft.

Weights: 206L – Empty 844kg (1861kg), max takeoff 1814kg (4000lb). 206L-1 – Empty 980kg (2160lb), max takeoff 1882kg (4150lb). 206L-3 – Empty 998kg (2200lb), max takeoff 1882kg (4150lb), or 1927kg (4250lb) with external sling load. 206L-4 – Empty 1031kg (2274lb), max takeoff 2018kg (4450lb), or 2064kg (4550lb) with external sling load.

Dimensions: Main rotor diameter 11.28 (37ft 0in), fuselage length 206L & 206L-1 10.13m (33ft 3in), 206L-3 10.44m (34ft 3in), 206L-4 – 9.81m (32ft 2in), height 3.14m (10ft 4in). Main rotor disc area 99.9m^2 (1075.2 sq ft).

Capacity: Total seating for seven, including five passengers in main rear cabin, or four in an optional executive layout. Can accommodate two stretchers and two medical attendants in aerial ambulance configuration. External sling load capacity of 907kg (2000lb).

Production: More than 1200 LongRangers have been delivered including a small number for military customers.

History: Bell developed the LongRanger to fill a market gap between its light 206 JetRanger and medium lift 205 and 212 Twin Twelve.

Bell announced it was developing a stretched JetRanger in September 1973, the subsequent Model 206L flew for the first time on September 11 1974, and production began in early 1975. The stretched LongRanger seated a further two passengers over the JetRanger from which it was derived, and featured a more powerful engine and Noda-Matic transmission suspension system for greater passenger comfort.

Subsequent versions have been the 206L-1 LongRanger II, introduced in 1978, the 206L-3 LongRanger III, and the current 206L-4 LongRanger IV, introduced in 1992. Each subsequent version features increasingly more powerful engines and other minor improvements. LongRanger production, along with the JetRanger, was transferred to Mirabel in Canada in 1986.

The LongRanger has found favour not only as a corporate transport, but with police and medical services worldwide, its extra cabin size providing a very useful boost in capacity. Bell now builds a twin engined LongRanger, the TwinRanger, while a US company offers the twin engine Gemini ST conversion of the LongRanger, and these are described separately in the next entry.

Photo: A longer cabin is the primary visual difference between the JetRanger and the LongRanger. Pictured is a LongRanger IV used at the Atlanta Olympic Games on support duties. (Bell)

Bell TwinRanger & Tridair Gemini ST

Countries of origin: United States of America & Canada

Type: Twin engine light utility helicopters

Powerplant: Two 335kW (450shp) takeoff rated Allison 250-C20R turboshafts, driving a two blade main rotor and two blade tail rotor.

Performance: 206LT – Max cruising speed 217km/h (117kt), economical cruising speed 200km/h (108kt). Service ceiling 10,000ft. Hovering ceiling in ground effect 10,000ft, out of ground effect 6900ft. Range with max fuel and no reserves at long range cruising speed 463km (250nm). 206L-3ST – Max cruising speed 217km/h (117kt). Initial rate of climb 1550ft/min. Service ceiling 20,000ft. Hovering ceiling in ground effect 15,800ft. Range with max payload and max internal fuel 643km (347nm).

Weights: 206LT – Standard empty 1246kg (2748lb), max takeoff 2018kg (4450lb), or 2064kg (4550lb) with an external sling load. 206L-3ST – Empty 1175kg (2590lb), max takeoff 1928kg (4250lb).

Dimensions: Main rotor diameter 11.28m (37ft 0in), length overall 13.02m (42ft 9in), fuselage length 9.81m (32ft 3in), height 3.14m (10ft 4in). Main rotor disc area 99.9m^2 (1075.2sq ft).

Capacity: Typical seating for seven, plus pilot, in three rows (3+2+3). Executive configuration has club seating for four in main cabin.

Production: Conversions to Gemini ST configuration commenced in early 1994. Deliveries of new build 206LTs began in early 1994.

History: Bell's 206LT TwinRanger, is, as its name suggests, a new build twin engined development of the 206L LongRanger, while Tridair helicopters in the USA offers its twin engine Gemini ST conversion for existing LongRangers.

The name TwinRanger predates the current 206LT to the mid 1980s when Bell first looked at a developed twin engine version of the LongRanger. The Model 400 TwinRanger actually flew (maiden flight was on April 4 1984) and featured two Allison 250 turboshafts, the four blade main rotor developed for the military Bell 406/OH-58 Kiowa and a reprofiled fuselage, but development was later suspended.

The current 206LT TwinRanger is based on Tridair Helicopters' Gemini ST conversion program. Tridair announced it was working on a twin engine conversion of the LongRanger in 1989, and the prototype flew for the first time on January 16 1991. Full FAA certification was awarded in November and covers the conversion of LongRanger 206L-1s, L-3s and L-4s to Gemini ST configuration.

In mid 1994 the Gemini ST made history when it was certificated as the first Single/Twin aircraft, allowing it to operate either as a single or twin engine aircraft throughout all phases of flight. This unique certification allows it to operate with a single engine for maximum economy (for ferrying etc), with the extra redundancy and performance of a twin available when required.

Bell's 206LT TwinRanger is a new build production equivalent to Tridair's Gemini ST, based on the LongRanger IV. The first example was delivered in January 1994.

The TwinRanger will be replaced by the 427 which is currently under development.

Photo: The reprofiled engine/transmission coaming is the most notable difference between the TwinRanger/Gemini ST and the single engine LongRanger. (Bell)

Bell 204, 205 & 214B

Country of origin: United States of America

Type: Medium lift utility helicopter

Powerplant: 204B – One 820kW (1100shp) Lycoming T5311A turboshaft driving a two blade main rotor and a two blade tail rotor. 205A-1 – One 932kW (1250shp) T5313B Lycoming turboshaft derated from 1050kW (1400shp).

Performance: 204B – Max speed 222km/h (120kt), max cruising speed 217km/h (117kt). Initial rate of climb 1600ft/min. Range with reserves 370km (200nm). 205A-1 – Max speed 204km/h (110kt), cruising speed 180km/h (97kt). Initial rate of climb 1680ft/min. Range 553km (300nm) at 8000ft.

Weights: 204B – Empty 2085kg (4600lb), max takeoff 4310kg (9500lb). 205A-1 – Empty 2414kg (5323lb), max takeoff 4765kg (10,500lb) with external load.

Dimensions: 205B – Main rotor diameter 14.63m (48ft 0in), fuselage length 12.69m (41ft 8in), height 4.45m (14ft 7in). Main rotor disc area 168.0m^2 (1808sq ft). 205A-1 – Same except for fuselage length 12.65m (41ft 6in).

Capacity: 204B – Total accommodation for 10 people, including one or two pilots, or 1360kg (3000lb) of freight. 205A-1 – Total accommodation for 15 including one or two pilots plus 1815kg (4000lb) of cargo internally, or 2270kg (5000lb) externally on a sling load. Air ambulance configuration for six stretchers and one or two medical attendants.

Production: Over 60 civil Model 204Bs were delivered by 1967, while further examples were built by Agusta-Bell up until 1973. 12,000 Model 205s (including civil 205A-1s) have been built by Bell and Agusta-Bell up to the early 1980s.

History: The Bell Model 204B and 205A-1 are the civil counterparts to the highly successful UH-1B and UH-1H Iroquois military helicopters.

Bell designed the Model 204 in response to a 1955 US Army requirement for a multi purpose utility helicopter. The 204 was something of a quantum leap forward in helicopter design as it was one of the first to be powered by a turboshaft. The turboshaft engine radically improved the practicality of the helicopter due to its lower maintenance and operating costs, lower fuel consumption and high power output. The use of a turboshaft in the 204 allowed it to carry a useful payload over respectable ranges and at reasonable speeds, which resulted in the 204 and 205 series becoming the most successful western helicopter in terms of numbers built.

The UH-1B, from which the 204B was derived, was first delivered March 1961. The subsequent Model 205A-1 is based on the UH-1H, which, when compared to the B model, is greater in length and capacity, has better performance and a more powerful engine.

In civil guise the 204 and 205 have been operated in a number of utility roles.

The 214B Biglifter is based on the 205 but is powered by a massive 2185kW (2930shp) Lycoming LTC4B turboshaft (with more than twice the power of the 205's T53). Its main use is as an aerial crane. Iran's Army took delivery of 287 during the 1970s while smaller numbers were built for civil customers through to 1981.

Photo: A firefighting configured 205. (David Neafsey)

Bell 212 Twin Two-Twelve

Countries of origin: United States of America and Canada

Type: Medium lift utility helicopter

Powerplant: One 1340kW (1800shp) (derated to 960kW/1290shp) Pratt & Whitney Canada PT6T-3 or PT6T-3B Turbo Twin-Pac, comprising of two coupled PT6 turboshafts sharing a common gearbox with a single output shaft, driving a two blade main rotor and two blade tail rotor.

Performance: Max speed 206km/h (111kt), long range cruising speed 193km/h (104kt). Initial rate of climb 1320ft/min. Range with standard fuel at long range cruising speed 450km (243nm).

Weights: Empty VFR configuration 2765kg (6097lb), IFR configuration 2847kg (6277lb); max takeoff (with or without an external load) 5080kg (11,200lb).

Dimensions: Main rotor diameter 14.69m (48ft 2in), length overall 17.46m (57ft 3in), fuselage length 12.92m (42ft 5in), height 4.53m (14ft 10in). Main rotor disc area 168.1m^2 (1809.6 sq ft).

Capacity: Total seating for 15, including one or two pilots. Max weight on an external sling load 2270kg (5000lb).

Production: Approximately 650 212s, including military aircraft, had been delivered by 1996. Production totals augmented by Agusta-Bell examples, although these are mainly military versions. Bell production transferred to Canada in 1988.

History: The Model 212 is a twin engined derivative of Bell's earlier and highly successful Model 204 and 205 series.

Bell announced its decision to develop the Model 212 in early May 1968, following successful negotiations with Pratt & Whitney Canada and the Canadian government, in large part in response to a Canadian Armed Forces requirement for a twin engined development of the CUH-1H (Model 205) then entering military service in that country. Development of the Model 212 was a joint venture between Bell, Pratt & Whitney Canada and the Canadian government, the latter providing financial support. The resulting helicopter (designated CUH-1N in Canadian and UH-1N in US military service) first flew in 1969 and was granted commercial certification in October 1970.

The most significant feature of the Twin Two-Twelve is the PT6T Twin Pac engine configuration. This consists of two PT6 turboshafts mounted side by side and driving a single output shaft via a combining gearbox. The most obvious benefit of the new arrangement is better performance due to the unit's increased power output. However, the Twin Pac engine system has a major advantage in that should one engine failure, sensors in the gearbox instruct the remaining operating engine to develop full power, thus providing a true engine out capability.

Aside from the twin engines, the 212 features only minor detail changes over the earlier Model 205 and UH-1H, including a slightly reprofiled nose. The 212 is also offered with a choice of IFR or VFR avionics suites. Production was transferred to Bell's Canadian factory in August 1988.

Photo: A 212 in rescue/medevac configuration. Another common 212 mission is oil rig support. (Dan White)

Bell 214ST

Country of origin: United States of America

Type: Medium transport helicopter

Powerplants: Two 1215kW (1625shp) General Electric CT7-2A turboshafts linked through a combining gearbox driving a two blade main rotor and two blade tail rotor.

Performance: Max cruising speed 260km/h (140kt) at 4000ft, or 264km/h (143kt) at sea level. Max initial rate of climb 1780ft/min. Service ceiling with one engine out 4800ft. Hovering ceiling in ground effect 6400ft. Ferry range with auxiliary fuel 1020km (550nm), range with standard fuel and no reserves 805km (435nm).

Weights: Empty 4300kg (9481lb), max takeoff 7938kg (17,500lb).

Dimensions: Main rotor diameter 15.85m (52ft 0in), length overall rotors turning 18.95m (62ft 2in), fuselage length 15.03m (49ft 4in), height overall 4.84m (15ft 11in). Main rotor disc area 197.3m^2 (2124sq ft).

Capacity: Pilot and copilot and up to 16 or 17 passengers. Freight volume of 8.95m^3 (316cu ft). Can carry an external sling freight load of 3630kg (8000lb).

Production: The 214ST was in production during 1980 and 1990, during which time 100 were built.

History: Despite sharing a common model number with the 214 Huey Plus and Big Lifter (described separately), the Bell 214ST is actually a much bigger helicopter.

Bell's biggest helicopter yet was developed in response to an Iranian requirement for a larger transport helicopter with better performance in its hot and high environment than its 214 Isfahans. Bell based its proposal on the 214 but made substantial design changes, resulting in what is essentially an all new helicopter with little commonality with the smaller 214 series.

The 214ST featured two General Electric CT7 turboshafts (the commercial equivalent of the military T700), a stretched fuselage seating up to 17 in the main cabin and stretched main rotor blades from the 214 with composite construction. The 214ST designation originally stood for Stretched Twin, reflecting the changes over the 214, but this was later changed to stand for Super Transporter.

The 214ST was to have been built under licence in Iran as part of that country's plans to establish a large army air wing (other aircraft ordered in large numbers under this plan were the 214A Isfahan and AH-1J SeaCobra, but the Islamic revolution and fall of the Shah in 1979 put paid to these plans).

Undeterred, Bell continued development of the 214ST for civil and military customers. The 214ST flew for the first time on July 21 1979 and 100 production aircraft were built through to 1990.

Most 214ST sales were to military customers. Ironically, Iraq was the 214ST's largest customer, taking delivery of 45 during 1987 and 1988, some most likely seeing service in the Gulf War.

Civil applications are numerous, including oil rig support, where its twin engine configuration and 17 passenger main cabin are big assets.

Photo: The 214ST is Bell's largest helicopter, and differs considerably from the similarly designated 214A and 214B. (Robert Wiseman)

Bell 412

Countries of origin: United States of America and Canada

Type: Medium lift utility helicopter

Powerplants: 412 – One 1350kW (1800shp) (derated to 980kW/1308shp for takeoff) Pratt & Whitney Canada PT6T-3B Turbo Twin Pac, consisting of two PT6 turboshafts linked through a combining gearbox, driving a four blade main rotor and two blade tail rotor. 412SP – One 1044kW (1400shp) takeoff rated PT6T-3B-1 Turbo Twin Pac. 412HP – One 1342kW (1800shp) takeoff rated PT6T-3BE Turbo Twin Pac.

Performance: 412 – Max speed 240km/h (130kt) at sea level, cruising speed 235km/h (127kt). Max range 455km (245nm), or 835km (450nm) with auxiliary tanks. 412SP – Max speed 260km/h (140kt), max cruising speed 230km/h (124kt). Initial rate of climb 1350ft/min. Range with max payload and reserves 695km (374nm), max range with standard fuel 656km (354nm). 412HP – Max cruising speed 230km/h (124kt), long range cruising speed 241km/h (130kt). Range with standard fuel and no reserves 745km (402nm).

Weights: 412 – Empty equipped 2753kg (6070lb), max takeoff 5216kg (11,500lb). 412SP – Empty equipped (IFR) 3001kg (6616lb), max takeoff 5397kg (11,900lb). 412HP – Empty equipped (IFR) 3066kg (6759lb), max takeoff 5397kg (11,900lb).

Dimensions: Main rotor diameter 14.02m (46ft 0in), fuselage length 12.70m (41ft 9in), height 4.57m (15ft 0in). Main rotor disc area 154.4m^2 (1662sq ft).

Capacity: Total seating for 15, including one or two pilots. Maximum weight of an external sling load 2040kg (4500lb).

Production: Over 400 Bell 412s of all models, civil and military, have been built.

History: The 412 family is a development of the 212, the major change being an advanced smaller diameter four blade main rotor in place of the 212's two blade unit.

Development of the 412 began in the late 1970s and two 212s were converted to the new standard to act as development aircraft for the program. The first of these flew in August 1979, and the 412 was awarded VFR certification in January 1981. That same month the first delivery occurred. Subsequent development led to the 412SP, or Special Performance, with increased fuel capacity, higher takeoff weight and more optional seating arrangements. The 412HP, or High Performance, superseded the 412SP in production in 1991. Features include improved transmission for better hovering performance. Production of the 412 switched to Bell's Canadian plant in February 1989.

The current standard production model is the 412EP, or Enhanced Performance. The 412EP features a PT6T-3D engine and a dual digital automatic flight control system fitted as standard, with optional EFIS displays.

Like the 212, the 412 is in widespread use for a number of utility roles, including EMS and oil rig support, its twin engine configuration being an asset, particularly in the latter role. It too is in military service, Canada once again being a major customer.

Photo: An Indonesian licence built and registered NBell-412. Note the inflatable floats on the skids. IPTN has a licence to build up to 100 NBell-412s. (Bell)

Bell 407

Countries of origin: Canada and the United States of America

Type: Seven place utility helicopter

Powerplants: One 605kW (814shp) takeoff rated, 520kW (700shp) max continuous rated Allison 250-C47 turboshaft, driving a four blade main rotor and two blade tail rotor.

Performance: Max cruising speed at sea level 237km/h (128kt), max cruising speed at 3950ft 243km/h (131kt), economical cruising speed at sea level 213km/h (115kt), at 3950ft 211km/h (114kt). Service ceiling 18,690ft. Hovering ceiling in ground effect 12,100ft, out of ground effect 10,400ft. Max range 575km (312nm).

Weights: Empty equipped 1178kg (2598lb), max takeoff with internal load 2268kg (5000lb), max takeoff with sling load 2495kg (5500lb).

Dimensions: Main rotor disc diameter 10.67m (35ft 0in), length overall rotors turning 12.70m (41ft 8in), fuselage length 9.77m (32ft 1in), height overall 3.56m (11ft 8in). Main rotor disc area 89.4m^2 (962.1sq ft).

Capacity: Typical seating configuration for seven comprising pilot and passenger, with five passengers in main cabin. Max hook capacity 1200kg (2645lb).

Production: By late 1996 over 200 customers had ordered the 407. First deliveries in early 1996. Production rate of 10 per month by mid 1996.

History: Bell's 407 is the long awaited successor to its JetRanger and LongRanger light singles.

Development work on Bell's New Light Aircraft replacement for the LongRanger and JetRanger dates back to 1993. The result was the 407, an evolutionary development of the LongRanger.

A modified 206L-3 LongRanger served as the concept demonstrator 407 and first flew in this form on April 21 1994, while the 407 was first publicly announced at the Las Vegas Heli-Expo in January 1995.

The 407 concept demonstrator mated the LongRanger's fuselage with the tail boom and dynamic system of the military OH-58D Kiowa (which has a four blade main rotor). Fake fairings were used to simulate the wider fuselage being developed for the production standard 407. The first preproduction 407 flew in June 1995.

Compared with the LongRanger, the 407 features the four blade main rotor developed for the OH-58. This features composite construction and the blades and hub have no life limits. Benefits of the four blade main rotor include improved performance and better ride comfort.

The other big change over the LongRanger is the 18cm (8in) wider cabin, increasing internal cabin width and space, plus 35% larger main cabin windows. Power is from a more powerful Allison 250-C47 turboshaft fitted with FADEC, allowing an increase in max takeoff weight and improving performance at hotter temperatures and/or higher altitudes. The tail rotor is made from carbonfibre composites, while Bell is also studying a shrouded tail rotor.

Bell looked at the 407T twin 407 for a time, but instead is now developing the substantially revised PW206D powered 427.

Photo: An early production 407

Bell 427

Countries of origin: USA, Canada and South Korea

Type: Light twin utility helicopter

Powerplants: Two 456kW (611shp) takeoff rated, 405kW (543shp) max continuous rated Pratt & Whitney Canada PW206D turboshafts driving a four blade main rotor and two blade tail rotor.

Performance: Provisional – Max cruising speed at sea level 252km/h (136kt), normal cruising speed 233km/h (126kt). Hovering ceiling in ground effect 14,000ft, out of ground effect 10,500ft. Range at sea level 653km (353nm). Endurance 4hr.

Weights: Provisional – Empty 1580kg (3485lb), max takeoff 2720kg (6000lb).

Dimensions: Main rotor diameter 11.28m (37ft 0in), fuselage length approx 10.11m (33ft 2in). Main rotor disc area 99.9m^2 (1075.2sq ft).

Capacity: Pilot and up to seven passengers (in a 2+3+3 arrangement), or pilot and passenger side by side with seating for four in a club configuration in main cabin. In medevac configuration two stretcher patients and two medical attendants.

Production: Unit price in 1996 approx $US1,875,000. Certification and first production deliveries planned for late 1998.

History: Bell's latest helicopter, the 427 is a replacement for the 206LT TwinRanger and the cancelled 407T, which was to be a twin engine 407 (described separately).

When Bell first looked at a twin engine version of its new 407 light single, the company originally anticipated developing the 407T which would have been a relatively straightforward twin engine development (with two Allison-250C22Bs). However, Bell concluded that the 407T would not offer sufficient payload/range performance, and so began studies of a new, more extensively modified twin 407.

The result of these studies was the 427, which Bell announced at the 1996 Heli Expo in Dallas in February. Prior to this announcement Bell had signed a collaborative partnership agreement with South Korea's Samsung Aerospace Industries covering the 427. Samsung's role on the 427 program is significant, the South Korean company will build the 427's fuselage and tailboom, and will also assemble any 427s sold in South Korea and China at its Sachon plant. Samsung already builds the left and right fuselage halves and the tailboom for the Bell 212 and 412. Bell will build the 427's flight dynamics systems at Fort Worth in Texas, with final assembly planned for Bell's Mirabel, Quebec plant.

The 427 is based on the 407, but will feature some important changes – foremost the two Pratt & Whitney Canada PW206 turboshafts. The PW206s will power the composite four blade main rotor and two blade tail rotor (based on those on the OH-58D Kiowa) through a new combining gearbox. The main rotor's soft-in-plane hub features a composite flexbeam yoke and elastomeric joints, eliminating the need for lubrication and any form of maintenance. Other changes include the 33cm (13in) stretched fuselage and a revised profile, more pointed nose.

Bell hopes to achieve FAR Part 27 certification for the 427 in late 1998, with deliveries commencing soon after. FAR Part 29 certification is also planned.

Photo: An artist's impression of how the new 427 will look in flight.

Bell 222 & 230

Countries of origin: United States of America and Canada

Type: Twin engine light utility helicopters

Powerplants: 222B – Two 505kW (680shp) Avco (Textron) Lycoming LTS 101-750C turboshafts, driving a two blade main rotor and two blade tail rotor. 230 – Initially two 520kW (700shp) takeoff rated Allison 250-C30G2 turboshafts.

Performance: 222B – Max cruising speed 240km/h (130kt). Initial rate of climb 1730ft/min. Hovering ceiling in ground effect 10,300ft. Range with no reserves 724km (390nm). 230 – Max cruising speed (with wheels) 261km/h (141kt), economical cruising speed (with wheels) 256km/h (138kt). Service ceiling 15,500ft. Hovering ceiling in ground effect 12,400ft. Range at economical cruising speed, with standard fuel, wheels and no reserves 558km (301nm), or 713km (385nm) with skids; range with wheels and auxiliary fuel, no reserves 702km (380nm).

Weights: 222B – Empty equipped 2076kg (4577lb), max takeoff 3472kg (8250lb). 230 – Empty with wheels 2312kg (5097lb), max takeoff 3810kg (8400lb).

Dimensions: 222B – Main rotor diameter 12.80m (42ft 0in), fuselage length 12.85m (42ft 2in), height 3.51m (11ft 6in). Main rotor disc area 128.7m^2 (1385.4sq ft). 230 – Main rotor diameter 12.80m (42ft 0in), length overall 15.23m (50ft 0in), fuselage length with wheels 12.87m (42ft 3in), with skids 12.81m (42ft 0in), height overall with skids 3.20m (12ft 2in). Main rotor disc area 128.7m^2 (1385.4sq ft).

Capacity: Standard seating for eight, including pilot, in four rows. Alternatively four in main cabin in club configuration.

Production: 184 Bell 222s built. Bell built 38 230s between 1992 and August 1995.

History: Bell announced development of the all new 222 twin in 1974, following the positive response generated by a mockup proposal displayed at that year's Helicopter Association of America convention.

Having taken note of potential customers' preferences and suggestions, Bell modified its design accordingly, and the subsequent development effort led to the Model 222's first flight in August 1976. A number of advanced features were designed into the 222, including the Noda Matic vibration reduction system developed for the 214ST, stub wings housing the retractable undercarriage, provision for IFR avionics, and dual hydraulic and electrical systems.

The 222 was awarded FAA certification in December 1979. Production deliveries commenced in early 1980. Subsequent development led to the more powerful 222B with a larger diameter main rotor, introduced in 1982, and the essentially similar 222UT Utility Twin, which features skid landing gear in place of wheels.

The Bell 230 is a development of the 222 with two Allison 250 turboshafts instead of the 222's LTS 101s plus other refinements. First flight of a 230, a converted 222, took place on August 12 1991, and Transport Canada certification was awarded in March 1992. The first delivery of a production 230 occurred that November and customers had a choice of skid or wheel undercarriage. Production ceased in 1995 and the type has been replaced by the stretched, more powerful 430, described separately.

Photo: A Macau operated Bell 222UT. (Bell)

Bell 430

Countries of origin: Canada and the United States of America

Type: Twin engine intermediate size helicopter

Powerplants: Two 605kW (811shp) TO rated, 535kW (715shp) max continuous rated Allison 250-C40 turboshafts, driving a four blade main rotor and two blade tail rotor.

Performance: Max cruising speed at sea level 260km/h (140kt), economical cruising speed 240km/h (130kt). Service ceiling 18,340ft. Hovering ceiling in ground effect 11,350ft, out of ground effect 8750ft. Max range with reserves and standard fuel 607km (328nm). Max endurance 3hr 48min.

Weights: Empty equipped 2397kg (5285lb), max takeoff with internal load 4082kg (9000lb), max takeoff with sling load 4220kg (9300lb).

Dimensions: Main rotor disc diameter 12.80m (42ft 0in), length overall rotors turning 15.39m (50ft 6in), fuselage length inc tailskid 13.44m (44ft 1in), height to top of rotor head with wheels 3.71m (12ft 2in), with skid undercarriage 3.86m (12ft 8in). Main rotor disc area 129m^2 (1385.4sq ft)

Capacity: Typical seating configuration for 10 comprising pilot and passenger, with eight passengers in main cabin behind them in three rows of seats. Six and eight place executive layouts offered. In EMS role can carry one or two stretcher patients with four or three medical attendants respectively. Max hook capacity 1585kg (3500lb).

Production: First deliveries from June 1996. Annual production rate of 55 aircraft planned from 1998.

History: Bell's 430 intermediate twin helicopter is a stretched and more powerful development of the 230.

Bell began preliminary design work on the 430 in 1991, even though the 230 itself had only flown for the first time in August that year. The 430 program was formally launched in February 1992. Two prototypes were modified from Bell 230s, and the first of these flew in its new configuration on October 25 1994. The second prototype featured the full 430 avionics suite, its first flight was on December 19 1994.

The first 430 production aircraft was completed in 1995, while Canadian certification was awarded on February 23 1996, allowing first deliveries from mid that year. Meanwhile 230 production wound up in August 1995, making way for the 430.

Compared with the 230, the 430 features several significant improvements. Perhaps the most important of these is the new four blade, bearingless, hingeless, composite main rotor. Other changes include the 46cm (1ft 6in) stretched fuselage, allowing seating for an extra two passengers, 10% more powerful Allison 250 turboshafts (with FADEC) and a modern EFIS flightdeck. As well as the EFIS displays the 430 features a Rogerson-Kratos Integrated Instrument Display System (IIDS), comprising two LCD displays to present engine information. The 430 is offered with skids or retractable wheeled undercarriage.

Between August 17 and September 3 1996 Americans Ron Bower and John Williams broke the round the world helicopter record with a Bell 430, flying westwards from England.

Photo: The around the world Bell 430.

Bell Boeing 609

Country of origin: United States of America

Type: Six/nine seat corporate/utility tiltrotor

Powerplants: Two 1380kW (1850shp) Pratt & Whitney Canada PT6C-67A turboprops driving three blade proprotors.

Performance: Provisional – Max cruising speed 510km/h (275kt), normal cruising speed 465km/h (260kt). Operational ceiling 25,000ft. Range with a 2500kg (5500lb) useful load at 465km/h (260kt) 1400km (755nm).

Weights: Provisional – Max takeoff 7265kg (16,815lb).

Dimensions: Provisional – Proprotor diameter 7.9m (26ft), wing span 10m (33ft), fuselage length 13.3m (44ft), width overall rotors turning 18.3m (60ft).

Capacity: To be certificated for single pilot IFR operation. Main cabin seats six to nine passengers depending on configuration. Could also be configured for search and rescue/medevac with stretchers and medical attendants.

Production: First deliveries planned for early 2001. Unit price $US8-10m depending on configuration. Manufacturers estimate potential market at up to 1000 over the next two decades.

History: The Bell Boeing 609 is set to become the first civil application of the revolutionary tiltrotor technology, taking advantage of the partner companies' experience with the military V-22 Osprey.

Bell pioneered the tiltrotor concept with the experimental XV-3 which first flew as early as 1957 and then with NASA developed the XV-15 experimental demonstrator which first flew in 1977.

In 1982 the US Department of Defense contracted Bell and Boeing to build six full scale development V-22s. Subsequently the partners were awarded an engineering and manufacturing development contract, and now the first production V-22 Ospreys are due to be delivered to the US Marines in 1999.

In late 1996 Bell and Boeing announced that they intended to use their expertise and experience with the V-22 to develop a nine seat civil tiltrotor. The Bell Boeing 609 was formally unveiled on November 18 1996. First flight is planned for mid 1999 with certification and first deliveries scheduled for 2001. (The US FAA is drawing up a new certification category for tiltrotors and a new pilot type rating.)

The benefits of a tiltrotor are that it has the vertical takeoff, landing and hovering abilities of a helicopter combined with fixed wing turboprop speed and performance. As such Bell Boeing anticipates that the 609 will compete against helicopters such as the Sikorsky S-76 and turboprops such as Beech's King Air. As well as point to point corporate transport Bell Boeing envisages that the 609 will be used for offshore oil rig support, search and rescue and medevac missions, where its unique capabilities would be particularly useful.

The 609 will incorporate advanced technologies such as a glass cockpit, fly-by-wire flight controls and a composite construction fuselage. Power will be from two PT6C-67A turboprops.

The 609 could form the basis for a family of civil tiltrotors. Bell has a 51% share of the 609 and program leadership, Boeing would have leadership on any civil tiltrotors of 20 seats and over.

Photo: An artist's impression of the 609. (Bell Boeing)

Beriev Be-32

Country of origin: Russia

Type: Commuter airliner and utility transport

Powerplants: Two 754kW (1011shp) Mars (Omsk) TVD-10B turboprops, driving three blade constant speed propellers.

Performance: Max cruising speed 440km/h (237kt), economical cruising speed 375km/h (202kt). Initial rate of climb 1475ft/min. Range with 17 passengers 600km (323nm), with 14 passengers 960km (518nm), or with seven passengers 1750km (944nm).

Weights: Empty 4760kg (10,495lb), max takeoff 7300kg (16,090lb).

Dimensions: Wing span 17.00m (55ft 9in), length 15.70m (51ft 6in), height 5.52m (18ft 2in). Wing area 32.0m^2 (344.45sq ft).

Capacity: Flightcrew of two. Typical passenger arrangements for 14 to 17 at two abreast. Corporate shuttle configuration seats seven. Ambulance configuration accommodates nine stretcher patients, six seated patients and one medical attendant.

Production: Eight Be-30s were built in the late 1960s before program terminated. One of the original Be-30s converted to operate as the Be-32 demonstrator. Moscow Airways announced an order for 50 Be-32s in 1993.

History: The Beriev Be-32 is a modern incarnation of the Be-30 commuter that was originally developed for Aeroflot in the late 1960s.

The original Beriev Be-30 was designed against an Aeroflot requirement for a twin turboprop airliner and utility transport in the late 1960s. The prototype first flew on March 3 1967. Eight development aircraft were built in the late 1960s, but the project was cancelled when Aeroflot chose the Czech L 410 (described separately) in preference to Beriev's design. Since then the Be-30 lay dormant until Beriev resurrected it as the Be-32, firstly to claim time to height records in the mid 1970s, and then in the early 1990s in a bid to attract new business and gain scarce hard currency.

Beriev exhibited the improved Be-32 at the 1993 Paris Salon, the design bureau claiming that the Be-32 incorporated a number of improvements, including more powerful engines. The actual aircraft demonstrated was one of the original Be-30s modified to the new configuration.

The basic Be-32 is now fairly dated. It is of conventional design and construction. Features of this high wing unpressurised commuter include Mars (formerly Omsk) TVD-10B turboprops, use of Glass Fibre Reinforced Plastics in the wingtips, tail surfaces and wing/fuselage fillets and honeycomb panelling covering sections of the wing and tail. Floats and skis will be offered as options.

Work is now concentrating on the Pratt & Whitney Klimov PK6A powered Be-32K, which first flew on August 15 1995. The 820kW (1100shp) PK6A-65B is a Russian built version of Pratt & Whitney Canada's successful PT6A.

Moscow Airways has placed an order for 50 Be-32s, and the design bureau is hopeful of selling more. Be-32 production machines will be built at the Irkutsk Aviation Production Plant (where the Be-200 amphibian, refer next entry, is also scheduled to be built).

Photo: The Be-32 first appeared in the mid to late 1970s to claim time to height records. (Beriev)

Beriev Be-200

Country of origin: Russia

Type: Firefighting and multirole amphibian

Powerplants: Two 73.6kN (16,550lb) ZMKB Progress D-436T turbofans.

Performance: Max speed 720km/h (388kt), max cruising speed 700km/h (377kt). Initial rate of climb 2755ft/min. Service ceiling 36,090ft. Range with four tonne (8820lb) payload 2100km (1130nm), range with max fuel 4000km (2160nm). With full fuel load on firefighting mission, Be-200 can drop a total of 320 tonnes (705,465lb) of water in successive flights when water source is 200km (110nm) from operating base and 10km (6nm) from the fire front.

Weights: Max takeoff 36,000kg (79,365lb).

Dimensions: Wing span 31.88m (104ft 7in), length 32.05m (105ft 2in), height 8.90m (29ft 3in). Wing area 117.4m^2 (74.92sq ft).

Capacity: Flightcrew of two. In firefighting configuration can uplift 12 tonnes (26,460lb) of water. Alternative passenger seating for 68 economy class, or 10 to 32 first class, with a seating pitch up to 102cm (40in). Ambulance configuration seats seven medical attendants and 30 stretcher patients. Can carry 12 tonnes (26,460lb) of freight in cargo configuration.

Production: First prototype nearing completion in late 1996. Orders reportedly held for more than 100 Be-200s.

History: The unique Beriev Be-200 jet powered multirole amphibian is based on the larger military A-40 Albatross.

Beriev has extensive and unique experience in building large amphibious aircraft. The turboprop ASW Be-12 Tchaika was built in fairly large numbers from the mid 1960s (approx 150) for the Soviet Navy. The Be-42 Albatross meanwhile (which has the NATO reporting name 'Mermaid') first flew in prototype form in December 1986 and 20 are on order for the Russian navy for maritime surveillance and ASW.

The Be-200 is based on the Be-42. It uses many of the design features and technologies developed for the Be-42, but is smaller overall and designed for civil roles, in particular firefighting. Aerodynamically the Be-200 is very similar to its larger forebear, with the same overall proportions. The all metal hull design is based on the Be-42's, and the Be-200 has a mildly swept wing with winglets, above fuselage mounted turbofan engines and a swept T-tail. The airframe is strengthened to cope with the demands of water operations and firebombing and there is some use of advanced aluminium lithium alloys. Russian avionics with a two crew cockpit is standard, but an ARIA-2000 suite is offered. ARIA is a collaboration between the Russian avionics research institute and AlliedSignal. The ARIA-2000 suite includes specialist firefighting functions including an automatic glidescope and water source/drop zone memorisation.

The Be-200 is being developed by Betair, a collaboration between Beriev and Irkutsk in central Russia where the aircraft will be built, and Swiss company ILTA Trade Finance, which is providing marketing and financing support.

The Be-200 is being built to meet western certification requirements. First flight is planned for early 1997.

Photo: The Be-200 prototype was publicly displayed in October 1996 but was then still some months away from flying.

Boeing 707

Country of origin: United States of America

Type: Medium to long range commercial transport

Powerplants: 707-120B – Four 76.2kN (17,000lb) Pratt & Whitney JT3D-1 turbofans. 707-320B – Four 80kN (18,000lb) Pratt & Whitney JT3D-3s or four 84.4kN (19,000lb) P&W JT3D-7s.

Performance: 707-120B – Max speed 1010km/h (545kt), max cruising speed 1000km/h (540kt), economical cruising speed 897km/h (484kt). Range with max payload 6820km (3680nm), range with max fuel 8485km (4580nm). 707-320B – Max speed 1009km/h (545kt), max cruising speed 974km/h (525kt), long range cruising speed 885km/h (478kt). Range with max passenger load 6920km (3735nm), range with max fuel and 147 passengers and reserves 9265km (5000nm).

Weights: 707-120B – Operating empty 55,589kg (122,533lb), max takeoff 116,575kg (257,000lb). 707-320B – Empty 66,406kg (146,400lb), max takeoff 151,315kg (333,600lb).

Dimensions: 707-120B – Wing span 39.90m (130ft 10in), length 44.07m (144ft 6in), height 12.94m (42ft 5in). Wing area 226.3m^2 (2433sq ft). 707-320B – Wing span 44.42m (145ft 9in), length 46.61m (152ft 11in), height 12.93m (42ft 5in). Wing area 283m^2 (3050sq ft).

Capacity: Flightcrew of three or four. 707-120 max seating for 179, or 110 in two classes (44 first and 66 economy). 707-320B – Max seating for 219, or 189 single class at 81cm (32in) pitch, or 147 in two classes. Convertible or freighter versions – 13 A type containers.

Production: Production of commercial 707s ended in 1978 after 878 had been built. Limited production of military variants continued until 1990. Approximately 130 remain in commercial service.

History: The 707 revolutionised airliner travel when introduced into service in 1958, bringing with it great improvements in range, speed, capacity and relative affordability. The 707 also laid the foundations for Boeing's quarter century dominance of the jet airliner market.

Like many outstanding successes, the 707 resulted in a great financial gamble on Boeing's part. Recognising the potential that the jet engine had for commercial aviation, Boeing decided to develop a jet powered transport that could fulfil military tanker transport roles and could be easily adapted for airliner production. The resulting prototype, known as the Dash 80, flew for the first time on July 16 1954, and it was this aircraft that helped Boeing gain massive orders from the US Air Force for the similar KC-135 Stratotanker, and paved the way for the commercial 707.

The first passenger carrying production 707 (a 707-120 for Pan Am) flew on December 20 1957, and entered service later the following year. Developments of the 707-120 include the similar 707-220, the shorter -138 for Qantas and the stretched 707-320, which flew in July 1959. The 707-320 and -120 were later re-engined with JT3D turbofans (in place of the original JT3 turbojets) to become the 707-320B, the definitive 707 model, and the 707-120B respectively. The similar 707-420 was powered by Rolls-Royce Conways, while the proposed CFM56 powered 707-700 upgrade was flight tested but never entered production.

Most 707s in service today have been converted to freighters, while others are used as corporate transports.

Photo: A 707-320 freighter of Nigeria's Merchant Express. (Dave Fraser)

Boeing 720

Country of origin: United States of America

Type: Medium range medium capacity airliner

Powerplants: 720B – Four 75.6kN (17,000lb) Pratt & Whitney JT3D-1 or four 80kN (18,000lb) JT3D-3 turbofans.

Performance: Max speed 1009km/h (545kt), max cruising speed 983km/h (530kt), economical cruising speed 896km/h (484kt). Range with maximum payload and no reserves 6687km (3610nm).

Weights: Operating empty 51,203kg (112,883lb), max takeoff 106,140kg (234,000lb).

Dimensions: Wing span 39.88m (130ft 10in), length 41.68m (136ft 9in), height 12.66m (41ft 7in). Wing area 234.2m^2 (2521sq ft).

Capacity: Flightcrew of three comprising two pilots and a flight engineer. Typical seating for 122 in two classes (14 first and 74 economy).

Production: Between 1959 and 1969 only 154 Boeing 720s were built. Small numbers are used as corporate transports.

History: Although being close to identical to the Boeing 707-120 in dimensions, only subtle external differences belie the fact that the 720 is structurally quite different to the heavier 707. This fact is backed by the different 720 designation, rather than a 707 based model number, and completely different empty and operating weights.

Boeing developed the 720 in response to a perceived need for an intermediate range airliner for domestic and regional routes, based on the successful 707. Similar in length to the 707-120, the external differences were subtle and few. These included a reprofiled wing with increased sweepback and changes to the leading edge and decreased thickness chord ratio. The structural weight was reduced significantly as the 720's medium range requirement meant that less fuel needed to be carried, thus allowing the structure to be lightened. Many components however were interchangeable between the 720 and 707, while inside the cabin the 720 and 707 share the same passenger interior and flightdeck.

The initial 720 model was powered by JT3 turbojets, and first flew on November 23 1959. Certification was awarded on June 30 1960, and entry into service with United Airlines was on July 5 that year.

The availability of the far more fuel efficient Pratt & Whitney JT3D turbofan resulted in the 720B, which was powered by either JT3D-1s or -3s. First flight of the 720B was on October 6 1960, with certification awarded on March 3 1961. Major operators of the 720 included American Airlines (a number of its 720s were converted to 720Bs with turbofan engines), United, Eastern, Northwest Orient and Western, while non US operators included Lufthansa and Avianca.

Today just one 720 is believed to be in commercial service, although others are used as corporate transports. Pratt & Whitney Canada meanwhile operates a modified 720B as an engine testbed.

Photo: This US registered JT3D turbofan powered 720B is used as a corporate transport. It is pictured here in Australia when it was used to transport the Croatian President. (Keith Myers)

Boeing 727-100

Country of origin: United States of America

Type: Short to medium range airliner

Powerplants: 727-100 – Three 62.3kN (14,000lb) Pratt & Whitney JT8D-7 turbofans.

Performance: Max speed 1017km/h (549kt), max cruising speed 960km/h (518kt), economical cruising speed 917km/h (495kt). Range with max payload 5000km (2700nm).

Weights: 727-100 – Empty equipped 36,560kg (80,602lb), max takeoff 72,570kg (160,000lb).

Dimensions: 727-100 – Wing span 32.92m (108ft 0in), length 40.59m (133ft 2in), height 10.36m (34ft 0in). Wing area 157.9m^2 (1700sq ft).

Capacity: Flightcrew of three (two pilots and flight engineer). Typical two class seating for 94, max seating for 131.

Production: Of the 582 727-100s built, over 300 remained in commercial service in late 1996.

History: The 727 began life as a short to medium range medium capacity airliner to slot beneath the Boeing 707 and 720 and went on to become the second most successful jet airliner built.

Initial design studies began as early as 1956, although for a time it appeared that a new medium range airliner would not be built at all due to Boeing's financial position before sales of the 707 had taken off. There was also the deterrent of an already competitive marketplace with the Electra and Caravelle available and the DC-9 on offer. Boeing persisted however, and the 727 was launched on the strength of launch orders for 80 from Eastern and United in 1960.

The resulting Boeing Model 727's power was supplied by three specially designed rear mounted Pratt & Whitney JT8D turbofans, although Rolls-Royce Speys were originally considered. The trijet design was settled upon as it gave the redundancy of three engines, good climb performance and better operating economics than a four engine jet. The 727 also featured an advanced wing design with the first airliner application of triple slotted Krueger flaps, the 707's fuselage cross section, but with a redesigned smaller lower fuselage due to the need to carry less baggage on shorter range flights, and limited commonality with the 707 and 720. It was also the first Boeing airliner to feature an APU (auxiliary power unit).

The prototype 727 flew for the first time on February 9 1963, and certification was granted in December that year. The first 727 entered service with Eastern on February 9 the following year.

Development of the initial 727-100 resulted in a small family of sub variants, including higher gross weight options for the basic passenger carrying 727, the 727-100C Convertible and 727-200QC Quick Change, both of which were fitted with a large freight door on the forward left hand side of the fuselage. The stretched 727-200 meanwhile is described separately.

Production of the 727-100 ceased in 1973 but one recent notable development is that Dee Howard in the USA has upgraded a number of 727-100s for freight operator UPS. The major feature of the upgrade is re-engining with Rolls-Royce Tays, which improves performance, reduces fuel consumption and more importantly, allows the aircraft to meet Stage III noise requirements.

Photo: An Aerolineas Argentinas 727-100. (Gary Gentle)

Boeing 727-200

Country of origin: United States of America

Type: Short to medium range airliner

Powerplants: Three 64.4kN (14,500lb) Pratt & Whitney JT8D-9 turbofans, or three 67.2kN (15,000lb) JT8D-11s, or three 68.9kN (15,500lb) JT8D-15s or three 71.1kN (16,000lb) JT8D-17s, or three 77.3kN (17,400lb) JT8D-17Rs.

Performance: Advanced 727-200 – Max speed 1017km/h (549kt), max cruising speed 953km/h (515kt), economical cruising speed 865km/h (467kt). Range with max payload 3965km (2140nm), range with max fuel 4450km (2400nm).

Weights: Advanced 727-200 – Operating empty 45,360kg (100,000lb), max takeoff 95,030kg (209,500lb).

Dimensions: Wing span 32.92m (108ft 0in), length 46.69m (153ft 2in), height 10.36m (34ft 0in). Wing area 157.9m^2 (1700sq ft).

Capacity: 727-200 – Max seating for 189 at six abreast and 76cm (30in) pitch, typical two class seating for 14 premium class and 131 economy class passengers. 727-200F – Typical max payload comprises 11 2.23m x 3.17m (7ft 4in x 10ft 5in) pallets.

Production: Sales of 1831 727s of all models completed before production ceased in 1984, including 1249 -200s. Approximately 990 727-200s remained in service at late 1996.

History: The 727-100 had been in service barely a year when Boeing began giving serious consideration to a stretched development.

The result was the 727-200, which Boeing announced it was developing in August 1965. The 727-200 was essentially a minimum change development of the -100, the only major change being the 6.10m (20ft) fuselage stretch, which increased maximum seating out to 189 passengers. The 727-200's stretch consisted of two 3.05m (10ft) plugs, one forward and one rear of the wing. Otherwise the 727-100 and -200 were quite similar, as they share common engines, fuel tankage and maximum takeoff weight.

The first flight of the 727-200 occurred on July 27 1967, with certification granted in late November that year. The type was placed into service by launch customer Northeast Airlines (this airline was later acquired by Delta) the following month, by which time total 727 orders for both models had exceeded 500.

The 727-200 helped broaden the sales appeal of the 727 considerably and snared a significant number of sales. However the 727-200 was restricted by its relatively short range, due to it having the same fuel capacity as the 727-100, despite being a heavier aircraft. Spurred on by Australian airlines Ansett-ANA and TAA, Boeing developed the Advanced 727-200. First flown in March 1972 changes introduced on the Advanced model included increased fuel capacity, and thus range, more powerful engines, quieter engine nacelles and strengthened structure. The Advanced remained the primary 727-200 production model until production ceased in 1984.

Valsan converted 23 727s to its Stage III compliant Quiet 727 standard. The Valsan retrofit included installing JT8D-217s on the outer engines and acoustic treatment of the centre engine. Nacelle manufacturer Rohr relaunched the Valsan conversion under the name Super 27 in late 1996. Rohr saw a market for 50 to 100 Super 27 conversions.

Photo: A 727-200 of short lived Kiwi International. (John Ruming)

Boeing 737-100 & 737-200

Country of origin: United States of America

Type: Short range airliner

Powerplants: 737-100 – Two 62.7kN (14,000lb) Pratt & Whitney JT8D-7 turbofans. 737-200 – Two 64.5kN (14,500lb) JT8D-9As, or two 68.95kN (15,500lb) JT8D-15s, or two 71.2kN (16,000lb) JT8D-17s, or two 77.4kN (17,400lb) JT8D-17Rs with automatic reverse thrust.

Performance: 737-100 – Max speed 943km/h (509kt), economical cruising speed 852km/h (460kt). Range with max fuel 2855km (1540nm). 737-200 – Max speed 943km/h (509kt), max cruising speed 927km/h (500kt), economical cruising speed 796km/h (430kt). Range with 115 passengers and reserves between 3520km (1900nm) and 4260km (2300nm) depending on weight options and engines.

Weights: 737-100 – Empty 25,878kg (57,000lb), max takeoff 49,940kg (110,000lb). 737-200 – Operating empty 27,448kg (60,600lb), max takeoff 52,390kg (115,500lb), or optionally 58,740kg (129,500lb).

Dimensions: 737-100 – Wing span 28.35m (93ft 0in), length 28.67m (94ft 0in), height 11.29m (37ft 0in). Wing area 91.1m^2 (980sq ft). 737-200 – Same except for length 30.53m (100ft 2in), height 11.28m (37ft 0in).

Capacity: Flightcrew of two. 737-100 – Typical single class seating for 100. 737-200 – Typical single class seating for 115, max seating for 130 at 74cm (29in) pitch. 737-200C & QC payload 15,545kg (34,270lb), consisting of pallets or containers.

Production: Total of 1144 737-100s and 200s built, comprising 30 -100s, and 1114 -200s, including various military models. Approximately 18 -100s and 925 737-200s remained in service in late 1996.

History: The 737-100 and -200 are the first generation production models of the world's most successful jet airliner.

The 737 was conceived as a short range small capacity airliner to round out the Boeing jet airliner family, slotting beneath the 727, 720 and 707. Announced in February 1965, the 737 was originally envisioned as seating between 60 to 85, although following consultation with launch customer Lufthansa, a 100 seat design was settled upon. Design features included two underwing mounted turbofans and 60% structure and systems commonality with the 727.

The first 737-100 made its first flight on April 9 1967, and the type entered service in February 1968. By this time however development of the larger capacity 1.93m (6ft 4in) stretched 737-200 was well advanced, and the first 737-200 flew for the first time on August 8 1967. Developments of the -200 include the -200C convertible and quick change -200QC, while a unprepared strip kit was also offered. The definitive Advanced 737-200 appeared in 1971, featuring minor aerodynamic refinements and other improvements.

Sales of the 737-200 far exceeded that of the shorter -100 and the 737-200 remained in production until 1988, by which time it had been superseded by the improved 737-300.

Photo: An Air New Zealand 737-200 fitted with Nordam Stage III hushkits and wearing the airline's new 'Pacific Wave' livery introduced in 1996. (Peter Clark)

Boeing 737-300

Country of origin: United States of America

Type: Short range airliner

Powerplants: Two 88.97kN (20,000lb) CFM International CFM56-3B-1 turbofans, or optionally two 97.9kN (22,000lb) CFM56-3B-2s.

Performance: Max cruising speed 908km/h (491kt), long range cruising speed 794km/h (429kt). Range with 128 passengers and standard fuel 3362km (1815nm), range with 128 pax and max fuel 4973km (2685nm). High gross weight version max range 6300km (3400nm) with 140 passengers.

Weights: Operating empty 31,895kg (70,320lb), or 32,459kg (71,560lb) long range option, max takeoff 56,472kg (124,500lb) or 62,823kg (138,500lb).

Dimensions: Wing span 28.88m (94ft 9in), length 33.40m (109ft 7in), height 11.13m (36ft 6in). Wing area 105.4m^2 (1135sq ft).

Capacity: Flightcrew of two. Typical two class seating for 128 (8 premium class four abreast and 120 economy six abreast), standard one class seating for 141 at six abreast and 81cm (31in) pitch, max seating for 149 at 76cm (30in) pitch.

Production: Grand total 737 orders stand at over 3490, of which over 1900 are for the -300, -400, -500 family. Approximately 963 737-300s were in service at late 1996 out of 1095 on order.

History: The success of the second generation Boeing 737 family pushed sales of the mark to over 3000, a record for a commercial jetliner. The 737-300 forms the backbone of many airline fleets worldwide and continues to sell strongly.

Boeing announced it was proceeding with development of a new 737-300 in March 1981. This new variant started off as a simple stretch over the 737-200 but Boeing decided to adopt the CFM International CFM56 high bypass turbofan (jointly developed by General Electric and SNECMA) to both reduce fuel consumption and comply with the then proposed International Civil Aviation Organisation Stage III noise limits.

Despite the all new engines and the 2.64m (104in) fuselage stretch, the 737-300 retains 80% airframe spares commonality and shares the same ground handling equipment with the 737-200. A number of aerodynamic improvements were incorporated to further improve efficiency including modified leading edge slats and new dorsal fin extending to the tail. Another feature was the uniquely shaped oval engine nacelles, while the nosewheel leg was extended to increase ground clearance for the new engines. Other internal changes include materials and systems improvements first developed for the 757 and 767 programs.

The first 737-300 flew for the first time on February 24 1984, while first deliveries were from November 1984. Since that time the 737-300 has sold in large numbers (it will soon account for more 737 sales than any other model) and forming the backbone of many airlines' short to medium range fleets.

The subsequent stretched 737-400 and shortened 737-500 are described separately.

Photo: The 737-300 is fast approaching the 1114 sales mark of the 737-200, currently the most popular 737 model. (Rob Finlayson)

Boeing 737-400

Country of origin: United States of America

Type: Short haul airliner

Powerplants: Two 97.9kN (22,000lb) CFM International CFM56-3B-2 turbofans, or optionally two 104.5kN (23,500lb) CFM56-3C-1s.

Performance: Max cruising speed 912km/h (492kt), long range cruising speed 813km/h (439kt). Standard version range with max payload 4005km (2160nm), typical range with 146 passengers 5000km (2700km). High gross weight option range with 146 passengers 5930km (3200nm).

Weights: Standard version operating empty 33,435kg (73,710lb), max takeoff 62,820kg (138,500lb). Optional high weight long range version operating empty 34,270kg (75,555lb), max takeoff 68,040kg (150,000lb).

Dimensions: Wing span 28.88m (94ft 9in), length 36.45m (119ft 7in), height 11.13m (36ft 6in). Wing area 105.4m^2 (1135sq ft).

Capacity: Flightcrew of two. Typical two class seating for 146 (eight premium, 138 economy), typical all economy for 159 at 81cm (32in) pitch, or max seating for 188.

Production: Orders for the 737-400 stood at 447 at late 1996, of which approximately 406 were in airline service.

History: Boeing announced it was developing a new higher capacity version of the fast selling 737-300 in June 1986.

The new aeroplane, the 737-400, was developed as a 150 seat 727 replacement. Although Boeing had initially developed the 180 to 200 seat 757 to replace the successful 727, there still existed a considerable market for a near direct replacement for the trijet. By also developing the 737-400 as a minimum change stretch of the 737-300, Boeing was also able to offer considerable commonality, and thus cost, benefits to operators already with the 737-300, and to a lesser extent, the 737-200 in their fleets.

The major change of the 737-400 over the smaller -300 is a 3.05m (10ft 0in) fuselage stretch, consisting of a 1.83m (6ft 0in) stretch forward and a 1.22m (4ft 0in) plug rear of the wing. The stretch increases maximum passenger seating to 188. To cope with the increased weights, more powerful CFM56s are fitted. Other changes are minor, such as a tail bumper fitted to protect against over rotation at takeoff, something that could have become a problem due to the increased fuselage length.

A higher gross weight longer range version is offered. It features increased fuel capacity, and strengthened undercarriage and structures, but is otherwise identical to the standard 737-400.

The maiden flight of a 737-400 occurred on February 19 1988 and entered airline service in October that year with Piedmont. Of the current 737 family the -400 has proven the most successful member behind the -300, its larger capacity and transcontinental US range meaning it has found a very useful market for Boeing as a 727 replacement. However the 737-400 does face stiff competition from the similar size Airbus A320, which has higher levels of technology, longer range and is faster.

Photo: South Korea's Asiana ordered a total of 20 737-400s. Apart from the longer fuselage the 737-400 can be identified from the -300 by its two above wing emergency exits, rather than one. (Boeing)

Boeing 737-500

Country of origin: United States of America

Type: Short range airliner

Powerplants: Two 88.97kN (20,000lb) CFM International CFM56-3B-1 turbofans, optionally derated to 82.3kN (18,500lb).

Performance: Max cruising speed 912km/h (492kt), economical cruising speed 795km/h (430kt). Higher gross weight option range with 108 passengers 4485km (2420nm).

Weights: Standard aircraft operating empty 30,960kg (68,240lb), max takeoff 52,390kg (115,500lb). Optional long range high gross weight version operating empty 31,515kg (69,480lb), max takeoff 60,554kg (133,500lb).

Dimensions: Wing span 28.88m (94ft 9in), length 31.01m (101ft 9in), height 11.13m (36ft 6in). Wing area 105.4m^2 (1135sq ft).

Capacity: Flightcrew of two. Typical two class seating for 108, or max single class seating for 132.

Production: Some 375 737-500s had been ordered by late 1996, of which an estimated 310 were in airline service.

History: The tubby looking 737-500 rounds out the current generation 737 family of airliners, and is Boeing's smallest airliner currently on offer.

Originally when the new stretched 737-300 appeared, this new generation version of the popular twinjet was intended to supplement, rather than replace, the then current 737-200. However the development of the 737 logically and inevitably led to the development of a new replacement model comparable in size to the 737-200, but offering better fuel economy, and extensive commonality with the new 737 models. Boeing announced it was developing the resulting 737-500, then known as the 737-1000, on May 20 1987.

Like the preceding 737-300 and 737-400, the 737-500 is powered by CFM International CFM56s turbofans, in this case optionally derated down to 82.3kN (18,500lb) thrust. All three share extensive systems and structure commonality, and a common type rating. These benefits offer great cost savings to an airline when two or more variants are operated within the same fleet.

Reversing the trend of the -300 and -400 though the 737-500 is 31.01m (101ft 9in) in length, closely matching the 30.53m (100ft 2in) length of the 737-200, and as such is a direct replacement for the earlier type. Like the -300 and -400, a higher gross weight longer range version is offered, featuring auxiliary fuel tanks and uprated engines.

The 737-500's first flight occurred on June 30 1989, FAA certification was awarded on February 12 1990, with service entry later that same month.

The 737-500's main appeal is for operators of large 737-400 and 737-300 fleets, as because the -500 is a shortened development of the -300, it still carries much of the structural weight needed for the higher weight models. This makes it less efficient than if it was designed specifically for its size category, however for operators of large 737-300/-400 fleets, the extensive commonality benefits more than compensate for this.

Photo: Although the smallest of the second generation 737 family, the -500 is still slightly bigger than the -200. (Boeing)

Boeing 737-600/-700/-800

Country of origin: United States of America

Type: Medium range medium capacity airliners

Powerplants: 737-600 – Two 82kN (18,500lb) CFM International CFM56-7 turbofans, or two 89kN (20,000lb) or 98kN (22,000lb) CFM56-7s on high gross weight version. 737-700 – Two 89kN (20,000lb) CFM56-7s or 98kN (22,000lb) or 107kN (24,000lb) CFM56-7s on HGW version. 737-800 – Two 107kN (24,000lb) CFM56-7s, or two 117kN (26,400lb) CFM56-7s on HGW version.

Performance: Typical cruising speed Mach 0.785. Service ceiling 41,000ft. 737-600 – Range with 108 pax 2790km (1505nm) or 5920km (3195nm) for HGW version. 737-700 – Range with 128 pax 2935km (1585nm) or 5930km (3200nm) for HGW version. 737-800 – Range with 162 pax 3565km (1925nm) or 5375km (2900nm) for HGW.

Weights: 737-600 – Max takeoff 56,240kg (124,000lb), high gross weight max takeoff 65,090kg (143,500lb). 737-700 – Max takeoff 60,320kg (133,000lb), HGW MTOW 69,400kg (153,500lb). 737-800 – Max takeoff 70,530kg (155,500lb), HGW MTOW 78,240kg (172,500lb).

Dimensions: 737-600 – Wing span 34.31m (112ft 7in), length 31.24m (102ft 6in), height 12.58m (41ft 3in). Wing area 125.0m^2 (1344sq ft). 737-700 – Same except length 33.63m (110ft 4in), height 12.56m (41ft 2in). 737-800 – Same as -700 except length 39.20m (128ft 6in).

Capacity: Flightcrew of two. 737-600 – 108 in two classes or 132 in a single class. 737-700 – 128 in two classes or 144 in a single class. 737-800 – 162 in two classes or up to 189 in a single class.

Production: At late 1996 501 firm orders were held.

History: The upgraded Next Generation 737-600/-700/-800 series are the latest additions to the best selling 737 family.

The improved Boeing 737 family originally were covered by the 737-X designation. Boeing and 30 customer airlines participated in definition design of the 737-X series, with the airlines requesting that the basic 737 design be changed only if it involved specific improvements to range, speed, noise or seating capacity.

The Next Generation 737s feature more efficient CFM56-7 turbofans. The CFM56-7s combine the core of the CFM56-5 with the CFM56-3's low pressure compressor and a 1.55m (61in) fan. The 737's new wing has greater chord, span and wing area. The tail surfaces are also larger.

The new engines and wings will allow the 737 to cruise at Mach 0.78 to Mach 0.80, a useful speed increase over current generation 737s, while the larger wing allows greater fuel tankage and transcontinental USA range. Other features include a 777 style six LCD EFIS flightdeck which can be programmed to present information as on the 777 or as on current 737s and the 757/767.

The 737-700 was the first member of the new family to be launched, and is based on the 737-300. The 737-800 is a stretched version of the 737-400 capable of seating up to 189, while the 737-600 is based on the 737-500. Boeing is also marketing the 737 Business Jet, a 11,120km (6000nm) range 737-700 corporate jet.

The first 737-700 rolled out on December 7 1996, with first deliveries planned for late '97. The 737-800 is planned to rollout in mid '97. First 737-600 deliveries are planned for late 1998.

Photo: The 737-700 prototype. (Boeing)

Boeing 747-100 & -200

Country of origin: United States of America

Type: Long range high capacity widebody airliners

Powerplants: 747-100 – Four 208.9kN (46,950lb) Pratt & Whitney JT9D-7A turbofans or four 213.5kN (48,000lb) JT9D-7Fs or 206.8kN (46,500lb) General Electric CF6-45A2s. 747-200B – Four 243.5kN (54,750lb) JT9D-7R4G2s, or four 233.5kN (52,500lb) CF6-50E2s, or four 236.5kN (53,110lb) Rolls-Royce RB211-524D4s.

Performance: 747-100 – Max level speed 967km/h (522kt), economical cruising speed 907km/h (490kt). Range with 385 pax and reserves 9045km (4880nm). 747-200B – Max level speed 981km/h (530kt) (with RR engines), economical cruising speed 907km/h (490kt). Range with 366 pax and reserves 12,778km (6900nm). 747-200F – Speeds same. Range with 90,270kg (200,000lb) payload 9075km (4900nm) with CF6-80C2s.

Weights: 747-100 – Empty 162,386kg (358,000lb), max takeoff 340,195kg (750,000lb). 747-200 – Operating empty with JT9Ds 169,960kg (374,400lb), with CF6-80C2s 172,730kg (380,800lb), with RB211s 174,000kg (383,600lb). Max takeoff 377,840kg (833,000lb). 747-100SR – Operating empty 162,430kg (358,100lb), max takeoff 272,155kg (600,000lb). 747-200F – Operating empty with JT9Ds 155,220kg (342,200lb), max takeoff 377,840kg (833,000lb).

Dimensions: Wing span 59.64m (195ft 8in), length 70.66m (231ft 10in), height 19.33m (63ft 5in). Wing area 511m^2 (5500sq ft).

Capacity: Flightcrew of three (two pilots and a flight engineer). 747-100 & -200 – Seating arrangements include 397 passengers in three classes, 452 passengers in two classes (32 first & 420 economy), all economy seating for 447 nine abreast or up to 500 ten abreast. 747-200F – Max payload of 112,400kg (247,800lb) consisting of freight containers, pallets and/or igloos.

Production: 747-100/-200 in production to 1991. 167 -100s, 9 -100Bs, 224 -200Bs, 13 -200Cs, 73 -200Fs and 77 -200Ms built. Approx 145 -100s and 355 -200s in service in late 1996.

History: Like the 707 before it, the 747 revolutionised airline transport. A massive increase in size on anything before it, the 747 introduced significant reductions in operating costs and thus cut the cost of long haul international airline travel.

The 747 was conceived in the mid 1960s, following Boeing's failure to secure a US Air Force contract for an ultra large strategic transport (which resulted in the Lockheed C-5 Galaxy), and an identified need for a new high capacity "jumbo jet". Design experience with the USAF transport was transferred to the new airliner, which was launched on July 25 1966. First flight occurred on February 9 1969, certification was awarded on December 30 that year.

The basic 747-100 entered service with PanAm in January 1970. Progressive development of the 747 led to the 747-200B with higher weights, more powerful engines and longer range. This aircraft first flew in October 1970, while nine higher weight 747-100Bs were built.

Developments include the 747-200F freighter, the SR (short range) optimised for high cycle short sector operations and the C (Combi).

Photo: A JT9D powered Trans World 747-100. The 747 revolutionised airline travel by making it much more affordable. (TWA)

Boeing 747SP

Country of origin: United States of America

Type: Long range high capacity widebody airliner

Powerplants: Four 218.4kN (48,750lb) Pratt & Whitney JT9D-7AW turbofans, or four 222.8kN (50,100lb) Rolls-Royce RB211-524B or 229.5kN (51,600lb) RB211-524Cs, or four 206.8kN (46,500lb) General Electric CF6-45A2s or CF6-50E2-F.

Performance: Max speed 1000km/h (540kt). Range with 331 passengers and baggage 10,840km (5855nm), range with 276 passengers 12,325km (6650nm), ferry range with max fuel and 13,610kg (30,000lb) payload 15,400km (8315nm).

Weights: Operating empty 147,420kg (325,000lb), max takeoff 317,515kg (700,000lb).

Dimensions: Wing span 59.64m (195ft 8in), length 56.31m (184ft 9in), height 19.94m (65ft 5in). Wing area 511m^2 (5500sq ft).

Capacity: Flightcrew of three comprising two pilots and one flight engineer. Max high density single class seating for 440, typical two class seating for 28 first class and 288 economy class passengers

Production: Just 45 747SPs were built, of which approximately 30 remain in service.

History: Thus far the tubby long range 747SP is the only 747 model to feature a changed fuselage length compared with the 747-100.

The SP suffix in 747SP stands for Special Performance, and points to the ultra long range abilities of this 747 variant that preceded the current 747-400 by 15 years. The abilities of the 747SP are best described by the spate of long range distance records set in the mid 1970s. The most prominent of those was the delivery flight of a South African Airways SP, which over March 23/24 1976 flew nonstop with 50 passengers from Paine Field in Washington State to Cape Town, South Africa, a distance of 16,560km (8940nm). Needless to say this was a world nonstop record for a commercial aircraft.

While shortening the 747's fuselage increased the fuel fraction and thus range, it also meant that seating capacity was reduced, making the 747SP suitable for lower density routes than that plied by the standard fuselage 747s. The fuselage is shortened by 14.35m (47ft 1in), while the vertical tail was increased in height to compensate for the reduced moment arm of the shorter fuselage. Structurally the 747SP has been lightened in some areas because of the significant reduction in gross weights. Overall though the 747SP retained 90% commonality of components with the 747-100 and -200.

First delivery of the 747SP occurred in March 1976, this being preceded by the type's first flight on July 4 1975 and the granting of certification on February 4 1976. Sales of the 747SP were slow despite the increased range, one penalty being poorer operating economics than the 747-200. However the 747SP did pioneer a number of long range nonstop services that are now commonly flown by the 747-400.

Notable SP customers included South African Airways, who found the SP's extended range a great asset in bypassing Black African nations that denied it landing rights while apartheid policies were in place, Qantas and PanAm, the latter pioneering nonstop Los Angeles/Sydney services.

Photo: The sole 747SP of South African based Alliance, leased from South African Airways. (Keith Anderson)

Boeing 747-300 & -400

Country of origin: United States of America

Type: Long range high capacity widebody airliners

Powerplants: 747-300 – Four 245.2kN (54,750lb) Pratt & Whitney JT9D-7R4G2 turbofans, or four 246.4kN (55,000lb) Rolls-Royce RB211-524D4s, or four 235.2kN (52,500kN) General Electric CF6-50E2s. 747-400 – Four 252.39kN (56,750lb) Pratt & Whitney PW4056s, or four 257.5kN (57,900lb) General Electric CF6-80C2B4s, or four 258kN (58,000lb) Rolls-Royce RB211-524Gs.

Performance: 747-300 – Max speed 982km/h (530kt), max cruising speed 939km/h (507kt), economical cruising speed 907km/h (490kt), long range cruising speed 898km/h (485kt). Range with max payload 11,040km (5960nm), range with max fuel 13,850km (7480nm). 747-400 – Max cruising speed 939km/h (507kt), long range cruising speed 907km/h (490kt). Range with 420 three class passengers 13,270km (7165nm) with PW4000s, 13,390km (7230nm) with GEs, 13,150km (7100nm) with RB211s.

Weights: 747-300 – Operating empty 176,847kg (389,875lb), max takeoff 377,850kg (833,000lb). 747-400 – Operating empty 182,255kg (401,800lb) with RB211s, 180,985kg (399,000lb) with PW4056s, 181,030kg (399,100lb) with CF6s. Max takeoff options of 362,875kg (800,000lb), or 385,555kg (850,000lb), or 394,625kg (870,000lb), regardless of engine choice.

Dimensions: 747-400 – Wing span 64.44m (211ft 5in), length 70.66m (231ft 10in), height 19.33m (63ft 5in). Wing area 524.9m^2 (5650sq ft).

Capacity: 747-300 – Flightcrew of three, two pilots and one flight engineer. 747-400 – Flightcrew of two. Typical three class arrangement for 34 first class, 76 business and 302 economy class passengers. Maximum permissible seating for 660 at 86cm (34in) pitch, eleven abreast in the main cabin. 747-400F – Payload comprising 30 pallets or 32 containers on main deck.

Production: 81 747-300s delivered between 1983 and 1990. 79 747-300s in service in late 1996. Orders for the 747-400 as of late 1994 stood at 510, of which 362 were in service. Total 747 sales 1252.

History: The 747-300 and 747-400 share the same basic airframe with the distinctive stretched upper deck, but are otherwise quite different aircraft.

The 747-300 is essentially little changed from the 747-200, and principally differs only in the stretched upper deck. The upper deck capacity is raised to 69 passengers at six abreast. The Extended Upper Deck (EUD) has also been offered as a conversion for current 747-100s and -200s, although the only airline to take up this option was KLM. The first 747-300 was delivered in March 1983.

The 747-400 goes much further in being a comprehensive update of the 747 based on the -300. Its features include drag reducing wingtip winglets, an advanced two crew EFIS glass flightdeck, new engine options, an 11 tonne empty weight saving and a 13,150km (7100nm) plus design range. It, like other 747 derivatives, is offered in Short Range SR, Combi and Freighter forms. The EUD is an option for 747-400F freighter aircraft.

The 747-400 was announced in October 1985 and first flew on April 29 1988. It has been the only 747 model on offer since 1990.

Photo: A British Airways 747-400.

Boeing 747-500X & -600X

Country of origin: United States of America

Type: Long range high capacity widebody airliners

Powerplants: 747-500X – Four 305 to 315kN (68 to 70,000lb) thrust class General Electric/Pratt & Whitney GP7000 or Rolls-Royce Trent 976 turbofans. 747-600X – Four 340 to 350kN (76 to 78,000lb) thrust class General Electric/Pratt & Whitney GP7000 or Rolls-Royce Trent 976 turbofans.

Performance: 747-500X – Cruising speed Mach 0.85 or 965km/h (521kt) plus. Cruising altitude 41,000ft. Design range 16,100km (8700nm). 747-600X – Cruising speed Mach 0.85 or 965km/h (521kt) plus. Cruising altitude 41,000ft. Design range 14,350km (7750nm).

Weights: 747-500X – Max takeoff 528,900kg (1,166,000lb). 747-600X – Max takeoff 538,000kg (1,186,000lb).

Dimensions: 747-500X – Wing span 77.7m (255ft), length 76m (249ft), height 21m (70ft). Interior cross section width 6.1m (20ft). 747-600X – Same except for a length of 84.5m (277ft).

Capacity: Flightcrew of two. 747-500X – Typical three class seating arrangement for 462. In combi configuration could carry 321 passengers and seven freight pallets on the main deck. 747-600X – Typical three class seating arrangement for 548.

Production: Boeing has forecast a market for approximately 400 aircraft in this size class. First deliveries would be in 2001.

History: In late 1996 Boeing looked set to go-ahead with these two stretched developments of the 747 as its answer to world airline demand for a Very Large Aircraft 500 plus seat airliner. The result will be the world's largest airliner growing even larger.

Boeing had first studied a VLA in the early 1990s under the VLCT (Very Large Commercial Transport) design study, which also involved Airbus Industrie's individual partners – BAe, DASA, Aerospatiale and CASA – and Japanese companies Fuji and Mitsubishi. The VLCT partners studied an all new design which would have featured twin decks. However the VLCT was shelved in mid 1995, allowing Boeing to concentrate instead on stretching the 747, which was always going to be a cheaper VLA solution.

Boeing had been studying stretched developments of the 747, dubbed the 747X, concurrently alongside the VLCT. Early studies focused on stretching the fuselage and joining an all new wing, based on that developed for the 777. Power would have been supplied by existing engines such as the CF6, PW4000 and Trent.

Design development in close co-operation with potential customers continued through to September 1996, when Boeing announced it had firmed up its designs, and hoped for a launch in 1997.

The 747-500X would feature a 5.6m (16.4ft) stretch over the 747-400 (giving a length of 76m/250ft) and seating for 462. The larger 747-600X would be further stretched to 85m (279ft) and seat 548. Both will feature a new 777 style flightdeck, fly-by-wire controls, a new wing and new engines, in the form of the Trent 900 or the all new GP7000 being developed by General Electric and Pratt & Whitney.

At late 1996 Boeing was actively marketing the 747-500X/-600X with a program launch possible in 1997. First flight is planned for 2000, with customer deliveries from as early as late 2001.

Photo: An artist's impression of the 747-500X and -600X. (Boeing)

Boeing 757-200

Country of origin: United States of America

Type: Medium range narrowbody airliner

Powerplants: Two 166.4kN (37,400lb) Rolls-Royce RB211-535C turbofans, or two 178.4kN (40,100lb) RB211-535E4s, or two 170kN (38,200lb) Pratt & Whitney PW2037s, or two 185.5kN (41,700lb) PW2040s.

Performance: Max cruising speed 914km/h (493kt), economical cruising speed 850km/h (460kt). Range with P&W engines and 186 passengers 5520km (2980nm), with RR engines 5225km (2820nm). Range at optional max takeoff weight with P&W engines 7410km (4000nm), with RR engines 6857km (3700nm). 757-200PF – Speeds same. Range with 22,680kg payload and P&W engines 7200km (3885nm), with RR engines 6857km (3700nm).

Weights: Operating empty with P&W engines 57,039kg (125,750lb), with RR engines 57,180kg (126,050lb). Medium range max takeoff weight 104,325kg (230,000lb), long range max takeoff weight 113,395kg (250,000lb).

Dimensions: Wing span 38.05m (124ft 10in), length 47.32m (155ft 3in), height 13.56m (44ft 6in). Wing area 185.3m^2 (1994sq ft).

Capacity: Flightcrew of two. 757-200 – Typical passenger arrangements vary from 178 two class (16 first & 162 economy), or 202 (12 first & 190 economy) or 208 (12 first and 196 economy) or 214 to 239 in all economy class. 757-200PF – Maximum of 15 standard 2.24 x 2.74m (88 x 108in) freight pallets on main deck.

Production: 858 757-200s had been ordered by late 1996, of which over 700 were in service.

History: After a slow sales start, the medium range single aisle 757 has become yet another sales success story for Boeing.

Boeing considered a number of proposals for a successor to the 727 trijet during the 1970s, many of these designs featuring the nose and T-tail of the earlier jet. It was not until later in that decade however that Boeing settled on a more conventional design featuring the same cross section as the 727 (as well as the 737, 707 and 720) but with the fuselage considerably longer in length, an all new wing, fuel efficient high bypass turbofan engines and a new nose section housing an advanced cockpit.

Boeing launched development of the 757 in March 1979 following orders from British Airways and Eastern, to be developed in tandem with the larger widebody 767. The 767 first flew a few months earlier, but the two types share a number of systems and technologies, including a common flightdeck.

First flight was on February 19 1982 and the 757 entered service in January the following year. Subsequent versions to appear are the 757-200PF Package Freighter, a pure freighter, and the 757-200M Combi. The standard passenger aircraft is designated the 757-200, there being no -100. The stretched 757-300 is described separately.

Initial sales of the 757 were fairly slow, however orders picked up significantly in the mid to late 1980s as traffic on routes previously served by smaller 727s and 737s grew to require the 757's extra capacity. Today 757 sales comfortably exceed those of the 767, a position that was reversed until the late 1980s.

Photo: A RB211 powered 757 of Airtours International. (Keith Gaskell)

Boeing 757-300

Country of origin: United States of America

Type: Medium range narrowbody airliner

Powerplants: Two 180kN (40,100lb) Rolls-Royce RB211-535E4 turbofans, or two 186kN (41,700lb) Pratt & Whitney PW2040s or PW2043s.

Performance: Speeds similar to 757-200. Design range 6500km (3500nm).

Weights: Max takeoff 122,580kg (270,000lb).

Dimensions: Wing span 38.05m (124ft 10in), length 54.47m (178ft 7in), height 13.56m (44ft 6in). Wing area 185.3m^2 (1994sq ft).

Capacity: Flightcrew of two. Typical two class arrangement seats 240 passengers, comprising 16 premium class at 91cm (36in) pitch and 224 economy class at 81cm (32in) pitch. Max seating for 289 passengers in a high density configuration

Production: The 757-300 was launched in September 1996 with an order for 12 and 12 options from Condor. Certification and first deliveries are planned for 1999.

History: The stretched, 240 seat Boeing 757-300 is the first significant development of the basic 757-200.

Although design work on the original 757 began in the late 1970s and its entry into service was in 1983, it wasn't until over a decade later in the mid 1990s that Boeing began to study a stretched development of its popular narrowbody twin. This new 757 stretch was covered by the 757-300X designation until its launch at the Farnborough Airshow in England in September 1996.

The 757-300's launch customer is Condor, the charter subsidiary of German flag carrier Lufthansa. Condor's order for 12 with options on 12 was the only contract placed for the new 757 model at the time of writing, but Boeing was confident that other airlines, particularly charter operators, would follow suite. One of the 757-300's biggest selling points is its 10% lower seat kilometre costs compared with the 757-200.

The most obvious change over the 757-200 is the -300's 54.4m (178ft 7in) long fuselage, which is 7.1m (23ft 4in) longer than the standard aircraft (and only fractionally shorter than the 767-300). This fuselage stretch allows a 20% increase in seating to 225 to 285 passengers, depending on the interior configuration. Lower hold freight capacity is also increased by 40% over the 757-200 by virtue of the longer fuselage.

Another feature of the 757-300 is its new interior which is based on that developed for the new generation 737 models. Features include a new sculptured ceiling, larger overhead bins, indirect overhead lighting and vacuum toilets.

The 757-300 will share the -200's cockpit, wing, tail and powerplant options, although the -300 will feature strengthened structure and landing gear to cope with the increased weights, new wheels, tyres and brakes and a tailskid.

At late 1996 Boeing anticipated the 757-300 receiving certification and entering airline service in 1999.

Photo: A retouched photo of how the 757-300 will look in flight. The 757-300 is the same length as the 767-300 and has the same seating capacity as the 767-200. (Boeing)

Boeing 767-200

Country of origin: United States of America

Type: Medium to long range widebody airliner

Powerplants: 767-200 – Two 213.5kN (48,000lb) Pratt & Whitney JT9D-7R4D turbofans, or two 223.3kN (50,200lb) PW4050s, or two 233.5kN (52,500lb) General Electric CF6-80C2B2s. 767-200ER – Two 252.4kN (56,750lb) PW4056s, or two 257.7kN (57,900lb) CF6-80C24B turbofans.

Performance: 767-200 – Max cruising speed 914km/h (493kt), economical cruising speed 854km/h (461kt). Range of basic aircraft with JT9Ds 5855km (3160nm), medium range version with CF6s 7135km (3850nm). 767-200ER – Speeds same. Range with PW4056s 12,545km (6770nm), with CF6s 12,610km (6805nm).

Weights: 767-200 – Empty with JT9Ds 74,752kg (164,800lb), with CF6s 74,344kg (163,900lb). Operating empty with JT9Ds 80,920kg (178,400lb), with CF6s 80,510kg (177,500lb). Max takeoff with JT9Ds 136,078kg (300,000lb), with CF6s 142,881kg (315,000lb). 767-200ER – Empty with PW4056s 76,566kg (168,800lb), with CF6-80C2B4s 76,476kg (168,600lb), operating empty with PW4056s 83,780kg (184,700lb), with CF6-80C2B4s 83,690kg (184,500lb). Max takeoff with PW4056s or CF6-80C2B4s 175,540kg (387,000lb).

Dimensions: Wing span 47.57m (156ft 1in), length 48.51m (159ft 2in), height 15.85m (52ft 0in). Wing area 283.3m^2 (3050sq ft).

Capacity: Flightcrew of two, or optionally three. Typical two class seating for 18 premium and 198 economy class pax. Max seating for 290 at eight abreast and 76cm (30in) pitch. Underfloor cargo holds can accommodate up to 22 LD2 containers.

Production: Total 767 sales at late 1996 717.Total 767-200/200ER orders stood at 229, of which all but three had been delivered.

History: The narrowest widebody in service, the 767 started life as an advanced technology mid to large size airliner in the late 1970s.

Launched in July 1978, the 767 was developed in tandem with the narrowbody 757. Although differing in physical configuration, the two types share a common two crew flightdeck and systems. Differences though are many, and the 767 features a unique width fuselage typically seating seven abreast in economy, and a different wing design with greater sweepback and high altitude cruise in mind. The 767 program also features a high degree of international participation, with Japanese companies in particular having a large share of construction.

Initially Boeing intended to offer two versions, the longer 767-200 and short fuselage 767-100. The -100 was not launched, being too close in capacity to the 757, and the 767-200 became the standard model. The first 767 flew on September 26 1981, entering service 12 months later. The longer range 767-200ER (Extended Range) version features higher weights and an additional wing centre section fuel tank and first flew on March 6 1984, and service entry, with Ethiopian Airlines, was two months later. The -200ER accounts for a large percentage of 767-200 sales as its extended range increases the 767's utility greatly, something that Boeing had not foreseen when the type was first launched.

Photo: An Air Canada 767-200 on approach to Toronto. Air Canada flies 14 -200s. (Gary Gentle)

Boeing 767-300

Country of origin: United States of America

Type: Medium to long range widebody airliner

Powerplants: Two 213.5kN (48,000lb) Pratt & Whitney JT9D-7R4 turbofans or two 222.4kN (50,000lb) JT9D-7R4Es, or two 222.4kN (50,000lb) PW4050, or two 52,000lb (233.5kN) PW4052s, or two 213.5kN (48,000lb) General Electric CF6-80As or two 213.5kN (48,000lb) CF6-80A2s, or two 231.3kN (52,500lb) CF6-80C2B2s, or two 257.5kN (57,900lb) CF6-80C2B4s or two 269.9kN (60,000lb) Rolls-Royce RB211-524Gs. 767-300ER – Same options or two 252.4kN (56,750lb) PW4056s or two 60,000lb (266.9kN) CF6-80C2B6s.

Performance: Max cruising speed 900km/h (486kt), economical cruising speed 850km/h (460kt). Higher gross weight version range with design payload and PW4050s 7840km (4260nm), with CF6-80C2B2s 7895km (4260nm). 767-300ER – Range with design payload with PW4060s 11,230km (6060nm), with CF6-80C2B4s 10,674km (5760nm).

Weights: 767-300 – Empty with PW4050s 79,560kg (175,400lb), with CF6-80C2B2s 79,379kg (175,000lb). Operating empty with PW4050s 87,135kg (192,100lb), with CF6-80C2B2s 86,955kg (191,700lb). Higher gross weight version max takeoff with PW4050s or CF6-80C2B2s 159,210kg (351,000lb). 767-300ER – Empty with PW4060s 81,374kg (179,400lb), with CF6-80C2B4s 80,603kg (177,700lb). Operating empty with PW4060s 89,900kg (198,200lb), with CF6-80C2B4s 89,130kg (196,500lb). Max takeoff with PW4060s 181,440kg (400,000lb), with CF6-80C2B4s 175,540kg (387,000lb).

Dimensions: Wing span 47.57m (156ft 1in), length 54.94m (180ft 3in), height 15.85m (52ft 0in). Wing area 283.3m^2 (3050sq ft).

Capacity: Flightcrew of two. Typical three class layout for 210, max seating for 290 at seven abreast. Underfloor capacity for 20 LD2s.

Production: 488 767-300s (including ERs) had been ordered by late 1996, of which 407 were in service.

History: Boeing announced that it was developing a stretched development of the 767-200 in February 1982.

The resulting 767-300 features a 6.42m (21ft 1in) stretch consisting of fuselage plugs forward (3.07m/10ft 1in) and behind (3.35m/11ft) the wing centre section. The flightdeck and systems were carried directly over from the 767-200, the only other changes were minor, and related to the increased weights of the new version. The max takeoff weight was the same as the later 767-200ER.

The 767-300 flew for the first time on January 30 1986, and was certificated and entered service in September that year. The higher weight Extended Range ER version flew on December 19 1986, while Rolls-Royce RB211-524G engines became available from 1989. The range of the 767-300ER has proven to be very popular with a number of airlines using them for long range low density flights.

In 1993 Boeing launched the 767-300ER Freighter. Changes include strengthened undercarriage and wing structure, a cargo handling system, no cabin windows and a main deck freight door. Capacity is 24 containers.

In late '96 Boeing revealed it was studying a stretched 767-300ER, the 767-400ERX. It would be 6.43m (21ft) longer, seat an extra 50 passengers, fly 11,100km (6000nm) and feature wingtip extensions and canted winglets. This wing could also be fitted to a longer range 767-300ER.

Photo: Air Pacific's 767-300ER cleans up after takeoff. (John Ruming)

Boeing 777-200

Country of origin: United States of America

Type: Medium to long range high capacity widebody airliner

Powerplants: 777-200 – Two 332kN (74,000lb) Pratt & Whitney PW4074 turbofans, or two 336kN (75,000lb) General Electric GE90-75Bs, or two 336kN (75,000lb) Rolls-Royce Trent 875s. 243 tonne MTOW version – Two 345kN (77,000lb) PW4077s, or two 340kN (76,000lb) GE90-76Bs or two 345kN (77,000lb) Trent 877s. 777-200IGW – Two 376kN (84,000lb) PW4084s, or two 381kN (85,000lb) GE90-85Bs, or two 376kN (84,000lb) Trent 884s.

Performance: Typical cruising speed 905km/h (490kt). 777-200 – Range 230 tonne MTOW 7278km (3930nm), 233 tonne MTOW 7778km (4200nm), 243 tonne MTOW range 8860km (4785nm). 777-200IGW – 263 tonne MTOW range 11,170km (6030nm), 286 tonne MTOW range 13,670km (7380nm).

Weights: 777-200 – Empty weight in lightest version 135,580kg (298,000lb), max takeoff optionally 229,520kg (506,000lb), or 233,600kg (515,000lb), or 242,670kg (535,000lb). 777-200IGW – Empty 138,100kg (304,510lb), max takeoff optionally 263,000kg (580,000lb), 268,000kg (590,000lb), or 286,897kg (632,500lb).

Dimensions: Wing span 60.93m (199ft 11in), or folded 47.32m (155ft 3in), length 63.73m (209ft 1in), height 18.51m (60ft 9in). Wing area 427.8m^2 (4605sq ft).

Capacity: Flightcrew of two. Passenger accommodation for between 305 in three classes through to maximum seating of 440. Underfloor capacity for LD3 containers or standard pallets.

Production: Total orders received as of late 1996 301, of which 260 were for the 777-200. Over 35 delivered by late 1996.

History: Almost definitely the last all new western airliner to be rolled out this century, Boeing's new big twin incorporates more advanced technologies than any other previous Boeing airliner.

The 777 was designed to fill the last major gap in the Boeing product line, between the mid size 767 and the 747. Originally conceived as a stretched 767, airline resistance to such a configuration led to Boeing adopting an all new design. Notable design features include Boeing's first application of fly-by-wire, an advanced technology glass cockpit, comparatively large scale use of composites and advanced and extremely powerful engines.

The basic 777-200 as launched in October 1990 is offered in two versions, the basic 777-200 (initially called the A-Market) and the increased weight longer range 777-200IGW (Increased Gross Weight, initially designated the B-Market).

The first 777-200 first flew on June 14 1994, with joint FAA/JAA certification awarded on April 19 1995. Soon after the FAA awarded full 180 minutes ETOPS clearance for PW4074 powered 777-200s.

The first significant 777 development is the stretched 777-300, described separately. The 777-100X meanwhile was a proposed shortened ultra long range (8635nm/16,000km) model, although airline preference seems to be for versions of the 777-200 which would have similar range performance but the 777-200's fuselage.

Photo: One of 18 777-200s ordered by Japan's All Nippon Airways, pictured at Tokyo's Haneda airport. (Rob Finlayson)

Boeing 777-300

Country of origin: United States of America

Type: Medium to long range high capacity widebody airliner

Powerplants: Two 374kN (84,000lb) Pratt & Whitney PW4074 turbofans, or two 374kN (84,000lb) Rolls-Royce Trent 884s, or two 378kN (85,000lb) General Electric GE90-85Bs, or two 400kN (90,000lb) Trent 890s, or two 436kN (98,000lb) PW4098s or two 445kN (100,000lb) GE90-100Bs.

Performance: Typical cruising speed 905km/h (490kt). Design range from 7030km (3400nm) to 10,460km (5650nm).

Weights: Operating empty 157,215kg (346,600lb), max takeoff 263,080kg (580,000lb) to 299,380kg (660,000lb).

Dimensions: Wing span 60.93m (199ft 11in), or folded 47.32m (155ft 3in), length 73.86m (242ft 4in), height 18.51m (60ft 9in). Wing area 427.8m^2 (4605sq ft).

Capacity: Flightcrew of two. Typical passenger accommodation for 368 to 394 in three class arrangements, 451 to 479 in two class arrangements of up 550 in an all economy configuration. Underfloor capacity for 20 standard LD3 containers or eight 2.55m x 3.17m (96in x 125in) pallets.

Production: Total orders as of late 1996 stood at 41, first customer delivery expected late May 1998.

History: Boeing's 777-300 will be the world's largest twin engined aircraft, powered by the world's most powerful turbofan engines, and when it enters service will be the world's longest and second largest airliner.

The stretched 777-300 is designed as replacement for early generation 747s (747-100s and -200s). Compared to the older 747s the stretched 777 will have nearly the same passenger capacity and range capability, but will burn one third less fuel and feature 40% lower maintenance costs.

Compared with the baseline 777-200 the -300 will feature a 10.13m (33ft 3in) stretch, comprising plugs fore and aft of the wings. The longer fuselage allows seating for up to 550 passengers in a single class configuration. To cope with the stretch and the up to 13 tonne (28,600lb) increased max takeoff weight the -300 will feature a strengthened undercarriage, airframe and inboard wing. Other changes compared with the 777-200 include a tailskid and ground manoeuvring cameras mounted on the horizontal tail and wing/fuselage fairing.

Boeing publicly announced it was developing the 777-300 at the Paris Airshow in mid June 1995 where it announced it had secured 31 firm orders from All Nippon, Cathay Pacific, Korean Airlines and Thai Airways. Later that month Boeing's board authorised production of the new aircraft. Japan Airlines ordered five 777-300s later that year, while Malaysia Airlines' early 1996 order for 777s may include some 777-300s.

The 777-300 is due to roll out in late August 1997, with first flight following that October. FAA certification and first customer deliveries are planned for May 1998.

Photo: An artist's impression of the 777-300, the world's largest twin-jet airliner. (Boeing)

Boeing Stearman

Country of origin: United States of America

Type: Two seat sport, utility and agricultural biplane

Powerplant: One 170kW (225hp) Lycoming R-680 seven cylinder radial piston engine driving a two blade fixed pitch propeller, or alternatively a 165kW (220hp) Continental W-670-6 or 170kW (225hp) Jacobs R-755-7 piston radial. Many later converted with a 335kW (450hp) Pratt & Whitney R-985-A6-1 radial piston engine.

Performance: Max cruising speed 200km/h (108kt), typical cruising speed range 148 to 170km/h (80 to 92kt). Initial rate of climb 1000ft/min. Service ceiling 11,200ft. Range with max fuel at 148km/h (80kt) cruising speed 605km (325nm).

Weights: Basic operating 940kg (2075lb), max takeoff 1275kg (2810lb), or max takeoff in ag configuration 2040kg (4500lb).

Dimensions: Wing span 9.80m (32ft 2in), length 7.62m (25ft 0in), height 2.79m (9ft 2in). Wing area 27.6m^2 (297.4sq ft).

Capacity: Typical seating for two in tandem, or single pilot only when used for agricultural work.

Production: Total production 8584. Postwar more than 2100 were converted for agricultural spraying and today small numbers survive in this role. Several hundred fly with private owners.

History: The Boeing Stearman is perhaps the most widely known and recognised biplane in the USA, as it was that country's primary basic trainer throughout World War 2.

This famous biplane began life as a design of the Stearman Division of United Aircraft (at that time United Aircraft also owned Boeing and United Airlines), which Boeing acquired as a wholly owned subsidiary in 1934. At the time of the takeover development on the X75 training biplane was well advanced, and Stearman continued work on the type under Boeing ownership. The prototype Stearman Model 75, as the X75 became, flew for the first time in 1936. That year Stearman delivered the first production Model 35s, as the PT-13, to the US Army Air Corp. That service immediately found the Lycoming R-680 powered PT-13 to be an ideal basic trainer, the airframe was rugged and forgiving, and the slow turning radial engine reliable and reasonably economical.

America's entry into World War 2 brought with it massive requirements for pilot training and the US Army and Navy went on to buy thousands of PT-13s and Continental engined PT-17 Kaydets (the Kaydet name was later adopted for all aircraft in the series). During the WW2 almost all American pilots undertook basic training on the PT-13 or PT-17, and the type was exported to Canada, Britain and other nations.

Postwar, the Stearman's rugged construction and good low speed handling saw the type converted en masse for agricultural spraying work. Many conversions involved replacing the Stearman's fabric covering with metal (to avoid problems with chemical contamination), while many were fitted with more powerful 335kW (450hp) P&W R-985-A6-1 radials.

Today few Stearmans are used for ag work, but, like its British equivalent the Tiger Moth, many hundred are still flown in private hands.

Photo: Stearmans are easily recognised by their large radial engine and biplane configuration. (Lance Higgerson)

Boeing C-97 Stratofreighter

Country of origin: United States of America

Type: Medium range utility freighter

Powerplants: KC-97G – Four 2610kW (3500hp) Pratt & Whitney R-4360-59B Wasp Major 28 cylinder radial piston engines, driving four blade constant speed propellers.

Performance: KC-97G – Max speed 603km/h (325kt), cruising speed 482km/h (260kt). Service ceiling 35,000ft. Range with max fuel 6920km (3735nm).

Weights: KC-97G – Empty 37,450kg (82,500lb), max takeoff 79,450kg (175,000lb).

Dimensions: KC-97G – Wing span 43.05m (141ft 3in), length 35.81m (117ft 5in), height 11.67m (38ft 3in). Wing area 164.5m^2 (1769sq ft).

Capacity: Flightcrew of two pilots, flight engineer, and, in military service, a navigator and radio operator. When configured for passengers can seat more than 100 (Stratocruisers in airline service typically seated 55). All surviving Stratofreighters used as freighters.

Production: Total military Model 367 production of 27 C-97s and 808 KC-97s, in addition to which 55 civil Model 377 Stratocruisers were built. A handful of Stratofreighters remained in commercial use in 1996.

History: Boeing's Stratofreighter formed the backbone of the US Air Force's Military Airlift Transport Service (MATS) during the early 1950s, and more than 800 were built for use as freighters and air-to-air refuellers.

The Model 367 Stratofreighter is based on the Boeing B-29 Superfortress, the Allies' most technologically advanced bomber to see service in World War 2, and an aircraft famous (or infamous) for dropping the only atomic bombs used operationally in warfare on Japan in the closing stages of that conflict. The B-29 flew for the first time in September 1942 by which time Boeing had already studied a transport version, utilising the B-29's wing, engines, tail and lower fuselage, combined with a new upper fuselage section. The new double lobe fuselage shape was very distinctive, and also formed the basis for future Boeing jet airliner fuselage cross sections.

The US Army Air Force was impressed with Boeing's proposals and ordered three prototypes be built, the first of which flew on November 15 1944. Ten development YC-97s were subsequently ordered, the last of which represented production aircraft, featuring the more powerful R-4360 engines and taller tail developed for the B-50, an improved B-29. The first production C-97A was delivered in October 1949.

Development of the C-97 led to the C-97C, which was used for casualty evacuation, and the KC-97E, KC-97F and KC-97G aerial tankers. More than 590 KC-97Gs were built. The KC-97 was the US Air Force's primary tanker until replaced by the jet powered KC-135, the predecessor to the Boeing 707. Small numbers of 377 Stratocruiser airliners were also built, but the last of these have long been retired.

Many Stratofreighters survived their military service to be acquired by civilian operators for use as freighters but few survived to see service into the 1990s.

Photo: One of a small number of C-97s still flying in commercial service comes in to land.

Boeing Vertol (Kawasaki) BV 107

Country of origin: United States of America

Type: Large airliner and utility helicopter

Powerplants: Two 930kW (1250shp) General Electric CT58-110-1 or Ishikawajima-Harima built CT58-IHI-110-1 turboshafts, driving two three blade rotors.

Performance: KV 107/II-2 – Max speed 270km/h (146kt), economical cruising speed 232km/h (125kt). Initial rate of climb 1440ft/min. Hovering ceiling out of ground effect 8800ft. Range with a three tonne (6600lb) payload and reserves 175km (95kt).

Weights: KV 107/II-2 – Empty equipped 4868kg (10,723lb), max takeoff 8618kg (19,000lb).

Dimensions: Diameter of each rotor 15.24m (50ft 0in), fuselage length 13.59m (44ft 7in), height 5.09m (16ft 9in). Main rotor disc area (total) 364.6m^2 (3925sq ft).

Capacity: Flightcrew of two. Typical seating for 23 to 25 passengers in airliner configuration, or 12 passengers and freight in combi configuration. Executive configuration seats six to 11 passengers in main cabin.

Production: Total BV/KV 107 production approximately 650, with almost all for military customers. Small numbers remained in commercial service in late 1996.

History: Boeing Vertol's Model 107 is best known as the military CH-46 Sea Knight, but small numbers were built as airliners and utility transports for commercial customers.

The then independent Vertol company (previously Piasecki) designed the 107 in the late 1950s as a medium lift helicopter for US Army evaluation. Three prototype Lycoming turboshaft powered Vertol 107s were built (the Army ordered 10) and designated YHC-1As, first flight occurred on August 27 1958. By that time though the Army's interest had switched to what would become the Chinook and it placed no orders. However in February 1961 Vertol (Boeing acquired Vertol in 1960) won a US Marine Corps competition with a developed General Electric T58-GE-8 powered version of the BV 107, and the type was ordered into production as the CH-46A Sea Knight.

The commercial 107 is based on the CH-46A powered by the civilianised CT-58-110 (equivalent to the T58-GE-8). The first commercial 107 to fly was one of the three original development aircraft built for the US Army and converted to the new standard, its first flight in the new configuration was on October 25 1960. Offered in two forms, the KV 107/II-1 utility transport and KV 107/II-2 airliner, only the latter was built. KV 107/II-2 customers included New York Airlines, who ordered three configured to seat 25, Columbia Helicopters in the US (Columbia still operates KV 107s) and Japan's Air Lift. A more powerful 1045kW (1400shp) CT58-140-1 powered longer range KV 107/II-A-17 was offered and one was built for the Tokyo Police.

Japan's Kawasaki built all commercial 107s, and has held manufacturing rights to the 107 since 1965. Kawasaki has also built KV 107s for the Japanese military and Saudi Arabia.

Photo: This Japanese KV 107 is pictured in Australia where it was used in support of testing of a space re-entry vehicle. (Richard Koehne)

Boeing Commercial Chinook

Country of origin: United States of America

Type: Heavylift commercial and airliner transport helicopter

Powerplants: Two 3040kW (4075shp) takeoff rated Lycoming AL 5512 turboshafts, driving two three blade rotors.

Performance: LR, MLR & ER – Max speed 278km/h (150kt), max cruising speed 270km/h (145kt), long range cruising speed 250km/h (135kt). Max initial rate of climb at MTOW 1180ft/min. Range – LR & MLR with max fuel 1150km (620nm), ER with max fuel 1918km (1035nm). UT – Max speed 260km/h (140kt), max cruising speed 260km/h (140kt), long range cruising speed 250km/h (135kt). Max initial rate of climb at MTOW 1500ft/min. Range with max internal load 425km (230nm).

Weights: LR – Empty 11,748kg (25,900lb), max takeoff 22,000kg (48,500lb), or 23,133kg (51,000lb) with an external load. ER – Empty 12,020kg (26,500lb), max takeoff same. MLR – Empty 11,113kg (24,500lb), max takeoff same. UT – Empty 9797kg (21,600lb), max takeoff 19,051kg (42,000lb), or 23,133kg (51,000lb) with an external sling load.

Dimensions: Rotor diameter (both) 18.29m (60ft 0in), length overall 30.18m (99ft 0in), fuselage length 15.87m (52ft 1in), height 5.68m (18ft 8in). Total rotor blade area 525.4m^2 (5655sq ft).

Capacity: Two pilots on flightdeck. Seating for 44 at four abreast in main cabin. Combi versions seat between eight and 32 with rear cabin loaded with freight, or between 22 and 32 with freight on one side of main cabin. Max internal load of LR and MLR models 9070kg (20,000lb), ER and UT models 8730kg (19250lb). Max external sling load 12,700kg (28,000lb).

Production: Approximately a dozen Commercial Chinooks have been built thus far (mainly LRs), most of which remain in service.

History: The Boeing Helicopters Model 234 Commercial Chinook is, as its name suggests, the commercial variant of the successful military airlifter, the CH-47 Chinook.

The original military Chinook as developed for the US Army first flew in September 1961, and has been developed into a number of progressively improved variants. The Commercial Chinook was not launched until 1978, following a British Airways Helicopters order for three for North Sea oil rig support missions. The Commercial Chinook's first flight occurred on August 19 1980, certification was granted in June 1981, and service entry was the following month.

Largely identical in configuration to the CH-47, the Commercial Chinook retains the former's rear cargo ramp, but has a slightly reprofiled nose, commercial avionics and large passenger windows along both sides of the main cabin.

The initial orders were for the 234 LR Long Range, which compared with the CH-47 has roughly twice the fuel load, plus a 44 seat passenger interior based on that used in Boeing jetliners. A number of other versions have been offered and these are the 234 ER Extended Range with additional tankage, the 234 UT Utility, and 234 MLR Multi purpose Long Range which can be used for passenger or freight operations, or a combination of both.

Photo: One of two Boeing 234 Commercial Chinooks which were used for a time by Trump Air. (Boeing)

Bombardier Aerospace is
all about group dynamics. The coming
together of designers, engineers and
Global Express*
manufacturers powered by innovation. Sharing technology and ideas.
Challenger*
Shaping the future with a singular vision of excellence.
Learjet*
Ultralong-range executive jets. Widebody intercontinental
Canadair Regional Jet*
business jets. High-performance light and mid-size jets. Pioneering
de Havilland Dash 8*
regional jetliners. Reliable commuter turboprops. The world's finest waterbombers
CL-415
and more. Bombardier Aerospace is the future in motion.
BOMBARDIER
Bombardier Aerospace
For more information, call (514) 855-7983
*Trademarks of Bombardier Inc.

Bombardier Global Express

Country of origin: Canada

Type: Ultra long range, high speed, high capacity corporate jet

Powerplants: Two 65.3kN (14,690lb) BMW Rolls-Royce BR710-48-C2 turbofans.

Performance: (Preliminary performance targets) High speed cruise Mach 0.88, normal cruising speed Mach 0.85, long range cruising speed Mach 0.80. Range with eight passengers, four crew and reserves at long range cruising speed 12,040km (6500nm), at normal cruising speed 11,720km (6330nm), at high speed cruise 9260km (5000nm).

Weights: Typical operating empty 22,000kg (48,500lb), max takeoff 41,278kg (91,000lb).

Dimensions: Wing span 28.00m (91ft 11in), length 30.20m (99ft 0in), height 7.40m (24ft 4in).

Capacity: Flightcrew of two and one or two flight attendants. Executive configuration fitted with a galley, crew rest station, work stations, a conference/lounge/dining area, a stateroom with a fold out bed, toilet, shower and wardrobe. Alternative 18 seat and high density 30 seat corporate shuttle configurations offered.

Production: Canadair held more than 40 firm orders at late 1996.

History: The ultra long range Global Express looks set to become the ultimate purpose designed corporate jet, rivalled only by the Gulfstream V (described separately).

The Global Express is a high speed long range corporate jet, intended to transport senior directors of large corporations over transcontinental ranges, and as such should prove an effective replacement for converted airliners currently operating in this role. The Global Express' range is such that it can fly between any two points on the globe, such as Sydney to London, and need only one refuelling stop, while from London it can fly nonstop to Singapore or Tokyo, or from Los Angeles to Auckland or Moscow at Mach 0.80.

Canadair announced development of the Global Express in October 1991 at the annual NBAA conference in the USA. It flew for the first time on October 13 1996, with certification and production deliveries scheduled for 1998.

The unique Global Express is based loosely on Canadair's Regional Jet airliner, featuring the same fuselage cross section and similar length. However despite the size similarities the two aircraft are very different due to the nature of their intended roles. The Global Express features an advanced all new supercritical wing with a 35° sweep and winglets, plus a new T-tail. The engines, two BMW Rolls-Royce BR710s, promise to be the most advanced engines in their class. The flightdeck should be one of the most advanced offered on any aircraft in any class, with six screen EFIS displays and two Heads Up Displays.

Besides Canadair, a number of other aerospace firms participate in the Global Express program. Canadair's Bombardier partner Shorts is responsible for the design and manufacture of the engine nacelles and parts of the fuselage, while Mitsubishi Heavy Industries will build the wing and centre fuselage sections.

Photo: High cruise speed, a spacious interior and very long range are the primary selling points of the Global Express. Pictured is the prototype on its first flight. (Bombardier)

Brantly B-2 & 305

Country of origin: United States of America

Type: Light piston powered utility helicopters

Powerplant: B-2B – One 135kW (180hp) Textron Lycoming IVO-360-A1A fuel injected flat four piston engine, driving a three blade main rotor and two blade tail rotor. 305 – One 225kW (305hp) Textron Lycoming IVO-540-B1A fuel injected flat six.

Performance: B-2B – Max level speed 161km/h (87kt), max cruising speed (at 75% power) 145km/h (78kt). Initial rate of climb 1900ft. Service ceiling 10,800ft. Hovering ceiling in ground effect 6700ft. Range with max fuel and reserves 400km (217nm). 305 – Max speed 193km/h (104kt), max cruising speed 177km/h (96kt). Initial rate of climb 975ft/min. Service ceiling 12,000ft. Hovering ceiling in ground effect 4080ft. Range with max fuel and reserves 354km (191nm).

Weights: B-2B – Empty 463kg (1020lb) or 481kg (1060lb) with floats, max takeoff 757kg (1670lb). 305 – Empty 815kg (1800lb), max takeoff 1315kg (2900lb).

Dimensions: B-2B – Main rotor diameter 7.24m (23ft 9in), length overall 8.53m (28ft 0in), fuselage length 6.62m (21ft 9in), height 2.06m (6ft 9in). Main rotor disc area 41.2m^2 (443.0sq ft). 305 – Main rotor diameter 8.74m (28ft 8in), length overall 10.03m (32ft 11in), fuselage length 7.44m (24ft 5in), height 2.44m (8ft 1in). Main rotor disc 60.0m^2 (654.4sq ft).

Capacity: B-2 series has seating for two side by side. 305 has seating for five with two forward individual seats and rear bench seat for three.

Production: Exact production unknown, but includes more than 400 B-2 series. Production has ceased.

History: The Brantly B-2 series of light helicopters first flew in the early 1950s, yet remained in production until the early 1990s, while the larger five seat 305 dates to the early 1970s.

The original B-2 two seat light helicopter was designed and built by Mr N Brantly, and flew for the first time on February 21 1953. Certification was awarded in April 1959 allowing production deliveries to get underway soon after. The initial production B-2 model featured a 135kW (180hp) VO-360-A1A flat four, the same basic powerplant that powered the B-2 series through to the 1990s. The initial B-2 was followed by the improved B-2A with a redesigned cabin and the B-2B, which became the definitive production model.

Brantly also developed a larger five seat Model 305 based on the B-2, with a larger cabin and more powerful VO-540 engine. The 305 first flew in January 1964 and was certificated in July the following year.

Brantly ceased trading in the early 1970s after more than 400 B-2s were built. However production resumed in 1976 when the Hynes company acquired the design and production rights to what became the Brantly-Hynes B-2 and 305.

Brantly-Hynes continued low rate manufacture of both models through to the mid 1980s when it too ceased production. Finally in 1989 James Kimura formed Brantly Helicopter Industries to build both models, and low rate production resumed. However Brantly Helicopter Industries has since ceased production.

Photo: A three blade rotor system and distinctive 'tadpole' fuselage are the primary design features of the Brantley B-2. (Tony Arbon)

Bristol 170 Freighter

Country of Origin: United Kingdom

Type: Short range freighter/utility transport

Powerplant: Mk 31 – Two 1475kW (1980hp) Bristol Hercules 734 14-cylinder sleeve valve radial piston engines, driving four blade propellers.

Performance: Mk 31 – Max cruising speed 311km/h (168kt) at 10,000ft, economical cruising speed 262km/h (141kt). Range with max payload 1320km (715nm), range with max fuel 2785km (1505nm).

Weights: Mk 31 – Empty 12,247kg (27,000lb), max takeoff 19,958kg (44,000lb).

Dimensions: Mk 31 – Wing span 32.92m (108ft 0in), length 20.83m (68ft 4in), height 6.56m (21ft 6in). Wing area 138.0m^2 (1487sq ft).

Capacity: Mk 31 payload of 5670kg (12,500lb), or alternatively seating for 15 to 23 passengers, depending on configuration. Mk 32 could seat up to 60 passengers.

Production: Total Bristol 170 production 214 aircraft. In late 1996 a lone example survived in commercial service in Canada.

History: Design of the Bristol Freighter began in 1944 in anticipation of demand for a rugged airliner and freighter once WW2 was over, plus potential military requirements.

Bristol's Type 170 started out as a private venture design and was developed under the leadership of technical director L G Frise (who also designed the Frise aileron). Design features of the 170 include its slab sided fuselage, fixed taildragger undercarriage, clamshell style nose doors, raised flightdeck, and a relatively large wing with swept back leading edge and straight trailing edge of two spar construction. As originally proposed the 170 was to be powered by improved sleeve valve Bristol Perseus radials.

Although conceived as a private venture the 170 soon caught the British Air Staff's attention who thought the design would be well suited for use in the India-Burma theatre carrying supplies and vehicles to jungle strips. Two prototypes were ordered with a slightly enlarged fuselage and more powerful Hercules 630 radials.

The 170 made its first flight from Filton on December 2 1945 and while it was too late to be ordered into production for military service in WW2 the type's potential had been ably demonstrated. The second prototype, configured in 32 seat Wayfarer airliner form (without the nose freight doors), flew the following April. Civil certification was granted in June 1946.

Early production was of the Mk I Freighter and Mk II Wayfarer. The Mark XI (later the Mk 21) was unveiled at the 1947 SBAC airshow and introduced rounded wingtips and more powerful Hercules 672 engines, allowing an increase in gross weight by 1360kg (3000lb). The Mk 31 introduced more powerful engines and remained in production until 1950.

The final 170 model is the Mk 32, developed at the request of Silver City Airways. The Mk 32 featured a lengthened nose which allowed it to carry three cars, rather than two, in a car ferry configuration.

Photo: The world's last known surviving Bristol Freighter in commercial service, flying in Canada.

Britten-Norman Trislander

Country of origin: United Kingdom

Type: Commuter airliner

Powerplants: Three 195kW (260hp) Lycoming 0-540-E4C5 flat six piston engines driving two blade constant speed Hartzell propellers. An optional 1.56kN (350lb) auxiliary rocket engine for use on takeoff was also offered.

Performance: Max level speed 290km/h (156kt), cruising speed at 75% power 267km/h (144kt), cruising speed at 50% power 241km/h (130kt). Initial rate of climb 980ft/min. Service ceiling 13,150ft. Max range 1610km (868nm).

Weights: Empty equipped without electronics 2650kg (5843lb), max takeoff 4536kg (10,000lb).

Dimensions: Wing span 16.15m (53ft 0in), length 15.01m (49ft 3in), height 4.32m (14ft 2in). Wing area 31.3m^2 (337.0sq ft).

Capacity: Usually one pilot and passenger on flightdeck. Seating for 16 passengers two abreast at 79cm (31in) pitch in main cabin.

Production: UK production amounted to 73. Plans were held to produce 12 from British components in Florida as the Tri-Commutair, and at one stage to undertake production in Australia.

History: The uniquely configured three engined Trislander takes its inspiration from trijets such as the L-1011 and DC-10 in its answer to the need for more power for a stretched version of the Islander (described separately under Pilatus Britten-Norman).

Britten-Norman research showed that there existed sufficient market demand to warrant the development of a stretched Islander, and the company concluded that any stretched version would need to offer a 50% increase in internal capacity. The company's novel approach to the need for more power was to add a third engine, rather than two engines of increased power output. A nose mounted engine in the fashion of the Ju 52 was considered, but due to the Islander's nose configuration, Britten-Norman settled on mounting the engine on the vertical tail, resulting in the BN-2A Mk III Trislander.

The tail mounted engine involved significant modification to the tail and strengthening of the rear fuselage. Other changes over the Islander include a 2.29m (7ft 6in) fuselage stretch forward of the wing, new main landing gear and larger diameter wheels and tyres.

The first Trislander was in fact converted from the second Islander prototype, and it made the type's first flight on September 11 1970. Early production Trislanders were also conversions of Islanders, while subsequent Trislanders were built on the same production line as the Islander. The first production Trislander flew on March 6 1971, certification was granted on May 14, and first deliveries to a customer occurred on June 29 that year.

Britten-Norman Trislander production ceased in 1982 after 73 were ordered (by which stage the company had been acquired by Pilatus). Plans to produce the Trislander in the USA as the Tri-Commutair by the International Aviation Corporation, and in Australia never came to fruition. However one of 12 kits built for the Tri-Commutair project was assembled in Guernsey in the UK and flew in March 1996.

Photo: This nose on shot of the Trislander shoes to good effect its unusual engine configuration. (Lance Higgerson)

Canadair CL-44 & Yukon

Country of origin: Canada

Type: Medium to long range airliner and freighter

Powerplants: CL-44D-4 – Four 4270kW (5730shp) Rolls-Royce Tyne 515/50 turboprops, driving four blade variable pitch propellers.

Performance: CL-44D-4 – Max cruising speed 647km/h (647kt), cruising speed 621km/h (335kt). Service ceiling 30,000ft. Range with max payload 4625km (2500nm), range with max fuel 8990km (4855nm).

Weights: CL-44D-4 – Operating empty 40,345kg (88,952lb), max takeoff 95,250kg (210,000lb).

Dimensions: CL-44D-4 – Wing span 43.37m (142ft 4in), length 41.73m (136ft 11in), height 11.18m (36ft 8in). Wing area 192.7m^2 (2075sq ft).

Capacity: Flightcrew of two pilots and one flight engineer. CL-44D-4 – Max single class seating for 178 passengers (or 214 in the CL-44J). Max payload 29,959kg (66,048kg).

Production: A total of 27 civil CL-44s built (including one CL-400 conversion), and 12 military CC-106 Yukons, many of which later entered civil service. Three remained in service in 1996 as freighters.

History: Based on the Bristol Britannia, the CL-44 resulted from a mid 1950s Royal Canadian Air Force requirement for a maritime patrol aircraft.

What resulted was the CP-107 Argus. The Argus differed in a number of significant respects from the Britannia in that it was powered by Wright Turbo Compound radial engines (selected in place of turboprops to give better endurance at low level), and a redesigned unpressurised fuselage incorporating a weapons bay. With Canadair already producing the Argus, it was a relatively simple matter to offer a Britannia based design to meet an RCAF requirement for a freighter.

The freighter became the CC-106 Yukon (or to Canadair the CL-44D). Twelve were built, featuring Rolls-Royce Tyne turboprops, lengthened fuselage and wings and a conventional side loading large freight door. The first Yukon flew on November 15 1959.

Canadair then began to offer the Yukon to commercial customers and developed the CL-44D-4, which featured the hinged tail which considerably simplified loading. The first CL-44D-4 flew on November 16 1960, and at that time the model was the largest commercial freighter on offer in the world.

While most CL-44s in civil service have been used as freighters, an Icelandic airline operated three CL-44D-4s plus a single CL-44J in a passenger configuration. The J, or the CL-400, differed from the D-4s in that it featured a 4.62m (15ft 2in) fuselage stretch, and only one was built. Meanwhile one CL-44 was converted by Conroy Aircraft in the US as a large volume freighter with a new voluminous cargo hold (similar to the Boeing 337 Super Guppy conversions), and it flew after conversion for the first time on November 26 1969. Several ex military Yukons found their way into civil service after retirement in 1973, but only a handful of these and commercial CL-44s remain in service.

Photo: HeavyLift operated this Conroy converted CL-44. (Bill Lines)

Canadair CL-215, CL-215T & CL-415

Country of origin: Canada

Type: Firebomber and utility amphibian

Powerplants: CL-215 – Two 1565kW (2100hp) Pratt & Whitney R-2800-CA3 18 cylinder radial piston engines driving three blade constant speed propellers. CL-415 – Two 1775kW (2380shp) Pratt & Whitney Canada PW123AF turboprops driving four blade constant speed Hamilton Standard props.

Performance: CL-215 – Max cruising speed 290km/h (157kt). Initial rate of climb 1000ft/min. Range at max cruising speed 1715km (925nm), at long range cruising speed 2095km (1130nm). CL-415 – Max cruising speed 376km/h (203kt), long range cruising speed 270km/h (145kt), patrol speed 240km/h (130kt). Initial rate of climb 1375ft/min. Ferry range with 500kg (1100lb) payload 2430km (1310nm).

Weights: CL-215 firebomber – Empty 12,220kg (26,941lb); max takeoff from water 17,100kg (37,700lb), from land 19,730kg (43,500lb). CL-415 firebomber – Operating empty 12,333kg (28,353lb); max takeoff from land 19,890kg (43,850lb), from water 17,168kg (37,850lb).

Dimensions: CL-215 – Wing span 28.60m (93ft 10in), length 19.82m (65ft 1in), height on land 8.98m (29ft 6in). Wing area 100.3m^2 (1080sq ft). CL-415 – Same except wing span over wingtips 28.63m (93ft 11in).

Capacity: Flightcrew of two, plus accommodation in special missions variants for a third flightdeck member, a mission specialist and two observers. Passenger configuration for 30 at 79cm (31in) pitch, or in a combi configuration for 11, with firebombing tanks retained and freight in forward fuselage. Fire retardant payload capacity of 6123kg (13,500lb).

Production: Total CL-215 production of 125. As of late 1996 24 CL-415s had been ordered. First deliveries were made in April 1994.

History: The CL-215 was designed as a specialist firebomber, particularly suited to Canada and other heavily forested regions.

The resulting amphibious aircraft is powered by two Pratt & Whitney R-2800 radials, and it is capable of scooping up 5455 litres (1200Imp gal/1440US gal) of water in 12 seconds from its water source. The CL-215 first flew on October 23 1967, and first delivery was to the French civil protection agency in June 1969. Production of batches of CL-215s continued right through to 1990.

Originally the subsequent CL-215T was to be a simple turboprop powered development of the CL-215, and Canadair converted two aircraft in 1989 to act as development aircraft. The first of these flew on June 8 that year. Retrofit kits for CL-215s to the new standard are offered, but Canadair elected not to build new CL-215Ts, and instead developed the CL-415.

The primary improvement added to the CL-415 is (compared to the CL-215T) an EFIS cockpit, while other improvements, some of which first appeared on the CL-215T, include winglets and finlets, higher weights and an increased capacity firebombing system. Like the CL-215 its principle mission is that of a firebomber, but various special mission (including SAR and maritime patrol) and transport configurations are available.

The first CL-415 flew in December 1993.

Photo: A CL-415 demonstrator demonstrates its water dumping capabilities. (David Neafsey)

Canadair CL-600 Challenger

Country of origin: Canada

Type: Medium to long range widebody corporate jet

Powerplants: Two 33.6kN (7500lb) Avco Lycoming ALF 502L turbofans.

Performance: Max speed 904km/h (488kt), max cruising speed 890km/h (480kt), long range cruising speed 800km/h (432kt). Max operating altitude 45,000ft. Range with reserves (latter build aircraft) 6300km (3402nm), or 5925km (3200nm) (earlier build aircraft).

Weights: Early build aircraft – Operating empty 10,353kg (22,825lb), max takeoff 18,325kg (40,400lb). Later build aircraft – Empty 8369kg (18,450lb), operating empty 10,285kg (22,675lb), max takeoff weight 18,201kg (40,125lb).

Dimensions: Wing span 18.85m (61ft 10in), length 20.85m (68ft 5in), height 6.30m (20ft 8in). Wing area 41.8m^2 (450sq ft).

Capacity: Flightcrew of two. Various customer seating options including 14, 15, 17 or 18 passenger configurations.

Production: 83 Challenger CL-600s were built between 1978 and 1983. Production of the Challenger continues as the CL-601, described separately.

History: The CL-600 Challenger is the first production model of what is now a successful business jet family, but as a stand alone aircraft it had a troubled early history.

Canadair purchased the exclusive production, development and marketing rights to an all new business jet developed by Bill Lear, original designer of the Learjet, in 1976. Known as the LearStar 600, this design was notable for its large size cabin, and promised long range and good operating economics. As the CL-600 Challenger, Canadair launched development of the LearStar design on October 29 1976 with 53 firm orders. Canadair made a small number of changes to the design including repositioning the horizontal tailplane to the top of the fin rather than on the fuselage.

Three development Challengers were built, the first of which flew for the first time on November 8 1978, the others flying in March and July the following year. The first aircraft however crashed in a deep stall accident and while certification was granted in August 1980, temporary restrictions limited maximum takeoff weight to 14,970kg (33,000lb) and maximum speed to 587km/h (317kt), while flight into known icing conditions and the use of thrust reversers was prohibited.

A major weight and drag reduction program pared back the Challenger's weight, improving range. The addition of General Electric CF34 turbofans as options as the CL-601, described separately, further addressed performance shortfalls and negated problems with the troubled ALF 502 turbofan.

One version that failed to see the light of day was the CL-610 Challenger E, this would have featured a fuselage stretch allowing seating for 24 passengers, but development was suspended in 1981.

Production of the CL-600 ceased in 1983, having switched to the much improved CL-601.

Photo: The primary visual difference between the original 600 model and later versions is the engines (using different nacelles) and lack of winglets, although some 600s have had this latter feature retrofitted on in later life.

Canadair 601 & 604 Challenger

Country of origin: Canada

Type: Long range widebody corporate jets

Powerplants: 601 – Two 40.66kN (9140lb) General Electric CF34-3A turbofans. 604 – Two GE CF34-3Bs flat rated to 38.8kN (8729lb).

Performance: 601-1A – Max cruising speed 851km/h (460kt), typical cruising speed 819km/h (442kt), long range cruising speed 786km/h (424kt). Max operating altitude 45,000ft. Range with max fuel and reserves 6208km (3352nm). 601-3A – Normal cruising speed 851km/h (460kt). Service ceiling 41,000ft. Range with max fuel, five pax and reserves 6236km (3365nm). 601-3A/ER – Speeds same. Service ceiling 41,000ft. Range with max fuel, five pax and reserves 6643km (3585nm). 604 – Range with max fuel, five pax and reserves 7408km (4000nm).

Weights: 601-3A – Empty 9049kg (19,950lb), operating empty 11,605kg (25,585lb), max takeoff 19,550kg (43,100lb). 601-3A – Empty 9292kg (20,485lb), operating empty 11,566kg (25,500lb), max takeoff 19,550kg (43,100lb) or optionally 20,457kg (45,100lb). 601-3A/ER – Empty 9405kg (20,735lb), operating empty 11,685kg (24,760lb), max takeoff 20,230kg (44,600lb) or optionally 20,457kg (45,100lb). 604 – Max takeoff 21,636kg (47,700lb).

Dimensions: Wing span 19.61m (64ft 4in), length 20.85m (68ft 5in), height 6.30m (20ft 8in). Wing area 48.3m^2 (520.0sq ft).

Capacity: Flightcrew of two. Various seating options available depending on customer preference, maximum permissible seating for 19.

Production: Production of 601-1As completed after 66 delivered. 601-3A and 601-3A/ER production of over 130. First 604 delivered in early 1996.

History: Through addressing the original CL-600's weight problems and replacing the troubled ALF 502 turbofans, the Challenger 601 has become a highly successful top of the range corporate jet.

Troubles with the Avco Lycoming powered CL-600 Challenger led Canadair to develop a vastly improved variant in the form of the General Electric CF34 (which also powers the military Fairchild A-10 Thunderbolt II and the Lockheed S-3 Viking) powered Challenger 601. Other detail changes included winglets, which are also offered as a retrofit to earlier aircraft. The 601 first flew on April 10 1982 and for a time was offered alongside the CL-600. The CL-600 was dropped from the model line in 1983.

Subsequent development of the Challenger led to the 601-3A. First flying in 1987, this variant features an EFIS glass cockpit and upgraded engines. The 601-3A/ER meanwhile is an extended range model with higher weights, the range increase available as a retrofit to earlier 601-3As.

Further improvements to the basic design led to the Challenger 604. Improvements include an advanced Collins Pro-Line IV avionics system including a late generation glass cockpit, higher weights, CF34-3B turbofans and increased fuel tankage. First flight with CF34-3A engines was in September 1994, first flight with the CF34-3B engines was on March 17 1995, with Transport Canada certification granted that September. First deliveries occurred in 1996.

Photo: A Portuguese registered Challenger 601. Note the winglets and GE engines. (Keith Anderson)

Canadair Regional Jet

Country of origin: Canada

Type: Regional jet airliner

Powerplants: 100 – Two 41.01kN (9220lb) General Electric CF34-3A1 turbofans. 200 – Two 41.0kN (9220lb) CF34-3B1s.

Performance: 100 – High speed cruise 851km/h (459kt), typical cruising speed 786km/h (424kt). Range with max payload at long range cruising speed with reserves 1815km (980nm). 200LR – Speeds same. Range with max payload at long range cruising speed and reserves over 3520km (1900nm).

Weights: 100 – Empty 13,236kg (29,180lb), operating empty 13,653kg (30,100lb), max takeoff 21,523kg (47450lb). 200LR – Empty 13,243kg (29,195lb), operating empty 13,740kg (30,292lb), max takeoff 24,040kg (53,000lb).

Dimensions: Wing span 21.21m (69ft 7in), length 26.77m (87ft 10in), height 6.22m (20ft 5in). Wing area 54.0m^2 (581.1sq ft).

Capacity: Flightcrew of two. Typical one class seating for 50 at four abreast and 79cm (31in) pitch. Max seating for 52. Various corporate configurations can seat from 15 to 50.

Production: Total Regional Jet orders received by late 1996 totalled 171, of which 120 had been built and were in service.

History: The 50 seat Regional Jet was the first of an entirely new class of airliner to emerge, and is now selling strongly.

The Regional Jet is designed to offer the high speed advantages of much larger jets, with similar standards of service while at the same time offering operating economics, particularly over longer stage lengths, close to that of comparable size high speed turboprops. Canadair promotes the Regional Jet as a hub buster, able to fly longish stage lengths linking secondary ports directly while bypassing congested major airports, something which now seems to be appealing strongly to North American operators.

The concept of a stretched airliner derivative of the Challenger is not new, Canadair originally studied a 24 seat stretched development of the CL-600 up to 1981. Design studies for a stretched airliner based on the CL-601 however were first undertaken in 1987, leading Canadair to launch the Regional Jet program on March 31 1989. The first of three development aircraft took to the skies for the first time on May 10 1991, while certification was awarded in January 1993.

Major changes over the Challenger apart from the stretched fuselage include a new advanced wing optimised for airline operations, higher design weights, new undercarriage, additional fuel capacity and slightly more powerful CF34 engines.

The original RJ 100 series – the 100, 100ER and 100LR – was replaced by the 200 series (with more efficient engines) in 1995. Corporate shuttle configurations are also available as the Corporate Jetliner and the SE.

In 1996 Canadair was close to launching a 4.72m (15ft 6in) stretched 70 seat RJ derivative under the designation CRJ-X. Canadair owner Bombardier hopes to make a decision whether to launch the CRJ-X by later 1996 or early 1997 if sufficient orders are received, and it could be available by 1998. Engines would be in the form of two 58kN (13,070lb) CF34-8C1s.

Photo: An RJ of Comair, the largest RJ operator in the USA. (Gary Gentle)

CASA C-212 Aviocar

Country of origin: Spain

Type: STOL turboprop airliner and utility transport

Powerplants: C-212C – Two 580kW (775shp) Garrett AiResearch (now AlliedSignal) TPE331-5-251C turboprop engines driving four blade propellers. Series 200 – Two 670kW (900shp) TPE311-10-501Cs. Series 300 – Two 670kW (900shp) TPE331-10R-513Cs.

Performance: C-212C – Max speed 370km/h (199kt), max cruising speed 359km/h (194kt), economical cruising speed 315km/h (170kt). Range with max fuel and 1045kg (2303lb) payload 1760km (950nm), range with max payload 480km (258nm). Series 200 – Max cruising speed 365km/h (197kt), cruising speed 346km/h (187kt). Range with max payload 408km (220nm), range with max fuel 1760km (950nm). Series 300 – Max operating speed 370km/h (200kt), max cruising speed 354km/h (191kt), economical cruising speed 300km/h (162kt). Range with 25 passengers and reserves at max cruising speed 440km (237nm), with 1700kg (3770lb) payload 1435km (775nm).

Weights: C-212C – Empty 3700kg (8157lb), max takeoff 6300kg (13,890lb). Series 200 – Empty 3780kg (8333lb), max takeoff 7450kg (16,425lb). Series 300 – Empty 3780kg (8333lb), operating empty 4560kg (10,053lb), max takeoff 7700kg (16,975lb).

Dimensions: C-212C & Series 200 – Wing span 19.00m (62ft 4in), length 15.20m (49ft 11in), height 6.30m (20ft 8in). Wing area 40.0m^2 (430.6sq ft). Series 200 – Same except length 15.16m (49ft 9in). Series 300 – Wing span 20.28m (66ft 7in), length 16.15m (53ft 0in), height 6.60m (21ft 8in). Wing area 41.0m^2 (441.3sq ft).

Capacity: Flightcrew of two. Max passenger seating for 26, typical layout for 22 passengers at three abreast. Freighter version can accommodate three LD3 containers or two LD2s or two LD727/DC-8s. Max payload 2700kg (5950lb).

Production: Over 430 Aviocars of all models built, including 170 for commercial operators and 260 for military customers. IPTN in Indonesia has built over 90 NC-212s under licence.

History: Initially conceived as a light STOL transport for the Spanish Air Force, the CASA C-212 has found a handy market niche and is quite popular in underdeveloped regions.

Designed to replace the Spanish air force's mixed transport fleet of Douglas C-47 Dakotas and Junkers Ju 52s still in service in the 1960s, the C-212 was also developed with the intention of offering a civil variant. Design work began in the late 1960s, the first prototype made the type's first flight on March 26 1971. Pre-production examples followed, then the type entered air force service in 1974. The first commercial version meanwhile was delivered in July 1975.

The basic civil version was designated the C-212C, the military version the C-212-5. Production of these models ceased in 1978, CASA switching to the Series 200 with more powerful engines and higher operating weights. The first Series 200, a converted C-212C prototype, flew for the first time in its new configuration on April 30 1978.

A third development of the Aviocar is the Series 300 which first flew in 1984 and was certificated in late 1987. Improvements to this model are newer engines and winglets.

Photo: A CASA C-212-300 demonstrator in company livery. (Jim Thorn)

Cessna 150 & 152

Country of origin: United States of America

Type: Two seat primary and aerobatic capable trainer

Powerplants: 150 & 150 Commuter II – One 75kW (100hp) Continental O-200-A flat four piston engine, driving a two blade fixed pitch prop. A152 Aerobat – One 80kW (108hp) Lycoming O-235-N2C.

Performance: 150 – Max speed 200km/h (108kt), optimum cruising speed 196km/h (106kt). Initial rate of climb 640ft/min. Service ceiling 15,300ft. Range 563km (304nm). Commuter II – Max speed 201km/h (109kt), max cruising speed 196km/h (106kt), economical cruising speed 153km/h (83kt). Initial rate of climb 670ft/min. Service ceiling 14,000ft. Max range with no reserves 1062km (573nm), or 1650km (891nm) with optional fuel. A152 – Max speed 200km/h (108kt), cruising speed 195km/h (105kt). Initial rate of climb 715ft/min. Range 575km (310nm).

Weights: 150 – Empty 447kg (985lb), max takeoff 681kg (1500lb). Commuter II – Empty 492kg (1085lb), max takeoff 726kg (1600lb). A152 – Empty 513kg (1131lb), max takeoff 760kg (1675lb).

Dimensions: 150 – Wing span 10.17m (33ft 4in), length 6.56m (21ft 6in), height 2.11m (6ft 11in). Wing area 14.8m^2 (159.5sq ft). Commuter II – Wing span 10.11m (33ft 2in), length 7.29m (23ft 11in), height 2.59m (8ft 6in). Wing area 14.6m^2 (157sq ft). A152 – Wing span 10.17m (33ft 4in), length 7.25m (24ft 1in), height 2.59m (8ft 6in). Wing area 14.8m^2 (159.5sq ft).

Capacity: Typical seating for two side by side.

Production: Total 150 and 152 production amounts to 31,289 aircraft over 27 years, comprising 7449 US built 152s, 589 French built 152s, 22,082 US built 150s and 1758 French built 150s.

History: The introduction of the Cessna 150 marked Cessna's return to the two seat trainer market after a six year absence and resulted in the most prolific and successful two seat trainer line in history.

Development of the original 150 began in the mid 1950s, resulting in a first flight in September 1957. This modern, all new aircraft followed the Cessna conventions then gaining favour of a strut braced high wing, all metal construction and tricycle undercarriage. Production began in September 1958.

What followed was a continuous process of product improvement, although throughout the 150 model life the Continental O-200-A powerplant remained unchanged. One of the significant model changes included the 150D of 1964 which introduced the wraparound rear window. Most versions were built in Standard, Commuter and Trainer forms with differing equipment levels, while licence production in France was undertaken by Reims. Aerobat versions were stressed for limited aerobatic work.

The 152 was a response to availability problems with 80/87 octane fuel, and used the 150 fuselage coupled with a Lycoming O-235 running on 100 Octane. The 152 replaced the 150 from 1977 and remained in production until late 1985. It too was progressively updated and also built in France.

Photo: The world's most successful light trainer, the 150/152 will no doubt remain in service in large numbers well into the 21st century. (Gerard Frawley)

Cessna 170

Country of origin: United States of America

Type: Four seat light aircraft

Powerplant: 170 – One 110kW (145hp) Continental C145-2 flat six piston engine driving a two blade fixed pitch McCauley propeller. 170B – One 110kW (145hp) Continental O-300-A.

Performance: 170 – Max speed 225km/h (122kt), max cruising speed 195km/h (106kt). Initial rate of climb 690ft/min. Service ceiling 15,000ft. Range 952km (514nm) 170B – Max speed 230km/h (124kt), max cruising speed 195km/h (106kt). Initial rate of climb 690ft/min. Service ceiling 15,500ft. Range 950km (513nm).

Weights: Empty 554kg (1220lb), max takeoff 998kg (2200lb). 170B – Empty 547kg (1205lb). 170B – Empty 547kg (1205lb), max takeoff 998kg (2200lb).

Dimensions: Wing span 10.97m (36ft 0in), length 7.61m (24ft 11.5in), height 2.01m (6ft 7in). Wing area 16.2m^2 (174sq ft).

Capacity: Typical seating for four.

Production: In production between 1948 and 1957, a total of 5173 Cessna 170s were built, including 730 170s and 1537 170As.

History: A larger four seat development of the earlier Cessna Model 120 and 140, the four seat 170 was in production for almost a decade, and is the predecessor to the successful and long running 172 series.

The prototype Cessna 170 (NX41691) flew for the first time in September 1947. Notable features included the six cylinder 110kW (145hp) Continental C145 engine, extensive metal construction and the characteristic Cessna braced high wing. The first production Cessna 170s were delivered from March 1948, but this model was soon replaced by the improved 170A. The primary improvement with the 170A was metal instead of fabric covered wings, but it also featured increased tail area.

The third and final major variant appeared in 1953. The Cessna 170B featured the most significant revisions to the line, including the large wing flaps (first developed for the military L-19 Bird Dog) that were to become characteristic of later single engine Cessna models, revised tail wheel steering, larger rear windows and revised and lengthened engine cowling.

The 170 remained in production until 1957, however, by this time its popularity had waned somewhat as the essentially similar, but tricycle undercarriage, 172 had become an instant sales success for Cessna and had bitten into 170 sales.

It is interesting to note that the 170 laid the foundation stone for two of Cessna's most successful single engine lines, the 172 and 182, as well as the 180 and 185. The 172 originally started life as a tricycle undercarriage version of the 170. The 180 meanwhile began as a more powerful, higher performance version of the 170, while the 182 was originally a tricycle undercarriage development of the 180.

Photo: Many 170s are today being refurbished as valuable collectors items. Pictured is a 170A. (Bill Lines)

Cessna 172 Skyhawk (early models)

Country of origin: United States of America

Type: Four seat light aircraft

Powerplants: 172 – One 110kW (145hp) Continental O-300-A flat six piston engine driving a two blade fixed pitch McCauley propeller. 175A – One 120kW (175hp) Continental GO-300-C geared flat six. 172F – One 110kW (145hp) Continental O-300-C.

Performance: 172 – Max speed 217km/h (117kt), cruising speed 200km/h (108kt). Initial rate of climb 660ft/min. Service ceiling 15,100ft. Range with no reserves 1000km (539nm). 175A – Max speed 236km/h (128kt), max cruising speed 225km/h (121kt), long range cruising speed 170km/h (91kt). Initial rate of climb 850ft/min. Service ceiling 15,900ft Range with no reserves 957km (517nm). 172F – Max speed 222km/h (120kt), max cruising speed 211km/h (114kt), long range cruising speed 164km/h (88kt). Initial rate of climb 645ft/min. Service ceiling 13,100ft. Max range with no reserves 1158km (625nm).

Weights: 172 – Empty 572kg (1260lb), max takeoff 998kg (2200lb). 175A – Empty 607kg (1339lb), max takeoff 1066kg (2350lb). 172F – Empty 599kg (1320lb), max takeoff 1043kg (2300lb).

Dimensions: 172 – Wing span 10.92m (35ft 10in), length 8.20m (26ft 11in), height 2.59m (8ft 6in). Wing area 16.2m^2 (175sq ft). 175A – Wing span 10.97m (36ft 0in), length 8.08m (26ft 6in), height 2.72m (8ft 11in). 172F – Wing span 11.02m (36ft 2in), length 8.07m (26ft 6in), height 2.72m (8ft 11in).

Capacity: Typical seating for four in all models.

Production: Total Cessna 172 family production over 42,000, of which the civil Continental powered models account for about 15,800. Production ran from 1955 to 1967. Approximately 2190 Skylarks built.

History: The Cessna 172 is without doubt the most successful mass produced light aircraft in history. From 1955 through to 1967 the Skyhawk was powered by the six cylinder Continental O-300, before this engine was replaced by the four cylinder Lycoming O-320.

The Cessna 172 started life as a relatively simple tricycle undercarriage development of the taildragger 170, with a fairly basic level of equipment. First flight was in November 1955. The 172 became an overnight sales success and over 1400 were built in its first full year of production (1956).

The basic 172 remained in production until replaced by the 172A of early 1960. The 172A introduced a swept back tail and rudder, while the 172B of late 1960 introduced a shorter undercarriage, equipment changes and for the first time the Skyhawk name.

The 172D of 1963 introduced the cut down rear fuselage with wraparound rear window. The 172F introduced electric flaps (and was built in France by Reims Cessna as the F172 through to 1971). The 172G of 1966 introduced a more pointed spinner, while the 172H was the last Continental powered 172.

The 175 Skylark meanwhile was powered by a 130kW (175hp) geared GO-300, the GO-300 powered P172D Powermatic of 1963 had a constant speed prop. The 1966 R172E had a Continental IO-360 and a constant speed prop. It was built in France as the FR172.

Photo: The basic 172 model was in production from 1955 to 1960. (Bill Lines)

Cessna 172 Skyhawk (later models)

Country of origin: United States of America

Type: Four seat light aircraft

Powerplants: 172N – One 120kW (160hp) Lycoming O-320-H2AD flat four piston engine driving a two blade fixed pitch propeller. R172 Hawk XP – One 145kW (195hp) Continental IO-360-KB fuel injected flat six driving a two blade constant speed propeller.

Performance: 172N – Max speed 232km/h (125kt), max cruising speed 226m/h (122kt). Initial rate of climb 770ft/min. Service ceiling 14,200ft. Max range with 45min reserves and standard fuel 1065km (575nm), with optional fuel 1390km (750nm). R175A – Max speed 246km/h (133kt), max cruising speed 241km/h (130kt), long range cruising speed 177km/h (95kt). Initial rate of climb 870ft/min. Service ceiling 17,000ft. Max range with 45min reserves and standard fuel 1065km (575nm), with optional fuel 1510km (815nm).

Weights: 172N – Empty 649kg (1430lb), max takeoff 1043kg (2300lb). R172 – Empty 710kg (1565lb), max takeoff 1157kg (2550lb).

Dimensions: 172N – Wing span 10.92m (35ft 10in), length 8.21m (26ft 11in), height 2.68 (8ft 10in). Wing area 16.3m^2 (175sq ft). R172 – Wing span 10.92m (35ft 10in), length 8.28m (27ft 2in), height 2.68m (8ft 10in).

Capacity: Typical seating for four in all models.

Production: Total Cessna 172 family production over 42,000, of which about 22,000 were basic Lycoming powered 172s built 1968/1985.

History: In the late 1960s Cessna re-engined its already highly successful 172 four seater with the four cylinder Lycoming O-320. These models were the most successful to bear the Skyhawk name, as they were in production during GA's golden years, the 1970s.

Cessna re-engined the 172 with the Lycoming O-320-E as compared with the O-300 it had two less cylinders (and thus lower overhaul costs), a 200 hour greater TBO, improved fuel efficiency and more power. Even so, Cessna thought 172 production would be shortlived as the similarly powered but more modern 177 Cardinal was released at the same time. In spite of the Cardinal the Lycoming powered 172 was a runaway success and easily outsold its intended replacement.

The first O-320 Skyhawk was the 172I introduced in 1968. The 1969 172K introduced a redesigned fin, reshaped rear windows and optional increased fuel capacity, while 1970's 172K sported conical camber wingtips and a wider track undercarriage. The 172L in production in the 1971/72 model years was the first to feature the enlarged dorsal fin fillet.

The 172M of 1973/76 gained a drooped wing leading edge for improved low speed handling. The 172M was also the first to introduce the optional 'II' package of higher standard equipment. Also in 1976 Cessna stopped marketing the aircraft as the 172.

The 172N was powered by a 120kW (160hp) O-320-H designed to run on 100 octane fuel, but the engine proved troublesome and was replaced by the similarly rated O-320-D in the 172P of 1981. The P was the last basic 172 model, remaining in production until 1985.

Higher performance 172s include the R172 Hawk XP, powered by a 145kW (195hp) Continental IO-360 and the 135kW (180hp) Lycoming O-360 powered, retractable undercarriage 172RG Cutlass.

Photo: A Cessna 172N, the last major Skyhawk model. (Keith Myers)

Cessna 172R Skyhawk

Country of origin: United States of America

Type: Four seat light aircraft

Powerplants: 172R – One 120kW (160hp) Textron Lycoming IO-320-L2A fuel injected flat four piston engine driving a two blade fixed pitch McCauley propeller.

Performance: 172R – Max cruising speed at sea level 228km/h (123kt), cruising speed at 75% power at 8000ft 222km/h (120kt). Initial rate of climb from sea level 750ft/min. Service ceiling 13,500ft. Range 1260km (680nm).

Weights: 172R – Empty 730kg (1608lb), max ramp 1115kg (2457lb).

Dimensions: 172R – Wing span 10.98m (36ft 0in), length 8.21m (26ft 11in), height 2.72m (8ft 11in).

Capacity: Typical seating for four.

Production: Total Cessna 172 family production over 42,000. Cessna 172R production restarted in 1996, with first deliveries in early 1997. Cessna plans to build 600 new Skyhawks in 1997 and over 1000 in 1998.

History: The Cessna 172R Skyhawk is possibly the most important light aircraft to enter production in the 1990s as it is the modern day development of the most popular GA aircraft in history.

Recession and crippling product liability laws in the USA (where US aircraft manufacturers were regularly being sued if one of their aircraft crashed) forced Cessna to stop production of light aircraft, including the 172, altogether in 1985. It was not until the signing of the General Aviation Revitalisation Act by the US President in August 1994 that Cessna announced it would resume light aircraft production.

Earlier in the previous year Cessna had established a Single Engine Restart Taskforce to investigate the possibility of returning some of its piston single designs to production. With the passing of the act Cessna announced it would initially begin building the 172 Skyhawk, 182 Skylane and T206 Turbo Stationair.

The new 172 Skyhawk model is designated the 172R. Based on the 172N (the last major Skyhawk production model), the 172R's major change is a fuel injected Textron Lycoming IO-320-L2A engine. Cessna says this engine is significantly quieter than earlier O-320s as it produces its max horsepower at only 2400rpm.

Other changes include a new interior with contoured front seats which adjust vertically and recline, an all new multi level ventilation system, standard four point intercom, interior soundproofing, and energy absorbing 26g seats with inertia reel harnesses.

The C172R features as standard epoxy corrosion proofing and stainless steel control cables, a dual vacuum pump system, tinted windows, long range fuel tanks, backlit instruments with non glare glass and an annunciator panel. The basic flyaway price in 1996 was $US124,500.

172R options include two avionics packages (one with GPS, the other with IFR GPS and a single axis autopilot) and wheel fairings.

An engineering prototype 172R (a converted 1978 172N) powered by an IO-360 first flew in April 1995, while the first new build pilot production 172R first flew on April 16 1996. This aircraft was built at Wichita, while new production 172Rs are being built at an all new factory in Independence, Kansas.

Photo: A Cessna 172R (Cessna)

Cessna 177 Cardinal

Country of origin: United States of America

Type: Four seat light aircraft

Powerplant: 177 – One 110kW (150hp) Lycoming O-320-E2D flat four piston engine driving a two blade fixed pitch McCauley propeller. 177B – One 135kW (180hp) Lycoming O-360-A1F6D driving a two blade constant speed McCauley prop. 177RG – One 150kW (200hp) Lycoming IO-360-A1B6 fuel injected flat four.

Performance: 177 – Max speed 227km/h (123kt), cruising speed 210km/h (113kt). Initial rate of climb 670ft/min. Service ceiling 12,700ft. Range 1215km (655nm). 177B – Max speed 250km/h (136kt), cruising speed 230km/h (124kt). Initial rate of climb 840ft/min. Service ceiling 14,600ft. Range 1120km (604nm). 177RG – Max speed 290km/h (156kt), long range cruising speed 223km/h (120kt). Initial rate of climb 925ft/min. Service ceiling 17,100ft. Max range with reserves 1657km (895nm).

Weights: 177 – Empty 608kg (1340lb), max takeoff 1067kg (2350lb). 177B – Empty 680kg (1495lb), max takeoff 1135kg (2500lb). 177RG – Empty 800kg (1671lb), max takeoff 1270kg (2800lb).

Dimensions: 177 – Wing span 10.85m (35ft 7.5in), length 8.22m (26ft 11.5in), height 2.77m (9ft 1in). Wing area 16.2m² (174sq ft). 177B – Wing span 10.82m (35ft 6in), length 8.44m (27ft 8in), height 2.62m (8ft 7in). Wing area 16.2m² (174sq ft). 177RG – Same except for length 8.31m (27ft 3in).

Capacity: Typical seating for four.

Production: Total 177 Cardinal production of 4240 between 1968 and 1978.

History: The all new Cessna 177 Cardinal was developed in the mid 1960s as a replacement for the ubiquitous 172 family.

Announced in late 1967, this new aircraft featured a wide and fairly spacious cabin, a rear set flush riveted high wing which offered good visibility in turns, a single piece all moving tailplane, a high standard of equipment level and the 110kW (150hp) O-320-E recently installed on the 172 driving a fixed pitch prop. Offered in two versions, the standard 177 and up-spec Cardinal, it entered the marketplace costing around 10% more than the then current 172 model.

While not a failure, the 177 failed to attract anywhere near the sales volume of the 172. A shortcoming of the initial model was a perceived lack of power, this was addressed with the 135kW (180hp) O-360-A powered 177A in 1969.

The 177B appeared in 1970 and featured a revised aerofoil, conical camber wingtips, cowl flaps and a constant speed propeller. An up market version known as the Cardinal Classic appeared in 1978 with full IFR instrumentation and luxury fittings.

The 177RG also appeared in 1970, and, as its designation suggests, featured retractable undercarriage and a 150kW (200hp) fuel injected IO-360-A engine and a constant speed prop.

Both the 177B and 177RG remained in production until 1978.

Photo: While it deserved to sell better than it did, the sleek Cardinal never really became the marketing success that Cessna had hoped for. Pictured is a 177B.

Cessna 180 & 185

Country of origin: United States of America

Type: Four to six seat utility light aircraft

Powerplant: 180 – One 170kW (225hp) Continental 0-470-A flat six piston engine driving a two blade constant speed McCauley prop. 180G – One 170kW (230hp) 0-470-R. A185F – One 225kW (300hp) fuel injected IO-520-D driving a three blade constant speed prop.

Performance: 180 – Max speed 267km/h (144kt), cruising speed 260km/h (140kt). Initial rate of climb 1150ft/min. Service ceiling 20,000ft. Range 1247km (673nm). 180G – Max speed 273km/h (147kt), max cruising speed 260km/h (141kt), long range cruising speed 195km/h (105kt). Initial rate of climb 1090ft/min. Service ceiling 19,600ft. Range with no reserves 1490km (804nm). A185F – Max speed 283km/h (153kt), max cruising speed 272km/h (147kt), long range cruising speed 207km/h (111kt). Initial rate of climb 1075ft/min. Service ceiling 17,900ft. Range with reserves 1575km (850nm).

Weights: 180 – Empty 690kg (1520lb), max takeoff 1158kg (2550lb). 180G – Empty 692kg (1525lb), max takeoff 1270kg (2800lb). A185F – Empty 783kg (1727lb), max takeoff 1520kg (3350lb).

Dimensions: 180 – Wing span 10.98m (36ft 0in), length 7.98m (26ft 2in), height 2.29m (7ft 6in). Wing area 16.2m^2 (174sq ft). 180G – Wing span 11.02m (36ft 2in), length 7.77m (25ft 6in), height 2.29m (7ft 6in). Wing area 16.2m^2 (174sq ft). A185F – Wing span 10.92m (35ft 10in), length 7.81m (25ft 8in). Wing area 16.2m^2.

Capacity: 180 has standard seating for four, 180 Skywagon and 185 have seating for six. 180H has optional 1360kg (3000lb) cargo pod. Often used with rear seats removed for cargo work. 185 Ag Carryall is fitted with a 571 litre (126Imp gal/151US gal) chemical hopper.

Production: Total 180 production amounted to 6210. Total 185 production 4339 aircraft including 265 U-17A and 215 U-17B military variants and 109 Ag Carryalls.

History: The 180 started life as a more powerful development of the 170, and evolved into a family of useful utility aircraft that were in production for over three decades.

The first 180s were essentially Model 170s with a more powerful 170kW (225hp) 0-470-A engine. The first of the type flew in 1952 and deliveries began in February the following year. The 180's career as a high performance single was short lived due to the arrival of the tricycle 180 based 182 in 1956, but by then the type had established itself a useful niche as a utility aircraft.

Progressive updating of the line led to a range of updated models including the 170kW (230hp) 180A, and 180G with a third cabin window, and from 1966 it was offered as a six seater, by then having the same fuselage as the more powerful 185. The Skywagon name was applied to the 180 in 1969. The 180 remained in production until 1981.

The first 185 Skywagon flew in July 1960. It differed from the 180 in having a more powerful engine (195kW/260hp) and larger cabin, allowing six seats. Updated models include the 225kW (300hp) A185E from 1967 and the Ag Carryall capable of chemical spraying.

Photo: A most useful light aircraft, the 180/185 series was also one of Cessna's best sellers. Pictured is an A185E. (Bill Lines)

Cessna 182 Skylane

Country of origin: United States of America

Type: High performance four seat light aircraft

Powerplants: 182 – One 170kW (230hp) Continental 0-470-R flat six piston engine, driving a two blade constant speed McCauley propeller. TR182 – One 175kW (235hp) Lycoming 0-540-L3C5D turbocharged flat six. 182S – One 170kW (230hp) Textron Lycoming IO-540-AB1A5.

Performance: 182 – Max speed 257km/h (140kt), cruising speed 253km/h (136kt). Initial rate of climb 1200ft/min. Service ceiling 20,000ft. Range 1078km (582nm). TR182 – Max speed 346km/h (187kt), economical cruising speed 232km/h (125kt). Initial rate of climb 1040ft/min. Service ceiling 20,000ft. Range 1870km (1010nm). 182S – Max cruising speed 270km/h (146kt), cruising speed at 75% power 260km/h (140kt). Initial rate of climb 865ft/min. Service ceiling 14,900ft. Range 1530km (825nm).

Weights: 182 – Empty 735kg (1621lb), max takeoff 1160kg (2550lb). TR182 – Empty 837kg (1845lb), max takeoff 1406kg (3100lb). 182S – Empty 794kg (1747lb), max takeoff 1411kg (3105lb).

Dimensions: 182 – Wing span 10.98m (36ft 0in), length 25.17m (25ft 2in), height 2.80m (9ft 2in). Wing area 16.2m^2 (174sq ft). TR182 – Wing span 10.92m (35ft 10in), length 8.53m (28ft 0in), height 2.82m (9ft 3in). Wing area 16.2m^2 (174sq ft). 182S – Wing span 10.98m (36ft 0in), length 8.54m (28ft 0in), height 2.82m (9ft 3in).

Capacity: Typical seating for four. Some models had optional jump seat for an extra two children.

Production: Total 182 production reached 21,864, including 169 R182s built in France by Reims. Production restarting at 300 per year.

History: Yet another successful single engined Cessna, the 182 began life as a tricycle development of the 180 (which itself is a more powerful development of the 170).

The first Model 182 appeared in 1956 and was essentially the Model 180 with a tricycle undercarriage. The Skylane name was first introduced with the 182A development, denoting a higher level of equipment. Major changes were introduced with the 182C, including a third window on each side of the cabin and a swept vertical tail. Other improvements introduced over the 182's lifespan included shorter undercarriage, reprofiled cowling, wrap around rear cabin window, progressively higher takeoff weights and improved wing root, fintip, and rudder fairings.

The retractable undercarriage Skylane RG arrived in 1977, giving a significant speed increase. A further performance boost came with the introduction of the turbocharged 175kW (235hp) Lycoming 0-540-L engine on the T182RG, which became available from 1979. The AiResearch turbocharger meant that maximum power could be delivered right up to the 182's service ceiling of 20,000ft. A turbocharged fixed gear model was also offered for a time, but only a small number were built.

Cessna 182 production initially ceased in 1985.

In 1994 Cessna announced plans to return the 182 to production, following the success of product liability law reforms in the USA. The new 182S prototype first flew in July 1996. Improvements include a IO-540-AB1A5 engine, new interior and avionics panel.

Photo: Cessna aims to build 300 new 182S Skylanes during 1997.

Cessna 188 Ag Wagon series

Country of origin: United States of America

Type: Agricultural aircraft

Powerplant: Ag Truck – One 225kW (300hp) Continental IO-520-D fuel injected flat six piston engine, driving a two blade fixed pitch McCauley propeller or three blade constant speed prop. Ag Husky – One 230kW (310hp) Continental TSIO-520-T turbocharged and fuel injected flat six, driving a three blade constant speed McCauley prop.

Performance: Ag Truck – Max speed 196km/h (106kt), max cruising speed 187km/h (101kt). Initial rate of climb 465ft/min. Service ceiling 7800ft/min. Range with max fuel and reserves at 75% power 465km (252nm). Ag Husky – Max speed 209km/h (113kt), max cruising speed (75% power) 196km/h (106kt). Initial rate of climb 510ft/min. Certificated service ceiling 14,000ft. Range with max fuel and reserves at max cruising speed 402km (217nm).

Weights: Ag Truck – Empty 1015kg (2235lb), max takeoff 1495kg (3300lb), max takeoff restricted ag category 1905kg (4200lb). Ag Husky – Empty 1045kg (2305lb), max takeoff restricted ag category 1995kg (4400lb).

Dimensions: Ag Truck – Wing span 12.70m (41ft 8in), length 7.90m (25ft 11in), height 2.49m (8ft 2in). Wing area 19.1m^2 (205sq ft). Ag Husky – Same except for length 8.08m (26ft 6in).

Capacity: Pilot only in all models. Standard hopper capacity of 757 litres (166Imp gal/200US gal) for Ag Wagon & Ag Pickup; Ag Truck & Ag Husky have a 1059 litres (233Imp gal/280US gal).

Production: Approximate total of 3975 including 53 Ag Pickups, 1589 Ag Wagons, 1949 Ag Trucks and 385 Ag Huskies.

History: The successful Ag Wagon 188 series of agricultural aircraft were Cessna's only purpose designed ag-planes.

Cessna's Model 188 resulted from extensive research and consultation with agricultural aircraft operators conducted in the early 1960s. The design Cessna settled upon was of the conventional agricultural aircraft arrangement with a braced low wing (making it the only Cessna single to be so configured) with seating for the pilot only. Like other ag aircraft the chemical hopper is of fibreglass and the rear fuselage is of semi monocoque construction and sealed to reduce the potential for damage from chemical contamination.

The prototype Cessna 188 Ag Wagon flew for the first time on February 19 1965, and type approval was awarded the following February. The 188 was initially offered in two forms, the 170kW (230hp) Continental 0-470-R powered 188 (which was named the Ag Pickup from 1972) and the 250kW (300hp) Continental IO-520-D powered 188A Ag Wagon.

The 1972 model year also saw the introduction of the most successful 188 model, the Ag Truck. The Ag Truck has the same powerplant as the Ag Wagon, but a larger hopper and a higher max takeoff weight. The ultimate 188 model is the Ag Husky, which was introduced in 1979. It features a turbocharged TSIO-520-T and a further increased max takeoff weight.

Production of the Ag Pickup was suspended in 1976, the Ag Wagon in 1981 and the Ag Truck and Ag Husky in 1985, when all Cessna light aircraft production ceased.

Photo: An A188B Ag Truck at rest, note heavy wing strut and large single place cockpit. (Bill Lines)

Cessna 205, 206 & 207

Country of origin: United States of America

Type: Six seat utility light aircraft

Powerplant: 205 – One 195kW (260hp) Continental IO-470-S fuel injected flat six piston engine, driving a two blade constant speed McCauley prop. TU206F – One 210kW (285hp) Continental TSIO-520-C turbocharged and fuel injected flat six driving a two or three blade c/s prop. 207A – One 225kW (300hp) Continental IO-520-F fuel injected flat six driving a three blade c/s McCauley prop.

Performance: Max speed 278km/h (150kt), max cruising speed 262km/h (140kt), long range cruising speed 183km/h (99kt). Initial rate of climb 965ft/min. Service ceiling 16,100ft. Range with no reserves 2050km (1110nm). TU206F – Max speed 321km/h (174kt), max cruising speed 296km/h (160kt), long range cruising speed 274km/h (148kt). Initial rate of climb 1030ft/min. Service ceiling 26,300ft. Range at long range cruising speed 1327km (717nm). 207A – Max speed 278km/h (150kt), max cruising speed 266km/h (144kt), long range cruising speed 220km/h (118kt). Initial rate of climb 810ft/min. Service ceiling 13,300ft. Range with standard fuel and reserves 870km (470nm), with optional fuel and reserves 1280km (690nm).

Weights: 205 – Empty 795kg (1750lb), max takeoff 1497kg (3300lb). TU206F – Empty 880kg (1940lb), max takeoff 1634kg (3600lb). 207A – Empty 951kg (2095lb), max takeoff 1730kg (3812lb).

Dimensions: 205 – Wing span 11.15m (36ft 7in), length 8.46m (27ft 9in), height 2.75m (9ft 0in). Wing area 16.3m^2 (175.5sq ft). TU206F – Wing span 10.92m (35ft 10in), length 8.54m (28ft 0in), height 2.95m (9ft 8in). Wing area 16.2m^2 (174sq ft). 207A – Same as 206 except for length 9.80m (32ft 2in).

Capacity: 205 & 206 have seating for six, 207 seating for seven or eight.

Production: 574 205s, 7556 206s and 790 207s were built.

History: In concept the 205/206/207 line began life as a six seat utility flying station wagon.

In its initial form the 205 was very much a fixed undercarriage derivative of the 210B Centurion, optimised for utility roles. Introduced to the Cessna lineup in 1962, the 206 was powered by the same IO-470 engine as the 210B and featured an additional small cargo door on the left side of the fuselage to allow access to the rear seats for their removal and the baggage compartment.

The 205 lasted in production until 1964 when it was replaced by the more powerful 206, which featured larger double cargo doors on the right fuselage side and was known as the Super Skywagon. Continuous product improvement followed, including adding a turbocharged and fuel injected model, while the prefix 'Super' was dropped in 1969, and the Stationair name was adopted in 1971. Production originally ceased in 1985.

The 207 Skywagon meanwhile featured a 1.07m (3ft 6in) fuselage stretch (allowing seating for seven) and became available from 1969. Known as the Stationair 7 from 1978, it was replaced by the 207A Stationair 8 from 1979 which had seating for an eighth occupant. Production ended in 1984.

Cessna is re-introducing the Turbo 206 Stationair to production during mid 1997 and aims to build 400 during 1998.

Photo: The new Cessna T206 on its first flight on August 28 1996.

Cessna 208 Caravan & Grand Caravan

Country or origin: United States of America

Type: Single turboprop utility transport

Powerplant: 208 & 208B – One 450kW (600shp) Pratt & Whitney Canada PT6A-114 turboprop driving a three blade variable pitch Hartzell propeller. Grand Caravan – One 505kW (675shp) PT6A-114A.

Performance: 208A – Max cruising speed 340km/h (184kt). Initial rate of climb 1215ft/min. Range with max fuel and reserves 1797km (970nm), range with max fuel and reserves 2066km (1115nm). 208B – Max cruising speed 317km/h (171kt). Max initial rate of climb 770ft/min. Range with max fuel and reserves 2000km (1080nm). Grand Caravan – Max cruising speed 337km/h (182kt). Max initial rate of climb 975ft/min. Range with max fuel and reserves 1667km (900nm).

Weights: 208A – Empty 1725kg (3800lb), max takeoff 3310kg (7300lb). 208B – Empty 2073kg (4570lb), max takeoff 3970kg (8750lb). Grand Caravan – Empty equipped 2250kg (4965lb), max takeoff 3970kg (8750lb).

Dimensions: 208A – Wing span 15.88m (52ft 1in), length 11.46m (37ft 7in), height 4.32m (14ft 2in). Wing area 26.0m^2 (279.4sq ft). 208B – Same except for length 12.67m (41ft 7in).

Capacity: 208A – Pilot and typically nine passengers, or up to 14 with an FAA FAR Part 23 waiver. Cargo capacity 1360kg (3000lb) of freight. 208B – Passenger accommodation same. Cargo capacity for 1587kg (3500lb). Grand Caravan – One pilot and up to 14 passengers.

Production: Production continues and at the time of writing more than 750 had been delivered.

History: With sales exceeding the 750 mark (including more than 300 for Federal Express alone) the useful Caravan has become a popular utility workhorse worldwide.

Design work for the Caravan dates back to the early eighties. First flight of a prototype occurred on December 9 1982 and certification was granted on October 1984. When production began the following year it became the first all new single engine turboprop powered aircraft to achieve production status.

The Caravan has had a close association with US package freight specialist Federal Express (FedEx), on whose request Cessna especially developed two pure freight versions. The first of these was the Cargomaster based on the basic 208A, the second the stretched 208B. The first 208B flew in 1986, the type entering FedEx service as the Super Cargomaster. It features a 1.22m (4ft) stretch, greater payload capacity, including an under fuselage cargo pannier, and FedEx aircraft do not have fuselage windows.

A military/special missions version of the 208A and 208B, dubbed the U-27, is also on offer.

The Grand Caravan first flew in 1990 and is a further stretched version of the basic Caravan powered by a 505kW (675shp) PT6A-114. It can seat up to 14 passengers.

Underbelly cargo pods, floats and skis are offered as options on the Caravan family, and the type is easily converted from freight to passenger configurations.

Photo: A short fuselage Caravan I. (Cessna)

Cessna 210 Centurion

Country of origin: United States of America

Type: High performance four seat light aircraft

Powerplant: 210L – One 225kW (300hp) Continental IO-520-L fuel injected flat six piston engine driving a three blade constant speed McCauley prop. T210M – One 230kW (310hp) fuel injected and turbocharged TSIO-520R, driving a constant speed three blade prop. P210R – One 240kW (325hp) turbocharged and fuel injected TSIO-520-CE.

Performance: 210L – Max speed 324km/h (175kt), max cruising speed 317km/h (171kt), long range cruising speed 249km/h (134kt). Initial rate of climb 950ft/min. Service ceiling 17,300ft. Max range with reserves 1972km (1065nm). T210M – Max speed 380km/h (205kt), max cruising speed 367km/h (198kt), long range cruising speed 260km/h (140kt). Initial rate of climb 1030ft/min. Service ceiling 28,500ft. Range at long range cruising speed 1455km (785nm). P210R – Max speed 417km/h (225kt) at 20,000ft, max cruising speed 394km/h (213kt) at 23,000ft. Initial rate of climb 1150ft/min. Service ceiling 25,000ft. Range with reserves and optional fuel 2205km (1190nm).

Weights: 210L – Empty 1015kg (2238lb), max takeoff 1724kg (3800lb). T210M – Empty 1022kg (2250lb), max takeoff 1725kg (3800lb). P210R – Empty 1120kg (2470lb), max takeoff 1860kg (4100lb).

Dimensions: 210 – Wing span 11.15m (36ft 9in), length 8.59m (28ft 2in). Wing area 16.3m^2 (175.5sq ft). T210M – Wing span 11.21m (36ft 9in), length 8.59m (28ft 2in), height 2.87m (9ft 5in). Wing area same. P210R – Wing span 11.84m (38ft 10in), length 8.59m (28ft 2in), height 2.95m (9ft 8in). Wing area 17.2m (185.5sq ft).

Capacity: Typical seating for four with optional seating for extra two children in some models, or seating for six adults in later versions.

Production: Total 210, T210 and P210 production reached 9240.

History: During its production life the Cessna 210 was at the top of the Cessna single piston engine model lineup, slotting between the 182 and the 310 twin.

First flight of the 210 occurred in January 1957. This new aircraft featured retractable undercarriage and swept back vertical tail surfaces for the first time on a Cessna aircraft. The 210 entered production in late 1959, and from that time the line was constantly updated. Notable early upgrades include the 210B which introduced the wraparound rear windows, the 210D with a more powerful (210kW/285hp) engine and introduced the Centurion name, and the turbocharged T210F. The 210G introduced a new strutless cantilever wing, increased fuel capacity, restyled rear windows and enlarged tail surfaces. Continual development of the 210 and T210 range continued through until production ceased in 1985.

A significant development of the T210 was the high performance, pressurised P210 which first appeared in 1978. The pressurisation system meant that the cabin's internal altitude was equivalent to 8000ft, while the aircraft was actually at 17,350ft.

Photo: The Centurion quickly became the flagship of Cessna's single engine line. Pictured is a 210L Centurion II. (Bill Lines)

Cessna T303 Crusader

Country of origin: United States of America

Type: Six seat corporate and utility transport

Powerplants: Two 185kW (250hp) Continental TSIO-520-AE turbocharged and fuel injected flat six piston engines driving three blade constant speed counter rotating McCauley propellers.

Performance: Max speed 400km/h (216kt) at 18,000ft, max cruising speed 363km/h (196kt), economical cruising speed 333km/h (180kt). Initial rate of climb 1480ft/min. Service ceiling 25,000ft. Range with max fuel and reserves at 71% power at 20,000ft 1658km (895nm), at economical cruising speed and 10,000ft 1890km (1020nm).

Weights: Empty 1526kg (3364lb), max takeoff 2336kg (5150lb).

Dimensions: Wing span 11.90m (39ft 0.5in), length 9.27m (30ft 5in), height 4.06m (13ft 4in). Wing area 17.6m^2 (189.2sq ft).

Capacity: Normal seating for pilot and five passengers with central aisle between seats. Can be configured with a club seating arrangement for four in the main cabin, or for aerial ambulance or freighter work.

Production: In production between 1981 and 1985, 297 Crusaders were sold.

History: Cessna's original Model 303 started life as a four seat twin, intended for the hotly contested light transport and training role.

One four seat 303 was flown for a time from February 14 1978. Powered by two 120kW (160hp) Lycoming O-320 engines it would have competed against the Beech Duchess, Grumman GA-7 (Cougar) and Piper Seminole. However, a reappraisal of market demand for aircraft in this already crowded class led to Cessna rethinking the 303 design, and resulted in a larger aircraft. Instead the resulting six seater aircraft was intended to replace Cessna's 310, then nearing the end of its production life.

The new model, designated the T303 for its turbocharged (and fuel injected) Continental TSIO-520 engines, flew for the first time on October 17 1979. Certification was granted in August 1981, and first production deliveries commenced in October 1981. For a time the T303 was named the Clipper, but this was changed to Crusader as PanAm held rights to the Clipper name.

In its definitive form the T303 incorporated a number of advanced features, being the first entirely new piston twin from Cessna in over a decade. Features included bonded structures around the integral fuel tank, a supercritical wing section and counter rotating propellers, while integral airstairs and a full IFR avionics suite was fitted as standard equipment (Cessna claimed the latter as a first for its class).

Production of the Crusader wound up in 1985 as part of the general decline in light aircraft sales during that period, terminating prematurely what looked to be a successful program. The cancellation also put paid to rumours that Cessna planned to develop a pressurised version of the aircraft.

Photo: Although a good design, the Crusader was ultimately beaten by a declining market and the decimation of the US GA market by that country's product liability laws. (Bill Lines)

Cessna 310 & 320

Country of origin: United States of America

Type: Four to six seat light piston twin

Powerplants: 310B – Two 180kW (240hp) Continental O-470-M flat six piston engines, driving two blade constant speed McCauley propellers. 320D – Two 195kW (260hp) turbocharged and fuel injected TSIO-470-Ds. 310R – Two 210kW (285hp) Continental IO-520-MB fuel injected piston engines.

Performance: 310B – Max speed 383km/h (207kt), cruising speed 291km/h (157kt). Initial rate of climb 1800ft/min. Service ceiling 19,800ft. Range with no reserves 1617km (873nm). 320D – Max speed 423km/h (228kt), max cruising speed 394km/h (213kt), long range cruising speed 288km/h (156kt). Initial rate of climb 1820ft/min. Service ceiling 28,100ft. Range with no reserves and standard fuel 1640km (886nm), with optional fuel 2134km (1152nm). 310R – Max speed 383km/h (207kt), max cruising speed 360km/h (195kt), long range cruising speed 267km/h (144kt). Initial rate of climb 1662ft/min. Service ceiling 19,750ft. Max range with reserves 1170km (632nm), with reserves and optional fuel 2840km (1535nm).

Weights: 310B – Empty equipped 1436kg (3166lb), max takeoff 2190kg (4830lb). 320D – Empty 1480kg (3260lb), max takeoff 2360kg (5200lb). 310R – Empty equipped 1480kg (3260lb), max takeoff 2495kg (5500lb).

Dimensions: 310B – Wing span 10.88m (35ft 8.5in), length 8.23m (27ft 0in), height 3.20m (10ft 6in). Wing area 16.3m^2 (175sq ft). 320D – Wing span 11.25m (36ft 11in), length 8.99m (29ft 6in), height 3.20m (10ft 6in). Wing area 16.3m^2 (175sq ft). 310R – Wing span 11.25m (36ft 11in), length 9.74m (31ft 11.5in), height 3.25m (10ft 8in). Wing area 16.6m^2 (179sq ft).

Capacity: Typical seating for four or five, with an optional sixth seat.

Production: Total 310 and 320 production was 6013 aircraft, of which 575 were 320s and 196 were for the US military.

History: The sleek Cessna 310 was the first twin engine design from Cessna to enter production since WW2.

The first 310 took to the skies for the first time on January 3 1953. The modern rakish lines of the new twin were backed up by such innovative features as engine exhaust thrust augmentor tubes and the storage of all fuel in tip tanks.

The first significant upgrade to the 310 line came with the 310C of 1959, which introduced more powerful 195kW (260hp) IO-470-D engines. The 310D of 1960 featured swept back vertical tail surfaces. An extra cabin window was added with the 310F. A development of the 310F was the turbocharged 320 Skyknight, with TSIO-470-B engines and a fourth cabin side window. The Skyknight was in production between 1961 and 1969 (the 320E was named the Executive Skyknight), when it was replaced by the similar Turbo 310.

The 310G introduced the 'stabila-tip' tip tanks, while the 310K replaced the rear two windows on each side with a single unit. Subsequent significant developments include the 310Q and turbocharged T310Q with redesigned rear cabin with a skylight window, and the final 310R and T310R, identifiable for their lengthened nose. Production ended in 1980.

Photo: A Cessna 310B. (Bill Lines)

Cessna 336 and 337

Country of origin: United States of America

Type: Four to six seat light piston twin

Powerplants: 336 – Two 145kW (195hp) Continental IO-360-A fuel injected flat six piston engines, driving two blade constant speed propellers. T337G – Two 170kW (225hp) turbocharged and fuel injected TSIO-360-Cs.

Performance: 336 – Max speed 294km/h (160kt), max cruising speed 278km/h (150kt), long range cruising speed 198km/h (107kt). Initial rate of climb 1340ft/min. Service ceiling 19,000ft. Range with no reserves and standard fuel 1520km (820nm), with optional fuel 2116km (1143nm). T337G – Max speed 402km/h (217kt), max cruising speed 380km/h (205kt), long range cruising speed 273km/h (147kt). Initial rate of climb 1250ft/min. Operational ceiling 20,000ft. Range with no reserves 2422km (1308nm) at 16,000ft.

Weights: 336 – Empty 1052kg (2320lb), max takeoff 1770kg (3900lb). T337G – Empty 1444kg (3184lb), max takeoff 2132kg (4700lb).

Dimensions: 336 – Wing span 11.58m (38ft 0in), length 9.02m (29ft 7in), height 2.90m (9ft 6in). Wing area 18.7m^2 (201sq ft). T337G – Wing span 11.63m (38ft 2in), length 9.07m (29ft 9in), height 2.84m (9ft 4in). Wing area 18.8m^2 (202.5sq ft).

Capacity: Typical seating for six. Optional underbelly cargo pod.

Production: 336 total production of 195 between 1962 and 1964. 337 production comprised 1859 337s, 332 pressurised 337s and 513 military versions. Reims built 67 standard and 27 pressurised 337s.

History: Through their push-pull engine configuration the Cessna 336 and 337 were designed to overcome the conventional twins' problems of poor engine out asymmetric flight handling characteristics .

Cessna called the layout concept Centre Line Thrust, as the nose mounted tractor and rear fuselage mounted pusher engine eliminated asymmetric handling problems normally experienced when one of a twin's engines fails. The concept was recognised by the US FAA which created a new centre thrust rating for pilots rated on the type. Another unusual feature of the Skymaster was the twin boom tail layout.

The Model 336 took to the skies for the first time on February 18 1961, but significant improvements to the design were made before production aircraft were delivered. Changes included more powerful engines, a larger fuselage, and revised wing, tail and rear engine cowling. The first production 336 was delivered in mid 1963 and production lasted until late 1964 when it was replaced by the improved and updated 337.

The improved 337 featured retractable undercarriage, more powerful 160kW (210hp) engines, a dorsal air intake for the rear engine, variable cowl flaps, repositioned forward engine and cowl for improved visibility and higher weights. It was known initially as the Super Skymaster, but Super was later dropped from the name. Subsequent development resulted in the turbocharged T337, while the ultimate 337 was the T337G Pressurised Skymaster. Development of the 337 continued in France by Reims after Cessna production ended in 1980, resulting in the FTB337 STOL and the military FTMA Milirole. Cessna also built more than 500 337s as O-2s for the US Air Force, used largely in the Forward Air Control role.

Photo: A 337F Super Skymaster. (Bill Lines)

Cessna 340 & 335

Country of origin: United States of America

Type: Six seat business twins

Powerplants: 340A – Two 230kW (310hp) Continental TSIO-520-NB turbocharged and fuel injected flat six piston engines, driving three blade constant speed McCauley propellers. 335 – Two 225kW (300hp) TSIO-520-EBs.

Performance: 340A – Max speed 452km/h (244kt), max cruising speed 425km/h (230kt), economical cruising speed 315km/h (170kt) at 25,000ft. Initial rate of climb 1650ft/min. Service ceiling 29,800ft. Range with reserves at economical cruising speed 2603km (1405nm), at max cruising speed 774km (418nm). 335 – Max speed 425km/h (230kt), max cruising speed 390km/h (211kt), economical cruising speed 313km/h (169kt). Initial rate of climb 1400ft/min. Service ceiling 26,800ft. Range at max cruising speed 2016km (1088nm), range at economical cruising speed 2542km (1372nm).

Weights: 340A – Empty 1778kg (3921lb), max takeoff 2717kg (5990lb). 335 – Empty equipped 1800kg (3963lb), max takeoff 2719kg (5990lb).

Dimensions: Wing span 11.62m (28ft 1in), length 10.46m (34ft 4in), height 3.84m (12ft 7in). Wing area 17.1m^2 (184sq ft).

Capacity: Typical seating for six, including one pilot.

Production: 1287 340s and 64 335s were built. The 340 was in production between 1971 and 1984, the 335 between 1979 and 1981.

History: When released, the Cessna 340 joined the Beechcraft Duke as the only other six seat pressurised piston twin from a major manufacturer, slotting into Cessna's product line between the 310 and the eight seat 414 and 421.

Development of the 340 began in 1969, but the loss of the prototype early in 1970 set back the development program so that production deliveries did not begin until early 1971. The resulting aircraft borrowed heavily from other Cessna twins of the time including the wings from the 414 and the 310's undercarriage and a similar tail unit. Design features of the new aircraft included a pressurisation system with a differential of 0.29bars (4.2psi) that kept the cabin's internal altitude at 8000ft while the aircraft was at 20,000ft, an all new fail safe fuselage and an integral airstair door.

Initial production 340s were powered by two 210kW (285hp) turbocharged Continental TSIO-520-K engines, but these were replaced on the improved 340A, which was first introduced in 1976. Power for the 340A was supplied by two 230kW (310hp) TSIO-520-NBs, while other improvements included reduced diameter props and a slight increase in weights. The 340A was offered in optional 340A II and 340A III forms with various levels of IFR avionics fitted.

The Cessna 335 is an unpressurised lighter weight and thus lower cost development of the 340. Available from 1979, aside from being unpressurised it differed in having 225kW (300hp) TSIO-520-EB engines. Although claimed by Cessna as the lowest priced cabin class business twin on the market, just 64 335s were built before production was terminated in 1980.

Production of the 340 continued until 1984.

Photo: A Cessna 340. (Lance Higgerson)

Cessna 404 Titan

Country of origin: United States of America

Type: Ten place corporate, commuter and freighter transport

Powerplants: Two 280kW (375hp) Continental GTSIO-520-M geared, turbocharged and fuel injected flat six piston engines, driving three blade constant speed McCauley propellers.

Performance: Max speed 430km/h (238kt), max cruising speed 402km/h (217kt) at 20,000ft, economical cruising speed 302km/h (163kt) at 20,000ft. Initial rate of climb 1940ft/min. Service ceiling 30,200ft. Range at economical cruising speed 2748km (1483nm), at max cruising speed 1633km (882nm).

Weights: Empty 2192kg (4834lb) for Ambassador, 2205kg (4861lb) for Courier, 2133kg (4702lb) for Freighter, max takeoff (all variants) 3810kg (8400lb).

Dimensions: Wing span 14.12m (46ft 4in) or 14.23m (46ft 8in) in late production aircraft, length 12.04m (39ft 6in), height 4.04m (13ft 3in). Wing area 22.5m^2 (242sq ft).

Capacity: Pilot and copilot on flightdeck, seating for eight in main cabin.

Production: In production between 1976 and 1982, a total of 378 Titans were built.

History: In July 1975 Cessna announced it was developing a new piston twin suitable for airline, freight and corporate work, capable of taking off with a 1560kg (3500lb) payload from a 770m (2530ft) strip, similar in concept to the successful 402, but much larger overall.

The resulting aircraft was the Model 404 Titan, Cessna's largest piston engined twin developed thus far. It shares the same basic fuselage as the turbine powered 441 Conquest which was developed concurrently, however it differs in having geared 280kW (375hp) piston engines and it is unpressurised. Other features include a bonded wet wing (then appearing on a number of 400 series Cessna twins) and the trailing link main undercarriage design shared with the Conquest.

The first Titan took to the skies for the first time on February 26 1975, production deliveries got underway in October the following year. Throughout the Titan's model life (Cessna dropped references to the 404 model number in the late 1970s) it was offered in three major versions, each differing in internal equipment fit. The base aircraft was the Titan Ambassador, configured for passenger operations, while the Titan Courier was convertible from passenger to freight configurations, and the Titan Freighter was a pure cargo aircraft. The Titan Freighter was specially equipped for freight operations with a strengthened floor, cargo doors and walls and a ceiling made from impact resistant material. All were offered with II and III avionics equipment levels (as with other Cessna twins).

The Titan underwent minor modification from 1980 when the wing span was increased and the wingtips redesigned, but production was to last for only another two years until 1982.

Photo: Titans are popular workhorses among commuter, charter and special mission operators worldwide. (Bill Lines)

Cessna 411, 401 & 402

Country of origin: United States of America

Type: Freighter, 10 seat commuter, or six to eight seat business twins

Powerplants: 411A – Two 255kW (340hp) Continental GTSIO-520-C turbocharged, geared and fuel injected flat six piston engines, driving three blade constant speed propellers. 402C – Two 240kW (325hp) turbocharged and fuel injected TSIO-520-VBs.

Performance: 411A – Max speed 431km/h (233kt), max cruising speed 396km/h (214kt), long range cruising speed 283km/h (153kt). Initial rate of climb 1900ft/min. Service ceiling 26,000ft. Range with no reserves and standard fuel 2003km (1081nm), with optional fuel 2310km (1247nm). 402C – Max speed 428km/h (230kt), max cruising speed 394km/h (213kt), long range cruising speed 304km/h (164kt). Initial rate of climb 1450ft/min. Service ceiling 26,900ft. Range with reserves at economical cruising speed 2360km (1273nm).

Weights: 411A – Empty 1973kg (4350lb), max takeoff 2948kg (6500lb). 402C – Empty (Businessliner) 1845kg (4069lb), max takeoff 3107kg (6850lb).

Dimensions: 411 – Wing span 12.15m (39ft 10in), length 10.20m (33ft 6in), height 3.52m (11ft 7in). Wing area 18.6m^2 (200sq ft). 402C – Wing span 13.45m (44ft 2in), length 11.09m (36ft 5in), height 3.49m (11ft 6in). Wing area 21.0m^2 (225.8sq ft).

Capacity: 411 & 401 – Standard seating for six with a centre aisle between the four main cabin seats. 402 – Six to eight seats in corporate configured Businessliner, 10 seats or freight in Utililiner.

Production: 301 Cessna 411s, 401 Cessna 404s and 1535 Cessna 402s were built.

History: The 411 was Cessna's entry into the eight seat cabin class twin market that had previously been dominated by the Beech Queen Air.

Much more modern than the Queen Air, the 411 was lighter, smaller and faster. The prototype first flew in July 1962 and differed from the following production aircraft in having two blade props and direct drive engines (as opposed to the geared GTSIO-520-C engines of production aircraft). Production deliveries commenced in October 1964, and optional features for corporate configured aircraft included folding tables, a toilet and refreshment centre. The 411 was followed up by the 411A from 1967 with lighter and more efficient props and optional extra fuel capacity.

The 411 was soon after replaced by the 401 and 402, which had first been introduced in late 1966. These developments of the 411 were lighter, less powerful and had direct drive engines, and thus were less costly to operate. While the 401 and 402 were essentially the same aircraft, the 401 was optimised for corporate transport and was fitted with fewer seats than the 402, which was optimised for commuter and freighter work. A number of versions of both models were developed with minor refinements, including the 402A, which had a lengthened nose, square windows and an optional 10th seat.

The 402 replaced the 401 from mid 1972, and, as the 402B, was offered in Businessliner corporate configured, and Utililiner convertible passenger or freighter aircraft. The 402C appeared in late 1978 and featured the longer span wings from the 414A and 421C, and more powerful engines. It remained in production until 1985.

Photo: A 401 in charter/regional airline colours. (Bill Lines)

Cessna 421 & 414

Country of origin: United States of America

Type: Pressurised six to eight seat cabin twins

Powerplants: 421A – Two 280kW (374hp) Continental GTSIO-520-D geared, turbocharged and fuel injected flat six piston engines, driving three blade constant speed McCauley propellers. 414A – Two 230kW (310hp) TSIO-520-NBs.

Performance: 421A – Max speed 444km/h (240kt), max cruising speed 420km/h (227kt), long range cruising speed 364km/h (197kt). Initial rate of climb 1680ft/min. Service ceiling 27,000ft. Range with no reserves and standard fuel 1570km (847nm), with optional fuel 2756km (1488nm). 414A – Max speed 436km/h (235kt), cruising speed 420km/h (224kt), economical cruising speed 340km/h (183kt). Initial rate of climb 1520ft/min. Service ceiling 30,800ft. Range with reserves at economical cruising speed 2460km (1327nm), at max cruising speed 2036km (1100nm).

Weights: 421A – Empty equipped 2132kg (4700lb), max takeoff 3103kg (6840lb). 414A – Empty 1976kg (4356lb), max takeoff 3062kg (6750lb).

Dimensions: 421A – Wing span 12.15m (39ft 10in), length 10.29m (33ft 9in), height 3.56m (11ft 8in). Wing area 18.6m^2 (200sq ft). 414A – Wing span 13.45m (44ft 2in), length 11.09m (36ft 5in), height 3.49m (11ft 6in). Wing area 21.0m^2 (225.8sq ft).

Capacity: Standard seating for six, optional seating for eight in 421 and 411A, seven in 411.

Production: 1901 Model 421s and 1055 Model 414s were built, production of both ceased in 1985.

History: The lineage of the 421 and 414 traces back to the 411, the 421 beginning life as a pressurised development of the 411.

The prototype 421 took to the skies for the first time in October 1965 (three years after the 411). In comparison to the 411 on which it was based, the 421 featured a cabin pressurisation system, more powerful geared and turbocharged GTSIO-520-D engines and a higher max takeoff weight. Deliveries of production 421s began in May 1967, Cessna at the time claiming it as the cheapest pressurised twin on the market.

First improvements to the 421 were offered with the 421A of 1969, but the 421B Golden Eagle of 1970 featured a number of significant improvements including lengthened nose and wing span, while the engines retained their power to higher altitudes than before. The final expression of the 421 was the 421C available from late 1975, with a bonded wet wing and no tip tanks, higher vertical tail, more efficient props and new trailing link undercarriage.

The 414 was developed as a less powerful, lighter, simpler and lower cost 421. First flown in 1968, it entered production in 1969. It features the wings and fuselage of the 401 and 402 (themselves lighter developments of the 411), plus direct drive, rather than geared engines. The improved 414A Chancellor appeared in 1978, introducing the bonded wet wing without tip tanks. It remained in production until 1985.

Photo: A 421 Golden Eagle. The 421 is pressurised and has geared engines. (David Daw).

Cessna Corsair, Conquest I & II, & Caravan II

Country of origin: United States of America

Type: Turboprop powered executive transports

Powerplants: 425 – Two 335kW (450shp) Pratt & Whitney Canada PT6A-112 turboprops, driving three blade wide chord constant speed Hartzell propellers. 441 – Two 474kW (636shp) Garrett TPE331-8-410S/402S turboprops, driving either Hartzell or McCauley props.

Performance: 425 – Max cruising speed 490km/h (264kt) at 17,700ft. Initial rate of climb 2027ft/min. Service ceiling 34,700ft. Range with max payload 1252km (676nm), max range 3050km (1647nm). 441 – Max speed 547km/h (295kt), max cruising speed 543km/h (293kt). Initial rate of climb 2435ft/min. Service ceiling 37,000ft. Max range with reserves at long range cruising speed 3048km (1646nm), range with max payload and reserves 2724km (1471nm).

Weights: 425 – Empty equipped 2210kg (4870lb), max takeoff 3710kg (8200lb). 441 – Empty 2588kg (5706lb), max takeoff 4468kg (9850lb).

Dimensions: 425 – Wing span 13.45m (44ft 2in), length 10.93m (35ft 10in), height 3.84m (12ft 7in). Wing area 20.9m^2 (224.98sq ft). 441 – Wing span 15.04m (49ft 4in), length 11.89m (39ft 0in), height 4.01m (13ft 1in). Wing area 23.6m^2 (253.6sq ft).

Capacity: 425 – Typical accommodation one or two pilots and four passengers in corporate configured main cabin, optional passenger seating for six. 441 – One or two pilots and up to nine passengers.

Production: Over 230 Corsair/Conquest Is delivered by end of 1987 by which time production had been suspended, and 370 Model 441s were built. Over 70 F406-5s built thus far.

History: The Corsair and Conquest I, and the 441 Conquest II are the turboprop powered equivalents of the 421 Golden Eagle and 404 Titan respectively.

The Model 441 Conquest was the first to be developed, it was designed concurrently with the piston engined 404 Titan in the mid 1970s. Cessna announced it was developing the 441 in November 1974, and the first flight occurred in August 1976. First customer deliveries were from September 1977. The 441 shares a common fuselage with the Titan, but has longer span (bonded and wet) wing, a pressurised fuselage, and most significantly, Garrett TPE331 turboprop engines. A PT6A powered 441, designated the 435, flew during 1986, but it did not enter production.

The 425 Corsair meanwhile was introduced to the Cessna model lineup from 1980. Based on the Model 421 Golden Eagle, it differs from its donor aircraft in having turboprop engines (in this case PT6As). Design work on the Corsair began in 1977, first flight was on September 12 1978 and first production deliveries took place in November 1980.

From 1983 Cessna renamed the Corsair the Conquest I, while the Conquest became the Conquest II. Production of both lines ceased in 1986.

The French built Reims Cessna F406 Caravan II meanwhile is something of a hybrid, incorporating 373kW (500shp) PT6A-112s, the unpressurised fuselage of the Titan, and the Conquest II's wings. First delivered in late 1984, the Caravan II is the only Cessna turboprop twin currently in production.

Photo: A Reims Cessna Caravan II. (Paul Howard)

Cessna Citation & Citation I

Country of origin: United States of America

Type: Light corporate jet

Powerplants: Citation – Two 9.77kN (2200lb) Pratt & Whitney JT15D-1 turbofans. Citation I – Two 9.77kN (2200lb) JT15D-1A1Bs.

Performance: Citation – Max speed 647km/h (350kt), max cruising speed 644km/h (348kt). Initial rate of climb 3350ft/min. Service ceiling 38,400ft. Range with eight people on board and reserves at high speed cruise 2250km (1215nm). Citation I – Cruising speed 662km/h (357kt). Initial rate of climb 2720ft/min. Range with max fuel 710kg (1560lb) payload and reserves 2460km (1328nm).

Weights: Citation – Empty 2455kg (5408lb), max takeoff 4920kg (10,850lb). Citation I – Empty equipped 3008kg (6631lb), max takeoff weight 5380kg (11,850lb).

Dimensions: Citation – Wing span 13.32m (43ft 9in), length 13.26m (43ft 6in), height 4.36m (14ft 3in). Wing area 24.2m^2 (260sq ft). Citation I – Same except for wing span 14.35m (47ft 1in). Wing area 25.9m^2 (278.5sq ft).

Capacity: Two pilots for Citation and Citation I, single pilot for Citation I/SP. Optional main cabin layouts for five, six or seven passengers.

Production: In production between 1971 and 1985 over 690 Citations, Citation Is and I/SPs were built.

History: The highly popular Citation and Citation I introduced a whole new market to jet aviation, and spawned the world's largest family of small to medium size corporate jets.

Cessna became the first of the big three American manufacturers (Piper, Beech and Cessna) to develop a jet powered transport. Cessna announced its decision to build a new eight place jet powered business aircraft that would be capable of operating into most airfields in October 1968. Dubbed the Fanjet 500, the prototype flew for the first time on September 15 1969. Soon after the new little jet was named the Citation.

A relatively long development program followed, during which time a number of key changes were made to the design including a longer forward fuselage, repositioned engine nacelles, greater tail area and added dihedral to the horizontal tail. In this definitive form the Citation was granted FAA certification on September 9 1971.

Improvements including higher gross weights and thrust reversers were added to the line in early 1976, followed shortly after by the introduction of the enhanced Citation I late that same year. Features of the Citation I were higher weights, JT15D-1A engines and an increased span wing. A further model to appear was the Citation I/SP, which is certificated for single pilot operation. The I/SP was delivered in early 1977.

Production of the Citation I ceased in 1985, its place in the Citation line left vacant until the arrival of the CitationJet (described separately) some years later.

Photo: The original Citation and Citation I ushered in a new era in corporate transportation. This shot shows to good effect the type's low ground clearance and tailplane dihedral.

Cessna CitationJet

Country of origin: United States of America

Type: Entry level corporate jet

Powerplants: Two 8.45kN (1900lb) Williams Rolls-Royce FJ44 turbofans.

Performance: Max cruising speed 704km/h (380kt). Initial rate of climb 1070ft/min. Certificated ceiling 41,000ft. Range with one pilot, four passengers and reserves 2780km (1500nm).

Weights: Empty 2794kg (6160lb), max takeoff 4717kg (10,400lb).

Dimensions: Wing span 14.26m (46ft 10in), length 12.98m (42ft 7in), height 4.18m (13ft 8in). Wing area 22.3m^2 (240.0sq ft).

Capacity: Two flightdeck positions, one for pilot, other optionally for copilot or passenger. Main cabin seats five in standard layout.

Production: First delivered in March 1993, at the time of writing more than 150 CitationJets had been ordered.

History: The new baby of Cessna's successful Citation family of business jets, the Model 525 CitationJet was developed as a replacement for the earlier Citation and Citation I.

Production of the Citation I ended in 1985 after nearly 700 Citations and Citation Is had been built, virtually assuring the new entry level CitationJet a large market for replacement aircraft. With this in mind Cessna launched the new Model 525 at the annual National Business Aircraft Association convention in the USA in 1989. First flight of the new jet occurred on April 29 1991, while FAA certification was awarded on October 16 1992 and first deliveries occurred in the first half of 1993.

While clearly a member of the Citation family, the CitationJet features a number of new design features for the range, the most noteworthy being the laminar flow wing. Cessna aimed for an extra 20 to 30km/h (10 to 15kt) increase in cruising speed for a given thrust through having the air passing over the wing in a laminar state for 30 to 35% of the wing chord. This was achieved by using a thicker skin wing which decreases dimpling and buckling of the wing's skin. Cessna however did not include the performance benefits of the laminar flow wing into certification testing as the laminar flow can be easily disturbed by foreign particles, ice and rain.

The powerplants are also notable for their simplicity, comprising just 700 parts each. They were designed by a partnership between Rolls-Royce and Williams International, the latter firm has previous experience in building jet engines for cruise missiles. The engines also feature unusual paddles for thrust reversal.

Unlike the Citation I, the 525 features a T-tail, mounted on an all new tailplane. The CitationJet's forward fuselage meanwhile is based on that of the Citation II.

Cessna marketing for the CitationJet targets operators currently equipped with turboprops, saying the CitationJet offers similar purchase and operating costs but with the high speed benefits of a jet. It predicts a total market for 1000 over the next decade.

Photo: The CitationJet combines jet speed with very good field performance. (Cessna)

Cessna Citation II & Bravo

Country of origin: United States of America

Type: Small to mid size corporate jets

Powerplants: S/II – Two 11.1kN (2500lb) Pratt & Whitney Canada JT15D-4Bs turbofans. Bravo – Two 12.2kN (2750lb) Pratt & Whitney Canada PW503As.

Performance: S/II – Cruising speed 746km/h (403kt). Initial rate of climb 3040ft/min. Range with two crew, four passengers and reserves 3223km (1739nm). Range with max fuel 3700km (1998nm). Bravo – Max cruising speed 743km/h (401kt). Max initial rate of climb 2980ft/min. Max certificated altitude 43,000ft. Range with four passengers and reserves 3520km (1900nm).

Weights: S/II – Empty equipped 3655kg (8060lb), max takeoff 6850kg (15,100lb). Bravo – Empty 3820kg (8423lb), max takeoff 6485kg (14,300lb).

Dimensions: S/II – Wing span 15.91m (52ft 3in), length 14.39m (47ft 3in), height 4.57m (15ft 0in). Wing area 31.8m² (342.6sq ft). Bravo – Wing span 15.90m (52ft 2in), length 14.39m (47ft 3in), height 4.57m (15ft 0in). Wing area 30.0m² (322.9sq ft).

Capacity: S/II – Flightcrew of two. Main cabin can be optionally configured to seat 10, but standard interior layout for six. Can be configured as an air ambulance with one or two stretchers and up to four medical attendants. Bravo – Standard seating for seven with max seating for 10 in main cabin.

Production: A total of 689 Citation IIs and 161 S/IIs built through to late 1994. Bravo deliveries due to start in early 1997.

History: The early success of the original Citation led Cessna to develop a larger capacity Citation model in the mid 1970s.

Cessna announced it was developing a stretched Citation in September 1976. The fuselage was extended by 1.14m (3ft 9in) to increase maximum seating capacity to 10, while more powerful Pratt & Whitney Canada JT15D-4 engines and greater fuel tankage meant higher cruise speeds and longer range. Increased baggage capacity and increased span wings were also added.

The new Model 550 Citation II took to the skies for the first time on January 31 1977 and FAA certification for two pilot operation was awarded in March 1978. The II/SP is the single pilot version.

Major improvements were made to the design with the arrival of the Model S550 Citation S/II. Announced in October 1983, this improved version first flew on February 14 1984. Certification, including an exemption for single pilot operation, was granted that July. Improvements were mainly aerodynamic, including a new wing designed using supercritical technology developed for the Citation III (described separately), plus JT15D-4B turbofans. The S/II initially replaced the II in production from 1984, but the II returned to the line-up from late 1985, and both variants remain in production.

The latest version of the Citation II is the Bravo, which features new P&WC PW530A turbofans, modern avionics with EFIS (including two primary flight display screens), a revised interior based on those in the Citation Ultra and other improvements. The Bravo made its first flight on April 25 1995 and was granted FAA certification in August 1996. First deliveries are planned for early 1997.

Photo: The Citation II series is the world's most successful biz jet family.

Cessna Citation V & Ultra

Country of origin: United States of America

Type: Small to midsize corporate jet

Powerplants: V – Two 12.9kN (2900lb) Pratt & Whitney Canada JT15D-5A turbofans. Ultra – Two 13.6kN (3045lb) JT15D-5Ds.

Performance: V – Cruising speed 790km/h (427kt). Initial rate of climb 3650ft/min. Range with six passengers, two crew and reserves 3558km (1920nm). Ultra – Max cruising speed 796km/h (430kt). Max initial rate of climb 4100ft/min. Max certificated altitude 45,000ft. Range with five passengers 3630km (1960nm).

Weights: V – Empty equipped 4004kg (8828lb), max takeoff 7212kg (15,900lb). Ultra – Empty 4196kg (9250lb), operating empty 4377kg (9650lb), max takeoff 7393kg (16,300lb).

Dimensions: V & Ultra – Wing span 15.91m (52ft 3in), length overall 14.90m (48ft 11in), height 4.57m (15ft 0in). Wing area 31.8m² (342.6sq ft).

Capacity: V – Typical seating for eight passengers. Ultra – Standard seating arrangements for seven or eight passengers, depending on configuration.

Production: By late 1996 over 300 Citation Vs and Citation V Ultras had been ordered, including 262 Citation Vs built through to mid 1994 when production ceased.

History: The Citation V and Citation Ultra are the largest straight wing members of Cessna's highly successful Citation family.

Cessna publicly announced it was developing a stretched development of the Citation II at the annual NBAA convention in New Orleans in 1987. Earlier in August that year the first engineering prototype Model 560 Citation V had successfully completed the type's maiden flight. A preproduction prototype flew in early 1996, while US FAA certification was granted on December 9 1988. Deliveries of production aircraft began in April the following year.

The Citation V was based on the Citation II/SP, but differences over the smaller jet include more powerful Pratt & Whitney Canada JT15D-5A turbofans and a slight fuselage stretch, allowing seating in a standard configuration for eight passengers. The Citation V proved quite popular, and 262 were built through to mid 1994, before production switched to the modernised Ultra.

Cessna announced development of an upgraded Citation V in September 1993. FAA certification for the new aircraft, the Ultra, was granted in June 1994, allowing for deliveries of production aircraft to commence soon after.

Compared with the Citation V, the Ultra features more powerful 13.6kN (3045lb) Pratt & Whitney Canada JT15D-5D engines and Honeywell Primus 1000 EFIS avionics with three CRT displays (two primary flight displays and one multifunction display).

Notable Citation Ultra customers include Korean Air Lines which ordered three for pilot training (one of these, delivered in mid 1996, was the 300th Citation V/Ultra delivered), Executive Jets, who ordered 25 for its fractional ownership scheme, the USAF which has ordered five as APG-66 radar equipped OT-47Bs, and the US Army, which selected the type to fulfil its 35 aircraft C-XX medium range transport requirement.

Photo: A Citation Ultra demonstrator. (Gerard Frawley)

Cessna Citation Excel

Country of origin: United States of America

Type: Small to mid size corporate jet

Powerplants: Two 16.2kN (3640lb) Pratt & Whitney Canada PW545A turbofans.

Performance: Max cruising speed 797km/h (430kt). Initial rate of climb 3640ft/min. Max certificated altitude 45,000ft. Range at economical cruising speed with two crew, four passengers and reserves 3810km (2055nm), range with full fuel load at max cruising speed 2965km (1600nm) plus.

Weights: Approximate empty 4945kg (10,900lb), max takeoff 8482kg (18,700lb).

Dimensions: Wing span 16.98m (55ft 9in), length overall 15.79m (51ft 10in), height 5.24m (17ft 3in). Wing area $34.4m^2$ (369.7sq ft).

Capacity: Flightcrew of two. Various interior configurations offered with seating typically for six, seven or eight passengers in main cabin.

Production: Over 100 Excels ordered by late 1996 with first deliveries planned for early 1998.

History: Cessna's latest in a now fairly extensive line of Citation business jets, the Citation Excel combines the cabin width and comfort of the Citation X with similar performance to the Citation V Ultra.

The new Excel resulted from extensive customer consultation over what they wanted in a light corporate jet and advances in engine and airframe technology. The basis of the Excel is a shortened Citation X fuselage (the same fuselage cross section as used in the Citation III, VI and VII), combined with a modified unswept supercritical wing based on the Citation V Ultra's, the V's cruciform tail configuration and new Pratt & Whitney Canada PW500 series turbofans. Other design features include trailing link main undercarriage units and a standard three screen EFIS avionics package with pedestal mounted GPS and V_{NAV}, based on the Honeywell Primus 1000 package developed for the Citation Ultra.

The Citation X based fuselage offers perhaps the largest usable fuselage volume of any light business jet, with stand up headroom and a dropped aisle than runs the length of the main cabin. Seated head and elbow room will be more than that in the Citation II and V, while the cabin length is similar to the Citation II, VI and VII.

The Excel is one of the first applications for the new generation PW500 series engines. The Excel's 16.2kN (3640lb) PW545As (derated from 19.9kN/4450lb, with a TBO of 5000 hours) are fitted with Nordam thrust reversers as standard and the engines allow it to climb to 43,000ft at maximum takeoff weight in 25 minutes and cruise at 797km/h (430kt) over 2965km (1600nm).

Cessna announced it was developing the Excel at the NBAA conference in October 1994. The Excel is due to be certificated in mid 1997, with first customer deliveries in early 1998. Cessna plans to build 30 Excels during 1998, with production scheduled to increase to four per month in 1999.

Photo: The prototype Citation Excel takes off on its first flight on February 29 1996. (Cessna)

Cessna Citation III, VI & VII

Country of origin: United States of America

Type: Medium size corporate jets

Powerplants: III & VI – Two 16.2kN (3650lb) Garrett TFE731-3B-100S turbofans. VII – Two 17.8kN (4000lb) AlliedSignal TFE731-4R-2Ss.

Performance: III & VI – Max cruising speed 874km/h (472kt). Initial rate of climb 805ft/min. Range with two crew and four passengers and reserves 4348km (2346nm). VII – Max cruising speed 885km/h (478kt). Initial rate of climb 830ft/min. Range with reserves 4075km (2200nm).

Weights: III & VI – Empty 5357kg (11,811lb), operating empty 5534kg (12,200lb), max takeoff 9980kg (22,000lb). VII – Empty 5301kg (11,686lb), max takeoff 10,183kg (22,450lb).

Dimensions: Wing span 16.31m (53ft 6in), length 16.90m (55ft 6in), height 5.12m (16ft 10in). Wing area $29.0m^2$ (312.0sq ft).

Capacity: Flightcrew of two. Typical main passenger cabin seating for six, or optionally up to nine.

Production: Total of 202 Citation IIIs delivered when production ceased in 1992. A total of 39 Citation VIs had been built when production ceased in 1995, while over 60 VIIs had been built by late 1996.

History: The all new Cessna Model 650 Citation III was designed as a high performance, mid size long range corporate jet to supplement the popular Citation I and II.

Development of this very different Citation began in 1978. As it evolved, the III had in little in common with the previous Citation models other than the name. The new design featured a swept supercritical wing optimised for high speed long range flight, new Garrett TFE731 turbofans, a T-tail, and a new lengthened fuselage. The new jet made its first flight on May 30 1979 with a second prototype flying on May 2 1980. Certification was granted on April 30 1982, first customer deliveries occurring the following year. The Citation III set two time to height records for its class in 1983 and a class speed record by flying from Gander to Le Bourget in 5hr 13min.

Production improvements to the Citation III were first proposed in the failed Citation IV. This model was announced in 1989 and was to feature longer range through greater fuel tankage, and better short field performance. In its place instead Cessna developed the Citation VI and VII. The Citation VI was offered as a low cost development of the III with a different avionics package and a standard interior layout, with customised interiors unavailable. First flight of the Citation VI took place in 1991 but only 39 were built when production was wound up in May 1995.

The Citation VII meanwhile features a number of improvements including more powerful engines for improved hot and high performance. The first Citation VII prototype flew in February 1991. The Citation VII remains in production as the only member of the Citation III/VI/VII currently available new build.

Photo: The Citation III (pictured), forms the basis for the current production Citation VII. (Cessna)

Cessna Citation X

Country or origin: United States of America

Type: Long range, high speed, mid size executive jet

Powerplants: Two 28.5kN (6400lb) Allison AE 3007C turbofans.

Performance: Max cruising speed Mach 0.88 (934km/h/504kt) at 37,000ft. Initial rate of climb 4000ft/min. Max operating altitude 51,000ft. Range with reserves 6115km (3300nm).

Weights: Standard empty 8340kg (18,390lb), max takeoff 16,010kg (35,300lb).

Dimensions: Wing span 19.48m (63ft 11in), length 22.00m (72ft 2in), height 5.77m (18ft 11in). Wing area 49.0m^2 (527.0sq ft).

Capacity: Flightcrew of two. Main cabin seating for up to 12 passengers seated on individual seats and couches in a high density configuration. Other interiors to customer preference, including eight passenger seats in a double club arrangement.

Production: First production Citation X delivered in June 1996.

History: The Citation X is Cessna's largest, fastest and longest range aircraft yet, and Cessna has claimed it to be the fastest commercial transport other than the supersonic Concorde.

The Citation X (or Cessna Model 750) is also the largest member of one of business aviation's biggest corporate jet families, the Citation. The design objectives driving Cessna's largest project to date includes transcontinental USA and trans Atlantic range in a mid size package that cruises faster than any other business jet available. This high speed cruise capability, which Cessna says is 105 to 210km/h (55 to 113kt) faster than other mid size corporate jets, means it can save up to one hour flight time on transcontinental US flights, flying from Los Angeles to New York with normal wind conditions in 4 hours 10 minutes. Because of its ability to cruise at high speed at high altitudes, Cessna also says the Citation X will consume less fuel than current jets on such a transcontinental flight.

To achieve such an ambitious design objective, Cessna arrived at an aircraft that at some angles at least is regarded as awkward. The two new advanced technology Allison AE 3007A turbofans are very large for an aircraft of the X's size, while the highly swept (37°) wings are also long in span. The Citation X is the first application for the AE 3007, which, like the Saab 2000's AE 2100 turboprop, is based upon the core of the T406 turboshaft developed for the V-22 Osprey.

Other design features of the Citation X include the fuselage cross section of the Citation III, VI and VII but with more efficient use of internal space that allows greater head and shoulder room, plus trailing link main undercarriage units and a modern EFIS glass cockpit.

Cessna announced that it was developing the Citation X in October 1990 at that year's NBAA conference. The prototype was publicly rolled out in September 1993 and flew for the first time on December 21 that year. Certification was granted on June 3 1996, with the first customer delivery that month.

Photo: Highly swept wings, a rakish T-tail and unusually large nacelles are visual hallmarks of Cessna's most ambitious jet project to date. (Cessna)

Chichester-Miles Leopard

Country of origin: United Kingdom

Type: High performance four seat jet powered light aircraft

Powerplants: Prototype – Two 1.33kN (300lb) Noel Penny NPT 301 turbofans. Production aircraft – Two 4.23kN (950lb) Williams International FJX turbofans.

Performance: Prototype aircraft – Max cruising speed 655km/h (354kt). Initial rate of climb 2350ft/min. Range with no reserves 1300km (700nm). Production aircraft – Max speed 870km/h (470kt), max and economical cruising speed at 45,000ft 804km/h (434kt). Initial rate of climb 6430ft/min. Service ceiling 55,000ft. Range with max payload and reserves 2780km (1500nm), range with max fuel 3547km (1915nm).

Weights: Prototype – Basic empty 795kg (1750lb), max takeoff 1155kg (2550lb). Production aircraft – Empty equipped 1000kg (2200lb), max takeoff 1815kg (4000lb).

Dimensions: Wing span 7.16m (23ft 6in), length 7.54m (24ft 9in), height 2.06m (6ft 9in). Wing area 5.9m^2 (62.9sq ft).

Capacity: Standard seating for four, but could alternatively be equipped for the medevac role with a pilot, stretcher patient and medical attendant.

Production: Prototype only built at the time of writing, with design of production aircraft continuing.

History: The sleek Leopard is arguably the most advanced and innovative light aircraft yet designed and flown.

Despite this advancement, the Leopard dates back over a decade to the early 1980s when Ian Chichester-Miles, a former Chief Research Engineer at BAe Hatfield, established Chichester-Miles Consultants. CMC completed construction of a Leopard mockup in early 1982 and then contracted Designability Ltd to perform detail design work and build a prototype. CMC originally hoped that the prototype Leopard would fly for the first time in early 1987, however various delays meant that it did not fly for the first time until December 12 1988. Since then development has progressed fairly slowly, and the prototype ceased test flying while it was fitted with a redesigned tailplane fitted with a liquid anti icing system.

The program then suffered a further setback when the Leopard's engine supplier Noel Penny ceased trading, and all flying stopped while a pre production aircraft powered by Williams International FJX turbofans was designed and built. This aircraft was displayed at the 1996 Farnborough Airshow and CMC also plans that production aircraft be powered by the FJX powerplant.

Production Leopards will incorporate a number of advanced design features including all composite construction, supercritical, laminar flow, swept wings; liquid deicing and decontamination system along the wings and tailplane; and EFIS avionics (the current prototype features simpler avionics and pressurisation systems and liquid deicing on the tailplane only). The Leopard also does not feature spoilers or ailerons, instead roll, pitch and yaw control is provided by the all moving fin and differentially actuated tailplanes.

Photo: The Leopard's clean, uncluttered lines and tiny jet engines are apparent in this shot of the No 2 proof of concept prototype. (Paul Merritt)

Cirrus Design Cirrus SR20

Country of origin: United States of America

Type: Four seat light aircraft

Powerplant: One 150kW (200hp) Teledyne Continental IO-360-ES fuel injected flat six piston engine driving a two or three blade Hartzell propeller.

Performance: Max cruising speed 295km/h (160kt). Initial rate of climb 1000ft/min. Max range 1480km (800nm).

Weights: Standard empty 790kg (1740lb), max takeoff 1315kg (2900lb).

Dimensions: Wing span 10.67m (35ft 0in), length 7.63m (25ft 0in), height 2.81m (9ft 2in). Wing area 12.6m^2 (135sq ft).

Capacity: Typical seating for four.

Production: Over 100 orders placed by late 1996, with first deliveries due late 1997.

History: Cirrus Design intends that its Cirrus SR20 become the first model in a family of advanced new technology general aviation aircraft.

Cirrus Design Corporation began life as a designer and manufacturer of kit aircraft. The company's piston or turbine powered kit built VK30 four seater in fact forms the basis of the SR20 design, although the two aircraft are very different, particularly as the VK30 features a pusher engine. The VK30 first flew in February 1988 but kit production ceased in 1993 to allow Cirrus to relocate its manufacturing facilities to Duluth, Minnesota, and to specifically concentrate on designing and manufacturing a family of fully certificated and factory built GA aircraft.

Details of the SR20 were publicly revealed at the Oshkosh EAA Convention in July 1994. What was revealed is arguably the most advanced four seater in production or under serious development. The SR20 features composite construction, advanced Trimbal supplied avionics, and what Cirrus calls "simple, modern systems to make the aircraft easier to fly than any other four passenger aircraft." The SR20 will also be fitted standard with a Ballistic Recovery System (BRS) parachute (Cirrus claims it will be the first manufacturer to offer this), while various energy absorbing features have been designed into the airframe to reduce deceleration loads and increase its ability to absorb energy in the event of an impact. Power is supplied by a 150kW (200hp) six cylinder Teledyne Continental IO-360-ES.

Apart from its high levels of technology, Cirrus claims that the SR20 will offer significant improvements over current four seaters in performance, interior cabin space and internal noise levels. The cockpit interior design will be based on modern car designs and will feature side mounted control yokes.

The SR20 prototype made its first flight on March 31 1995. Full FAA FAR Part 23 certification is planned for late 1997. Cirrus had earlier hoped to have achieved certification in time for it to make first customer deliveries at the 1997 EAA Oshkosh convention but was forced to accept a delay when it decided to lower stall speeds and improve lateral control up to and in the stall.

A number of developments of the SR20 are planned including a more basic version optimised for the vast flying training market, powered by a 120kW (160hp) engine and possibly a high performance version powered by a 185 to 225kW (250 to 300hp) engine.

Photo: The four seat SR20 in flight.

Commander 114B

Country of origin: United States of America

Type: Four seat high performance light aircraft

Powerplant: 114B – One 195kW (260hp) Textron Lycoming IO-540-T4B5 flat six piston engine driving a three blade constant speed McCauley propeller.

Performance: 114B – Max speed 304km/h (164kt), performance cruising speed at 75% power 296km/h (160kt), economical cruising speed at 65% power 287km/h (155kt), long range cruising speed at 55% power 276km/h (149kt). Initial rate of climb 1070ft/min. Range at performance cruising speed 1165km (630nm), range at economical cruising speed 1305km (705nm), range at long range cruising speed 1345km (725nm).

Weights: 114B – Empty 928kg (2044lb), max takeoff 1475kg (3250lb).

Dimensions: Wing span 9.99m (32ft 9in), length 7.60m (24ft 11in), height 2.57m (8ft 5in). Wing area 14.1m^2 (152sq ft).

Capacity: Typical seating for four.

Production: Production commenced in 1992, and by late 1996 approximately 140 Commander 114Bs had been built. Rockwell built over 1000 112s and 114s (described separately) for which Commander has service responsibility.

History: The Commander 114B is a new build, modernised development of the original Rockwell Commander 114.

The Rockwell Commander 114 was itself a more powerful development of the Commander 112 of 1970, one of only two new GA designs from Rockwell. Unfortunately for Rockwell, the 150kW (200hp) powered 112 was widely regarded as underpowered. To address concerns with the 112, Rockwell developed the 114 which incorporated a number of improvements plus most importantly a 195kW (260hp) six cylinder engine.

The 112 and 114 remained in production with Rockwell until 1979. In 1981 Rockwell's General Aviation Division was sold to Gulfstream Aerospace. Gulfstream held the manufacturing rights for the Commander family but never built the 112 or 114, instead selling the rights to the newly formed Commander Aircraft Company in 1988.

Under the Commander Aircraft Company's stewardship, the basic 114 design was improved and updated considerably. The main changes to the Commander 114B over the original 114 include a restyled engine cowling to reduce drag and other aerodynamic improvements, and a quieter and more efficient three blade McCauley Black Mac propeller. Other changes in the pipeline include further aerodynamic improvements.

The new Commander company originally intended leasing new build aircraft to save on product liability insurance premiums, but such a scheme never gained favour and Commander switched to conventional marketing. The revised Commander 114B was issued a new Type Certificate on May 4 1992 and the first was delivered later that year. Commander also offers the 114AT optimised for pilot training and the turbocharged 200kW (270hp) TIO-540 powered 114TC.

Photo: The reprofiled nose identifies the Commander 114B from earlier Rockwell built 114s (refer separate entry).

Convair CV-240, 340 & 440

Country of origin: United States of America

Type: Short haul commercial transports

Powerplants: CV-240 – Two 1490kW (2000hp) Pratt & Whitney R-2800-CA18 Double Wasp piston radial engines driving three blade constant speed propellers. CV-340 – Two 1790kW (2400hp) R-2800-CB16 Double Wasps. CV-440 – Two 1865kW (2500hp) R-2800-CB16 or -CB17 Double Wasps.

Performance: CV-240 – Cruising speed 435km/h (235kt). Range with max fuel 2900km (1565nm). CV-340 – Cruising speed 457km/h (247kt). Typical range with max payload 935km (505nm). CV-440 – Max cruising speed 483km/h (261kt), economical cruising speed 465km/h (250kt). Service ceiling 24,900ft. Range with max payload 756km (408nm), range with max fuel 3106km (1677nm).

Weights: CV-240 – Empty 12,520kg (27,600lb), max takeoff 18,956kg (41,790lb). CV-340 – Empty 13,375kg (29,486lb), max takeoff 21,320kg (47,000lb). CV-440 – Empty 15,110kg (33,314lb), max takeoff 22,544kg (49,700lb).

Dimensions: CV-240 – Wing span 27.97m (91ft 9in), length 22.76m (74ft 8in), height 8.20m (26ft 11in). Wing area 75.9m² (817sq ft). CV-340 – Wing span 32.12m (105ft 4in), length 24.13m (79ft 2in), height 8.58m (28ft 2in). Wing area 85.5m² (920sq ft). CV-440 – Same as CV-340 except for length 24.84m (81ft 6in).

Capacity: CV-240 – Flightcrew of two or three. Passenger seating for up to 40, or a 4240kg (9350lb) payload. CV-340 – Flightcrew of two or three. Passenger seating for up to 52, or a 6075kg (13,391lb) payload. CV-440 – Flightcrew of two or three. Passenger seating for up to 52 or a 5820kg (12,836lb) payload.

Production: 176 CV-240s, 133 civil and 99 military (C-131 Samaritan) CV-340s and 153 CV-440s were built.

History: The Convair CV-240, 340 and 440 were perhaps the closest designs to come near to being a Douglas DC-3 replacement as despite a glut of cheap DC-3s in the postwar years this family of airliners achieved considerable sales success.

Design of the original CV-110 was initiated in response to an American Airlines request for a DC-3 replacement. American found the CV-110 (which first flew on July 8 1946) to be too small and asked that the CV-110 be scaled up in size, and this resulted in the CV-240 ConvairLiner. The CV-240 was arguably the most advanced short haul airliner of its day, and first flew on March 16 1947 and entered service on June 1 1948. The success of the CV-240 led to the 1.37m (4ft 6in) stretched CV-340, which first flew on October 5 1951, and the CV-440 (often called the Metropolitan) which incorporated some aerodynamic improvements and first flew on October 6 1955.

The CV-240, CV-340 and CV-440 sold in large numbers, mainly to airlines in North America, and formed the backbone of many airlines' short to medium haul fleets. Today the small number that remain in service are mainly used as freighters.

Many of the surviving aircraft have been converted with turboprops, and these conversions are discussed in the following entry.

Photo: An American registered Convair in a corporate configuration. (Gordon Reid)

Convair CV-540, 580, 600, 640 & CV5800

Country of origin: United States of America

Type: Short haul turboprop converted commercial transports

Powerplants: CV-580 – Two 2800kW (3750shp) Allison 501-D13H turboprops driving four blade constant speed propellers. CV-640 – Two 2255kW (3025hp) Rolls-Royce R.Da.10/1 Darts. CV5800 – Two 3430kW (4600shp) 501-D22Gs.

Performance: CV-580 – Max cruising speed 550km/h (297kt) at 20,000ft. Range with 2270kg (5000lb) payload 3650km (1970nm), range with max fuel 4773km (2577nm). CV-640 – Cruising speed 483km/h (260kt). Range with max payload 1979km (1069nm), range with max fuel 3138km (1695nm).

Weights: CV-580 – Operating empty 13,732kg (30,275lb), max takeoff 26,371kg (58,140lb). CV-640 – Operating empty 13,733kg (30,275lb), max takeoff 25,855kg (57,000lb). CV5800 – Operating empty 15,043kg (33,166lb), max takeoff 28,576kg (63,000lb).

Dimensions: CV-580 – Wing span 32.12m (105ft 4in), length 24.84m (81ft 6in), height 8.89m (29ft 2in). Wing area 85.5m² (920sq ft). CV5800 – Same except for length 29.18m (95ft 9in).

Capacity: Flightcrew of two or three. Passenger seating for up to 56 at four abreast and 76cm (30in) pitch. CV5800 – Passenger seating for 76.

Production: 170 CV-340s and CV-440s converted to CV-580s, 38 CV-240s converted to CV-600s, 27 CV-340s and CV-440s converted to CV-640s. 80 converted Convairs remained in commercial service in late 1996. In addition there has been one CV5800 conversion.

History: The original piston Convairs have been the subject of a number of turboprop modification programs, the line's inherent strength and reliability making it a popular choice for conversions.

As early as 1950 the potential of turboprop powered CV-240s was recognised leading to the first flight and development of the CV-240 Turboliner, while an Allison 501D powered YC-131 conversion took to the skies for the first time on June 19 1954. One other early conversion occurred in 1954 when D Napier and Sons in Britain converted CV-340s with that company's 2280kW (3060hp) Eland N.El.1 turboprops as the CV-540. Six such aircraft were converted for Allegheny Airlines in the USA, although these aircraft were later converted back to piston power. Canadair meanwhile built 10 new aircraft with Eland engines for the Royal Canadian Air Force.

The most popular Convair conversions were those done by PacAero in California for Allison, and this involved converting CV-340s and CV-440s with Allison 501D turboprops, plus modified tail control surfaces and a larger tail area to CV-580s. The first such conversion flew on January 19 1960, although it was not until June 1964 that a converted aircraft entered service.

Convair's own conversion program involved Rolls-Royce Darts, and the first of these flew on May 2 1965. Thus converted CV-240s became CV-600s, while CV-340s and CV-440s became CV-640s.

Kelowna Flightcraft in Canada has offered the most ambitious Convair conversion program, having stretched a CV-580 by 4.34m (14ft 3in) and reverting to the CV-440's original tail unit. Production conversions would also have the options of a new freight door and new avionics.

Photo: A Convair CV-580 freighter. (Gary Gentle)

Curtiss C-46 Commando

Country of origin: United States of America

Type: Ex military freighter and airliner

Powerplants: C-46 – Two 1495kW (2000hp) Pratt & Whitney R-2800-34 piston radial engines driving three blade constant speed propellers. C-46R – Two 1565kW (2100hp) Pratt & Whitney R-2800 C or CA series radial pistons.

Performance: C-46 – Typical cruising speed 300km/h (162kt). Range with 2585kg (5700lb) payload 1880km (1017nm). C-46R – Max speed 435km/h (235kt), max cruising speed 378km/h (204kt). Service ceiling 22,000ft. Range with max fuel 2897km (1564nm).

Weights: C-46 – Operating empty 14,970kg (33,000lb), max payload 5265kg (11,630lb), max takeoff 21,772kg (48,000lb). C-46R – Empty 13,290kg (29,300lb), max takeoff 22,680kg (50,000lb).

Dimensions: Wing span 32.92m (108ft 0in), length 23.27m (76ft 4in), overall height 6.60m (21ft 8in). Wing area 126.2m^2 (1358sq ft).

Capacity: Flightcrew of two pilots and optional flight engineer. Typical accommodation for freight, but in an airliner configuration can seat 36, or in military configuration 50 troops.

Production: 3182 Commandos built for US armed forces (as the C-46 for the USAAF and R5C for the USN). Many hundreds subsequently converted for civil service. Approximately 20 remain in service as of late 1996.

History: The Curtiss Commando came into widespread civilian service as both an airliner and a freighter after a large number were built as transports for the US military during World War 2, although the original Curtiss design was intended as an airliner.

Originally intended as a competitor to the highly successful Douglas DC-3, which was the pre-eminent airliner of the time, the Curtiss CW-20 was designed to operate on routes of up to 1000km (540nm), which at the time accounted for 90% of the US domestic airline system. This design featured two Wright R-2600 Twin Cyclone radial engines of 1270kW (1700hp), twin vertical tails and a pressurised double lobe, or 'double bubble' fuselage. Accommodation would have been for 36 passengers plus four crew.

Later in timing than the DC-3, the first CW-20 took to the skies for the first time on March 26 1940. In July that year an impressed US Army Air Force ordered 20 unpressurised CW-20s, which it named the C-46 Commando. The first production aircraft was completed in May 1942, by which time the powerplant choice had been switched to P&W R-2800s, and the first deliveries to the US Army occurred in July. Initially the C-46 was troubled with reliability problems in military service, but these were soon overcome and the Commando proved to be a useful transport with its relatively cavernous freight hold.

A proposed postwar commercial version was the CW-20E, but it failed to attract customer interest and thus all Commandos to enter civilian service were ex military aircraft. Most were purchased by American operators for freight work. One postwar version though was the Riddles Airlines C-46R which had more powerful engines and better performance. Thirty or so were converted.

Photo: The C-46 features a cavernous fuselage making it well suited to freight operations. (Gordon Reid)

Dassault Mystère/Falcon 10 & 100

Country of origin: France

Type: Light corporate jet

Powerplants: 10 & 100 – Two 14.4kN (3230lb) Garrett TFE731-2 turbofans.

Performance: 10 – Max cruising speed 912km/h (492kt). Range with four passengers and reserves 3560km (1920nm). 100 – Max cruising speed same. Range with four passengers and reserves 3480km (1880nm).

Weights: 10 – Empty equipped 4880kg (10,760lb), max takeoff 8500kg (18,740lb). 100 – Empty equipped 5055kg (11,145lb), max takeoff 8755kg (19,300lb).

Dimensions: Wing span 13.08m (42ft 11in), length 13.86m (45ft 6in), height 4.61m (15ft 2in). Wing area 24.1m^2 (259sq ft).

Capacity: Flightcrew of two on flightdeck. Main cabin is typically configured to seat four in an executive club seating arrangement. Main cabin can seat up to seven in Falcon 10 or eight in Falcon 100 in a high density layout. Can be configured for air ambulance, aerial photography and navaid calibration missions.

Production: In addition to three prototypes, a total of 226 Falcon 10 and Falcon 100s (including seven military MERs & 31 Falcon 100s), were built between 1973 and 1990, of which over 200 remain in civilian service.

History: The baby of Dassault's corporate jet lineup, the Falcon 10 and Falcon 100 series (Mystère 10 and Mystère 100 in France) sold in good numbers over almost two decades.

In concept a scaled down Falcon/Mystère 20, the Falcon 10/100 is however basically an all new design except for similar wing high lift devices. Conceived in the late 1960s, the Falcon 10 was the second member of the Dassault Falcon family to be developed. Dassault originally intended the Falcon 10 be powered by two General Electric CJ610 turbojets, and a so powered prototype flew for the first time on December 1 1970. A longer than average flight test and development program followed however. Flight testing was delayed until May 1971 while changes were made to the wing design, including increasing the wing sweepback angle. The second prototype was the first to be powered by Garrett TFE731 turbofans, and it completed its first flight on October 15 1971. Flight testing was completed with the aid of a third prototype, and French and US certification was awarded in September 1973. Deliveries of production aircraft began that November.

While almost all production of Falcon 10s was for civil customers, the French navy ordered seven, designated the Mystère 10 MER, as multi purpose pilot trainers. Missions included simulation of targets for Super Etendard pilots, and conventional instrument training.

The improved Falcon 100 replaced the Falcon 10 in production in the early 1980s. Changes include an optional early EFIS glass cockpit, a higher maximum takeoff weight, a fourth cabin window on the right side and a larger unpressurised rear baggage compartment.

Production of the Falcon 100 ceased in 1990 with the last machine delivered that September.

Photo: A Falcon 100. Like the larger Falcon 50 and 900, the Falcon 10/100 is powered by the popular Garrett (now AlliedSignal) TFE731.

Dassault Mystère/Falcon 20 & 200

Country of origin: France

Type: Medium range corporate jet and multirole utility transport

Powerplants: 20 – Two 21.16kN (4500lb) General Electric CF700-2D-2 turbofans. 200 – Two 23.13kN (5200lb) Garrett ATF 3-6A-4Cs.

Performance: 20 – Max cruising speed 863km/h (466kt), economical cruising speed 750km/h (405kt). Service ceiling 42,000ft. Range with max fuel and reserves 3300km (1780nm). 200 – Max cruising speed 870km/h (470kt), economical cruising speed 780km/h (420kt). Service ceiling 45,000ft. Range with max fuel, eight pax and reserves 4650km (2510nm).

Weights: 20 – Empty equipped 7530kg (16,600lb), max takeoff 13,000kg (28,660lb). 200 – Empty equipped 8250kg (18,290lb), max takeoff 14,515kg (32,000lb).

Dimensions: Wing span 16.32m (53ft 7in), length 17.15m (56ft 3in), height 5.32m (17ft 6in). Wing area 41.0m^2 (441.33sq ft).

Capacity: Flightcrew of two. Typical main cabin seating for between eight and 10 passengers, optionally for as many as 14 in a high density configuration. Quick change and convertible versions have a usable freight volume of 6.7m^3 (235cu ft). Freighter (as used by Federal Express) payload of 3000kg (6615lb). Three stretchers can be fitted in an air ambulance configuration.

Production: Production ended in 1988 when the last Falcon 200 was delivered, by which time 35 200s and 473 20s had been built. The last 20 was completed in late 1983.

History: The Mystère or Falcon 20 and 200 constitutes Dassault's most successful business jet program thus far, with more than 500 built.

Development of the original Mystère 20 traces back to a joint collaboration between Sud Aviation (which later merged into Aerospatiale) and Dassault in the late 1950s. Development progressed to the stage where prototype construction began in January 1962, leading to a first flight on May 4 1963. This prototype shared with production aircraft the type's overall configuration, but differed in the powerplant. The prototype was initially powered by 14.78kN (3300lb) Pratt & Whitney JT12A-8 turbojets, whereas production Mystère 20s (or Falcon 20s outside France) were powered with General Electric CF700s. The first of these flew on New Year's Day 1965. Throughout the Mystère production life Aerospatiale remained responsible for production of the tail and rear fuselage.

In 1980 Dassault gained certification for a new version powered by more powerful yet more efficient Garrett AiResearch ATF 3-6A-4C turbofans. Known initially as the 20H, it was later redesignated the 200, and features greater fuel tankage and much longer range, redesigned wing root fairings and some systems and equipment changes. This version remained in production until 1988, while production of the 20 had ceased in 1983.

Photo: A Dassault owned Mystère 200, better known as the Falcon 200 outside France. (Dassault)

Dassault Falcon 50

Country of origin: France

Type: Long range mid size corporate jet

Powerplants: 50 – Three 16.5kN (3700lb) AlliedSignal TFE731-3 turbofans. 50EX – Three 16.5kN (3700lb) TFE731-40s.

Performance: 50 – Max cruising speed 880km/h (475kt), long range cruising speed 797km/h (430kt). Max operating altitude 45,000ft. Range at Mach 0.75 with eight passengers and reserves 6480km (3500nm). 50EX – Range with eight pax at Mach 0.80 5600km (3025nm), at Mach 0.75 6717km (3625nm).

Weights: 50 – Empty equipped 9150kg (20,170lb), standard max takeoff 17,600kg (38,800lb), or optionally 18,500kg (40,780lb). 50EX – Empty equipped 9603kg (21,270lb), max takeoff 18,005kg (39,700lb).

Dimensions: Wing span 18.86m (61ft 11in), length 18.52m (61ft 11in), height 6.97m (22ft 11in). Wing area 46.8m^2 (504.1sq ft).

Capacity: Flightcrew of two pilots. A number of cabin seating arrangements are available, depending on the toilet location. Seating for eight or nine with aft toilet, or for up to 12 with forward toilet. Can accommodate three stretchers, two medical attendants and medical equipment in a medevac role.

Production: More than 250 have been ordered since 1979.

History: The trijet Falcon 50 is a very substantial long range upgrade based on the earlier twinjet Mystère/Falcon 20 and 200 family.

The Dassault Falcon 50 was developed for long range trans Atlantic and transcontinental flight sectors, using the Falcon 20 as the design basis. To meet the 6440km (3475nm) range requirement though significant changes meant that the Falcon 50 is for all intents and purposes an all new aircraft. Key new features to achieve the range were the selection of three 16.58kN (3700lb) Garrett TFE731 turbofans, in place of the Falcon 20's two General Electric CF700s, mounted on a new area ruled tail section, plus a new supercritical wing of greater area than that on the 20 and 200. Three engines also offers greater redundancy for flight over oceans and uninhabited regions. Some Falcon 20 components were retained however, the most obvious of these being the nose and fuselage cross section.

The first flight of the prototype Falcon 50 occurred in November 1976, though it wasn't until March 7 1979 that FAA certification was granted. In the meantime the design had been changed to incorporate a supercritical wing, although the original wing's basic planform was retained. A second prototype first flew on February 18 1978, and the first preproduction aircraft on June 13 1978. First customer deliveries began in July 1979.

In April 1995 Dassault announced the long range Falcon 50EX with more fuel efficient TFE731-40 turbofans, 740km (400nm) greater range (at Mach 0.80) than the base Falcon 50 and a new EFIS flightdeck based on the Falcon 2000's with Collins Pro-Line IV avionics. The 50EX also features as standard equipment items offered as options only on the standard Falcon 50.

The Falcon 50EX's maiden flight was on April 10 1996, with first deliveries scheduled for mid 1997.

Photo: A Falcon 50 demonstrator. The Falcon 50 is particularly popular as a government transport. (Dassault)

Dassault Falcon 900

Country of origin: France

Type: Large size transcontinental range corporate jet

Powerplants: 900 – Three 20kN (4500lb) Garrett TFE731-5AR-1C turbofans. 900B – Three 21.1kN (4750lb) AlliedSignal TFE731-5BRs.

Performance: 900 – Max cruising speed 927km/h (500kt), economical cruising speed Mach 0.75. Range with max payload and reserves 6412km (3460nm), with 15 passengers and reserves 6968km (3760nm), with eight pax and reserves 7227km (3900nm). 900B – Same except for range with 15 pax and reserves 7116km (3840nm).

Weights: Empty equipped 10,240kg (22,575kg), max takeoff 20,640kg (45,500lb).

Dimensions: Wing span 19.33m (63ft 5in), length 20.21m (66ft 4in), height 7.55m (24ft 9in). Wing area 49.0m² (527.43sq ft).

Capacity: Flightcrew of two. Main passenger cabin accommodation for between eight and 15 passengers, or up to 18 in a high density configuration.

Production: More than 175 Falcon 900s have been ordered, many of which are in military or government service as VIP transports.

History: As the Falcon 50 was derived from the Falcon/Mystère 20 & 200, the Falcon 900 long range trijet is a substantially revised development of the Falcon 50.

Dassault announced it was developing a new intercontinental range large size business jet based on its Falcon 50 on May 27 1983 at the Paris Airshow. Development culminated in the prototype, *Spirit of Lafayette*, flying for the first time on September 21 1984. A second prototype flew on August 30 1985, and this aircraft demonstrated the type's long range potential by flying nonstop from Paris to Little Rock, Arkansas in the USA for a demonstration tour. French certification was awarded on March 14 1986, FAA certification followed on March 21, and first customer deliveries occurred in December that year.

While of similar overall configuration to the Falcon 50, the Falcon 900 features an all new wider and longer fuselage, which can seat three passengers abreast. The main commonality with the Falcon 50 is the wing, which despite being designed for a considerably lighter aircraft, was adapted almost directly unchanged (and incidentally also appears on the Falcon 2000). The design of the Falcon 900 made use of computer aided modelling, while the aircraft's structure incorporates a degree of composite materials.

From 1991 the standard production model was the Falcon 900B, which differs from the earlier 900 in having more powerful engines, increased range, the ability to operate from unprepared strips and Category II visibility approach clearance. Earlier production 900s can be retrofitted to 900B standard.

The Falcon 900EX is a longer range development launched in October 1994. It features TFE731-60s, a Honeywell Primus 4000 EFIS avionics suite, increased fuel capacity and greater range. Its first flight was on June 1 1995 and first delivery was in May 1996.

Like the smaller Falcon 50, the 900 is used widely as a government VIP transport by a number of nations. Its transcontinental range has also meant it has found a welcome home in the bizjet fleets of a number of large multinational companies.

Photo: The Falcon 900EX. (Dassault)

Dassault Falcon 2000

Country of origin: France

Type: Transcontinental range mid to large size corporate jet

Powerplants: Two 25.6kN (5725lb) CFE (General Electric & Allied-Signal) CFE738-1-1B turbofans.

Performance: Cruising speed 890km/h (480kt). Max certificated altitude 47,000ft. Range at 0.80 Mach cruising speed 5560km (3000nm).

Weights: Empty equipped 9030kg (19,980lb), max takeoff 15,890kg (35,000lb).

Dimensions: Wing span 19.34m (63ft 5in), length 20.23m (66ft 4in), height 7.06m (23ft 2in). Wing area 49.0m² (527.66sq ft).

Capacity: Flightcrew of two. Main cabin seating typically for eight passengers, or up to 12 in a high density layout.

Production: First customer delivery occurred in March 1995. Over 70 on order.

History: In simple terms the Falcon 2000 is a twin engine development of Dassault's successful long range Falcon 900, but a number of crucial design changes ensure that this modern twinjet is quite a different aircraft to its trijet brethren.

The Falcon 2000 is a direct descendant from the Falcon 900 and shares the 900's wing and forward fuselage, but there are a number of both obvious and unnoticeable design changes. From the start the Falcon 2000 was designed with a range of 5560km (3000nm) in mind, which is less than the transcontinental 900's range. This design range removed the need for the redundancy of three engines for long range overwater flights, allowing the two new engines to be fitted, which offer considerable maintenance and operating economics benefits. The twin engines were in fact developed specifically for the Falcon 2000 in a partnership between General Electric and AlliedSignal, known as CFE. The fuselage meanwhile houses less fuel, passengers and baggage than the 900.

Another noticeable design change between the 900 and 2000 is the area ruled rear fuselage. Dassault engineers found that the three engine layout of the 900 to be aerodynamically efficient, whereas the twin engine design of the 2000 would have been comparatively draggy. To combat this and reduce drag to desired levels Dassault designed an area ruled (or Coke bottle) rear fuselage, using its Catia three dimensional computer aided design program.

Minor modifications made to the wing include a modified leading edge and the inboard slats have been removed, while the cockpit features a Collins four screen EFIS system.

Dassault has a number of industry partners in the Falcon 2000 program, foremost of these being Alenia, which is a 25% risk sharing partner. Alenia in turn has subcontracted some work to Dee Howard and Piaggio.

Dassault announced it was developing the Falcon 2000, then known as the Falcon X, in June 1989. First flight occurred on March 4 1993 and certification was awarded in November 1994. The first customer delivery occurred in March 1995.

Photo: The transcontinental 2000 is the latest in a successful line of Dassault Falcon corporate jets. (Dassault)

De Havilland Canada DHC-1 Chipmunk

Country of origin: Canada

Type: Tandem seat basic trainer and sport aircraft

Powerplant: One 108kW (145hp) de Havilland Gipsy Major 8 four cylinder inverted inline engine, driving a two blade fixed pitch wooden propeller.

Performance: Max speed at sea level 223km/h (120kt), cruising speed 200km/h (108kt). Initial rate of climb 900ft/min. Service ceiling 17,200ft. Endurance 2.3 hours or a 450km (243nm) max range.

Weights: Empty 526kg (1158lb), max takeoff weight 914kg (2014lb).

Dimensions: Wing span 10.46m (34ft 4in), length 7.75m (25ft 5in), height 2.13m (7ft 0in). Wing area 15.9m^2 (172sq ft).

Capacity: Seating for two in tandem, usually pilot and trainee or pilot and passenger. Small numbers were modified for crop spraying and fitted with a chemical hopper in place of the front cockpit.

Production: A total of 1291 Chipmunks built, including 217 in Canada, 60 under licence in Portugal and 1014 in Britain. Most of these were built originally for military customers, but many now fly with private operators.

History: Known affectionately as the Chippie, de Havilland Canada's Chipmunk was primarily designed in response to a growing need to replace the Royal Air Force's then current two seat basic trainer, the ageing Tiger Moth biplane (described separately).

With a full design workload, courtesy of the revolutionary Comet jet airliner project among others, the de Havilland company decided to hand design responsibility for the new trainer to its Canadian subsidiary, de Havilland Canada. Design leadership for DHC's first aircraft was the responsibility of W J Jakimuk who had emigrated to Canada from Poland in 1940 and was previously responsible for the design of the PZL 24 and PZL 50 Jastrab fighters, and the DH.95 Flamingo airliner.

His new aircraft was designated the DHC-1 Chipmunk and flew for the first time on May 22 1946, and first deliveries took place the following year. Main Chipmunk models included the Canadian built DHC-1B-1 and DHC-1B-2 for the RCAF, these were known as the T.30 in British service, and many featured clear view blown canopies, while main British production models included the initial T.10 and T.20 for the RAF, and civilian T.21.

Civilianised versions of RAF aircraft became available in large numbers from the late 1950s, and the T.10 became the Mk.22 in civil service, while the Mk.22A was a modification to RAF T.10s with greater fuel capacity. Farm Aviation Services in the UK heavily modified Chipmunks with a hopper tank in place of the forward cockpit for spraying duties, these aircraft were designated Mk.23s. A small number of similar conversions were performed in Australia by Sasin/Aerostructures.

In civil service the Chipmunk is a very popular sport and private aircraft, while a number are still used for pilot training and tailwheel endorsements. Some have also been extensively modified with the installation of Lycoming or Continental engines.

Photo: Chipmunks nowadays are prized as classic aircraft appreciating in value. Large numbers have been restored. (Bill Lines)

De Havilland Canada DHC-2 Beaver

Country of origin: Canada

Type: STOL utility transport

Powerplant: Mk I – One 335kW (450hp) Pratt & Whitney R-985 Wasp Junior nine cylinder radial piston engine driving a two blade variable pitch Hamilton Standard propeller. Mk III – One 430kW (578eshp) Pratt & Whitney Canada PT6A-6 or PT6A-20 turboprop driving a three blade constant speed Hartzell propeller.

Performance: Mk I – Max speed 225km/h (121kt), max cruising speed 217km/h (117kt), normal cruising speed 201km/h (109kt). Initial rate of climb 1020ft/min. Service ceiling 18,000ft. Max range with reserves 1252km (676nm). Mk III – Max speed 274km/h (148kt), max cruising speed 253km/h (137kt), long range cruising speed 225km/h (122kt). Initial rate of climb 1185ft/min. Service ceiling 20,000ft. Max range with reserves 1090km (588nm).

Weights: Mk I – Empty 1293kg (2850lb), max takeoff 2313kg (5100lb). Mk I seaplane – Operating empty 1506kg (3316lb), max takeoff 2309kg (5090lb). Mk III – Empty 1175kg (2590lb), max takeoff 2436kg (5370lb).

Dimensions: Mk I – Wing span 14.63m (48ft 0in), length 9.25m (30ft 4in), height 2.75m (9ft 0in). Wing area 23.1m^2 (250sq ft). Mk I – seaplane – Same except for length 9.98m (32ft 9in), height 3.18m (10ft 5in). Mk III – Same as Mk I except for length 10.74m (35ft 3in).

Capacity: Pilot and passenger on flightdeck plus main cabin seating for six. The 'Ag-Beaver' is fitted with a 0.99m^3 (35cu ft) chemical hopper.

Production: In production between 1948 and 1968, 1692 Beavers of both versions were built, including approximately 60 Turbo Beavers, and 974 aircraft delivered to the US military and many others delivered to foreign military air arms. Several hundred remain in service with civilian operators.

History: De Havilland Canada's first purpose designed bush aircraft, the Beaver has the distinction of also being that company's most successful program sales wise (both military or civil), with almost 1700 built during a two decade production run.

Development work of de Havilland Canada's second indigenous design began in 1946. The Ontario Department of Lands and Forests had considerable input into the final design and configuration of this rugged and versatile utility. A prototype flew on August 16 1947, with seating for five or six, although the production Beaver grew slightly to seat an extra two passengers by the time civil certification was awarded in March 1948.

The only major development of the Beaver (aside from a one off powered by a 410kW/550hp Alvis Leonides 502/4 radial engine) was the Turbo Beaver. First flown in December 1963 it featured the Pratt & Whitney PT6A-6 turboprop, which offered lower empty and higher takeoff weights, and even better STOL performance. The Turbo Beaver's cabin was also longer, allowing maximum accommodation for 11, including the pilot. Externally, the Turbo Beaver had a much longer and reprofiled nose, and squared off vertical tail. DHC also offered conversion kits enabling piston powered Beavers to be upgraded to Turbo standard.

Photo: A PT6 powered Turbo Beaver floatplane. (Gary Gentle)

De Havilland Canada DHC-3 Otter

Country of origin: Canada

Type: STOL utility transport

Powerplant: One 447kW (600hp) Pratt & Whitney R-1340-S1H1-G or R-1340-S3H1-G nine cylinder radial piston engine driving a three blade Hamilton Standard constant speed propeller.

Performance: Max speed 257km/h (140kt), economical cruising speed at sea level 195km/h (105kt). Initial rate of climb 850ft/min. Service ceiling 18,800ft. Max range with reserves 1520km (820nm), range with a 950kg (2100lb) payload and reserves 1410km (760nm).

Weights: Landplane – Basic operating 2010kg (4431lb), max takeoff 3629kg (8000lb). Floatplane – Basic operating 2219kg (4892lb), max takeoff 3614kg (7967lb).

Dimensions: Wing span 17.69m (58ft 0in), length 12.80m (41ft 10in), height 3.83m (12ft 7in), floatplane height 4.57m (15ft 0in). Wing area 34.8m^2 (375sq ft).

Capacity: Flightcrew of two. Normal main cabin seating for nine passengers, max seating for 10. As an aerial ambulance can carry six stretchers and four passengers or three stretchers and seven passengers.

Production: A total of 460 Otters built including for military air arms in 11 nations.

History: Another in de Havilland Canada's successful line of rugged and useful STOL utility transports, the Otter was conceived to be capable of performing the same roles as the earlier and highly successful Beaver, but was bigger.

Using the same overall configuration of the earlier and highly successful DHC-2 Beaver, the Otter is much larger overall. The Otter in fact began life as the King Beaver, but compared to the Beaver is longer, has greater span wings and is much heavier. Seating in the main cabin is for 10 or 11, whereas the Beaver could seat seven. Power is supplied by a 450kW (600hp) Pratt & Whitney R-1340 Wasp radial. Like the Beaver the Otter can be fitted with skis and floats. The amphibious floatplane Otter features a unique four unit retractable undercarriage, with the wheels retracting into the floats.

De Havilland Canada began design work on the DHC-3 Otter in January 1951, the company's design efforts culminating in the type's first flight on December 12 1951. Canadian certification followed in November 1952.

De Havilland Canada demonstrated the Otter to the US Army, and subsequently that service went on to become the largest DHC-3 operator (as the U-1). Other military users included Australia, Canada and India.

Small numbers of Otters were converted to turbine power by Cox Air Services of Alberta, Canada. Changes included a Pratt & Whitney Canada PT6A turboprop, a lower empty weight of 1692kg (3703lb) and a higher maximum speed of 267km/h (144kt). It was called the Cox Turbo Single Otter, to avoid confusion with the Twin Otter.

The Otter found a significant niche as a bush aircraft, although today only small numbers remain in use.

Photo: The Otter is substantially larger than the Beaver despite similar overall configurations. (Lenn Bayliss)

De Havilland Canada DHC-4 Caribou

Country of origin: Canada

Type: STOL utility transport

Powerplants: DHC-4A – Two 1080kW (1450shp) Pratt & Whitney R-2000-7M2 14 cylinder twin row radial piston engines driving three blade propellers.

Performance: DHC-4A – Max speed 347km/h (187kt), normal cruising speed 293km/h (158kt). Initial rate of climb 1355ft/min. Service ceiling 24,800ft. Range with max payload 390km (210nm), range with max fuel 2105km (1135nm).

Weights: DHC-4A – Basic operating 8293kg (18,260lb), standard max takeoff 12,930kg (28,500lb), military overload max takeoff 14,195kg (28,500lb).

Dimensions: Wing span 29.15m (95ft 8in), length 22.13m (72ft 7in), height 9.68m (31ft 9in). Wing area 84.7m^2 (912sq ft).

Capacity: Flightcrew of two. Can carry almost four tonnes (8000lb) of cargo in freighter configuration. Can seat approximately 30 passengers.

Production: DHC-4 Caribou production ended in 1983 after 307 had been built, most of which were for military customers. A small number survived in commercial service in 1996.

History: De Havilland Canada's fourth design was a big step up in size compared with its earlier products, and was the first powered by two engines, but was similar in that it is a rugged STOL utility that in commercial service found itself a small niche.

De Havilland Canada originally designed the DHC-4 in response to a US Army requirement for a for a tactical airlifter to supply the battlefront with troops and supplies and evacuate casualties on the return journey. With assistance from Canada's Department of Defence Production DHC built a prototype demonstrator that flew for the first time on July 30 1958.

Impressed with the DHC-4's STOL capabilities and potential, the US Army ordered five for evaluation as the YAC-1. That service went on to become the largest Caribou operator, taking delivery of 159. The AC-1 designation was later changed to CV-2, and then C-7 when the US Army's CV-2s were transferred to the US Air Force in 1966. US and Australian Caribou saw extensive service during the Vietnam conflict. In fact some US Caribou were captured by North Vietnamese forces and remained in service with that country through the late 1970s. Other notable military operators included Canada, Malaysia, India and Spain.

The majority of Caribou production was for military operators, but the type's ruggedness and excellent STOL capabilities also appealed to a select group of commercial users. US certification was awarded on December 23 1960. Ansett-MAL, who operated a single example in the New Guinea highlands, and AMOCO Ecuador were early customers, as was Air America (a CIA front in South East Asia for covert operations). Other Caribou entered service after being retired from their military users.

Today only a handful are in civil use, the Caribou's thirsty twin row radial engines making commercial operations uneconomic where its STOL performance is not a factor.

Photo: The Caribou's unique design makes it an excellent airlifter where true STOL performance is required. (Paul Howard)

De Havilland Canada DHC-6 Twin Otter

Country of origin: Canada

Type: STOL turboprop airliner and utility transport

Powerplants: 100 – Two 431kW (578shp) Pratt & Whitney Canada (formerly United Aircraft of Canada) PT6A-20 turboprops driving three blade propellers. 300 – Two 460kW (620shp) P&WC PT6A-27s.

Performance: 100 – Max cruising speed 297km/h (160kt). Range with max fuel 1427km (771nm), range with 975kg (2150lb) payload 1344km (727nm). 300 – Max cruising speed 338km/h (182kt). Initial rate of climb 1600ft/min. Range with 1135kg (2500lb) payload 1297km (700nm), range with a 860kg (1900lb) payload and wing tanks 1705km (920nm).

Weights: 100 – Basic operating empty 2653kg (5850lb), max takeoff 4763kg (10,500lb). 300 – Operating empty 3363kg (7415lb), max takeoff 5670kg (12,500lb).

Dimensions: 100 – Wing span 19.81m (65ft 0in), length 15.09m (49ft 6in), height 5.94m (19ft 6in). Wing area 39.0m² (420sq ft). 300 – Same except for length 15.77m (51ft 9in), or 15.09m (49ft 6in) for seaplane variants.

Capacity: Flightcrew of two. Standard commuter interior seats 20 at three abreast and 76cm (30in) pitch. Can be configured as an executive transport, freighter, aerial ambulance and survey aircraft.

Production: Production has been completed, and comprised 115 Series 100 aircraft, 115 Series 200s and 614 Series 300s.

History: In terms of civil sales the versatile Twin Otter has been de Havilland Canada's most successful commercial design, in part due to the type's rugged construction and handy STOL performance.

Development of the Twin Otter dates back to January 1964 when de Havilland Canada started design work on a new STOL twin turboprop commuter airliner (seating between 13 and 18) and utility transport. The new aircraft was designated the DHC-6 and construction of the prototype began in November that year, resulting in the type's first flight on May 20 1965. Receiving certification in mid 1966, the first Twin Otter entered service with long time de Havilland Canada supporter the Ontario Department of Lands in Canada.

The first production aircraft were known as Series 100, design features including double slotted trailing edge flaps and ailerons on the wings that can act in unison to boost STOL performance. In comparison with the later Series 200 and 300s, the 100s are distinguishable by their shorter noses, while in common with the later aircraft skis and floats can be fitted.

The main addition to the Series 200, which was introduced in April 1968, was the extended nose, which, together with a reconfigured storage compartment in the rear cabin, greatly increased baggage stowage area. The Series 300 was introduced from the 231st production aircraft in 1969. It too featured the lengthened nose, but also introduced more powerful engines, thus allowing a 450kg (1000lb) increase in takeoff weight and a 20 seat interior. Production ceased in late 1988. Further, six 300S enhanced STOL performance DHC-6-300s were built in the mid 1970s.

Photo: A Series 300 Twin Otter floatplane on Vancouver Harbour. (Lenn Bayliss)

De Havilland Canada Dash 7

Country of origin: Canada

Type: STOL turboprop airliner

Powerplants: Four 835kW (1220shp) Pratt & Whitney Canada PT6A-50 turboprops driving four blade constant speed Hamilton Standard propellers.

Performance: Max cruising speed 428km/h (230kt), long range cruising speed 400km/h (215kt). Service ceiling 21,000ft. STOL takeoff distance at 18,600kg (41,000lb) TO weight 670m (2260ft). Range with 50 passengers and reserves 1270km (690nm), range with standard fuel and three tonne payload 2168km (1170nm). 150 – Range with 50 pax at max cruising speed 2110km (1140nm), with max fuel 4670km (2525nm).

Weights: 100 – Empty 12,247kg (27,000lb), operating empty 12,560kg (27,690lb), max takeoff 19,958kg (44,000lb). 150 – Operating empty 12,465kg (27,480lb), max takeoff 21,320kg (47,000lb).

Dimensions: Wing span 28.35m (93ft 0in), length 24.58m (80ft 8in), height 7.98m (26ft 2in). Wing area 79.9m² (860.0sq ft).

Capacity: Flightcrew of two. Max seating for 54 at four abreast and 74cm (29in) pitch, 50 passengers at 81cm (32in) pitch. In freighter configuration can carry five standard pallets.

Production: 111 Dash 7s were built between 1977 and 1988. Approximately 75 were in commercial service as of late 1996.

History: Despite being out of production for some years now, the four engine de Havilland Canada Dash 7 is still unrivalled in its STOL and low noise capabilities.

The Dash 7 (or DHC-7) was designed primarily as a specialised STOL 50 seat airliner capable of operating from strips as short as 915m (3000ft) in length. The main design features to achieve such a capability were an advanced wing and four Pratt & Whitney PT6A turboprops. Double slotted trailing edge flaps run the entire span of the high mounted wing, dramatically increasing the lifting surface available for takeoff. Extra lift is also generated through the air flowing over the wing from the relatively slow turning propellers. The wings also feature two pairs of spoilers each, the inboard pair of which also operate as lift dumpers, the outboard pair can also act differentially in conjunction with the ailerons to boost roll control.

Financial backing from the Canadian Government allowed the launch of the DHC-7 program in the early 1970s, resulting in the first flight of the first of two development aircraft on March 27 1975. The first production Dash 7 flew on March 3 1977, and the type entered service in February the following year. The standard passenger carrying Dash 7 is the Series 100, while the type was also offered in pure freighter form as the Series 101.

The only major development of the Dash 7 was the Series 150, which featured a higher max takeoff weight and greater fuel capacity, boosting range. The Series 151 was the equivalent freighter. Production of the Dash 7 ended in 1988, following Boeing's takeover of DHC.

Photo: The Dash 7 was the first aircraft licenced to use London City Airport. This is one of four operated by Brymon Aviation in British Airways Express livery. (Keith Gaskell)

De Havilland Dash 8-100 & -200

Country of origin: Canada

Type: Short range turboprop airliner

Powerplants: 100 – Two 1490kW (2000shp) Pratt & Whitney Canada PW120A turboprops driving four blade constant speed Hamilton Standard propellers. 100B – Two 1605kW (2150shp) PW121As. 200 – Two 1605kW (2150shp) PW123Cs in 200A, or two PW123Ds in 200B.

Performance: 100A – Max cruising speed 490km/h (265kt), long range cruising speed 440km/h (237kt). Initial rate of climb 1560ft/min. Range with full passenger load, fuel and reserves 1520km (820nm), range with a 2720kg (6000lb) payload 2040km (1100nm). 100B – Same except max cruising speed of 500km/h (270kt). 200A & 200B – Same except max cruising speed 555km/h (300kt).

Weights: 100A – Operating empty 10,250kg (22,600lb), max takeoff 15,650kg (34,500lb). 100B – Operating empty 10,273kg (22,648lb), max takeoff 16,465kg (36,300lb). 200A & 200B – Operating empty 10,380kg (22,886lb), max takeoff 16,465kg (36,300lb).

Dimensions: Wing span 25.91m (85ft 0in), length 22.25m (73ft 0in), height 7.49m (24ft 7in). Wing area 54.4m^2 (585.0sq ft).

Capacity: Flightcrew of two. Typical passenger seating for 37 at four abreast and 79cm (31in) pitch, max seating for 40.

Production: Over 290 Dash 8-100s had been ordered by late 1996, of which 270 were in service. 45 Dash 8-200s were on order.

History: The de Havilland Dash 8 has carved itself a substantial customer base in the fiercely competitive commuter airliner market.

De Havilland began development of the Dash 8 in the late 1970s in response to what it saw as a considerable market demand for a new generation 30 to 40 seat commuter airliner. Design efforts climaxed in the first flight of the first of two pre production aircraft on June 20 1983, and Canadian certification was awarded on September 28 1984. The first customer delivery was to norOntair of Canada on October 23 1984.

Like the Dash 7, the Dash 8 features a high mounted wing and T-tail, and has an advanced flight control system and large full length trailing edge flaps. Power meanwhile is supplied by two Pratt & Whitney Canada PW120 series (originally designated PT7A) turboprops.

Initial Dash 8 production was of the Series 100, which was followed by the Series 100A in 1990. The 100A features a revised interior with extra headroom and PW120A turboprops. The Series 100B has been on offer since 1992 and has more powerful PW121s for better climb and airfield performance.

Significant performance benefits are offered by the Series 200 which was announced in 1992 and has been available for delivery since 1994. It features more powerful PW123C engines, and thus has higher cruising speeds, plus greater commonality with the stretched Dash 8-300 (described separately). The 200B derivative has PW123Bs for better hot and high performance. Surveillance Australia launched the 200 with an order for three, equipped with search radar and FLIR for customs use. Another was ordered for use as a corporate shuttle in Columbia.

Photo: Qantas regional airlines Eastern, Southern and Sunstate between them operate 13 Dash 8-100s (pictured) and one Dash 8-200. (Rob Finlayson)

De Havilland Dash 8-300 & -400

Country of origin: Canada

Type: Short range turboprop commuter airliners

Powerplants: 300 – Two 1775kW (2380shp) Pratt & Whitney Canada PW123 turboprops, driving four blade Hamilton Standard propellers. 400 – Two 3600kW (4830shp) Pratt & Whitney Canada PW150 turboprops driving six blade Dowty composite propellers.

Performance: 300 – Max cruising speed 532km/h (287kt). Initial rate of climb 1800ft/min. Service ceiling 25,000ft. Range with full passenger load and reserves 1538km (830nm), with 2720kg (6000lb) payload 1612km (870nm). 400 – Max cruising speed 650km/h (350kt). Range at max cruising speed with 70 pax 2425km (1310nm).

Weights: 300 – Operating empty 11,657kg (25,700lb), standard max takeoff 18,642kg (41,100lb). 400 – Operating empty 16,105kg (35,500lb), standard max takeoff 26,990kg (59,500lb).

Dimensions: 300 – Wing span 27.43m (90ft 0in), length 25.68m (84ft 3in), height 7.49m (24ft 7in). Wing area 56.2m^2 (605sq ft). 400 – Wing span 28.42m (93ft 3in), length 32.99m (108ft 3in), height 8.28m (27ft 2in). Wing area 63.1m^2 (679.0sq ft).

Capacity: 300 – Flightcrew of two. Standard single class seating for 50 passengers at four abreast and 81cm (32in) pitch. 400 – Standard seating for 70, or up to 78 in a high density configuration.

Production: Total orders for Dash 8-300s stood at over 125 by late 1996, of which 110 were in service. 19 Dash 8-400s were on order.

History: Following the success of the Dash 8-100 series, stretched versions of greater capacity became logical developments.

De Havilland Canada (now de Havilland Inc) launched full scale development of a stretched version of its Dash 8 regional airliner during 1986, approximately two years after the standard fuselage length aircraft had entered service. The first series 300 aircraft was in fact the prototype Dash 8 converted to the new length, and it flew for the first time in its new configuration on May 15 1987. Flight testing culminated in the awarding of Canadian certification in February 1989, with the first delivery to Time Air following late that same month. US certification was awarded in June 1989.

The stretch comprises fuselage plugs forward and aft of the wing, an increase in length of 3.43m (11ft 3in). In addition, the wings are greater in span. The fuselage stretch increases typical seating capacity to 50, or for up to 56, putting it in the same class as the Fokker 50. Other changes compared with the Dash 8-100 were minor, but included a larger, repositioned galley, a new galley service door and optional APU.

The Dash 8-300 is offered in two basic forms, the standard 300, and the 300A, which introduced higher gross weights, interior improvements (as on the Dash 8-100A), and optional PW123B engines.

De Havilland launched a further stretch of the Dash 8, the Dash 8 Series 400, in June 1995. The Dash 8-400 will seat 70 passengers and have new 3600kW (4830shp) Pratt & Whitney PW1150 turboprops with FADEC and advanced six blade propellers, giving a max cruising speed of 650km/h (350kt). First flight is planned for December 1997, with first deliveries in early 1999. Mitsubishi Heavy Industries is a risk sharing partner, responsible for the design and manufacture of the fuselage and tail.

Photo: The 70 seat Dash 8-400 is due to fly in December 1997.

De Havilland DH.82 Tiger Moth

Country of origin: United Kingdom

Type: Two seat basic trainer and sport biplane

Powerplant: DH.82A – One 95kW (130hp) de Havilland Gipsy Major 1 inline and inverted four cylinder piston engine, driving a fixed pitch two blade wooden propeller.

Performance: DH.82A – Max speed 175km/h (95kt), max cruising speed 160km/h (87kt), economical cruising speed 145km/h (78kt). Initial rate of climb 673ft/min. Service ceiling 13,600ft. Range with max fuel 459km (248nm).

Weights: DH.82A – Empty 506kg (1115lb), max takeoff 828kg (1825lb).

Dimensions: Wing span 8.94m (29ft 4in), length 7.29m (23ft 11in), height 2.70m (8ft 10in). Wing area 22.2m² (239sq ft).

Capacity: Seating for two in tandem open cockpits. Pilot in command usually operates aircraft from rear cockpit.

Production: A total of 8492 Tiger Moths were built, including 5161 in the UK (including 1153 prewar), and 1747 in Canada, 1085 in Australia, 345 in New Zealand, 91 in Portugal, 37 in Norway and 23 in Sweden.

History: One of the most famous biplane and training aircraft in the world, the much loved Tiger Moth was produced in large numbers for wartime service as a basic pilot trainer, and today is a highly sought after private aircraft.

The DH.82 Tiger Moth is a development of de Havilland's successful and famous Moth line of biplanes. Based on the DH.60T Moth Trainer, the Tiger Moth flew for the first time on October 26 1931. Like the earlier Moth and Gipsy Moth the new aircraft was a two place biplane and featured a Gipsy Major engine and both wooden and metal construction. Difficulty bailing out in an emergency was a problem with the earlier aircraft, and this was addressed through repositioning the struts forward of the front cockpit. To counter centre of gravity problems that would have resulted, the wings were given a modest sweepback angle.

The DH.82 attracted the interest of Britain's Royal Air Force, with the first of what would ultimately be several thousand Tiger Moths entering service with the RAF in 1932. The initial production DH.82s were powered by 80kW (120hp) engines, while the DH.82A introduced in 1937 featured a 97kW (130hp) engine, and was the most produced version. Most prewar production was against military orders, although some civil machines were built. As Britain's standard basic pilot training aircraft, production of the Tiger Moth increased greatly during WW2, and some 4000 were built in the UK. During the war large numbers were also built in Canada (as the DH.82C with a Gipsy Major IC or 120kW/160hp Pirate D.4 engine), Australia and New Zealand.

Postwar, surplus military Tiger Moths proved extremely popular with private owners, a situation which continues to this day. Many examples were converted for agricultural work, particularly in Australia and New Zealand, while small numbers of the four seat Jackaroo conversion were built from 1957. Today the Tiger Moth remains very popular, and in some countries the Tiger Moth populations are actually growing as retired machines are restored and returned to the air.

Photo: This Tiger Moth is painted up in the Red Baron's famous blood red scheme as featured on his Fokker Triplane. (Peter Martinson)

De Havilland DH.104 Dove

Country or origin: United Kingdom

Type: Eight seat commuter airliner and executive transport

Powerplants: Dove 1 – Two 245kW (330hp) de Havilland Gipsy Queen 70-3 supercharged inverted six cylinder inline engines driving three blade constant speed propellers. Dove 8 – Two 300kW (400hp) Gipsy Queen 70 Mk.3s.

Performance: Dove 1 – Max speed 338km/h (182kt), max cruising speed 322km/h (174kt), long range cruising speed 266km/h (144kt). Initial rate of climb 750ft/min. Service ceiling 20,000ft. Max range 1610km (890nm). Dove 8 – Max speed 370km/h (200kt), max cruising speed 338km/h (183kt), long range cruising speed 300km/h (163kt). Initial rate of climb 1135ft/min. Service ceiling 21,700ft. Max range 1416km (765nm).

Weights: Dove 1 – Empty 2563kg (5650lb), max takeoff 3856kg (8500lb). Dove 8 – Empty 2869kg (6325lb), max takeoff 4060kg (8950lb).

Dimensions: Wing span 17.37m (57ft 0in), length 11.96m (39ft 3in), height 4.06m (13ft 4in). Wing area 31.1m² (335sq ft).

Capacity: Flightcrew of two pilots. Main cabin seating for eight passengers, max cabin seating for 11 in a modified cabin arrangement.

Production: 544 Doves were built, including 200 for military operators. A small number remain in commercial service.

History: The Dove was Britain's first successful post war civil aircraft, and one of the few successful Brabazon Committee projects.

The Brabazon Committee was established during WW2 to define requirements for British postwar civil aircraft. While the government established committee was responsible for a number of complete failures such as the Bristol Brabazon, its studies did result in the highly successful Vickers Viscount (described elsewhere) and the de Havilland Dove. The Dove was developed in response to a defined requirement for a small feederliner for UK and Commonwealth domestic services. The resulting aircraft featured new versions of the Gipsy Queen engine, a raised flightdeck and separate passenger cabin and all metal construction. The first DH.104 Dove flew for the first time on September 25 1945.

Steady sales success was boosted by significant military orders (RAF versions were known as the Devon, Royal Navy aircraft the Sea Devon). One other large market for the Dove was as an executive transport, a large number of thus configured aircraft were sold in the USA.

The Dove was in production until the mid 1960s (by which time it was a Hawker Siddeley product), and a number of variants were built. These were the initial Series 1, the executive interior Series 2, the military Series 4, the Series 5 with greater range and more powerful engines, the Series 6 (and 6A for the US) executive version of the Series 5, Series 6BA with more powerful engines, Series 7 (Series 7A for the US) with more powerful engines and raised Heron style flightdeck, and Series 8 (8A or Custom 800 in the US) with five seat interior.

In the USA Riley Aeronautics offered conversions of the Dove with two 300kW (400hp) Lycoming IO-720 flat eight piston engines. The conversion is known as the Riley 400, and aside from the engines, customers could fit a swept back tail, a new instrument panel and a steel spar capped wing. The first Riley 400 flew in 1963.

Photo: A Gipsy Queen powered Dove.

De Havilland DH.114 Heron

Country of origin: United Kingdom

Type: Four engined commuter airliner

Powerplants: Series 2 – Four 185kW (250hp) de Havilland (later Bristol Siddeley) Gipsy Queen 30 Mk 2 six cylinder inline piston engines, driving two blade de Havilland constant speed propellers. Series 2E/A1 – Four 215kW (290hp) Lycoming IO-540-B1A5 flat six piston engines driving three blade constant speed props.

Performance: Series 2 – Cruising speed 307km/h (166kt), economical cruising speed 295km/h (160kt). Initial rate of climb 1075ft/min. Service ceiling 17,200ft. Range with max fuel and reserves 2873km (1550nm).

Weights: Empty 3848kg (8484lb), max takeoff 6124kg (13,500lb).

Dimensions: Wing span 21.80m (71ft 6in), length 14.80m (48ft 6in), height 4.75m (15ft 7in). Wing area 46.4m^2 (499sq ft).

Capacity: Flightcrew of two. Typical main cabin seating for 14 at two abreast with a central aisle. Alternative seating for 15 or 17. Executive versions with seating for eight.

Production: 149 Herons built comprising 51 Series 1s and 98 Series 2. Conversions include 28 Riley Herons, six by Tawron, 29 by Prinair and 13 Saunders ST-27s. A handful remain in commercial service.

History: The DH.114 Heron is a stretched four engined development of de Havilland's successful DH.104 Dove.

Only a few years later in development than the Dove on which it was based, design work on the Heron began in the late 1940s, resulting in the prototype's first flight on May 10 1950 (the Dove first flew in 1945). In designing the Heron, de Havilland made as much use of Dove componentry as possible, and so both types feature the distinctive slightly raised cockpit and separate main cabin and metal construction. Initial Heron production aircraft also featured fixed undercarriage (unlike the retractable gear dove). Major differences though are the four 185kW (250hp) Gipsy Queen engines (as opposed to two 255 to 300kW/340 to 400hp Gipsy Queen 70s), greater span wings, a longer and taller fuselage and greater seating capacity. The first Series 1 production Herons were delivered to New Zealand National Airways in 1952.

Also in 1952 the first Series 2 Heron took to the skies for the first time, on December 14. The main improvement over the 1 was retractable undercarriage, which for a weight penalty of 75kg (165lb) increased cruising speed by 32km/h (17kt), while other standard and optional improvements were minor in nature. The Heron 2A was certificated for use in the USA, and an equivalent 2B executive version was also offered. The 2C and equivalent executive 2D have greater weights.

The Heron has been the subject of numerous conversion programs. In the USA Riley converted 20 to be powered by Lycoming IO-540s (eight more were converted in Australia), while Prinair converted a further 29 to Lycoming power.

The most ambitious Heron conversions were performed by Saunders, whose ST-27 conversions feature two Pratt & Whitney Canada PT6 turboprops and a stretched fuselage. In addition, Tawron converted six Series 1 Herons with Continental engines.

Photo: A Lycoming powered Heron.

Dornier Do 27

Country of origin: Germany

Type: Four to six seat STOL utility light aircraft

Powerplant: Do 27H-2 – One 255kW (340hp) Lycoming GSO-480-B1B6 flat six piston engine, driving a three blade Hartzell propeller. Do 27Q-5 – One 200kW (270hp) GSO-480-B1A6 driving a two blade prop.

Performance: Do 27H-2 – Max speed 245km/h (132kt), high speed cruise 212km/h (115kt), economical cruising speed 180km/h (97kt). Initial rate of climb 965ft/min. Service ceiling 22,000ft. Range with max fuel and no reserves 1360km (735nm). Do 27Q-5 – Max speed 232km/h (125kt), 75% power cruising speed 211km/h (114kt), 60% power cruising speed 190km/h (103kt), economical cruising speed 175km/h (95kt). Initial rate of climb 650ft/min. Service ceiling 10,800ft. Range with max fuel and no reserves 1102km (595nm).

Weights: Do 27H-2 – Empty equipped 1170kg (2580lb), max takeoff 1848kg (4070lb). Do 27Q-5 – Empty equipped 1130kg (2490lb), max takeoff 1848kg (4070lb).

Dimensions: Do 27H-2 & Q-5 – Wing span 12.00m (39ft 5in), length 9.60m (31ft 6in), height 2.80m (9ft 2in). Wing area 19.4m^2 (208.8sq ft).

Capacity: Pilot and passenger side by side with between four and six passengers behind them. Can be configured for freight.

Production: Total Do 27 production of 577, including 195 Do 27A-1s, 75 Do 27A-3s, 54 A-4s, 88 D-1s, 18 B-3s, one H-1, 12 H-2s, one Q-3, 34 Q-4s and one Q-5.

History: The Dornier Do 27 was the first military aircraft to be built in any numbers in the then West Germany since World War 2, but was also built for civil customers in limited numbers.

The Do 27 traces back to the Do 25, which Professor Claude Dornier (Dornier was responsible for the Do 17 medium bomber in WW2) designed in Spain for a Spanish military requirement for a light general purpose utility aircraft. Two prototype Do 25s were built, the first was powered by a 110kW (150hp) ENMA Tigre G-IVB engine and flew for the first time on June 25 1954. Subsequently CASA built 50 production aircraft as Do 27As for the Spanish air force (Spain designated the type the C-127).

Following this success the German military ordered the Do 27 in large numbers. A total of 428 were delivered to German forces from the mid 1950s to 1960, although these aircraft have now been retired. Small numbers were built for other military customers, and others for commercial use.

Features of the Do 27 design include a flat six Lycoming engine, a wide and relatively roomy cabin, wide track undercarriage and excellent STOL performance. The STOL performance in particular suited the Do 27 for use in undeveloped countries, and several have seen service in Africa and Papua New Guinea.

Models of the Do 27 include the initial Do 27A and dual control Do 27B for Germany; the Do 27-H series that was based on the A-4 but with a more powerful engine and three blade prop; and the Do 27Q series, equivalent to the Do 27A.

Photo: The Do 27 was postwar one of Germany's first major aircraft design and manufacturing programs. Shown is an A4. (Jim Thorn)

Dornier Do 28 & 128

Country of origin: Germany

Type: STOL utility transports

Powerplants: Do 28D-2 – Two 285kW (380hp) Lycoming IGSO-540-A1E flat six piston engines driving three blade constant speed Hartzell propellers. 128-6 – Two 300kW (400shp) Pratt & Whitney Canada PT6A-110 turboprops.

Performance: Do 28D-2 – Max speed 325km/h (175kt), max cruising speed 306km/h (165kt), economical cruising speed 241km/h (130kt). Max rate of climb 1160ft/min. Service ceiling 25,200ft. Range with max payload 1050km (566nm). 128-6 – Max speed 340km/h (183kt), max cruising speed 330km/h (178kt), econ cruising speed 256km/h (138kt). Initial rate of climb 1260ft/min. Service ceiling 32,600ft. Range with max fuel at econ cruising speed 1825nm (985nm), with a 805kg (1774lb) payload 1460km (788nm).

Weights: Do 28D-2 – Empty 2328kg (5132lb), max takeoff 3842kg (8470lb). 128-6 – Empty 2540kg (5600lb), max takeoff 4350kg (9590lb).

Dimensions: Do 28D-2 – Wing span 15.55m (51ft 0in), length 11.41m (37ft 5in), height 3.90m (12ft 10in). Wing area 29.0m^2 (312sq ft). 128-6 – Same except for wing span 15.85m (52ft 0in).

Capacity: One or two pilots on flightdeck and seating in main cabin for 10 or 12 seats two abreast with a centre aisle.

Production: Total Do 28 and 128-2 production was over 200 units including military orders, total 128-6 production approximately 25.

History: The Do 28 Skyservant was the second aircraft to bear the Do 28 designation, but is similar only in overall configuration to the original Do 28.

Dornier's first Do 28 was first flown in 1959 and was a twin engined development of the high wing single engine Do 27 utility. The Do 28 Skyservant first flew on February 23 1966, and while it retained the earlier Do 28's high wing and unique side mounted engine configuration, was a completely new aircraft. Other design features of this unusual looking aircraft were the fixed tailwheel undercarriage, with the faired mainwheels mounted under the engines. FAA certification was granted on April 19 1968.

The Do 28 was developed into a number of progressively improved variants, from the original D, through the D-1 and D-2, to the 128-2, introduced in 1980. Each variant introduced a number of detail changes. Most Do 28 production was for military customers, notably Germany, although a small number were sold to commercial operators.

A turboprop version of the Do 28, designated the Do 28D-5X, first flew in April 1978, fitted with two Avco Lycoming LTP 101-600-1As derated to 300kW (400shp). Production turboprop Dornier 128-6s however feature Pratt & Whitney PT6As, the first such configured aircraft flying in March 1980. Only a small number were built between then and 1986, when production ceased, and again most aircraft were for military customers.

Photo: A Do 128 taxies past its larger brothers at Dornier's Munich facilities. (Dornier)

Douglas DC-3

Country of origin: United States of America

Type: Short range airliner and utility transport

Powerplants: Two 895kW (1200hp) Pratt & Whitney R-1830-S1C3G Twin Wasp 14 cylinder twin row radial piston engines driving three blade variable pitch propellers, or two 895kW (1200hp) Wright SGR-1820 Cyclones.

Performance: Max speed 346km/h (187kt), economical cruising speed 266km/h (143kt). Initial rate of climb 1130ft/min. Range with max fuel 2420km (1307nm), range with max payload 563km (305nm).

Weights: Typical operating empty 8030kg (17,720lb), max takeoff 12,700kg (28,000lb).

Dimensions: Wing span 28.96m (95ft 0in), length 19.66m (64ft 6in), height 5.16m (16ft 12in). Wing area 91.7m^2 (987sq ft).

Capacity: Flightcrew of two. Seating for between 28 and 32 passengers, four abreast.

Production: A total of 10,655 built in the USA, including 430 for commercial operators prior to US participation in WW2. 2000 or so built in Russia under licence. More than 400 remain in commercial service in 1996.

History: No greater accolade for the DC-3 exists than the fact that over six decades after its first flight more than 400 remain in commercial service worldwide. Durability, longevity and profitability are but three of this outstanding aircraft's virtues.

Development of the DC-3 traces back to the earlier one-off Douglas Commercial 1 (DC-1) and then the DC-2 which made their first flights in 1933 and 1934 respectively. In 1934 American Airlines requested that Douglas develop a larger more capable version of the DC-2 for transcontinental US sleeper flights. The resulting DC-3 (or DST – Douglas Sleeper Transport as it then was) flew for the first time on December 17 1935. An almost instant sales success, the DC-3 became the mainstay of US domestic airline traffic in the years prior to World War 2. Aside from passenger comfort and appeal, the DC-3 offered that most important of virtues, profitability, with the result that over 400 had been sold to airlines prior to late 1941.

The entry of the United States into WW2 in December 1941 had a profound effect on the fortunes of the already successful DC-3. The US Army Air Force's requirements for transport aircraft were admirably met by the in-production DC-3, with the result that as the C-47 Skytrain it became the standard USAAF transport during the war. More than 10,000 were built for service with US and allied air arms.

After the war many of these aircraft became surplus to requirements and were sold off at bargain prices. The result was that demilitarised C-47s became the standard postwar aircraft of almost all the world's airlines and the backbone of the world airline industry. Its availability and reliability meant it proved extremely popular. To this day hundreds remain in service.

A postwar update of the DC-3, the Super DC-3, involving a stretched airframe and more powerful engines, was commercially unsuccessful. This aircraft first flew in June 1949. A small number were built for the US Navy as the R4D-8 and a US domestic airline, and a few remain in service.

Photo: DC-3s are often used for charters and joyflights. (Mike Davidson)

Douglas DC-4

Country of origin: United States of America

Type: Short haul transport

Powerplants: Four 1080kW (1450shp) Pratt & Whitney R-2000-2SD-BG Twin Wasp radial piston engines, driving three blade constant speed propellers.

Performance: Max speed 451km/h (244kt), cruising speed 365km/h (197kt). Service ceiling 22,300ft. Range with a 5200kg (11,440lb) payload 4023km (2172nm).

Weights: Empty 19,460kg (43,300lb), max takeoff 33,112kg (73,000lb).

Dimensions: Wing span 35.81m (117ft 6in), length 28.60m (93ft 10in), height 8.38m (27ft 6in). Wing area 135.6m^2 (1460sq ft).

Capacity: Flightcrew of three, standard passenger seating for 44, max seating for 86. Most surviving aircraft configured as freighters.

Production: Total DC-4 production comprised one DC-4E, 78 commercial DC-4s, 1162 military C-54 Skymasters and 42 Canadair developed Merlin powered derivatives. Almost 80 remain in commercial service, most as freighters.

History: The history of the DC-4 dates back to when United Airlines devised a requirement for a four engine long range airliner.

Looking to Douglas to fulfil the requirement, the manufacturer devised the highly ambitious DC-4E (where the E stands for experimental). This four engined monster was flight tested in 1939. It was roughly three times the size of the DC-3 (its wingspan was 42.17m/138ft 3in, and length 29.76m/97ft 7in), had triple tail surfaces, tricycle undercarriage, was pressurised and potentially could fly nonstop from Chicago to San Francisco. Sadly all the ground breaking new technology on the DC-4E meant that it was costly, complex and had higher than anticipated operating costs, so Douglas thoroughly revised the design, resulting in the smaller and simpler definitive DC-4.

The new DC-4 was developed under the darkening clouds of WW2, and upon the USA's entry into war all DC-4s then on the production line were requisitioned for the US military. The result was that the first DC-4 flew for the first time on February 14 1942 in military markings (as the C54 Skymaster). The DC-4 was found to admirably suit the USAAF's requirement for a long range cargo transport, and 1162 were built through the war years.

As was the case with the DC-3, the end of war meant that much of that number were surplus and sold to the world's airlines. Further to this Douglas built an additional 78 DC-4s to new orders. Over the years the survivors have been past down to third level airlines, and just a few survive today in service as freighters.

Notable developments of the DC-4 include Aviation Trader's much modified Carvair freighter (described separately) while Canadair built a number with Rolls-Royce Merlin engines and pressurised fuselages. The DC-4 also formed the basis for the larger DC-6 and DC-7 (described separately). In fact the DC-4 was the first airliner to introduce a circular section, constant diameter fuselage which made stretching the basic aircraft reasonably simple.

Photo: Almost all DC-4s today soldier on as freighters. This well maintained example is based in Brisbane, Australia. (Rob Finlayson)

Douglas DC-6

Country of origin: United States of America

Type: Medium haul transport

Powerplants: DC-6 – Four 1340kW (1800hp) Pratt & Whitney Double Wasp R-2800-CA15 18 cylinder twin row radial piston engines with a maximum output rating of 1790kW (2400hp) with water injection, driving three blade constant speed Hamilton Standard propellers. DC-6B – Four 1685kW (2500hp) R-2800-CB17s.

Performance: DC-6 – Max speed 570km/h (425kt), cruising speed 501km/h (270kt). Initial rate of climb 1070ft/min. Max range 7376km (3983nm). DC-6B – Cruising speed 507km/h (274kt). Service ceiling 25,000ft. Range with max payload 4835km (2610nm), range with max fuel 7595km (4100nm).

Weights: DC-6 – Empty 23,840kg (52,567lb), max takeoff 44,129kg (97,200lb). DC-6B – Empty 25,110kg (55,357lb), max takeoff 48,534kg (107,000lb).

Dimensions: DC-6 – Wing span 35.81m (117ft 6in), length 30.66m (100ft 7in), height 8.66m (28ft 5in). Wing area 135.9m^2 (1463sq ft). DC-6B – Same except length 32.18m (105ft 7in), height 8.74m (28ft 8in).

Capacity: DC-6 – Flightcrew of three or four. Passenger accommodation typically for between 48 to 56, but aircraft now usually equipped to carry freight. DC-6B – Typical passenger seating for 54, with max seating for 102, but usually configured for freight.

Production: Total DC-6 production of 665, comprising 174 DC-6s, 73 DC-6As, 288 DC-6Bs, 105 C-118s and 25 R6Ds. Approximately 100 remain in service.

History: While the DC-3's and DC-4's civilian careers were interrupted by WW2, the opposite applies to the DC-6, which started off in response to a military airlift requirement, and went on to become Douglas's most successful four engined piston airliner in terms of civil sales.

During WW2 the USAAF's C-54 fleet's long range and payload capabilities so impressed the service that it ordered development of a larger and improved variant. Designated YC-112, this long range transport featured more powerful 1565kW (2100hp) R-2800-22W engines and a lengthened fuselage. The development timetable of the YC-112 though was that it did not fly for the first time until February 15 1946, by which time the war ended and the USAAF requirement no longer stood.

Instead Douglas continued development of the type as a long range airliner, resulting in the DC-6. The YC-112 served as the prototype for the DC-6 program, and the first civil production aircraft were delivered to US airlines in March 1947. Entry into service however was not smooth with the fleet grounded for four months from later that year after a spate of inflight engine fires.

Development of the DC-6 into the DC-6A also began in 1947. Main changes were a fuselage stretch and more powerful engines. The DC-6A was optimised for freight work, the equivalent passenger version was the DC-6B. The DC-6C was a convertible passenger/freight model. Renewed military interest in the DC-6 was sparked by the Korean War, with the result that large numbers of USAF C-118s and USN R6D-1s were built. Many of these aircraft later found their way into civil hands.

Photo: A DC-6 freighter. (Gordon Reid)

Douglas DC-7

Country of origin: United States of America

Type: Medium to long range airliner, freighter and utility transport

Powerplants: DC-7F & DC-7C – Two 2535kW (3400hp) Wright R-3350-EA1 or -EA4 Turbo Compound radial piston engines, driving four blade constant speed propellers.

Performance: DC-7F – Typical cruising speed 555km/h (300kt). Range with max fuel and no reserves 7130km (3850nm). DC-7C – Typical cruising speed 555km/h (330kt). Range with max payload 5810km (3135nm), range with max fuel and no reserves 9077km (4900nm).

Weights: DC-7F – Basic operating 30,030kg (66,200lb), max takeoff 57,153kg (126,000lb). DC-7C – Basic operating 36,287kg (80,000lb), max takeoff 64,865kg (143,000lb).

Dimensions: DC-7F – Wing span 35.81m (117ft 6in), length 33.24m (108ft 11in), height 8.90m (29ft 3in). Wing area 136.0m^2 (1463sq ft). DC-7C – Wing span 38.80m (127ft 6in), length 34.23m (112ft 3in), height 9.65m (31ft 8in). Wing area 152.0m^2 (1637sq ft).

Capacity: Flightcrew of three. In passenger configurations most standard length DC-7s sat 99 in a high density single class layout, stretched DC-7Cs sat up to 105 passengers. Capacity of DC-7F conversion of the DC-7B is 15,700kg (34,600lb).

Production: DC-7 production was 338, comprising 120 DC-7s, 97 DC-7Bs and 121 DC-7Cs. Approximately 40 remain in service.

History: Douglas' largest and last piston engined airliner, the DC-7 was one of the first airliners capable of nonstop trans Atlantic crossings between London and New York.

Previously the DC-7 designation had applied to a commercial development of the C-74 Globemaster I that PanAm had ordered. As it emerged though the DC-7 arose from an American Airlines requirement for a stretched longer range development of the DC-6. The resulting aircraft was based on the same wing of the DC-6 (the same basic wing designed for the DC-4), with a stretched DC-6 fuselage, more powerful Wright Turbo Compound engines and extra fuel allowing Douglas to guarantee it could offer nonstop US transcontinental range in both directions.

The prototype DC-7 flew for the first time on May 18 1953, and the type entered service with American that November. Production of the initial DC-7 was solely for US domestic operators. The improved DC-7B had the same dimensions as the DC-7, but carried extra fuel, allowing PanAm to inaugurate nonstop New York/London services from June 1955.

While the DC-7B could fly New York/London nonstop, weather conditions often forced reverse services to make a refuelling stop at Gander. This operational hurdle gave Douglas the impetus to develop the ultimate DC-7 model, the DC-7C 'Seven Seas'. The DC-7C featured extra fuel capacity, a 3.05m (10ft) fuselage stretch and more powerful engines. It entered service in April 1956, although sales were restricted by the coming availability of jets.

Today a small number DC-7s survive, mainly as freighters. Douglas offered DC-7F conversions from 1959 (the DC-7F described above is based on the DC-7B). Others are used for firefighting.

Photo: A DC-7 firebomber. (Gordon Reid)

Douglas DC-8 Series 10 to 50

Country of origin: United States of America

Type: Medium to long range airliner and freighter

Powerplants: Series 50 – Four 80.6kN (18,000lb) Pratt & Whitney JT3D-3 turbofans.

Performance: Series 50 – Max recommended cruising speed 933km/h (504kt). Range with max payload 9205km (4970nm), max range 11,260km (6078nm).

Weights: Series 50 – Operating empty 60,020kg (132,325lb), max takeoff 147,415kg (325,000lb).

Dimensions: Wing span 43.41m (142ft 5in), length 45.87m (150ft 6in), height 12.91m (42ft 4in). Wing area 257.6m^2 (2773sq ft) on early aircraft, or 266.5m^2 (2868sq ft) on later aircraft.

Capacity: Flightcrew of three. Mixed class seating for 132, typical all economy seating for 144, or up to 179 in high density single class layout. A number of aircraft are converted for VIP/executive use. Freighter versions can carry approximately 15 tonnes (34,000lb) of cargo consisting of pallets or containers.

Production: A total of 295 Series 10, 20, 30, 40 and 50 DC-8s were built between the late 1950s and late 1960s. Approximately 40 series DC-8-50s remain in service.

History: The DC-8 was Douglas' first jet powered airliner, and the USA's second successful jet powered transport, behind the Boeing 707.

Despite its stronghold on the world airliner market in the early 1950s, and the appearance of the jet powered de Havilland Comet in 1949, Douglas moved cautiously into the field of jet powered transports, an action which was to cost it in potential future sales over the following decades. Douglas announced it was developing a jet powered airliner under the designation DC-8 in June 1955, a full year after the first flight of the Boeing Model 367-80, the 707 predecessor. The first DC-8 did not take to the skies until May 30 1958, shortly before the 707 entered service with PanAm. A concentrated flight test program involving nine aircraft led to certification on August 31 1959, and entry into commercial service on September 18 that year, a year behind the 707.

Unfortunately for Douglas, Boeing had seized leadership of the jet engined airliner market, a position it has held ever since. The earlier availability of the 707 meant that initial sales of the DC-8 were relatively slow.

Versions of the initial short fuselage DC-8 were: the Series 10, the initial domestic version with 60.5kN (13,500lb) P&W JT3C-6 turbojets, 28 were built for Delta and United; the similar Series 20 but with more powerful 75.3kN (16,800lb) JT4A-9 turbojets; the intercontinental Series 30 and Series 40, powered by JT4A-11s or Rolls-Royce Conways respectively; and the Series 50, perhaps the definitive short fuselage model, with 80.6kN (18,000lb) JT3D-3 turbofans (the convertible 50CF, and pure freight 50AF Jet Trader versions were also offered).

The short fuselage DC-8s were replaced in production by the substantially larger stretched DC-8 Super Sixty series.

Photo: A Douglas DC-8-50 freighter in service with Zimbabwe's Affretair. (Rob Finlayson)

Douglas DC-8 Super 60 & 70 Series

Country of Origin: United States of America

Type: Long range medium capacity airliner

Powerplants: DC-8-61 & 62 – Four 80.6kN (18,000lb) Pratt & Whitney JT3D-3B turbofans. DC-8-63 – Four 85.1kN (19,000lb) JT3D-7s. DC-8-70 series – Four 97.9kN (22,000lb) CFM International CFM56-2C5s.

Performance: DC-8-60 – Max cruising speed 965km/h (521kt). Range with max payload DC-8-61 6035km (3256nm); DC-8-62 9620km (5210nm); DC-8-63 7240nm (3907nm). DC-8-70 – Max cruising speed 887km/h (479kt), economical cruising speed 850km/h (459kt). Range with max payload (Super 73) 8950km (4830nm).

Weights: DC-8-61 – Operating empty 67,538kg (148,897lb), max takeoff 147,415kg (325,000lb). DC-8-62 – Operating empty 64,366kg (141,903lb), max takeoff 151,950kg (335,000lb). DC-8-63 – Operating empty 69,739kg (153,749lb), max takeoff 158,760kg (350,000lb). DC-8-73 – Operating empty 75,500kg (166,500lb), max takeoff 162,025kg (355,000lb).

Dimensions: DC-8-61 & 71 – Wing span 43.41m (142ft 5in), length 57.12m (187ft 5in), height 12.92m (42ft 5in). Wing area 267.9m^2 (2884sq ft). DC-8-62 & 72 – Wing span 45.23m (148ft 5in), length 47.98m (157ft 5in), height 12.92m (42ft 5in). Wing area 271.9m^2 (2927sq ft). DC-8-63 & 73 – Wing span 45.23m (148ft 5in), length 57.12m (187ft 5in), height 12.92m (45ft 5in). Wing area 271.9m^2 (2927sq ft).

Capacity: Flightcrew of two. Max seating capacity 259 or standard seating for between 180 and 220 in Series 61, 63, 71 & 73. Super 62 & 72 standard seating arrangement for 189. Super 60 and 70 freighters have a cargo capacity between 40,405kg (89,000lb) and 49,585kg (109,217lb).

Production: Total Super 60 series production was 262. Approximately 115 Super 60s and 95 Super 70 CFM56 conversions remained in commercial service in late 1996.

History: The DC-8 Super 60 is a significantly stretched development of the DC-8 Series 50.

Douglas announced the DC-8 Super Sixty in April 1965. The first, a DC-8-61, took to the skies for the first time on March 14 1966, followed by the first flights of the DC-8-62 on August 29 1966, and the DC-8-63 on April 10 1967. The DC-8-61 differed from the earlier DC-8-50 in having two fuselage plugs which increased length by 11.18m (36ft 8in), increasing max seating capacity to 259 (the largest of any single aisle airliner prior to the 757-300), and underfloor freight capacity by 80%. Intended for domestic operations, its max takeoff weight was identical to the DC-8-50. The Super 62 was intended for long range operations and featured only a modest 2.04m (6ft 8in) stretch compared to the Series 50, greater wing span, revised engine nacelles and pylons and significantly increased fuel capacity. The Super 63 meanwhile combined the DC-8-61's fuselage with the DC-8-62's wings. It was the final DC-8 variant in production, the last was delivered in May 1972.

McDonnell Douglas initiated a re-engining program of Super 60 series aircraft with CFM International CFM56 engines in the early 1980s. Known as the Super 70 Series, the first converted airframe flew in August 1981. The Super 70 aircraft are considerably quieter than their predecessors, with better fuel economy and greater range.

Photo: A DC-8-62F of Arrow Air. (Peter Clark)

EH Industries EH 101 Heliliner

Countries of origin: Italy and United Kingdom

Type: Commuter, offshore oil rig support & utility helicopter

Powerplants: Three 1230kW (1649shp) max continuous rated General Electric CT7-6 turboshafts, driving a five blade main rotor and four blade tail rotor.

Performance: Typical cruising speed 278km/h (150kt), long range cruising speed 260km/h (140kt). Range with 30 passengers offshore IFR equipped, standard fuel and reserves 926km (500nm), with 30 pax, IFR equipped, auxiliary fuel and reserves 1158km (625nm), range from vertical takeoff 555km (300nm).

Weights: Basic empty 7120kg (15,700lb), operating empty (with IFR, offshore equipped) 8933kg (19,695lb), max takeoff 14,288kg (31,500lb).

Dimensions: Main rotor diameter 18.59m (61ft 0in), length with rotors turning 22.81m (74ft 10in), height with rotors turning 6.65m (21ft 10in). Main rotor disc area 271.5m^2 (2922.5sq ft).

Capacity: Flightcrew of two. Main cabin seating for 30 at four abreast and 76cm (30in) pitch. Equipped with galley and toilet.

Production: Thus far nine preproduction aircraft have been built, of which two, PP3 and PP8, are configured as civilian Heliliners and PP9 as a civil utility version with rear loading ramp. No commercial orders received as yet.

History: The Heliliner is the commercial development of the EH 101 EH Industries is primarily developing for use for the UK and Italian armed forces.

EH Industries is a collaborative venture between Westland of the UK and Agusta of Italy, and was formed to develop an anti submarine warfare helicopter for the Royal Navy and Italian Navy. The partnership was formed in 1980, and both companies have a 50% holding. Westland has design responsibility for the commercial Heliliner, the anti submarine warfare variant is being developed jointly, while Agusta heads development of military and utility transport versions with a rear loading ramp.

The development history of this aircraft is protracted and dates back to initial studies conducted during the early 1980s, while full scale program go ahead was announced in March 1984. The first flight of an EH 101 (the Westland built PP1) was on October 9 1987, while the first civil configured EH 101, PP3, flew for the first time on September 30 1988. Certification for the Heliliner was initially expected for late 1993, but was delayed until November 1994. At late 1996, no civil orders had been placed.

While the Royal Navy's EH 101s (named Merlins) will have Rolls-Royce Turboméca RTM322 engines, civil EH 101s will have General Electric CT7 engines. The 30 seat Heliliner is optimised either for offshore oil rig or airport to city centre transfers, and the rear freight door is offered as an option, while the civil utility version has the rear ramp fitted as standard.

Photo: Civil Heliliner demonstrator PP3. The EH 101 could find a useful market as a S-61 replacement used as an airliner and on oil rig support missions.

Embraer EMB-110 Bandeirante

Country of origin: Brazil

Type: Twin turboprop commuter

Powerplants: Two 560kW (750shp) Pratt & Whitney Canada PT6A-34 turboprops, driving three blade constant speed Hartzell propellers.

Performance: EMB-110P – Max speed 460km/h (248kt), max cruising speed 417km/h (225kt), economical cruising speed 326km/h (176kt). Initial rate of climb 1788ft/min. Service ceiling 22,500ft. Range at long range cruising speed with reserves 2000km (1080nm). EMB-110P2A/41 – Max cruising speed 413km/h (222kt), economical cruising speed 341km/h (184kt). Range with max fuel 1964km (1060nm).

Weights: EMB-110P2 – Empty equipped 3515kg (7751lb), max takeoff 5700kg (12,566lb). EMB-110P2A/41 – Operating empty 3590kg (7915lb), max takeoff 5900kg (13,010lb).

Dimensions: Wing span 15.33m (50ft 3in), length 15.10m (50ft 4in), height 4.92m (16ft 2in). Wing area 29.1m^2 (313sq ft).

Capacity: Flightcrew of two. Typical passenger seating for 18 at three abreast, max seating for 21 at 74cm (29in) pitch.

Production: Production of all EMB-110 reached 500, the last of which was delivered to the Brazilian military in 1990.

History: The Embraer EMB-110 Bandeirante, or 'Bandit', has thus far proven to be Embraer's most successful indigenous civil program.

Design of the EMB-110 was undertaken in response to a Brazilian Ministry of Aeronautics specification for a general purpose light transport suitable for both military and civilian duties. The new design was developed with the assistance of well known French designer Max Holste, and the first of three prototypes, designated YC-95s, flew for the first time on October 26 1968. Embraer (or Empresa Brasilera de Aeronáutica SA) was established the following year, and development and production of the YC-95 became one of the company's first responsibilities. The first production standard EMB-110 Bandeirante (or Pioneer) flew on August 9 1972, and the first entered airline service in April 1973.

Bandeirante models include the 12 seat transport EMB-110, the aerial photography EMB-110B and maritime patrol EMB-111 for the Brazilian air force; the initial airline version, the 15 seat EMB-110C; the seven seat EMB-110E executive transport; 18 seat enlarged EMB-110P; convertible passenger/freight EMB-110P1 with larger rear door; the EMB-110PA which replaced the -110P as the standard passenger aircraft from 1983 and introduced dihedral to the tailplane among other minor improvements; the EMB-110P1K and EMB-110K SAR military equivalents to the P1A; the EMB-110P2 commuter with seating for up to 21; the EMB-110P2A which replaced the P2 and introduced the same changes as the P1A; and the EMB-110P1A/41 and EMB-P2A/41 versions of the P1A and P2A recertificated to US FAA SFAR-41 standards with higher weights.

Production of the Bandeirante ceased in May 1990, the final aircraft being delivered to the Brazilian air force. Today the Bandeirante's virtues of reliability and good operating economics though means that it remains highly sought after.

Photo: The Bandeirante is a very popular 15/18 seat unpressurised regional airliner. (Rob Finlayson)

Embraer EMB-120 Brasilia

Country of origin: Brazil

Type: Twin turboprop regional airliner

Powerplants: Two 1340kW (1800shp) Pratt & Whitney Canada PW118 or PW118A turboprops, driving four blade Hamilton Standard propellers.

Performance: EMB-120 – Max cruising speed 555km/h (300kt) with PW118s, or 574km/h (310kt) with PW118As, long range cruising speed 482km/h (260kt). Initial rate of climb 2120ft/min. Service ceiling 30,000ft with PW118s, or 32,000ft with PW118As. Range with max passengers and reserves 1020km (550nm) with PW118s, or 926km (500nm) with PW118As. EMB-120ER – Max cruising speed 555km/h (300kt) with PW118s, or 580km/h (313kt) with PW118As, long range cruising speed 500km/h (270kt). Initial rate of climb 2500ft/min. Service ceiling 29,000ft with PW118s, or 32,000ft with PW118As. Range with max pax and reserves 1556km (840nm) with PW118s, or 1500km (810nm) with PW118As.

Weights: EMB-120 – Empty equipped 7100kg (15,655lb), max takeoff 11,500kg (25,353lb). EMB-120ER – Empty equipped 7140kg (15,741lb), max takeoff 11,990kg (26,433lb).

Dimensions: EMB-120 – Wing span 19.78m (64ft 11in), length 20.00m (65ft 8in), height 6.35m (20ft 10in). Wing area 39.4m^2 (424.42sq ft). EMB-120ER – Same except for length 20.07m (65ft 10in).

Capacity: Flightcrew of two. Standard main cabin seating for 30 at three abreast and 79cm (31in) pitch. Optional passenger seating for 24 or 26 with greater baggage/cargo space. Alternative interior arrangements for executive and cargo roles.

Production: Approximately 334 ordered by late 1996, including a small number of military orders, of which approximately 310 had been delivered.

History: The Brasilia seems to be following in the highly successful footsteps of the earlier and smaller Bandeirante, with this high speed yet relatively inexpensive to operate and purchase commuter proving to be a considerable sales success.

Embraer began design work on a new regional turboprop airliner in the late 1970s when the company investigated stretching its EMB-121 Xingu corporate turboprop to a 25 seat regional airliner. While this was the first aircraft to bear the EMB-120 designation (it was named the Araguia), the resulting EMB-120 is an all new aircraft. Design studies of the definitive EMB-120 began in September 1979, first flight of a PW115 powered prototype took place on July 27 1983, and entry into service was on October 1985.

Versions of the EMB-120 include: the initial production EMB-120; the current standard production Brasilia; the Reduced Takeoff weight EMB-120RT; the Extended Range EMB-120ER; the EMB-120 Cargo freighter; mixed passenger/freight EMB-120 Combi; and EMB-120 Convertible. Hot and high versions of these models have PW118A engines, which retain their power ratings to a higher altitude. The latest version is the EMB-120ER Advanced, which incorporates a range of external and interior improvements, while the fuselage of the EMB-120 also forms the basis for the EMB-145 regional jet.

Photo: A Brasilia in the colours of South African airline Sun Air. Sun Air no longer flies the type. (Lloyd Fox)

Embraer EMB-121 Xingu

Country of origin: Brazil

Type: Twin turboprop corporate transport

Powerplants: Xingu I – Two 505kW (680shp) Pratt & Whitney Canada PT6A-28 turboprops, driving three blade constant speed Hartzell propellers. Xingu II – Two 635kW (850shp) PT6A-42s, driving four blade constant speed Dowty props.

Performance: Xingu I – Max cruising speed 450km/h (243kt), economical cruising speed 365km/h (197kt). Initial rate of climb 1400ft/min. Service ceiling 26,000ft. Range with max fuel 2352km (1270nm). Xingu II – Max cruising speed 465km/h (251kt), economical cruising speed 380km/h (205kt). Initial rate of climb 1800ft/min. Range with max fuel 2278km (1230nm), with max payload 1630km (880nm).

Weights: Xingu I – Empty equipped 3620kg (7984lb), max takeoff 5670kg (12,500lb). Xingu II – Empty equipped 3500kg (7716lb), max takeoff 6140kg (13,536lb).

Dimensions: Xingu I – Wing span 14.45m (47ft 5in), length 12.25m (40ft 2in), height 4.74m (15ft 7in). Wing area 27.5m^2 (296.0sq ft). Xingu II – Wing span 14.83m (48ft 8in), length 13.44m (44ft 1in), height 4.74m (15ft 7in). Wing area 27.9m^2 (300.3sq ft).

Capacity: Xingu I – Flightcrew of one or two, plus typical main cabin seating for five or six passengers. Xingu II – Flightcrew of two. Main cabin seating for seven, eight or nine passengers, depending on customer preference.

Production: Total Xingu I & II production 105 aircraft, including military orders.

History: Produced in modest numbers, the sleek looking Xingu coupled the Bandeirante's wing and engines with an all new fuselage.

The Xingu flew for the first time on October 10 1976, with a production aircraft following on May 20 1977. The first customer delivery occurred later that same year (to the Copersucar-Fittipaldi Formula One racing team). The major customer for the Xingu I was the French military, with a total order for 41 (for aircrew training and liaison duties for the air force and navy) accounting for almost half of all EMB-121 production.

Several derivatives of the Xingu design were proposed, including the original EMB-120, the Araguia, a commuter airliner which would have seated 25, and the EMB-123 Tapajós. The Tapajós would have had more powerful 835kW (1120shp) PT6A-45 engines (which also would have powered the Araguia), increased wing span and a lengthened fuselage.

A more modest development did enter production, the EMB-121B Xingu II. This features more powerful engines, four blade props, increased fuel tankage and greater seating capacity courtesy of a slightly stretched fuselage. Similar in size, powerplant and performance to the Beech Super King Air B200, the Xingu II made its first flight on September 4 1981.

Production of the Xingu line ceased in August 1987 after only 105 had been built.

Photo: A Xingu II. Aside from production for the French military, most EMB-121s were sold to South American operators. (Embraer)

Embraer EMB-145

Country of origin: Brazil

Type: 50 seat regional jet airliner

Powerplants: Two 31.3kN (7040lb) Allison AE 3007A turbofans.

Performance: EMB-145 – Max cruising speed 797km/h (430kt), economical cruising speed 667km/h (360kt). Service ceiling 37,000ft. Range with 50 passengers and reserves 1480km (800nm), range with max fuel and 20 passengers 2575km (1390nm). EMB-145ER – Max cruising speed 771km/h (416kt). Range with 50 passengers and reserves 2220km (1200nm).

Weights: Basic operating empty 11,585kg (25,450lb), max takeoff 19,200kg (423,29lb). EMB-145ER – Max takeoff 20,600kg (45,415lb).

Dimensions: Wing span 20.04m (65ft 9in), length 29.87m (98ft 0in), height 6.71m (22ft 0in). Wing area 51.2m^2 (550.9sq ft).

Capacity: Flightcrew of two. Standard passenger accommodation for 50 at three abreast and 79cm (31in) pitch. Alternative seating for 48 or 49 with wardrobe fitted.

Production: First deliveries due December 1996. Production rate of four per month in 1997. At late 1996 firm orders held for 40, with 181 options.

History: One of two 50 seat regional jets (the other being Canadair's successful RJ), Embraer's EMB-145 has had by far a more chequered early development history.

Embraer has been working on 50 seat regional jet concepts since the late 1980s. The original EMB-145 concept was launched in mid 1989 and was essentially a stretched and jet engined EMB-120 Brasilia. Features of this design included a straight wing with winglets and the two turbofans mounted forward of the wing as on most low wing turboprops. This design would have seated 45 to 50 passengers and featured 75% commonality with the Brasilia. In that configuration cruising speed would have been 740km/h (400kt) and range with a 4500kg (9920lb) payload 2500km (1350nm).

But by 1990 Embraer was studying a modified design with less commonality to the Brasilia as wind tunnel testing revealed that the original configuration would not reach its design performance objectives. Changes to this interim design included a mildly swept wing (wing sweep of 22.3°) and conventional below wing mounted engines. Wind tunnel testing proved that this configuration met design objectives however it had a major drawback in that it would have needed an unusually high undercarriage. The longer undercarriage would have required a slightly longer fuselage and a redesign of the airstairs and emergency exit slides.

Thus in late 1991 Embraer froze the EMB-145 design with rear fuselage mounted engines, while the wing does not feature winglets. Other features include Allison AE 3007A turbofans (similar to those that power the Citation X) and a Honeywell Primus 1000 avionics suite. Two versions are on offer, the standard EMB-145 and the higher max takeoff weight longer range EMB-145ER.

The EMB-145's first flight took place on August 11 1995 with first deliveries expected from December 1996 to Continental Express. Continental Express's order for 25 firm and 175 options announced at the 1996 Farnborough Airshow was a major fillup for the EMB-145 program.

Photo: An inflight portrait of the second EMB-145. (Embraer)

Enstrom F28, 280 & 480

Country of origin: United States of America

Type: Three and four seat light helicopters

Powerplant: F28A – One 155kW (205hp) Lycoming HIO-360-C1B flat four piston engine driving a three blade main rotor and two blade tail rotor. 280FX – One 170kW (225hp) Textron Lycoming HIO-360-F1AD with Rotomaster turbocharger. 480 – One 215kW (285shp) takeoff rated Allison 250-C20W turboshaft.

Performance: F28A – Max cruising speed 161km/h (87kt). Initial rate of climb 950ft/min. Service ceiling 12,000ft. Hovering ceiling in ground effect 5600ft. Range with max fuel 380km (205nm). 280FX – Max cruising speed 172km/h (93kt). Initial rate of climb 1450ft/min. Certificated ceiling 12,000ft. Hovering ceiling out of ground effect 8700ft. Range with max fuel and no reserves 483km (260nm). 480 – Cruising speed 177km/h (96kt). Initial rate of climb 1583ft/min. Service ceiling 13,000ft. Hovering ceiling out of ground effect 12,000ft. Max range 620km (334nm).

Weights: F28A – Empty 657kg (1450lb), max takeoff 975kg (2150lb). 280FX – Empty equipped 719kg (1585lb), max takeoff 1179kg (2600lb). 480 – Empty 780kg (1720lb), max takeoff 1292kg (2850lb).

Dimensions: F28A – Main rotor diameter 9.75m (32ft 0in), length overall 8.94m (29ft 4in), height to top of rotor hub 2.79m (9ft 2in). Main rotor disc area 74.7m^2 (804sq ft). 280FX – Same except for length 8.92m (29ft 3in). 480 – Same as 280FX except for height to main rotor hub 2.92m (9ft 7in).

Capacity: Three seats in the F28 and 280, four seats in 480. Can also be fitted with agricultural spraying gear.

Production: Production of all versions exceeds 800. Approximately 20 480s built.

History: This long running line of three and four place light helicopters dates back to the late 1950s and is still in production.

The Enstrom Helicopter Corporation was first formed in 1959, and the three place F28 was its first product. The first F28 prototype made its maiden flight on November 12 1960, the production prototype of the F28 flying in May 1962. Since that time numerous developments of the basic design have appeared. These include the F28A which appeared in 1968. Next to appear, in 1973, was the Model 280 Shark, an improved version with a reprofiled airframe, it supplemented the F28A in production. The turbocharged F28C and 280C were certificated in 1975.

The first four seat version was the piston engined 280L Hawk. The Hawk's enlarged fuselage was also adopted for the Allison 250 turboshaft powered 480, which was first flown in 1988. The 480 also formed the basis of the TH-28 which Enstrom unsuccessfully entered in the US Army's competition for a new basic pilot training helicopter.

Current Enstrom production models are the F28F Falcon which first appeared in 1981, the FLIR pod equipped F28F-P Sentinel which is optimised for police work, the four seat 280FX which was certificated in early 1988, and the four seat turbine powered 480.

Photo: The Textron Lycoming HIO-360 powered Enstrom 280FX Shark. The 280FX features a more pointed nose compared with the F28F. (Dave Prossor)

Eurocopter AS 332 Super Puma

Country of origin: France

Type: Medium lift utility helicopter

Powerplants: AS 332L – Two 1325kW (1755shp) Turboméca Makila turboshafts driving a four blade main rotor and five blade tail rotor. AS 332L2 – Two 1375kW (1845shp) takeoff rated Turboméca Makila 1A2 turboshafts.

Performance: AS 332L – Max cruising speed 278km/h (150kt). Max inclined rate of climb 1810ft/min. Hovering ceiling in ground effect 9840ft. Range 850km (635nm). AS 332L2 – High speed cruise 277km/h (150kt), economical cruising speed 247km/h (133kt). Rate of climb at 130km/h (70kt) 1447ft/min. Hover ceiling in ground effect 9414ft. Range with max fuel, economical cruising speed and no reserves 1490km (805nm), with standard fuel and same conditions 850km (460nm).

Weights: AS 332L – Empty 4370kg (9635lb), max takeoff 9000kg (19,840lb). AS 332L2 – Empty 4660kg (10,274lb), max takeoff 9150kg (20,172lb), max flight weight with slung load 10,000kg (22,046lb).

Dimensions: AS 332L – Main rotor diameter 15.08m (49ft 6in), length overall rotors turning 18.70m (61ft 4in), fuselage length 15.52m (50ft 11in), height overall 4.92m (16ft 1in). AS 332L2 – Main rotor diameter 16.20m (53ft 2in), length overall rotors turning 19.50m (63ft 11in), height overall 4.97m (16ft 4in). Main rotor disc area 206.0m^2 (2217.4sq ft).

Capacity: Flightcrew of one (VFR ops), or two (IFR ops) pilots. AS 332 seating for 17, AS 332L and AS 332L2 max seating for 24.

Production: Military and civil orders for all variants of the Super Puma total more than 470.

History: A larger development of the Puma (described under Aerospatiale), the Super Puma is a practical and proven medium lift twin helicopter, particularly popular for offshore oil rig support work.

The original SA 330 Puma, on which the Super Puma is based, flew for the first time in April 1965. The first Super Puma meanwhile flew for the first time in September 1978 and was simply a more powerful version of the Puma, featuring 1270kW (1700shp) Turboméca Makila turboshafts, new avionics, composite rotor blades and an enlarged fuselage. For a time Aerospatiale planned to fit the Super Puma with a Fenestron shrouded tail rotor, but testing revealed no significant performance benefits. Commercial versions were designated AS 332Cs.

The AS 332L (or SA 332L before 1980) Super Puma introduced a stretched fuselage (by 76.5cm/2.5ft) and was first flown on October 10 1980. Certificated in 1983, this Super Puma was updated in 1986 as the AS 332L1 with Makila 1A1 engines. Bristow Helicopters ordered 31 specially customised AS 332Ls for its North Sea offshore oil rig work, and these are named Tiger.

The AS 332L remains in production but is progressively being replaced by the AS 332L2. The L2 Super Puma Mk II (known as the Cougar in military guise) features a further fuselage stretch permitting a further row of seats, EFIS flight instrumentation, spheriflex rotor heads and longer main rotor blades with parabolic tips. It was certificated in 1992.

Photo: One of Bristow Helicopters' specially customised AS 332L Tigers, used for North Sea oil rig support. (Keith Gaskell)

Eurocopter AS 350 Ecureuil

Country of origin: France

Type: Light general purpose helicopter

Powerplant: AS 350B – One 478kW (641shp) Turboméca Arriel turboshaft driving a three blade main rotor and two blade tail rotor. AS 350D – One 460kW (615shp) Textron (Avco) Lycoming LTS 101-600A2. AS 350B2 – One 546kW (732shp) Arriel 1D1.

Performance: AS 350B – Cruising speed 232km/h (125kt). Max inclined rate of climb 1555ft/min. Hovering ceiling in ground effect 9678ft. Range 700km (378nm). AS 350D – Max cruising speed 230km/h (124kt). Max inclined rate of climb 1575ft/min. Range with max fuel and no reserves 760km (410nm). AS 350B2 – Max cruising speed 246km/h (133kt). Max rate of climb 1750ft/min. Hovering ceiling out of ground effect 8350ft. Range with max fuel 666km (360nm).

Weights: AS 350B – Empty 1065kg (2348lb), max takeoff 1950kg (4300lb) or 2100kg (4630lb) with a sling load. AS 350D – Empty 1070kg (2359lb), max takeoff 1950kg (4300lb), or 2100kg (4630lb) with a sling load. AS 350B2 – Empty 1153kg (2542lb), max takeoff 2250kg (4960lb).

Dimensions: AS 350B2 – Main rotor diameter 10.69m (35ft 1in), length with rotors turning 12.94m (42ft 6in), fuselage length 10.93m (35ft 11in), height overall 3.14m (10ft 4in). Main rotor disc area 89.8m^2 (966.1sq ft).

Capacity: Standard seating for six, including two forward seats and a four place rear bench seat.

Production: Almost 2000 AS 350s of all types (including military aircraft) ordered as at late 1996. In addition Helibras in Brazil has built under licence 100 civil Esquilos.

History: Europe's most successful civil helicopters, the Ecureuil (or Squirrel) family is in extensive military and civil use worldwide, performing a variety of wide ranging missions.

Aerospatiale development of the AS 350 Squirrel in the early 1970s culminated in the first flights of the Avco Lycoming LTS 101 powered prototype on June 27 1974 and the Turboméca Arriel powered prototype on February 14 1975. These aircraft were followed by eight preproduction examples, the first of which flew in late 1977.

Production of an initial batch of 40 Ecureuils resulted in the first customer delivery occurring in April 1978. Initial models offered were the Arriel powered AS 350B, which was marketed outside North America, and the LTS 101 powered AS 350C Astar sold in the USA. The AS 350C was soon replaced by the D, with a more powerful engine.

Subsequent developments include the hot and high AS 350B1 with a 510kW (684shp) Arriel 1D; the AS 350BA which was certificated in 1991 and is fitted with the larger main rotors of the AS 350B2 (AS 350Bs can be retrofitted with the blades in the field); and the AS 350B2 (marketed in North America as the SuperStar) with a more powerful Arriel 1D1 turboshaft, and the main and tail rotors developed for the twin engine AS 355F Ecureuil 2 (described separately) and certificated in April 1989. Military Ecureuils are now marketed as the AS 550 Fennec.

Photo: An AS 350B Ecureuil/Squirrel. (Martin Grimm)

Eurocopter AS 355 Ecureuil 2

Country of origin: France

Type: Twin engined light utility helicopter

Powerplants: AS 355F – Two 315kW (420shp) Allison 250-C20F turboshafts, driving a three blade main rotor and two blade tail rotor. AS 355N – Two Turboméca TM 319 1M Arrius turboshafts.

Performance: AS 355F – Max cruising speed 224km/h (121kt). Initial rate of climb 1280ft/min. Hovering ceiling in ground effect 5900ft. Service ceiling 11,150ft. Range with max fuel and no reserves 703km (380nm). AS 355N – Max cruising speed 225km/h (120kt). Initial rate of climb 1340ft/min. Hovering ceiling out of ground effect 8530ft. Range with max fuel 722km (390nm).

Weights: AS 355F – Empty 1305kg (2877lb), max takeoff 2540kg (5600lb) or 2600kg (5732lb) with external sling load. AS 355N – Empty 1382kg (3046lb), max takeoff 2540kg (5600lb) or 2600kg (5732lb) with external sling load.

Dimensions: Main rotor diameter 10.69m (35ft 1in), length overall with rotors turning 12.94m (42ft 6in), fuselage length 10.91m (35ft 10in), height 3.14m (10ft 4in). Main rotor disc area 89.8m^2 (966.1sq ft).

Capacity: Standard seating for six, including two forward seats and a four place rear bench seat. Can be configured for police, ambulance, EMS and media missions with various appropriate internal configurations.

Production: Orders for military AS 555s and civil AS 355s total over 600, of which approx 470 are for civilian customers. Helibras of Brazil has built over 25 AS 355s under licence.

History: The twin engined version of the Ecureuil/Squirrel family, the AS 355 Ecureuil 2 offers greater performance, carrying capability and the safety benefits of twin engines compared to the single engined AS 350 (described separately).

Development of the first twin engine Ecureuil began early in the model's development life, with the first flying on September 28 1979. This prototype was powered by two Allison 250-C20F turboshafts, supplying power to the main and tail rotors through a combining gearbox. Put into production as the AS 350E, the Ecureuil 2 is essentially a twin engined version of the AS 350 with detail changes made to the fuselage structure, fuel system, transmission and main rotor blades to support the twin engine configuration. In common with the AS 350, the AS 355 features the maintenance free Starflex main rotor hub, and main rotor blades of composite construction.

The AS 355F replaced the AS 355E from early 1982, and introduced new wider chord main rotor blades and a higher max takeoff weight. The AS 355F was followed by the F1 in January 1984 and F2 in December 1985, which introduced progressively higher maximum takeoff weights.

The current production model is the AS 355N Ecureuil 2 which introduced the twin Turboméca TM 319 1M Arrius turboshafts. It was certificated in 1989 and first deliveries took place from early 1992. It is marketed in North America as the TwinStar. As with the single engined AS 550, the twin engine military AS 555 is known as the Fennec.

Photo: The primary visual difference between the single and twin engined Ecureuil/Squirrel is the enlarged engine fairings of the latter. Here a Police AS 355N patrols above London's Heathrow Airport.

Eurocopter AS 365 Dauphin 2

Country of origin: France

Type: Twin engine mid sized utility helicopter

Powerplants: SA 365C – Two 505kW (680shp) Turboméca Arriel turboshafts, driving a four blade main rotor and 11 blade Fenestron shrouded tail rotor. AS 365N2 – Two 550kW (739shp) Arriel 1C2s.

Performance: SA 365C – Max cruising speed 260km/h (140kt). Initial rate of climb 1653ft/min. Hovering ceiling in ground effect 15,000ft. Range 545km (295nm). AS 365N2 – Max cruising speed 285km/h (154kt), economical cruising speed 260km/h (140kt). Initial rate of climb 1380ft/min. Hovering ceiling in ground effect 8365ft, out of ground effect 5905ft. Range with standard fuel 900km (485nm).

Weights: SA 365C – Empty equipped 1806kg (3980lb), max takeoff 3400kg (7495lb). AS 365N2 – Empty 2240kg (4940lb), max takeoff 4250kg (9370lb).

Dimensions: SA 365C – Main rotor diameter 11.68m (38ft 4in), length (inc main rotor) 13.32m (43ft 9in), fuselage length 10.98m (37ft 7in). AS 365N2 – Main rotor diameter 11.94m (39ft 2in), length overall 13.68m (44ft 11in), height overall 3.98m (13ft 1in). Main rotor disc area 111.9m^2 (1205sq ft).

Capacity: One pilot (VFR) or two pilots (IFR), and max seating for 13 passengers (with one pilot). Standard passenger seating for eight or nine, executive and VIP configurations for five, six or seven. Can be configured for SAR, EMS (with two or four stretchers) and police work.

Production: Total orders, including HH-65s for the US Coast Guard and 50 Chinese (as Harbin Z-9 Haitun) licence built aircraft, total approximately 600.

History: One of Eurocopter's most successful designs, the Dauphin 2 has found widespread use in corporate, police, EMS and search and rescue missions worldwide.

The Dauphin 2 is a twin engined development of the original single Astazou powered SA 360 Dauphin (see under Aerospatiale). Compared with the SA 360, the AS 365 (originally the SA 365) features twin Arriel turboshafts and new engine fairing, the Starflex main rotor hub and a higher max takeoff weight.

The Dauphin 2's first flight was on January 24 1975, while production deliveries of SA 365Cs began in early 1978.

The SA 365 however was soon replaced by the much improved AS 356N, which introduced more powerful Arriel 1C turboshafts, enlarged tail surfaces, revised transmission, main rotor, rotor mast fairing and engine cowling, and retractable tricycle undercarriage. The US Coast Guard took delivery of 99 HH-65 Dolphins. These aircraft are powered by Textron (Avco) Lycoming LTS 101s and are optimised for Search and Rescue.

Current production is of the AS 365N2, deliveries of which commenced in 1990. It features upgraded Arriel 1C2 engines, improved gearbox, increased max takeoff weight, redesigned cabin doors, revised interior and optional EFIS instrumentation.

Dauphins have been configured for research work, one configured with fly-by-wire controls and another for high speed testing with a five blade main rotor. Military models of the Dauphin have also been built, current military machines are designated AS 565 Panthers.

Photo: An LTS 101 powered US Coast Guard HH-65 Dolphin.

Eurocopter BO 105 & EC Super Five

Country of origin: Germany

Type: Five place multi purpose light utility helicopter

Powerplants: BO 105 CBS & Super Five – Two 313kW (420shp) Allison 250-C20B turboshafts, driving a four blade main rotor and two blade tail rotor.

Performance: BO 105 CBS – Max cruising speed 242km/h (130kt), long range cruising speed 204km/h (110kt). Initial rate of climb 1457ft/min. Hovering ceiling out of ground effect 1500ft. Range with standard fuel and max payload 596km (320nm), ferry range with auxiliary fuel tanks 1020km (550nm). Super Five – Max cruising speed 243km/h (130kt). Initial rate of climb 1870ft/min. Hovering ceiling out of ground effect 7970ft. Range 575km (310nm).

Weights: BO 105 CBS – Empty 1300kg (2868lb), max takeoff 2500kg (5511lb).

Dimensions: Main rotor diameter 9.84m (32ft 4in), length including rotors 11.86m (38ft 11in), fuselage length 8.81m (28ft 11in), height to top of main rotor mast 3.02m (9ft 11in). Main rotor disc area 76.1m^2 (818.6sq ft).

Capacity: Total seating for five, including two pilots or one pilot and passenger in front bucket seats, and three passengers on rear bench seat. Can be configured for police, EMS (with two stretchers) and SAR work, among other roles. Behind rear seats and below the engine is a cargo compartment, accessible by two clamshell doors in the rear of the fuselage.

Production: Approximately 1350 BO 105s of all models, including military versions, delivered thus far, including licence production in Canada, Indonesia, the Philippines and Spain.

History: In widespread military and civilian service, the BO 105 is MBB's (now part of Eurocopter) most successful helicopter design.

Construction of the first of three prototypes began in 1964, the first of which made the type's first flight on February 16 1967. This aircraft was powered by 236kW (317shp) Allison 250-C18 turboshafts and featured a conventional main rotor hub, but the subsequent prototypes incorporated a new rigid hub with feathering hinges, plus composite blades and MAN-Turbo 6022 engines. The BO 105 reverted back to Allison 250 power with the second of two pre production aircraft, flying in this form in January 1971.

Initial production was of the BO 105C which was available from 1970. The Allison 250-C20 powerplant became standard from 1973. The BO 105 CB was introduced in 1975, and became the standard production model. It introduced uprated engines and a strengthened transmission. The BO 105 is now available in BO 105 CBS form with a slight 25cm (10in) fuselage stretch and extra window, allowing an extra passenger to be carried. Other models that have been offered include the BO 105D which has IFR instrumentation and was developed for the British offshore oil rig support market. The BO 105 L has more powerful engines and higher takeoff weight. The BO 105 LS is a hot and high version with Allison 250-C28C engines and built exclusively in Canada by Eurocopter Canada.

The EC Super Five is a high performance development of the BO 105 CBS with new main rotor blades. It was certificated in late 1993.

Photo: A Eurocopter BO 105 demonstrator.

Eurocopter/CATIC/STA EC 120

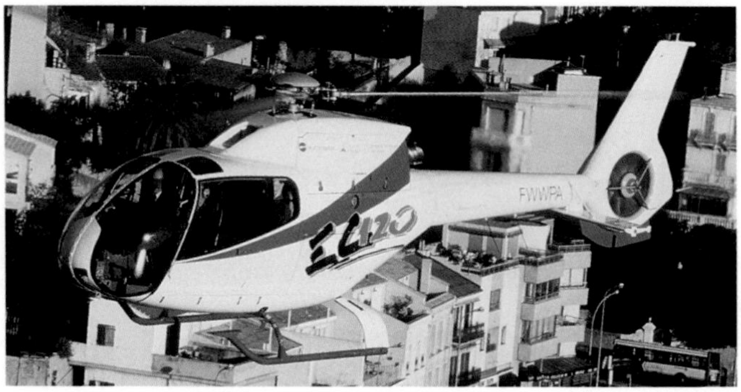

Countries of origin: France, Germany, China and Singapore

Type: Five place light utility helicopter

Powerplants: One 375kW (505shp) Turboméca TM 319 Arrius 1F turboshaft, driving a three blade main rotor and an eight blade Fenestron shrouded tail rotor.

Performance: Max cruising speed 235km/h (127kt). Service ceiling 16,000ft. Hovering ceiling out of ground effect 10,500ft at ISA or 4595ft at ISA + 20°. Range approximately 705km (380nm).

Weights: Standard empty 850kg (1875lb), max takeoff 1550kg (3417lb).

Dimensions: Main rotor diameter 10.00m (32ft 9in), length overall blades folded 9.60m (31ft 6in), height overall 3.27m (10ft 9in). Main rotor disc area 78.5m^2 (845.4sq ft).

Capacity: Typical seating for five, with pilot and passenger side by side with three passengers on rear bench seat. Could be configured for special missions roles. Max sling load 750kg (1653lb).

Production: First prototype only flying at the time of writing. Deliveries of production aircraft planned for late 1997 following certification. Eurocopter predicts sales of between 1600 and 2000 units during the EC 120's production life.

History: Eurocopter's solution to develop a replacement for its very successful Ecureuil lay in forming a partnership with CATIC (Harbin) of China and Singapore Technologies Aerospace of Singapore.

Eurocopter (then Aerospatiale), CATIC and STA launched definition development of their new light helicopter, then designated P 120L, in February 1990. The teaming arrangements for the helicopter saw Aerospatiale/Eurocopter with a 61% program share and leadership, CATIC with 24% and STA with 15%. A development go-ahead contract for the new aircraft was signed in October 1992 (by which time Aerospatiale's helicopter activities had been merged into Eurocopter) and the EC 120 designation was announced in January 1993. Design definition was completed in mid 1993.

Within the Eurocopter/CATIC/STA partnership, Eurocopter is responsible for the design and manufacture of the rotor system and transmission, final assembly, flight testing and certification. CATIC will build the EC 120's fuselage, landing gear and fuel system, while STA's areas of responsibility covers the tailboom, fin and doors.

Notable EC 120 design features include a three blade main rotor with a Spheriflex hub integrated with the driveshaft and transmission, composite main and tail rotor blades and skid landing gear, a metal construction fuselage and a new eight blade Fenestron shrouded tail rotor. At least the first 300 EC 120s will be powered by a Turboméca TM 319 Arrius 1F turboshaft. The new helicopter's cabin features standard seating for five including the pilot.

The first of three prototype EC 120s to be built flew for the first time on June 9 1995 from Eurocopter France's Marignane facility. Eurocopter and its partners are working towards certification in late 1997, with first customer deliveries following shortly afterwards. Final assembly of production EC 120s will be undertaken in either France or Germany. Eurocopter has forecast a market for up to 2000 EC 120s.

Photo: The EC 120 prototype. (Eurocopter)

Eurocopter/Kawasaki BK 117

Countries of origin: Germany & Japan

Type: Twin engine medium size utility helicopter

Powerplants: BK 117 A – Two 450kW (600shp) Avco (Textron) Lycoming LTS 101-650B-1 turboshafts driving a four blade main rotor and two blade tail rotor. BK 117 B-2 – Two 442kW (592shp) AlliedSignal LTS 101-750B-1s.

Performance: BK 117 A – Cruising speed 264km/h (143kt). Initial rate of climb 1970ft/min. Hovering ceiling in ground effect 13,450ft. Range with max payload 545km (295nm). BK 117 B-2 – Max cruising speed 250km/h (135kt). Initial rate of climb 2165ft/min. Hovering ceiling in ground effect 11,700ft. Range with standard fuel 540km (290nm).

Weights: BK 117 A – Empty 1520kg (3350lb), max takeoff 2800kg (6173lb). BK 117 B-2 – Empty 1727kg (3807lb), max takeoff 3350kg (7385lb).

Dimensions: Main rotor diameter 11.00m (36ft 1in), length overall 13.00m (42ft 8in) fuselage length 9.91m (32ft 6in), height rotors turning 3.85m (12ft 8in). Main rotor disc area 95.0m^2 (1023sq ft).

Capacity: One pilot and max seating for 10 passengers. Executive configuration seats six, standard MBB/Eurocopter configuration seats seven, standard Kawasaki version seats nine. Can be equipped for Search & Rescue, EMS, and police work with various appropriate internal configurations.

Production: Approximately 360 BK 117s built by both Eurocopter/MBB and Kawasaki, the break down comprising 260 from Eurocopter/MBB and 100 from Kawasaki.

History: The BK 117 was developed under a joint collaborative effort between MBB of Germany (now part of Eurocopter) and Kawasaki of Japan with production lines in both countries.

The BK 117 program replaced the independently developed BO 107 and Kawasaki KH-7 design studies. Retaining the former's overall configuration, Eurocopter is responsible for the helicopter's rotor system (which uses a scaled up version of the BO 105's four blade rigid main rotor), tail unit, hydraulic system and power controls, while Kawasaki has responsibility for the fuselage, transmission and undercarriage.

Development led to the BK 117's first flight on June 13 1979, the first production aircraft (built in Japan) flew December 1981, certification was awarded in December 1982, and first deliveries took place early in 1983. Initial production was of the BK 117 A-1, while the BK 117 A-3 with higher max takeoff weight and enlarged tail rotor with twisted blades was certificated in March 1985. The BK 117 A-4 introduced from 1987 features increased performance through an increased transmission limit at takeoff power, improved tail rotor head and, on German built aircraft, increased fuel.

The BK 117 B-1 (certificated in 1987) has more powerful engines and better performance, the BK 117 B-2 is currently in production and has an increased max takeoff weight. The BK 117 C-1 is a German development with a new cockpit and Turboméca Arriel engines. Indonesian licence built aircraft are known as the NBK-117. Research variants of the BK 117 include one built with composites, and one fitted with a fly-by-wire control system.

Photo: A New Zealand medevac BK 117. (Peter Clark)

Eurocopter EC 135

Countries of origin: Germany and France

Type: Seven place light twin turbine utility helicopter

Powerplants: Either two 435kW (583shp) takeoff rated Turboméca Arrius 2B or two 463kW (621shp) takeoff rated Pratt & Whitney Canada PW206B turboshafts, driving a four blade main rotor and 10 blade shrouded Fenestron tail rotor.

Performance: Max cruising speed 261km/h (141kt). Max initial rate of climb 1595ft/min. Service ceiling 20,000ft. Hovering ceiling in ground effect 15,585ft, out of ground effect 13,450ft. Range with standard fuel 715km (385nm), ferry range with long range tank 925km (500nm). Endurance with standard fuel 4hr.

Weights: Empty with Arrius 2Bs 1370kg (3020lb), empty with PW206s 1390kg (3064lb), max takeoff 2500kg (5511lb) or 2700kg (5952lb) with an external sling load.

Dimensions: Main rotor diameter 10.20m (33ft 5in), length overall 12.10m (39ft 9in), fuselage length 10.16m (33ft 4in), height to top of rotor head 3.35m (11ft 0in). Main rotor disc area 81.7m^2 (879.5sq ft).

Capacity: Designed for single pilot operation (including IFR ops). Alternative cabin layouts are for five (two forward & three rear) or seven (two + three + two) in passenger roles. Alternative EMS layouts for one stretcher, three medical attendants and the pilot, or two stretchers two attendants and pilot. Stretchers loaded through rear freight door.

Production: First deliveries in July 1996. Total forecast sales of 900 units.

History: The EC 135 is intended as a replacement for Eurocopter's successful BO 105 light twin, and is developed from the BO 108 technology demonstrator.

The original MBB BO 108 was intended as a high technology helicopter demonstrator, and as such incorporated a range of high technology features including a hingeless main rotor (Sikorsky and Boeing adopted this design for their military RAH-66 Comanche), all composite bearingless tail rotor, shallow transmission (allowing greater cabin height) with special vibration absorbers, composite structures, improved aerodynamics, modern avionics and EFIS instrumentation. The first BO 108 was powered by Allison 250-C20R-3 turboshafts and flew on October 15 1988.

The success of the BO 108 test program led to MBB's announcement in January 1991 that it would develop the 108 with Arrius or PW206 engines as a replacement for the BO 105, with certification planned for 1994, with deliveries in 1995. The formation of Eurocopter (via a merger of Aerospatiale's and MBB's helicopter operations in January 1992) gave the program access to Aerospatiale's Fenestron shrouded tail rotor technology.

The combination of the BO 108 and the Fenestron led to the definitive EC 135 flying for the first time on February 15 1994. German certification was granted on June 14 1996, while US approval was given on July 31 that year, the same day as the first customer delivery. Eurocopter forecasts sales of 900 EC 135s over the next decade, despite strong competition from the McDonnell Douglas Explorer.

Photo: The third pre production EC 135. Production aircraft feature an enlarged auxiliary fins and strake beneath the shrouded tail rotor. (Eurocopter)

Extra 230, 300 & 200

Country of origin: Germany

Type: Unlimited competition aerobatic aircraft

Powerplant: 230 – One 150kW (200hp) Textron Lycoming AEIO-360 flat four piston engine, driving a two blade c/s Mühlbauer propeller. 300 – One 225kW (300hp) Textron Lycoming AEIO-540-L1B5 flat six, driving a three (or optionally four) blade Mühlbauer c/s prop.

Performance: 230 – Max speed 352km/h (190kt). Initial rate of climb 2950ft/min. Endurance with max fuel 2hr 30min. 300 – Max speed 343km/h (185kt), max manoeuvring speed 293km/h (158kt). Initial rate of climb 3300ft/min. Range with reserves 974km (526nm).

Weights: 230 – Empty 440kg (970lb), max takeoff 560kg (1235lb). 300 – Empty 630kg (1389lb), max aerobatic takeoff 870kg (1918lb), max takeoff 950kg (2094lb).

Dimensions: 230 – Wing span 7.40m (24ft 3in), length 5.82m (19ft 2in), height 1.73m (5ft 8in). 300 – Wing span 8.00m (26ft 3in), length 7.12m (23ft 4in), height 2.62m (8ft 7in). Wing area 10.7m^2 (115.17sq ft). 300 S – Same except for wing span 7.50m (24ft 7in), length 6.65m (21ft 9in). Wing area 10.4m^2 (112sq ft).

Capacity: 300 and 200 seats two, 230 and 300 S seat pilot only.

Production: Extra 230 production ceased in 1990. Approximately 70 Extra 300s delivered since 1988, including six for the Chilean air force.

History: The Extra series of aerobatic light aircraft were designed from the outset for unlimited aerobatic competition flying.

The original wooden wing Extra 230 was designed by Extra founder, Walter Extra, to meet the requirements of competition pilots with the Swiss Aero Club. First flight occurred during 1983. Unusually for an aircraft of its type the Extra 230 features a wooden wing with dacron covering, while as on other aerobatic competition aircraft the 230's wing has 0° incidence for sustained inverted flight. Production ceased in 1990 when Extra was experiencing difficulties in sourcing the correct type of wood.

Design work on the larger, two seat Extra 300 began in early 1987, culminating in the first flight of a prototype on May 6 1988, and the awarding of certification in May 1990. Production began in October 1988.

A small number of Extra 260s were also built in the early 1990s. These aircraft were essentially downsized Extra 300s with seating for a pilot and powered by a 195kW (160hp) IO-540 flat six. The Extra 260 was not certificated, the six that were built were able to fly under special permits.

The single seat Extra 300 S meanwhile first flew on March 4 1992 and was certificated that same month. The 300 S differs from the 300 in having a single seat, shorter span wings and more powerful ailerons, while retaining the same powerplant and basic fuselage. The 300L has a low mounted wing.

As they are designed for aerobatics, both the 300 and 300 S are stressed for +10/-10 g flight with a single pilot, have additional transparencies in the lower sides of the fuselage below the wings for pilot visibility, and a single piece main canopy.

Extra's latest product is the 150kW (200hp) AEIO-360 powered Extra 200 two seater. It first flew in April 1996. Of similar construction to the 300, it replaces the earlier 230.

Photo: An Extra 300. (Julian Green)

Fairchild Dornier 228

Country of origin: Germany

Type: Commuter airliner and STOL utility transport

Powerplants: 100 – Two 535kW (715shp) Garrett TPE331-5 turboprops, driving four blade constant speed Hartzell propellers. 212 – Two 560kW (776shp) Garrett/AlliedSignal TPE331-5-252Ds.

Performance: 100 – Max cruising speed 432km/h (233kt). Initial rate of climb 2050ft/min. Service ceiling 29,600ft. Range at max cruising speed 1730km (934nm), or 1970km (1064nm) at long range cruising speed. 212 – Max cruising speed 434km/h (234kt), cruising speed 408km/h (220kt). Initial rate of climb 1870ft. Service ceiling 28,000ft. Range with max pax and reserves at max cruising speed 1037km (560nm), range with a 775kg (1710lb) payload and reserves at long range cruising speed 2445km (1320nm).

Weights: 100 – Operating empty 3235kg (7132lb), max takeoff 5700kg (12,570lb). 212 – Empty 3258kg (7183lb), operating empty 3739kg (8243lb), max takeoff 6400kg (14,110lb).

Dimensions: Wing span 16.97m (55ft 7in), length 15.03m (49ft 3in), height 4.86m (15ft 9in). Wing area 32.0m^2 (345sq ft). 212 – Same except for length 16.56m (54ft 4in).

Capacity: Flightcrew of two. 100 – Typical passenger seating for 15. 212 – Typical passenger seating for 19 two abreast at 76cm (30in) pitch. 228-212 based 228 Cargo has a max payload of 2340kg (5159lb). -212 based ambulance accommodates six stretchers and up to nine attendants or passengers.

Production: Approximately 230 Dornier 228s of all models ordered thus far, most of which have been delivered and are in service. Indian licence production of more than 55 228s.

History: In terms of civil sales the 228 series has been Dornier's most successful postwar design, with orders now in the region of 250.

The Dornier 228 incorporates the fuselage cross section of the earlier Do 28 and 128, combined with an all new high technology supercritical wing and TFE331 turboprops. Two fuselage length versions, the 100 and 200, were developed concurrently, the 100 offering better range, the 200 more payload. The 100 was the first to fly taking to the skies for the first time on March 28 1981, the first 200 followed on May 9 that year. The first 228 entered service in August 1982.

Composites were used in a number of secondary structure areas on the 228 including upper wing skins, nose and tail. At one stage Dornier also planned to offer the Pratt & Whitney Canada PT6A as an optional powerplant, but this never eventuated.

228 developments include the 228-101 with reinforced structure and landing gear for higher weights, the corresponding 228-201 version of the -200, the 228-202 version under licence production in India with HAL to meet that country's Light Transport Aircraft requirement, and the 228-212. The -212 is the current and only Dornier production aircraft, its improvements include higher operating weights, structural strengthening and a lower empty weight, improvements to enhance STOL performance, and modern avionics.

Photo: A 228-200 of Malaysia's Pelangi Air in flight. (Dornier)

Fairchild Dornier 328

Country of origin: United States of America

Type: High speed short range commuter airliner

Powerplants: Two 1625kW (2180shp) takeoff rated Pratt & Whitney PW119B turboprops, driving six blade Hartzell propellers.

Performance: 328-110 – Max cruising speed 620km/h (335kt). Design cruising altitude 25,000ft or optionally 31,000ft. Range with 30 passengers and reserves at max cruising speed at 25,000ft cruising altitude 1665km (900nm), at 31,000ft 1850km (1000nm).

Weights: 328-110 – Operating empty 8920kg (19,665lb), max takeoff 13,990kg (30,842lb).

Dimensions: Wing span 20.98m (68ft 10in), length 21.22m (69ft 8in), height 7.24m (23ft 9in). Wing area 40.0m^2 (430.6sq ft).

Capacity: Flightcrew of two. Typical passenger seating for 30 to 33 at three abreast, max seating for 39 at four abreast.

Production: At late 1996 orders stood at 98, of which 50 aircraft were in service.

History: The modern Dornier 328 is one of the most technologically advanced commuter airliners on the market offering high speed and advanced systems.

Development of the 328 traces back to Dornier's mid 1980s market research that indicated there existed a substantial market for commuter airliners in the 30 seat class through to 2005. Firm 328 development work began in December 1988, culminating in the first development aircraft (registered D-CHIC)'s first flight on December 6 1991. The development program was marked by some setbacks, including the loss of all six propeller blades (two penetrated the fuselage and entered the cabin) from the left side engine in December 1992 during a test flight. The 328 was awarded certification in October 1993. First customer deliveries also occurred in October 1993. A big setback for the program was the collapse of US carrier Midway which had ordered 33 328s.

The 328 design incorporates an all new fuselage section and shape coupled to the supercritical wing of the earlier Dornier 228. Clean aerodynamics give the 328 excellent high speed cruise and climb performance. Composite materials are used in a number of areas (particularly the tail) to reduce weight. The cockpit features a five screen EFIS system, while with a Head Up Display the 328 can be qualified for Cat IIIa landings.

Industrial participation on the 328 comes from Daewoo Heavy Industries (fuselage), Aermacchi (nose), Westland (nacelles) and Israel Aircraft Industries (wing), and accounts for 40% of the aircraft construction.

Dornier 328 variants are the initial production standard 328-100, the standard 328-110 with heavier weights and greater range, the 328-120 with improved short field performance and the 328-200 with progressive rudder authority reduction with increasing airspeed.

Plans for a stretched 50 seat 328 were initially dropped, but later revived in 1996 when Fairchild bought Dornier from DASA. Fairchild Dornier is seriously studying a jet powered 328, which could be launched by late 1996. Potential engines are the Pratt & Whitney Canada PW300, Textron Lycoming LF507 or the CFE738.

Photo: A 328 in the colours of Texas based Lone Star, which operates four. (Dornier)

Fairchild Dornier Metro II, III & 23

Country of origin: United States of America

Type: Commuter airliner

Powerplants: Metro II – Two 700kW (940shp) Garrett AiResearch TPE331-3UW-303G turboprops driving three blade constant speed propellers. 23 – Two 745kW (1000shp) AlliedSignal TPE331-11U-612Gs, or 820kW (1100shp) TPE331-12UARs.

Performance: II – Max cruising speed 473km/h (255kt), long range cruising speed 450km/h (242kt). Service ceiling 27,000ft. Range with 19 pax and reserves at max cruising speed 346km (187nm), with 15 pax and reserves at max cruising speed 1100km (595nm). 23 – Max cruising speed 542km/h (293kt). Service ceiling 25,000ft. Range with 19 passengers and reserves 2065km (1314nm), with 2268kg (5000lb) payload and reserves 988km (533nm).

Weights: II – Empty 3380kg (7450lb), max takeoff 5670kg (12,500lb). 23 – Operating empty 4309kg (9500lb), max takeoff 7484kg (16,500lb).

Dimensions: II – Wing span 14.10m (46ft 3in), length 18.09m (59ft 4in), height 5.08m (16ft 8in). Wing area 25.8m² (277.5sq ft). 23 – Same except for wing span 17.37m (57ft 0in). Wing area 28.7m² (309.0sq ft).

Capacity: Flightcrew of two. Passenger seating for 19 at two abreast and 76cm (30in) pitch. Merlin IV and 23 also seat 12 to 14 passengers in a corporate configuration. The Expediter I and 23 are freighters.

Production: Over 1000 Metros in service in late 1996.

History: Despite a slow start to sales in the early 1970s, the Metro series has become one of the most popular 19 seat commuters.

The Metro can trace its lineage back to the original Merlin I executive transport. From the Merlin I Swearingen developed the turboprop powered II and III which were to form the basis of the new Metro commuter airliner. Design work on Swearingen's first complete inhouse design began in the late 1960s, culminating in the SA-226TC Metro's first flight on August 26 1969. The design was similar in appearance and layout to the earlier Merlins, and featured a pressurised fuselage, TPE331 turboprop engines and double slotted trailing edge flaps. Certification was awarded in June 1970 and the first example entered commercial service in 1973.

The Metro II quickly superseded the I from 1975, its improvements focusing on reducing main cabin noise levels and revised flightdeck seating. The equivalent executive aircraft is the Merlin IV. Following the Metro II from 1981 was the III (by which time Fairchild had taken over Swearingen), which was certificated to SFAR-41B which allowed greater takeoff weights, while more efficient engines (including the option of Pratt & Whitney Canada PT6As on the IIIA) and greater wing span made the III more economical to operate. The Expediter freighter is based on the III.

The current Metro model is the 23. Certificated to FAR Part 23 standards (hence Metro 23 designation) it features a higher takeoff weight, more powerful engines and systems improvements first introduced on the military C-26. The Metro 23 EF has a bulged lower fuselage for greater baggage capacity, while the Merlin 23 and Expediter 23 models are also offered. In 1996 Fairchild was considering a Metro with a significantly higher fuselage (in the style of the Beech 1900D).

Photo: Metro IIIs. (Fairchild)

Fairchild (Swearingen) Merlin

Country of origin: United States of America

Type: Turboprop executive transport

Powerplants: IIB – Two 495kW (665shp) AiResearch (Garrett) TPE 331-1-151G turboprops, driving three blade constant speed propellers. IIIC – Two 670kW (900shp) Garrett TPE331-10U-503G turboprops, driving four blade constant speed Dowty propellers.

Performance: IIB – Max cruising speed 475km/h (257kt). Initial rate of climb 2570ft/min. Service ceiling 29,000ft. Range with max fuel 2872km (1550nm). IIIC – Max cruising speed 556km/h (300kt). Initial rate of climb 2650ft/min. Range with max standard fuel at max cruising speed with six people on board 3590km (1938nm).

Weights: IIB – Empty 2926kg (6452lb), max takeoff 4540kg (10,000lb). IIIC – Empty equipped 3695kg (8150lb), max takeoff 5670kg (12,500lb).

Dimensions: IIB – Wing span 13.98m (45ft 11in), length 12.22m (40ft 1in), height 4.37m (14ft 4in). Wing area 26.0m² (279.74sq ft). IIIC – Wing span 14.10m (46ft 3in), length 12.85m (42ft 2in), height 5.13m (16ft 10in). Wing area 25.8m² (277.5sq ft).

Capacity: IIB – Flightcrew of one or two, with typical main cabin seating for six in executive layout or up to eight. III – Seating in main cabin for up to 11, or eight in a corporate configuration. Merlin IV seats up to 12 passengers in main cabin in a corporate configuration.

Production: Includes 33 Merlin IIAs, 87 Merlin IIBs, 92 Merlin III and IIIAs and 10 Merlin 300s.

History: The Merlin series of turboprop executive transports was Swearingen's first manufacturing program, and laid the foundations for the successful Metro series of commuters.

Prior to the original Merlin II, Swearingen specialised in building conversions of existing aircraft into corporate transports. The Merlin II (or SA26-T) was an extension of this policy in that it is based on the Beech Queen Air and Twin Bonanza. The Merlin combines the wing of the Queen Air with the Twin Bonanza's undercarriage with an all new Swearingen designed pressurised fuselage and tail. The first Merlins were powered by two 300kW (400hp) Lycoming TIGO-540s, while the Merlin IIA was powered by Pratt & Whitney Canada PT6A-20 turboprops. The prototype IIA flew for the first time on April 13 1965 and 33 were built before production switched to the AiResearch TPE331 powered Merlin IIB.

The improved and slightly larger Merlin III combines the Merlin II's fuselage but slightly stretched, with a new tail; and the wings and landing gear of the Metro II airliner (described separately) and more powerful engines. The Merlin III (or SA226-T) was certificated on July 27 1970. The Merlin III was followed by the Merlin 300 (by which time Fairchild had acquired the Merlin and Metro lines) which introduced aerodynamic improvements including winglets. Only 10 were built.

The Merlin IV designation applies to corporate configured versions of the Metro series of commuter airliners. The Merlin IVA designation covers the corporate versions of the original Metro II (which used a stretched Merlin II's fuselage coupled with a new wing, undercarriage and tail), the IVB the executive equivalent of the Metro III, and the Merlin 23 equivalent of the Metro 23.

Photo: A Swearingen Merlin III. (Bill Lines)

FFA AS 202 Bravo

Country of origin: Switzerland

Type: Two seat basic trainer and aerobatic light aircraft

Powerplants: AS/202 15 – One 110kW (150hp) Lycoming O-320-E2A flat four piston engine, driving a two blade fixed pitch McCauley propeller. 18A4 – One 135kW (180hp) fuel injected Textron Lycoming AEIO-360-B1F, driving a two blade constant speed Hartzell propeller, or optionally a three blade Hoffmann prop.

Performance: 15 – Max cruising speed 210km/h (114kt), economical cruising speed 203km/h (110kt). Initial rate of climb 633ft/min. Service ceiling 14,000ft. Range with max fuel and no reserves 890km (480nm). 18A4 – Max speed 240km/h (130kt), max cruising speed 226km/h (122kt), economical cruising speed 205km/h (110kt). Initial rate of climb 800ft/min. Service ceiling 17,000ft. Range with max fuel and no reserves 1140km (615nm).

Weights: 15 – Empty equipped 630kg (1388lb), max takeoff 999kg (2202lb) for Utility category, 885kg (1951lb) for Aerobatic. 18A4 – Operating empty 710kg (1565lb), max takeoff 1080kg (2380lb) for Utility category, 1050kg (2315lb) for Aerobatic category.

Dimensions: Wing span 9.75m (32ft 0in), length 7.50m (24ft 7in), height 2.81m (9ft 3in). Wing area 13.9m^2 (149.2sq ft).

Capacity: Two pilots side by side, plus one passenger in rear.

Production: Orders received stand at over 34 15s and 180 18s, with approximately 170 of the latter in service, largely with military customers.

History: Although primarily in service with military air arms as a basic trainer, small numbers of the FFA Bravo are in also civilian service, both as aerobatic and basic pilot trainers.

Design of the Bravo dates back to the late 1960s, with original design work undertaken by SIAI Marchetti of Italy, but with production and subsequent development work the responsibility of FFA (a company originally established by Dornier as its Swiss subsidiary).

The first prototype to fly was Swiss built, it took to the air for the first time on March 7 1969. An Italian built prototype followed soon after on May 7, while the first production standard aircraft flew on December 22 1971.

Initial production concentrated on the AS 202/15 and 34 were built through to the early 1980s. The current production model is the AS 202/18A4, which first flew in August 1974 and received its certification in late 1975. This version differs from the original 15 in having a more powerful 135kW (180hp) engine. The principle civil Bravo operator is the British Aerospace Flying College in Scotland which operates 11 (named Wrens).

Two other models have been developed, although single aircraft of each have flown only. The first was the 195kW (260hp) Textron Lycoming AEIO-540 powered Bravo 26A1, which first flew in 1979, the second was the 240kW (320shp) Allison 250-B17C turbine powered Bravo 32TP which flew in 1991.

The Bravo is still offered for sale although none have been delivered since 1989.

Photo: An AS 202/18AF Bravo demonstrator awaiting takeoff at the 1992 Farnborough Airshow. (Paul Merritt)

Fokker F27 & Fairchild F-27 & FH-227

Country of origin: Netherlands

Type: Short range turboprop airliner

Powerplants: Mk 200 – Two 1730kW (2320ehp) Rolls-Royce Dart Mk 536-7R turboprops, driving four blade Dowty Rotol propellers. FH-227E – Two 1715kW (2300shp) Dart 532-7Ls.

Performance: Mk 200 – Normal cruising speed 480km/h (260kt). Service ceiling 20,000ft. Range with 44 passengers and reserves 1925km (1040nm). FH-227 – Max cruising speed 473km/h (255kt), economical cruising speed 435km/h (236kt). Range with max payload 1055km (570nm), range with max fuel 2660km (1440nm).

Weights: Mk 200 – Operating empty 12,011kg (26,480lb), max takeoff 20,410kg (44,996lb). FH-227 – Operating empty 10,398kg (22,923lb), max takeoff 20,639kg (45,500lb).

Dimensions: Mk 200 – Wing span 29.00m (95ft 2in), length 23.56m (77ft 4in), height 8.50m (27ft 11in). Wing area 70.0m^2 (754sq ft). FH-227 – Same except for length 25.50m (83ft 8in), height 8.41m (27ft 7in).

Capacity: Flightcrew of two. Seating for 44 at four abreast and 76cm (30in) pitch in original fuselage length versions (Mks 100, 200, 300, 400, 600 & F-27). Standard seating for 52, and max seating for 60 at 72cm (28.5in) pitch in Mk 500. FH-227 seats 52 at 79cm (31in) pitch, or a max of 56.

Production: Total of 581 F27s, 128 F-27s and 78 FH-227s built. Fokker production comprised 85 Mk 100s, 138 Mk 200s, 13 Mk 300s, 218 Mk 400 & 600s, 112 Mk 500s and six F27MPA Maritimes. Total in service in late 1996 stood at just over 300.

History: Perhaps the nearest yet to the fabled DC-3 replacement, the Fokker F27 Friendship series, together with the Fairchild built F-27 and FH-227, was built in greater numbers than any other western turboprop airliner.

The Fokker F27 began life as a 1950 design study known as the P275, a 32 seater powered by two Rolls-Royce Dart turboprops. With the aid of Dutch government funding the P275 evolved into the F27, which first flew on November 24 1955. This original prototype was powered by Dart 507s and would have seated 28, by the time the second prototype had flown (in January 1957) the fuselage length grew to allow seating for 32.

By this stage Fokker had signed an agreement that would see Fairchild build Friendships in the USA. The first aircraft to enter service was actually a Fairchild built F-27 in September 1958.

Fairchild F-27s differed from the initial Fokker F27 Mk 100s in having basic seating for 40, a lengthened nose capable of housing a weather radar, and additional fuel capacity.

Developments included the Mk 200/F-27A with more powerful engines, Mk 300/F-27B and primarily military Mk 400 Combi planes, the Mk 500 with a 1.50m (4ft 11in) fuselage stretch taking seating to 52, and Mk 600 quick change freight/pax aircraft.

Fairchild independently developed the stretched FH-227, which in fact appeared almost two years earlier than the Mk 500. The FH-227 featured a 1.83m (6ft 0in) stretch over standard length F27/F-27s, taking standard seating to 52.

Photo: An F27-600 quick change freighter/airliner. (David Daw)

Fokker 50

Country of origin: Netherlands

Type: Turboprop regional airliner

Powerplant: Series 100 – Two 1864kW (2500shp) Pratt & Whitney Canada PW125B turboprops, driving six blade Dowty propellers. Series 300 – Two 2050kW (2750shp) PW127Bs.

Performance: Series 100 – Max cruising speed 532km/h (287kt), economical cruising speed 454km/h (245kt). Max operating altitude 25,000ft. Range with 50 passengers and reserves 2055km (1110nm), or 2822km (1524nm) for optional high gross weight version. Series 300 – Typical cruising speed 526km/h (284kt). Range with 50 passengers and reserves at high speed cruise 2033km (1097nm), or 3017km (1628nm) for high gross weight option at long range cruise.

Weights: Series 100 & 300 – Operating empty 12,520kg (27,602lb), max takeoff 19,950kg (43,980lb), or optionally 20,820kg (45,900lb).

Dimensions: Wing span 29.00m (95ft 2in), length 25.25m (82ft 10in), height 8.32m (27ft 4in). Wing area 70.0m^2 (753.5sq ft).

Capacity: Flightcrew of two. Standard seating for 50 at four abreast and 81cm (32in) pitch. Max high density seating for 58. Available with convertible passenger/freight configurations.

Production: Approximately 220 Fokker 50s ordered at early 1996. Fokker due to wind up production in late 1996.

History: The Fokker 50 is the successor to Fokker's highly successful and long running F27 Friendship.

Fokker announced it was developing the 50 seat Fokker 50, together with the 100 seat jet powered Fokker 100 in November 1983. The Fokker 50 is based on the fuselage of the F27-500 Friendship, but embodies a number of key design changes. Foremost of the improvements was the new generation Pratt & Whitney Canada PW125 turboprops, driving advanced six blade props giving a 12% higher cruising speed and greater fuel economy, and thus range. Other improvements include new avionics and an EFIS glass cockpit, limited use of composites, small 'Foklet' winglets, and more, square, main cabin windows.

Two prototypes were built based on F27 airframes (despite the fact that over 80% of parts are new or modified), the first flying on December 28 1985. The first production aircraft flew on February 13 1987, certification being granted in May 1987, with first customer delivery, to Lufthansa Cityline, that August.

The basic Fokker 50 production model is the Series 100. With three, instead of four doors, the Series 100 is designated the Series 120. The hot and high optimised Series 300 has more powerful PW127B turboprops, and was announced in 1990. It has higher cruising speeds and better field performance, particularly at altitude.

Fokker studied stretched developments of the 50. A stretched version would have been capable of seating 68 and be named the Fokker 60. The Dutch manufacturer has already built stretched Fokker 60 Utility military freighters for the Netherlands air force.

Fokker collapsed due to financial problems on March 15 1996. While several buyers had shown interest in buying Fokker it is unlikely that the Fokker 50 would return to production under a new owner, given the proliferation of 50 seat regional airliners.

Photo: Philippine Airlines operates 10 Fokker 50s. (Fokker)

Fokker F28 Fellowship

Country of origin: Netherlands

Type: Short range regional jet airliner

Powerplants: Mk 3000 & 4000 – Two 44.3kN (9900lb) Rolls-Royce RB183-2 Spey Mk 555-15P turbofans.

Performance: 3000 – Max cruising speed 843km/h (455kt), economical cruising speed 678km/h (366kt). Range at high speed cruise with 65 passengers 2743km (1480nm), at long range cruise with 65 passengers 3170km (1710nm). 4000 – Speeds same. Range at high speed cruise with 85 passengers 1900km (1025nm), at long range cruising speed with 85 passengers 2085km (1125nm).

Weights: 3000 – Operating empty 16,965kg (37,400lb), max takeoff 33,110kg (73,000lb). 4000 – Operating empty 17,645kg (38,900lb), max takeoff 33,110kg (73,000lb).

Dimensions: 3000 – Wing span 25.07m (82ft 3in), length 27.40m (89ft 11in), height 8.47m (27ft 10in). Wing area 79.0m^2 (850sq ft). 4000 – Same except for length 29.61m (97ft 2in).

Capacity: Flightcrew of two. Max seating for 85 at five abreast and 74cm (29in) pitch in Mk 4000, or 65 in Mk 3000. Mk 3000 offered with a 15 seat executive interior.

Production: Total F28 sales of 241, including some military customers. As at late 1996 160 remained in commercial service.

History: The F28 Fellowship is Fokker's first jet engined airliner, and was developed to complement that company's highly successful F27 Friendship turboprop.

Fokker began development of the F28 in 1960 after perceiving a market requirement for a higher performance (ie jet engined) and greater capacity airliner in comparison with the F27. First details of the F28 were made public in April 1962, and production of the first development aircraft began in 1964. The first of three prototypes flew for the first time on May 9 1967, with certification and first customer delivery both occurring on February 24 1969.

The F28 was developed into a range of models, starting with the initial production model, the Mk 1000. The 1000 would typically seat between 55 and 65, and was powered by 44.1kN (9850lb) Spey Mk 555-15 turbofans. The Mk 2000 was essentially similar but featured a 2.21m (7ft 3in) fuselage stretch, increasing maximum seating to 79.

The Mks 5000 and 6000 were based on the 1000 and 2000 respectively, but introduced a longer span wing (by 1.49m/4ft 11in) and wing leading edge slats. Unfortunately neither version attracted serious sales interest, and no 5000s and just two 6000s were built. Another version that did not come to fruition was the Mk 6600, which would have been stretched by a further 2.21m (7ft 3in), allowing for seating for 100 in a high density layout. It was aimed specifically at Japanese airlines.

The final production models were the 3000 and 4000, again based on the 1000 and 2000 respectively. Both introduced a number of improvements, while the addition of two extra above wing emergency exits on the 4000 increased maximum seating to 85. Freight door equipped convertible versions of each model were offered, and are identified by a C suffix.

Photo: One of 16 Canadian Regional F28-1000s, pictured at Toronto's Pearson International Airport. (Gary Gentle)

Fokker 70

Country of origin: Netherlands

Type: 70 seat short range regional jetliner

Powerplants: Two 61.6kN (13,850lb) Rolls-Royce Tay Mk 620 turbofans.

Performance: High speed cruise Mach 0.77. Range with 79 passengers and baggage at standard weights 2010km (1085nm), or 3410nm (1840nm) for high gross weight option with extra fuel.

Weights: Operating empty 22,673kg (49,985lb), max takeoff standard aircraft 36,470kg (80,997lb), or optionally 38,100kg (83,996lb), or 39,915kg (87,997lb).

Dimensions: Wing span 28.08m (92ft 2in), length 30.91m (101ft 5in), height 8.50m (27ft 11in). Wing area 93.5m^2 (1006.4sq ft).

Capacity: Flightcrew of two. Standard single class passenger accommodation for 79 at five abreast at 81cm (32in) pitch. Fokker Executive Jet 70 interiors fitted to customer requirements.

Production: Approximately 50 Fokker 70s due to be completed before Fokker production winds up.

History: The Fokker 70 is a shortened development of the popular 100 seat class Fokker 100.

Fokker began development of the new derivative airliner in November 1992 despite the absence of firm orders, hopeful of snaring a large share of the forecast 2000 plus aircraft in the 70 to 125 seat class required through to 2010, and the replacement F28 market. The Fokker 70's 30.91m (101ft 4in) length is close to that of the F28-4000's 29.61m (97ft 2in), on which the Fokker 100 was originally based.

The first Fokker 70 was in fact originally the second Fokker 100 prototype which was modified to the new configuration by deleting two fuselage plugs – one forward and one rear of the wing. Construction on this aircraft began in October 1992 (before the November 1992 program go-ahead), resulting in the type's first flight on April 4 1993. The first production Fokker 70 flew for the first time in July 1994 and certification was awarded on October 14 1994. The first Fokker 70 (an Executive Jet 70) was delivered to Ford in the USA later that month.

A design aim of the Fokker 70 was to make it as little different from the larger Fokker 100 as possible. The result of this is that they share essentially identical wings, airframes (except for length, and the removal of two emergency overwing exits on the Fokker 70) and systems, plus similar EFIS cockpits. The Fokker 70 is actually offered with two cockpits, one optimised for the 70's regional airline operations, the other essentially identical to the Fokker 100's to give operators of both types a level of commonality. The Fokker 70 and 100 also share identical Tay Mk 620 powerplants, although the Tay Mk 650 that is offered for the 100 was not available on the 70. The high levels of commonality between the 70 and 100 also allowed them to be built on a common production line.

As with the Fokker 100, a Fokker Executive Jet 70 corporate shuttle was offered (and attracted a small number of orders). The Fokker 70A was optimised for US carriers, while the Fokker 70ER (announced in late 1994) has extra fuel tankage and extended range.

With Fokker's collapse in 1996, the Fokker 70/100 production line will close in early 1997.

Photo: An Air Littoral Fokker 70 in Air France/Air Inter Express colours. (Keith Gaskell)

Fokker 100

Country of origin: Netherlands

Type: Short to medium range airliner

Powerplants: Two 61.6kN (13,850lb) Rolls-Royce Tay Mk 620-15 or 67.2kN (15,100lb) Mk 650-15 turbofans.

Performance: Max cruising speed 845km/h (456kt), long range cruising speed 737km/h (453kt). Range with 107 passengers and Tay 620s 2505km (1323nm), or high gross weight version with Tay 650s 3167km (1710nm).

Weights: Tay 620 – Operating empty 24,375kg (53,738lb), max takeoff 43,090kg (95,000lb). With Tay 650s – Operating empty 24,541kg (54,103lb), max takeoff 45,810kg (101,000lb).

Dimensions: Wing span 28.08m (92ft 2in), length 35.53m (116ft 7in), height 8.50m (27ft 11in). Wing area 93.5m^2 (1006.4sq ft).

Capacity: Flightcrew of two. Max single class high density seating for 122. Standard single class seating for 107 at five abreast and 81cm (32in) pitch. Two class seating for 12 first class passengers at four abreast and 91cm (36in) pitch, and 85 economy class passengers; or 55 business class at five abreast and 86cm (34in) pitch, and 50 economy class pax. Fokker 100QC Quick Change max payload of 11,500kg (25,353lb), comprising five LD9/LD7 containers and one half size container, or up to 11 LD3 containers.

Production: Almost 300 Fokker 100s had been ordered before Fokker's collapse in March 1996. Production to cease early 1997.

History: Fokker's largest aircraft yet, the Fokker 100 is a 100 seat airliner based on the F28 Fellowship, but stretched and thoroughly modernised.

Fokker announced it was developing the Fokker 100 simultaneously with the Fokker 50 turboprop in November 1983. The Fokker 100 is based on the basic F28 airframe, with the most important and obvious change being the stretched fuselage, increasing maximum seating to 122, compared with 85 in the F28-4000 (on which the 100 is based). Other changes include more economical Rolls-Royce Tay turbofans (which, unlike the F28's Speys, conform to Stage III noise limits), revised wing design with greater span and aerodynamic efficiency (Fokker claimed it to be 30% more efficient than the F28's), a modern EFIS glass cockpit, redesigned cabin interior plus other systems and numerous equipment changes.

The Fokker 100's first flight occurred on November 30 1986, certification was awarded in November 1987 and the first customer delivery, to Swissair, occurred in February 1988.

The Fokker 100 was offered in a number of versions including higher gross weight options of the standard airliner, the Fokker 100QC Quick change airliner or freighter with a large forward freight door and the Fokker Executive Jet 100 corporate shuttle or VIP transport, fitted with luxury interiors to customer requirements. It also forms the basis for the Fokker Jetline family of jet airliners. The second Jetline member to be developed was the shorter Fokker 70, while a 130 seat class Fokker 130 had also been studied.

Photo: The Fokker 100 has comfortably outsold the entire family of F28 twinjets on which it is based. (Fokker)

Fuji FA-200 Aero Subaru

Country of origin: Japan

Type: Four seat light aircraft

Powerplant: FA-200-160 – One 120kW (160hp) Lycoming O-320-D2A flat four piston engine driving a two blade fixed pitch McCauley propeller. FA-200-180 – One 135kW (180hp) fuel injected IO-360-B1B driving a two blade constant speed McCauley prop.

Performance: FA-200-160 – Max speed 222km/h (120kt), max cruising speed 196km/h (106kt), long range cruising speed 164km/h (89kt). Initial rate of climb 680ft/min. Service ceiling 11,400ft. Max range with no reserves 1520km (820nm). FA-200-180 – Max speed 233km/h (126kt), max cruising speed 204km/h (110kt), long range cruising speed 167km/h (90kt). Initial rate of climb 760ft/min. Service ceiling 13,700ft. Range with no reserves 1400km (755nm).

Weights: FA-200-160 – Empty 620kg (1366lb), max takeoff 1059kg (2335lb). FA-200-180 – Empty 650kg (1433lb), max takeoff 1150kg (2535lb).

Dimensions: FA-200-160 – Wing span 9.42m (30ft 11in), length 7.96m (26ft 1in), height 2.02m (6ft 8in). Wing area 14.0m^2 (150.7sq ft). FA-200-180 – Same except for length 7.98m (26ft 2in).

Capacity: Typical seating for four.

Production: A total of 299 Aero Subarus built between 1965 and 1986. Series production lasted until 1977, before the Aero Subaru became available by firm order only.

History: The Fuji FA-200 Aero Subaru was the first wholly Japanese designed light aircraft to enter series production, with the majority of aircraft built for export orders.

A product of the Fuji Heavy Industries industrial conglomerate (formed through the merger of six different concerns, including WW2 fighter manufacturer Nakajima), design work on the FA-200 began in 1964. A prototype, the FA-200-II, took to the air for the first time on August 12 1965.

The basic FA-200 design was expected to form the basis of a whole family of light aircraft including the two seat side by side trainer FA-200-I powered by a 85kW (115hp) Lycoming O-235 and the single seat F-204 agricultural version. However only the four seat tourer, as represented by the prototype, entered production. This aircraft was of conventional low wing and fixed undercarriage design, and was aerobatic at reduced weights.

Three versions of the FA-200 were to enter production, the first being the 120kW (160hp) powered FA-200-160, which was also certificated with reduced weights in the Utility category with three seats, and the Aerobatic with two seats. The FA-200-180 was essentially similar but powered by a 135kW (180hp) fuel injected IO-360. Deliveries of both versions began in March 1968.

A third model joined the lineup from mid 1973, the FA-200-180AO. This was a reduced specification version of the FA-200-180 with a fixed pitch propeller and caburetted Lycoming O-360 engine.

The Aero Subaru remained in production until 1977 by which time 274 had been built. The type remained available to special order only through to 1986, by which time a further 25 had been built.

Photo: An Australian registered example of the Lycoming O-320 powered FA-200-160. (Bill Lines)

GAF N22 & N24 Nomad

Country of origin: Australia

Type: STOL utility transport

Powerplants: Two 313kW (420shp) Allison 250-B17C turboprops driving three blade Hartzell propellers.

Performance: Typical cruising speed 311km/h (168kt). Service ceiling N22B 21,000ft, N24A 20,000ft. Range with standard fuel, reserves and operating at 90% power 1352km (730nm). Search mission endurance at 259km/h (140kt) at 5000ft up to 8 hours.

Weights: N22B – Basic empty 2150kg (4741lb), max takeoff 3855kg (8500lb). N24A – Operating empty 2377kg (5241lb); max takeoff 4268kg (9400lb).

Dimensions: N22B – Wing span 16.52m (54ft 2in); length 12.56m (41ft 2in); height 5.52m (18ft 1.5in). Wing area 30.1m^2 (324.0sq ft). N24A – Same except for length 14.36m (47ft 1in).

Capacity: Flightdeck for two pilots although certificated for single pilot operation. Seating in main cabin at two abreast for 12 (N22) or 16 (N24). Searchmaster B patrol aircraft is fitted with a Bendix RDR 1400 search radar and has a normal crew of four. The more sophisticated Searchmaster L has a Litton LASR (AN/APS-504) search radar with 360 degree coverage in an undernose radar.

Production: By the time production ceased in late 1984 a total of 172 Nomads for both civil and military customers had been built, including two prototypes. Approximately 50 are in service with civilian operators.

History: The Nomad was conceived by Australia's Government Aircraft Factory during the late 1960s to help provide the facility with work after construction of licence built Mirage jet fighters was completed, and to offer a new rugged STOL utility transport suited to both military and civil operators.

First flight of the prototype Nomad N2 occurred on July 23 1971, this was followed by a second prototype which flew on December 5 that year. First deliveries of the production N22 aircraft (to the Philippines military) occurred in 1975.

Features of the new utility included retractable undercarriage, two Allison 250 turboprops, a braced high mounted wing with full span double slotted flaps and a squared sided fuselage.

The initial N22 was followed up by the N22B with an increased maximum takeoff weight, this version being certificated in 1975. The N22 also formed the basis for the Searchmaster coastal patrol aircraft which apart from military users also saw service with Australian and US customs services. The Floatmaster was a N22B fitted with Wipaire floats with retractable undercarriage.

Stretching of the N22 fuselage by 1.14m (3ft 9in) led to the N24. Aimed more at commuter airlines (known also as the Commuterliner) than utility operators, main cabin accommodation in this version increased to 16. Versions of the N24 offered included the Cargomaster freighter and the Medicmaster aerial ambulance.

Nomad production ceased in 1984, more due to mismanagement by the Australian government departments entrusted with its development, rather than any faults with the aircraft. The N24 in particular showed more promise than its production figures indicate.

Photo: This N24 Nomad is used to fly tourist sight seeing flights over Australia's famous Kakadu National Park.

Gippsland Aeronautics GA-8 Airvan

Country of origin: Australia

Type: Eight seat utility light aircraft

Powerplants: Prototype – One 185kW (250hp) Textron Lycoming 0-540 flat six piston engine driving a two blade constant speed propeller. Production aircraft – One 225kW (300hp) IO-550 fuel injected flat six driving a three blade constant speed propeller.

Performance: Max cruising speed 240km/h (130kt), economical cruising speed 222km/h (120kt). Max initial rate of climb 600ft/min. Service ceiling 20,000ft. Range with max fuel 1205km (650nm), range with max payload 185km (100nm).

Weights: Empty 862kg (1900lb), max takeoff 1815kg (4000lb).

Dimensions: Wing span 12.37m (40ft 7in), length overall 8.79m (28ft 10in), height 2.82m (9ft 3in). Wing area 19.3m^2 (208.0sq ft).

Capacity: Single pilot and passenger side by side with up to six passengers in the main cabin behind them. Main cabin also configured to carry freight

Production: Unit price approximately $US280,000. First deliveries expected 1997. Intended to capitalise on potentially lucrative Cessna 206 replacement market.

History: The second all new aircraft design from Australian manufacturer Gippsland Aeronautics, the GA-8 has been designed as a utility transport to replace the popular Cessna 206/207 series and others such as the de Havilland Canada Beaver.

Design work on the Airvan began in early 1994 and prototype construction commenced soon after. This prototype flew for the first time on March 3 1995 and publicly appeared at the Australian International Airshow and Aerospace Expo at Avalon later that month after having completed just eight flying hours.

At that time Gippsland Aeronautics anticipated that the Airvan could be certificated within 12 months, all being well. Unfortunately the prototype subsequently crashed, pushing back somewhat the planned certification and entry into service dates.

The prototype Airvan was powered by a 185kW (250hp) Textron Lycoming 0-540 driving a two blade propeller. Production aircraft meanwhile will feature a more powerful fuel injected 225kW (300hp) IO-550 driving a three blade constant speed propeller.

Apart from the engine, design features of the Airvan include its high mounted two spar wing which is based on the unit on the GA-200 ag aircraft, the square sided large volume fuselage with a large sliding freight door on the port side, and fixed landing gear designed for rough field operations. Wiplane floats will be offered as options.

With first customer deliveries planned for 1997 the Airvan will be a keenly priced competitor to Cessna's new production 206, which is expected to cost more, is slightly smaller and will not be available until later than the Australian aircraft. The Airvan is also seen as a worthy replacement for ageing 206/207s and DHC Beavers which have had to soldier on in service due to the lack of a suitable replacement type.

Photo: The first prototype GA-8 Airvan. (Gippsland Aeronautics)

Gippsland Aeronautics GA-200

Country of origin: Australia

Type: Two seat agricultural aircraft

Powerplant: One 195kW (260hp) Textron Lycoming 0-540-H2A5 flat six piston engine, driving a two blade fixed pitch McCauley propeller, or alternatively a 185kW (250hp) 0-540-A1D5.

Performance: Long range cruising speed 185km/h (100kt). Initial rate of climb 970ft/min.

Weights: Operating empty 770kg (1698lb), certificated max takeoff 1315kg (2899lb), max takeoff in agricultural operation 1700kg (3748lb).

Dimensions: Wing span 11.17m (36ft 7in) or optionally 11.93m (39ft 1in), length in flying attitude 7.48m (24ft 7in), height on ground over cockpit 2.33m (7ft 8in). Wing area 18.3m^2 (197.0sq ft).

Capacity: Seating for two side by side in enclosed cabin. Hopper capacity 800 litres (211US gal/176Imp gal).

Production: Approximately 40 built by late 1996.

History: The all new Gippsland Aeronautics GA-200 is one of only two aircraft in series production in Australia certificated to US FAR Part 23 standards.

The GA-200 is Gippsland Aeronautics' first indigenous design, and results from more than two decades of experience in modifying other aircraft. Gippsland Aeronautics has extensive experience in modifying the Piper Pawnee among other aircraft, but despite the visual similarity the GA-200 is an all new design.

Features of the GA-200 include a braced low mounted wing, a Textron Lycoming 0-540 flat six engine and 800 litre (211US gal/176Imp gal) chemical hopper.

Australian CAA certification in normal and agricultural categories to US airworthiness standards was awarded on March 1 1991. The GA 200 is currently offered in standard agricultural aircraft and Ag-trainer form. The Ag-trainer's role is self explanatory and is fitted with a smaller chemical hopper and dual flight controls.

Gippsland Aeronautics claims the GA-200 is currently the only ag aircraft of its size presently in production, and it has succeeded in snaring a number of export orders, the largest of which was for seven to China (further large orders from China are a strong possibility). Other aircraft are being built for customers in New Zealand, while interest has been shown by agricultural aircraft operators in Chile and South East Asia.

Gippsland Aeronautics has also studied a development of the GA-200 powered by an Australian developed magnesium block V8 engine that would run on unleaded mogas (the GA-200 already has Australian approval to operate using premium grade unleaded mogas for its 0-540). The V8 powered GA-200 would be developed to meet strict US EPA emission requirements due to be implemented late in the decade, something that few current US agricultural aircraft are capable of meeting.

Photo: The GA-200 seats two side by side in its relatively wide cabin.

Grob G 115

Country of origin: Germany

Type: Two seat basic and aerobatic trainer

Powerplant: G 115A – One 85kW (115hp) Textron Lycoming O-235-H2C flat four piston engine driving a two blade fixed pitch or optionally constant speed Hoffmann propeller. G 115D – One 135kW (180hp) Textron Lycoming fuel injected AEIO-360 driving a two blade constant speed prop.

Performance: G 115A – Max speed 220km/h (119kt), cruising speed 205km/h (110kt). Initial rate of climb 690ft/min. Range with max fuel 1000km (540nm). G 115D – Max speed 270km/h (146kt), cruising speed 250km/h (135kt). Initial rate of climb 1500ft/min. Range with no reserves 963km (520nm).

Weights: G 115A – Basic empty 590kg (1300lb), max takeoff 850kg (1874lb). G 115D – Basic empty 660kg (1455lb), max takeoff 920kg (2028lb).

Dimensions: G 115A – Wing span 10.00m (32ft 10in), length 7.36m (24ft 2in), height 2.75m (9ft 0in). Wing area 12.2m^2 (131.4sq ft). G 115D – Wing span 10.00m (32ft 10in), length 7.44m (24ft 5in), height 2.75m (9ft 0in). Wing area 12.2m^2 (131.4sq ft).

Capacity: Standard seating for two.

Production: 110 G 115s and G 115As built by late 1992. Production switched to G 115C and G 115D in late 1993. Approximately 180 have been built of all models.

History: Grob is a company well known for its sailplanes and powered gliders, having produced over 3500 aircraft since the early 1970s, so it is not surprising that the G 115 is the first aircraft made from Glass Fibre Reinforced Plastics to be certificated by the US FAA.

Development of the G 115, sometimes referred to as the T Bird, dates back to the early 1980s and Grob's two earlier two seat trainers. The initial G 110 first flew in 1982 and was built in small numbers, while the G 112 flew in 1984 in prototype form only. Nevertheless the two types formed the basis of the G 115, the prototype (powered by an O-235 engine) of which made its first flight in November 1985. The first prototype was representative of the production G 115 model, a second prototype differed in having a constant speed propeller, a taller fin and rudder and relocated tailplane, and represented the G 115A. The G 115 and G 115A remained in production until 1992 when the line was closed in anticipation of new production models.

The current Grob G 115 models are: the 115B, essentially a 115A with a more powerful 120kW (160hp) O-320 engine (which can be retrofitted to earlier A models); the G 115C with the same O-320, plus fuel in the wings and other minor improvements; and the fully aerobatic G 115D which features a more powerful aerobatic AEIO-360 engine of 135kW (180hp), also allowing it to be used as a glider tug. The G 115 Bavarian was built for a US flying club. It features fuel in the wing, a revised instrument panel and more glass.

Another aircraft to bear the G 115 designation is the G 115T, but this is similar to other G 115s in name and basic configuration only. Powered by a 195kW (260hp) AEIO-540, it was developed primarily for the US Air Force's Enhanced Flight Screener competition (won by the Slingsby Firefly), and no civil customers have yet come forward.

Photo: A Grob G 115D2.

Grob GF 200

Country of origin: Germany

Type: Four seat high performance light aircraft

Powerplants: GF 200 – One 230kW (310hp) Teledyne Continental TSIOL-550 turbocharged and fuel injected flat six piston engine driving a three blade constant speed Mühlbauer propeller.

Performance: GF 200 – Max cruising speed 370km/h (200kt), economical cruising speed 335km/h (181kt). Max initial rate of climb 1220ft/min. Max range with 45min reserves 1850km (1000nm).

Weights: GF 200 – Payload 600kg (1323lb), max takeoff 1600kg (3527lb).

Dimensions: GF 200 – Wing span 11.00m (36ft 1in), length 8.70m (28ft 6in), height 3.42m (11ft 3in). Wing area 12.5m^2 (134.9sq ft).

Capacity: GF 200 standard seating for four with bizjet style leather seats and interior. GF 200/6 to seat six, GF 300 to seat six, and GF 350 to seat six to eight.

Production: Certification and first deliveries planned for late 1996. Grob says there are over 200,000 aircraft worldwide in the four to six seat high performance class. The GF 200 is pitched to replace these aircraft.

History: Grob of Germany launched the GF 200 four/five seater to offer a modern, high performance alternative to the thousands of four/six seater business aircraft in use worldwide.

Initial design aims of the GF 200 were to create a comfortable and roomy pressurised four seater capable of cruising at 420km/h (225kt) at 26,000ft. Power was to be supplied by a Porsche piston engine, but Grob later switched to the turbocharged Textron Lycoming TIO-540 flat six. Another powerplant selection switch will see production aircraft powered by a Teledyne Continental TSIOL-550, also a turbocharged flat six.

A key feature of the GF 200 is its pusher engine installation. The engine, which is buried in the airframe and mounted on the aircraft's centre of gravity, drives a three blade constant speed propeller via a carbonfibre reinforced plastic shaft. Grob says the major advantage of the pusher configuration is that, unlike tractor aircraft, the airflow over the airframe is laminar.

Grob also claims the GF 200's composite airframe brings significant benefits in drag reduction compared with conventional construction. Other features of the aircraft include its advanced profile wing with winglets and retractable undercarriage.

The GF 200 was first conceived in 1983 by Grob's head of design K H Fischer, whose concept was to apply the company's extensive knowledge of composite construction to a new four place high performance four seater. The project was postponed until 1989 because of potential difficulties with certificating a composite aircraft. Serious design effort resumed with the assistance of the German Ministry for Research and Technology, resulting in the unpressurised prototype's first flight on November 26 1991. Design changes meant that certification and deliveries of the first unpressurised production aircraft was planned for late 1996.

Planned GF 200 developments include the stretched six seat turboprop powered GF 300 and the six seat twin turboprop powered (supplying power through a single driveshaft) GF 350.

Photo: The GF 300 prototype.

Grumman G-44 Widgeon

Country of origin: United States of America

Type: Light utility amphibian

Powerplants: G-44A – Two 150kW (200hp) Ranger 6-440C-5 six cylinder, inverted, inline piston engines, driving two blade propellers. Super Widgeon – Two 200kW (270hp) Lycoming GO-480-B1D flat sixes driving three blade constant speed Hartzell propellers.

Performance: G-44A – Max speed 257km/h (139kt), typical cruising speed 209km/h (113kt). Initial rate of climb 1000ft/min. Super Widgeon – Max speed 306km/h (165kt), typical cruising speed 282km/h (152kt). Initial rate of climb 1750ft/min. Service ceiling 18,000ft. Range with max fuel and reserves 1600km (865nm).

Weights: G-44A – Empty 1470kg (3240lb), max takeoff 2052kg (4525lb). Super Widgeon – Empty 1724kg (3800lb), max takeoff 2500kg (5500lb).

Dimensions: Wing span 12.19m (40ft 0in), length 9.47m (31ft 1in), height 3.48m (11ft 5in). Wing area 22.8m^2 (245sq ft).

Capacity: Maximum accommodation for six, including pilot.

Production: More than 266 Widgeons built, including 176 for military use during World War 2, and postwar 50 Grumman built G-44As and 40 SCAN-30 French built G-44As. McKinnon converted more than 50 G-44s to Lycoming powered Super Widgeon configuration.

History: The smallest of Grumman's amphibians developed for civil use, the Widgeon was conceived as a light personal and executive transport, following the success of the larger Goose.

The prototype Widgeon flew for the first time in July 1940, but America's impending entry into WW2 stalled plans for civilian production. The first production Widgeon was a military J4F-1, a three seat anti submarine patrol and utility version for the US Navy. The US Navy and US Army Air Force ordered large numbers of Widgeons throughout the war years, others saw service with the US Coast Guard and 15 were supplied to the Royal Navy, that service originally calling the aircraft Gosling. In all, 174 Widgeons were built for military service during the conflict.

After the War, Grumman refined the Widgeon for commercial markets by altering the hull profile for improved handling on water, and increased seating capacity, with seating for up to six. Grumman built 50 of these as the G-44A, while a further 40 were built in France as the SCAN-30. Most SCAN-30s were delivered to customers in the USA.

US firm McKinnon Enterprises offered conversions during the 1960s to both the Grumman Goose and Widgeon. McKinnon's Super Widgeon conversion involved fitting G-44As with Lycoming GO-480 flat six cylinder engines driving three blade propellers, which significantly boosted top speed, climb performance and range through improved fuel economy and extra fuel tankage. Other changes incorporated on the Super Widgeon were then modern IFR avionics, new wider cabin windows, more soundproofing, and an emergency escape hatch, and as an option retractable wingtip floats. Modifications to the hull and structure meanwhile allowed an increase in the Super Widgeon's maximum takeoff weight.

Small numbers of Widgeons and Super Widgeons still fly, mostly in private hands, with a few in commercial service.

Photo: An appropriately registered Super Widgeon. (Lenn Bayliss)

Grumman G-21 Goose

Country of origin: United States of America

Type: Eight seat utility amphibian

Powerplants: G-21A – Two 335kW (450hp) Pratt & Whitney R-985-AN-6 Wasp nine cylinder piston radial engines, driving two blade constant speed propellers. Turbo-Goose – Two 505kW (680shp) Pratt & Whitney Canada PT6A-27 turboprops, driving three blade props.

Performance: G-21A – Max speed 323km/h (175kt), cruising speed 307km/h (166kt). Initial rate of climb 1300ft/min. Service ceiling 22,000ft. Range with max fuel 1285km (695nm). Turbo-Goose – Max speed 390km/h (210kt). Service ceiling 20,000ft. Range with standard fuel 2575km (1390nm).

Weights: G-21A – Empty 2460kg (5425lb), max takeoff 3630kg (8000lb). Turbo-Goose – Empty equipped 3040kg (6700lb), max takeoff weight 5670kg (12,500lb).

Dimensions: G-21A – Wing span 14.95m (49ft 0in), length 11.70m (38ft 4in), height 3.66m (12ft 0in). Wing area 34.8m^2 (375sq ft). Turbo-Goose – Wing span 15.49m (50ft 10in), length 12.06m (39ft 7in). Wing area 35.1m^2 (377.6sq ft).

Capacity: Flightcrew of two. Main cabin passenger seating for six or seven in piston engined Goose, Turbo-Goose seats up to 12.

Production: Total Goose production exceeded 300 aircraft, much of which were originally delivered to military customers. Grumman production ceased in 1945. Small numbers of radial and turbine powered Gooses remain in service worldwide.

History: The Goose originally began life in the pre WW2 days as Grumman's first design intended for civilian use, but most of the type's production ultimately was against military orders during WW2.

The Goose's first flight occurred in June 1937. Grumman's already extensive experience in building fighters for the US Navy was reflected in the Goose's rugged construction, features of which included a braced tailplane, deep two step hull and retractable undercarriage. Initial civil production machines were designated the G-21A.

The arrival of WW2 saw the Goose (a name in fact bestowed on the aircraft by Britain's Royal Air Force) enter military service with a number of allied air arms, the largest operator being the US Navy. Military orders from the US, Britain and Canada accounted for much of the Goose's 300 unit production run.

Postwar, surplus Gooses found their way into service with commercial operators worldwide, their unique amphibious capability and rugged construction ensuring their popularity in the coming decades.

A number of Gooses have been converted to turboprop power, McKinnon Enterprises (initially based in the US, and then Canada) first fitting Gooses with four 255kW (340hp) Lycoming GSO-480 piston engines, and then with two Pratt & Whitney Canada PT6s. Two versions of the latter were developed, the Turboprop Goose and the G-21G Turbo-Goose, which also introduced enlarged cabin windows and retractable wingtip floats.

Photo: A US registered Goose. Note floats under each wing.

Grumman G-73 Mallard

Country of origin: United States of America

Type: Ten seat utility amphibious transport

Powerplants: G-73 – Two 450kW (600hp) Pratt & Whitney R-1340-S3H1 Wasp nine cylinder piston radial engines, driving three blade constant speed propellers. G-73T – Two 530kW (715shp) Pratt & Whitney Canada PT6A-27 turboprops.

Performance: Max speed 346km/h (187kt), cruising speed 290km/h (157kt). Initial rate of climb 1290ft/min. Service ceiling 23,000ft. Range with max fuel 2220km (1655nm).

Weights: Empty 4240kg (9350lb), max takeoff 5783kg (12,750lb). G73T – Max takeoff 6110kg (13,500lb).

Dimensions: Wing span 20.32m (66ft 8in), length 14.73m (48ft 4in), height on undercarriage 5.72m (18ft 9in). Wing area 41.3m^2 (444sq ft).

Capacity: Crew of two. Main cabin seating for up to 10 passengers. Many aircraft used as executive transports with customised interiors.

Production: Only 59 Mallards were built between 1946 and 1951. Small numbers later converted to turboprop power. Possibility of production being restarted in Czech Republic in late 1990s.

History: Following in the footsteps of the Goose and Widgeon before it, Grumman developed the Mallard amphibian for commercial use.

Developed in the immediate postwar years, the Mallard is of similar overall configuration to Grumman's earlier amphibious designs in that it features twin radial engines on a high mounted wing with wingtip floats, retractable undercarriage and an unswept tail unit. Unlike the earlier aircraft the Mallard features tricycle undercarriage, a stressed skin two step hull and fuel can be carried in the wingtip tanks.

The Mallard prototype first flew on April 30 1946, and the type entered service shortly afterwards in September that year with a Canadian operator. The Mallard was designed for regional airline operations with two pilots and 10 passengers, but most of the 59 delivered were for corporate use. Today only a small number remain in use, but their unique amphibious capability means they remain popular, particularly with tourist operators.

In common with the earlier Goose, the Mallard has been fitted with Pratt & Whitney Canada PT6A turboprops. Frakes Aviation in the USA re-engined a small number of Mallards as G-73Ts in the early 1970s, the PT6s substantially boosting performance and operating economy.

In early 1994 a plan emerged which would see the Mallard re-enter production in the Czech Republic. Aero and Levov of the Czech Republic, and Duncan Aviation of the USA hoped to raise the necessary capital to restart the line in the late 1990s. Aero currently builds the L-39 jet trainer and would be responsible for final assembly, while Duncan Aviation would be responsible for interior finish, painting and avionics. In 1996 no more had been heard of this ambitious plan.

Photo: Few, if any, aircraft exist nowadays with the Mallard's amphibian qualities and load carrying capability. This Mallard is powered by PT6 turboprops.

Grumman G-111 Albatross

Country of origin: United States of America

Type: Amphibious airliner & light utility transport

Powerplants: Two 1100kW (1475hp) Wright R-1820-982C9HE3 radial piston engines, driving three blade constant speed propellers.

Performance: Max speed 380km/h (205kt), max cruising speed 362km/h (195kt), long range cruising speed 200km/h (108kt). Initial rate of climb (with METO power) 1250ft/min. Range with 28 passengers and reserves 750km (405nm) from water or 505km (273nm) from land, max ferry range with no reserves 2740km (1480nm).

Weights: Operating empty 10,660kg (23,500lb), max takeoff from land 13,970kg (30,800lb), max takeoff from water 14,130kg (31,150lb).

Dimensions: Wing span 29.46m (96ft 8in), length 18.67m (61ft 3in), height 7.87m (25ft 10in). Wing area 96.2m^2 (1035sq ft).

Capacity: Flightcrew of two. G-111 conversion seats 28 passengers in main cabin at 81cm (32in) pitch.

Production: Production for military customers of 418, built between 1947 and 1961. Grumman purchased 57 ex military Albatrosses for conversion to civil G-111 configuration in the early 1980s, but only 12 were converted. Other ex USN Albatrosses fly in private hands.

History: The Albatross is easily the largest of Grumman's series of utility amphibians, and was the only one originally developed specifically for military service.

The Albatross resulted from a late 1940s US Navy requirement for a general purpose amphibious transport. The first Albatross prototype flew for the first time on October 24 1947, with more than 400 production HU-16s subsequently delivered to the US Navy, US Coast Guard and 12 other nations. Military Albatross missions included general reconnaissance, maritime patrol, anti submarine warfare (in which role it could be armed with torpedoes and depth charges) and search and rescue.

In the late 1970s, Grumman and major US flying boat operator Resorts International began work on a conversion program to develop the Albatross for civil airline service. The conversion incorporated numerous changes to the basic Albatross, including a 28 seat passenger interior, a galley and provision for a flight attendant, upgraded avionics and other improved systems. The airframes were also stripped down, inspected, components were replaced or repaired, and the whole airframe was zero timed. Military equipment was removed and the engines were stripped down and rebuilt. The first such G-111 Albatross conversion flew for the first time on February 13 1979 and US FAA certification was awarded in April 1980.

Grumman purchased 57 Albatrosses for conversion and foresaw a potential market for up to 200 modified amphibians, however this prediction proved very optimistic. In all only 12 aircraft were converted, all for Resorts International.

A more developed version powered by Garrett TPE331 turboprops and a firebomber were also studied but not developed. Later in 1986 Frakes International proposed re-engining Albatrosses with Pratt & Whitney Canada PT6A or PW120 turboprops, but this plan was also not pursued.

Photo: A civil registered ex US Navy Albatross. (Paul Merritt)

Grumman American AA-1

Country of origin: United States of America

Type: Family of two seat light aircraft

Powerplant: AA-1A – One 81kW (108hp) Lycoming 0-235-C2C flat four piston engine, driving a two blade fixed pitch propeller. AA-1C – One 85kW (115hp) 0-235-L2C.

Performance: AA-1A – Max speed 222km/h (120kt), max cruising speed 203km/h (110kt), long range cruising speed 180km/h (97kt). Initial rate of climb 765ft/min. Service ceiling 13,750ft. Range with no reserves 805km (435nm). AA-1C – Max speed 233km/h (126kt), max cruising speed 217km/h (117kt), long range cruising speed 178km/h (96kt). Initial rate of climb 700ft/min. Max range with reserves 648km (350nm).

Weights: AA-1A – Empty 442kg (975lb), max takeoff 680kg (1500lb). AA-1C – Empty 485kg (1066lb), max takeoff 726kg (1600lb).

Dimensions: Wing span 7.47m (24ft 6in), length 5.87m (19ft 3in), height 2.32m (7ft 7in). Wing area 9.4m^2 (101sq ft).

Capacity: Typical seating for two.

Production: Overall production totals 1100 of all models.

History: What became Grumman's first light aircraft is from the drawing boards of noted kit built aircraft designer Jim Bede.

The AA-1 began life as the Bede BD-1, a small and compact design using just 385 parts and with bonded honeycomb construction. The original BD-1 was powered by a 65kW (90hp) Continental C90-14, and first flew on July 11 1963. Unlike other Bede designs though the BD-1 was not intended for kit building, instead Bede renamed his company the American Aviation Corporation, and placed the BD-1 in series production at the company's Cleveland plant.

Production aircraft differed from the prototype in having a revised wing layout and vertical tail, a wider track undercarriage and a more powerful Lycoming 0-235 engine. First production aircraft were designated the AA-1 Yankee and the first were delivered in 1968, the last in 1971.

The Yankee was replaced in production by the AA-1A Trainer, with a modified wing and equipped for pilot training. A superior spec deluxe version of the AA-1A was the Tr-2 with upmarket interior trim, wheel fairings and more comprehensive standard avionics fit.

Following Grumman Corporation's acquisition of American Aviation, all AA-1s and Tr-2s were produced under the Grumman American Aviation Corporation banner. The first new development from the new company was the AA-1B, a revised version of the Trainer with greater takeoff weights. Grumman introduced the further improved AA-1C, T-Cat and Lynx in 1978, these aircraft boasted greater takeoff weights, a more powerful 0-235 engine and revised tail surfaces. The AA-1C was the standard production model, the T-Cat and Lynx offering progressively higher levels of standard equipment.

Gulfstream acquired Grumman American in 1978, and production of the AA-1 line was discontinued shortly afterwards.

Photo: A simple and well balanced design has made the two seat Grumman (in this case an AA-1B) a popular light trainer. (Jim Thorn)

Grumman American AA-5

Country of origin: United States of America

Type: Four seat light aircraft

Powerplants: AA-5 – One 110kW (150hp) Lycoming 0-320-E2G flat four piston engine, driving a two blade fixed pitch propeller. AG-5B – One 135kW (180hp) Textron Lycoming 0-360-A4K.

Performance: AA-5 – Max speed 240km/h (130kt), max cruising speed 225km/h (122kt), typical cruising speed 207km/h (112kt). Initial rate of climb 660ft/min. Service ceiling 12,650ft. Range with reserves 805km (435nm). AG-5B – Max cruising speed 265km/h (143kt). Service ceiling 13,800ft. Range with max fuel at 75% power 1020km (550nm).

Weights: AA-5 – Empty 545kg (1200lb), max takeoff 998kg (2200lb). AG-5B – Empty 595kg (1310lb), max takeoff 1088kg (2400lb).

Dimensions: Wing span 9.60m (31ft 6in), length 6.71m (22ft 0in), height 2.40m (8ft 0in). Wing area 13.0m^2 (140sq ft).

Capacity: Standard seating for four.

Production: Production totals include over 1000 Tigers, plus over 100 American General Aircraft AG-5Bs.

History: The four seat AA-5 series is the bigger brother to the two seat AA-1, sharing 60% structural commonality.

The first AA-5 prototype (built under the original American Aviation banner) flew on August 21 1970. Primary differences from the AA-1 included the stretched fuselage allowing seating for four, greater span wing, higher max takeoff weight and more powerful 110kW (150hp) 0-320 Lycoming engine. Production deliveries began in December 1971, at which time two basic models were offered, the standard AA-5 and the upmarket Traveler. The Traveler featured a comprehensive instrument fit with dual controls.

Significant improvements were added to the line when Grumman American (following Grumman's 1972 acquisition of American Aviation) released the AA-5B. Performance was boosted considerably with a more powerful 135kW (180hp) Lycoming 0-360 (giving performance more like 150kW/200hp powered retractable gear singles), while the maximum takeoff weight was increased. Other revisions included increased span horizontal tail surfaces, larger rear cabin windows, greater fuel capacity, revised wheel fairings and deletion of the ventral fin fitted to earlier Traveler models. An up spec model with a greater standard equipment list was also offered as the Tiger. The AA-5B was offered alongside the AA-5.

The basic AA-5 was modernised in 1976 with the aerodynamic improvements introduced on the AA-5B, optional extra fuel and other improvements to boost speed slightly. Base aircraft of this model were the AA-5A, the corresponding higher level standard equipment model known as the Cheetah.

Production of the AA-5A and AA-5B continued through the late 1970s, until 1978 when Gulfstream purchased Grumman American. The production rights to the series were then put up for sale. Over a decade later the American General Aircraft Corporation restarted production of a revised AA-5B in 1990 as the AG-5B. However American General ceased trading in mid 1994 due to poor sales and financial problems.

Photo: An AA-5 Traveller. (Bill Lines)

Grumman G-159 Gulfstream I

Country of origin: United States of America

Type: Corporate transport and regional airliner

Powerplants: Two 1485kW (1990hp) Rolls-Royce Dart Mk 529-8X or -8E turboprops, driving four blade Rotol propellers.

Performance: I – High speed cruise 560km/h (302kt), economical cruising speed 463km/h (250kt). Range with a 1245kg (2740lb) payload, max fuel and reserves 4087km (2206nm). I-C – Max cruising speed 555km/h (300kt). Range with max payload 805km (435nm).

Weights: I – Empty equipped 9942kg (21,900lb), max takeoff 15,935kg (35,100lb). I-C – Empty 10,747kg (23,639lb), max takeoff 16,300kg (36,000lb).

Dimensions: I – Wing span 23.92m (78ft 6in), length 19.43m (63ft 9in), height 6.94m (22ft 9in). Wing area 56.7m^2 (610.3sq ft). I-C – Same except for length 22.97m (75ft 4in), height 7.01m (23ft 0in).

Capacity: I – Flightcrew of two. Typical corporate layouts seat between 10 and 14 passengers. Commuter airliner seating for 19 or high density seating for up to 24. I-C – Flightcrew of two. Seating for between 32 and 38 at three abreast.

Production: 200 Gulfstream Is built when production ceased in 1969 in favour of the jet powered Gulfstream II. Five Gulfstream G-1C conversions performed.

History: Grumman set about developing a turbine powered executive transport to replace the many hundred war surplus piston twins performing such missions in the mid 1950s.

Design work began in 1956, with first flight of the Gulfstream I prototype occurring on August 14 1958 and deliveries of production aircraft followed from June 1959. As the first in the Gulfstream line, it established the basic fuselage shape and cross section that carries through today to the Gulfstream IV and V. Other features were the Rolls-Royce Dart turboprops which gave the I good high speed cruise performance, and an auxiliary power unit which allows independent operations from remote strips, providing power for the air conditioning and electrical systems prior to engine start.

While primarily designed as a corporate transport, a number of the standard fuselage Gulfstream Is were also used as commuter airliners, seating up to 24 passengers. Military Gulfstream Is were built for the US Navy (navigator training TC-4s) and US Coast Guard (VIP VC-4s). Production of the standard fuselage I ceased in 1969.

In 1979, by which time Grumman's design rights were purchased by the newly established Gulfstream American Corporation, Gulfstream began offering stretched airliner conversions of the base GI. These aircraft were stretched by 3.25m (10ft 8in), allowing seating for up to 38 passengers at three abreast. Known as the G-159C Gulfstream I-C the first conversion flew on October 25 1979, and production conversions were delivered from November 1980. However, only a small number were converted.

Photo: A US registered Gulfstream I. (Wally McLeod)

Grumman Gulfstream II & Gulfstream III

Country of origin: United States of America

Type: Long range full size corporate jet

Powerplants: Gulfstream II & III – Two 51.1kN (11,400lb) Rolls-Royce Spey turbofans.

Performance: GII – Max cruising speed 935km/h (505kt), economical cruising speed 795km/h (430kt). Initial rate of climb 4350ft/min. Range with max fuel and reserves 6880km (3715nm). GIII – Max cruising speed 928km/h (500kt), economical cruising speed 818km/h (442kt). Initial rate of climb 3800ft/min. Max operating ceiling 45,000ft. Range with eight passengers and reserves 7600km (4100nm).

Weights: GII – Operating empty 16,740kg (36,900lb), max takeoff 29,710kg (65,500lb). GIII – Empty 14,515kg (32,000lb), operating empty 17,235kg (38,000lb), max takeoff 31,615kg (69,700lb).

Dimensions: GII – Wing span 20.98m (68ft 10in), length 24.36m (79ft 11in), height 7.47m (24ft 6in). Wing area 75.2m^2 (809.6sq ft). GIII – Wing span 23.72m (77ft 10in), length 25.32m (83ft 1in), height 7.43m (24ft 5in). Wing area 86.8m^2 (933sq ft).

Capacity: Flightcrew of two. Main cabin seating for up to 19 in GII or 21 in GIII in a high density configuration, or eight to 12 in a typical corporate configuration.

Production: Total Gulfstream II and III production amounted to 464 aircraft, comprising 258 GIIs and 206 GIIIs.

History: Collectively the most successful members of the Gulfstream corporate aircraft family, the Gulfstream II and Gulfstream III are Spey powered developments of the original turboprop powered Gulfstream I.

The Rolls-Royce Dart turboprop powered Grumman Gulfstream I proved to be quite successful as a large long range corporate transport. The availability of a relatively small and economical turbofan in the form of the Rolls-Royce Spey meant that a jet powered successor to the Gulfstream I was a logical development. Grumman launched such an aircraft, named the Gulfstream II or GII, in May 1965.

While based on the original Gulfstream I – the GII shares the same forward fuselage and cross section – there are more differences than similarities. The most obvious difference is the two Spey turbofans, while being a jet the GII has a new swept wing and T-tail. A similar size fuselage to the GI seats 10 in a typical executive configuration.

No prototype of the GII was built, the first to fly was a production standard aircraft, with the first flight taking place on October 2 1966. Certification and first production deliveries occurred in October and December 1967 respectively.

The improved Gulfstream III followed Gulfstream American's purchase of Grumman's GA lines in 1978. The Gulfstream III first flew on December 2 1979. Changes compared with the GII include a revised wing of greater span and area with drag reducing winglets, more fuel tankage and thus range, and a 97cm (3ft 2in) fuselage stretch. Gulfstream IIBs meanwhile are GIIs retrofitted with the GIII's wing.

Production deliveries of GIIIs began in late 1980 and continued until 1986 when production ceased in favour of the Gulfstream IV.

Photo: A Gulfstream III on the ramp with its airstair deployed. The III featured winglets and minor internal improvements and both models used the RR Spey. (Gary Gentle)

Gulfstream Aerospace Gulfstream IV

Country of origin: United States of America

Type: Long range large corporate transport

Powerplants: Two 61.6kN (13,850lb) Rolls-Royce Tay Mk 611-8 turbofans.

Performance: IV – Normal cruising speed 850km/h (460kt). Initial rate of climb 4000ft/min. Range with max payload and reserves 6732km (3633nm), range with eight passengers and reserves 7820km (4220nm). IV-SP – Normal cruising speed 850km/h (460kt). Initial rate of climb 4120ft/min. Range with max payload and reserves 6186km (3338nm), range with eight passengers and reserves 7820km (4220nm).

Weights: IV – Empty 16,102kg (35,500lb), max takeoff 33,203kg (73,200lb). IV-SP – Max takeoff 33,838kg (74,600lb).

Dimensions: Wing span 23.72m (77ft 10in), length 26.92m (88ft 4in), height 7.45m (24ft 5in). Wing area 88.3m^2 (950.39sq ft).

Capacity: Flightcrew of two. Main cabin seating for between 14 and 19, plus flight attendant. SRA-4 special missions version can also be configured for freight work.

Production: Over 300 Gulfstream IVs and IV-SPs delivered by late 1996, including military C-20s for the US Air Force, Navy, Marines and Army.

History: The Gulfstream IV is a significantly improved, larger and advanced development of the earlier II and III.

Major improvements over the earlier Gulfstream models are the Rolls-Royce Tay turbofans, which bring significant fuel burn and noise emission improvements despite their higher output than the II and III's Speys (the IV continues a Gulfstream and Rolls-Royce association that dates back to the original Dart powered Gulfstream I). Other changes include a stretched fuselage and structurally revised wing with 30% fewer parts, greater fuel capacity (and hence range), increased span tailplane and an advanced EFIS glass cockpit and avionics.

Design work on the IV began in early 1983, with the first of four production prototypes making the type's first flight on September 19 1985. FAA certification was awarded on April 22 1987. The improved Gulfstream IV-SP, with higher weights and improved payload range performance, replaced the IV from September 1992.

A third development is the special mission SRA-4. Designed primarily for military roles (such as maritime patrol and electronic surveillance, depending on equipment fit) it is also offered as a freighter for priority cargo transport (the US Navy has ordered five GIV-SPs as C-20G operations support aircraft capable of accommodating 26 passengers or three freight pallets).

Both the Gulfstream IV and IV-SP have set a number of records. A Gulfstream IV flew west around the world over 36,800km (19,890nm) in June 1987 in a time of 45hr 25min, setting 22 world records, another flew east around the world in February 1988, setting 11 class world records. More recently a IV-SP set new world speed and distance records on a routine business flight from Tokyo to Alberquerque in the USA in March 1993.

Photo: High bypass RR Tay turbofans are the primary visual difference between the Gulfstream IV and III. This is a IV-SP (Gulfstream)

Gulfstream Aerospace Gulfstream V

Country of origin: United States of America

Type: Ultra long range large corporate transport

Powerplants: Two 65.3kN (14,680lb) BMW Rolls-Royce BR710 turbofans.

Performance: Max cruising speed 930km/h (501kt), design cruising speed 851km/h (459kt) or Mach 0.80 at 41,000ft. Initial rate of climb 4188ft/min. Initial cruise altitude 41,000ft. Max range with four crew and eight passengers and reserves at design cruising speed 12,045km (6500nm), flight time for which would be approximately 14hrs 28min.

Weights: Basic operating 21,228kg (46,800lb), max takeoff 40,370kg (89,000kg).

Dimensions: Wing span 28.50m (93ft 4in), length 29.41m (96ft 6in), height 7.47m (24ft 6in).

Capacity: Flightcrew of two. Typical passenger load of eight, but with a crew rest room, a business work station with SATCOM, computer and fax, a dining/conference area with seating for four, a three seat couch that converts into a bed, five other reclining seats, two galleys and a rest room fitted with a toilet and shower.

Production: Construction of parts for the first prototype began in September 1993. Initial deliveries are planned for 1996. In 1996 Gulfstream held approximately $US3bn worth of GV orders.

History: The Gulfstream V is the largest and latest development of the Gulfstream line of corporate transports, designed to fly intercontinental distances.

Gulfstream Aerospace first announced it was studying a stretched ultra long range corporate transport based on the Gulfstream IV at the annual NBAA convention in October 1989, while the program was officially launched at the 1992 Farnborough Airshow. First flight was on November 28 1995, with certification and first deliveries planned for late in 1996. Apart from long range and high speed cruise, design objectives included high speed climb, good low speed handling and high speed manoeuvrability.

Like all other Gulfstream corporate jets, the Gulfstream V can trace its original origins to the Grumman Gulfstream I (described separately), although the only similarity between the two is the fuselage cross section. The Gulfstream V uses the Gulfstream IV as its basis, but features a number of substantial changes to suit its different design objectives. The most obvious change is the stretched fuselage, the GV is 2.49m (8ft 2in) longer overall than the GIV

Perhaps the most important changes though are the advanced new wing design and new BMW Rolls-Royce BR710 turbofans. The GV is the first application for the new BR710 engine, the second aircraft to fly with the BR710 was the GV's main competitor, Bombardier's Global Express (described separately). The all new wing is being built by Vought, and is optimised for high speed flight. The wing was developed using Computer Aided Design and NASA developed computational fluid dynamics.

Wing manufacturer Northrop Grumman and Japan's ShinMaywa are also risk sharing partners in the GV program.

Photo: The first GV undergoing flight testing. (Gulfstream)

Handley Page Herald

Country of origin: United Kingdom

Type: Short range turboprop airliner and freighter

Powerplants: 200 – Two 1605kW (2150shp) Rolls-Royce Dart 527 turboprops driving four blade constant speed propellers.

Performance: 200 – Max cruising speed 440km/h (238kt), economical cruising speed 426km/h (230kt). Range with max payload 450km (280nm), range with max fuel 1400km (870nm).

Weights: 200 – Operating empty 11,700kg (25,800lb), max takeoff 19,505kg (43,000lb).

Dimensions: 200 – Wing span 28.88m (94ft 4in), length 23.01m (75ft 6in), height 7.34m (24ft 1in). Wing area 82.3m^2 (886sq ft).

Capacity: Flightcrew of two. Series 100 max passenger seating for 47, series 200 max seating for 56. Most now configured for freight work, max payload of series 200 5100kg (11,240lb).

Production: Total production of 50, comprising four Series 100, 38 Series 200 and eight Series 400 for the Royal Malaysian Air Force. Approximately nine remained in service in 1996.

History: A contemporary of the BAe 748 and Fokker F27 Friendship, the Handley Page Herald was an unsuccessful attempt at providing a replacement for the ubiquitous Douglas DC-3.

The Herald was designed by Handley Page's Reading facility, which was formerly the Miles Aircraft Company. Bearing a superficial resemblance to the smaller and older Miles Marathon, the Herald originally was powered by four 650kW (870hp) Alvis Leonides Major radial piston engines.

Handley Page optimised the design of the Herald for operations from underdeveloped airfields with operators which it thought would prefer piston rather than turbine power. The first Herald prototype flew on August 25 1955, and a second flew on August 3 1956.

However, by this time the Vickers Viscount had proven the reliability and economical operation of turboprops and consequently Handley Page made the decision to switch to turboprops in May 1957. Both of the original piston powered prototypes were converted with two Rolls-Royce Darts in place of the four Alvis Leonides Majors. The first flight of a Herald in the new configuration occurred on March 11 1958. The first Series 100 production Herald flew for the first time on October 30 1959.

Only four Series 100s were built before production switched to the larger capacity and stretched (by 1.09m/3ft 7in) Series 200 in late 1961. The prototype 200 flew for the first time on April 8 1961 and it became the major production model. The only other Herald derivative built was the Series 400, a military version of the 200 for Malaysia, which took delivery of eight.

The Herald failed to attract any significant sales success, its poor sales further contributing to the decline of Handley Page. Herald production ceased in August 1968, while Handley Page collapsed in late 1969.

Only a small number of Heralds remain in service with UK freight and charter operators. The largest Herald operator is Channel Express, with a fleet of seven.

Photo: A Herald of freight specialist Channel Express. (Dave Fraser)

Harbin Y-11 & Y-12

Country of origin: China

Type: Commuter airliner and utility transports

Powerplants: Y-11 – Two 210kW (285hp) Jia Hou-sai 6itsi (AI-14R) nine cylinder radial piston engines driving two blade constant speed propellers. Y-11B – Two 260kW (350hp) Teledyne Continental TSIO-550-B flat sixes, driving three blade variable pitch props. Y-12 (II) – Two 460kW (620shp) Pratt & Whitney Canada PT6A-27 turboprops driving three blade constant speed Hartzell props.

Performance: Y-11 – Max speed 220km/h (120kt), cruising speed at 57% power 165km/h (90kt). Service ceiling 13,120ft. Range 995km (515nm). Y-11B – Max speed 265km/h (143kt), max cruising speed 235km/h (127kt), economical cruising speed 200km/h (108kt). Initial rate of climb 1100ft/min. Service ceiling 19,685ft. Range with max payload 300km (163nm), with max fuel 1080km (590nm). Y-12 (II) – Max cruising speed 292km/h (157kt), economical cruising speed 250km/h (135kt). Initial rate of climb 1655ft/min. Service ceiling 22,960ft. Range at economical cruising speed with max fuel and reserves 1340km (725nm).

Weights: Y-11 – Empty 2050kg (4520lb), max takeoff 3500kg (7715lb). Y-11B – Empty equipped 2505kg (5250lb), max takeoff 3500kg (7715lb). Y-12 (II) – Max takeoff 5300kg (11,685lb).

Dimensions: Y-11 – Wing span 17.00m (55ft 9in), length 12.00m (39ft 5in), height 4.64m (15ft 3in). Wing area 34.0m^2 (366sq ft). Y-11B – Wing span 17.08m (56ft 1in), length 12.12m (39ft 9in), height 5.19m (17ft 0in). Wing area 34.2m^2 (367.7sq ft). Y-12 (II) – Wing span 17.25m (56ft 7in), length 14.86m (48ft 9in), height 5.68m (18ft 8in). Wing area 34.3m^2 (368.88sq ft).

Capacity: Flightcrew of two. Main cabin for six to eight passengers in Y-11. Y-12 can seat up to 17 at three abreast and 75cm (30in) pitch.

Production: Approximately 40 Y-11s, two prototype and one production Y-11Bs and over 100 Y-12s built by late 1996.

History: One of China's few indigenous civilian aircraft, the Y-11 and Y-12 series serve in modest numbers mainly in China.

Design of the type 11 transport aircraft, or Yun-shu 11 (Y-11) began during the mid 1970s as a replacement for the Antonov An-2 utility biplane in Chinese service (licence built as the Y-2 in China). A prototype was built and flown at Shenyang in 1975, while pre series and production aircraft are built at what is now the Harbin Aircraft Manufacturing Company. Production Y-11s were built from 1980 and features included two radial engines, capability for rough field operations and STOL performance. Y-11s have seen service as commuter airliners and have also been configured and used for ag spraying.

The Y-11B is an improved development powered by Teledyne Continental engines to overcome single engine altitude performance shortfalls. The first Y-11B flew for the first time on December 25 1990.

The Y-12 is a turboprop powered development and has been built in greater numbers than the Y-11. Work on a turboprop powered Y-11 began in the early 1980s, and a Pratt & Whitney Canada PT6A powered and enlarged cabin Y-12 prototype (previously the Y-11T) flew for the first time in August '84. Current production is of the Y-12 (II), while the further improved Y-12 (IV) was granted US certification in March '95.

Photo: Fiji Air's sole Y-12. (Julian Green)

Hawker Siddeley HS.125

Country of origin: United Kingdom

Type: Mid size corporate jet

Powerplants: Srs 400 – Two 15.5kN (3360lb) Rolls-Royce Viper 522 turbojets. Srs 600 – Two 16.8kN (3750lb) Rolls-Royce Viper 601 turbojets.

Performance: Srs 400 – Long range cruising speed 724km/h (390kt). Initial rate of climb 4800ft/min. Range with 454kg (1000lb) payload and reserves 2835km (990nm). Srs 600 – Long range cruising speed 810km/h (427kt). Initial rate of climb 4900ft/min. Range with max fuel and reserves 3020km (1630nm).

Weights: Srs 400 – Typical operating empty 5557kg (12,260lb), max takeoff 10,569kg (23,300lb). Srs 600 – Max takeoff 11,340kg (25,000lb).

Dimensions: Srs 400 – Wing span 14.32m (47ft 0in), length 14.42m (47ft 5in), height 5.26m (17ft 3in). Wing area 32.8m^2 (353sq ft). Srs 600 – Same except length 15.37m (50ft 6in).

Capacity: Flightcrew of two. Various optional interior configurations offered depending on customer preference. Max main cabin seating for 12 in Srs 400 or 14 in Srs 600.

Production: Total sales of HS.125s up to and including the Series 600 reached 358, including the Srs 2 Dominie for Britain's RAF.

History: One of the British aerospace industry's most successful postwar designs, and the most successful British civil jet, the Hawker Siddeley HS.125 was one of the most successful first generation business jets and in developed form remains in production with Raytheon (refer separate entry).

The HS.125 started life as a de Havilland project, before that company became part of the Hawker Siddeley group. As the DH.125 this mid size corporate jet flew for the first time on August 13 1962. For a time named the Jet Dragon, just eight initial Series 1 production aircraft were built before deliveries switched to the more powerful Series 1A (the A suffix denoting North America) and Series 1B (the B denoting sales for world markets). A total of 77 was built. The Series 2 meanwhile was a military derivative built for the RAF as the Dominie.

The improved Series 3A and 3B (29 built) had a higher gross weight, while the 3A-R and 3B-R (36 built) were heavier still with extra fuel for greater range.

With de Havilland merged into Hawker Siddeley the Series 4, which featured numerous minor refinements, was marketed as the Series 400A and 400B and 116 were built.

The final Viper turbojet powered 125 built was the Series 600A and 600B. The Series 600 features a stretched fuselage taking standard main cabin seating from six to eight, or up to 14 in a high density configuration. Other changes included more powerful Rolls-Royce Viper 601-22 turbojets, lengthened vertical tail and ventral fin and a fuel tank in the extended dorsal fin.

The 600 first flew on January 21 1971, and became the standard production model until the Garrett turbofan powered 700 series was introduced (described separately), in 1976.

Photo: A HS.125 Series 600B. The 600 introduced the stretched fuselage, allowing main cabin seating for eight.

Helio Courier

Country of origin: United States of America

Type: Four/six place STOL utility

Powerplants: H-250 – One 185kW (250hp) Lycoming O-540-A1A5 flat six piston engine driving a three blade constant speed propeller. H-295 – One 229kW (295hp) geared GO-480-G1D6.

Performance: H-250 – Max speed 257km/h (140kt), max cruising speed 245km/h (132kt), long range cruising speed 214km/h (116kt). Initial rate of climb 830ft/min. Service ceiling 15,200ft. Range with no reserves and standard fuel 1035km (560nm), with optional fuel 2073km (1120nm). H-295 – Max speed 270km/h (145kt), max cruising speed 265km/h (143kt), long range cruising speed 240km/h (130kt). Initial rate of climb 1150ft/min. Service ceiling 20,500ft. Range with standard fuel and no reserves 1060km (575nm), with optional fuel 2220km (1200nm).

Weights: H-250 – Empty 890kg (1960lb), max takeoff 1542kg (3400lb). H-295 – Empty 943kg (2080lb), max takeoff 1542kg (3400lb).

Dimensions: H-250 & H-295 – Wing span 11.89m (39ft 0in), length 9.45m (31ft 0in), height 2.69m (8ft 10in). Wing area 21.5m^2 (231sq ft).

Capacity: Early models up to the H-250 could seat four, the H-395 five or six, the H-250 and subsequent models six.

Production: More than 500 Couriers of all models built, including 130 U-10s for the US Air Force.

History: The Helio Courier has proven to be a highly versatile family of utility aircraft types, the entire range being renowned for its superb STOL abilities.

The Courier lineage traces back to a much modified experimental development of the two seat Piper Vagabond known as the Koppen-Bolinger Helioplane. This Helioplane featured numerous aerodynamic improvements to enhance low speed handling capabilities and STOL ability, and while the subsequent Courier was an all new and much larger design, it did incorporate features pioneered on the Helioplane.

The Courier was initially known as the Helioplane Four and first appeared in 1952, in its first form it was powered by a 197kW (264hp) Lycoming GO-435, and seated four. First flight occurred during 1953 and deliveries of the initial production model the H-391B got underway in 1954. Subsequent development led to a number of derivatives, beginning with the H-392 Strato Courier of 1957. Intended for high altitude photographic work, it was powered by a 255kW (340hp) supercharged GSO-435. The H-395, featuring a 220kW (295hp) GO-485 and seating for five or six, was the first major production version and it appeared in 1957. The H-395 was similar but its engine could operate on 80 octane fuel, making it suitable for operations in remote areas. Next came the H-250 (with a 185kW/250hp O-540) and H-295 Super Courier (220kW/295hp GO-480) from 1965, and the tricycle undercarriage HT-295 from 1974. The H-250 remained in production until 1972, the H-295 1976.

A development of the H-295 with an eight cylinder 300kW (400hp) Lycoming IO-720, the Courier 800, and the 260kW (350hp) TIO-540 powered Courier 700 were put into production by the newly established Helio Aircraft Company from 1983, but production was limited and ceased in the late 1980s.

Photo: A US registered Courier. (Jim Thorn)

Hiller UH-12

Country of origin: United States of America

Type: Light utility helicopter

Powerplant: UH-12E4T – One 315kW (420shp) Allison 250-C20B turboshaft, driving a two blade main rotor and two blade tail rotor. UH-12E – One 255kW (340hp) Textron Lycoming VO-540-C2A flat six piston engine.

Performance: UH-12E4T – Max speed 154km/h (83kt). Range with auxiliary tanks 565km (305nm). UH-12E – Max speed 154km/h (83kt), cruising speed 145km/h (78kt). Initial rate of climb 1290ft/min. Service ceiling 15,000ft. Hovering ceiling in ground effect 10,400ft. Range with reserves 278km (150nm), or 585km (316nm) with optional fuel.

Weights: UH-12E4T – Empty 750kg (1650lb), max takeoff 1406kg (3100lb). UH-12E – Empty 798kg (1759lb), max takeoff 1406kg (3100lb).

Dimensions: UH-12E4T – Main rotor diameter 10.80m (35ft 5in), length overall 12.41m (40ft 9in), fuselage length 9.08m (29ft 10in), height 3.08m (10ft 2in). Main rotor disc area 92.0m^2 (990.0sq ft). UH-12E – Same except fuselage length 8.69m (28ft 6in).

Capacity: Seating for three on a bench seat, or for four (two forward and two behind) on UH-12E4 and -12E4T. Many equipped with tanks and booms for aerial spraying work.

Production: Over 2300 of all versions built, including military.

History: The UH-12 series of light helicopters has one of the longest and probably most sporadic production runs in history.

The UH-12 first flew in 1948, the initial variant being the Model 12, powered by a 133kW (178hp) Franklin 6V4-178-B33 engine. The Model 12A followed from 1952, it introduced a semi enclosed cockpit, while the distinctive goldfish bowl cockpit first appeared on the 12C, which also introduced all metal rotor blades (the 12C, plus the 12A and 12B were powered by a 150kW/200hp or 155kW/210hp engines). The definitive UH-12E was first delivered from May 1959 and differs little from the UH-12E3 currently in production.

Developments on the UH-12E theme though include the four seat UH-12E4 with a stretched fuselage, and Allison 250 turboshaft powered UH-12ET and UH-12E4T. Kits were offered allowing the conversion of -12Es into -12E4s, while piston powered aircraft could be retrofitted with the Allison turboshaft. Large numbers of military versions were also built for the US military as the H-23 Raven.

The production history of the UH-12 is chequered, with design and initial production undertaken by the original Hiller company. Hiller, and then Fairchild Hiller, built over 2000 up until the late 1960s. The newly formed Hiller Aviation acquired design and production rights in 1973 and restarted UH-12E production. Hiller Aviation was then acquired by Rogerson Aircraft in 1984, the first UH-12Es manufactured under the new company banner coming off the line in mid 1984. Rogerson subsequently changed its name to Rogerson Hiller, and relaunched UH-12E production in 1991.

The final chapter of the UH-12 story thus far opened in mid 1994 when the original designer and owner Stanley Hiller, in conjunction with Thai investors, acquired the program from Rogerson. The new Hiller Aircraft Corporation is building 15 UH-12E3s for its Thai partners, and has also developed the five seat UH-12E5.

Photo: The UH-12E has proven successful worldwide. (Jim Thorn)

Hindustan Advanced Light Helicopter

Country of origin: India

Type: Medium utility helicopter

Powerplants: Two 745kW (1000shp) Turboméca TM 333-2B turboshafts, driving a four blade main rotor and a four blade tail rotor. Alternatively could be powered by two 970kW (1300shp) LHTEC CTS800s.

Performance: Max level speed 290km/h (156kt), max cruising speed 245km/h (132kt). Max initial rate of climb 2360ft/min. Service ceiling 19,685ft. Hovering ceiling in ground effect over 9850ft. Range with max fuel 800km (430nm), range with a 700kg (1543lb) payload 400km (215nm). Endurance 4hr.

Weights: Army version – Empty equipped 2500kg (5511lb), max takeoff 4000kg (8818lb). Naval version – Empty 2500kg (5511lb), max takeoff 5000kg (11,023lb).

Dimensions: Main rotor diameter 13.20m (43ft 4in), length overall rotors turning 15.87m (42ft 1in), fuselage length tail rotor turning 12.89m (42ft 4in), height overall tail rotor turning with skids 4.98m (16ft 4in), with wheels 4.81m (15ft 10in). Main rotor disc area 136.9m^2 (1473.0sq ft).

Capacity: Flightcrew of two. Main cabin seating for 10 to 14, depending on configuration. Max external sling load army variant 1000kg (2205lb), naval variant 1500kg (3307lb).

Production: The Indian government plans to buy 250 for that country's military. HAL foresees total civil and military domestic orders at around 650.

History: The Advanced Light Helicopter is the first indigenous helicopter of the growing Indian aircraft industry, and will be built in different versions for the Indian Army, Navy, Coast Guard and Air Force, as well as for civil customers.

In the early 1980s India approached Germany's MBB (now Eurocopter Deutschland) to help it design and build a midsize multirole helicopter for both military and civil use. Subsequently a co-operation agreement was signed in July 1984, covering design support, development and production. Actual design work began in November that year, while the first flight of the first of four prototypes was on August 20 1992.

ALH design features include, a hingeless four blade main rotor with swept back tips and composite construction main and tail rotor blades.

The Advanced Light Helicopter will be built in two distinct military versions, one for the Indian air force and army, and one for the navy. Army and air force versions will feature skids, and will be used for a number of missions including ground attack, troop transport and SAR. Naval versions will be fitted with retractable tricycle undercarriage and a folding tail boom. The civil version will feature tricycle landing gear and will be certificated to western standards. The first civil ALH was due to fly in late 1996 or early 1997. Series production is due to start in 1997.

The Indian Government plans to buy around 250 ALHs for its military, to replace a variety of helicopters including Chetaks and Cheetahs, although no firm orders had been placed by late 1996.

Photo: The first prototype ALH, Z 3182. (Hindustan)

IAI Arava

Country of origin: Israel

Type: STOL utility transport

Powerplants: 201 – Two 560kW (750shp) Pratt & Whitney Canada PT6S-34 turboprops, driving three blade constant speed Hartzell propellers.

Performance: 201 – Max speed 326km/h (176kt), max cruising speed 320km/h (172kt), economical cruising speed 310km/h (168kt). Initial rate of climb 1290ft/min. Service ceiling 25,000ft. Range with max payload and reserves 260km (140nm), max range with a 1585kg (3500lb) payload and reserves 1000km (540nm).

Weights: 201 – Operating empty 4000kg (8816lb), max takeoff 6804kg (15,000lb).

Dimensions: 201 – Wing span 20.96m (68ft 9in), length 13.03m (42ft 9in), height 5.21m (17ft 1in). Wing area 43.7m^2 (470.2sq ft).

Capacity: Flightcrew of two. Seating for 19 passengers four abreast in an airline configuration in 101B, 20 in 102 and 24 in 201. 201 can carry 2350kg (5184lb) of freight. 102 can carry up to 12 passengers in an executive configuration, other configurations offered include aerial ambulance, mapping and mineral exploration.

Production: Total Arava production of more than 90 mainly for military customers.

History: The Arava STOL utility transport was IAI's first design to enter production that was optimised for both military and civil customers, and was built in only small numbers.

IAI began design work on the Arava in 1966. Design objectives included STOL performance, the ability to operate from rough strips and carry 25 troops or bulky payloads. To achieve this the Arava design was of a fairly unusual configuration, featuring a barrel like short but wide fuselage, the rear of which is hinged and swings open for easy loading and unloading, long span wings, twin tails (to compensate for the loss of moment arm due to the short fuselage) mounted on booms that run from the engine nacelles and two Pratt & Whitney Canada PT6A turboprops.

The Arava first flew on November 27 1969, while a second prototype flew for the first time on May 8 1971. US FAA certification for the initial Arava 101 was granted in April 1972.

The Arava 101 was not put into production itself, but it formed the basis for the 101B, 102 and 201 production models. The 101B was marketed in the USA as the Cargo Commuterliner and differed from the 101 in having an improved 19 seat interior in passenger configuration and more powerful PT6A-36s. The 102 had a 20 seat passenger interior, or alternatively a 12 passenger executive interior or all freight configuration. The 201 is primarily a military version, and has sold in the most numbers, with more than 70 built, mainly for third world air forces. The final Arava development is the 202, which is easily recognised by its large Whitcomb winglets, boundary layer fences inboard of each wingtip and slightly stretched fuselage. The winglets and boundary layer fences were offered as a kit for retrofitting to existing Aravas.

Arava production ceased in the late 1980s.

Photo: Twin tail booms and a high wing configuration allow an unobstructed fuselage with rear loading capability. (IAI)

IAI Westwind

Country of origin: Israel

Type: Medium size corporate jet

Powerplants: 1123 – Two 13.8kN (3100lb) General Electric CJ610-9 turbojets. 1124A – Two 16.5kN (3700lb) Garrett TFE731-1-100G turbofans.

Performance: 1123 – Max cruising speed 870km/h (470kt), economical cruising speed 755km/h (408kt). Initial rate of climb 4040ft/min. Service ceiling 45,000ft. Max range 3410km (1840nm), range with max payload 2575km (1390nm). 1124A – Max speed 868km/h (469kt), economical cruising speed 723km/h (390kt). Range with max payload and reserves 4430km (2390nm), range with four passengers and max fuel 5385km (2905nm).

Weights: 1123 – Operating empty 5330kg (11,750lb), max takeoff 9390kg (20,700lb). 1124A – Operating empty 6010kg (13,250lb), max takeoff 10,660kg (23,500lb).

Dimensions: 1123 – Wing span 13.65m (44ft 5in), length 15.93m (52ft 3in), height 4.81m (15ft 10in). Wing area 28.6m^2 (308.3q ft). 1124A – Same.

Capacity: Flightcrew of two. Standard seating for seven in typical corporate layout, max seating for 10. Many configured as freighters.

Production: Westwind production ceased in 1987 after more than 250 were built, of which 36 were turbojet powered. Most turbofan powered aircraft remain in service.

History: The IAI Westwind has become one of the success stories of the small but effective Israeli aviation industry.

The Westwind started life as the Aero Commander 1121 Jet Commander or Commodore Jet, a General Electric CJ610 turbojet powered small executive jet based on Aero Commander's successful piston and turboprop twin line (described separately under Rockwell). The first 1121 flew on January 2 1963, with deliveries of production aircraft from early 1965. However North American shortly afterwards acquired Aero Commander, and as it was already building the Sabreliner (described under Rockwell), the Jet Commander line had to be disposed of because of anti-trust laws. Thus the design and production rights for the Jet Commander were sold to Israel Aircraft Industries (IAI) in 1968.

IAI completed production of the 1121 (total US/Israeli production was 150) before developing the basic design into the 1123 (Westwind) with a stretched fuselage allowing seating for 10 passengers, this aircraft flying for the first time in September 1970. Thirty six turbojet powered 1123s were built before production transferred to the Garrett TFE731 turbofan powered 1124 (known as the Westwind I from 1981), the first of which were delivered in mid 1976. The 1124N Sea Scan was announced in 1976 and is a radar equipped maritime patrol and surveillance derivative.

Successive development of the basic 1124 has led to the 1124A Westwind 2 with improved hot and high performance, better fuel economy and longer range. Delivered from May 1980, changes over the 1124 included a modified wing section, winglets, flat cabin floor and other interior improvements. Production ceased in 1987 in favour of the 1125 Astra (described separately).

Photo: A Westwind I. (IAI)

IAI 1125 Astra

Country of origin: Israel

Type: Small medium corporate jet

Powerplants: 1125 – Two 16.4kN (3650lb) Garrett TFE731-3B-100G turbofans. 1125SP – Two 16.6kN (3700lb) AlliedSignal TFE731-3C-200Gs.

Performance: 1125 – Max cruising speed 862km/h (465kt). Initial rate of climb 3560ft/min. Service ceiling 41,500ft. Range with two crew and five passengers at long range cruising speed 5760km (3110nm). 1125SP – Max cruising speed 858km/h (463kt), long range cruising speed 795km/h (430kt). Range with reserves 3200km (1730nm).

Weights: 1125 – Basic operating empty 5747kg (12,670lb), max takeoff 10,660kg (23,500lb). 1125SP – Basic operating empty 6005kg (13,225lb), max takeoff 10,670kg (23,500lb), or optionally 11,190kg (24,650lb).

Dimensions: Wing span 16.05m (52ft 8in), length 16.94m (55ft 7in), height 5.53m (18ft 2in). Wing area 29.4m^2 (316.6sq ft).

Capacity: Flightcrew of two. Typical executive arrangements for six passengers, with max seating for nine.

Production: Over 80 Astras delivered by mid 1996, most for use in the USA.

History: The IAI 1125 Astra is a comprehensive development of the successful 1124 Westwind, with a number of key changes to improve performance and increase cabin volume.

Israel Aircraft Industries began work on an improved development of its model 1124, initially known as the 1125 Westwind, in the early 1980s, with the first flight of the new type occurring on March 19 1984. A second prototype flew in October 1984, and a third was used for ground based static and fatigue testing. The first production Astra flew in March 1985, and the first customer delivery took place in mid 1986 after certification had been granted in August the previous year.

The Astra is based on the basic Westwind II fuselage and tail, mated with an all new high speed swept wing (which interestingly does not sport winglets, despite winglets being a feature of the Westwind 2). Aside from the aerodynamic and hence performance benefits of the new wing, it has also been repositioned low on the fuselage (as opposed to mid mounted on the Westwind), where it does not intrude on internal cabin space. The repositioned wing plus reshaped fuselage frames means that headroom was increased by 20cm (8in). Other changes include a lengthened nose for greater avionics space and more extensive use of composites (mainly for control surfaces).

The original 1125 Astra has since been replaced in production by the Astra SP. The SP was first announced in 1989 and features a revised cabin interior, upgraded avionics, EFIS cockpit and some minor aerodynamic refinements.

The latest Astra model is the SPX, which first flew in August 1994. It features 18.9kN (4250lb) TFE731-40R-200Gs, winglets and Collins Pro Line 4 avionics. Two have been ordered for the US Air National Guard as C-38s.

Photo: The Astra uses a modified Westwind fuselage and tail unit with a new wing, nose and improved systems. The cabin is also significantly larger than its forebear's.

IAI 1126 Astra Galaxy

Country of origin: Israel

Type: Mid size corporate transport

Powerplants: Two 25.4kN (5700lb) Pratt & Whitney Canada PW306A-5 turbofans.

Performance: Max cruising speed 915km/h (494kt), long range cruising speed 797km/h (430kt). Max operating altitude 45,000ft. Range with four passengers and reserves 6550km (3700nm).

Weights: Empty equipped 8060kg (17,770lb), max takeoff 15,175kg (33,450lb).

Dimensions: Wing span 17.42m (57ft 2in), length 18.96m (62ft 2in), height 6.40m (21ft 0in). Wing area 34.3m^2 (369sq ft).

Capacity: Flightcrew of two. Seating for eight or more in executive style arrangements, or up to 19 in corporate commuter arrangement with a single aisle.

Production: None built thus far as aircraft is still in the early phases of its development program. Four prototypes are planned.

History: Now due to fly during the course of 1996, the IAI Galaxy (originally the Astra IV) will be IAI's first all new corporate jet design.

The Galaxy is a part of IAI's long term strategy to develop a family of business aircraft, and will be produced alongside the current 1125 Astra SP. The new Galaxy features a wing design based on the swept high speed unit of the Astra, but otherwise is a completely new design. Key to the new design is the new 'widebody fuselage', significantly wider and longer than the Astra's, with stand up room for people up to 1.90m (6ft 3in) height. The rear fuselage is area ruled to reduce drag, while the wing features winglets (something the Astra's wing does not). The Galaxy will feature an EFIS Collins Pro Line IV cockpit and nonstop trans Atlantic and one stop trans Pacific range.

IAI selected the Pratt & Whitney Canada PW306A turbofans for the Galaxy in January 1993 after studying competing designs from Allison (the AE 3007) and AlliedSignal/General Electric (the CFE738). The PW306A is a growth development (with increased fan diameter, improved hot end material and a forced mixer in the exhaust) of the PW305 series that powers the Hawker 1000 and Learjet 60, and is due to be certificated in 1996.

The Galaxy is due to be certificated by late 1996, with first flight scheduled to occur before the end of 1995. First deliveries are expected in early 1998.

The Galaxy program was to be a unique partnership with Russian designer Yakovlev. IAI and the Russian company signed a co-operation agreement in 1993 that saw Yakovlev responsible for the design and manufacture of the Galaxy fuselage, while IAI would be the main contractor responsible for final assembly, integration and marketing. However in 1995 the program suffered a delay when IAI was forced to find a replacement company to build the fuselage. SOGERMA of France has since been selected.

Photo: An artist's rendering of the Galaxy illustrates the family resemblance to the company's Astra. (IAI)

Ilyushin Il-14

Country of origin: Russia

Type: Short range airliner and utility transport

Powerplants: Il-14M – Two 1415kW (1900hp) Shvetsov ASh-82T 14 cylinder radial piston engines driving four blade constant speed propellers.

Performance: Il-14M – Max cruising speed 350km/h (190kt), economical cruising speed 320km/h (173kt). Service ceiling 24,280ft. Range with max payload and reserves 400km (215nm), with max fuel and reserves 1750km (945kt).

Weights: Il-14M – Empty equipped 12,600kg (27,780lb), max takeoff 17,500kg (38,580lb).

Dimensions: Il-14M – Wing span 31.70m (104ft 0in), length 22.31m (73ft 2in), height 7.80m (25ft 7in). Wing area 100.0m^2 (1076.4sq ft).

Capacity: Standard passenger seating in Il-14P for 18 or 24, and 24 or up to 36 in Il-14M. Il-14G and Il-14T are freighters.

Production: Production of the Il-14 is estimated at over 3500, including 80 built in the former East Germany and 80 in the former Czechoslovakia. Small numbers remain in service.

History: Like many western aircraft of loosely similar size and configuration, the Il-14 was developed as a replacement for the then irreplaceable Douglas DC-3.

As with so many other countries around the world the Soviet Union's immediate postwar airline system was heavily dependant on war surplus DC-3s, and the Soviet licence built copy the Lisunov Li-2. In the late 1940s/early 1950s Aeroflot drafted up a requirement for a modern replacement of the Li-2 and the DC-3. Ilyushin responded with a low wing tricycle undercarriage design powered by two Shvetsov radials with maximum seating for 27. This aircraft was designated the Il-12.

The Il-14 is an improved development of the basic Il-12 design. The major improvement Ilyushin introduced was a new wing design featuring a more efficient aerofoil section, more powerful Shvetsov engines and a general clean up of the airframe.

Given the NATO reporting name 'Crate', the Il-14 is believed to have entered service in either 1954 or 1955. Initial service models were designated Il-14P (Passazhirskii or Passenger) and was configured to seat 18. Approximately two years after entry into service most Il-14Ps were configured to seat 24 passengers in a higher density configuration. By 1956 a slightly stretched development, the Il-14M (Modifikatsirovanny/modified) had appeared. Initially the Il-14M was configured to seat 24, but this was later changed to 36. Very few modifications were made to the Il-14 during its impressive 3500 plus production run, although many freighter Il-14Ts (Transportny/transport) were built, while many airliner Il-14s were later converted to freighters.

While most Il-14s were built in Russia, Il-14s were also built under licence in the former Eastern Germany by VEB Flugzeugwerke and the former Czechoslovakia by Avia. Approximately 80 VEB Il-14Ps and 80 Avia-14s were built.

Today few Il-14s remain in service, most are used for general freight and charter work.

Photo: One of the many east European airlines to operate the Il-14 was Hungary's Malev. (Gordon Reid)

Ilyushin Il-18

Country of origin: Russia

Type: Medium range turboprop airliner

Powerplants: Il-18D – Four 3170kW (4250shp) Ivchenko AI-20M turboprops, driving four blade constant speed propellers.

Performance: Max cruising speed 675km/h (365kt), economical cruising speed 625km/h (337kt). Range with max payload and reserves 3700km (1995nm), with max fuel and reserves 6500km (3510nm).

Weights: Empty equipped (with 90 seats) 35,000kg (77,160lb), max takeoff 64,000kg (141,095lb).

Dimensions: Wing span 37.40m (122ft 9in), length 35.90m (117ft 9in), height 10.17m (33ft 4in). Wing area 140m^2 (1507sq ft).

Capacity: Flightcrew of five comprising two pilots, flight engineer, navigator and radio operator. Initial Il-18s seated 75, the Il-18B 84, Il-18C 90 to 100, Il-18D and Il-18E 110 or max 122.

Production: Estimated production of over 600 aircraft for civilian operators, all initially delivered to airlines in the former Soviet Union, Eastern Europe, China, Cuba and various client states in Africa and Asia. Over 100 remain in service.

History: Enjoying one of the longest production runs of any turboprop airliner in the world, the Ilyushin Il-18 played a significant role in developing air services in Russia's remote regions in the 1960s and 1970s.

The Il-18 (and Antonov An-10) was developed in response to a mid 1950s Aeroflot requirement for an economical 75 to 100 seat medium range airliner. The prototype Il-18 (named *Moskva*) was powered by four 2985kW (4000shp) Kuznetsov SN-4 turboprops and flew for the first time on July 4 1957. The first Il-18 entered Aeroflot service on April 20 1959.

Initial production aircraft could seat 75 passengers and were powered by the Kuznetsov engines, but only the first 20 aircraft built were so powered before 2985kW (4000shp) Ivchenko AI-20 became the standard powerplant. From there on only minor changes were to characterise the Il-18's development life. The first new production model was the Il-18B which had a reconfigured interior to seat 84 passengers.

The Il-18V entered service in 1961. It became the standard Aeroflot version and could seat 90 to 100 passengers, depending on configuration. The Il-18I introduced more powerful 3170kW (4250ehp) AI-20Ms, while seating could be increased to 122 in summer with the deletion of the rear closet (so essential in Russian winters) and fitting extra seats. The Il-18D is similar to the I but has extra fuel capacity with an additional centre section tank. On the Il-18D and Il-18I the APU is in the belly of the fuselage, rather than in the tail.

The Il-18 has the NATO reporting name of 'Coot'.

Most Il-18s in service with Aeroflot are now flown on secondary routes and on charters as they have been replaced by more modern and efficient jet equipment on primary routes. Most east European Il-18 operators meanwhile use their aircraft for charters or have retired them altogether.

Photo: The Il-18 was a contemporary of the British Vanguard and the US Electra. Like the latter aircraft it also became a maritime surveillance/ASW platform (as the Il-38 'May').

Ilyushin Il-62

Country of origin: Russia

Type: Medium to long range medium capacity airliner

Powerplants: Il-62 – Four 103kN (23,150lb) Kuznetsov NK-8-4 turbofans. Il-62M – Four 107.9kN (24,250lb) Soloviev D-30KU turbofans.

Performance: Il-62 – Cruising speed 820 to 900km/h (440kt to 485kt). Range with max payload and reserves 6700km (3610nm), range with 10 tonne (22,045lb) payload 9200km (4965nm). Il-62M – Speeds same. Range with max payload 7800km (4210nm), range with 10 tonne (22,045lb) payload 10,000km (5400nm).

Weights: Il-62 – Empty 66,400kg (146,390lb), operating empty 69,400kg (153,000lb), max takeoff 162,200kg (375,150lb). Il-62M – Operating empty 71,500kg (157,360lb), max takeoff 165,500kg (363,760lb).

Dimensions: Wing span 43.20m (141ft 9in), length 53.12m (174ft 4in), height 12.35m (40ft 6in). Wing area 279.6m^2 (3009sq ft).

Capacity: Flightcrew of five comprising two pilots, flight engineer, navigator and radio operator. Max seating for 174 in Il-62M, 186 Il-62 and 195 in Il-62MK at six abreast in two cabins. Alternative configurations include 114 at five abreast, and 85 first class passengers.

Production: Over 250 of all models built, of which over 75 were exported. Low rate production of Il-62M is believed to have ceased during 1994. Over 160 remain in service.

History: The four engined Il-62 was the Soviet Union's first long range jetliner designed for intercontinental flights such as Moscow to New York nonstop.

The prototype Il-62 was first unveiled in September 1962. Due to the unavailability of the chosen Kuznetsov turbofans this aircraft made the type's first flight powered by four 75.0kN (16,750lb) Lyulka AL-7 turbojets. Other design features of this new jet included wing sweep of 35°, three section ailerons, double slotted trailing edge flaps, two upper surface spoilers and fixed drooping leading edge extension on the outer two thirds of the wings to combat limited control at low speed, a characteristic of T-tail aircraft. Like its contemporary the British Vickers VC10, the four engines are rear mounted either side of the fuselage in pairs. Only the outer two engines are fitted with thrust reversers.

The Il-62 did not enter passenger revenue service until March 1967, with its first long range intercontinental service taking place in September 1967 when an example flew from Moscow to Montreal.

The improved Il-62M appeared in 1971 and features more economical Soloviev D-30KU turbofans, increased fuel capacity and modified mechanised cargo holds capable of housing containers. The Il-62M entered service in 1974. Announced in 1978, a third Il-62 model is the Il-62MK, whose higher max takeoff weight of 167,000kg (368,170lb) allows a maximum of 195 passengers to be carried.

Low rate production of the Il-62 ceased during 1994, although the type remains an important part of many former Soviet airlines' fleets, including Aeroflot Russian Airlines.

Photo: An Aeroflot Il-62M retracts its landing gear soon after takeoff. (John Ruming)

Ilyushin Il-86

Country of origin: Russia

Type: Medium range widebody airliner

Powerplants: Four 127.5kN (28,660lb) KKBM (Kuznetsov) NK-86 turbofans.

Performance: Max cruising speed 950km/h (512kt), typical cruising speed between 900km/h (485kt) and 950km/h (515kt). Design range with 40 tonne (88,185lb) payload 3600km (1945nm), with max fuel 4600km (2480nm).

Weights: Max takeoff 208,000kg (458,560lb).

Dimensions: Wing span 48.06m (157ft 8in), length 59.94m (195ft 4in), height 15.81m (51ft 10in). Wing area 320m^2 (3444sq ft).

Capacity: Flightcrew of three comprising two pilots and flight engineer, with provision for a navigator. Max seating for 350 at nine abreast. Mixed two class seating for 234 comprising 28 six abreast in forward cabin and 206 eight abreast in other two cabins. Lower deck freight holds can accommodate up to 16 standard LD3 containers if some lower deck carry on baggage racks are omitted.

Production: A total of 103 built (including four military command posts) and over 90 in service, all with Russian and CIS operators and one Chinese airline.

History: Russia's first widebody airliner has experienced a very chequered career. It has suffered from poor fuel economy, reports of failing to meet its design range, and has been produced in only relatively modest numbers.

Development of the Soviet Union's first widebody airliner was announced at the Paris Airshow in 1971. But a protracted development program followed and the first examples did not enter service until almost a decade later in late 1980. Antonov, Tupolev and Ilyushin were all asked to respond to Aeroflot's requirement for a widebody airliner, with Ilyushin's design proving successful.

The Il-86 initially was similar in configuration to the narrowbody Il-62, with four rear mounted turbofans and a T-tail. However the same problems that affects most T-tail designs such as poor low speed handling, plus the heavy structural weight needed to support the four engines caused a rethink, resulting in the conventional tail and wing mounted engine design that was first unveiled in prototype form in 1976.

Although basically of conventional design, one unusual feature of the Il-86 is that passengers can board the aircraft via airstairs leading to a lower deck baggage stowage area, before climbing a fixed internal staircase to the main passenger cabin. This feature however is of use only where aerobridges are not provided.

The first of two Il-86 prototypes flew for the first time on December 22 1976, the first production aircraft flew on October 24 1977 and airline service began in December 1980 (Aeroflot had previously hoped to have it in service in time for the 1980 Moscow Olympic Games). About 100 were built when production ended in 1994.

Plans to equip aircraft with CFM International CFM56 turbofans to dramatically improve fuel economy (thus boosting range) and reducing noise levels to within ICAO Stage III limits have been discussed at various times, but cost may prove to be too big an obstacle.

Photo: An Aeroflot Il-86.

Ilyushin Il-96-300

Country of origin: Russia

Type: Long range widebody airliner

Powerplants: Four 156.9kN (35,275lb) Aviadvigatel (Soloviev) PS-90A turbofans.

Performance: Cruising speed 850 to 900km/h (460 to 485kt). Range with max payload and reserves 7500km (4050nm), with 30 tonne (66,140lb) payload 9000km (4860nm), with 15 tonne (33,070lb) payload 11,000km (5940nm).

Weights: Operating empty 117,000kg (257,940lb), max takeoff 216,000kg (476,200lb).

Dimensions: Wing span over winglets 60.11m (197ft 3in), length 55.35m (181ft 7in), height 17.57m (57ft 8in). Wing area 391.6m^2 (4215sq ft).

Capacity: Flightcrew of three, comprising two pilots and flight engineer. Basic single class seating for 300 at nine abreast in two cabins. Three class arrangement seats 235 comprising 22 first class at six abreast and 102cm (40in) pitch, 40 business class at eight abreast and 90cm (35in) pitch, and 173 economy class at nine abreast and 87cm (34in) pitch. Forward lower freight hold accommodates six LD3 containers or pallets, rear hold accommodates 10 LD3s or pallets.

Production: Approximately 15 Il-96-300s have been built, of which six are in service with Aeroflot and three with other Russian airlines.

History: Despite resembling the larger Il-86, the Il-96-300 is basically a new design, incorporating a number of advanced technologies and new engines aimed at improving on the uncompetitive Il-86.

Development of Russia's second widebody airliner began in the mid 1980s, resulting in the Il-96's first flight on September 28 1988. Two other flying prototypes were built, as were two airframes to be used for static and ground testing. Commonality in some areas with the Il-86 allowed a 1200 flight hour certification program, resulting in Russian certification being awarded on December 29 1992. The first Il-96-300 entered service with Aeroflot Russian International Airlines the following year.

The Il-96-300 is based on the older and larger Il-86, but it features a number of new technologies previously the exclusive domain of modern western built airliners. These include fly-by-wire flight controls, a six screen EFIS cockpit (flightcrew however is for three and not two as on most modern western designs), some composite construction (including the flaps and main deck floors), and winglets. The PS-90 turbofans are designed to comply with ICAO Stage III noise limits (something the Il-86 cannot conform to) and the Il-86's unique lower deck airstair design has been deleted.

Perhaps the Il-96-300's greatest claim to fame though is that it forms the basis for the stretched and westernised Il-96M, described separately, which could result in a Russian airliner equal to its western counterparts, at least in the areas of technology and performance.

Photo: The visual differences between the Il-86 and -96 are the latter's shorter fuselage, larger engines and winglets.

Ilyushin Il-96M

Country of origin: Russia

Type: Long range widebody airliner

Powerplants: Four 164.6kN (37,000lb) Pratt & Whitney PW2337 turbofans.

Performance: Cruising speed 850 to 870km/h (460 to 470kt). Range with 30 tonne (66,138lb) payload and reserves 11,500km (6200nm).

Weights: Operating empty 132,400kg (291,887lb), max takeoff 270,000kg (595,238lb).

Dimensions: Wing span over winglets 60.11m (197ft 3in), length 63.94m (209ft 9in), height 15.72m (51ft 7in). Wing area 391.6m^2 (4215sq ft).

Capacity: Flightcrew of two. Three class seating for 18 first class passengers at 152cm (60in) pitch, 44 business class at 92cm (36in) pitch and 250 economy class at 86cm (34in) pitch. Two class seating for 85 business class and 250 economy class passengers. Single class seating for 375 passengers in three separated cabins seating 124, 162 and 89. Underfloor freight holds can accommodate up to 32 standard LD3 containers. Il-96T Freighter can carry max payload of 92 tonnes (202,820lb) with international standard containers of pallets.

Production: Over 40 unconfirmed orders held, while most of the remaining Il-96-300 orders (for 100) expected to be switched to the Il-96M. Deliveries were scheduled to begin in 1996.

History: The Ilyushin Il-96M represents the pinnacle of east and west co-operation in airliner design, and perhaps offers the Russian aerospace industry its best hope yet in the medium term of securing crucially needed sales from western markets.

The Il-96M uses the standard Russian Il-96-300 as its basis, but features a host of improvements and the incorporation of much western technology. Most obvious is the fuselage stretch taking max single class passenger accommodation back to 350 (as on the Il-86). The longer fuselage also means that the Il-96M's vertical tail can be smaller. Perhaps most important of the changes are the Pratt & Whitney PW2337 turbofans giving greater fuel economy and reliability and, perhaps just as importantly from a sales aspect, reputation than Russian engines. The Il-96M also features Rockwell Collins avionics including a modern two crew six screen EFIS cockpit.

The first Il-96M to fly was the Il-96MO prototype, a conversion of an Il-96-300, its first flight occurring on April 6 1993. The first new build production Il-96M will be a Il-96T freighter, destined for the type's first western customer, Dutch firm Partnairs. Production aircraft will be built at the newly established Ilyushin Aircraft Production Association plant in Voronezh and certification, both western and Russian, is planned, but had not been achieved by late 1996.

Possible developments of the Il-96M under study include the Il-96MK, which would be powered with ducted engines in the 175 to 195kN (38,000 to 43,000lb) thrust class, and the twin engine Il-98, which would be powered by western turbofans such as the GE90, Trent 800 or P&W PW4000 series.

Photo: The Il-96MO prototype. Note the winglets and the third main undercarriage unit. (Paul Merritt)

Ilyushin Il-76

Country of origin: Russia

Type: Medium to long range freighter

Powerplants: Four 117.7kN (26,455lb) Aviadvigatel (Soloviev) D-30KP turbofans. Il-76MF – Four 156.9kN (35,275lb) Aviadvigatel PS-90ANs.

Performance: Il-76T – Max speed 850km/h (460kt), cruising speed 750 to 800km/h (405 to 430kt). Max range with reserves 6700km (3615nm), range with 40 tonne (88,185lb) payload 5000km (2700nm). Il-76TD – Speeds same. Range with max payload 3650km (1970nm), with 20 tonne (44,090lb) payload 7300km (3940nm). Il-76MF – Range with 40 tonne (88,185lb) payload 5200km (2805nm).

Weights: Il-76T – Max takeoff 170,000kg (374,785lb). Il-76TD – Max takeoff 190,000kg (418,875lb). Il-76MF – Operating empty 101,000kg (222,665lb), max payload 52,000kg (114,640lb), max takeoff 200,000kg (440,925lb).

Dimensions: Wing span 50.50m (165ft 8in), length 46.59m (152ft 10in), height 14.76m (48ft 5in). Wing area 300.0m^2 (3229.2sq ft). Il-76MF – Same except for length which is approx 53m (174ft).

Capacity: Flightcrew of five including two pilots, flight engineer, navigator and radio operator, plus two freight handlers. Il-76MP firefighting conversion can carry 44 tonnes (97,000lb) of fire retardant in two tanks.

Production: Over 800 Il-76s of all models built, most for the Russian military, but over 320 in service with Aeroflot and other civilian operators.

History: The Ilyushin Il-76 (which has the NATO reporting name of 'Candid') was developed as a replacement for the turboprop powered Antonov An-12, mainly for military use.

Development under the design leadership of G V Novozhilov in the late 1960s resulted in the type's first flight on March 25 1971. Series production commenced in 1975 and the first examples entered Aeroflot service that year. In the now classic military freighter configuration, the Il-76 features a high mounted wing passing above the fuselage, four engines, T-tail, rear loading ramp and freight doors.

The Il-76 was also designed with short field performance in mind, operating from austere strips. To this end the Il-76 features wide span triple slotted trailing edge flaps, upper surface spoilers and near full span leading edge slats for short field performance, while the aircraft rides on a total of 20 low pressure tyres, the front nose unit featuring four wheels, the main wheel bogies having two rows of four tyres each. Freight handling is largely mechanised, requiring only two freight handlers which can be carried as part of the standard crew complement of seven.

Civil versions developed from the basic Il-76 include the Il-76T with additional fuel; the Il-76TD with increased takeoff and payload weights, while its D-30KP-2s retain their power output to higher altitudes; and finally the Il-76MP firefighter. The stretched PS-90 powered Il-76MF, which first flew on August 1 1995, will be built in Tashkent. Ilyushin also plans to build a CFM56 powered version of this aircraft.

Photo: The Il-76MF prototype makes a fly-by.

Ilyushin Il-103

Country of origin: Russia

Type: Two and five seat light aircraft

Powerplants: One 157kW (210hp) Teledyne Continental IO-360ES2B fuel injected flat six piston engine, driving a two blade variable pitch Hartzell propeller.

Performance: Il-103 trainer – Max speed 265km/h (143kt), cruising speed 235km/h (127kt). Initial rate of climb 1575ft/min. Endurance 2 hours. Il-103 tourer – Max speed 250km/h (135kt), max cruising speed 225km/h (120kt). Initial rate of climb 1080ft/min. Range with three passengers 1240km (670nm).

Weights: Il-103 trainer – Empty 720kg (1587lb), max takeoff 965kg (2127lb). Il-103 tourer – Empty 765kg (1686lb), max takeoff 1460kg (3218lb).

Dimensions: Wing span 10.56m (34ft 5in), length 8.00m (26ft 3in), height 3.13m (10ft 4in). Wing area 14.7m^2 (158.4sq ft).

Capacity: Il-103 trainer – Seating for two (typically instructor and student) side by side. Il-103 tourer – Seating for four or five, with rear bench seat for either two or three.

Production: Russian certification was granted in early 1996, with first deliveries to Russian customers shortly after. Western certification and sales are planned.

History: The Il-103 is one of the Russian aerospace industry's first attempts at designing and building a light aircraft for both eastern and western certification.

The Il-103 was originally conceived in response to a Russian requirement for 500 military and civil basic trainers. Development of Ilyushin's new tourer and trainer dates back to 1990 when program go-ahead was given. First flight was originally planned for the second half of 1993, and although this was delayed somewhat, the first Il-103 prototype successfully took to the skies on May 17 1994.

The smart looking Il-103 is one of the first all new four seat piston engine light aircraft to be developed in over a decade. Optimised for western markets, it is powered by a six cylinder Teledyne Continental IO-360, while western avionics equipment is available optionally. Ilyushin is marketing tourer and trainer versions which differ only in seating capacity, the trainer seats two, the tourer four or five.

Ilyushin hopes to receive both Russian and US FAA FAR Part 23 certification. Russian AP-23 certification was awarded in February 1996, with first deliveries to local customers taking place later that year.

The Il-103 is one of a small number of promising Russian designs that looks capable of realistically achieving sales success in western markets. Not surprisingly, Ilyushin plus a number of other Russian design bureaux and manufacturers look upon the development and sale of light aircraft for international markets as a relatively inexpensive means of earning much wanted foreign currency.

Time will tell how will this promising design sells in the west, but if the price (and product) is right, and it is backed up by credible sales and support, it might just make it.

Photo: As one of the few all new light aircraft of the past decade, the Il-103 could do well if it flys as good as it looks. (Ilyushin)

Ilyushin Il-114

Country of origin: Russia

Type: Turboprop regional airliner

Powerplants: Two 1840kW (2466shp) Klimov TV7-117 turboprops driving six blade constant speed propellers

Performance: Cruising speed 500km/h (270kt). Range with 5400kg (11,905lb) payload and reserves 1000km (540nm), with 3600kg (7935lb) payload 2850km (1540nm), with 1500kg (3300lb) payload 4800km (2590nm).

Weights: Operating empty 15,000kg (33,070lb), max takeoff 22,700kg (50,045lb).

Dimensions: Wing span 30.00m (98ft 5in), length 26.88m (88ft 2in), height 9.32m (30ft 7in).

Capacity: Flightcrew of two. Seating for 64 at four abreast and 75cm (30in) pitch.

Production: Original requirement for 350 from various successors to Aeroflot in Russia.

History: The Ilyushin Il-114 has been designed to fill what should ultimately be a very large requirement to replace ageing fleets of turboprop airliners, including the Antonov An-24, in service on regional routes within Russia and other CIS states.

While only just entering service now, Ilyushin finalised the Il-114's basic design and configuration in 1986. However the first prototype did not fly until March 29 1990. In total, three prototypes were built plus two static test airframes, with the original intention being to achieve certification and service entry in 1993. However the test program was delayed somewhat, caused at least in part by the crash of one of the prototypes on takeoff during a test flight in mid 1993.

The Il-114 is of conventional configuration, but 10% of its structure by weight is of composites and advanced metal alloys, including titanium. It features low noise six blade propellers, and it can operate from unpaved airfields.

Two new versions of the Il-114 have been proposed so far. The Il-114M will feature more powerful YV7M-117 engines and increased max takeoff weight allowing a payload of 7000kg (15,430lb) to be carried. Like many current Russian airliner programs, a westernised version of the Il-114 is under development. This is the Pratt & Whitney Canada PW127 powered Il-114PC, which is intended primarily for export.

The Il-114 has also been designed with a possible stretch in mind. The original design allows for the Il-114 to be easily stretched to seat 70 to 75 in a future development.

Although a Russian design, the Il-114 is assembled in Tashkent in Uzbekistan as well as by the Moscow Aircraft Production Group, while Romania, Polish and Bulgarian aerospace companies are also responsible for some component manufacture.

Photo: The Il-114 holds the possibility of substantial long term sales within the CIS. (Rob Finlayson)

IPTN N-250

Country of origin: Indonesia

Type: 64/68 seat turboprop regional airliner

Powerplants: Two 2385kW (3200shp) Allison AE 2100C turboprops, driving six blade constant speed Dowty propellers.

Performance: N-250-50 – Max cruising speed 610km/h (330kt), economical cruising speed 555km/h (300kt). Initial rate of climb 1970ft/min. Service ceiling 25,000ft. Range with 50 passengers and standard fuel 1480km (800nm), range with 50 passengers and optional fuel 2040km (1100nm).

Weights: N-250-50 – Operating empty 13,665kg (30,125lb), max takeoff 22,000kg (48,500lb). 250-100 – Max takeoff 24,800kg (54,675lb).

Dimensions: N-250-50 – Wing span 28.00m (91ft 11in), length 26.30m (86ft 4in), height 8.37m (27ft 6in). Wing area 65.0m^2 (700sq ft). 250-100 – Same except length 28.15m (92ft 5in), height 8.79m (28ft 10in).

Capacity: Flightcrew of two. Typical accommodation in N-250-50 for 50 to 54. N-250-100 will seat up to 68 passengers at four abreast and 76cm (30in) pitch, or 64 at 81cm (32in) pitch.

Production: Prototype only built with deliveries of production aircraft scheduled from mid to late 1997. At late 1996 firm orders stood at 28 with 191 on option.

History: The advanced N-250 is by far Indonesia's infant aerospace industry's most ambitious project yet.

The N-250 airliner is the third plank in Indonesian technology minister Dr B J Habibie's long term strategy for that country's aerospace industry. Dr Habibie was the driving force in the establishment of IPTN in the mid 1970s, and since then IPTN has licence built Bell 412s, Eurocopter BO 105s and Super Pumas and CASA Aviocars, and partnered CASA in development and construction of the Airtech CN-235 transport. The N-250 is Dr Habibie's third stage of IPTN's development, the fourth is the proposed N-2130 130 seat jet airliner.

IPTN announced development of the N-250 at the 1989 Paris Airshow. Prototype construction began in 1992 but by this stage calculations showed that the 50 seater would be overweight, and so IPTN decided to stretch the basic aircraft to seat 64 to 68 passengers. At the time only the prototype was to be built to the 50 seat N-250 standard, subsequent aircraft would have been to the larger N-250-100 specification. However the 50 seat N-250-50 is once again on offer alongside the larger N-250-100.

First flight was on August 10 1995. Indonesian certification is scheduled for mid 1997, US certification for late 1997, and first deliveries in early 1998. IPTN says it will breakeven after 259 aircraft are built, while it predicts a production run of up to 700 aircraft.

IPTN is actively marketing the N-250 offshore, and with General Electric has established the American Regional Aircraft Industry (AMRAI) to build the type in the USA at Mobile, Alabama. AMRAI will build the 3m (10ft) further stretched 70 seat N-270, which is due to fly in late 1998.

Features of the N-250 include fly-by-wire, a glass EFIS Rockwell Collins Pro Line IV avionics system, and Allison AE 2007 turboprops.

Photo: The N-250-50 prototype. (IPTN)

Israviation ST-50

Countries of origin: Israel and the United States of America

Type: Five place pressurised corporate turboprop

Powerplants: One 373kW (500shp) Pratt & Whitney Canada PT6A-135/7 turboprop, driving a three blade constant speed propeller.

Performance: Max cruising speed at 30,000ft 518km/h (280kt). Max initial rate of climb 1800ft/min. Max operating altitude 31,000ft. Max range with standard fuel and 45min reserves 2035km (1100nm).

Weights: Standard empty 1383kg (3050lb), max takeoff 2268kg (5000lb).

Dimensions: Wing span 11.89m (39ft 0in), length 7.92m (26ft 0in), height 3.56m (11ft 8in). Wing area 15.3m^2 (165.0sq ft).

Capacity: Standard seating configuration of five, comprising pilot and passenger side by side, with three passengers behind them on a bench seat.

Production: In 1996 one proof of concept demonstrator flying with two preproduction prototypes under construction. Certification planned for early 1997, after which series production would commence. Orders claimed for 50 aircraft.

History: The Israviation ST-50 is an all new five place composite, pressurised, turboprop business aircraft which has been designed in the USA but will be built in Israel.

The Cirrus Design Corporation announced it was working on the ST-50 in 1993. In designing the ST-50, Cirrus was able to draw upon its design experience with its four/five place VK30 high performance kit built aircraft. The ST-50 is similar in configuration to the VK30, but is larger and is powered by a PT6 turboprop (the VK30 is powered by a IO-550 flat six or an Allison 250). Cirrus ceased manufacturing the VK30 to allow it to concentrate on factory production of certificated aircraft such as the ST-50 and the SR20 (described under Cirrus).

Although Cirrus sold the ST-50's development rights to Israeli company Israviation, Cirrus continued to develop the aircraft and built the first proof of concept demonstrator with the aid of Israviation engineers.

This aircraft completed its first flight on December 7 1994 in the US. Following shipping to Israel the prototype reflew in May the following year, and this aircraft is due to be joined by two Isravaition built certification and production prototypes. Certification testing is being performed in Israel, with the aim of achieving simultaneous Israeli and US certification to FAR Part 23. Production will be undertaken in Israel once certification is granted.

Key ST-50 design features include its composite airframe construction, three LCDs in the cockpit, and the mid mounted PT6 turboprop which drives the rear mounted three blade propeller via a driveshaft passing through the tail. A ventral inlet supplies air to the engine. The aircraft is pressurised and designed for single pilot IFR operations.

Photo: The Cirrus built ST-50 proof of concept aircraft on its first flight in the USA. This aircraft was shipped to Israel in 1995. (Cirrus)

Kaman K-2100 K-Max

Country of origin: United States of America

Type: Aerial crane and utility helicopter

Powerplant: One 1120kW (1500shp) AlliedSignal T53-17A-1 turboshaft, flat rated to 1005kW (1350shp) for takeoff and 1000kW (1340shp) max continuous operation driving two intermeshing two blade main rotors.

Performance: Max normal operating speed 185km/h (100kt) or 130km/h (75kt) with an external load. Initial rate of climb 2500ft/min. Hovering ceiling out of ground effect with 2270kg (5000lb) sling load 8000ft.

Weights: Operating empty 2132kg (4700lb), max takeoff without jettisonable load 2721kg (6000lb), with jettisonable external load 5216kg (11,500lb).

Dimensions: Rotor diameter (each) 14.73m (48ft 4in), length overall rotors turning 15.85m (52ft 0in).

Capacity: Accommodates pilot only. Designed to lift external loads such as Bambi firefighting buckets. The K-Max's maximum hook lifting capability is 2720kg (6000lb).

Production: The first K-Max was delivered in January 1994. Over two dozen sold by late 1996.

History: Kaman's first civil helicopter since the Ka-225 was certificated in 1949, the K-Max is a specialised helicopter designed specifically for aerial crane work, and other than the pilot's cockpit has no internal cabin.

The unusual looking K-Max is easily identified by its characteristic intermeshing main rotors. The two main rotors have the dual advantages of allowing a low rotor disc area loading and that all the engine's power produces lifted, and is not 'wasted' on an anti torque tail rotor. The two main rotors are also fitted with trailing edge servo flaps that control the blades' angle of attack, negating the need for hydraulic power.

Power is supplied by a AlliedSignal (formerly Lycoming) T53-17A-1 turboshaft, the T53 also powers the Bell UH-1 Iroquois series (and the equivalent commercial Bell 204 & 205, described separately). The extremely high power to weight ratio of the K-Max means it can lift loads of up to 2720kg (6000lb).

Kaman has been developing the K-Max since the early 1990s and the prototype first flight took place on December 23 1991. Certification was delayed somewhat by an early decision to improve the rotor system to increase performance margins, changes including lengthening the main rotors' diameters and increasing the rating of the transmission. US FAA certification was awarded in September 1994.

Recognising that the K-Max's high power to weight ratio may place inexperienced operators in difficult situations, Kaman took a very cautious approach to marketing the aircraft and leased out the first six production aircraft while flight experience was gained.

As an aerial crane the K-Max is suited to firefighting operations carrying various size Bambi buckets, logging, construction, surveying and aerial spraying. It has also been demonstrated to the US Navy in the vertrep (vertical replenishment) role.

Photo: Intermeshing twin rotors eliminate the need for a tail rotor on the purpose designed K-Max.

Kamov Ka-26

Country of origin: Russia

Type: Light twin engine utility and training helicopter

Powerplants: Two 240kW (325hp) Vedeneyev M-14V-26 radial piston engines driving two counter rotating main rotors.

Performance: Max level speed 170km/h (90kt), max cruising speed 150km/h (80kt), economical cruising speed 90 to 110km/h (60 to 70kt), typical agwork operating speeds 30 to 115km/h (15 to 60kt). Service ceiling 9840ft. Range with seven passengers and reserves 400km (215nm), max range with auxiliary fuel tanks 1200km (647nm). Endurance at economical cruising speed 3hr 40min.

Weights: Basic aircraft operating empty 1950kg (4300lb), max takeoff 3250kg (7165lb).

Dimensions: Main rotor diameter (each) 13.00m (42ft 8in), fuselage length 7.75m (25ft 5in), height 4.05m (13ft 4in). Disc area of each main rotor 132.7m^2 (1430sq ft).

Capacity: Seating for eight including one pilot and passenger separated from modular main cabin which seats six. For agwork can be fitted with a 900kg (1985lb) capacity hopper and spraybars in place of cabin. In air ambulance configuration can accommodate two stretchers and three seated casualties or medical attendants. For freight work it can carry a sling load or be operated with an open platform in place of the cabin module.

Production: Estimated 850 built for civil and military roles, with operators in over 15 countries.

History: The unusually configured but useful Kamov Ka-26 remains in widespread civil service in many former Soviet states and throughout eastern Europe.

The Ka-26 (which has the NATO code name 'Hoodlum') first flew in prototype form in 1965, but it did not enter service until 1970. However since then approximately 850 have been built for mainly civil service, making it one of the most produced helicopters in the world.

The uniquely configured Ka-26 features two counter rotating main propellers, a Kamov characteristic that negates the need for an anti torque tail rotor. Other features include the two podded radial piston engines mounted either side of the fuselage, and the removable and exchangeable rear fuselage.

The interchangeable cabin means that the Ka-26 can perform a wide variety of missions, including passenger and freight transport, air ambulance, aerial survey, and search and rescue among others with a special mission specific rear fuselage pod fitted as needed. The fuselage pod can also be removed and the aircraft instead equipped with a chemical hopper and booms for crop spraying, or it can work as an aerial crane and can also carry sling loads of freight.

The Ka-26 is no longer in production, although it has been developed into the turbine powered and modernised Ka-126 which first flew in 1986.

Photo: Ka-26s at a Romanian airfield. Note that the fuselage pod has been removed from these aircraft. (Eastavia)

Kamov Ka-32

Country of origin: Russia

Type: Medium size utility helicopter

Powerplants: Ka-32T – Two 1635kW (2190shp) Klimov (Isotov) TV3-117V turboshafts, driving two counter rotating three blade main rotors.

Performance: Ka-32T – Max speed 250km/h (135kt), max cruising speed 230km/h (125kt). Service ceiling 16,400ft. Hovering ceiling out of ground effect 11,480ft. Range with max fuel 800km (430nm). Endurance with max fuel 4hr 30min.

Weights: Ka-32T – Empty 6500kg (14,330lb), normal loaded 11,000kg (24,250lb), max flight weight with sling load 12,600kg (27,775lb).

Dimensions: Ka-32T – Main rotor diameter (each) 15.90m (52ft 2in), fuselage length 11.30m (37ft 1in), height 5.40m (17ft 9in). Rotor disc area (each) 198.5m^2 (2138sq ft).

Capacity: Pilot and navigator on flightdeck. Main cabin seats 16 passengers, or can be configured for freight carriage or as an air ambulance. Max internal payload is 4000kg (8820lb), max sling load weight is 5000kg (11,025lb).

Production: Currently in production, approximately 170 Ka-32s have been delivered, mainly to Russian civil operators.

History: An increasingly common sight in many western countries, the Kamov Ka-32 (NATO reporting name 'Helix-C') is a multi purpose civil utility helicopter based upon the military Ka-27.

Kamov began design work on the Ka-27 in 1969, its principle design objective being to provide a shipborne anti submarine warfare helicopter to replace the Ka-25 ('Hormone'). The Ka-27 prototype first flew in December 1974 and served as a prototype for the planned military and civil (Ka-32) variants. The Ka-27 was first noted in Soviet navy service in 1981, the same year that the first civil Ka-32 was publicly exhibited at Minsk. The Ka-27/32 both feature the pod powerplant/gearbox and twin tails fuselage configuration of the Ka-25, and the Kamov trademark counter rotating main propellers (negating the need for a tail rotor).

A number of versions of the basic Ka-32 have appeared thus far. The Ka-32T is the standard utility version, and is in use for a range of missions including passenger transport, air ambulance or flying crane. Although it features only basic avionics, it has been produced in greater numbers than the other Ka-32 derivatives. The Ka-32S meanwhile is fitted with a comprehensive IFR avionics suite for operations in poor weather conditions. Equipped for maritime operations, it is used from icebreakers, for maritime search and rescue, and offshore oil rig support, among other tasks. The Ka-32K is optimised for use as a flying crane and features a retractable gondola (with better forwards and below visibility) underneath the fuselage for a second pilot who can manoeuvre the aircraft when positioning it. The Ka-32A is similar to the Ka-32T but is certificated to a different standard.

The Ka-32 has primarily been delivered to Russian operators, but a number have been leased by western companies and others operate in the west on charter from their Russian owners.

Photo: Although complex in an engineering sense, the counter rotating main rotors (a long time Kamov hallmark) negate the need for a tail rotor. Pictured is a Ka-32A. (Lance Higgerson)

Kestrel KL-1

Country of origin: United States of America

Type: Four to six place light aircraft

Powerplants: KL-1A – One 120kW (160hp) Textron Lycoming O-320-D2G flat four piston engine, driving a two blade fixed pitch propeller.

Performance: KL-1A – Cruising speed at 75% power 230km/h (124kt), cruising speed at 65% power 200km/h (108kt). Max initial rate of climb 700ft/min. Service ceiling 13,000ft. Range with no reserves at 8000ft 1750km (945nm).

Weights: KL-1A – Empty 624kg (1375lb), max takeoff 1135kg (2500lb).

Dimensions: KL-1A – Wing span 11.20m (36ft 9in), length overall 8.15m (26ft 9in), height overall 2.73m (9ft 0in). Wing area 16.7m^2 (179.6sq ft).

Capacity: KL-1A – Typical seating for four. KL-1D – Seating for six or freight.

Production: Deliveries will commence once US FAA certification is awarded, planned for 1996. Production rate in first full year planned for 120 aircraft.

History: Kestrel's KL-1 is an all new, composite construction entry into the four place light aircraft market, and in its base KL-1A form is an almost direct competitor to Cessna's new 172R.

Oklahoma based Kestrel was founded by a former Cessna sales manager Donald L Stroud in 1991. The KL-1A is its first aircraft, with a family of developments of the basic aircraft to follow. The KL-1A's basic price is expected to be around $US90,000, considerably cheaper than other new build four seaters

The prototype KL-1A was rolled out on April 21 1995, with first flight occurring later that same year, on November 19. Certification to FAR Part 23 in utility and normal categories was planned for 1996, with deliveries of the first production aircraft following some time later.

Design features of the basic KL-1A include its graphite composite construction fuselage, while power is from a 120kW (160hp) Textron Lycoming O-320 flat four driving a two blade prop.

The KL-1A is due to be followed by a family of developments, offering greater performance and/or capacity. The KL-1B will be powered by a 140kW (190hp) fuel injected Textron Lycoming IO-360ES driving a three blade constant speed propeller. The KL-1R will be similarly powered but compared with the KL-1B will have a retractable undercarriage. The high performance KL-1C will also feature a three blade prop, but power will be from a 170kW (230hp) Textron Lycoming IO-540.

At the top of the planned family tree will be the six seat utility KL-1D, which will feature a Textron Lycoming TSIO-550-B derated to 240kW (325hp) driving a three blade constant speed propeller.

Kestrel has also proposed a military observation/forward air control variant of the KL-1A, which would feature a pylon under each wing for light weapons and additional observation windows.

Photo: The KL-1A prototype as rolled out in April 1995. This aircraft is similar in power and performance to Cessna's new production 172R. (Kestrel)

Lake LA-4, Buccaneer & Renegade

Country of origin: United States of America

Type: Four/six place amphibious light aircraft

Powerplant: LA-4 – One 135kW (180hp) Lycoming O-360-A1A flat four piston engine driving a two blade fixed pitch propeller. LA-4-200 – One 150kW (200hp) fuel injected IO-360-A1B. Turbo 270 – One 185kW (250hp) turbocharged Textron Lycoming TIO-540-AA1AD flat six.

Performance: LA-4 – Max speed 217km/h (117kt), max cruising speed 210km/h (114kt), typical cruising speed 200km/h (109kt). Initial rate of climb 800ft/min. Service ceiling 14,000ft. Max range 1010km (545nm). LA-4-200 – Max speed 248km/h (134kt), max cruising speed 240km/h (130kt), long range cruising speed 213km/h (115kt). Initial rate of climb 1200ft/min. Service ceiling 14,700ft. Max range 1327km (717nm). Turbo 270 – Max cruising speed 287km/h (155kt). Service ceiling 23,800ft. Max range with no reserves at 55% power 2075km (1120nm).

Weights: LA-4 – Empty 715kg (1575lb), max takeoff 1090kg (2400lb). LA-4-200 – Empty 705kg (1555lb), max takeoff 1220kg (2690lb). Turbo 270 – Empty equipped 875kg (1930lb), MTOW 1383kg (3050lb).

Dimensions: LA-4 & LA-4-200 – Wing span 11.58m (38ft 0in), length 7.59m (24ft 11in), height 2.84m (9ft 4in). Wing area 15.8m^2 (170.0sq ft). Turbo 270 – Wing span 11.68m (38ft 4in), length 8.64m (28ft 4in), height 3.05m (10ft 0in). Wing area 15.2m^2 (164.0sq ft).

Capacity: Normal seating for four in LA-4 and Buccaneer; Renegade and Turbo Renegade seat six.

Production: Over 1000 built, including over 300 Renegades. Licence assembly of Renegades in China planned.

History: This successful family of light amphibians has been by far the largest selling series of its type since Republic's Seabee, and one of a very small number of such aircraft to even enter production.

The LA-4 series dates back to the Colonial C-1 Skimmer, a three place light amphibian which first flew in July 1948. The C-1 eventually entered production powered by a 110kW (150hp) Lycoming O-320 in 1955, and small numbers of it and the four seat 135kW (180hp) O-360 powered C-2 Skimmer IV were built before Lake Aircraft purchased the manufacturing and design rights in October 1959.

Lake's prototype LA-4P was a development of the Skimmer IV, and first flew in November 1959. Put into production in August 1960, the production LA-4 differed from the Skimmer IV in having greater wing span, strengthened structure and higher weights. The LA-4 remained in production until 1972 (small numbers of seaplane only LA-4Ts were built), by which stage the improved LA-4-200 Buccaneer had been in production for two years. The main difference in the two models was the LA-4-200's more powerful engine, extra fuel and higher weights.

Further development led to the LA-250 Renegade being certificated in 1983. It introduced a number of changes over the Buccaneer including the more powerful six cylinder IO-540 engine and a stretched fuselage with seating for six. It and the turbocharged (TIO-540-AA1AD powered) Turbo 270 Renegade remain in production. The Special Edition Seafury and Special Edition Turbo Seafury are based on the Renegade and Turbo Renegade respectively, and feature enhancements for salt water operations.

Photo: An LA-250 Renegade. (Lake)

Learjet 23, 24, 25, 28 & 29

Country of origin: United States of America

Type: Light corporate jets

Powerplants: 23 – Two 12.8kN (2850lb) General Electric CJ610-4 turbojets. 25D & 29 – Two 13.1kN (2950lb) CJ610-8As.

Performance: 23 – Max speed 860km/h (465kt), max cruising speed 850km/h (460kt), economical cruising speed 817km/h (440kt). Range with max fuel and reserves 2660km (1440nm). 25D – Cruising speed 860km/h (465kt). Range with two crew, four passengers and reserves 2663km (1437nm). 29 – Max speed 883km/h (477kt), max cruising speed 836km/h (452kt), economical cruising speed 756km/h (408kt). Service ceiling 51,000ft. Range with two crew, four pax, max fuel and reserves 2550km (1376nm).

Weights: 23 – Empty 2974kg (6550lb), max takeoff 5675kg (12,500lb). 25D – Empty equipped 3465kg (7640lb), max takeoff 6804kg (15,000lb). 29 – Empty 3730kg (8224lb, max takeoff 6805kg (15,000lb).

Dimensions: 23 – Wing span 10.84m (35ft 8in), length 13.18m (43ft 3in), height 3.73m (12ft 3in). Wing area 21.5m^2 (231.77sq ft). 25D – Same except for length 14.50m (47ft 7in). 29 – Same as 25 except for wing span 13.35m (43ft 10in). Wing area 24.6m^2 (264.5sq ft).

Capacity: 23 & 24 – Flightcrew of two. Max seating in main cabin for six, typical seating for four. 25 & 28 – Flightcrew of two. Main cabin seating for up to eight passengers. 29 – Flightcrew of two and seating for six passengers.

Production: 745 turbojet power Learjets were built, comprising 363 23/24s; 373 25s; five 28s and four 29s.

History: One of the world's largest, fastest, best selling and well known series of business jets, the Learjet family began with the original six to eight seat Learjet 23 which first flew on October 7 1963.

The 23 was designed and conceived by William (Bill) Lear in Switzerland as the SAAC-23. The diminutive Model 23 pioneered an entirely new market segment for the light business jets, and it and its successors achieved sales figures that reflect this. The first production 23 was delivered in October 1964, but was replaced by the improved Model 24 in 1966 after 104 had been built. The 24, which introduced uprated engines and a number of detail changes, first flew in February 1966 and was delivered from the middle of that year. Developments of the 24 included the 24D, E and F, introducing improvements such as increased weights, thrusts, and range.

The Learjet 25 introduced a 1.27m (4ft 2in) fuselage stretch allowing seating for up to eight passengers and was first flown on August 12 1966, and, like the 24, a number of subsequent developments were built, including the B, D, F and G.

The unsuccessful Learjet 28 and 29 Longhorns are based on the 25 but introduced a new increased span wing fitted with winglets, which improved fuel efficiency and overall performance, particularly payload range and fuel economy. The Longhorn 28 seats up to eight passengers, the similar dimensions Longhorn 29 sacrifices two seats for extra range. Production of the family ceased in 1982.

Photo: A Learjet 24. The Lear 24 introduced uprated engines and a number of detail changes. (Bill Lines)

Learjet 35, 36 & 31

Country of origin: United States of America

Type: Light twin turbofan corporate jets.

Powerplants: Two 15.6kN (3500lb) Garrett (now AlliedSignal) TFE731-2-2B turbofans.

Performance: 35A & 36A – Max speed 872km/h (470kt), max cruising speed 852km/h (460kt), economical cruising speed 774km/h (418kt). Service ceiling 41,000ft. Range with four passengers, max fuel and reserves 4070km (2195nm) for 35A, 4673km (2522nm) for 36A. 31A – Cruising speed 832km/h (450kt). Service ceiling 51,000ft. Range with two crew, four passengers and reserves 3075km (1660nm), or 3515km (1897nm) for 31A/ER.

Weights: 35A and 36A – Empty equipped 4590kg (10,120lb), max takeoff 8300kg (18,300lb). 31A – Empty 4575kg (10,087lb), operating empty 4758kg (10,847lb), max takeoff 7030kg (15,500lb).

Dimensions: Wing span (over tip tanks) 12.04m (39ft 6in), length 14.83m (48ft 8in), height 3.73m (12ft 3in). Wing area 23.5m^2 (253.3sq ft). 31A – Same except for wing span 13.33m (43ft 9in). Wing area 24.6m^2 (264.4sq ft).

Capacity: Flightcrew of two. Seating for up to eight in main cabin in 35 and 31, or up to six in 36A. Some aircraft configured as package freighters.

Production: A total of 676 Learjet 35s and 36s delivered. US Air Force and Air National Guard ordered 84 Learjet 35As as C-21s. More than 100 31s built.

History: The Learjet 35 and 36 are larger, turbofan powered developments of the initial Learjet models, the 23, 24 and 25.

The availability of the Garrett AiResearch TFE731 turbofan in the late 1960s led to a development of the Learjet 25 that was initially known as the 25B-GF (Garrett Fan). A testbed Lear 25 with a TFE731 on its left engine nacelle flew in May 1971, while the definitive Learjet 35 prototype first flew on August 22 1973.

Aside from turbofans, the 35 and longer range 36 differ from the earlier Learjet 25 in having a 0.33m (1ft 1in) fuselage stretch, and five windows (instead of four) on the right side of the fuselage. The Learjet 35 has seating for up to eight, but has less fuel than the longer range 36, which can only seat up to six, as both types share the same maximum takeoff weight. The 35 and 36 were certificated in July 1974.

Improvements to the two models led to the 35A and 36A from 1976, with higher standard max takeoff weights. Both models remained in production until 1994.

Development of the 35 and 36 range was taken one step further with the Learjet 31, which combines the 35/36's fuselage and powerplants, with the more modern wing of the 55 (now also on the 60) and delta fins under the tail. A 31 development aircraft first flew in May 1987, and certification was awarded in August 1988. The improved 31A and 31A/ER are the current production models, the 31A/ER being an extended range variant with a higher maximum takeoff weight and more fuel. A new interior with increased headroom was introduced in 1995.

Photo: A Learjet 31A in flight. Major visual differences between the 30 series and the earlier 20s are turbofan engines and stretched fuselages with extra windows. (Learjet)

Learjet 45

Country of origin: United States of America

Type: Mid size corporate jet

Powerplants: Two 15.7kN (3500lb) AlliedSignal TFE731-20 turbofans.

Performance: Max cruising speed 860km/h (464kt), economical cruising speed 753km/h (406kt). Service ceiling 51,000ft. Initial rate of climb 3200ft/min. Max range with four passengers and reserves 4074km (2200nm).

Weights: Empty 5307kg (11,700lb), max takeoff 8845kg (19,750lb).

Dimensions: Wing span 14.56m (47.82ft), length 17.68m (57.99ft), height 4.29m (14.06ft).

Capacity: Flightcrew of two. Main cabin seating for eight to 10 passengers in a corporate configuration. Singapore Airlines plans to use Learjet 45s as pilot trainers with a secondary freight function at night, equipped with a special mail pallet.

Production: Over 100 Learjet 45s sold with first deliveries scheduled for early 1997.

History: The all new Learjet 45 is the company's latest entry into the medium size corporate jet market sector.

Learjet announced it was developing the Model 45 at the US National Business Aircraft Association's annual convention in Dallas in September 1992. First flight was on October 7 1995, and certification to the latest US FAA and European JAA certification standards is planned for late 1996.

The 45 is of classical Learjet design and layout. However a number of key design changes were made early into the 45's design life including a larger fin and rudder, extended engine pylons, smaller delta fins, full span elevators, and single piece flaps.

Fractionally larger than the Learjet 35/36, and slightly smaller than the 60, Learjet states that the 45's 1.50m (4.9ft) high and 1.55m (5.1ft) wide cabin will provide more head and shoulder room than any other aircraft in its class. The cabin is designed to accommodate double club seating, a galley and a full width aft rest room, while eight windows line each side of the cabin.

The -20 version of the proven AlliedSignal TFE731 engine was developed in co-operation with Learjet for the 45 and incorporates 60 design changes to increase fuel economy and reduce operating and maintenance costs.

Learjet sees a market for as many as 1000 45s, and is confident of snaring a large share of the estimated 7000 turboprop business aircraft market over the next 15 to 20 years, given that the 45's unit cost is claimed to be only slightly higher than that of the top end turboprops.

While Learjet retains overall 45 program leadership, and is responsible for the aircraft's design, other Bombardier Group companies are participating in Learjet 45 construction. De Havilland Inc in Canada is responsible for wing construction, while Shorts of Northern Ireland in the UK will build the fuselage and empennage. Learjet will be capable of building 60 45s annually if demand dictates.

Photo: The Learjet 45's first flight on October 7 1995 was the 32nd anniversary of the original Lear 23. (Learjet)

Learjet 55 & 60

Country of origin: United States of America

Type: Small to mid size corporate jets

Powerplants: 55 – Two 16.5kN (3700lb) Garrett TFE731-3A-2B turbofans. 60 – Two 20.6kN (4600lb) Pratt & Whitney Canada PW305A turbofans.

Performance: 55C – Max level speed 884km/h (477kt), max cruising speed 843km/h (455kt), economical cruising speed 776km/h (420kt). Service ceiling 51,000ft. Range with two crew, four passengers and reserves 4442km (2397nm) for 55C/LR. 60 – Max cruising speed 858km/h (463kt). Service ceiling 51,000ft. Range with two crew, four pax and reserves 5075km (2740nm).

Weights: 55C – Empty 5832kg (12,858lb), operating empty 6013kg (13,258lb), max takeoff 9525kg (21,000lb). 60 – Empty 6278kg (13,840lb), max takeoff 10,320kg (22,750lb) or optionally 10,478kg (23,100lb).

Dimensions: 55 – Wing span 13.34m (43ft 9in), length 16.79m (55ft 1in), height 4.47m (14ft 8in). Wing area 24.6m^2 (264.5sq ft). 60 – Wing span 13.34m (43ft 9in), length 17.88m (58ft 8in), height 4.47m (14ft 8in).

Capacity: 55 – Flightcrew of two. Six different main cabin arrangements offered with seating ranging from four to eight. 60 – Flightcrew of two. Optional seating arrangements for six to nine passengers.

Production: Production of the Model 55 ceased in 1990 after 147 had been built. Deliveries of Model 60 began in January 1993, with more than 90 delivered by late 1996.

History: The Learjet 55 and its follow-on successor, the Learjet 60, are the largest members of the Learjet family, and date back to development work undertaken in the late 1970s.

In designing the 55, Learjet (or Gates Learjet as the company was then known as) took the wing of the earlier Longhorn 28/29 series and married it to an all new larger 10 seat fuselage. The original Model 55 Longhorn prototype first flew on November 15 1979. The production aircraft meanwhile flew on August 11 1980, with the first delivered in late April 1981 (after FAA certification was granted in March that year).

Development of the 55 led to a number of sub variants, including the 55B which introduced a digital flightdeck, modified wings, improved interior, and most importantly, the previous optional higher takeoff weights becoming standard. The 55C introduced 'Delta Fins' which gave a number of performance and handling advantages, the 55/ER is an extended range version with additional fuel in the tail cone (the additional tank can be retrofitted to earlier aircraft), while the 55C/LR introduced more fuel capacity.

The Learjet 60 first flew in its basic definitive form in June 1991 (the modified Learjet 55 prototype for the 60 earlier served as a proof of concept aircraft with Garrett engines). It differs from the 55 in having a 1.09m (43in) fuselage stretch, and new Pratt & Whitney Canada PW305 turbofans. Certification of the 60 was awarded in January 1993, with first deliveries following shortly afterwards.

Photo: This Learjet 55 was the first business jet delivered to a private owner in China, in April 1995 . (Learjet)

Let L-40 Meta-Sokol

Country of origin: Czech Republic

Type: Three/four seat light aircraft

Powerplant: Late production aircraft – One 85kW (115hp) with 5 min supercharged 105kW (140hp) rating Walter M332 inline inverted four cylinder piston engine, driving a two blade constant speed propeller.

Performance: Late production aircraft – Max speed 237km/h (128kt), max cruising speed 208km/h (112kt). Initial rate of climb 630ft/min. Service ceiling 14,765ft. Max range 850km (460nm).

Weights: Late production aircraft – Empty 520kg (1147lb), max take-off 920kg (2030lb).

Dimensions: Late production aircraft – Wing span (without wingtip tanks) 10.00m (32ft 10in), length 7.54m (28ft 9in), height 2.47m (8ft 1in). Wing area 14.6m^2 (156sq ft).

Capacity: Initial production aircraft had seating for three with a single passenger seated behind pilot and passenger. Late production had seating for four.

Production: Approximately 200 Meta-Sokols were built between 1954 and 1961. Almost all production was of the four seat model, only small numbers of the initial three seat model were built.

History: One of the more obscure light aircraft to emerge from behind the Iron Curtain, the unusually configured Meta-Sokol three/four seat light aircraft was a development of the original Let Mraz M.1 Sokol.

The M.1 Sokol was a three seat light aircraft developed in the late 1940s. It was used in a variety of roles, mainly for training and a number were built for Czechoslovak flying schools. The M.1 Sokol was of wooden construction, featured tail dragger undercarriage and a 80kW (105hp) Walter Minor 4-III inline inverted four cylinder engine.

Like the M.1 Sokol, early production Meta-Sokols sat three passengers and were powered by the same 80kW (105hp) Walter Minor engine. However the Meta-Sokol introduced a number of new features and design changes compared with the M.1. Changes included metal construction, a rear sliding cockpit canopy, a very tall vertical tail that extends from the fuselage at almost a right angle, and unique undercarriage system. The Meta-Sokol's undercarriage is of a reverse tricycle arrangement, with the main undercarriage legs extending from the front of the wing, with the third leg extending from under the fuselage. Unlike the original fixed undercarriage M.1 Sokol, the Meta-Sokol's undercarriage retracts, although the rearward retracting main landing gear remains exposed in flight.

The prototype L-20 Meta-Sokol flew for the first time during 1954. This original three seat model was built in only small numbers before superseded by the definitive four seater, which also introduced a more powerful M332 engine. The M332 engine was notable in that its normal maximum power output could be boosted for up to five minutes with supercharging.

Like the majority of eastern bloc aircraft of its time, most Meta-Sokols were exported to countries within the Soviet sphere of influence, although a number were sold in western Europe, North America and Australia.

Photo: An L-40 Meta-Sokol. Note the reverse tricycle undercarriage, rear sliding canopy and tall vertical tail. (Bill Lines)

Let L-200 Morava

Country of origin: Czech Republic

Type: Four/five seat light twin

Powerplants: L-200A – Two 155kW (210hp) Walter Minor M337 fuel injected inverted inline piston engines, driving two blade variable pitch propellers. L-200D – Same except for three blade constant speed props.

Performance: L-200A – Max speed 305km/h (165kt), max cruising speed 293km/h (158kt), long range cruising speed 256km/h (138kt). Initial rate of climb 1150ft/min. Service ceiling 20,340ft. Range with max fuel 1770km (955nm). L-200D – Max speed 290km/h (157kt), max cruising speed 282km/h (152kt), long range cruising speed 256km/h (138kt). Initial rate of climb 1260ft/min. Service ceiling 18,700ft. Range with max fuel 1710km (923kt).

Weights: L-200A – Empty 1275kg (2810lb), max takeoff 1950kg (4300lb). L-200D – Empty 1330kg (2932lb), max takeoff 1950kg (4300lb).

Dimensions: Wing span 12.31m (40ft 5in), length 8.61m (28ft 3in), height 2.25m (7ft 4in). Wing area 17.3m^2 (186sq ft).

Capacity: Typical accommodation for four or five, with pilot and passenger in individual seats and two or three passengers on rear bench seat.

Production: Total L-200 production over 1000, including approximately 160 L-200As.

History: One of the few light aircraft to be exported from behind the Iron Curtain during the Cold War, albeit in small numbers, the Let L-200 Morava is a retractable four seat light twin.

Ladislav Smrek of the Czechoslovak State Aircraft Factory designed the L-200 in the mid 1950s in response to a requirement to replace the early postwar vintage Aero 45 and 145 light twins. His resulting design is similar in many ways to its contemporary western twins, with a four or five place cabin, a low wing, wingtip tanks, metal construction and retractable undercarriage. However the Morava is distinguishable by its twin tails, standard thermal wing de-icing equipment and inverted inline engines.

The prototype Morava was designated XL-200 and flew for the first time on April 8 1957. The XL-200 and a series of preproduction L-200s were powered by 120kW (160hp) Walter Minor 6-III inline sixes. Initial production was of the L-200A, which differed from the L-200 in being powered by two 155kW (210hp) fuel injected M337s, greater weights, a reprofiled cabin and hydraulically (rather than electrically) operated undercarriage and flaps. After Let built 160 L-200s production switched to the improved L-200D. Features of the L-200D include a strengthened undercarriage, improved hydraulic and electrical systems and constant speed three blade propellers. The L-200D remained in production until 1969, and a number were licence built in Slovenia (then part of Yugoslavia). A turboprop powered development was also studied, but was not built.

Most L-200 production was for customers within the Soviet Bloc, Aeroflot operated several hundred in a range of roles including air taxi, air ambulance and communications duties. Small numbers though were exported to western Europe, the USA and other countries.

Photo: An L-200A. (Bill Lines)

Let L 410 & L 420

Country of origin: Czech Republic

Type: 19 seat twin turboprop commuter airliners

Powerplants: L 410 UVP-E – Two 560kW (750shp) Motorlet M 601 E turboprops, driving five blade Avia Hamilton Avia 510 propellers. L 420 – Two 580kW (775shp) M 601 Fs.

Performance: L 410 UVP-E – Max cruising speed 380km/h (205kt), economical cruising speed 365km/h (197kt). Initial rate of climb 1420ft/min. Service ceiling 19,700ft. Range with max fuel (including wingtip tanks), 920kg (2030lb) payload and reserves 1318km (707nm). 420 – Max cruising speed 390km/h (210kt). Initial rate of climb 1400ft/min. Range with 17 passengers (without tip tanks) and reserves 680km (367nm), range with max fuel and reserves 1366km (737nm).

Weights: L 410 UVP-E – Empty (without tip tanks) 4020kg (8662lb), max takeoff 6400kg (14,109lb). L 420 – Empty (with tip tanks) 4125kg (9094lb), max takeoff 6600kg (14,550lb).

Dimensions: Wing span (with tip tanks) 19.98m (65ft 7in), length 14.42m (47ft 4in), height 5.83m (19ft 2in). Wing area 34.9m^2 (375.2sq ft).

Capacity: Flightcrew of two. Typical commuter passenger seating for 17 or 19 at three abreast. Executive version seats 15 plus flight attendant. Cargo version equipped to handle special containers. Air ambulance version configured for six stretcher patients and six sitting passengers, either injured or medical attendants.

Production: Over 1100 L 410s of all variants built, including 31 L 410As, 110 L 410Ms and 560 L 410 UVP-Es, with over 400 in service and more than 40 on order. One L 420 built.

History: This very successful Czech commuter was first built in response to Soviet requirements, but it is now also being developed to meet western certification.

First design studies of the original 15 seat L 410 began in 1966. The resulting design, named the Turbolet, was conventional, and was designed with operations from unprepared strips in mind. Powerplant chosen was the all new Walter or Motorlet M 601, but this engine was not sufficiently developed enough to power the prototypes, and Pratt & Whitney Canada PT6A-27s were fitted in their place. First flight occurred on April 16 1969, and series production began in 1970. Initial production L 410s were also powered by the PT6A, and it was not until 1973 that production aircraft featured the M 601, these being known as the L 410M.

The L 410 was first superseded from 1979 by the L 410 UVP with a slight 47cm (1ft 7in) fuselage stretch, M 601B engines and detail refinements. The UVP was in turn replaced by the UVP-E in which the toilet and baggage compartments were repositioned allowing more efficient seating arrangements for up to 19 passengers, and M 601E powerplants were introduced. The UVP-E is the current production version.

The L 420 is an improved variant with more powerful M 601F engines, higher weights and improved performance designed to meet western certification requirements. The L 420 first flew on November 10 1993.

Photo: A Let L 410UVP-E 19 seater. This model remains in production. (Let)

Let L 610

Country of origin: Czech Republic

Type: 40 seat regional airliner

Powerplants: L 610G – Two 1305kW (1750shp) General Electric CT7D-9D turboprops, driving four blade constant speed Hamilton Standard HS14 RF-23 propellers.

Performance: L 610G – Max cruising speed 438km/h (237kt), long range cruising speed 282km/h (152kt). Initial rate of climb 1675ft/min. Service ceiling 26,000ft. Range with 40 passengers and reserves 1230km (615nm), range with max fuel 2370km (1280nm).

Weights: L 610G – Empty 8950kg (19,713lb), operating empty 9220kg (20,327lb), max takeoff 14,500kg (31,967lb).

Dimensions: Wing span 25.60m (84ft 0in), length 21.4m (70ft 3in), height 8.19m (26ft 11in). Wing area 56.0m^2 (602.8sq ft).

Capacity: Flightcrew of two. Standard basic passenger seating for 40, at three abreast and 76cm (30in) pitch. Combi mixed passenger/freight and all freight layouts available, the latter can carry six pallets.

Production: Four L 601Gs built thus far with orders and options held for 16 L 610Gs from airlines in Norway, Bolivia and India. Small numbers of L 610s were delivered to Aeroflot.

History: The Let L 610 is a stretched development of the earlier L 410 commuter, and although originally designed for a Soviet requirement, in its westernised form is now marketed worldwide.

The L 610 was conceived in the mid 1980s to meet a Soviet Union requirement for a new 40 seat turboprop airliner. A production run of 500 was envisaged for primary customer Aeroflot, and the L 610's design was optimised to suit that carrier's requirements (including operations from austere airfields). The basic L 610M for Aeroflot is conceptually a stretched 40 seat development of the L 410 powered by two 1358kW (1822shp) Motorlet M 602 turboprops. The L 610M flew for the first time on December 28 1988, and a small number were actually delivered to Aeroflot during 1991 before Let suspended deliveries, stating that they would not resume unless western currency was used for payment.

As a result of the dissolution of the Soviet Union and the collapse of communism throughout eastern Europe, Let began development of a westernised version intended to significantly widen the type's sales appeal. Known as the L 610G, it is optimised for world markets and features General Electric CT7 turboprops and Collins Pro Line II digital avionics. First flight of the L 610G prototype occurred on December 18 1992 (four years after the L 610M), and US FAA certification is planned for 1997. The first customer delivery was due to take place by mid 1995.

Let has high hopes that the L 610 will crack the potentially lucrative, although very crowded, western market for 40 seat airliners. Sales for the L 610 thus far have been fairly limited, although the Czech Republic's lower labour costs should see it priced competitively compared with its western competitors. Undoubtedly, sales interest will increase once western certification is awarded.

Photo: The L 610 is being marketed in the West as a rugged, austere operations commuter. The family resemblance to the L 410 is obvious. (Let)

Lockheed Electra

Country of origin: United States of America

Type: Short to medium range turboprop airliner and freighter

Powerplants: L-188C – Four 2800kW (3750shp) Allison 501-D13 turboprops, driving four blade constant speed propellers.

Performance: L-188C – Max cruising speed 652km/h (352kt), economical cruising speed 602km/h (325kt). Service ceiling 27,000ft. Range with max payload 3450km (1910nm), with max fuel 4023km (2180nm).

Weights: L-188C – Operating empty 27,895kg (61,500lb), max takeoff 52,664kg (116,000lb).

Dimensions: Wing span 30.18m (99ft 0in), length 31.81m (104ft 6in), height 10.01m (32ft 10in). Wing area 120.8m^2 (1300sq ft).

Capacity: Normal flightcrew of three. Single class seating for up to 104. Most aircraft currently configured as freighters, max payload weight is approximately 12 tonnes (26,000lb).

Production: Total Electra production of 170, including 55 L-188Cs. More than 55 remained in commercial service as at late 1996.

History: Modestly successful in terms of sales, the Electra was many airlines' introduction to turbine powered aircraft.

The Lockheed L-188 Electra evolved from an American Airlines requirement for a domestic short to medium range airliner. In June 1955 Lockheed was awarded an order for 35 such aircraft. Lockheed's design, designated the L-188, was of a low wing, four turboprop powered configuration. Many other airlines shared American's enthusiasm for the L-188, and by the time the first prototype flew on December 6 1957, the type had gained 144 orders. Service entry was with Eastern Airlines on January 12 1959.

However, any optimism Lockheed would have felt about a rosy sales future would have been short lived, as the onset of the jet age and two mysterious crashes soon after the Electra had entered service contributing to the order book suddenly drying up.

As an interim measure following the crashes, speed restrictions were imposed on Electras while the problem was resolved. Strengthened nacelles, nacelle mountings and a beefier wing structure overcame the problems, but it was not until 1961 that the speed restrictions were lifted.

Two basic versions of the Electra were built. The L-188A was the basic production aircraft, and accounted for most Electra sales. The L-188C entered service with KLM in 1959 and had greater fuel capacity and higher weights, and thus improved payload range performance. The Electra also forms the basis for the hugely successful P-3 Orion long range maritime surveillance aircraft of which more than 600 have been built.

Most Electras currently in service are configured as freighters. From 1967 Lockheed converted 41 Electras to freighters or convertible freighter/passenger aircraft, fitting a strengthened floor and a large cargo door forward of the wing on the left side. Other companies have also converted Electras to freighters. A small number do remain in airline service though, mainly in South America.

Photo: An Irish registered L-188CF Electra of Hunting Cargo. (Keith Gaskell)

Lockheed JetStar

Country of origin: United States of America

Type: Four engined corporate transport

Powerplants: JetStar – Four 14.7kN (3300lb) Pratt & Whitney JT12A-6 turbojets. JetStar II – Four 16.5kN (3700lb) Garrett TFE731-3 turbofans.

Performance: JetStar – Max speed 920km/h (498kt), max cruising speed 823km/h (445kt). Range with a 910kg (2000lb) payload and reserves 4585km (2476nm). JetStar II – Max cruising speed 880km/h (475kt), economical cruising speed 817km/h (440kt). Max initial rate of climb 4200ft. Service ceiling 36,000ft. Range with max fuel and reserves 5132km (2770nm), range with max payload and reserves 4818km (2600nm).

Weights: JetStar – Empty 8376kg (18,450lb), max takeoff 17,678kg (38,940lb). JetStar II – Operating empty 10,967kg (24,178lb), max takeoff 19,844kg (43,750lb).

Dimensions: JetStar – Wing span 16.37m (53ft 8in), length 18.42m (60ft 5in), height 6.23m (20ft 5in). Wing area 50.4m^2 (542.5sq ft). JetStar II – Same except wing span 16.60m (54ft 5in). Wing area 50.4m^2 (542.5sq ft).

Capacity: Flightcrew of two. Normal seating for eight to 10 passengers, but this can be varied to suit individual operators' requirements.

Production: A total of 164 turbojet powered JetStars built by mid 1973. Lockheed built 40 new build turbofan powered JetStar IIs from 1976, while Garrett converted an additional 53 to JetStar II configuration.

History: The four engined JetStar was initially designed as a private venture but was also selected to fulfil a US Air Force requirement for a multi engined light transport and crew trainer.

The first JetStar prototype flew for the first time on September 4 1957. Two prototypes were built powered by Bristol Siddeley Orpheus turbojets, one of these was re-engined with four Pratt & Whitney JT12s in 1959. The JT12 was selected for production aircraft, and the first of these flew in mid 1960. The Jetstar entered service with the USAF as the C-140 navaid calibration aircraft and the VC-140 VIP transport . Given its design origins the JetStar was naturally suited to be a private business/commercial transport, and the first civil configured aircraft was delivered in early 1961. The JetStar was thus the first business jet to enter service.

The turbojet powered JetStar remained in production until mid 1973, by which time development of the turbofan powered JetStar II had been announced. The JetStar II differs from the earlier aircraft primarily in its four Garrett (previously AiResearch and now AlliedSignal) TFE731 turbofans with their significantly improved fuel consumption, resulting in substantial improvements in operating costs range and lower noise levels, while more power allows a higher maximum takeoff weight.

The first JetStar II flew on August 18 1976, with certification following in December that year. The II remained in production until 1979.

AiResearch meanwhile had already flown its own TFE731 powered conversion of the JetStar, this flying in July 1974. The first production AiResearch 731 Jetstar conversion flew in March 1976.

Photo: Today most surviving JetStars are Garrett turbofan powered examples. (Bill Lines)

Lockheed Martin L-100 Hercules

Country of origin: United States of America

Type: Medium range freighter

Powerplants: L-100-30 – Four 3490kW (4680shp) Allison 501-D22A turboprops driving four blade constant speed propellers. L-100J – Four 3425kW (4591shp) Allison AE 2100D3s driving six blade constant speed Dowty propellers.

Performance: L-100-30 – Max cruising speed 571km/h (308kt). Range with max payload 2526km (1363nm), range with max fuel 9227km (4980nm). L-100J – Max cruising speed approx 685km/h (370kt). Range 3700km (2000nm).

Weights: L-100-30 – Operating empty 35,235kg (77,680lb), max takeoff 70,310kg (155,000lb). L-100J – Operating empty 34,438kg (75,923lb), max takeoff 70,310kg (155,000lb).

Dimensions: L-100-30 – Wing span 40.41m (132ft 7in), length 34.37m (112ft 9in), height 11.66m (38ft 3in). Wing area 162.1m^2 (1745sq ft). Adv L-100 – Same except for length 29.79m (97ft 9in).

Capacity: L-100-30 – Flightcrew of three or four. Payload of 23,158kg (51,054lb) comprising pallets or containers. Adv L-100 – Flightcrew of two. Payload of 20,533kg (45,312lb) in pallets.

Production: Approximately 55 civil standard L-100s were in commercial service, while others had been built for military use. No Advanced L-100s had been ordered at the time of writing.

History: The L-100 series of freighters are the civil equivalents of the venerable military C-130 Hercules family, and have proven themselves to be of immense utility, particularly in undeveloped countries.

Lockheed initiated design of the Hercules in response to a 1951 US Air Force requirement for a turboprop powered freighter. This resulted in the C-130 Hercules, which first flew in prototype form on August 23 1954. The USAF ordered the C-130 into series production in September 1952, and since that time 2200 have been built.

The C-130's obvious appeal to freight operators led Lockheed to develop a civil version. The first commercial versions were based on the C-130E model, and a demilitarised demonstrator first flew in April 1964. This initial civil development, the Model 382, was awarded civil certification in February 1965. This model was soon followed up by the 382B, or the L-100, which featured an improved freight handling system.

Sales of these initial versions were slow, leading Lockheed to develop the 2.54m (8ft 4in) stretched L-100-20 (Model 382E), which offered better freight capacity and operating economics. The L-100-20 was certificated in October 1968, but was soon followed by the even longer L-100-30. At 2.03m (6ft 8in) longer than the -20, the -30 first flew in August 1970, and was delivered from December that year. Most civil Hercules sales have been of the L-100-30 variant.

The L-100J is a commercial derivative of the new generation C-130J Hercules II currently under development. Improvements include new AE 2100 advanced turboprop engines with six blade props, two crew EFIS cockpit and significantly lower maintenance and operating costs. The C-130J first flew on April 5 1996, while US FAA certification is planned for early 1997. Both standard (described above) and stretched -30 length fuselage L-100J versions are on offer.

Photo: A L-100-30 of HeavyLift. The L-100-30 is comparable to the military C-130-30. (Les Bushell)

Lockheed TriStar

Country of origin: United States of America

Type: Medium range widebody airliner

Powerplants: L-1011-1 – Three 187kN (42,000lb) Rolls-Royce RB211-22B turbofans. L-1011-200 – Three 215kN (48,000lb) RB211-524s.

Performance: L-1011-1 – Max cruising speed 973km/h (526kt), economical cruising speed 890km/h (463kt). Max range 5760km (3110nm). L-1011-200 – Speeds same. Range with max pax payload 6820km (3680nm), range with max fuel 9111km (4918nm).

Weights: L-1011-1 – Operating empty 109,045kg (240,400lb), max takeoff 195,045kg (430,000lb). L-1011-200 – Operating empty 112,670kg (248,000lb), max takeoff 211,375kg (466,000lb).

Dimensions: Wing span 47.34m (155ft 4in), length 54.17m (177ft 8in), height 16.87m (55ft 4in). Wing area 320.0m^2 (3456sq ft).

Capacity: Flightcrew of three. Max seating for 400 in an all economy configuration at 10 abreast and 76cm (30in) pitch. Typical two class seating for 256, with six abreast seating in first class and nine abreast in economy. Underfloor holds can accommodate 16 standard LD3 containers.

Production: Total TriStar production of 250, of which 200 were standard fuselage length -1, -100, -200 and -250 models. Approximately 165 TriStars remained in service in 1996, of which 135 were standard fuselage models.

History: The Lockheed TriStar was the second widebody airliner to be launched, and although it was dogged with early financial and development problems, particularly with the engine, it eventually gained an excellent reputation in service for its reliability, economy of operation and low noise emissions.

The last Lockheed airliner to be developed, the L-1011 TriStar was launched in March 1968 in response to an American Airlines requirement (that also resulted in the DC-10) for a large capacity medium range airliner. Lockheed initially studied a twin engined layout, but it was felt that three engines would be necessary to ensure it could takeoff at max weights from existing runways.

Construction work on the L-1011 prototype began early in 1969, resulting in a November 16 1970 first flight. The engine choice of Rolls-Royce's advanced three shaft design RB211 however was to dog the TriStar's early career. Rolls-Royce went bankrupt in February 1970 largely due to higher than estimated RB211 development costs, severely damaging the TriStar program and surrendering many potential sales to the rival DC-10 (described separately) until state aid guaranteed the supply of production engines. Despite some initial development problems the RB211 proved to be extremely reliable and efficient in service.

The first L-1011s that entered service with Eastern and TWA in April 1972 were the initial -1 models. Subsequent variants to be developed were the -100 with more fuel and higher weights, the -200 with higher thrust engines, and the long range -500, described separately. The -250 was a conversion of the -1 with RB211-524B4 engines (as on the -500) for US carrier Delta.

Photo: One of three Royal L-1011-100 TriStars. (Gary Gentle)

Lockheed L-1011-500 TriStar

Country of origin: United States of America

Type: Long range widebody airliner

Powerplants: Three 222.4kN (50,000lb) Rolls-Royce RB211-524B or -525B4 turbofans.

Performance: Max cruising speed 960km/h (518kt), economical cruising speed 894km/h (483kt). Range with max pax payload 9905km (5345nm), range with max fuel 11,260km (6100nm).

Weights: Operating empty 111,310kg (245,500lb), max takeoff 231,330kg (510,000lb).

Dimensions: Wing span 50.09m (164ft 4in), length 50.05m (164ft 3in), height 16.87m (55ft 4in). Wing area 329.0m^2 (3540sq ft).

Capacity: Flightcrew of three. Max seating for 330 in a single class 10 abreast layout at 76cm (30in) pitch. Typical two class seating for 24 first class at six abreast and 222 economy at nine abreast. Underfloor cargo holds can accommodate 19 standard LD3 containers.

Production: 50 sold when production ceased in 1984, of which 30 were in service in late 1996.

History: The L-1011-500 TriStar was developed as a long range, smaller capacity derivative of the -200 series TriStar.

Launched in August 1976, the key changes incorporated in the -500 over the standard L-1011s are the 4.11m (13ft 6in) shorter fuselage, greater takeoff weights, more powerful engines and increased span wings. The shortened fuselage reduces seating capacity to a maximum of 330, 70 less than the standard length TriStars, while the below deck galleys that had been a feature of the family were replaced with conventional main deck units. Increased fuel capacity, higher weights, the shorter fuselage, and more powerful engines combine to give the -500 a maximum range of 11,260km (6100nm), approximately 2000km (1300nm) further than the long range -200. Other improvements include improved wing to fuselage and fuselage to rear engine intake fairings.

The -500 also introduced the active aileron improvements first pioneered on the Advanced TriStar. The original prototype TriStar was given this name after being fitted with a number of advanced features intended for introduction to the TriStar production line. The Advanced TriStar incorporated increased span wings to reduce drag, but instead of beefing up the wing structure to cope with their increased weight and increased aerodynamic loads, active, or automatic operation of the ailerons were used to compensate. Other features included the more powerful RB211-524 engines, automatic braking and automatic thrust control.

The first L-1011-500 flew on October 16 1978, while the first -500 with active ailerons and extended wingtips flew in November 1979. Before then the -500 had entered service without the active ailerons with British Airways in May 1979. Production ceased in 1984 after 50 had been built.

Nine ex PanAm and British Airways -500s are operated by Britain's Royal Air Force as long range tanker/transports.

Photo: An L-1011-500 in the colours of Tajikistan International. Note the shortened fuselage by comparison with the earlier TriStars and the revised fuselage/air intake fairing. (Keith Gaskell)

Luscombe Model 8 Silvaire

Country of origin: United States of America

Type: Two seat light aircraft

Powerplant: 8A – One 50kW (65hp) Continental A-65 flat four piston engine, driving a two blade fixed pitch propeller. 8F Special – One 65kW (90hp) Continental C-90 flat four.

Performance: 8A – Max speed 185km/h (100kt), cruising speed at 75% power 165km/h (90kt). Initial rate of climb 900ft/min. Service ceiling 15,000ft. Range 595km (320nm). 8F – Max speed 206km/h (111kt), max cruising speed 193km/h (104kt). Initial rate of climb 900ft/min. Range 804km (435nm).

Weights: 8A – Empty 302kg (665lb), max takeoff 545kg (1200lb). 8F Special – Empty 395kg (870lb), max takeoff 635kg (1400lb).

Dimensions: 8A & 8F Special – Wing span 10.68m (35ft 0in), length 6.10m (20ft 0in), height 1.78m (5ft 10in). Wing area 13.0m^2 (140sq ft).

Capacity: Seating for two in tandem except in the Sedan, which seats four.

Production: Several thousand aircraft of all models have been built, including 1200 before the United States' entry into World War 2.

History: The Luscombe 8 Silvaire was one of a number of highly successful two seat high wing light aircraft built in the years surrounding World War 2, and today remains popular as a classic aircraft.

Prior to introducing the Silvaire into production in 1937 Luscombe had built a small number of two seat high wing light aircraft, the most popular of which was the Phantom, which was powered by a 108kW (145hp) Warner Super Scarab radial engine. The initial Model 8A Silvaire was similar to the Phantom in overall configuration but differed in that it was powered by a 50kW (65hp) Continental A65 engine. A more up market model was also built from 1939, featuring a higher level of standard equipment and improved cabin trim. The 8B was similar to the 8A other than it was powered by a 50kW (60hp) Lycoming engine.

In 1941 Luscombe released the 8C which featured a 55kW (75hp) Continental engine, and the 8D, which differed in having wingtip fuel tanks. A total of 1200 Model 8s were built through to early 1942 when production ceased because of the United States' entry into WW2.

Shortly after the end of the war in late 1945 Luscombe resumed Silvaire production to meet the booming demand experienced by all US light aircraft manufacturers as returned military pilots wanted to continue flying in civilian life. From 1946 all Luscombes featured a new metal wing with a single strut. The first Silvaire to feature the new wing was the 8E, which was powered by a 65kW (85hp) Continental C-85-12 engine.

The final Silvaire production model was the 8F, which featured a 65kW (90hp) Continental C-90. The 8A Sky Pal meanwhile was a lower powered variant of the 8F with a Continental C-65, while small numbers of the four seat Continental E-165 powered Sedan were also built.

Financial difficulties forced Luscombe to cease trading in 1949. US company Temco took over production and built a small number before it too ceased production in 1950. Finally, some Silvaires were built in Colorado between 1955 and 1960.

Photo: A pristine Silvaire at Oshkosh. (Jim Thorn)

Maule M-4 to M-7

Country of origin: United States of America

Type: Family of STOL capable 4/5 seat light aircraft

Powerplant: M-4C – One 108kW (145hp) Continental O-300-A flat six piston engine, driving a two blade constant speed propeller. MX-7-235 – One 175kW (235hp) Textron Lycoming O-540-J1A5D flat six, or fuel injected IO-540-W1A5D driving a two or three blade prop.

Performance: M-4C – Max speed 245km/h (132kt), max cruising speed 233km/h (125kt). Initial rate of climb 700ft/min. Service ceiling 12,000ft. Max range with no reserves 1130km (610nm). MX-7-235 (with IO-540) – Max speed 273km/h (147kt), max cruising speed 257km/h (140kt). Initial rate of climb 2000ft/min. Service ceiling 20,000ft. Range with standard fuel 790km (425nm), range with auxiliary fuel 1496km (807nm).

Weights: M-4C – Empty 500kg (1100lb), max takeoff 953kg (2100lb). MX-7-235 – Empty 669kg (1475lb), max takeoff 1247kg (2750lb).

Dimensions: M-4C – Wing span 9.04m (29ft 8in), length 6.71m (22ft 0in), height 1.89m (6ft 3in). Wing area $14.2m^2$ (152.5sq ft). MX-7-235 – Wing span 9.40m (30ft 10in), length 7.16m (23ft 6in), height 1.93m (6ft 4in). Wing area $15.4m^2$ (165.6sq ft).

Capacity: Standard seating for four, M-7-235 has seats for five.

Production: More than 2000 of all variants produced.

History: The originator of this rugged series of STOL capable light aircraft was the Bee Dee M-4 (named after its designer Belford D Maule), which first flew on September 8 1960.

Although it was originally intended to offer the M-4 as a kitbuilt aircraft, instead it was placed into series production and spawned a prolific series of variants and sub variants.

The first of the line was the M-4 series, which remained in production between 1962 and 1973. The initial M-4, or later M-4C Jetasen, was quite basic, featuring a 108kW (145hp) O-300 and fixed pitch prop; other M-4 variants were the 155kW (210hp) Continental IO-360 powered M-4-210C Rocket and the 118kW (220hp) Franklin 6A-350 powered M-4-220C Strata-Rocket.

The M-5 series which went into production in 1973 introduced a large swept back vertical tail surface, four cabin doors, optional extra fuel and the cambered wingtips first introduced on later series M-4s. Variants included the Franklin powered M-5-220C and Lycoming O-540 powered M-5-225C Lunar Rockets; the Continental powered M-5-210C and M-5-180C (with a four cylinder O-360); and the turbocharged Lycoming TIO-360 powered M-5-210TC.

The M-6 was only built in small numbers due to its lack of aileron response and poor low speed handling, but introduced changes such as greater wing span and fuel tankage.

The M-7 followed from 1984 and forms the basis of a prolific family of subvariants. Current production models include the tricycle undercarriage MXT Trainer (available in 120kW/160hp and 135kW/180hp forms); MX-7-180A Sportplane; MXT-7-180A Trainer; MX-7-180B Star Rocket; MXT-7-180 Star Craft; M-7-235 Super Rocket five seater and MT-7-235 with tricycle undercarriage and the MX-7-235 Super Rocket four seater. The MX-7/MXT-7/M-7 Star Craft models were Allison 250 turboprop powered.

Photo: Pleasure craft surround this MX-7-235 on floats. (John Ruming)

McDonnell Douglas DC-9-10, -20 & -30

Country of origin: United States of America

Type: Short range airliners

Powerplants: -10 – Two 54.5kN (12,250lb) Pratt & Whitney JT8D-5 turbofans. -30 – Two 64.5kN (14,500lb) JT8D-9s, or two 66.7kN (15,000lb) JT8D-11s, or two 71.2kN (16,000lb) JT8D-17s.

Performance: -10 – Max cruising speed 903km/h (488kt), economical cruising speed 885km/h (478kt). Range with max payload 1055km (570nm). -30 – Max cruising speed 907km/h (490kt), long range cruise 798km/h (430kt). Range at high speed cruise with 64 passengers and reserves 2150km (1160nm), range at long range cruise with 80 passengers and reserves 3095km (1670nm).

Weights: -10 – Operating empty 22,635kg (49,900lb), max takeoff 41,140kg (90,700lb). -30 – Empty 25,940kg (57,190lb), max takeoff 54,885kg (121,000lb).

Dimensions: -10 – Wing span 27.25m (89ft 5in), length 31.82m (104ft 5in), height 8.38m (27ft 6in). Wing area $86.8m^2$ (934sq ft). -30 – Same except for length 36.37m (119ft 4in), wing span 28.47m (93ft 5in). Wing area $93.0m^2$ (1000.7sq ft).

Capacity: Flightcrew of two. -10 – Seating for 80 in a single class at five abreast and 86cm (34in) pitch. Max seating for 90. -30 – Max seating for 115 in a single class, five abreast and 81cm (32in) pitch, standard single class seating for 105. DC-9-30CF can carry over eight cargo pallets.

Production: 976 DC-9s of all models built including 137 -10s, 10 -20s and 662 -30s (including military C-9s). 495 DC-9-30s in service at late '96.

History: No other airliner in history has undergone more development than the DC-9/MD-80/MD-90 series, which started life with the diminutive DC-9-10 of the early sixties.

The DC-9 was developed as a short range airliner complementing the much larger DC-8, and filling a market sector that at the time Boeing had been neglecting. Development was launched on April 8 1963, with a launch order from Delta following soon after. The DC-9 was an all new design, featuring rear fuselage mounted engines, a T-tail, moderately swept wings and seats for up to 90 passengers. Construction of the prototype began in July 1963 and the first flight occurred on February 25 1965. Certification and service entry occurred on November 23 and December 8 1965, respectively.

The DC-9 had been designed with stretched larger capacity developments in mind, and such versions of the basic DC-9-10 soon followed. The first stretch resulted in the highest selling member of the family, the 4.54m (14ft 11in) longer, 105 seat DC-9-30, which entered service with Eastern on February 1 1967. Subsequent stretched versions are described separately.

Small numbers of developed versions of the DC-9-10 were also built. The DC-9-20 featured the DC-9-10's fuselage with the -30's more powerful engines and longer span wings, giving better hot and high performance. The DC-9-15 was basically a -10 but with more fuel and higher weights. Factory built convertibles and pure freighters were also offered, while a number of DC-9-30s have been converted to freighters, and/or are having Stage III hushkits fitted, further extending their useful service lives.

Photo: A hushkitted DC-9-30 freighter. (Rob Finlayson)

McDonnell Douglas DC-9-40 & -50

Country of origin: United States of America

Type: Short to medium range airliners

Powerplants: -40 – Two 64.5kN (14,500lb) Pratt & Whitney JT8D-9 turbofans, or two 69.0kN (15,500lb) JT9D-15s, or two 71.2kN (16,000lb) JT8D-17s. -50 – Two 69.0kN (15,500lb) JT8D-15s, or two 71.2kN (16,000lb) JT8D-17s.

Performance: -40 – Max cruising speed 898km/h (485kt), long range cruising speed 820km/h (443kt). Range at high speed cruise with 70 passengers and reserves 1725km (930nm), range with 87 passengers and reserves at long range cruising speed 2880km (1555nm). -50 – Speeds same except for max speed 926km/h (500kt). Range at long range cruising speed with 97 passengers and reserves 3325km (1795nm).

Weights: -40 – Empty 26,612kg (58,670lb), max takeoff 54,885kg (121,000lb). -50 – Empty 28,068kg (61,880lb), max takeoff 54,885kg (121,000lb).

Dimensions: -40 – Wing span 28.47m (93ft 5in), length 38.28m (125ft 7in), height 8.53m (28ft 0in). Wing area 93.0 m^2 (1000.7sq ft). -50 – Same except for length 40.30m (132ft 0in).

Capacity: Flightcrew of two. -40 – Seating for up to 125 passengers at five abreast. -50 – Seating up to 139 passengers at five abreast and 79cm (31in) pitch.

Production: Total DC-9 production of 976, including 71 Series 40s and 96 Series 50s. Approximately 60 -40s and 85 -50s remained in service in late 1994.

History: The DC-9-40 and DC-9-50 are the longest and largest members of the DC-9 family, slotting in between and -10 and -30, and the later MD-80 and MD-90 series.

The DC-9-40 was initially developed in response to a Scandinavian Airline System's specific requirement for a larger capacity development of the DC-9. Compared with the DC-9-30, the DC-9-40 is 1.87m (6ft 4in) longer, raising seating capacity in a single class configuration to 125. Apart from the fuselage stretch and more powerful engine options, the -40 was the much the same as the -30. First flight occurred on November 28 1967, and the type entered service with SAS on March 12 the following year.

The DC-9-50 is the largest member of the DC-9/MD-80/MD-90 family to bear the DC-9 designation. Launched in mid 1973, the DC-9-50 is a further 1.87m (6ft 4in) longer than the DC-9-40, or 4.34m (14ft 3in) longer than the DC-9-30, and has maximum seating for 139 passengers. Delivered from August 1975, the DC-9-50 introduced a new look cabin interior designed to make more efficient use of the space available and give the impression of a more spacious widebody interior, and other improved features such as an improved anti skid braking system and quieter engine nacelles compared with the DC-9-40.

Compared with the rest of the DC-9 based family, the -40 and -50 sold only in fairly modest numbers. The largest DC-9-40 customer was SAS, while Northwest Airlines operates a large fleet of DC-9-40s and DC-9-50s (it is in fact the largest DC-9 operator in the world).

Photo: A DC-9-40 of SAS at Frankfurt. Visually, there is very little difference between the -40 and -50. (Gerard Frawley)

McDonnell Douglas MD-80

Country of origin: United States of America

Type: Short to medium range airliner

Powerplants: MD-81 – Two 82.3kN (18,500lb) Pratt & Whitney JT8D-209 turbofans. MD-88 – Two 93.4kN (21,000lb) JT8D-219s.

Performance: MD-81 – Max speed 925km/h (500kt), long range cruising speed 813km/h (440kt). Range with 155 passengers and reserves 3020km (1630nm). MD-88 – Speeds same. Range with 155 passengers and reserves 4850km (2620nm).

Weights: MD-81 – Operating empty 35,239kg (77,888lb), max takeoff 63,503kg (140,000lb), or 67,810kg (149,500lb) with JT8D-217As. MD-88 – Operating empty 35,369kg (77,976lb), max takeoff 67,810kg (149,500lb).

Dimensions: Wing span 32.87m (107ft 10in), length 45.06m (147ft 10in), height 9.19m (30ft 2in). Wing area 115.1m^2 (1239sq ft).

Capacity: Flightcrew of two. Seating for up to 172 passengers at five abreast and 78cm (31in) pitch. Two class seating for 142, comprising 14 premium class and 128 economy class passengers.

Production: Total MD-80 series orders for over 1170 aircraft, of which over 1120 were in service at late 1996. Low rate production in China.

History: The MD-80 series is a stretched and improved development of the DC-9, and sold in particularly large numbers during the 1980s.

The MD-80 series began life as the DC-9 Super 80, and before that the DC-9-55. The origins of the line lie in 1975 testing where a standard DC-9 was fitted with refanned JT8D turbofans known as the JT8D-200 series, which resulted in quieter, more efficient and more powerful engines. McDonnell Douglas originally proposed fitting the new engines to a development designated the DC-9-55, which would have featured two JT8D-209s and a 3.86m (12ft 8in) stretched fuselage over the -50. Instead this concept evolved into the DC-9 Super 80 (or DC-9-80), which had the new engines, a further stretched fuselage, greater wing span and other improvements. Launched in October 1977, the expected first flight date of July 1979 was delayed somewhat until October 18 that year. Certification for the initial Super 80 model, the 81, was granted in July 1981. The first customer delivery was to Swissair in September 1980.

The DC-9-80 became the MD-80 in 1983. The MD-80 designation however broadly applies to a family of developments, and does not specifically apply to a certain model type. The specific MD-80 models are the initial MD-81, the MD-82 with more powerful JT8D-217s, the extended range MD-83 with extra fuel and more efficient JT8D-219s, and the MD-88 (first flight August 1987) with the JT8D-217s of the MD-83 with an EFIS cockpit and redesigned cabin interior, with other improvements. The shorter fuselage but longer range MD-87 is described separately.

Initial sales of the Super 80 were sluggish until American Airlines placed a massive initial order for 67 MD-82s (with options on 100) in early 1984 (American now operates a fleet of 260 MD-80s), boosting what has now become MDC's most successful airliner program since the DC-3. A small number of MD-82s have also been built under licence in China. The 1000th MD-80 was delivered in March 1992.

Photo: One of three MD-83s of Turkish charter operator Sunway Intersun. (Keith Gaskell)

McDonnell Douglas MD-87

Country of origin: United States of America

Type: Short to medium range airliner

Powerplants: Two 68.9kN (20,000lb) Pratt & Whitney JT8D-217C turbofans. Other JT8D-200 series engines available optionally.

Performance: Max speed 925km/h (500kt), long range cruising speed 811km/h (438kt). Range with 130 passengers and reserves 4457km (2405nm), or optionally 5326km (2874nm).

Weights: Operating empty with standard fuel 33,237kg (73,274lb), operating empty with optional fuel 33,965kg (74,880lb), max takeoff 63,503kg (140,000lb).

Dimensions: Wing span 32.86m (107ft 10in), length 39.75m (130ft 5in), height 9.50m (31ft 2in). Wing area 115.1m^2 (1239sq ft).

Capacity; Flightcrew of two. Max seating for 139 passengers at five abreast at 81cm (32in) pitch). Two class seating for 117.

Production: Of total MD-80 sales of over 1400, over 130 were for MD-87s. Most were in airline service at late 1996.

History: The MD-87 is a shortened version of McDonnell Douglas' successful MD-80 series.

A reversal of the trend from the DC-9 to the MD-80 series, the MD-87 combines the advanced features introduced on the MD-80 (most notably the Pratt & Whitney JT8D-200 engines) into a 5.3m (17ft 5in) shorter length fuselage similar to the DC-9-30. The DC-9-30 was the most successful of the DC-9 family, and McDonnell Douglas no doubt hoped to capitalise on what appeared to be a large replacement market.

The MD-87 features the 39.75m (130ft 5in) fuselage length; plus an EFIS cockpit (the MD-87 was the first aircraft of the MD-80 series to feature an EFIS cockpit) and a Head Up Display as standard; Pratt & Whitney JT8D-217C turbofans (which are approximately 2% more efficient than the -217A); the cruise performance package improvements introduced on late production MD-80s, including the extended low drag tail cone; and increased height fin to compensate for the loss of moment arm due to the shorter fuselage.

The MD-87 is optionally available with extra front and rear cargo compartment auxiliary fuel tanks to extend range, and other engines in the JT8D-200 series. In other respects the MD-87 is essentially identical to the MD-80 series.

McDonnell Douglas' airliner arm, Douglas Aircraft Company, announced it had launched development of the MD-87 on January 3 1985, following launch orders from Finnair and Austrian in December 1984. First flight took place on December 4 1986, certification was granted on October 21 1987.

Unfortunately for MDC, sales have been relatively small, and mainly to traditional Douglas customers. Notable operators include Iberia (with 24), SAS (18) and Japan Air System (eight). Smaller operators include Finnair, Aero Llyod, Aeromexico, Great American, Austrian and Reno Air.

Photo: A shortened MD-80, the -87 is dimensionally similar to the older DC-9-40 and 50 series. SAS, the national airline of Sweden, Norway and Denmark, operates 18 MD-87s alongside MD-80s and DC-9-20s and -40s. (Keith Gaskell)

McDonnell Douglas MD-90

Country of origin: United States of America

Type: Short to medium range airliner

Powerplants: MD-90-30 – Two 111.2kN (25,000lb) International Aero Engines IAE V2525-D5 turbofans. MD-90-55 – Two 124.5kN (28,000lb) V2528-D5s.

Performance: MD-90-30 – Typical cruising speed 809km/h (437kt). Range with 153 passengers and reserves 4215km (2275nm). MD-90-55 – Speeds same. Range with 187 passengers and reserves 5005km (2700nm).

Weights: MD-90-30 – Operating empty 39,915kg (88,000lb) max takeoff 70,760kg (156,000lb). MD-90-55 – Operating empty 41,685kg (91,900lb), max takeoff 78,245kg (172,500lb).

Dimensions: Wing span 32.87m (107ft 10in), length 46.51m (152ft 7in), height 9.33m (30ft 7in). Wing area 112.3m^2 (1209sq ft).

Capacity: Flightcrew of two. Two class seating for 12 premium class and 141 economy class passengers in MD-90-30, or max single class seating for 172. MD-90-55 has max single class seating for 187.

Production: At late 1996 MD-90 orders stood at 120, of which approximately 20 were in airline service.

History: Over the years the MD-90 designation has been applied to a number of DC-9/MD-80 series developments, among them the DC-9-30 in the early 1980s, and then the Unducted Fan powered series of airliners in vogue in the late 1980s. In the end though, like the MD-80 was to the DC-9, the MD-90 is a stretched and re-engined development of the MD-80.

Most important of the changes introduced on the MD-90 are the two International Aero Engines IAE V2500 turbofans. At 111kN (25,000lb) on the MD-90-30, the V2500s are the largest, heaviest and most powerful engines to be rear mounted on any airliner yet. More importantly though, the V2500 is recognised as the most efficient and economical engine in its thrust class. Other changes to the MD-90 include the 1.4m (4ft 6in) fuselage stretch forward of the wing, allowing seating for an extra 10 passengers (in a two class arrangement) over the MD-80, making it a true 150 seater, and a realistic 727 replacement. The stretch is forward of the wing to compensate for the extra weight of the rear mounted engines. The MD-90 also features an EFIS glass cockpit based on that in the MD-88, and other detail improvements.

Launched in November 1988, first flight occurred on February 22 1993, and certification was awarded on November 16 1994. Launch customer was Delta, which has 31 on firm order, while other major customers are Saudi Arabian Airlines and Japan Air System.

The basic MD-90 model is the MD-90-30 (Chinese built Trunkliners are designated the MD-90-30T, and will feature double bogey main landing gear). The MD-90-50 is an extended range version with a higher maximum takeoff weight and extra fuel, the MD-90-55 is a high capacity variant capable of seating 187 in a single class (more than double the max seating of the original DC-9-10), with two extra doors in the forward fuselage to meet emergency evacuation requirements.

Photo: The MD-90 is the ultimate development of the DC-9 line. (Rob Finlayson)

McDonnell Douglas MD-95

Country of origin: United States of America

Type: 100 seat short range airliner

Powerplants: Two 82.9kN (18,500lb) BMW Rolls-Royce BR715 turbofans.

Performance: MD-95-30 – Cruising speed 811km/h (438kt). Range with reserves 3155km (1705nm). MD-95-30ER – Range with reserves 3430km (1850nm).

Weights: MD-95-30 – Operating empty 29,890kg (65,900lb), max takeoff 51,710kg (114,000lb). MD-95-30ER – Operating empty 30,255kg (66,700lb), max takeoff 51,710kg (114,000lb).

Dimensions: Wing span 28.50m (93ft 5in), length 36.37m (119ft 4in), height 8.60m (28ft 6in). Wing area 93.0m^2 (1000.7sq ft).

Capacity: Flightcrew of two. Typical two class seating for 106 passengers at five abreast in main cabin.

Production: Launch order for 50 MD-95s placed by Valujet in October 1995, with first delivery scheduled for mid 1999. McDonnell Douglas has forecast sales of 200 to 300 MD-95s .

History: The 100 seat class MD-95 will combine a fuselage similar in length to the DC-9-30 with advanced technologies developed for the MD-90 and all new BMW Rolls-Royce BR715 engines.

When McDonnell Douglas originally announced that it planned developing the MD-95 at the Paris Airshow in June 1991 the company anticipated a program launch by late 1991, a first flight in July 1994 and deliveries of production MD-95s from October 1995. As it happened this schedule proved to be optimistic. MDC was authorised to offer the MD-95 to potential customers in mid 1994, although official program launch was not until October 1995 when US discount airline ValuJet ordered 50 and optioned 50. First flight is planned for 1998, with certification and service entry scheduled for mid 1999.

When the MD-95 was announced MDC initially proposed powering the aircraft with Pratt & Whitney JT8D-218s or Rolls-Royce Tays. In February 1994 however McDonnell Douglas announced it had chosen the new BMW Rolls-Royce BR715 over the JT8D and an engine from the proposed 'Project Blue' teaming of General Electric, SNECMA, MTU and P&W.

Other than the advanced engines, the MD-95 will feature a fuselage 1.45m (4ft 9in) longer than the DC-9-30's, a wing based on the DC-9-34's, and a six screen Honeywell EFIS flightdeck and cabin interior to that developed for the MD-90. It will be offered in standard MD-95-30 and extended range MD-95-30ER form. A stretched, 130 seat MD-95-50 has also been seriously studied.

Companies selected to participate in MD-95 construction include Alenia who will build the fuselage, Sth Korea's Halla Engineering and Heavy Industries and McDonnell Douglas Canada the wings, ShinMaywa of Japan the engine pylons and horizontal stabilizers, and Israel Aircraft Industries the undercarriage. In late 1994 MDC announced that Dalfort Aviation would undertake MD-95 final assembly in Dallas, Texas under subcontract, however MDC will now assemble the MD-95 itself.

Photo: An artist's impression of a MD-95 in ValuJet colours.

McDonnell Douglas DC-10

Country of origin: United States of America

Type: Medium to long range widebody airliner

Powerplants: DC-10-10 – Three 178kN (40,000lb) General Electric CF6-6D turbofans, or three 182.4kN (41,000lb) CF6-6D1s. DC-10-30 – Three either 218kN (49,000lb) CF6-50As, 226.9kN (51,000lb) CF6-50Cs, or 233.5kN (52,500lb) CF6-50C1s or C2s, or 240.2kN (54,000lb) CF6-50C2Bs. DC-10-40 – Three 219.6kN (49,400lb) Pratt & Whitney JT9D-20s, or 235.8kN (53,000lb) JT9D-59As.

Performance: DC-10-30 – Max speed 982km/h (530kt), max cruising speed 908km/h (490kt). Range with max fuel and no payload 12,055km (6505nm), range with max payload 7415km (4000nm). DC-10-40 – Speeds same. Range with max fuel and no payload 11,685km (6305nm), range with max payload (& JT9D-59As) 7505km (4050nm).

Weights: DC-10-30 – Empty 121,198kg (267,197lb), max takeoff 263,085kg (580,000lb). DC-10-40 – Empty 122,951kg (271,062lb), max takeoff 259,450kg (572,000lb).

Dimensions: Wing span 50.40m (165ft 5in), length 55.50m (182ft 1in), height 17.70m (58ft 1in). Wing area 367.7m^2 (3958sq ft).

Capacity: Flightcrew of three. Max seating for 380 passengers at 10 abreast and 81cm (32in) pitch. Mixed class seating arrangements vary between 250 and 270 passengers. Underfloor hold accepts 14 LD3 containers or pallets. DC-10-30F – Main deck accommodates 23 standard pallets.

Production: Of the 386 civil DC-10s built, 295 remained in service at late 1996.

History: Designed in response to the same American Airlines requirement as the Lockheed TriStar, the DC-10, despite a sometimes troubled past, was the more successful of the two widebody trijets.

The DC-10 program was launched in February 1968 with orders from American and United. Although originally conceived as a twinjet, the DC-10 gained a third engine at the base of the vertical tail to meet American's requirement that the aircraft be capable of operating from existing runways. Construction of the prototype began in January 1969, and first flight took place on August 29 1970.

The first DC-10s entered service with American and United in August 1971. These aircraft were the initial US domestic DC-10-10 version, and already work was progressing on the longer transcontinental range DC-10-30 version against orders from European airlines. Fitted with additional fuel tanks and more powerful engines, the -30 differs little from the -10 except for its greater range and a third main undercarriage unit.

Most DC-10 production was of the -30 model, while convertible -30CF and pure freight -30Fs were built. One further -30 development is the -40, a Pratt & Whitney JT9D powered variant operated by Northwest and JAL. Sixty GE powered DC-10s were also built as KC-10 tanker transports for the USAF during the mid to late eighties.

A number of major and catastrophic accidents marred the DC-10s service record in the mid to late 1970s, but the various causes of these accidents were overcome and the DC-10 continues to operate reliably. Production ceased in 1989.

The MD-10 conversion for Federal Express involves fitting DC-10's with the DC-11's two crew cockpit.

Photo: An AOM French Airlines DC-10-30. (John Adlard)

McDonnell Douglas MD-11

Country of origin: United States of America

Type: Long range widebody airliner

Powerplants: Either three 266.9kN (60,000lb) Pratt & Whitney PW4460s or 273.6kN (61,500lb) General Electric CF6-80C2D1F turbofans.

Performance: MD-11 – Max cruising speed 945km/h (510kt), economical cruising speed 876km/h (473kt). Range with 323 passengers and reserves 12,566km (6790nm). MD-11F – Speeds same. Range 6710km (3626nm). MD-11 Combi – Speeds same. Range with 214 passengers, six freight pallets and reserves 11,610km (6273nm). MD-11ER – Speeds same. Range 13,340km (7200nm).

Weights: MD-11 – Operating empty 131,035kg (288,880lb) with CF6s, 155,620kg (288,180lb) with PW4460s. Max takeoff 283,725kg (625,500lb). MD-11F – Operating empty 113,630kg (250,510lb), max takeoff same. MD-11 Combi – Operating empty 129,590kg (285,700lb), max takeoff same. MD-11ER – Max takeoff 286,250kg (630,500lb).

Dimensions: Wing span 51.77m (169ft 10in), length 61.64m (200ft 11in) with PW4460s, 61.37m (201ft 4in) with CF6s, height 17.60m (57ft 9in). Wing area 338.9m^2 (3648sq ft).

Capacity: Flightcrew of two. MD-11 – Max single class seating for 405 at 10 abreast and 81cm (32in) pitch. Typical two class seating for 323 passengers, three class seating for 293. MD-11F – Pallets and/or containers on main and lower decks. MD-11 Combi – Typical two class seating for 213 and six pallets on main deck.

Production: Total MD-11 orders for over 175, with more than 155 in service in late 1996.

History: Despite being the first new entrant in the 300 to 350 seat class ahead of the Airbus A330 and Boeing 777, the MD-11 has been only modestly successful, with few new sales now expected.

The MD-11 is a modernised, slightly stretched and re-engined development of the DC-10 trijet. Launched on December 30 1986 (following a launch order from British Caledonian for three earlier that month), the MD-11 was the result of a two year study to find a replacement for the DC-10. First flight occurred on January 10 1990, certification was granted in November that year, with service entry that December.

Compared to the DC-10, the MD-11 features a 5.71m (18ft 9in) fuselage stretch, winglets, modified tail with less sweepback, an advanced two crew six screen EFIS flightdeck, restyled main cabin interior and new engine options. Variants on offer include the longer range MD-11ER with extra fuel and slightly lower drag and available from early 1996; the pure freight MD-11F, and the MD-11 Combi. McDonnell Douglas has at various times proposed a number of other MD-11 developments aimed at increasing passenger capacity through fuselage stretches and underfloor panorama deck seating.

For a time the designation MD-12 applied to a significantly stretched MD-11. Subsequently the MD-12 designation applied to an all new 747 size quad jet that was not launched, while in 1996 MDC looked closely at the MD-XX, MD-11 variants with a new wing. Two versions were proposed, one with the standard MD-11 fuselage and a 15,565km (8400nm) range, the other a stretched 375 seater. These were not launched.

Photo: An American Airlines MD-11. (Rob Finlayson)

McDonnell Douglas MD 500 & Hughes 500

Country of origin: United States of America

Type: Light utility helicopters

Powerplant: 500C – One 207kW (278shp) Allison 250-C20 turboshaft, driving a four blade main rotor and two blade tail rotor. MD 530F – One 260kW (350shp) Allison 250-C30 driving a five blade main rotor and two or optionally four blade tail rotor.

Performance: 500C – Max cruising speed 232km/h (125kt), long range cruising speed 217km/h (117kt). Initial rate of climb 1700ft/min. Hovering ceiling in ground effect 13,000ft. Range 605km (325nm). MD 530F – Max cruising speed 246km/h (133kt), economical cruising speed 228km/h (123kt). Initial rate of climb 2070ft/min. Service ceiling 16,000ft. Range with standard fuel and no reserves 422km (228nm).

Weights: 500C – Empty 493kg (1088lb), max takeoff 1157kg (2550lb). MD 530F – Empty 717kg (1580lb), max (overload) takeoff 1610kg (3550lb), max operating weight with sling load 1700kg (3750lb).

Dimensions: 500C – Main rotor diameter 8.03m (26ft 4in), fuselage length 7.01m (23ft 0in), height 2.48m (8ft 2in). MD 530F – Main rotor diameter 8.33m (27ft 4in), length overall 8.97m (29ft 5in), fuselage length 7.49m (24ft 7in), height 2.67m (8ft 9in). Main rotor disc area 54.6m^2 (597.5sq ft).

Capacity: Typical seating for five, two in front bucket seats (including pilot), and three on rear bench seat. Alternatively can accommodate two stretchers and medical attendant, plus pilot.

Production: Approximately 4675 Hughes 500s and MD 500s have been built, including large numbers for military customers.

History: One of the world's most successful and useful light turbine helicopters, the Hughes/McDonnell Douglas 500 series began life in response to a US Army requirement for a light observation helicopter.

Hughes won the US Army observation helicopter contest against competition from Bell and Hiller, resulting in the Allison 250 powered OH-6 Cayuse, which first flew in February 1963. Prior to that Hughes announced it was developing a civil version, to be marketed as the Hughes 500 (Hughes Model 369). It was offered in basic five and seven seat configurations, and a 500U, later 500C, utility version with a more powerful engine.

From 1976 deliveries were of the 500D, an improved version with a more powerful engine, a T-tail, and new five blade main and optional four blade tail rotors. The 500D was followed by the 500E from 1982 with recontoured nose, and various interior improvements including greater head and leg room. The 530F is a more powerful version optimised for hot and high work.

McDonnell Douglas acquired Hughes Helicopters in January 1984, and since August 1985 the 500E and 530F have been built under the McDonnell Douglas banner as the MD 500E and MD 530F Lifter.

Military variants are marketed under the MD 500 Defender name.

The MD 500 also forms the basis for the NOTAR equipped MD 520N, which is described separately.

Photo: This Hughes 500 is used for agricultural spraying in New Zealand by Wanganui Aero Work. (Peter Clark)

McDonnell Douglas MD 520N

Country of origin: United States of America

Type: Light utility helicopter

Powerplant: One 280kW (375shp) Allison 250-C20R turboshaft, driving a five blade main rotor.

Performance: Max cruising speed 250km/h (135kt). Initial rate of climb 1850ft/min. Service ceiling 14,175ft. Hovering ceiling in ground effect 9043ft. Range 402km (217nm).

Weights: Empty 742kg (1636lb), max takeoff 1520kg (3350lb), or 1745kg (3850lb) with an external sling load.

Dimensions: Main rotor diameter 8.33m (27ft 4in), length overall 8.69m (28ft 6in), fuselage length 7.62m (25ft 0in), height 2.74m (9ft 0in), or 3.01m (9ft 11in) on extended skids. Main rotor disc area $54.5m^2$ (586.8sq ft).

Capacity: Standard seating for pilot and four passengers, with pilot and passenger on front bucket seats, and three passengers on rear bench seat.

Production: Orders and options held for over 200 MD 520Ns, with more than 80 delivered.

History: The MD 520N represents a major revolution in helicopter design, as it dispenses with a conventional tail rotor in favour of McDonnell Douglas' unique NOTAR (NO TAil Rotor) system.

The MD 520N is the first application of NOTAR technology. Based on the earlier conventional MD 500E, McDonnell Douglas' original intention was to develop the standard MD 520N alongside the more powerful hot and high optimised MD 530N (both were launched in January 1989). The MD 530N was the first to fly, on December 29 1989, the MD 520N first flew on May 1 1990. Development of the MD 530N was suspended when it was found that the MD 520N met most customer requirements for the 530N. Certification of the MD 520N was awarded on September 13 1991, and the first was delivered on December 31 that year.

Development of the revolutionary NOTAR system dates back to late 1975 when Hughes engineers began initial concept development work. In December 1981 Hughes flew an OH-6A fitted with NOTAR for the first time. A more heavily modified prototype demonstrator first flew in March 1986 (by which time McDonnell Douglas had acquired Hughes Helicopters).

Although the concept, known as the Coanda effect, took some time to refine, the NOTAR system is quite simple and works the same way as a wing develops lift to provide directional control. Low pressure air is forced through two slots on the right side of the tailboom, causing the downwash from the main rotor to hug the tailboom, producing lift, and thus a measure of directional control. This is augmented by a direct jet thruster and vertical stabilisers.

The NOTAR system offers a number of benefits including far lower external noise (at the time of writing it was the quietest certificated helicopter in the world), increased safety due to the removal of the tail rotor, improved handling and performance, reduced vibration and easier maintainability.

The stretched eight place MD 600N is described separately.

Photo: A MD 520N in operation with the Los Angeles County Sheriff. The MD 520N's low noise signature is proving popular with police.

McDonnell Douglas MD 600N

Country of origin: United States of America

Type: Eight place light turbine helicopter

Powerplants: MD 600N – One 590kW (791shp) Allison 250-C47 turboshaft, derated to 445kW (600shp) for takeoff driving a six blade main rotor.

Performance: MD 600N – Max cruising speed to 5000ft 248km/h (134kt). Max initial rate of climb 1700ft/min. Max operating altitude 20,000ft. Hovering ceiling in ground effect 10,500ft, out of ground effect 6800ft. Max range at 5000ft 740km (400nm) or 620km (335nm) at sea level.

Weights: MD 600N – Empty 875kg (1930lb), max takeoff with internal load 1860kg (4100lb), max takeoff with sling load 2205kg (4860lb).

Dimensions: MD 600N – Main rotor disc diameter 8.38m (27ft 6in), length overall rotors turning 11.25m (36ft 11in), fuselage length 9.30m (30ft 6in), height to top of rotor head 2.65m (8ft 9in), or 2.96m (9ft 9in) with extended skids. Main rotor disc area $55.2m^2$ (594.0sq ft)

Capacity: Typical seating for eight, with pilot and passenger on bucket seats, and two bench seats for three people each in the main cabin. Can be configured for a variety of missions including medevac, with customised interior.

Production: Three prototypes flying by late 1996, with first production deliveries planned for late 1996. McDonnell Douglas Helicopters estimated demand for 180 to 200 MD 600Ns through to 2000.

History: The MD 600N is a stretched eight seat development of the five seat MD 520N Notar helicopter.

McDonnell Douglas Helicopter Systems first announced it was developing a stretched MD 520N in late 1994, but surprised the world helicopter community the following year when it unveiled the first flying prototype of the new helicopter, at that time designated the MD 630N, at the Heli Expo in Las Vegas in January 1995. This prototype, actually a modified MD 530F, had made its first flight on November 22 1994. The MD 630N created high levels of interest at the Heli Expo and McDonnell Douglas gave the go-ahead for the production aircraft, redesignated the MD 600N, in March '96.

The prototype was modified to MD 600N standard with a production standard engine and tail boom and flew in November 1995, followed the next month by the first MD 600N production prototype. Unfortunately this second prototype MD 600N was destroyed by fire following a forced landing in May 1996, caused by the main rotor contacting the tail boom during extreme control reversal tests.

Thus the third prototype, which first flew on August 9 1996, featured modifications to increase the main rotor-tail boom clearance. Despite the setback McDonnell Douglas Helicopters was still planning for certification and first customer deliveries in late 1996.

McDonnell Douglas stretched the MD 520N fuselage by inserting a plug aft of the cockpit/cabin bulkhead and stretching the NOTAR tail boom. The larger fuselage allows for an extra (middle) row of seats. Other differences compared with the MD 520N include a new six blade main rotor (the MD 520N has a five blade unit) and a more powerful Allison 250 turboshaft.

Photo: The first MD 600N prototype. This particular aircraft was converted from the MD 530N demonstrator. (MDHS)

McDonnell Douglas MD Explorer

Country of origin: United States of America

Type: Executive and utility helicopter

Powerplants: MD 900 – Two 469kW (629shp) (takeoff rating) Pratt & Whitney Canada PW 206B turboshafts, driving a five blade main rotor, or two 478kW (641shp) (takeoff rating) Turboméca TM319-2 Arrius 2Cs.

Performance: MD 900 with PW 206Bs – Max cruising speed 274km/h (148kt). Initial rate of climb 2800ft/min. Service ceiling 18,000ft. Hovering ceiling out of ground effect 11,300ft. Max range 585km (315nm).

Weights: MD 900 – Standard empty 1481kg (3265lb), max takeoff 2722kg (6000lb), or 3057kg (6740lb) with external sling load.

Dimensions: Main rotor diameter 10.31m (33ft 10in), length overall 11.85m (38ft 10in), fuselage length 9.85m (32ft 4in), height 3.66m (12ft 0in). Main rotor disc area 83.5m^2 (899.04sq ft).

Capacity: One pilot and passenger or two pilots on front bucket seats, with six passengers in main cabin in club seating arrangement. Max seating for 10 (including pilot). Alternatively can be configured with stretchers and seating for medical attendants.

Production: Production began late 1994. At late 1996 MDHS had delivered 25 MD 900 Explorers.

History: The first all new helicopter to be developed by McDonnell Douglas (in fact the first all new civil McDonnell Douglas aircraft since the DC-10), the MD Explorer is also the first all new design to incorporate the unique NOTAR (NO TAil Rotor) system.

McDonnell Douglas Helicopters launched the Explorer as the MDX in January 1989, pitching it into the hotly contest light twin turbine helicopter market. Later designated the MD 900, MD 901 and later just the MD Explorer, first flight took place on December 18 1992. VFR certification for the PW206B powered version was granted in October 1994.

One of the most advanced helicopters in its market segment, the MD Explorer features McDonnell Douglas's unique NOTAR anti torque system (described in detail under the MD 520N entry), whose benefits include increased safety, far lower noise levels and performance and controllability benefits.

The design also features an advanced bearingless five blade main rotor system with composite blades, and extensive use of composites, mainly carbonfibre, in the fuselage and tail. Initial aircraft will be powered by two Pratt & Whitney Canada PW206s (the Explorer is the first application of the PW200 series), while Turboméca Arrius TM319-9 2C powered versions of the Explorer will also be available from the 129th production aircraft.

In 1996 McDonnell Douglas announced the development of a improved version of the Explorer, the MD 902, which will replace the MD 900 in production in 1997. Features of the MD 902 will include PW206E engines with higher one engine operative ratings (the Arrius remains an option), revised engine air inlets, improved NOTAR inlet design and a more powerful stabiliser control system. Benefits include a 578km (312nm) range (up 7%), a 3.3hr endurance (up 4%) increased payload (up 109kg/240lb) and lower operating costs.

Photo: Low operating costs and a minimal noise footprint are hallmarks of the Explorer. (MDHS)

Mil Mi-8, Mi-17 & Mi-171

Country of origin: Russia

Type: Medium lift utility helicopters

Powerplants: Mi-8T – Two 1250kW (1677shp) Klimov (Isotov) TV2-117A turboshafts, driving a five blade main rotor and three blade tail rotor. Mi-171 – Two 1545kW (2070shp) TV3-117M turboshafts.

Performance: Mi-8T – Max speed 260km/h (140kt), max cruising speed 220km/h (120kt). Service ceiling 14,765ft. Hovering ceiling in ground effect 6235ft. Range with 24 passengers and reserves 500km (270nm). Mi-171 – Max speed 250km/h (135kt), max cruising speed 230km/h (124kt). Service ceiling 18,700ft. Range with reserves 570km (307nm), range with two external tanks 1065km (575nm).

Weights: Mi-8T – Empty 6800kg (14,990lb), max takeoff (for vertical takeoff) 12,000kg (26,455lb). Mi-171 – Empty equipped 7055kg (15,555lb), max takeoff 13,000kg (28,660lb).

Dimensions: Mi-8T – Main rotor diameter 21.29m (69ft 10in), length overall 25.24m (82ft 10in), fuselage length 18.17m (59ft 8in), height 5.65m (18ft 7in). Main rotor disc area 356m^2 (3932sq ft). Mi-171 – Same except for length overall 25.35m (83ft 2in), fuselage length 18.42m (60ft 6in).

Capacity: Flightcrew of two, with provision for flight engineer. Primarily used for cargo transport, both internal or with external sling loads. Can carry up to 32 passengers in Mi-8, or 24 in Mi-8T. Mi-8 Salon executive version seats 11 passengers. As air ambulance can accommodate 12 stretchers.

Production: Over 12,000 Mi-8s, Mi-17s and Mi-171s built, but majority for military service.

History: Produced in greater numbers than any other helicopter built in Russia, the Mi-8/Mi-17/Mi-171 series (NATO codename 'Hip') was designed primarily as a military assault transport, but is also in widespread civil use.

The Mi-8 was designed as a replacement for the piston engined Mi-4, with design work beginning in May 1960. First flight of the prototype (powered by a single Soloviev turboshaft driving a four blade main rotor) occurred in June 1961, while a production standard Mi-8 flew in August 1962 and production began shortly afterwards. Civil versions of the Mi-8 have square windows and include the Mi-8 passenger version, Mi-8T utility transport, Mi-8TM passenger transport with weather radar and Mi-8 Salon executive transport.

Production of the Mi-8 ceased in favour of the re-engined Mi-17, which was first publicly revealed to the west at the 1981 Paris Airshow. The main improvement in the Mi-17 is the TV3 turboshafts which give better overall performance. Civil versions include the base Mi-17, and the essentially similar Mi-171 and Mi-17M, which both feature more powerful TV3-117VM turboshafts, and are built by Ulan-Ude Aviation and Kazan Helicopters respectively. Both companies are actively marketing their types in the west. Kazan's Mi-172 is designed to meet western certification standards.

Photo: An Mi-172. The Mi-8 and Mi-17/-171/-172 differ in having their tail rotor on the starboard and port sides of the tailboom respectively. (Keith Anderson)

Mil Mi-26

Country of origin: Russia

Type: Ultra heavy lift utility helicopter

Powerplants: Two 7460kW (10,000shp) ZMKB Progress (Lotarev) turboshafts, driving an eight blade main rotor and five blade tail rotor.

Performance: Max speed 295km/h (160kt), typical cruising speed 255km/h (137kt). Service ceiling 15,100ft. Hovering ceiling in ground effect 14,765ft. Range with max internal fuel at max takeoff weight with reserves 800km (432nm), range with four auxiliary fuel tanks 1920km (1036nm).

Weights: Empty 28,200kg (62,170lb), normal takeoff 49,600kg (109,350lb), max takeoff 56,000kg (123,450lb).

Dimensions: Main rotor diameter 32.00m (105ft 0in), length overall 40.03m (131ft 4in), fuselage length 33.73m (110ft 8in), height to top of rotor head 8.15m (26ft 9in). Main rotor disc area 804.3m^2 (8657sq ft).

Capacity: Flightcrew of four comprising two pilots, flight engineer and navigator, plus loadmaster. Four seat passenger compartment behind flightdeck. Main cabin typically accommodates freight (max payload 20 tonnes/44,090lb), but can seat 63 passengers at four abreast. Firefighting version can carry 7500 litres (1650Imp gal/1980US gal) of fire retardant. Medical version comprehensively equipped with operating theatre and accommodation for stretcher patients and medical attendants.

Production: Approximately 70 built, mostly for military use.

History: One word aptly describes the Mi-26 (NATO codename 'Halo') .... big. The largest helicopter in the world by a large margin, the Mi-26 has a maximum takeoff weight greater than that of the Fokker 100 and an internal freight hold close in size to that in the L-100 Hercules.

Development of the Mi-26 began in the early 1970s and resulted in a first flight on December 14 1977. Although mainly in military use, the original design requirement stated that the helicopter would be for civil use, and that it should have a maximum takeoff weight one and a half times that of any previous helicopter. Preproduction machines were built from 1980, and production machines sometime after that. The first Mi-26s are understood to have become operational with the Soviet military during 1985.

Notable for its eight blade main rotor, powerful turboshaft engines and massive size, several civil versions have been developed or proposed. These include the basic freighter Mi-26T, Mi-26A with automated approach and descent avionics, Mi-26MS medevac version, Mi-26P 63 passenger airliner, Mi-26TM flying crane with undernose gondola to allow supervision of sling operations, and Mi-26TZ fuel tanker. The improved Mi-26M is under development and features new 10,440kW (14,000shp) class ZMKB Progress D-127 turboshafts, better hot and high performance, increased maximum payload, composite main rotor blades, improved aerodynamics and EFIS cockpit displays.

Photo: An Mi-26T demonstrator. Note the eight blade main rotor and military freighter style rear freight doors. (Paul Merritt)

Mil Mi-34 & Mi-34 VAZ

Country of origin: Russia

Type: Two/four place light helicopter

Powerplants: Mi-34 – One 240kW (320hp) Vedeneyev/VOMKB M-14V-26 nine cylinder radial piston engine driving a four blade main rotor and two blade tail rotor. Mi-34 VAZ – Two 200kW (265hp) VAZ-430 twin chamber rotary engines.

Performance: Mi-34 – Max speed 210km/h (113kt), max cruising speed 180km/h (97kt), normal cruising speed 160km/h (86kt). Service ceiling 14,765ft. Hovering ceiling 4920ft. Range with 165kg (363lb) payload 180km (97nm), or 360km (195nm) with 140kg (309lb) payload. Mi-34 VAZ – Max level speed 210km/h (113kt), normal cruising speed 185km/h (100kt). Range with 400kg (880lb) payload and reserves 300km (160nm), range with max internal fuel 480km (260nm), range with auxiliary fuel 980km (530nm).

Weights: Mi-34 – Max takeoff 1350kg (2975lb). Mi-34 VAZ – Max takeoff 1960kg (4320lb).

Dimensions: Main rotor diameter 10.00m (32ft 10in), length of fuselage 8.71m (28ft 7in). Main rotor disc area 78.5m^2 (845sq ft).

Capacity: Typical seating for four, including one pilot. Mi-34 VAZ can accommodate stretcher in rear cabin instead of seats.

Production: Production of the Mi-34 began during 1993, but a planned production rate of 50 in 1994 was not achieved due to a lack of funding. Development Mi-34 VAZ aircraft only built, series production due to begin in 1996/97.

History: At the time of its first flight, the Mi-34 was the smallest helicopter yet designed by Mil.

Despite only entering series production in 1993, the Mi-34 development story dates back to the mid 1980s, with a first flight in 1986. The Mi-34 was first exhibited to the west at the Paris Airshow in 1987 and has made a number of appearances at major airshows, including Farnborough, since that time.

The Mi-34 is the first helicopter designed in a former eastern bloc country that can loop and roll. More than 60 had been delivered by mid 1996, with missions including pilot training, observation and liaison missions. Many have been delivered to Russian government agencies and the police.

Power for the Mi-34 is supplied by the same M-14 radial that powers the Su-26, Su-29 and Su-31 series (described separately) among other Russian light aircraft designs. Mil is also studying powering the Mi-34 with a Textron Lycoming TIO-540 flat six piston engine or an Allison 250-C20R turboshaft (as the Mi-34A).

The twin engine Mi-34 VAZ meanwhile was announced in mid 1993 along with a number of other Mil civil and military helicopters. Currently under development, the Mi-34 VAZ is essentially similar to the standard Mi-34 but for its twin VAZ-430 rotary engines. While a rotary is perhaps an unusual choice of powerplant, the Mi-34 VAZ is being built by the VAZ car factory, which may explain the engine choice. The Mi-34 VAZ also features a new carbonfibre star plate based rotor head. VAZ aimed to have the helicopter in production in 1996 or 1997.

Photo: A mockup of the Allison 250 powered Mi-34A, displayed at the 1995 Moscow Airshow. (Alex Radetski)

Millicer M9-200 Shrike

Country of origin: Australia

Type: Four seat light aircraft

Powerplants: M9-200 – One 150kW (200hp) Textron Lycoming IO-360-A1B6 flat four fuel injected piston engine, driving a two blade constant speed Hartzell propeller.

Performance: M9-200 – Cruising speed at 75% power at 5000ft 267km/h (145kt). Max initial rate of climb 1000ft/min.

Weights: M9-200 – Approx operating empty 680kg (1500lb), max certificated takeoff 1145kg (2520lb).

Dimensions: M9-200 – Wing span 7.92m (26ft 0in), length 7.06m (23ft 2in), height 2.59m (8ft 6in). Wing area 12.0m^2 (129sq ft).

Capacity: Typical seating for four.

Production: The original Aircruiser prototype still survives in Australia. First Shrike due completion mid '97 with deliveries scheduled soon after.

History: The Millicer M9-200 Shrike is a reborn modern incarnation of the promising Victa Aircruiser.

The original Victa Aircruiser was designed by Dr Henry Millicer, who had earlier designed the two seat Victa Airtourer (described separately), which was without doubt the most popular light aircraft designed and built in Australia. With Airtourer production in full swing in the early 1960s Victa commissioned Dr Millicer to develop a four seat light aircraft based on the Airtourer. This resulted in the Aircruiser 210 CS, which flew for the first time on July 17 1966. The Aircruiser was later awarded full Australian certification equivalent to US FAR 23 standard.

The Aircruiser showed considerable promise and looked a worthy competitor to American four seaters, however Victa withdrew from light aircraft production in January 1967 due to the Airtourer's inability to compete on price against alleged dumped imports, and the design and production rights to the Airtourer and Aircruiser were sold to AESL of New Zealand in 1970. AESL continued to build the Airtourer and used the Aircruiser as its basis for the CT-4 Airtrainer (described separately) military trainer but did not put the Aircruiser into production.

In 1990 Tony Peters, a flying school proprietor in Mount Gambier in South Australia commissioned a market study to determine the demand for new build two and four seat light aircraft. This survey indicated demand for 780 new build light aircraft in Australia alone through to 2000, and this result gave Peters the impetus to form Millicer Aircraft (named after Dr Millicer) to place a modernised Aircruiser into production in Australia as the M9-200 Shrike.

In mid 1996 Millicer Aircraft was able to announce it had acquired the design and manufacturing rights and Australian type certificate for the Aircruiser. A production line is being established in Sale in Victoria to build the aircraft, with the first Shrike expected to be completed in July 1997, with first deliveries soon after.

Millicer Aircraft claims the Shrike is inherently more efficient than other four seaters, and that for example it will cruise 37km/h (20kt) faster than the new 172 for the same fuel consumption rate.

Compared with the Aircruiser, the Shrike will feature a fuel injected IO-360 engine, standard GPS, new wheels, brakes and controls. A retractable undercarriage variant may later be offered.

Photo: The original Victa built Aircruiser prototype.

Mitsubishi MU-2

Country of origin: Japan

Type: Twin turboprop utility transport

Powerplants: MU-2B – Two 430kW (575shp) Garrett AiResearch TPE331-25A turboprops, driving three blade constant speed propellers. Marquise – Two 535kW (715shp) Garrett TPE331-10-501Ms driving four blade constant speed propellers.

Performance: MU-2B – Max cruising speed 500km/h (270kt), economical cruising speed 440km/h (237kt). Initial rate of climb 2220ft/min. Max range with reserves 1930km (1040nm). Marquise – Max cruising speed 571km/h (308kt), economical cruising speed 547km/h (295kt). Service ceiling 29,750ft. Range with max fuel and reserves 2585km (1395nm).

Weights: MU-2B – Empty 2422kg (5340lb), max takeoff 4050kg (8930lb). Marquise – Empty equipped 3470kg (7650lb), max takeoff 5250kg (11,575lb).

Dimensions: MU-2B – Wing span 11.94m (39ft 2in), length 10.13m (33ft 3in), height 3.94m (12ft 11in). Wing area 16.5m^2 (178sq ft). Marquise – Same except for length 12.01m (39ft 5in), height 4.17m (13ft 8in).

Capacity: Flightcrew of one or two. Short fuselage models had typical seating for seven in main cabin, longer fuselage models up to 11. Many aircraft in various corporate configurations, or used as freighters.

Production: Over 800 built. Production comprised three MU-2As, 34 MU-2Bs, four military MU-2Ds, 18 MU-2Ds, 16 military SAR MU-2Es, 95 MU-2Fs, 46 MU-2Gs, 108 MU-2Js, 83 MU-2Ks, 36 MU-2Ls, 27 MU-2Ms, 36 MU-2Ns, 31 MU-2Ps, 130 plus Marquise and 60 plus Solitaires.

History: One of postwar Japan's most successful commercial aircraft types sales wise, its popularity has in recent years been marred by a series of crashes.

Development of the MU-2, Mitsubishi's first indigenous postwar design, began in the late 1950s. Designed as a light twin turboprop transport suitable for a variety of civil and military roles, the MU-2 first flew on September 14 1963. This first MU-2 and the handful of MU-2As built were powered by Turboméca Astazou turboprops, all other models from the MU-2B onwards had Garrett TPE331s.

The MU-2 lineup can be divided up into two basic types, the standard fuselage and stretched fuselage models. The MU-2B, E, F, K, M, P and Solitaire feature the short fuselage, the others, including the Marquise, the stretched fuselage. The first stretched fuselage MU-2G flew on January 10 1969.

As can be gathered by the proliferation of models, the MU-2 was progressively improved and upgraded throughout its production life. Notable changes include improved and more powerful engines, and four blade props from the N and P models.

Mitsubishi established a production facility for MU-2s in San Angelo, Texas in the USA in 1967 to build MU-2s for the North American and world markets. The San Angelo Mitsubishi International facility became the sole source of MU-2 production until 1986 when the line finally closed.

Photo: A short fuselage Solitaire (foreground) formates with its stablemate, the Marquise.

Mooney M-20A to M-20F

Country of origin: United States of America

Type: Four seat light aircraft

Powerplant: M-20C – One 135kW (180hp) Lycoming O-360-A1D flat four piston engine driving a two blade constant speed propeller. M-20E – One 150kW (200hp) Lycoming IO-360-A1A fuel injected flat four.

Performance: M-20C – Max speed 288km/h (156kt), max cruising speed 272km/h (147kt), economical cruising speed 236km/h (127kt). Initial rate of climb 800ft/min. Service ceiling 17,200ft. Range with reserves 1464km (790nm). M-20E – Max speed 317km/h (171kt), max cruising speed 301km/h (163kt), economical cruising speed 270km/h (146kt). Initial rate of climb 1120ft/min. Service ceiling 19,500ft. Max range with no reserves 1648km (890nm).

Weights: M-20C – Empty 692kg (1525lb), max takeoff 1168kg (2575lb). M-20E – Empty 714kg (1575lb), max takeoff 1168kg (2575lb).

Dimensions: M-20C – Wing span 10.67m (35ft 0in), length 7.06m (23ft 2in), height 2.54m (8ft 4in). Wing area 15.5m^2 (167sq ft). M-20E – Same as M-20C.

Capacity: Typical seating for four.

Production: Over 5000 early model M-20 series aircraft built from the mid 1950s to the mid 1970s.

History: Mooney's first design (as Culver) in 1948 was the wooden single seat M-18 Mite, but design work was soon underway on a much larger four seater of metal, wood and fabric covered construction.

The resulting Mooney M-20 first flew on August 10 1953, was powered by a 78kW (145hp) six cylinder Continental O-300 engine, had retractable undercarriage and the distinctive forward swept tail. Placed into production soon after with a 110kW (150hp) Lycoming O-320, a prolific series of developments followed.

These included the 700 plus M-20As with a 135kW (180hp) O-360, and the similarly powered M-20C Mark 21. Very successful with 400 built in its first year, the Mark 21 featured an all metal structure and higher takeoff weight. A lower spec fixed undercarriage version, the M-20D Master was also offered. The subsequent M-20E Super 21 flew for the first time in July 1963 and featured a more powerful fuel injected 150kW (200hp) IO-360 engine, combining the M-20E's clean aerodynamics and the more powerful engine to give a claimed top speed of 317km/h (171kt). From the mid 1960s all models gained a small fin fillet and a larger squared off rear cabin window.

The M-20F Executive 21 of 1965 was based on the M-20E Super 21 and had a 25cm (10in) fuselage stretch and an extra cabin window on each side, new cabin fittings and extra fuel. In 1967 the range was renamed, the M-20C becoming the Ranger, the M-20F continued as the Executive, the M-20E was discontinued for a time until reappearing as the Chaparral, and a new model, the M-20G Statesman (with the Executive's fuselage and a 135kW/180hp engine) appeared (although only 183 were built).

For a time from 1970 Mooney was known as the Aerostar Aircraft Corporation, and the Ranger became the Aerostar 200, the Chaparral the 201 and Executive the 220. However this company ceased production in early 1972, and it was not until 1973 that revised models were built under the Mooney banner (described separately).

Photo: A Mooney M-20F Executive. (Lance Higgerson)

Mooney M-20J to M-20R

Country of origin: United States of America

Type: High performance four seat light aircraft

Powerplant: TLS – One 200kW (270hp) Textron Lycoming TIO-540-AF1A turbocharged and fuel injected flat six piston engine driving a three blade constant speed propeller. 205 MSE – One 150kW (200hp) IO-360-A3B6D fuel injected flat four driving a two blade c/s prop.

Performance: TLS – Max cruising speed 413km/h (223kt). Initial rate of climb 1230ft/min. Service ceiling 25,000ft. Range with max fuel 1983km (1070nm). MSE – Max speed 325km/h (175kt), max cruising speed 311km/h (168kt), economical cruising speed 282km/h (152kt). Initial rate of climb 1030ft/min. Service ceiling 18,600ft. Range at economical cruising speed 1960km (1060nm).

Weights: TLS – Empty 913kg (2012lb), max takeoff 1451kg (3200lb). MSE – Empty 809kg (1784lb), max takeoff 1243kg (2740lb).

Dimensions: TLS – Wing span 11.00m (36ft 1in), length 8.15m (26ft 9in), height 2.51m (8ft 3in). Wing area 16.2m^2 (174.8sq ft). MSE – Same except for length 7.52m (24ft 8in), height 2.54m (8ft 4in).

Capacity: Typical seating for four.

Production: Over 2150 of all models delivered since the mid 1970s.

History: Mooney's new owners, the Republic Steel Company, placed the M-20 line back into production in late 1973.

All three then current models, the Ranger, Chaparral and Executive, were returned to production, but new design efforts centred around the M-20F Executive design. The first model developed was the M-20J 201, its main improvements were aimed at reducing drag (including a redesigned engine cowling, flush rivetting and a new windscreen shape), giving a theoretical top speed of 323km/h (175kt), or 201mph. The 201 entered production in 1976, replacing the Executive, while the Ranger remained in production until 1979.

Subsequent models included the M-20K 231 from late 1978, powered by a turbocharged Continental TSIO-360 six cylinder engine, and the 201LM (Lean Machine) from 1986 with only basic options. The 201 evolved into the M-20J 205 with rounded cabin windows and redesigned wingtips, giving a slight increase in top speed. A Special Edition 'SE' luxury options package was also offered. The M-20K 252TSE (Turbo Special Edition) was a development of the 231 with a top speed of 405km/h (220kt), or 252mph, and combined the 205's airframe mods with a 155kW (210hp) turbocharged, intercooled Continental TSIO-360. The Porsche PFM 3200 powered M-20L was built between 1987 and 1991.

Current production includes the M-20M TLS (Turbo Lycoming Sabre) which was introduced in 1989 and features a slightly stretched fuselage, a turbocharged and intercooled Textron Lycoming TIO-540 and three blade prop. The M-20J MSE 205 development is powered by a 150kW (200hp) Textron Lycoming IO-360-A3B6D. Introduced in mid 1994, the M-20R Ovation is based on the TLS and powered by a 210kW (280hp) Continental IO-550G flat six. The Ovation slots in between the MSE and TLS in terms of performance and capabilities.

In 1997 Mooney plans to introduce the 370km/h (200kt) cruise Encore, powered by the turbocharged and intercooled TSIO-360, effectively a replacement for the out of production TLS.

Photo: The prototype M-20R Ovation, which first flew in May 1994.

Mudry CAP 10, 20, 21, 231 & 232

Country of origin: France

Type: Single and two seat aerobatic light aircraft

Powerplant: 10B – One 135kW (180hp) Textron Lycoming AEIO-360-B2F fuel injected flat four piston engine, driving a two blade fixed pitch Hoffmann propeller. 21 – One 150kW (200hp) AEIO-360-A1B driving a two blade variable pitch Hartzell prop. 231 – One 225kW (300hp) AEIO-540-L1B5D flat six, driving a two blade constant speed Hartzell or three blade constant speed Mühlbauer prop.

Performance: 10B – Max speed 270km/h (146kt), max cruising speed at 75% power 250km/h (135kt). Initial rate of climb 1575ft/min. Service ceiling 16,400ft. Range with max fuel 1000km (540nm). 21 – Max cruising speed at 75% power 265km/h (143kt). Initial rate of climb 2755ft/min. Endurance with max fuel for two hours. 231 – Max speed 330km/h (162kt). Range with max fuel 360km (195nm).

Weights: 10B – Empty equipped 550kg (1213lb), max takeoff in aerobatic category 760kg (1675lb), or 830kg (1829lb) in utility category. 21 – Empty 500kg (1103lb), max takeoff 620kg (1367lb). 231 – Empty 630kg (1390lb), max takeoff aerobatic category 730kg (1610lb), max takeoff normal category 820kg (1807lb).

Dimensions: 10B – Wing span 8.06m (26ft 5in), length 7.16m (23ft 6in), height 2.55m (8ft 5in). Wing area 10.9m^2 (116.8sq ft). 21 – Wing span 8.08m (26ft 6in), length 6.46m (21ft 3in), height 1.52m (5ft 0in). Wing area 9.2m^2 (99.0sq ft). 231 – Wing span 8.08m (26ft 6in), length 6.75m (22ft 2in), height 1.90m (6ft 3in). Wing area 9.9m^2 (106.1sq ft).

Capacity: Seating for two side by side in CAP 10, all others pilot only.

Production: Approximately 275 CAP 10s and 10Bs, 40 CAP 21s, and approximately 30 231s and 231 EXs.

History: The successful Mudry series of two seat trainers and single seat aerobatic trainers dates back to the Piel C.P.30 Emeraude of the early 1960s.

Claude Piel designed the two seat Emeraude in France in the early 1960s for kit builders, but more than 200 were built in four different factories across Europe. The Emeraude first flew in 1962 and was built in basic 50kW (65hp) Continental A65 power C.P.30 form and 65kW (90hp) Continental C90 C.P.301 Super Emeraude form.

One of the companies to build the Emeraude was CAARP, a company owned by Auguste Mudry. CAARP used the basic Emeraude design as the basis for the CAP 10, which was a similar aircraft other than its 135kW (180hp) Lycoming IO-360 engine and stressing for aerobatic flight. The prototype CAP 10 first flew in August 1968. CAARP built 30 CAP 10s for the French air force before Mudry started production for civil orders in 1972 at his other aviation company, Avions Mudry.

The CAP 10 remains in production today in 10B form with an enlarged tail. The CAP 20 meanwhile was a single seat development with a 150kW (200hp) AIO-360 engine.

The updated CAP 21 replaced the CAP 20 in 1981. The CAP 21 combined the fuselage of the CAP 20 with an all new wing and new undercarriage, and forms the basis for the similar CAP 231, CAP 231 EX (with a carbon fibre wing) and CAP 232.

Photo: An Australian Aviation College CAP 10, used for initial pilot training. (Garry Veroude)

NAMC YS-11

Country of origin: Japan

Type: Twin turboprop regional airliner

Powerplants: YS-11A-200 – Two 2280kW (3060shp) Rolls-Royce Dart 542-10K turboprops, driving four blade constant speed propellers.

Performance: -200 – Max cruising speed 470km/h (253kt), economical cruising speed 452km/h (244kt). Range with max payload and no reserves 1090km (590nm), range with payload and no reserves 3215km (1736nm).

Weights: -200 – Operating empty 15,419kg (33,993lb), max takeoff 24,500kg (54,010lb).

Dimensions: Wing span 32.00m (105ft 0in), length 26.30m (86ft 4in), height 8.98m (29ft 6in). Wing area 94.8m^2 (1020.4sq ft).

Capacity: Flightcrew of two. Typical single class seating in main cabin for 60 at four abreast and 86cm (34in) pitch. The combi YS-11A-300 accommodates freight in the forward fuselage and seating for 46 behind that.

Production: Total YS-11 production was 182 comprising two prototypes, 48 series 100s, 83 Series 200s, 31 series 300s, eight series 400s, two series 500s, and eight series 600s. Production total includes 23 for Japanese defence forces. Approximately 70 remained in service at late 1996.

History: The only Japanese airliner to enter production since WW2, the YS-11 achieved a small degree of success in both its domestic market and North America.

The YS-11 was a product of the Nihon Aircraft Manufacturing Company (or NAMC), a consortium of Fuji, Kawasaki, Mitsubishi, Nippi, Shin Meiwa and Showa which formed on June 1 1959 to design and develop a short to medium range airliner, with particular attention being paid to meeting the specific operating requirements of the Japanese domestic airlines.

For the new airliner, NAMC selected the Rolls-Royce Dart over the Allison 501. Fuji was given responsibility for the tail unit, Kawasaki the wings and engine nacelles, Mitsubishi the forward fuselage, and final assembly, Nippi the ailerons and flaps, Shin Meiwa the rear fuselage and Showa the light alloy honeycomb structural components.

The YS-11 first flew on August 30 1962 (a second prototype flew that December), and was awarded Japanese certification in August 1964. By that time the first production aircraft were under construction, and the type entered service with Toa Airways (now JAS) in April 1965. Initial production was of the YS-11-100, the follow up YS-11A-200 (first flight November 1967) was designed for export markets and featured an increased max takeoff weight. The YS-11A-300 was a combi passenger/freight model, while the YS-11A-400 was a pure freighter with a forward freight door.

The YS-11A-500, -600 and -700 were equivalent to the -200, -300 and -400, but with a 500kg (1100lb) greater max takeoff weight. Production ceased in February 1974.

Almost 70 YS-11s remained in service in 1996, the largest operators being All Nippon and Japan Air Commuter (JAC).

Photo: About 70 of the 182 NAMC YS-11s built remain in operation. The type was noteworthy for employing the most powerful version of the RR Dart to go into operation. (Jim Thorn)

Navion Rangemaster

Country of origin: United States of America

Type: High performance four/five seat light aircraft

Powerplant: Super 260 – One 195kW (260hp) Lycoming GO-435-C2 flat six piston engine, driving a two blade propeller. Model H – One 215kW (285hp) Continental IO-520-B fuel injected flat six piston engine, driving a two blade constant speed McCauley prop.

Performance: Super 260 – Max speed 280km/h (151kt). Model H – Max speed 307km/h (166kt), max cruising speed at 75% power 298km/h (161kt). Initial rate of climb 1300ft/min. Service ceiling 21,500ft. Range with max fuel 2560km (1397nm).

Weights: Super 260 – Max takeoff 1293kg (2850lb). Model H – Empty 882kg (1945lb), max takeoff 1504kg (3315lb).

Dimensions: Super 260 – Wing span 10.19m (33ft 5in), length 8.38m (27ft 6in). Model H – Wing span 10.59m (34ft 9in), length 8.38m (27ft 6in), height 2.54m (8ft 4in). Wing area 17.1m^2 (184.34sq ft).

Capacity: North American and Ryan Navions typically sat four, while Navion Rangemasters typically seat pilot and four passengers.

Production: Approximately 2500 aircraft of all models built, including 1100 North American NA-145 Navions, 1000 Ryan built Navion 205s and 240 Super 260s, and small numbers of Rangemasters. Small numbers also converted to Twin Navions.

History: The Navion was designed in the late 1940s and built by four different companies through until the mid 1970s.

The company responsible for the original Navion was North American Aviation, a company made famous by the WW2 P-51 Mustang fighter. The end of WW2 saw massive military contracts cancelled en masse and so North America designed the original four seat NA-145 to diversify out military production. The NA-145 Navion was powered by a 140kW (185hp) Continental and North American built more than 1100 in 1946 and 1947. North American also built a number of L-17 observation aircraft based on the Navion for the US military.

Production and development of the Navion then transferred to Ryan. The standard Ryan production model was the Navion 205 or Navion A, which differed from the North American NA-145 in that it was powered by a 155kW (205hp) Continental E-185. More than 100 were built between 1948 and 1950. Ryan also built a few hundred Navion Super 260s or Navion Bs between 1950 and 1951, these aircraft were powered by a 195kW (260hp) Lycoming GO-435. In addition Ryan also built almost 200 L-17s (some saw military service in Korea).

The basic Navion design resurfaced in 1960 when the Navion Aircraft Company developed a five seater variant called the Rangemaster. The Rangemaster was powered by the same 195kW (260hp) Lycoming engine as the Navion Super 260, but instead of the rear sliding canopy of earlier Navions, the Rangemaster had a reprofiled, more streamlined five seat cabin. Later production Rangemasters had a smaller tail.

The Rangemaster was last built by the Navion Rangemaster Aircraft Corporation between 1974 and 1976 in improved G and H form.

Camair in the USA also converted a small number of Navions of various models to twin engine configuration, the first flew in 1953.

Photo: North American and Ryan built Navions feature a rear sliding cockpit canopy.

Noorduyn Norseman

Country of origin: Canada

Type: Ten place utility transport

Powerplants: Norseman V – One 450kW (600hp) Pratt & Whitney R1340-AN-1 Wasp driving a three blade propeller.

Performance: V – Normal cruising speed 238km/h (128kt). Time to climb to 5000ft 6.5min, time to climb to 15,000ft 28.5min. Service ceiling 17,000ft. Range at 75% power cruising speed with max fuel 1850km (998nm).

Weights: V – Empty 2007kg (4420lb), loaded 3360kg (7400lb).

Dimensions: V – Wing span 15.75m (51ft 8in), length 9.85m (32ft 4in), height 3.12m (10ft 3in).

Capacity: V – Pilot and up to nine passengers on bench seats. Often configured for freight.

Production: Norseman production ran from the late 1930s through until 1946 with Noorduyn, and then with Canadian Car and Foundry until 1959, by which time 904 had been built by both manufacturers. Approximately 20 remain in use in Canada, while one or two may be flying in other countries.

History: The rugged Norseman bush aircraft first flew in the mid 1930s, and so its longevity in service record is only matched by that of the legendary DC-3.

The Norseman was designed by Robert Noorduyn, who was born in Holland and later worked for several then prominent aircraft companies in England and the USA, including Armstrong Whitworth, British Aerial Transport Sopwith, Fokker (in the USA where he worked on the F.VII/3m), Bellanca and Pitcairn. In 1934 Noorduyn formed Noorduyn Aircraft Ltd (Noorduyn Aviation from 1938). Later in 1934 Noorduyn began work on the Norseman, resulting in the first flight of the float equipped prototype Norseman I from the St Laurence River on November 14 1935.

The Norseman I was powered by a 315kW (420hp) Wright Whirlwind, featured spruce wing spars and a metal tubing fuselage frame with fabric covering. It was the first Canadian aircraft with flaps.

Further development resulted in the heavier Norseman II and the 335kW (450hp) P&W Wasp Junior powered Norseman III. The 415kW (550hp) Norseman IV was the subject of significant Royal Canadian Air Force and civil orders in 1938.

The USA's entry into WW2 in late 1941 saw the US Army Air Force take deliveries of 746 Norsemans in C-64A, UC-64A and C-64B variants. These aircraft operated in many theatres and were often equipped with floats as skis. The Norseman V is the civil equivalent of the C-64A.

With the aircraft no longer needed for war, Noorduyn production ceased in 1945 and its Cartierville plant was taken over by Canadair. However through to 1959 Canadian Car and Foundry built small numbers of Norseman Vs for civil customers.

After the war many ex military Norsemans found gainful use with civil operators, and even to this day approximately 20 fly in Canada.

Photo: A surprising number of Norsemans remain in commercial use, primarily in Canada. This float equipped example is pictured as it appeared in service with KayAir of Ear Falls, Ontario in 1993. (Rodney Kozar)

Pacific Aerospace CT-4 Airtrainer

Country of origin: New Zealand

Type: Two/three seat basic trainer

Powerplant: CT-4A – One 155kW (210hp) Teledyne Continental IO-360-D fuel injected flat six piston engine, driving a two blade constant speed propeller. CT-4B – One 155kW (210hp) IO-360-HB9.

Performance: CT-4A – Max speed 285km/h (155kt), cruising speed 240km/h (130kt), long range cruising speed 235km/h (127kt). Initial rate of climb 1345ft/min. Range at long range cruising speed 1300km (700nm). CT-4B – Max speed 267km/h (144kt), 75% power cruising speed 260km/h (140kt). Initial rate of climb 1250ft/min. Range with max fuel at normal cruising speed 1110km (600nm).

Weights: CT-4A – Empty 690kg (1520lb), max takeoff 1090kg (2400lb) or 1203kg (2650lb). CT-4B – Max takeoff 1202kg (2650lb).

Dimensions: Wing span 7.92m (26ft 0in), length 7.06m (23ft 2in), height 2.59m (8ft 6in). Wing area 12.0m^2 (129.0sq ft).

Capacity: Normally two seats side by side, with space for optional third seat or baggage behind.

Production: 112 CT-4s of all models built, mainly for military orders. The largest civil user is the British Aerospace Flight Training Australia academy (formerly the BAe/Ansett Flying College) which operates 12 CT-4Bs. Many (30+) ex RAAF CT-4As now flying in civil hands mainly in Australia, some in New Zealand and the USA.

History: Affectionately dubbed the Plastic Parrot in Royal Australian Air Force service, the CT-4 Airtrainer was primarily designed as a military trainer, but is now in small scale civilian use.

The CT-4 was developed from the Australian Victa Airtourer series (described separately). Victa had developed the four place Aircruiser based on the Airtourer, but development work was not continued with and instead the production rights for the Aircruiser were purchased by Aero Engine Services Ltd (or AESL) of New Zealand in 1969, which already had the rights to the Airtourer series.

AESL made a number of changes to the basic Aircruiser design, including a new clamshell canopy, structural strengthening for aerobatic work, and stick controls, making it suitable for military basic training. The first such CT-4A Airtrainer flew on February 23 1972. Primary customers were the Australian, New Zealand and Thai air forces. Production by NZAI (New Zealand Aircraft Industries), as AESL had become, continued until 1977.

In 1990 Pacific Aerospace Corporation (the successor to NZAI) resumed production of the improved CT-4B against an order from the BAe/Ansett Flying College in Tamworth, Australia, providing the impetus for further developments of the line, although no sales were achieved for the new variants. A turboprop Allison 250 powered CT-4C flew on January 21 1991, and a retractable undercarriage version, the CT-4CR was proposed. Development of the 225kW (300hp) IO-540 powered CT-4E was aimed for the US Air Force's Enhanced Flight Screening competition.

During late 1994 Pacific Aerospace announced it would cease aircraft production unless fresh orders were forthcoming.

Photo: PAC's CT-4E demonstrator at its home base of Hamilton New Zealand. The CT-4E features a more streamlined nose compared with the CT-4A and CT-4B. (Peter Clark)

Pacific Aerospace Fletcher FU-24 & Cresco

Country of origin: New Zealand

Type: Agricultural aircraft

Powerplant: FU-24-954 – One 300kW (400hp) Textron Lycoming IO-720-A1A or -A1B fuel injected flat eight piston engine, driving a three blade constant speed Hartzell propeller. Cresco 08-600 – One 450kW (600shp) Textron Lycoming LTP 101-700A-1A turboprop.

Performance: FU-24-954 – Max speed 233km/h (126kt), max cruising speed 209km/h (113kt), typical operating speed range 165 to 210km/h (90 to 115kt). Initial rate of climb 805ft/min. Service ceiling 16,000ft. Range with max payload and reserves 709km (383nm). 08-600 – Max speed 274km/h (148kt), max cruising speed 246km/h (133kt). Initial rate of climb 1245ft. Service ceiling 18,000ft. Range with max fuel and no reserves 850km (460nm).

Weights: FU-24-954 – Empty equipped 1188kg (2620lb), max takeoff 2465kg (5430lb). 08-600 – Empty equipped 1270kg (2800lb), max takeoff 3175kg (7000lb).

Dimensions: FU-24-954 – Wing span 12.81m (42ft 0in), length 9.70m (31ft 10in), height 2.84m (9ft 4in). Wing area 27.3m^2 (294.0sq ft). 08-600 – Same except for length 11.07m (36ft 4in), height 3.63m (11ft 11in).

Capacity: Typical arrangement seats pilot and passenger, and chemical hopper (capacity 1210 litres/265Imp gal/319US gal in FU-24-954, 1780 litre/390Imp gal/470US gal in 08-600). Can also be configured for freight and general utility work, or as a passenger aircraft can seat six in rear compartment (earlier models seat five or six passengers).

Production: Almost 300 FU-24s built in the USA and New Zealand (70 in US, balance in NZ) since 1955. Twenty Crescos built.

History: Fletcher in the USA originally developed the FU-24 largely for New Zealand agwork.

Flying for the first time in June 1954, production and deliveries began during 1955, following certification on July 22. Seventy 195kW (260hp) Continental IO-470-D powered FU-24s and slightly larger FU-24As were built in the USA before Fletcher ceased production in 1964, and Air Parts (now Pacific Aerospace) of New Zealand acquired the production rights.

Initial New Zealand production was of two models, one powered by a 215kW (285hp) Continental, the other a 250kW (300hp) unit. The subsequent FU-24-950 was powered by a 300kW (400hp) eight cylinder Lycoming IO-720, and was followed up by the similarly powered FU-24-954 from 1979. In 1994 a New Zealand Fletcher operator announced its plans to fit 375kW (500hp) V8 car engines to its FU-24 fleet.

Like many ag aircraft, the Fletcher was a natural candidate for conversion to turboprop power. The resulting Cresco first flew on February 28 1979 powered by a 450kW (600shp) Avco Lycoming (now Textron Lycoming) LTP 101. Nine such aircraft were built, while a tenth was fitted with a 560kW (750shp) Pratt & Whitney Canada PT6A-34AG.

Although PAC announced it would cease aircraft manufacture in 1994, PAC's new owners have placed the Cresco back into production. At late 1996 10 new Crescos had been built, with five more sold.

Photo: The Cresco displays the characteristics of most ag aircraft – a large fuselage, low wings and all aerodynamic surfaces optimised for low speed, low level manoeuvring. (Mike Davidson)

Partenavia P.68

Country of origin: Italy

Type: Six/seven place light twin

Powerplants: P.68B – Two 150kW (200hp) Lycoming IO-360-A1B fuel injected flat four piston engines, driving two blade constant speed propellers. P.68TC – Two 155kW (210hp) Textron Lycoming TIO-360-C1A6Ds.

Performance: P.68B – Max speed 322km/h (174kt), max cruising speed 306km/h (165kt), economical cruising speed 295km/h (160kt). Initial rate of climb 1600ft/min. Service ceiling 20,000ft. Range at economical cruising speed 1700km (920nm). P.68C – Max speed 352km/h (190kt), max cruising speed 324km/h (175kt), economical cruising speed 278km/h (150kt). Initial rate of climb 1550ft/min. Service ceiling 27,000ft. Range with max payload 555km (300nm), range with max fuel 1924km (1040nm).

Weights: P.68B – Empty 1200kg (2645lb), max takeoff 1960kg (4321lb). P.68TC – Empty equipped 1300kg (2866lb), max takeoff 1990kg (4387lb).

Dimensions: P.68B – Wing span 12.00m (39ft 5in), length 9.35m (30ft 8in), height 3.40m (11ft 2in). Wing area 18.6m^2 (200sq ft). P.68TC – Same except for length 9.55m (31ft 4in).

Capacity: Standard seating arrangement for seven, comprising one pilot and six passengers, or two pilots and five passengers.

Production: Approximate total 400, including 13 preproduction P.68As and 150 P.68B Victors. At late 1996 production was temporarily suspended.

History: Partenavia developed the P.68 as a multirole twin capable of performing a number of utility roles in a low maintenance aerodynamically efficient package.

The resulting P.68 Victor first flew on May 25 1970, and demonstrated performance similar to that of aircraft in its class (such as the Seneca) which had retractable undercarriage, but without the added weight and complexity of retractable gear. The high wing design also incorporated a large degree of glass fibre reinforced plastic construction in non load bearing areas. Thirteen preproduction P.68As were built between 1971 and 1973, before improved production standard P.68Bs, with a longer cabin, increased takeoff weight and redesigned instrument panel, were delivered from 1974. A retractable undercarriage variant, the P.68R was trialled over 1976/77, but did not enter production.

The P.68C replaced the B in 1979, and introduced a longer nose to house weather radar and more avionics, more fuel, revised cabin interior and redesigned wheel fairings. The turbocharged TC was first introduced in 1980 and features two turbocharged 157kW (210hp) TIO-360s. Observer versions of both the P.68B and P.68C have been built, these featuring a clear nose section for helicopter-like visibility.

A turboprop development, the AT.68TP-300 Spartacus first flew in 1978, and led to the larger AP.68TP Viator, which is in Italian government service.

Photo: A rakish low drag design is the primary visual hallmark of Partenavia's P.68. Pictured is a P.68B. (Bill Lines)

Piaggio P.166

Country of origin: Italy

Type: Commuter airliner and utility transport

Powerplants: P.166 – Two 255kW (340hp) Lycoming GSO-480-B1C6 geared and supercharged flat six piston engines, driving three blade constant speed propellers. P.166DL3SEM – Two 450kW (600shp) AlliedSignal LTP 101-700 turboprops.

Performance: P.166 – Max speed 357km/h (193kt), max cruising speed 333km/h (180kt), economical cruising speed 280km/h (151kt). Initial rate of climb 1240ft/min. Service ceiling 25,000ft. Max range 1930km (1040nm). P.166-DL3SEM – Max speed 400km/h (215kt). Range with max payload 1390km (750nm), range with max fuel 2130km (1150nm).

Weights: P.166 – Empty 2350kg (5180lb), max takeoff 3680kg (8115lb). P.166-DL3SEM – Empty equipped 2688kg (5926lb), max takeoff 4300kg (9480lb).

Dimensions: P.166 – Wing span (without tip tanks) 14.25m (46ft 9in), length 11.61m (38ft 1in), height 5.00m (16ft 5in). Wing area 26.6m^2 (286sq ft). P.166-DL3SEM – Same except for wing span over tip tanks 14.69m (48ft 3in), length (including chin mounted radar) 11.88m (39ft 0in).

Capacity: Flightcrew of one or two and standard seating for eight or nine in main cabin in airliner configuration. Max seating for 12 in P.166C. Executive configuration seats five or six with toilet and bar. Air ambulance can carry two stretchers and two medical attendants.

Production: Approximately 145 P.166s of all models built, including many for government and military customers. New production aircraft built on demand.

History: Affectionately dubbed the Pig, the Piaggio P.166 has been built in only small numbers but has been in more or less continuous, although limited production since the late 1950s.

Intended for civil use when designed in the late 1950s, the P.166 features a large cabin which has been put to use in a variety of civil, military and quasi military roles, while its gull wing with tip tanks and pusher engines, inherited from the P.132 amphibian, ensures it is easily identified.

The prototype P.166 first flew on November 16 1957, and deliveries of the initial P.166 production model took place from April 1959. Just 23 were built before production switched to the P.166B Portofino, which featured more powerful 285kW (380hp) engines and an increased max takeoff weight of 3800kg (8377lb). Five Portofinos were built, while several earlier P.166s were converted to that standard with the more powerful engines.

With its larger cabin and 3950kg (8708lb) max takeoff weight, the P.166C, introduced in 1964, could seat 12 passengers. Only two were built.

The turboprop LTP 101 powered P.166.DL3 first flew in 1976 and was certificated in 1978. Alitalia has taken delivery of several for use as crew trainers, but most have been for the Italian government and military. Production of the radar and FLIR equipped P.166-DL3SEM continued into the 1990s for the Italian Coast Guard and it remains available on demand.

Photo: An Australian registered P.166. (Bill Lines)

Piaggio P.180 Avanti

Country of origin: Italy

Type: Twin turboprop executive transport

Powerplants: Two 635kW (850shp) Pratt & Whitney Canada PT6A-66 turboprops, driving five blade constant speed Hartzell propellers.

Performance: Max speed 732km/h (395kt), max cruising speed 644km/h (348kt). Initial rate of climb 2950ft/min. Service ceiling 41,000ft. Range with one pilot, six passengers and reserves 3150km (1700nm).

Weights: Empty equipped 3400kg (7500lb), max takeoff 5240kg (11,550lb).

Dimensions: Wing span 14.03m (46ft 1in), length 14.41m (47ft 4in), height 3.94m (12ft 11in). Wing area 16.0m^2 (172.2sq ft).

Capacity: Flightcrew of one or two (certificated for single pilot operation). Max seating in main cabin for nine in high density airliner configuration. Standard seating for seven in individual seats. Executive/VIP seating for five.

Production: Orders placed for approximately 40 Avantis (including three for the Italian air force for use as regional transports), with 30 delivered at late 1994.

History: The innovative Avanti has, unfortunately for its financially troubled manufacturer, been a slow seller despite its modern features, and jet like performance but turboprop like operating costs.

Development of the Avanti dates back to program launch in 1981. For a time Gates Learjet participated in the development from 1983 and would have built the Avanti's forward fuselage, but that company withdrew from the program in January 1986. Not deterred by Gates' withdrawal, Piaggio assumed total control of the program, and all tooling for what would have been the Learjet P.180 was transferred to Italy.

Piaggio flew the first of two P.180 prototypes on September 23 1986, the second flew in May 1987. Italian certification was granted in March 1990, the first production Avanti flew that May and the first customer delivery took place in September 1990.

The unorthodox Avanti is unique for a corporate aircraft in that it features three flying surfaces – the canard foreplane, wing and tail. This arrangement not only offers the benefits of the canard, but meant the wing could be positioned in the rear of the fuselage, so that it didn't intrude on available interior cabin space. The small natural laminar flow wing was designed by the Ohio State University. The pusher engine configuration was chosen to reduce cabin noise.

Composites are used in a number of areas, including the tail, engine nacelles, canards, outboard wing flaps, landing gear doors and the tail cone, but generally, unlike the Starship, most construction is conventional. A three screen Collins EFIS flightdeck is standard, a five screen flightdeck is offered as an option.

No major developments of the Avanti are planned, although twice Piaggio has increased the P.180's maximum weight, thus improving its payload range.

Photo: An Avanti development aircraft. Production aircraft feature a single piece windscreen. (Piaggio)

Pilatus Britten-Norman Islander

Country of origin: United Kingdom

Type: Commuter airliner and light utility transport

Powerplants: BN-2A – Two 195kW (260hp) Lycoming O-540-E4C flat six piston engines, driving two blade constant speed propellers. BN-2B-20 – Two 225kW (300hp) Textron Lycoming IO-540K1B5s.

Performance: BN-2A – Max speed 273km/h (147kt), max cruising speed 257km/h (140kt), economical cruising speed 246km/h (133kt). Initial rate of climb 970ft/min. Service ceiling 13,200ft. Range at economical cruising speed 1400km (755nm). BN-2B-20 – Max speed 280km/h (150kt), max cruising speed 264km/h (142kt), economical cruising speed 245km/h (132kt). Initial rate of climb 1130ft/min. Service ceiling 17,200ft. Range at economical cruising speed and standard fuel 1136km (613nm), with optional fuel 1965km (1060nm).

Weights: BN-2A – Empty equipped 1627kg (3588lb), max takeoff 2993kg (6600lb). BN-2B-20 – Empty equipped 1925kg (4244lb), max takeoff 2993kg (6600lb).

Dimensions: Wing span 14.94m (49ft 0in), length 10.86m (35ft 8in), height 4.18m (13ft 9in). Wing area 30.2m^2 (325.0sq ft).

Capacity: Flightcrew of two pilots or pilot and passenger on flightdeck, with seating for eight in main cabin. Air ambulance accommodates three stretcher patients and two medical attendants.

Production: Over 1200 delivered since 1969, including production in the UK and Romania. Approximately 65 BN-2Ts built.

History: With over 1200 aircraft sold to date, the Pilatus Britten-Norman Islander is western Europe's best selling commercial aircraft.

The BN-2 Islander was Britten-Norman's second original design, work on which began during 1963. Developed as a Dragon Rapide replacement, the emphasis was on producing a rugged and durable aircraft that had good field performance, low operating costs and was easy to maintain. One unusual feature is that there is no centre aisle between seats in the main cabin, instead there are three doors along each side of the fuselage for passenger boarding. The prototype BN-2 Islander was powered by two 155kW (210hp) IO-360s and first flight was on June 13 1965.

The first production machines were powered by 195kW (260hp) IO-540s and were simply designated the BN-2, the first flew in 1967. A small number were built before production switched to the BN-2A which introduced fairings to the main undercarriage legs, wing leading edge and flap droop, and increased max takeoff weight. From 1970 the base A model was the BN-2A-6 and the BN-2A-7 had extended wingtips, while the BN-2A-2 and BN-2A-3 were powered by the 225kW (300hp) IO-540, the latter with the extended wingtips.

Appearing in 1972 were the 195kW (260hp) powered BN-2A-26 and BN-2A-27 with extended wingtips, and the 225kW (300hp) BN-2A-20 and BN-2A-21 with extended wingtips, all four models having higher weights. Further improvements came with the BN-2B range with higher weights, improved interior and instrument panel and shorter diameter props. The -26, -27, -20 and -21 variants were available as before. The -27 and -21 were later dropped while the -20 and -26 remain in production. The turboprop (Allison 250) powered BN-2T has been built since 1981.

Photo: One of six Australian Customs Islanders. (PBN)

Pilatus PC-6 Porter & Turbo Porter

Country of origin: Switzerland

Type: STOL utility transport

Powerplant: PC-6-H2 – One 255kW (340hp) Lycoming GSO-480-B1A6 geared and supercharged six cylinder piston engine, driving a three blade constant speed propeller. PC-6/B2-H4 – One 410kW (550shp) Pratt & Whitney Canada PT6A-27 turboprop.

Performance: PC-6-H2 – Max speed 233km/h (126kt), max cruising speed 216km/h (117kt), economical cruising speed 190km/h (103kt). Initial rate of climb 550ft/min. Service ceiling 17,400ft. Max range with no reserves 1500km (810nm). PC-6/B2-H4 (Utility version) – Economical cruising speed 213km/h (115kt). Initial rate of climb 940ft/min. Range with max payload at economical cruising speed and no reserves 730km (395nm), range with max internal fuel 925km (500nm), with external fuel 1610km (870nm).

Weights: PC-6-H2 – Empty 1250kg (2755lb), max takeoff 2200kg (4850lb). PC-6/B2-H4 – Empty 640kg (1411lb), max takeoff 920kg (2028lb).

Dimensions: PC-6-H2 – Wing span 15.14m (49ft 8in), length 10.20m (33ft 6in), height 3.20m (10ft 6in). Wing area 28.8m² (310sq ft). PC-6/B2-H4 – Wing span 15.87m (52ft 1in), length 11.00m (36ft 1in), height tail down 3.20m (10ft 6in). Wing area 30.2m² (324.5sq ft).

Capacity: Pilot and passenger on flightdeck, with max seating for 11 in main cabin. Standard seating for six in main cabin. Alternative layouts include two stretchers and three medical attendants, or 10 parachutists. Some aircraft equipped for agricultural spraying.

Production: Over 500 Porters of all versions built, including 100 under licence in the USA and various military orders.

History: Known for their exceptional STOL performance and low speed handling, the Pilatus Porter and Turbo Porter STOL utilities have proven to be highly successful sales wise in a number of fields.

The high wing taildragger Porter was designed to be capable of performing a range of utility roles, and flew for the first time on May 4 1959. The first production aircraft built, delivered from 1960 were powered by the six cylinder GSO-480 piston engine, but it was not long after that a turboprop powered development flew. The first PC-6/A Turbo Porter flew in May 1961, powered by a 390kW (523shp) Turbo-méca Astazou II turboprop. The majority of PC-6s are PC-6/Bs, powered by the ubiquitous Pratt & Whitney Canada PT6A. PC-6/Cs are powered by a 310kW (575shp) AiResearch TPE331, and were first delivered in 1965.

Smaller numbers of piston powered Porters have been built with Lycoming GSO-480s and IGO-540s in parallel with Turbo Porters.

The PC-6/B was first delivered from 1964, and remains in production today. Initial models were powered by the 410kW (550shp) PT6A-6 or -20. The PC-6/B2-H2 was first flown in 1970 and introduced the PT6A-27 and an increased maximum takeoff weight. Current production is of the PC-6/B2-H4 with a further increase in max takeoff weight, larger dorsal fin fillet, revised wingtips, strengthened airframe structure and improved undercarriage.

Photo: A ski equipped Turbo Porter of New Zealand's Mount Cook Airline. (David Eyre)

Pilatus PC-12

Country of origin: Switzerland

Type: Light utility and business transport

Powerplant: One 895kW (1200shp) Pratt & Whitney Canada PT6A-67B turboprop, driving a four blade constant speed Hartzell propeller.

Performance: Max cruising speed 500km/h (270kt), economical cruising speed 430km/h (232kt). Initial rate of climb 2040ft/min. Service ceiling 25,000ft. Range at economical cruising speed with reserves 2965km (1600nm).

Weights: PC-12 – Empty 2386kg (5260lb), max takeoff 4000kg (8818lb).

Dimensions: Wing span 16.08m (52ft 9in), length 14.38m (47ft 2in), height 4.26m (14ft 0in). Wing area 25.8m² (277.8sq ft).

Capacity: Flightcrew of one or two pilots and one passenger on flightdeck. Max seating for nine in commuter airliner configuration. Corporate/executive transport configurations typically seat six. Combi passenger/freight version seats four passengers in main cabin plus freight pallet.

Production: First production aircraft delivered second half 1994, orders and options held for over 60 PC-12s at late 1996.

History: The latest in a line of single engined PT6 powered Pilatus products, the PC-12 is a new generation utility aimed at fulfilling commuter, executive and freight transport missions.

Pilatus announced it was developing a new single engine multi purpose transport at the National Business Aircraft Association's annual convention in October 1989. First flight of the first of two prototypes occurred on May 31 1991, this aircraft entering a flight test program that originally envisaged achieving Swiss certification in mid 1993, with first deliveries later that year. However the development program was delayed somewhat when Pilatus redesigned the wing to feature winglets to meet performance guarantees. The improvements were successful, but the delays meant that the PC-12 was not certificated until mid 1994, with first deliveries following soon after.

Currently regulations in the US, Europe and Australia prevent single engine IFR (Instrument Flight Rules) RPT (Revenue Public Transport) flights with single engine aircraft. However moves underway in the US and Australia in particular could significantly improve the sales prospects of the PC-12 (and also the TBM 700 and Cessna Caravan) if it can be demonstrated that single engine turboprop aircraft can meet the reliability standards of twins. If these moves are successful, as they have been in Canada, there appears to be fairly good sales prospects for all three types to replace the now fairly elderly piston twins such as the Piper Navajo and Chieftain and Cessna 400 series.

The PC-12 is offered in standard nine passenger combi form and in a six seat executive configuration. The PC-12F Freighter is no longer offered, while the PC-12 Eagle is a special missions variant, pitched at military and government requirements.

One interesting customer for the PC-12 is Australia's Royal Flying Doctor Service which operates an emergency aerial ambulance and clinic service in the Australian outback. Others are bound for charter, freight and corporate operators.

Photo: The PC-12 has a King Air sized cabin. (Gerard Frawley)

Piper Cub

Country of origin: United States of America

Type: Two seat light aircraft

Powerplant: J-3C-65 – One 50kW (65hp) Continental A-65-1 flat four piston engine, driving a two blade fixed pitch propeller. PA-12 – One 75kW (100hp) Lycoming O-235 flat four.

Performance: J-3C-65 – Max speed 148km/h (80kt), typical cruising speed 132km/h (71kt). Initial rate of climb 450ft/min. Service ceiling 12,000ft. Range 402km (217nm). PA-12 – Max speed 183km/h (99kt), normal cruising speed 170km/h (90kt). Service ceiling 12,600ft. Range 580km (313nm).

Weights: J-3C-65 – Empty 290kg (640lb), max takeoff 500kg (1100lb). PA-12 – Empty 430kg (950lb), max takeoff 795kg (1750lb).

Dimensions: Wing span 10.75m (35ft 3in), length 6.79m (22ft 3in), height 2.03m (6ft 8in). Wing area 16.6m^2 (178.5sq ft). PA-12 – Wing span 10.83m (35ft 6in), length 6.74m (22ft 1in), height 2.08m (6ft 10in). Wing area 16.7m^2 (179.3sq ft).

Capacity: Typical seating for two in tandem in the Cub, Cub Coupe and Cub Special, three in the Cub Cruiser and Super Cruiser, and four in the Family Cruiser.

Production: Production includes 5795 prewar J-3s, 8252 postwar J-3C-65s, 1248 J-4 Cub Coupes, more than 1410 J-5 Cub Cruisers, more than 430 PA-11 Cub Specials, 3761 PA-12 Super Cruisers and 521 PA-14 Family Cruisers. Wartime construction of 5687 L-4s.

History: The simple and economical Piper Cub is one of the most famous light aircraft of all time, and helped make flying an affordable pastime for thousands of pilots in the years surrounding World War 2.

The Piper Cub began life as the Taylor E-2 Tiger Kitten, which was powered by a tiny 15kW (20hp) Brownbach engine. The Tiger Kitten was grossly underpowered and the Taylor Brothers' Airplane Company went bankrupt before a more powerful engine could be found. Businessman William Piper, who had made large profits from the oil industry, purchased a majority holding in the Taylor company for $US1000 in 1931. The company continued building derivatives of the E-2 under the Taylor banner through the 1930s. The first aircraft to be called Cubs were E-2s powered by a Continental A-40 and small numbers were built from 1931.

In 1937 Piper adopted his own name for the company, and the first J-3 Cubs were built. The J-3 was an improved J-2, which resulted from a redesign from the three cylinder radial powered H-2 by Walter Janouneay. The affordable J-3 Cub became a runaway sales success and several thousand were sold before the USA's entry into WW2 saw all J-3 production requisitioned for the US Army as the L-4. Prewar Piper also built the J-4 Cub Coupe with side by side seating and the three seat J-5 Cub Cruiser.

Postwar Piper reverted to civilian production, the J-3 later becoming the PA-11 Cub Special. Late build PA-11s were powered by 65kW (90hp) Continental C-90s and had increased range. The PA-12 Super Cruiser has seating for three and a more powerful Lycoming O-235 engine, while the four seat PA-14 Family Cruiser forms the basis for the Super Cub.

Photo: Piper J-3 Cubs were built in their thousands and painted in this distinctive yellow scheme with black lightning strike. (Bill Lines)

Piper PA-18 Super Cub

Country of origin: United States of America

Type: Two seat utility light aircraft

Powerplant: PA-18-95 – One 65kW (90hp) Continental C90-12F or -8F flat four piston engine, driving a two blade fixed pitch propeller, PA-18-150 – One 110kW (150hp) Lycoming O-320.

Performance: PA-18-95 – Max speed 180km/h (97kt), max cruising speed 161km/h (87kt). Initial rate of climb 710ft/min. Service ceiling 15,750ft. Max range with no reserves 580km (313nm). PA-18-150 – Max speed 210km/h (113kt), max cruising speed 185km/h (100kt), economical cruising speed 170km/h (90kt). Initial rate of climb 960ft/min. Service ceiling 19,000ft. Range at max cruising speed and no reserves 740km (400kt).

Weights: PA-18-95 – Empty 367kg (910lb), max takeoff 680kg (1500lb). PA-18-150 – Empty 429kg (946lb), max takeoff 794kg (1750lb).

Dimensions: PA-18-95 – Wing span 10.73m (35ft 3in), length 6.83m (22ft 5in), height 2.02m (6ft 9in). Wing area 16.6m^2 (178.5sq ft). PA-18-150 – Same except for length 6.88m (22ft 7in).

Capacity: Typical seating for two in tandem.

Production: Almost 7500 Super Cubs (including 1700 military) built until 1981 when production originally ceased. Piper production for WTA between 1982 and 1988 totalled 250. Piper production since 1988 of approximately 100.

History: The Super Cub is one of Piper's most successful and long lived aircraft programs, with production spanning over four decades.

The PA-18 Super Cub was the ultimate development of Piper's original aircraft, the J-3 Cub (described separately). The four seat development of the Cub, the PA-14 Cub Cruiser, was the basis for the Super Cub, but the later differed in having seating for two in tandem (as on the Cub), all metal wings and, in its initial form, a 65kW (90hp) Continental C90 in the PA-18-90 or a 80kW (108hp) Lycoming O-235 engine in the PA-18-105. The Super Cub flew for the first time in 1949, and certification was awarded on November 18 that year. The first production Super Cubs were delivered from late 1949, the type replacing the PA-11 Cub Special on Piper's production lines.

The 100kW (135hp) Lycoming O-290 powered PA-18-135 appeared in 1952, while the definitive 110kW (150hp) Lycoming O-320 powered PA-18-150 was certificated on October 1 1954 and delivered from the following year.

The Super Cub remained in production with Piper through until 1981, when almost 7500 had been built over an uninterrupted 42 year production run. Piper continued building Super Cubs on behalf of Texas based WTA who acquired the manufacturing and marketing rights in 1981 through until 1988. In 1988 Piper resumed marketing responsibility for the Super Cub and continued low rate production. Financial troubles meant that Super Cub production ceased in 1992, before resuming once more the following year. Finally in late 1994 Piper announced that the Super Cub would not form part of its model line for 1995 and that it would cease production after the last of 24 on order for distributor Muncie Aviation were completed.

Photo: Compared with the Cub, the Super Cub has a similar overall configuration, but is larger and more powerful. (Gary Gentle)

Piper PA-20 Pacer & PA-22 Tri-Pacer & Colt

Country of origin: United States of America

Type: Two and four seat light aircraft

Powerplant: PA-22-108 Colt – One 80kW (108hp) Lycoming 0-235-C1B flat four piston engine, driving a two blade fixed pitch propeller. PA-22-160 Tri-Pacer – One 120kW (160hp) Lycoming 0-320-B2A.

Performance: PA-22-108 – Max speed 193km/h (104kt), max cruising speed 173km/h (93kt). Initial rate of climb 610ft/min. Service ceiling 12,000ft. Max range with no reserves 1110km (600nm). PA-22-160 – Max speed 227km/h (123kt), max cruising speed 216km/h (117kt). Initial rate of climb 800ft/min. Service ceiling 16,500ft. Range with standard fuel and no reserves 862km (465nm), or with optional fuel 1055km (570nm).

Weights: PA-22-108 – Empty 447kg (985lb), max takeoff 748kg (1650lb). PA-22-160 – Empty 503kg (1110lb), max takeoff 907kg (2000lb).

Dimensions: PA-22-108 – Wing span 9.14m (30ft 0in), length 6.10m (20ft 0in), height 1.91m (6ft 3in). Wing area 13.7m^2 (147sq ft). PA-22-160 – Wing span 8.92m (29ft 3in), length 6.28m (20ft 7in), height 2.53m (8ft 4in). Wing area 13.7m^2 (147.5sq ft).

Capacity: Pacer and Tri-Pacers (including Caribbean) typically seat four, while the Colt seats two side by side. Seaplane versions of the Tri-Pacer could seat three.

Production: Total PA-22 production of 9495 comprising 7688 Tri-Pacers and 1827 Colts, while 1699 PA-20 Pacers were built.

History: The Pacer and Tri-Pacer designs were Piper's volume selling four seaters from 1949 through to the introduction of the Comanche and Cherokee in the early 1960s, while the Colt was a two seat training derivative of the Tri-Pacer.

The original tail dragger PA-20 Pacer was introduced in 1949 alongside the two seat Super Cub, and was powered by a 85kW (115hp) Continental engine. Improvements were made in 1950, including a larger tail, while a 93kW (125hp) variant was added. From 1952 to 1954 when production ceased the Pacer was offered in 93kW (125hp) and 100kW (135hp) variants.

The tricycle undercarriage Tri-Pacer (with the same engine options) initially augmented the Pacer in production from 1950 until Pacer production ceased in 1954. The Tri-Pacer gained a 110kW (150hp) engine and a higher takeoff weight from 1955, and a 120kW (160hp) 0-320 from 1957. From 1958 Piper offered a lower spec less expensive version of the Tri-Pacer in the form of the PA-22-150 Caribbean.

The two seat Colt was derived from the Tri-Pacer but had a less powerful 85kW (108hp) engine, lower maximum takeoff weight, no rear cabin windows, the removal of a rear door and less fuel capacity, but otherwise the two airframes were identical. Piper introduced the Colt to its lineup in late 1960, and the type remained in production for just over two years until the two seat Cherokee could be introduced. Colt production ceased in 1963 after almost 2000 had been built.

The Tri-Pacer and Colt were Piper's only high wing tricycle undercarriage aircraft, and the last in production to feature metal tubing and fabric covering construction.

Photo: The PA-20/22 series are now collectors' items and valued classic aircraft. Pictured is a Tri-Pacer. (Eric Allen)

Piper PA-23 Apache & Aztec

Country of origin: United States of America

Type: Four seat light twins

Powerplant: PA-23-160 Apache G – Two 120kW (160hp) Lycoming 0-320-B flat four piston engines, driving two blade constant speed Hartzell propellers. PA-23-250T Aztec F – Two 185kW (250hp) turbocharged and fuel injected Lycoming TIO-540-C1As.

Performance: PA-23-160 – Max speed 294km/h (160kt), max cruising speed 278km/h (150kt), long range cruising speed 240km/h (130kt). Initial rate of climb 1260ft/min. Service ceiling 17,000ft. Max range with no reserves 2028km (1095nm). PA-23-250T – Max speed 408km/h (220kt), max cruising speed 390km/h (211kt), economical cruising speed 335km/h (181kt). Initial rate of climb 1470ft/min. Service ceiling 24,000ft. Range at max cruising speed 1797km (970nm), at economical cruising speed 2309km (1246nm).

Weights: PA-23-160 – Empty 1035kg (2280lb), max takeoff 1725kg (3800lb). PA-23-250T – Empty 1508kg (3323lb), max takeoff 2360kg (5200lb).

Dimensions: PA-23-160 – Wing span 11.28m (37ft 0in), length 8.27m (27ft 2in), height 2.90m (9ft 6in). Wing area 19.0m^2 (204sq ft). PA-23-250T – Wing span 11.39m (37ft 4in), length 9.53m (31ft 3in), height 3.08m (10ft 1in). Wing area 19.3m^2 (207sq ft).

Capacity: Apache seats four. Aztec As seat five, later Aztecs seat six.

Production: Total PA-23 production was almost 7000, comprising 2047 Apaches and 4929 Aztecs, including a small number of military sales.

History: The origins of the portly Apache (one of the first widely available GA twins and Piper's first 'Indian') and the larger and more powerful Aztec lie in the early postwar Twin Stinson design.

Piper acquired the assets of Consolidated Vultee's Stinson Aircraft division in 1948, and inherited a design study for a modern four place light twin. Piper left the design dormant for a few years until 1952 when it built a prototype aircraft, designated 23-01, based on the Stinson design. The low wing four seat twin was powered by 93kW (125hp) engines, had fabric covering, fixed undercarriage and a twin fin tail design. Unsatisfactory flight trials led Piper to substantially redesign the 23-01, introducing more powerful 110kW (150hp) engines, metal construction, retractable undercarriage and a conventional tail unit. Designated the PA-23 Apache, the redesigned twin flew for the first time on March 2 1952, and production deliveries occurred from March 1954.

Apache A, B, C, D and E subvariants of the initial PA-23-150 were built before production switched to the more powerful PA-23-160 Apache F in late 1958. Subsequent Apache developments were the Apache F with a third cabin window, and Apache 235, a lower powered development of the Aztec A.

The Aztec is an enlarged and more powerful development of the Apache, powered by two six cylinder 185kW (250hp) 0-540s, and was first delivered from early 1960. The Apache B introduced a longer nose, the Apache C fuel injected engines, and optional Apache C Turbo was turbocharged, while the Apache D, E and F and corresponding turbo models introduced detail changes. Production ceased in 1982.

Photo: This Interlsland Airways Aztec is pictured in the Dominican Republic. (Gary Gentle)

Piper PA-24 Comanche

Country of origin: United States of America

Type: Four seat high performance light aircraft

Powerplant: PA-24-250 – One 185kW (250hp) Lycoming 0-540-A1A5 flat six driving a constant speed propeller. PA-24-400 – One 300kW (400hp) Lycoming IO-720-A1A flat eight driving a three blade constant speed prop. PA-24-260 T – One 200kW (260hp) turbocharged and fuel injected IO-540-R1A5 flat six driving a two blade constant speed prop.

Performance: PA-24-250 – Max speed 306km/h (165kt), max cruising speed 291km/h (157kt). Initial rate of climb 1350ft/min. Service ceiling 20,000ft. Max range with optional fuel 2665km (1440nm). PA-24-400 – Max speed 360km/h (194kt), max cruising speed 343km/h (185kt). Initial rate of climb 1600ft/min. Service ceiling 19,500ft. Range with standard fuel 2012km (1086nm), with optional fuel 2478km (1338nm). PA-24-260 T – Max speed 390km/h (210kt), max cruising speed 318km/h (172kt). Initial rate of climb 1320ft/min. Operating ceiling 25,000ft. Max range 2052km (1108nm), with optional fuel 2398km (1295nm).

Weights: PA-24-250 – Empty 767kg (1690lb), max takeoff 1315kg (2900lb). PA-24-400 – Empty 957kg (2110lb), max takeoff 1633kg (3600lb). PA-24-260 T – Empty 860kg (1894lb), max TO 1450kg (3200lb).

Dimensions: PA-28-2250 – Wing span 10.97m (36ft 0in), length 7.59m (24ft 11in), height 2.29m (7ft 6in). Wing area 16.5m² (178sq ft). PA-28-400 – Wing span 10.97m (36ft 0in), length 7.84m (25ft 8in), height 2.39m (7ft 10in). Wing area 16.5m² (178sq ft). PA-28-260 T – Wing span 10.97m (36ft 0in), length 7.62m (25ft 0in), height 2.29m (7ft 6in). Wing area 16.5m² (178sq ft).

Capacity: Standard seating for four, Comanche 260C had an optional six seat arrangement.

Production: Total PA-24 production 4856, including 1143 180s, 2537 250s, 1028 260s and 260 Ts, and 148 400s.

History: Piper's PA-28 Comanche was very much a hot ship, a high performance retractable undercarriage single designed to knock the established high performance Beech Bonanza off its perch.

Piper's first low wing single engine design, the Comanche featured a retractable tricycle undercarriage, swept back tail, flying tail or stabilators, laminar flow wing and all metal construction, a stark contrast to Piper's earlier high wing fabric covered designs. The Comanche first flew on May 24 1956, and was delivered to customers from late 1957 in PA-24-180 form.

Since then through to the cessation of production in June 1972 (due to flooding of Piper's Lock Haven plant), a number of progressively higher performance variants were developed. These included 1958's 185kW (250hp) PA-24-250, and the 300kW (400hp) PA-24-400. Just 148 400s were built, despite Piper claiming it to be the fastest production four seat single available. Its massive eight cylinder engine consumed fuel at a prodigious rate, meaning that it was relatively expensive to operate, and there were problems with cooling the rear cylinders. Today though it has something of a mini cult status.

Following the PA-24-400 was the PA-24-260 from 1964, with a 195kW (260hp) O-540 or IO-540, and finally the Rajay turbocharger fitted PA-24-260 T, available from 1970.

Photo: A PA-24-250 Comanche at rest. (Bill Lines)

Piper PA-28 Cherokee Series

Country of origin: United States of America

Type: Two and four seat light aircraft

Powerplant: PA-28-161 Warrior II – One 110kW (160hp) Lycoming O-320-A2B flat four piston engine, driving a two blade fixed pitch propeller. PA-28-181 Archer III – One 135kW (180hp) Textron Lycoming O-360-A4M flat four.

Performance: PA-28-161 – Max speed 235km/h (1127kt), max cruising speed 233km/h (126kt), long range cruising speed 195km/h (105kt). Initial rate of climb 644ft/min. Service ceiling 11,000ft. Max Range with reserves 1185km (637nm). PA-28-181 – Max speed 246km/h (133kt), normal cruising speed 237km/h (128kt). Max initial rate of climb 667ft/min. Service ceiling 13,240ft. Range with reserves at normal cruise power 685km (370nm).

Weights: PA-28-161 – Empty 613kg (1352lb), max takeoff 1105kg (2440lb). PA-28-181 – Empty equipped 752kg (1658lb), max takeoff 1155kg (2550lb).

Dimensions: PA-28-161 – Wing span 10.67m (35ft 0in), length overall 7.25m (23ft 10in), height 2.22m (7ft 4in). Wing area 15.8m² (170sq ft). PA-28-181 – Same as PA-28-161.

Capacity: Most versions typically seat four, while some dedicated trainer versions had seating for two only.

Production: Over 30,000 fixed undercarriage PA-28 Cherokee series built, including approximately 10,100 PA-28-140s, 10,000 PA-28-180s & -181s, 5000 PA-28-151 & -161s, and 2800 PA-28-235 & 236s.

History: The initial PA-28-150 and PA-28-160 Cherokees were introduced in 1961 as replacements for Piper's PA-22 Tri-Pacer and Colt.

Unlike the PA-22 series the new PA-28 was a low wing design with metal construction. The prototype Cherokee was powered by a 120kW (160hp) engine, and flew for the first time on January 14 1960. Production aircraft were powered by either 110kW (150hp) or 120kW (160hp) engines and were delivered from early 1961.

From 1962 a 135kW (180hp) version was added to the lineup. The 127kW (235hp) flat six Lycoming O-540 was introduced in 1963, while the two seat trainer optimised Colt replacement PA-28-140 entered the marketplace in 1964. With these models in place the basic PA-28 lineup (the retractable PA-28R and larger PA-32 are described separately) was in place.

Subsequent variants include the Cherokee B and Cherokee C, the 180D, 235C, 140 Flite Liner two seat trainer PA-28-140, 180F, 235E, PA-28-180 Cherokee Challenger and PA-28-235 Cherokee Charger, the PA-28-180 Cherokee Archer and PA-28-235 Cherokee Pathfinder, PA-28-151 Cherokee Warrior which introduced the new tapered wing that would become a feature of subsequent PA-28s, PA-28-181 Cherokee Archer II and PA-28-236 Dakota (the Cherokee prefix was later dropped for the Archer II and Warrior), the PA-28-161 Warrior II, PA-28-236T Turbo Dakota and PA-28-161 Cadet.

The Archer II and Dakota were returned to low rate production in 1994, while the latest releases are the PA-28-181 Archer III (detailed above), which features a new, streamlined cowling, and the PA-28-161 Warrior III, which features a new instrument panel.

Photo: The Archer III, note the revised nose cowling. (Bob Grimstead)

Piper PA-28R Cherokee Arrow

Country of origin: United States of America

Type: Four seat light aircraft

Powerplant: PA-28R-180 – One 135kW (180hp) Lycoming IO-360-B1E fuel injected flat four piston engine, driving a two blade constant speed Hartzell propeller. PA-28R-201T – One 150kW (200hp) Continental TSIO-360-FB turbocharged and fuel injected flat six.

Performance: PA-28R-180 – Max speed 274km/h (148kt), typical cruising speed 260km/h (140kt), long range cruising speed 230km/h (124kt). Initial rate of climb 875ft/min. Service ceiling 15,000ft. Range at economical cruising speed 1600km (865nm). PA-28R-201T – Max speed 330km/h (178kt), max cruising speed 320km/h (172kt), long range cruising speed 284km/h (153kt). Initial rate of climb 940ft/min. Range with reserves 1667km (900nm).

Weights: PA-28R-180 – Empty 626kg (1380lb), max takeoff 1134kg (2500lb). PA-28R-201T – Empty 786kg (1732lb), max takeoff 1315kg (2900lb).

Dimensions: PA-28R-180 – Wing span 9.14m (30ft 0in), length 7.38m (24ft 3in), height 2.44m (8ft 0in). Wing area 14.2m^2 (160sq ft). PA-28R-201T – Wing span 10.80m (35ft 5in), length 8.33m (27ft 3in), height 2.52m (8ft 3in). Wing area 15.9m^2 (170sq ft).

Capacity: Typical seating for four.

Production: Approximately 6000 PA-28Rs of all models built, including 81 PA-28R-180Bs, 1664 PA-28R-200s and -201s, and 1291 PA-28R-201Ts and PA-28RT-201Ts.

History: The PA-28R originally began life as a retractable undercarriage variant of the PA-28 Cherokee, augmenting the higher performance Comanche.

The original PA-28-180R Cherokee Arrow was a relatively simple adaptation of the existing PA-28-180 Cherokee D, but incorporated a electro-hydraulically operated retractable undercarriage (complete with a self lowering system that safeguarded against the pilot failing to do so, automatically lowering when airspeed reached 170km/h/91kt and a certain engine manifold pressure), a fuel injected version of the PA-28-180's O-360, a constant speed propeller and an increased max takeoff weight.

Production switched to the PA-28R-180 and more powerful (150kW/200hp IO-360-C1C powered) PA-28R-200 Cherokee Arrow II. Changes included the same 12.7cm (5in) stretched fuselage introduced on the Cherokee Challenger and Cherokee Charger, with greater rear legroom and baggage capacity, plus larger horizontal tail and dorsal fin fillet.

The PA-28R-201 Arrow III first flew in September 1975, and was introduced from 1976. The major change (also introduced on the fixed undercarriage PA-28s at that time) was a new longer tapered span wing, while the maximum takeoff weight increased. The turbocharged PA-28R-201T was also offered.

The PA-28RT-201 and -201T Arrow IV introduced a new all moving T-tail. Production of the Arrow IV ceased in 1982, and resumed again in 1989, but ceased once more in 1992. The Arrow III was also placed into production in 1990 for a few months, and is once again on offer.

Photo: A PA-28R-200 Cherokee Arrow II. (Bill Lines)

Piper Cherokee Six, Lance & Saratoga

Country of origin: United States of America

Type: Six seat light aircraft

Powerplant: PA-32RT-300 Lance II – One 225kW (300hp) Lycoming IO-540-K1G5 fuel injected flat six piston engine, driving a two blade constant speed propeller. PA-32R-301 Saratoga II HP – One 225kW (300hp) Textron Lycoming IO-540-K1G5 driving a three blade prop.

Performance: PA-32RT-300 – Max speed 306km/h (165kt), max cruising speed 293km/h (158kt), long range cruising speed 258km/h (139kt). Initial rate of climb 1000ft/min. Service ceiling 14,600ft. Max range with reserves 1600km (865nm). PA-32R-301 – Max speed 314km/h (170kt), normal cruising speed 302km/h (163kt). Max initial rate of climb 1116ft/min. Service ceiling 15,590ft. Range at normal cruising speed with reserves 1370km (740nm).

Weights: PA-32RT-300 – Empty 912kg (2011lb), max takeoff 1633kg (3600lb). PA-32R-301 – Empty equipped 1072kg (2364lb), max takeoff 1633kg (3600lb).

Dimensions: PA-32RT-300 – Wing span 9.99m (32ft 10in), length 8.44m (27ft 9in), height 2.90m (9ft 6in). Wing area 16.2m^2 (174.5sq ft). PA-32T-301 – Wing span 11.02m (36ft 2in), length 8.23m (27ft 0in), height 2.59m (8ft 6in). Wing area 16.6m^2 (178.3sq ft).

Capacity: Standard seating for six, some an optional seventh seat.

Production: Approximately 700 PA-32s of all versions have been built, including new production of the Saratoga II HP.

History: What began life as the PA-32 Cherokee Six was a significantly modified development of the ubiquitous PA-28 Cherokee series.

While similar in configuration to the Cherokee, the Cherokee Six differed in a number of major areas. Two of the big differences were implied in its name, a six cylinder O-540 or IO-540 powerplant, and the six seat configuration. While the wing was based on the Cherokee's, the fuselage was substantially larger, with a strengthened undercarriage and larger tail.

First flight of the Cherokee Six was on December 6 1963, and deliveries of production PA-32-260 aircraft took place from mid 1965. From then continual development led to a range of improved models, starting with the 225kW (300hp) fuel injected IO-540 powered Cherokee Six-300 (PA-32-300). Production of the -260 and -300 ended in the late 1970s, but in the meantime they had been joined by the Cherokee Lance. The Cherokee Lance, or just Lance from mid 1977 with the introduction of the improved Lance II, was a retractable undercarriage development. The Lance II and turbocharged PA-32R-300T Turbo Lance also introduced T-tail, and these two models remained in production to late 1979.

Taking the Lance II and Cherokee Six's place was the Saratoga family. Available in fixed or retractable undercarriage form, with standard or turbocharged powerplants, the major change was the new increased tapered span wing, which was also introduced on the PA-28 and PA-28R series. Production of the Saratoga ceased in 1985, but has since been restarted, with the current model being the Saratoga IIHP (detailed above) with aerodynamic improvements and a revised instrument panel and interior.

Photo: The current production model of the six place PA-32 line, the Saratoga IIHP. (Piper)

Piper Pawnee & Pawnee Brave

Country of origin: United States of America

Type: Agricultural aircraft

Powerplant: PA-25-235 – One 175kW (235hp) Lycoming O-540-B2B5 flat six piston engine, driving a two blade fixed pitch McCauley propeller. PA-36-375 – One 280kW (375hp) Lycoming IO-720-DICD fuel injected flat eight driving a three blade constant speed Hartzell prop.

Performance: PA-25-235 – Max speed 188km/h (102kt), cruising speed 170km/h (91kt), typical spraying speed 145km/h (78kt). Initial rate of climb 630ft/min. Service ceiling 13,000ft. PA-36-325 – Max speed 216km/h (116kt), cruising speed 210km/h (113kt), spraying speed range 161 to 193km/h (87 to 104kt). Initial rate of climb 550ft/min. Service ceiling 15,000ft. Range 772km (417nm).

Weights: PA-25-235 – Empty 585kg (1288lb), max takeoff 1317kg (2900lb). PA-36-375 – Empty 1162kg (2560lb), max takeoff 2180kg (4800lb).

Dimensions: PA-25-235 – Wing span 11.02m (36tft 2din), length 7.55m (24ft 9in), height 2.19m (7ft 2in). Wing area 17.0m^2 (183sq ft). PA-36-375 – Wing span 11.82m (38ft 10in), length 8.39m (27ft 6in), height 2.29m (7ft 6in). Wing area 21.0m^2 (225.65sq ft).

Capacity: Seating for pilot only, but can be fitted with an optional jump seat. PA-25-235 – Hopper capacity 568 litres (150US gal/125Imp gal), or 545kg (1200lb). PA-36-375 – Hopper capacity 454 litres (120US gal/100Imp gal), or 1000kg (2200lb).

Production: Total PA-25 Pawnee production 5015. PA-36 Pawnee Brave production ceased in 1982.

History: The Piper Pawnee was one of the first single seat light aircraft to be specifically designed and built for agricultural spraying and dusting, and was one of the most successful, with several thousand built, and with licence production in a number of countries.

The PA-25 Pawnee was originally designed by Fred Weick as the Ag-3, and flew in prototype form during 1957. The design was originally powered by a 110kW (150hp) Lycoming O-320, the fuselage structure was designed to absorb impact forces in a crash, the high cockpit had excellent all round vision, the braced wing was fitted with spray bars, while a jump seat could be fitted in the hopper.

Initial production was of the 110kW (150hp) powered Pawnee, which was delivered from August 1959. The Pawnee was replaced by the 175kW (235hp) powered Pawnee B with an enlarged hopper, the Pawnee C followed with oleo type shock absorbers, while the ultimate Pawnee model, the Pawnee D had a 195kW (260hp) O-540. Production ceased in 1982.

The PA-36 Pawnee Brave meanwhile was a much larger new design, although of the same overall configuration to the Pawnee. The result of Piper research on Pawnee operations, the Pawnee Brave (originally the Pawnee II) was available from 1971. Initial production was of the 210kW (285hp) Continental O-285 Tiara powered PA-36-285. The 225kW (300hp) Lycoming IO-540 powered Brave 300, 280kW (375hp) IO-720 powered Brave 375 and 300kW (400hp) IO-720 powered Brave 400 followed. Production ceased in 1982.

Photo: A spray bar equipped PA-36-285 Pawnee Brave. (Lance Higgerson)

Piper PA-30 & PA-39 Twin Comanche

Country of origin: United States of America

Type: Six place light twin

Powerplants: PA-30-160 – Two 120kW (160hp) Lycoming IO-320-B1A fuel injected flat four piston engines driving two blade constant speed Hartzell propellers. PA-39T – Two 120kW (160hp) counter rotating Lycoming IO-320-C1A.

Performance: PA-30-160 – Max speed 330km/h (178kt), max cruising speed 312km/h (168kt), long range cruising speed 267km/h (144kt). Initial rate of climb 1460ft/min. Service ceiling 18,600ft. Max range with no reserves and standard fuel 1795km (970nm), or with tip tanks 2190km (1182nm). PA-39T – Max speed 376km/h (203kt), max cruising speed 357km/h (193kt), economical cruising speed 327km/h (177kt). Initial rate of climb 1460ft/min. Service ceiling 25,000ft. Range at max cruising speed 2373km (1282nm), range at economical cruising speed 2582km (1395nm).

Weights: PA-30-160 – Empty 1002kg (2210lb), max takeoff 1633kg (3600lb), or 1690kg (3725lb) with tip tanks. PA-30-160 – Empty 1097kg (2416lb), max ramp 1690kg (3725lb).

Dimensions: Wing span 10.97m (36ft 0in) or 11.22m (36ft 10in) with tip tanks, length 7.67m (25ft 2in), height 2.49m (8ft 2in). Wing area 16.5m^2 (178sq ft).

Capacity: Typical seating for four, including pilot in Twin Comanche. Up to six, including one pilot in Twin Comanche B.

Production: Total Twin Comanche production was 2156, comprising 2001 PA-30s and 155 PA-39s.

History: As its name implies, the Twin Comanche is a twin engine development of the PA-24 Comanche, and while it was in production, it was Piper's premier four/six seat light twin, slotting beneath the larger and more powerful Aztec, and replacing the Apache 235.

The Twin Comanche was originally proposed as early as 1956, when the single engine Comanche was undergoing initial development, however the project was delayed while Piper worked on the Comanche and the Aztec twin. Thus it was not until 1962 that a Comanche was converted to a twin with two 120kW (160hp) IO-320s (originally two 110kW/150hp engines were planned), with the first flight occurring on November 7 1962. First flight of a production Twin Comanche occurred in May 1963, with first deliveries later that year.

The Twin Comanche differed little from its single engine brethren other than changes associated with its twin layout, and the type quickly proved to be relatively inexpensive and very popular. Improvements to the PA-30 resulted in the introduction of the Twin Comanche B in 1965, which introduced a stretched fuselage allowing seating for up to six, as on the equivalent Comanche single, while turbocharged engines and wingtip tanks were offered as options. From 1970 the Twin Comanche C featured a slightly higher cruising speed and interior improvements, while the PA-39 Twin Comanche C/R was fitted with counter rotating engines.

Production of the Twin Comanche ceased in 1972, by which time only the PA-39 was available, due to the flooding of Piper's Lock Haven factory.

Photo: The Twin Comanche's Comanche origins are fairly obvious. Pictured is a Twin Comanche C. (Bill Lines)

Piper PA-34 Seneca

Country of origin: United States of America

Type: Six place light twin

Powerplants: PA-34-200 Seneca – Two 150kW (200hp) Lycoming IO-360-A1A fuel injected flat four piston engines, driving two blade constant speed propellers. PA-34-220T Seneca IV – Two 165kW (220hp) Continental TSIO-360-KB turbocharged and fuel injected flat sixes driving three blade constant speed McCauley propellers.

Performance: PA-34-200 – Max speed 314km/h (170kt), max cruising speed 300km/h (160kt), long range cruising speed 267km/h (144kt). Initial rate of climb 1360ft/min. Service ceiling 19,400ft. Max range with no reserves 1818km (982nm). PA-34-220T – Max speed 363km/h (193kt), max cruising speed 358km/h (193kt), long range cruising speed 311km/h (168kt). Initial rate of climb 1400ft/min. Operational ceiling 25,000ft. Max range with reserves and standard fuel 1170km (632nm), with optional fuel 1673km (903nm).

Weights: PA-34-200 – Empty 1190kg (2623lb), max takeoff 1905kg (4200lb). PA-34-220T – Empty 1450kg (3195lb), max takeoff 2155kg (4750lb).

Dimensions: Wing span 11.85m (38ft 11in), length 8.69m (28ft 6in), height 3.02m (9ft 11in). Wing area 19.2m^2 (206.5sq ft). PA-34-220T – Wing span 11.85m (38ft 11in), length 8.72m (28ft 8in), height 3.02m (9ft 11in). Wing area 19.4m^2 (208.7sq ft).

Capacity: Typical seating for six.

Production: Approximately 4500 Senecas have been built, with production of the Seneca IV continuing. Seneca II also licence built in Poland by PZL Mielec as the M-20 Mewa.

History: The most successful aircraft in the twin engine six seat class since its introduction, the Seneca is a twin engine development of the Cherokee Six.

Perhaps surprisingly, the Seneca actually began life as a trimotor when Piper trialled a Cherokee Six, designated PA-32-3M, fitted with additional 85kW (115hp) Lycomings O-235 on either wing. Needless to say, the cost and complexity of a trimotor saw any plans for production dropped, and the twin engine Cherokee Six, or Twin Six was born.

The prototype PA-34 Seneca first flew fitted with two 135kW (180hp) Lycomings, but by the time the definitive standard third Seneca prototype first flew in October 1969 power was supplied by fuel injected 150kW (200hp) IO-360s. Production deliveries of the initial PA-34-200 began in late 1971 and the type proved very popular.

Handling and performance criticisms were addressed from the 1974 model year with the PA-34-200T Seneca II which introduced changes to the flight controls, and more importantly two turbocharged Continental TSIO-360-Es. Piper originally planned that the follow-on Seneca III would feature a T-tail, but these plans were dropped and the main changes introduced were counter rotating 165kW (220hp) TSIO-360s and a revised interior and instrument panel. Introduced in 1981, the Seneca III was replaced by the improved Seneca IV in 1994 with aerodynamic refinements, axisymetric engine inlets and a revised interior.

Photo: Unrivalled in its class, the six place Seneca (such as this PA-34-220T Seneca IV) has sold well to private and charter operators. (David Tarbutt)

Piper PA-38 Tomahawk

Country of origin: United States of America

Type: Two seat light aircraft and basic trainer

Powerplant: PA-38-112 – One 85kW (112hp) Avco Lycoming O-235-L2A or -L2C flat four piston engine, driving a two blade fixed pitch Sensenich propeller.

Performance: Max speed 202km/h (109kt), max cruising speed 200km/h (108kt), normal cruising speed 185km/h (100kt). Initial rate of climb 718ft/min. Service ceiling 13,000ft. Max range with reserves 867km (468nm).

Weights: Empty 512kg (1128lb), max takeoff 757kg (1670lb).

Dimensions: Wing span 10.36m (34ft 0in), length 7.04m (23ft 1in), height 2.77m (9ft 1in). Wing area 11.6m^2 (124.7sq ft).

Capacity: Typical seating for two side by side, usually comprising instructor and student.

Production: Total Tomahawk production stands at 2497, built between 1978 and 1983.

History: Piper's Tommy, or PA-38 Tomahawk, was the first all new trainer built by one of the USA's big three in close to 30 years when introduced.

The Tomahawk was designed as a relatively inexpensive to acquire and operate two seat trainer to tackle the firmly established definitive basic trainer in the 1970s, the Cessna 150 and 152, and to take over the spot in Piper's model range then occupied by two seat variants of the PA-28 Cherokee series.

Design input for the Tomahawk came from a questionnaire Piper distributed randomly to 10,000 flight instructors during the 1970s. With their responses in mind, Piper developed the PA-38. The resulting aircraft featured a T-tail and low set wing of constant chord and thickness, a cabin design with 360° vision and an economical Lycoming O-235 powerplant, while many parts, such as the main undercarriage wheels and elevators were interchangeable.

Piper announced the development of the Tomahawk during late 1977 and first deliveries were made in early 1978. Despite an initial mixed reaction to the new trainer from the flying public, the Tomahawk was an instant sales success. Unlike the similar Beech Skipper (described elsewhere), the PA-38 was almost instantly in great demand, and over 1000 were built in the first year of production alone. In service the Tomahawk has proven to be economical to operate, with a number of features, including its 1.07m (42in) wide cabin, all round vision, comfort and good handling, ensuring its popularity.

Flow strips were added to the wing on late production Tomahawk Is to improve stall performance, while a number of other criticisms levelled against the Tomahawk including poor quality control were addressed in the improved Tomahawk II, which was introduced for the 1981 model year. Improvements included better sound proofing, windscreen defrosting, door latching and the nose wheel design. Piper also improved the Tomahawk's much criticised stalling characteristics with the Tomahawk II.

Piper ceased production of the Tomahawk during 1983.

Photo: A Tomahawk in a distinctive military-like high-vis colour scheme. (Glenn Alderton)

Piper PA-31 Navajo

Country of origin: United States of America

Type: Six/eight seat corporate twin and commuter airliner

Powerplants: PA-31-310 – Two 230kW (310hp) Lycoming TIO-540-A turbocharged and fuel injected flat six piston engines, driving three blade constant speed propellers. PA-31P – Two 317kW (425hp) Lycoming TIGO-541-E1A geared, turbocharged and fuel injected engines.

Performance: PA-31-310 – Max speed 420km/h (227kt), max cruising speed 404km/h (218kt), long range cruising speed 273km/h (147kt). Initial rate of climb 1445ft/min. Service ceiling 27,300ft. Range with reserves 2398km (1295nm). PA-31P – Max speed 451km/h (244kt), max cruising speed 428km/h (231kt), long range cruising speed 306km/h (165kt). Initial rate of climb 1740ft/min. Operational ceiling 29,000ft. Range with reserves 2150km (1160nm).

Weights: PA-31-310 – Empty equipped 1843kg (4062lb), max takeoff 2950kg (6500lb). PA-31P – Empty equipped 2380kg (5250lb), max takeoff 3540kg (7800lb).

Dimensions: PA-31-310 – Wing span 12.40m (40ft 8in), length 9.94m (32ft 8in), height 3.97m (13ft 0in). Wing area 21.3m^2 (229sq ft). PA-31P – Same except for length 10.52m (34ft 6in), height 4.04m (13ft 3in).

Capacity: Configured to seat six including pilot in standard and executive layouts, and eight in commuter layout.

Production: Total PA-31 Navajo production of 2044, including 259 Pressurised Navajo PA-31Ps.

History: The highly successful Navajo six/eight seat cabin class light twin has been adapted to a number of commuter, charter, air taxi, light freight and executive transport roles, and has spawned a series of developments that ultimately led to Cheyenne 400LS.

The PA-31 was developed at the beckoning of the William T Piper, and the development program for a roomy twin was given the project name Inca. The prototype PA-31 made its first flight on September 30 1964, and was Piper's largest aircraft to be built to that time. A small number of initial 225kW (300hp) PA-31-300s were built before production switched to the definitive PA-31-310, with five cabin windows per side, Piper's distinctive Tiger Shark engine nacelles with optional nacelle lockers, 230kW (310hp) TIO-540 engines and a higher max takeoff weight. The PA-31-310 was further improved in Navajo B and C developments, and the Navajo C/R with counter rotating engines.

The Pressurised Navajo PA-31P had three windows per side of the cabin, geared, turbocharged and fuel injected TIGO-541-E1A engines, a higher takeoff weight and strengthened structure and undercarriage, optional extra fuel, a lengthened nose, and most importantly a cabin pressurisation system. First flown in March 1968, first deliveries took place from 1970, and it remained in production until 1984.

Production of the PA-31-310 had meanwhile ceased in 1983. Further developments of the Navajo, including the Chieftain, Mojave and Cheyenne, are described separately.

Photo: The Navajo remains popular worldwide for charter work, despite its age, as there is no direct new build replacement for the type. (David Daw)

Piper PA-31 Mojave & Chieftain

Country of origin: United States of America

Type: Eight/10 seat corporate twin and commuter airliner

Powerplants: PA-31P-350 Mojave – Two 260kW (350hp) Lycoming TIO-540-V2AD turbocharged and fuel injected flat six piston engines, driving three blade constant speed Hartzell propellers. PA-31-350 Chieftain – Two 260kW (350hp) Lycoming TIO-540-J2BD turbocharged and fuel injected flat sixes.

Performance: PA-31P-350 – Max speed 447km/h (241kt), max cruising speed 435km/h (235kt), long range cruising speed 361km/h (195kt). Initial rate of climb 1220ft/min. Service ceiling 30,400ft. Max range with reserves 2260km (1220nm). PA-31-350 – Max speed 428km/h (231kt), max cruising speed 254km/h (137kt), long range cruising speed 320km/h (173kt). Initial rate of climb 1120ft/min. Operational ceiling 24,000ft. Max range with reserves and standard fuel 1760km (950nm), with optional fuel 2390km (1290nm).

Weights: PA-31P-350 – Empty equipped 2495kg (5500lb), max takeoff 3265kg (7200lb). PA-31-350 – Empty equipped 1988kg (4383lb), max takeoff 3175kg (7000lb).

Dimensions: PA-31P-350 – Wing span 13.56m (44ft 6in), length 10.52m (34ft 6in), height 3.96m (13ft 0in). Wing area 22.0m^2 (237sq ft). PA-31-350 – Wing span 12.40m (40ft 8in), length 10.55m (34ft 8in), height 3.96m (13ft 0in). Wing area 21.3m^2 (229sq ft).

Capacity: Standard seating in Mojave for seven, including one pilot and passenger, or two pilots on flightdeck, with seating for five behind them. Chieftain has max seating for 10.

Production: Mojave production of approximately 50. Total Chieftain production of 1825.

History: The PA-31P-350 Mojave was the last pressurised version of the PA-31 series to be built, while the larger Chieftain consolidated on the Navajo's success in the commuter and charter roles.

The stretched Navajo Chieftain first appeared in 1973, after Piper began design work in 1971 (delays were caused by the destruction of the second prototype and early production aircraft due to flooding at Piper's Lock Haven plant in June 1972). Originally dubbed the Navajo II, the Navajo Chieftain was intended to compete against the Cessna 402 and to a lesser extent the turboprop powered Beech 99. Changes over the basic Navajo were many, including a 61cm (2ft) fuselage stretch, six side cabin windows, larger doors (an extra crew door was optional), and more powerful and counter rotating 260kW (350hp) IO-540 engines. From the 1980 model year the PA-31-350 became known simply as the Chieftain, and the type remained in production until October 1984.

Small numbers were also built of the airline optimised T-1020 and Pratt & Whitney Canada PT6 powered P-1040 'airliner'.

The Mojave was a development of the PA-31P, and its airframe was essentially similar to the turboprop powered PA-31T Cheyenne I. Changes included less powerful 260kW (350hp) counter rotating IO-540-V2As, a lower pressure differential and longer span wings. Mojaves were built between 1983 and 1986.

Photo: Most Chieftains are employed in the third level regional/commuter airline environment as single pilot nine passenger airliners. (Rob Finlayson)

Piper PA-31T Cheyenne

Country of origin: United States of America

Type: Light business and executive turboprop transport

Powerplants: PA-31T Cheyenne – Two 460kW (620shp) Pratt & Whitney Canada PT6A-28 turboprops, driving three blade constant speed Hartzell propellers. PA-31T2-620 Cheyenne II XL – Two 460kW (620shp) PT6A-135s.

Performance: PA-31T – Max speed 516km/h (280kt), max cruising speed 516km/h (280kt), economical cruising speed 452km/h (244kt). Initial rate of climb 2800ft/min. Service ceiling 29,000ft. Range at max cruising speed 1555km (840nm). PA-31T2-620 – Max speed 510km/h (275kt), max cruising speed 500km/h (270kt), economical cruising speed 385km/h (208kt). Service ceiling 32,400ft. Range at max cruising speed 2608km (1408nm), at economical cruising speed with max fuel 2740km (1478nm).

Weights: PA-31T – Empty equipped 2260kg (4983lb), max takeoff 4082kg (9000lb). PA-31T2-620 – Empty equipped 2580kg (5680lb), max takeoff 4335kg (9540lb).

Dimensions: PA-31T – Wing span 13.01m (42ft 8in), length 10.57m (34ft 8in), height 3.89m (12ft 9in). Wing area 21.3m^2 (229sq ft). PA-31T2-620 – Same except for length 11.10m (36ft 8in).

Capacity: Cheyenne II, I, IA, and II XL typically seat six, including pilot, or optionally eight.

Production: Total PA-31T Cheyenne production of approximately 825, comprising 526 Cheyenne IIs, 215 Cheyenne I & IIAs and 82 Cheyenne II XLs.

History: The Piper Cheyenne name originally applies to a turboprop development of the popular Navajo, but now covers a family of two quite distinct variants, the second of which, the PA-42, is described separately.

Although it was not until mid 1974 that the first Cheyenne was delivered, work on a turboprop version of the Pressurised Navajo dates back almost a decade earlier to the mid 1960s. The prototype of the Cheyenne flew for the first time on August 29 1969. Piper had to redesign the flight control systems to handle the increased loads on the airframe due to the turboprops' higher speeds, but certification was granted in mid 1972. However, production deliveries were delayed due to flooding at Piper's Lock Haven plant, the first production aircraft not flying until October 22 1973.

Piper introduced the lower powered and less expensive Cheyenne I in 1978, and renamed the original Cheyenne the Cheyenne II. Refinements to the Cheyenne I made in 1983, including more powerful engines, revised cowlings and interior, resulted in the Cheyenne IA.

Meanwhile the stretched Cheyenne II XL had been introduced in 1979. Compared with the standard length Cheyennes, the II XL was 61cm (2ft) longer, featured an extra cabin window on the left side, and slightly higher weights. An improved II XLA was planned, but did not enter production.

The further stretched and T-tail PA-42 was also introduced in 1978, and is described separately.

Photo: The II XL variant featured the largest cabin in the Cheyenne I & II family. (Gary Gentle)

Piper PA-42 Cheyenne III, IIIA & 400LS

Country of origin: United States of America

Type: Twin turboprop executive transports

Powerplants: PA-42-720 Cheyenne III – Two 535kW (720shp) Pratt & Whitney Canada PT6A-41 turboprops, driving three blade constant speed Hartzell propellers. PA-42-1000 Cheyenne 400LS – Two 1225kW (1645shp) derated to 745kW (1000shp) Garrett TPE331-14A/Bs driving four blade Hartzell props.

Performance: PA-42-720 – Max speed 537km/h (290kt), max cruising speed 461km/h (250kt), economical cruising speed 413km/h (223kt). Initial rate of climb 2235ft/min. Service ceiling 33,000ft. Range at max cruising speed 3100km (1675nm). PA-42-1000 – Max speed 650km/h (351kt), max cruising speed 594km/h (320kt), economical cruising speed 506km/h (273kt). Initial rate of climb 3242ft/min. Range at max cruising speed 3015km (1630nm), range at economical cruising speed 3500km (1890nm).

Weights: PA-42-720 – Empty 2900kg (6389lb), max ramp weight 5125kg (11,285lb). PA-42-1000 – Empty 3412kg (7522lb), max takeoff 5466kg (12,050lb).

Dimensions: PA-42-720 – Wing span (over tip tanks) 14.53m (47ft 8in), length 13.23m (43ft 5in), height 4.50m (14ft 9in). Wing area 27.2m^2 (293.0sq ft). PA-42-1000 – Same except for height 5.18m (17ft 0in).

Capacity: One or two pilots on flightdeck, with main cabin seating for between six and nine passengers. Typical seating for six in main cabin in corporate configuration.

Production: PA-42 Cheyenne production totals approximately 185 aircraft, of which approximately 145 are Cheyenne IIIs and IIIAs.

History: Aimed directly at Beech's successful and entrenched Super King Air twin turboprop series, the larger PA-42 Cheyennes are developments of the earlier PA-31T Cheyennes, which themselves were turboprop developments of the PA-31 Navajo.

The PA-42 Cheyenne III first appeared in 1979, and was an enlarged development of the PA-31T. However Piper originally planned for the PA-42/31T to be a pressurised piston twin that would have been approximately 2.73m (9ft) longer than the Cheyenne II. As it evolved however the PA-42 was instead about 1m (3ft) longer than the Cheyenne II, had turbine power and a T-tail, the latter the most obvious external difference between the PA-31T and PA-42. Named the Cheyenne III, production of the PA-42 began in 1980.

Development and improvement of the III led to the PA-42-720 Cheyenne IIIA, with more powerful PT6A-61 engines, a higher service ceiling and revised systems and interior.

The higher powered and significantly faster PA-42-1000 is basically similar to the PA-42-720 except for its far more powerful 745kW (1000hp) Garrett TPE331 turboprops and four blade propellers. Piper's largest and fastest production aircraft to date, the PA-42-1000 was initially called the Cheyenne IV, before becoming known as the Cheyenne 400LS, and then simply the Cheyenne 400. First flown in 1983, the Cheyenne 400 was delivered from late 1984. Both the Cheyenne IIIA and 400 were available on special order through to the early 1990s.

Photo: The top of the line Cheyenne 400 in flight. (Piper)

Piper PA-44 Seminole

Country of origin: United States of America

Type: Four seat light twin

Powerplants: PA-44-180 – Two 135kW (180hp) Lycoming 0-360-E1AD flat four piston engines, driving two or optionally three blade constant speed Hartzell propellers. PA-44-180T – Two 135kW (180hp) Lycoming TO-360-E1A6D turbocharged flat fours driving two blade constant speed props.

Performance: PA-44-180 – Max speed 311km/h (168kt), max cruising speed 309km/h (167kt), long range cruising speed 280km/h (151kt). Initial rate of climb 1200ft/min. Service ceiling 17,100ft. Range with reserves 1630km (880nm). PA-44-180T – Max speed 363km/h (196kt), max cruising speed 343km/h (185kt), long range cruising speed 293km/h (158kt). Initial rate of climb 1290ft/min. Range with reserves 1520km (820nm).

Weights: PA-44-180 – Empty 1070kg (2360lb), max takeoff 1723kg (3800lb). PA-44-180T – Empty 1116kg (2461lb), max takeoff 1780kg (3925lb).

Dimensions: Wing span 11.77m (38ft 8in), length 8.41m (27ft 7in), height 2.59m (8ft 6in). Wing area 17.1m^2 (183.8sq ft).

Capacity: Typical seating for four.

Production: Total Seminole production through to 1990 amounted to 469, including 87 Turbo Seminoles.

History: The Seminole was developed during the heyday of the GA industry in the late 1970s, only to fall victim to the depressed market form the early 1980s plus the growing reliability and popularity of high performance big singles, and thus was built in only fairly modest numbers.

The contemporary of the Gulfstream GA-7 Cougar and Beechcraft Duchess, the Seminole was conceived in part as a Twin Comanche replacement, aimed at the self flying businessman, plus the twin engine training market. Developed from the mid 1970s, the Seminole is a twin engined development of the PA-28R Archer series, with the Archer's single engine replaced by two counter rotating 135kW (180hp) Lycoming 0-360s, plus a new T-tail and semi tapered wings. The first flight of the prototype was made during May 1976, and production machines, designated PA-44-180, were delivered from May 1978.

The turbocharged PA-44-180T was introduced from 1980. Aside from turbocharged TO-360s, the Turbo Seminole introduced prop deicing and an oxygen system. Just 87 PA-44-180Ts were built when Piper ceased production for the first time in late 1981. Piper reopened the Seminole line in 1988, with 30 non turbocharged PA-44s being built before Piper once more cancelled production, with the last rolling of the line in 1990, due to Piper's parlous financial position at the time.

Once again the PA-28-180 Seminole is back in production, with manufacture restarting in 1995. The Seminole will enjoy the new build four place light twin market all to itself until Socata's Tangara enters production in 1997. Interestingly it is also the only T-tail Piper in production, even though in the late 1970s most Piper aircraft had been modified to feature a T-tail.

Photo: Seminoles are widely used in the twin engine training role. Pictured is a new production PA-44-180. (Piper)

Piper PA-46 Malibu & Malibu Mirage

Country of origin: United States of America

Type: High performance six seat light aircraft

Powerplant: PA-46-310P – One 230kW (310hp) Continental TSIO-520-BE turbocharged and fuel injected flat six piston engine, driving a two blade constant speed Hartzell propeller. PA-46-350P – One 260kW (350hp) Textron Lycoming TIO-540-AE2A.

Performance: PA-46-310P – Max speed 434km/h (234kt), max cruising speed 398km/h (215kt), long range cruising speed 363km/h (196kt). Initial rate of climb 1170ft/min. Service ceiling 25,000ft. Max range at long range cruising speed and altitude with reserves 2880km (1555nm). PA-46-350P – Max speed 430kt (232kt), max cruising speed 417km/h (225kt), normal cruising speed 398kt (215kt) long range cruising speed 311km/h (168kt). Initial rate of climb 1220ft/min. Service ceiling 25,000ft. Range at max cruising speed with reserves 1833km (990nm), range at normal cruising speed 1955km (1055nm), range at long range cruising speed 2685km (1450nm).

Weights: PA-46-310P – Empty 1066kg (2350lb), max takeoff 1860kg (4100lb). PA-46-350P – Empty 1265kg (2790lb), max takeoff 1950kg (4300lb).

Dimensions: PA-46-310P – Wing span 13.11m (43ft 0in), length 8.66m (28ft 5in), height 3.44m (11ft 4in). Wing area 16.3m^2 (175sq ft). PA-46-350P – Same except for length 8.72m (28ft 7in), height 3.51m (11ft 6in).

Capacity: Typical seating for pilot and five passengers.

Production: Approximately 650 PA-46s delivered, comprising 402 PA-46-310Ps and the remainder PA-46-350Ps.

History: The all new Piper Malibu, according to Piper, was the first pressurised cabin class piston single, promised to be one of the first of a new generation of light aircraft introduced from the early 1980s, before recession and oppressive liability laws in the USA strangled the GA industry. Nevertheless, the PA-46 remains in production today, and is currently one of the few single engine six seaters available.

Announced in November 1982, the Malibu was intended to compete against Cessna's pressurised P210 Centurion, plus older light business twins. Designed with the aid of CAD/CAM (Computer Aided Design/ Computer Aided Manufacture), the prototype first flew in 1980. Certification was awarded in September 1983, with production deliveries from that November.

Features of the first production model PA-46-310P included the specially developed turbocharged Continental TSIO-520, a longish span high aspect ratio wing, a relatively roomy cabin with club seating for four behind the pilot, a rear airstair style door, IFR avionics as standard, and cabin pressurisation.

The improved PA-46-350P Malibu Mirage replaced the -310P Malibu in production from October 1988. The major change introduced on the Malibu Mirage was the 260kW (350hp) Textron Lycoming TIO-540-AE2A, while other changes included a new electrical system and revised interior.

In 1996 the Malibu Mirage had a list price of $US750,000. Current production is 40 to 50 aircraft per year.

Photo: A 1994 production Malibu Mirage. Note the high aspect ratio wings, sleek overall appearance and long nose. (Piper)

Piper PA-60 Aerostar

Country of origin: United States of America

Type: Six seat high performance light twin

Powerplants: 600A – Two 215kW (290hp) Lycoming IO-540-K1J5 fuel injected flat six piston engines, driving three blade constant speed Hartzell propellers. PA-60-700P – Two 260kW (350hp) turbocharged and counter rotating TIO-540-U2As.

Performance: 600A – Max cruising speed 408km/h (220kt), long range cruising speed 357km/h (193kt). Initial rate of climb 1800ft/min. Service ceiling 21,200ft. Max range with reserves 2225km (1200nm). PA-60-700P – Max speed 490km/h (264kt), max cruising speed 484km/h (261kt), economical cruising speed 390km/h (211kt). Initial rate of climb 1755ft/min. Service ceiling 25,000ft. Range at max cruising speed 1250km (675nm), at economical cruising speed with max fuel 2150km (1160nm).

Weights: 600A – Empty 1695kg (3757lb), max takeoff 2495kg (5500lb). PA-60-700P – Empty 1940kg (4275lb), max takeoff 2864kg (6315lb).

Dimensions: 600A – Wing span 10.41m (34ft 2in), length 10.61m (34ft 10in), height 3.89m (12ft 1in). Wing area 15.8m^2 (170sq ft). PA-60-700P – Same except for wing span 11.18m (36ft 8in). Wing area 16.6m^2 (178.2sq ft).

Capacity: Typical seating for six.

Production: Total Aerostar production approximately 1010, including 512 built by Piper.

History: The Aerostar – which in its higher powered forms can claim to be the fastest piston twin GA aircraft built – was designed by Ted Smith, who was also responsible for the Aero Commander twins.

Smith's original intention in designing the Aerostar was to develop a family of single and piston twins, twin turboprop and even twin jet powered versions of the same basic aircraft. However the Aerostar appeared in piston twin configuration only. Smith began design work on the Aerostar in late 1964, with a prototype making its first flight two years later in November 1966.

The prototype was powered by 120kW (160hp) Lycoming IO-320s, but the Aerostar was placed into production from 1968 as the Aerostar 600 with 215kW (290hp) IO-540s. The turbocharged Aerostar 601 followed the 600 into production shortly afterwards, while the turbocharged and pressurised 601P went into production in 1972. By this time Butler Aviation had acquired the production rights of the Aerostar in 1970, producing a small number as Butler Aerostars. Smith bought the line back again in 1972, and his company continued to manufacture Aerostars, including the improved 601B with the same span wings as on the 601P, until Piper acquired the Aerostar line in March 1978.

Piper continued production of the 600A, 601B and 601P at Ted Smith's Santa Maria plant, and introduced the 602P with low compression TIO-540-AA1A5 engines. When Piper transferred production to its new Vero Beach, Florida factory in early 1982, only the 602P was in production, and this was redesignated the PA-60-602P. The PA-60-700P was the last Aerostar version, and just 25 were built. In production between 1983 and 1985, the 700P has more powerful engines, a higher max takeoff weight and optional fuel.

Photo: A Ted Smith built Aerostar 601B in a freighter configuration. (Keith Myers)

PZL Mielec M-18 Dromader

Country of origin: Poland

Type: Ag spraying and firefighter aircraft

Powerplant: One 745kW (1000hp) PZL Kalisz (Shvetsov) ASz-62IR supercharged nine cylinder radial piston engine, driving a four blade constant speed propeller.

Performance: M-18 & M-18A (with ag equipment) – Max cruising speed 237km/h (128kt), typical operating speed range 170 to 190km/h (90 to 103kt). Initial rate of climb 1115ft/min. Service ceiling 21,235ft. Max range with no reserves with max fuel and no ag equipment 970km (520nm). M-18A (without ag equipment) – Max speed 256km/h (138kt), cruising speed 205km/h (110kt), typical operating speed 230km/h (124kt). Initial rate of climb 1360ft/min. Service ceiling 21,235ft. Max range with no reserves with max fuel and no ag equipment 970km (520nm).

Weights: M-18A – Empty 2690kg (5930lb), max takeoff 4700kg (10,360lb) but restricted to 4200kg (9230lb) under FAR Pt 23.

Dimensions: M-18A – Wing span 17.70m (58ft 1in), length 9.47m (31ft 3in), height over tail 3.70m (12ft 2in). Wing area 40.0m^2 (430.5sq ft).

Capacity: M-18 seats pilot only, M-18A has second seat for a ground loader or mechanic, M-18AS has second seat with cockpit instrumentation for an instructor. M-18A hopper capacity of 2500 litres (550Imp gal) of liquid or 1350kg (2975lb) of dry chemicals.

Production: Since 1979 over 670 Dromaders of all models have been built, 90% of which have been delivered outside Poland. Production of the single seat M-18 ceased in 1984 after 230 had been built, but it remains available to order.

History: The M-18 Dromader has been one of Poland's most successful aircraft exports to non eastern bloc countries.

PZL Swidnik designed the Dromader in collaboration with Rockwell International in the US during the mid 1970s with the aim of meeting western certification standards from the outset. The first prototype of the basic single seat M-18 first flew on August 27 1976, a second prototype flew that October. Poland awarded certification for the Dromader during September 1978, and series production began the following year. The basic design was of conventional agricultural aircraft configuration, with power supplied by a nine cylinder radial engine, while the outer wing panels are in fact based on the Rockwell Thrush Commander (described separately under Ayres).

Several versions of the M-18 have been built. The basic single seat M-18 was in production for five years until 1984 when it was replaced by the two seat M-18A, but has been available to special order since. The two seat M-18A was developed to allow the carriage of either a mechanic or chemical loader to austere fields. In the meantime PZL Mielec had developed a firebombing derivative which first flew in 1978. The M-18AS development of the M-18 has a second set of instruments for flight instruction. The M-18B has a 5300kg (11,684lb) max takeoff weight, in M-18C is similar but for its 895kW (1200hp) Kalisz K-9 engine.

In the USA, Melex (part owned by PZL Mielec) developed a PT6A turboprop development dubbed the T45 Turbine Dromader. The Turbine Dromader first flew during 1985 and the US FAA issued it a Supplementary Type Certificate in April 1986.

Photo: An M-18A Dromader. (Bill Lines)

PZL Swidnik (Mil) Mi-2 & Kania

Countries of origin: Poland & Russia

Type: Light twin turboshaft utility helicopter

Powerplants: Mi-2 – Two 300kW (400shp) Isotov designed Polish built GTD-350 turboshafts, driving a three blade main rotor and two blade tail rotor. Kania – Two 315kW (720shp) Allison 250-C20B turboshafts, driving a three blade main and two blade tail rotor.

Performance: Mi-2 – Max cruising speed 200km/h (108kt), long range cruising speed 190km/h (102kt). Max rate of climb 885ft/min. Service ceiling 13,125ft. Hovering ceiling in ground effect 6560ft. Range with max payload and reserves 170km (91nm), range with max fuel 440km (237nm), range with optional fuel 580km (313nm). Kania – Max cruising speed 215km/h (116kt), economical cruising speed 190km/h (102kt). Initial rate of climb 1725ft/min. Service ceiling 13,125ft. Hovering ceiling out of ground effect 4510ft/min. Range with standard fuel and reserves 430km (232nm), with max fuel and reserves 800km (432nm). Endurance with auxiliary fuel 4hr.

Weights: Mi-2 – Empty equipped 2402kg (5295lb) in passenger version, or 2372kg (5229lb) in transport version; max takeoff 3550kg (7825lb). Kania – Basic empty 2000kg (4410lb), max takeoff 3550kg (7826lb).

Dimensions: Mi-2 – Main rotor diameter 14.50m (47ft 7in), length overall 17.48m (57ft 4in), fuselage length 11.94m (39ft 2in), height (no tail rotor) 2.70m (8ft 10in). Main rotor disc area 166.4m^2 (1791.1sq ft). Kania – Same except for fuselage length 12.03m (29ft 6in).

Capacity: Mi-2 – Two pilots or one pilot and passenger on flightdeck, and main cabin seating for seven. Ambulance configurations can accommodate four stretchers and one medical attendant or two stretchers and two attendants. Kania – Pilot and eight passengers in passenger configuration, pilot and five passengers in corporate configuration. Two stretchers one seated patient and two medical attendants in ambulance configuration. Ag version capacity 1000kg (2205lb) of chemicals.

Production: More than 5500 mainly military Mi-2s built since 1965. Over 10 Kanias have been built thus far.

History: Poland's most massed produced helicopter was originally developed in Russia by Mil, and in its Allison powered Kania (Kitty Hawk) version, has achieved US certification.

Mil originally designed the light utility Mi-2 in Russia during the early 1960s, resulting in a first flight in September 1961. In January 1964 an agreement between the USSR and Poland transferred development and production to the latter country, which commenced in 1965. The Mi-2 has evolved since that time and remains in low rate production today. The main civil variant is simply designated Mi-2, Swidnik has also developed a diverse number of military variants.

The Kania is a substantial upgrade of the basic Mi-2, and features Allison 250-C20B turboshafts, western avionics, composite main and tail rotor blades, and has won US FAR Pt 29 certification. Developed in co-operation with Allison, the Kania first flew on June 3 1979, and US certification was granted in February 1986. The Kania has never entered full scale production but remains on offer, both as new build aircraft and upgrades of existing Mi-2s.

Photo: The Allison 250 powered Kania. (PZL Swidnik)

PZL Swidnik W-3 Sokol

Country of origin: Poland

Type: Mid size twin engine utility helicopter

Powerplants: Two 670kW (900shp) takeoff rated WSK-PZL Rzeszów PZL-10W turboshafts, driving a four blade main rotor and three blade tail rotor.

Performance: Max cruising speed 250km/h (135kt), economical cruising speed 240km/h (130kt). Initial rate of climb 1673ft/min. Hovering ceiling (at max takeoff weight) out of ground effect 6225ft. Service ceiling 19,680ft. Max range with no reserves at economical cruising speed 760km (410nm).

Weights: W-3A – Operating empty 3850kg (8488lb), max takeoff 6400kg (14,110lb).

Dimensions: Main rotor diameter 15.70m (51ft 6in), length overall 18.79m (61ft 8in), fuselage length 14.40m (47ft 3in), height overall 5.14m (16ft 10in), height to top of rotor mast 4.20m (13ft 9in). Main rotor disc area 193.6m^2 (2034sq ft).

Capacity: Two pilots or pilot and flight engineer or passenger on flightdeck. Main cabin seating for 12 in passenger configuration, or three medical attendants and eight rescued survivors in SAR Anaconda version, or four stretchers and medical attendant in ambulance configuration, one stretcher and medical attendants in critical care EMS version, or five/six passengers in executive configuration. Can carry a 2100kg (4630lb) sling load.

Production: Approximately 90 Sokols of all models have been built, including for Polish military orders.

History: The multi purpose W-3 Sokol, or Falcon, is the first helicopter to be fully designed and built in Poland, and is PZL Swidnik's most promising sales prospect in the near to medium future.

Developed during the mid 1970s, the Sokol made its first flight on November 16 1979, and has the distinction of being certificated in Poland, Russia, the US and Germany. Following a fairly protracted development program, low rate production of the Sokol commenced during 1985. Initial sales of the general purpose Sokol were within Poland and in the eastern block, before the collapse of communism allowed PZL Swidnik to broaden its sales base. To do this PZL Swidnik developed the improved W-3A Sokol aimed at achieving western certification. Certification to US FAR Pt 29 standards was granted in May 1993, while German certification was granted in December that year.

So far sales of the Sokol to operators either in the east or west have been slow, largely due to a recessed helicopter industry worldwide, but one has been sold to German police, while Swidnik has leased 18 Sokols for use as firefighters in Spain. Others are flying in Myanmar, Nigeria and South Korea.

The Sokol is of conventional design and construction, with two PZL-10W turboshafts, which are based on the Russian designed TVD-10B turboprops that power the Polish built An-28. Composites are used in the tail and main rotor blades.

The Sokol is offered in a number of variants and is capable of performing a typical range of helicopter missions, including passenger transport, VIP, cargo, EMS, medevac, firefighting and search and rescue (the W-3 RM Anaconda).

Photo: A German Police W-3A Sokol. (Grzegorz Holdanowicz)

PZL Swidnik SW-4

Country of origin: Poland

Type: Light utility helicopter

Powerplants: One 335kW (450shp) Allison 250-C20R/2 turboshaft driving a three blade main rotor and two blade tail rotor. Option of one 460kW (615shp) Pratt & Whitney Canada PW200/9 turboshaft.

Performance: Allison engine – Max speed 245km/h (132kt), max cruising speed at 70% power 240km/h (130kt). Max initial rate of climb 1965ft/min. Service ceiling 19,680ft. Hovering ceiling in ground effect 11,480ft, out of ground effect 9515ft. Max range with standard fuel and reserves 900km (485nm). Endurance 5hr 30min.

Weights: Empty 850kg (1874lb), max takeoff (internal load) 1600kg (3527lb), max takeoff with sling load 1800kg (3968lb).

Dimensions: Main rotor disc diameter 9.00m (29ft 6in), length overall rotors turning 10.55m (34ft 8in), fuselage length 8.24m (27ft 1in), height overall 2.94m (9ft 8in). Main rotor disc area 63.6m^2 (684.8sq ft).

Capacity: Standard seating for four or five (including pilot). In medevac configuration accommodation for one stretcher patient and two medical attendants. Max sling load 750kg (1655lb).

Production: One non flying and one flying prototype built by late 1996. Production future unclear at that time.

History: PZL Swidnik's SW-4 was the first new Eastern European aircraft to fly since the collapse of communism in 1989, although the origins of this utility helicopter date back to the early 1980s.

Swidnik began development of a new four/five place light utility helicopter in 1981. This original SW-4 was to have been powered by a 300kW (400shp) PZL Rzeszow GTD-350 turboshaft and was built in mock-up form. It would have had a top speed of 240km/h (130kt) and a max range with auxiliary fuel of 900km (485nm).

The collapse of the Iron Curtain allowed Swidnik to substantially redesign the SW-4, based around the Allison 250 turboshaft. Aside from the powerplant, design changes included a more streamlined fuselage and revised tail and tailboom.

The first prototype, a non flying ground test aircraft, was rolled out in December 1994. Three flying prototypes are scheduled to be built, the first of which was completed in 1996, allowing a first flight on October 26 that year.

PZL Swidnik aims to attain US FAA FAR Part 27 certification for the SW-4, but late in 1996 the company was seeking Polish government funding to achieve this. The SW-4 program has been about one fifth government funded.

Once the SW-4 is certificated and in production PZL Swidnik aims to offer a Pratt & Whitney Canada PW200 powered variant. A twin engine model is also planned to allow the helicopter to meet forthcoming European regulations which will restrict single engine helicopter operations under some conditions.

The SW-4 is expected to be able to fulfil a range of utility missions ranging from executive transport to medevac and police roles. Border patrol and military pilot training are other planned missions.

The helicopter features Bendix King avionics, including an optional IFR instrument package.

Photo: The non flying SW-4 prototype. The flying SW-4 prototype completed its much delayed maiden flight in October 1996.

PZL Warszawa-Okecie PZL-104 Wilga

Country of origin: Poland

Type: Four seat light utility aircraft

Powerplant: 35A – One 195kW (260hp) PZL AI-14RA nine cylinder radial piston engine, driving a two blade constant speed propeller.

Performance: 35A – Max speed 194km/h (105kt), cruising speed at 75% power 157km/h (85kt). Initial rate of climb 905ft/min. Service ceiling 13,250ft. Range with max fuel and reserves 510km (275nm).

Weights: 35A – Empty equipped 870kg (1918lb), max takeoff 1300kg (2866lb).

Dimensions: 35A – Wing span 11.12m (36ft 6in), length 8.10m (26ft 7in), height 2.96m (9ft 9in). Wing area 15.5m^2 (166.8sq ft).

Capacity: Typical seating for four including pilot when configured for passengers. Rear two seats can be replaced with fuel tank. In ambulance configuration accommodates two stretchers and medical attendants.

Production: More than 950 Wilgas of all models built since the mid 1960s. Many hundred were built for east European and Russian markets, but also for customers in various western countries.

History: With almost 1000 built since the late 1960s, the rugged STOL PZL-104 Wilga has been one of Poland's most successful light aircraft exports with sales to both east and west markets.

Poland's Light Aircraft Science and Production Centre in Warsaw began development of the Wilga in the early 1960s as a replacement for the general purpose Czechoslovak L-60 Brigadyr utility. The prototype Wilga 1 was powered by a 135kW (180hp) Narkiewicz WN-6B radial and flew for the first time on April 24 1962. A fairly extensive redesign of the basic aircraft followed, and a modified Wilga 2 with a new fuselage and tail and a 145kW (195hp) WN-6RB engine flew in August 1963. That December the 170kW (225hp) Continental 0-470 powered Wilga C or (Wilga 32) flew and Lipnur Gelatnik later built 39 in Indonesia.

Poland's first production Wilgas were the 3A four seat utility and 3S ambulance, these aircraft introducing the definitive 195kW (260hp) Ivchenko designed AI-14 radial. It was not long though until PZL reconfigured the Wilga's cabin and landing gear, resulting in the definitive production version, the Wilga 35. The prototype Wilga 35 first flew on July 28 1967.

The Wilga 35 remains in production in 1996 basically unchanged, and several variants have been offered, while the Wilga 80 is identical to the 35 other than its further rear positioned carburettor air intake. The Wilga 35A and 80A are designed for flying club operations and are fitted with a hook for glider towing, the 35H and 80H are float equipped, the 35P is usually fitted with four seats, the 35R and 80R are agricultural aircraft fitted with a 270kg (595lb) under fuselage chemical hopper and spray bars, and the 35P is an ambulance variant capable of carrying two stretchers.

In the United States, PZL's subsidiary Melex has worked on the 225kW (300hp) Teledyne Continental IO-550 flat six powered Wilga 80-550. The 80-550 flew in 1992, and Melex will supply kits to PZL for new build 80-550s and convert existing 80s to the new standard. The 80-550 Blue Shield is an electronic surveillance development.

Photo: Unusual in appearance, the Polish Wilga (here a Wilga 80) has been designed with function ahead of form. (Robert Wiseman)

PZL Warszawa-Okecie PZL-110 Koliber

Country of origin: Poland

Type: Four seat light aircraft

Powerplant: Series I/II – One 95kW (125hp) PZL-F (Franklin) flat four piston engine, driving a two blade ground adjustable pitch propeller. 150/150A – One 110kW (150hp) Textron Lycoming O-320-E2A flat four piston engine, driving a two blade fixed pitch Sensenich prop.

Performance: Series I – Max speed 195km/h (105kt), max cruising speed 170km/h (92kt). Initial rate of climb 560ft/min. Service ceiling 11,480ft. Range with max fuel 730km (395nm). 150A – Max cruising speed 190km/h (102kt), economical cruising speed 170km/h (92kt). Initial rate of climb 665ft/min. Service ceiling 12,140ft. Range with max fuel 830km (448nm).

Weights: Series I – Empty equipped 516kg (1137lb), max takeoff 850kg (1874lb). 150A – Empty 548kg (1208lb), max takeoff 850kg (1874lb).

Dimensions: 150/150A – Wing span 9.75m (32ft 0in), length 7.37m (24ft 2in), height 2.80m (9ft 2in). Wing area 12.7m^2 (136.5sq ft).

Capacity: Typical seating for four, or seating for two in flight training role.

Production: Total Franklin powered Series I, II and III production approximately 40 units. Lycoming powered Koliber 150 and 150A currently in production.

History: The Koliber (Humming bird) is a licence built development of one of Europe's most successful two/four seat light aircraft families, the Socata Rallye.

The Rallye was still in production when PZL Warszawa-Okecie acquired a licence to build and develop the Rallye 100ST in Poland. The prototype Koliber was powered by a 87kW (116hp) PZL-F (Franklin) four cylinder engine (Poland having previously purchased the design and production rights to Franklin engines) and first flew on April 18 1978. Subsequent production aircraft featured the 86kW (116hp) engine, later aircraft a more powerful 95kW (125hp) Franklin engine. Franklin powered versions of the Koliber were the Series I, the initial production model of which just 10 were built and first flight occurred in May 1979; the Series II was developed for Polish aero clubs and was capable of limited aerobatics and 25 were built; and the improved Series III, of which 45 were built.

Current Koliber production is of the Textron Lycoming O-320 powered 150, and the Koliber 150A, which was developed for export. The Koliber 150A (Koliber II in the USA) was granted US FAA FAR Part 23 certification in early 1994. According to the type's US and Asia Pacific distributor Cadmus, this was the first time that a four place fixed undercarriage light aircraft had been fully certificated in the USA in over a decade. The first Koliber 150A delivery was made to a US customer in mid 1994, while Koliber 150s have been delivered to a number of European countries.

The PZL-111 Koliber 235 is a more powerful, higher performance development, powered by a 175kW (235hp) Textron Lycoming O-540. It first flew in September 1995.

Photo: The Koliber is a development of the 'light series' Rallye airframe. (PZL Warszawa-Okecie)

Raytheon Hawker 800 & BAe 125-700

Countries of origin: United Kingdom and USA

Type: Twin turbofan executive jet

Powerplants: 700 – Two 16.6kN (3700lb) Garrett TFE731-3-RH turbofans. 800XP – Two 20.7kN (4660lb) AlliedSignal TFE731-5BR-1Hs.

Performance: 700 – Max cruising speed 808km/h (436kt), economical cruising speed 723km/h (390kt). Service ceiling 41,000ft. Range with max fuel, payload and IFR reserves 4725km (2550nm). 800XP – Max speed and cruising speed 845km/h (456kt), economical cruising speed 740km/h (400kt). Max initial rate of climb 3100ft/min. Service ceiling 43,000ft. Range with max payload 4780km (2580nm), range with max fuel and VFR reserves 5230km (2825nm).

Weights: 700 – Empty 5825kg (12,845lb), max takeoff 11,567kg (25,500lb). 800XP – Empty 7075kg (15,600lb), max takeoff 12,700kg (28,000lb).

Dimensions: 700 – Wing span 14.33m (47ft 0in), length 15.46m (50ft 9in), height 5.36m (17ft 7in). Wing area 32.8m^2 (353.0sq ft). 800XP – Wing span 15.66m (51ft 5in), length 15.60m (51ft 2in), height 5.36m (17ft 7in). Wing area 34.8m^2 (374.0sq ft).

Capacity: Flightcrew of two. Typical seating for eight in corporate layout, or max seating for 14.

Production: 215 125-700s built between 1976 and 1984, when replaced by 125-800, now Hawker 800, of which sales exceed 250. Total 125 series production of over 850 aircraft including military versions.

History: The 125-700 and Hawker 800 are two more recent versions of the world's longest running corporate jet production program.

The 125-700 and Hawker 800 are direct developments of the DH.125, (later the HS.125) which first flew in August 1962. This aircraft was developed into a number of variants through to the HS.125-600, all of which are powered by the Rolls-Royce Viper turbojet and are described separately under Hawker Siddeley.

The introduction of the BAe 125-700 in 1976 brought with it significant performance and fuel economy benefits as it incorporated Garrett TFE731 turbofans (which use less fuel in cruise flight than some of the earlier 125's Vipers do at idle!). Other detail changes introduced on the 700 were aimed at passenger comfort and fuel economy. The first 125-700 flew for the first time on June 19 1976, and the model remained in production until it was replaced by the 125-800 in 1984.

The 125-800 first flew on May 26 1983 and it introduced a number of improvements. Aerodynamic changes included a reprofiled nose and windscreen, extended fin leading edge, and greater span wing which decreased drag and increased both lift and fuel capacity. Range was boosted further by a larger ventral fuel tank. More powerful TFE731s were incorporated to boost field performance, while a redesigned interior made more efficient use of the space available. The 800 was also the first corporate jet to feature an EFIS cockpit. The 800A is specifically designed for the US market, the 800B for non US markets. The 800XP (Extended Performance) has improved engines giving better climb and cruise performance, and is the current production model.

The 125-800 became the Hawker 800 from mid 1993 when Raytheon purchased BAe's Corporate Jets division. From 1997 all Hawker production will take place in Wichita in the USA.

Photo: A Hawker 800XP. (Raytheon)

Raytheon Hawker 1000

Countries of origin: United Kingdom and USA

Type: Long range corporate jet

Powerplants: Two 23.1kN (5200lb) Pratt & Whitney Canada PW305 turbofans.

Performance: Max cruising speed 867km/h (468kt), economical cruising speed 745km/h (402kt). Service ceiling 43,000ft. Range with max payload and VFR reserves 5750km (3105nm), range with max fuel and VFR reserves 6205km (3350nm).

Weights: Empty 7810kg (17,220lb), max takeoff 14,060kg (31,000lb).

Dimensions: Wing span 15.66m (51ft 4in), length 16.42m (53ft 10in), height 5.21m (17ft 1in). Wing area 34.8m^2 (374.0sq ft).

Capacity: Flightcrew of two. Standard main cabin seating for eight comprising four single club seats at the front of the cabin, a three seat couch and a single seat. Max seating for 15.

Production: Over 50 ordered at late 1996.

History: The Hawker 1000 is the latest and largest member of the DH/HS/BAe 125/Hawker 800 series of corporate jets.

The Hawker 1000 is based on the smaller Hawker 800, and at one stage the two types were in production side by side in the famous de Havilland plant in Hatfield. The 1000 differs from the 800 in a number of respects though, the most obvious being the stretched fuselage. The 1000 is identifiable via its seven main cabin windows per side, whereas the 800 has six, and the 0.84m (2ft 9in) stretch (achieved by small fuselage plugs in front of and behind the wing) allowing an increase in max seating to 15. However as it is optimised for long range intercontinental work, the typical Hawker 1000 configuration actually seats one less than the smaller Hawker 800.

Other important changes include the Pratt & Whitney Canada PW305 turbofans (in place of the AlliedSignal TFE731 on the Hawker 800), extra fuel in the extended forward wing fairing, new lightweight systems, revised and more efficient cabin interior with increased headroom, EFIS cockpit and certification to the latest US FAA FAR and European JAA JAR requirements.

British Aerospace launched the BAe 1000 program in October 1989. The first BAe 1000 development aircraft first flew on June 16 1990, with a second following on November 26 that year. These two were followed by the first production aircraft which participated in an 800 hour flight test development program, culminating in the type being granted certification on October 21 1991 in the UK (FAA certification followed on October 31 1991). The first production aircraft was delivered in December 1991.

As is the case with the BAe 125-800, the BAe 1000 became the Hawker 1000 from mid 1993 when Raytheon purchased British Aerospace's Corporate Jets division. Production began to be transferred to the USA in 1995, and was due to be completed in 1997. Raytheon built a new 41,800m^2 plant at Wichita especially for Hawker 800 and Hawker 100 production.

Photo: Although it looks similar to its predecessors, the Hawker 1000 is recognisable by its stretched fuselage and larger engine nacelles. (Raytheon)

Raytheon Hawker Horizon

Country of origin: United States of America

Type: Large midsize corporate jet

Powerplants: Two 29.3kN (6575lb) Pratt & Whitney Canada PW308A turbofans.

Performance: Max cruising Mach 0.84, normal cruising speed Mach 0.8. Service ceiling 45,000ft. Range at Mach 0.8 cruising speed 6100km (3295nm), range at Mach 0.82 cruising speed 5730km (3095nm).

Weights: Max takeoff 16,300kg (35,940lb).

Dimensions: Wing span 18.91m (62ft 1in), length overall 19.98m (65ft 7in).

Capacity: Flightcrew of two. Typical main cabin layout will seat eight, with a toilet in the aft fuselage. Fuselage diameter 2.13m (7ft) with standup headroom.

Production: Certification and first deliveries planned for the second quarter of 2001. Launched in late 1996 with a $US14.5m pricetag.

History: Raytheon's Hawker Horizon is an all new 'super midsize' corporate jet being developed to replace the Hawker 1000.

Design work on what became the Horizon was already underway when Raytheon Corporate Jets and Beech merged in early 1995. The new design, initially labelled the PD 376, was one of three projects the new Raytheon Aircraft was working on, along with what became the Premier I. Raytheon worked closely with potential customers for the replacement Hawker 1000 in the design definition stage, and their input directly influenced the direction of the new aircraft. For a time this initial design was designated the Model 4000.

Raytheon formally announced the Hawker Horizon immediately prior to the National Business Aircraft Association's annual convention in November 1996. The development schedule announced at that time will see the Horizon make its first flight in late 1999, followed by certification and first deliveries in the second quarter of 2001.

One of Raytheon's design philosophies in developing the Horizon is to combine the earlier Hawkers' popular characteristics with advanced technologies. Experienced Hawker designers form the core of the Horizon's design team and the aircraft has been deliberately designed to look and feel like a Hawker (the most obvious example of this is the nose).

Compared to the Hawker 1000 the Horizon will have a wider, 2.13m (7ft), slightly longer fuselage with a flat floor and stand up headroom and a two tonne heavier max takeoff weight. The Horizon will feature an all composite fuselage which will be manufactured using the automated fibre placement technology developed for the Premier I. Power will be from two digitally controlled Pratt & Whitney Canada PW308A turbofans. P&WC is a risk sharing partner in the program, as is avionics integrator Honeywell (the Horizon will feature Honeywell's Primus Epic system with five flat panel colour LCDs). The Horizon's new supercritical wing will pass beneath the fuselage.

Photo: The Raytheon Hawker Horizon is due to make its first flight in late 1999. The Horizon will be larger and faster than the Hawker 1000 which it will replace. (Raytheon)

Raytheon Beechjet 400

Country of origin: United States of America

Type: Light corporate transport

Powerplants: Two 12.9kN (2900lb) Pratt & Whitney Canada JT15D-5 turbofans.

Performance: 400 – Max speed 837km/h (452kt), cruising speed 748km/h (404kt). Range with four pax, max fuel and reserves 3572km (1929nm). 400A – Max speed 865km/h (467kt), cruising speed 834km/h (450kt), long range cruising speed 732km/h (395kt). Range with four pax, max fuel and reserves 3537km (1909nm).

Weights: 400 – Basic empty 4225kg (9315lb), max takeoff 7158kg (15,780lb). 400A – Operating empty (including crew) 4817kg (10,620lb), max takeoff 7303kg (16,100lb).

Dimensions: Wing span 13.25m (43ft 6in), length 14.75m (48ft 5in), height 4.19m (13ft 9in). Wing area 22.4m^2 (241.4sq ft).

Capacity: Flightcrew of one or two pilots, with standard passenger arrangement for eight in main cabin (provision for a ninth passenger in toilet compartment optional).

Production: Total Beechjet 400 production 64, with approximately 150 400As delivered by late 1996.

History: The little Beechjet traces its origins back to the unsuccessful Mitsubishi Diamond 2 bizjet, the rights of which were acquired by Beechcraft in the mid 1980s.

The original Mitsubishi MU-300 Diamond 1 flew for the first time in August 1978, powered by two 11.1kN (2500lb) P&WC JT15D-4 turbofans. The subsequent Diamond 2 flew on June 20 1984, with the first production aircraft flying in January 1985. Only 11 Diamond 2s were built before Beech purchased the rights, resulting in the Model 400 Beechjet. Beech re-engined the Diamond 2 with the current P&WC JT15D-5 turbofans, developed a new interior, and incorporated a number of other minor refinements. Deliveries of the Beechjet began in June 1986, with low rate production continuing until that model was replaced by the Model 400A.

The new 400A incorporated a number of improvements over its predecessor, its increased weights and operating ceiling conveying a number of performance improvements. Repositioning the rear fuselage fuel tank increased the cabin volume, while the flightdeck features Collins Pro Line IV EFIS.

The Beechjet 400A also serves as the basis for the military T-1 Jayhawk tanker and transport trainer, for which the USAF has a requirement for 211. The Japan Air Self Defence Force has also taken delivery of three T-400 trainers with options on three more. This large military requirement will no doubt bring down the 400A's unit cost considerably.

Larger than the entry level CitationJet, Raytheon is promoting the Beechjet as having operating economics in the class of comparable sized turboprops, with the advantages of jet speed.

Photo: A significant feature of the Beechjet is its relatively large cabin for a small jet of this class. (Raytheon)

Raytheon Premier I

Country of origin: United States of America

Type: Light corporate jet

Powerplants: Two 10.2kN (2300lb) Williams-Rolls FJ44-2A turbofans.

Performance: Max cruising speed 853km/h (461kt). Max certificated operating altitude 41,000ft. Takeoff length at MTOW at S/L less than 915m (3000ft). Max range at long range cruising speed with reserves 2780km (1500nm).

Weights: Empty and max takeoff weights not published at late 1996.

Dimensions: Wing span 13.56m (44ft 6in), length overall 13.81m (45ft 4in), height 4.66m (15ft 4in).

Capacity: One or two pilots on flightdeck. Main cabin seats six in standard configuration with four seats in a club arrangement and two seats behind them. Toilet in rear fuselage. Baggage compartments in nose and tail.

Production: First deliveries planned for late 1998. Launched in mid 1995 with a $US3.9m pricetag. Initial production of 40 aircraft per year planned.

History: The Premier I is the first all new product of the Raytheon Aircraft Beech/Hawker combine, and is a new entry level corporate jet designed to compete head on with Cessna's highly successful CitationJet.

Design work on the Premier I began in early 1994 under the designation PD374. Development go-ahead was authorised in early 1995, and initial details of the new jet were released in mid 1995. Raytheon publicly launched the Premier I at the NBAA (National Business Aircraft Association) convention in Las Vegas in September 1995, where a full size cabin mock-up was on display.

Construction of the first Premier I began in late 1996, at which time Raytheon anticipated a first flight in the third quarter of 1997, with certification and first deliveries planned for late 1998.

Design features of the Premier I include its composite carbonfibre/epoxy honeycomb fuselage, swept wings, T-tail and two Williams-Rolls FJ44 turbofans.

The composite fuselage is an important feature for a number of reasons. Firstly, advanced production techniques (using computer controlled automated machines) means a Premier I fuselage can be constructed in just one day, whereas a conventional airframe would require one to two weeks to complete. The composite construction also allows greater (approx 13%) internal cabin space compared with a conventional construction fuselage of the same external dimensions.

The Premier I will be certificated for single pilot operations. The flightdeck will feature the new Collins Pro Line 21 EFIS avionics suite with two 20 x 25cm (8 x 10in) flat panel LCDs.

Raytheon intends that the Premier I forms the basis of a new family of business jets. The stretched Premier II and Premier III are due to be launched in 1997 and 1998 respectively.

Photo: The Raytheon Premier I is due to make its first flight in the third quarter of 1997. Raytheon has been able to draw upon its experience with the Starship 2000 in developing the composite fuselage new light corporate jet. (Raytheon)

Republic RC-3 Seabee

Country of origin: United States of America

Type: Four seat amphibious light aircraft

Powerplant: One 160kW (215hp) Franklin 6A8-215-B8F six cylinder inline piston engine, driving a two blade propeller.

Performance: Max speed 193km/h (104kt), max cruising speed 166km/h (90kt). Initial rate of climb 700ft/min. Service ceiling 12,000ft. Range 900km (485nm).

Weights: Empty 885kg (1950lb), max takeoff 1360kg (3000lb).

Dimensions: Wing span 11.48m (37ft 8in), length 8.51m (27ft 11in), height 2.92m (9ft 7in). Wing area 18.2m^2 (196sq ft).

Capacity: Typical seating for four.

Production: Total Seabee production of 1060 between 1946 and 1947.

History: One of the few light amphibians to be produced in any sort of numbers, the Seabee was built by the same company that was responsible for the legendary World War 2 P-47 Thunderbolt fighter.

The Seabee was conceived during the latter stages of World War 2 when Republic began to look beyond its massive wartime contracts to a basis for sustained peacetime production. The original concept was one that was quite popular during the 1940s – to provide a four seat light aircraft that would cost little more to purchase and operate than a family car. To an extent Republic succeeded in its aims, more than 1000 Seabees were built in just one year of production.

The original prototype Seabee was designated the RC-1 (Republic Commercial design number one) and first appeared during 1944. The RC-1 was a three seat design powered by a 130kW (175hp) six cylinder Franklin 6ALG-365 piston engine. Successfully flown for the first time during November 1944, the RC-1 was dubbed for a time the Thunderbolt Amphibian. It was of conventional all metal construction.

A comprehensive testing and development program ensued, during which the RC-1 was punishingly tested. One test that exhibited that the design encompassed Republic's aircraft's legendary abilities to absorb punishment involved deliberating making a wheels-up landing on a concrete runway. The RC-1 passed with flying colours, the only damage being a small metal shaving from the keel.

While the RC-1's structural integrity was beyond dispute, Republic nevertheless decided to redesign the RC-1, mainly to significantly reduce production and acquisition costs. What evolved was the RC-3 Seabee, a four seater powered by a 160kW (215hp) Franklin 6A8-215-B8F piston engine. Aside from the increased seating capacity, the Seabee differed from the RC-1 in being lighter, built with far fewer components (450 compared with 1800 in the RC-1), required 25% less tooling to manufacture and, most importantly, had an acquisition cost half that of what the RC-1's would have been.

Seabee production began in mid 1946, but lasted only until October 1947, when ironically Republic decided to concentrate on its once more lucrative military business, despite healthy Seabee sales.

The decision to cease Seabee production also terminated development plans for twin engined and landplane developments.

Photo: This photograph shows to good effect the Seabee's stepped hull, outrigger floats and undercarriage. (Randall Krebbs)

Robin DR 400

Country of origin: France

Type: Four/five seat light aircraft

Powerplant: DR 400/120 Dauphin – One 84kW (112hp) (Textron) Lycoming O-235-L2A flat four, driving a two blade fixed pitch propeller. DR 400/180 – One 135kW (180hp) Textron Lycoming O-360-A.

Performance: DR 400/120 – Max speed 241km/h (130kt), max cruising speed 215km/h (116kt). Initial rate of climb 600ft/min. Service ceiling 12,000ft. Range with standard fuel and no reserves at max cruising speed 860km (465nm). DR 400/180 – Max speed 278km/h (150kt), max cruising speed 260km/h (140kt), economical cruising speed 245km/h (132kt). Initial rate of climb 825ft/min. Service ceiling 15,475ft. Range at economical cruising speed 1450km (783nm).

Weights: DR 400/120 – Empty equipped 535kg (1180lb), max takeoff 900kg (1985lb). DR 400/180 – Empty equipped 600kg (1320lb), max takeoff 1100kg (2425lb).

Dimensions: Wing span 8.72m (28ft 7in), length 6.96m (22ft 10in), height 2.23m (7ft 3in). Wing area 13.6m^2 (146.39sq ft).

Capacity: DR 400/120 seats two adults and two children, most other DR 400 models typically seat four adults.

Production: Over 1200 DR 400s of all variants built.

History: The Robin DR 400 series of light aircraft owes its origins to the original Jodel series of wooden construction aircraft.

Avions Pierre Robin was formed by Pierre Robin and the principle designer of Jodel Aircraft, Jean Delemontez, in October 1957 as Centre Est Aeronautique. The company's initial production was of developments of the basic Jodel series of tail draggers, and it was these aircraft that evolved into the DR 400 series. Initial production was of the DR 100 and the DR 1050/1051, while the DR 220, DR 221 and DR 250 featured the Jodel's basic wing with a four seat fuselage. The final link between the Jodels and the DR 400 were the DR 253 and DR 300 series, tricycle developments of the DR 220 series.

First flight of the DR 400 occurred during June 1972, both a DR 400/125 and a DR 400/180 taking flight that month.

Since that time a number of developments have been offered. The least powerful version is the DR 400/120, and it remains in production today as the DR 400/120 Dauphin 2+2. Powered by a 84kW (112hp) O-235, the DR 400/210 is really a two seater, although it can seat two children on a rear bench seat. A more powerful version of the Dauphin, the DR 400/140 Dauphin is powered by a 120kW (160hp) O-320 and is a full four seater. The four seat DR 400/160 Chevalier meanwhile also features a 120kW (160hp) Lycoming O-320 and seats four. It first flew in June 1972, and with improvements became the DR 400/160 Major from 1980. It differs from the DR 400/140 in having a different prop, fuel capacity and slightly different wing.

The four/five seat DR 400/180 Regent and DR 400 Remo 180R are powered by the 135kW (180hp) (Textron) Lycoming O-360, the Remo being optimised for glider towing. Also optimised for glider tug work is the DR 400/200R Remo 200, the most powerful DR 400 model (powered by a 150kW/200hp IO-360, driving a constant speed prop). The three blade prop, Teledyne Continental IO-240 powered DR 400/125i flew in prototype form in 1995.

Photo: The DR 400/125i. (Paul Merritt)

Robin HR 200 & R 2000 Alpha series

Country of origin: France

Type: Two seat aerobatic light aircraft

Powerplant: HR 200 Club – One 80kW (108hp) Lycoming O-235-C2A flat four piston engine, driving a two blade fixed pitch propeller. R 2160 Alpha Sport – One 120kW (160hp) Lycoming O-320-D.

Performance: HR 200 – Max speed 230km/h (124kt), max cruising speed 215km/h (116kt). Initial rate of climb 670ft/min. Service ceiling 13,000ft. Range with max fuel 1078km (582nm). 2160 – Max speed 257km/h (138kt), max cruising speed 242km/h (130kt), cruising speed 234km/h (126kt). Initial rate of climb 1025ft/min. Service ceiling 15,000ft. Range with max fuel 795km (430nm).

Weights: HR 200 – Empty 500kg (1100lb), max takeoff 760kg (1670lb). 2160 – Empty 550kg (1213lb), max takeoff 800kg (1765lb).

Dimensions: HR 200 – Wing span 8.40m (27ft 7in), length 6.68m (21ft 11in), height 2.18m (7ft 2in). Wing area 12.6m^2 (135.6sq ft). 2160 – Wing span 8.33m (27ft 4in), length 7.10m (23ft 4in), height 2.14m (7ft 0in). Wing area 13.0m^2 (140sq ft).

Capacity: Typical seating for two, side by side.

Production: Approx 150 200s and 120 R 2000s built.

History: This series of light two seat aerobatic aircraft was designed during the 1970s specifically for flying school use, and has been developed in two major variants, both of which are back in production.

The original HR 200 was the second all metal aircraft designed for Robin by Christophe Heintz (previous Robins had been designed by Jean Delemontez, who was also responsible for the earlier Jodel series). It first flew on July 19 1971 powered by a 80kW (108hp) O-235, the first production aircraft flew in April 1973. Three initial versions were built, the 80kW (108hp) powered Club or HR 200/100, the more powerful Acrobin 125 or HR 200/125 (with a 95kW/125hp O-235) and the Acrobin 160 or HR 200/160 (with a 120kW/160hp IO-320). The more powerful Acrobins were developed to exploit the full aerobatic potential of the basic HR 200 airframe. The HR 200 remained in production until the late 1970s, and is once again on offer. Robin has now recommenced production of the HR 200/120 as the Robin 200, with power supplied by a 88kW (118hp) Textron Lycoming O-235-L2A.

The R 2000 Alpha series meanwhile was a redevelopment of the HR 200. The HR 200's basic fuselage was retained, but changes included an all new wing and a enlarged rudder and vertical tail to improve spinning characteristics. The prototype R 2000 was powered by a 135kW (160hp) IO-320 and flew for the first time on January 15 1976. Deliveries of production aircraft began in 1977.

Three developments of the R 2000 series were built, the R 2100, the R 2112 and R 2160 Alpha Sport, with the main differences between the three being the powerplant fitted. The R 2100 is powered by a 80kW (108hp) O-235, the R 2112 has a 84kW (112hp) O-235, and the R 2160 has a 120kW (160hp) O-320. Of the three, the R 2160 Alpha Sport has been the most popular, and has seen fairly widespread use as a basic and aerobatic trainer. Production of the R 2000 series (by Robin factories in France and Canada) originally ceased in 1983, however Robin restarted production of the R 2160 in 1994.

Photo: An R 2160 Alpha Sport, the flagship of the Robin 2000 series. Note large strake. (Bill Lines)

Robin R 3000

Country of origin: France

Type: Two/four seat light aircraft

Powerplant: R 3000/100 – One 87kW (116hp) Lycoming O-235 flat four piston engine, driving a two blade fixed pitch propeller. R 3000/160 – One 135kW (180hp) Lycoming O-320-A flat four.

Performance: R 3000/100 – Max speed 230km/h (124kt), max cruising speed 210km/h (113kt), normal cruising speed 200km/h (108kt). Initial rate of climb 590ft/min. Service ceiling 13,000ft. Range with standard fuel and no reserves 1120km (605nm), with optional fuel 1420km (767nm). R 3000/160 – Max speed 270km/h (146kt), max cruising speed 255km/h (138kt), economical cruising speed 238km/h (128kt). Initial rate of climb 875ft/min. Service ceiling 15,000ft. Range with standard fuel at max cruising speed 1490km (804nm), at economical cruising speed 1610km (868nm).

Weights: R 3000/100 – Empty 580kg (1280lb), max takeoff 900kg (1985lb). R 3000/160 – Empty 650kg (1433lb), max takeoff 1150kg (2535lb).

Dimensions: Wing span 9.81m (32ft 2in), length 7.51m (24ft 8in), height 2.66m (8ft 9in). Wing area 14.5m^2 (155.75sq ft).

Capacity: Seating for two in R 3000/100, three in R 3000/120 and four in R 2000/140 and R 3000/160.

Production: Approximately 75 examples of the two versions of the R 3000 had been delivered by late 1996.

History: Although only built in small numbers, the R 3000 series has the distinction of being in production during the late 1980s, a rare occurrence for a fixed undercarriage light aircraft.

Robin began development of the R 3000 in the late 1970s as part of a model range modernisation drive. Robin originally proposed offering a wide range of R 3000 models, although only a few have actually been built. Models that were proposed but never saw the light of day included the R 3180S with a turbocharged engine and retractable undercarriage; the fixed gear, but turbocharged R 3180T; the R 3180GT1 and R 3180GT2 with a larger cabin (the GT1 was to be turbocharged, the GT2 turbocharged with retractable gear); and the R 3140T with a solid cabin roof.

A 1981 agreement saw Aerospatiale, GA manufacturer Socata's parent, become responsible for R 3000 marketing between 1983 and 1987, which meant that Robin concentrated on lower power models so as to not compete with Socata's own range (described separately), and plans for the higher performance models were dropped.

The R 3000 features a Jodel based wing and forward sliding cockpit canopy and an aerodynamically efficient airframe, although it is distinguishable by its T-tail. The first R 3000 model to fly was the R 3140, its first flight occurred on December 8 1980, a second prototype flew in June 1981 and introduced the definitive tapered wings. Production aircraft have been delivered since 1985.

The R 3140, now the R 3000/140, has been joined in production by the two seat 87kW (116hp) O-235 powered R 3000/100; the three seat R 3120; four seat 105kW (140hp) powered R 3000/140; and the 135kW (180hp) R 3000/180R glider tug. Current production is of the R 3000/140 and R 3000/160, a development of the R 3000/120.

Photo: Note large forward sliding canopy in this pic of a R 3000-120.

Robinson R22

Country of origin: United States of America

Type: Two seat piston engined light helicopter

Powerplant: R22 – One 93kW (124hp) Lycoming 0-360-A2B flat four piston engine, driving a two blade main rotor and two blade tail rotor. R22 Beta – One 120kW (160hp) Textron Lycoming 0-320-B2C.

Performance: R22 – Max speed 180km/h (97kt), 75% power cruising speed 174km/h (94kt), economical cruising speed 153km/h (82kt). Initial rate of climb 1200ft/min. Service ceiling 14,000ft. Hovering ceiling in ground effect 6500ft. Range with max payload and no reserves 385km (207nm). R22 Beta – Max speed 180km/h (97kt), 75% power cruising speed 177km/h (97kt), economical cruising speed 153km/h (82kt). Initial rate of climb 1200ft/min. Hovering ceiling in ground effect 6970ft. Range with max payload, auxiliary fuel and no reserves 590km (320nm).

Weights: R22 – Empty 361kg (796lb), max takeoff 590kg (1300lb). R22 Beta – Empty 379kg (835lb), max takeoff 620kg (1370lb).

Dimensions: Main rotor diameter 7.67m (25ft 2in), length overall 8.76m (28ft 9in), fuselage length 6.30m (20ft 8in), height 2.67m (8ft 9in). Main rotor disc area 46.2m^2 (497.4sq ft).

Capacity: Typical seating for two, side by side. R22 Agricultural is fitted with a 150 litre (33Imp gal) capacity chemical tank.

Production: Over 2700 R22s of all versions have been delivered (including some against military orders).

History: Since its introduction in the late 1970s, the Robinson R22 has become the fastest selling helicopter in the world.

The R22 was designed by the founder of the Robinson Helicopter Company, Frank Robinson. The R22 was conceived to be an efficient, cheap to acquire (with a purchase cost comparable to two/four seat light aircraft), reliable and economical to operate multi purpose two seat helicopter. To this end Robinson has been highly successful, with over 2700 delivered.

Design work on the R22 began in the 1970s, and an 85kW (115hp) Lycoming 0-235 powered prototype flew for the first time on August 28 1975. Certification of the R22 was delayed somewhat to March 1979 however by the loss of the prototype. Despite this setback though the R22 was an overnight success, several hundred had been ordered by the time the first were delivered from October 1979.

A number of variants and developments of the R22 have been offered. These include the improved R22 Alpha introduced in 1983, and more powerful R22 Beta from 1985. The R22 Mariner is equipped with floats, the R22 Police version is fitted with special communications gear, a searchlight, siren and loudspeaker, the R22 Agricultural is fitted with tanks and booms for agricultural spraying, while the R22 IFR is fitted with IFR instrumentation for helicopter IFR flight training.

The latest R22 model is the R22 Beta II, powered by a derated 120kW (160hp) 0-360. The Beta II was introduced into production in 1995 and certificated in early 1996.

The R22 is widely used for helicopter pilot training and cattle mustering, traffic reporting and police work.

Photo: The diminutive R22 is widely used in the training and personal transport roles. (Peter Martinson)

Robinson R44

Country of origin: United States of America

Type: Four place piston engine light helicopter

Powerplant: One 195kW (260hp) Textron Lycoming 0-540 flat six piston engine derated to 165kW (225hp) for takeoff and 153kW (205hp) for continuous operation driving a two blade main rotor and two blade tail rotor.

Performance: Cruising speed at 75% power 209km/h (113kt). Initial rate of climb over 1000ft/min. Service ceiling 14,000ft. Hovering ceiling in ground effect 6100ft. Max range with no reserves 645km (350nm).

Weights: Empty equipped 635kg (1400lb), max takeoff 1090kg (2400lb).

Dimensions: Main rotor diameter 10.07m (33ft 0in), length overall 11.65m (38ft 2in), height 3.28m (10ft 9in). Main rotor disc area 79.5m^2 (855.3sq ft).

Capacity: Typical seating for four, with two passengers on bench seat behind pilot and passenger.

Production: Over 200 R44s have been delivered since production began in late 1992.

History: While bearing a resemblance with the earlier R22, the piston engine powered four seat R44 is a much larger aircraft being almost as long as the turbine powered Bell JetRanger.

The comparison with the JetRanger is useful as it provides a good illustration of Robinson's design philosophy in developing the R44. The aim in developing the R44 was to provide a relatively fast (205 to 215km/h [110 to 115kt] cruising speed) and useful four seat helicopter that had performance close to that of turbine powered aircraft, yet with an acquisition cost of just a third of those machines and vastly reduced maintenance costs. The R44 also uses the same simple design, construction and operating philosophies behind the design of the smaller two place R22.

Robinson Helicopter Company president and founder Frank Robinson first began design work on a light four seat piston engined helicopter during 1986. First flight occurred on March 31 1990 following extensive structural and dynamic component fatigue testing. US FAA certification was awarded on December 10 1992, with deliveries commencing soon after. The R44 is now also offered as the float equipped R44 Clipper.

The R44's early in service career was tarnished by the unexplained loss of an early production machine in July 1993. Cracking in the cyclic stick was found to be a possible cause, and in response Robinson voluntary redesigned and strengthened the cyclic stick assembly. Subsequent investigations, including a Special Certification Review conducted by the FAA at the behest of the US National Transportation Safety Board, found that it could not be proven that the fracture of the stick caused the accident and was not a result of it, and cleared both the original and redesigned cyclic sticks.

With the cyclic stick controversy behind it, Robinson is now focusing on increasing production at its new Torrance California plant, to meet growing demand for this increasingly popular helo.

Photo: The R44 is a surprisingly big helicopter, its most noteworthy visual feature is the large rotor mast fairing. Pictured is the float equipped R44 Clipper. (Robinson)

Rockwell Darter & Lark Commanders

Country of origin: United States of America

Type: Four seat light aircraft

Powerplant: Darter – One 110kW (150hp) Lycoming 0-320-A flat four piston engine, driving a two blade fixed pitch propeller. Lark – One 135kW (180hp) 0-360-A2F.

Performance: Darter – Max speed 214km/h (115kt), max cruising speed 206km/h (111kt). Initial rate of climb 785ft/min. Service ceiling 11,000ft. Range at max cruising speed 820km (443nm). Lark – Max speed 222km/h (120kt), max cruising speed 212km/h (114kt). Initial rate of climb 750ft/min. Service ceiling 13,000ft. Range at max cruising speed 845km (456nm).

Weights: Darter – Empty 580kg (1280lb), max takeoff 1020kg (2550lb). Lark – Empty 658kg (1450lb), max takeoff 1110kg (2450lb).

Dimensions: Darter – Wing span 10.67m (35ft 0in), length 6.86m (22ft 6in), height 2.84m (9ft 4in). Wing area 16.8m^2 (181sq ft). Lark – Same except for length 7.59m (24ft 11in), height 3.07m (10ft 1in).

Capacity: Typical seating for four.

Production: Approximately 200 Model 100s/Darter Commanders and 250 Lark Commanders built.

History: Aero Commander developed the high wing four seat 100 series in a bid to expand its product range away from its very successful series of light twins.

What evolved into the Aero Commander 100 originally began life as a three seat design from Volaircraft of Aliquippa, Pennsylvania in the USA. The basic design was known as the Volaire 10 and flew for the first time during 1960. Features include a high wing, 360° all round visibility and metal construction. A handful of production aircraft, the 1035 powered by 100kW (135hp) 0-290 and the four seat 110kW (150hp) 0-320 powered 1050 were built before Aero Commander purchased the design and manufacturing rights for both the 1035 and 1050 in 1965.

Aero Commander only made a small number of changes before the 1035 and 1050 were placed into production as the Aero Commander 100A and 100 respectively in the second half of 1965. In 1966 Aero Commander incorporated a small number of changes including revised windscreen and rear cabin window designs and other mods.

By the time the first major changes to the design were introduced to the basic design, Aero Commander had been taken over by North American Rockwell, and the aircraft was renamed the Darter Commander. North American Rockwell introduced the improved 100-180 Lark Commander in 1967 (FAA Type Approval was awarded on Sept 26 that year). Changes introduced on the Lark Commander included a more powerful 135kW (180hp) 0-360-A2F piston engine, a swept back fin and reprofiled cowling. The aerodynamic changes gave the Lark Commander a much more sleeker appearance, and the more powerful engine boosted performance. However Rockwell dumped production in 1971, the Lark Commander being outsold and out performed by the less powerful Piper Cherokee and Cessna 172.

Rockwell then sold design and production rights for both the Darter (which had been out of production since 1969) and the Lark to Phoenix Aircraft, but the latter company did not continue production.

Photo: An Aero Commander 100. (Stewart Wilson)

Rockwell Commander 112 & 114

Country of origin: United States of America

Type: Four seat light aircraft

Powerplant: 112B – One 140kW (200hp) Lycoming IO-360-C1D6 fuel injected flat four piston engine, driving a two blade constant speed propeller. 114 – One 195kW (260hp) Lycoming IO-540-T4A5D fuel injected flat six, driving a three blade constant speed prop.

Performance: 112B – Max speed 277km/h (150kt), max cruising speed 251km/h (135kt), long range cruising speed 222km/h (120kt). Initial rate of climb 880ft/min. Service ceiling 15,200ft/min. Max range with reserves 1085km (585nm), or 1647km (890nm) with optional fuel. 114 – Max speed 307km/h (166kt), max cruising speed 290km/h (157kt), long range cruising 254km/h (137kt). Initial rate of climb 1088ft/min. Service ceiling 17,400ft. Max range with reserves 1355km (730nm).

Weights: 112B – Empty 804kg (1773lb), max takeoff 1270kg (2800lb). 114 – Empty 885kg (1885lb), max takeoff 1425kg (3140lb).

Dimensions: Wing span 10.85m (35ft 8in), length 7.63m (25ft 1in), height 2.57m (8ft 5in). Wing area 15.2m^2 (164sq ft). 114 – Same except wing span 9.98m (32ft 9in). Wing area 14.1m^2 (152sq ft).

Capacity: Typical seating for four.

Production: Production of the 112 and 114 series ceased in 1979.

History: The Rockwell Commander 112 and 114 were Rockwell's only forays into the design of four seat single engine light aircraft.

Rockwell's General Aviation Division began development of the original Commander 111 and 112 during the late 1960s, and announced its new range in late 1970. Of conventional construction and low wing configuration the 111 was the fixed undercarriage model while the 112 had retractable gear. The prototype 112 flew for the first time on December 4 1970, and was powered by a 135kW (180hp) Lycoming 0-360, while a prototype 111 flew for the first time late in 1971. The loss of the 112 prototype during flight testing due to the structural failure of the tail unit delayed certification and production of both models somewhat until a fix was found. Deliveries of production aircraft eventually took place from late 1972.

Production 111s were powered by 135kW (180hp) 0-360s, production 112s were powered by more powerful 150kW (200hp) IO-360s. Only a few 111s were built before Rockwell decided to concentrate on the higher performance retractable gear 112, continued development of which led to the 112A. The 112A appeared in 1974 with a higher max takeoff weight, improved cabin ventilation and detail refinements, while the turbocharged 112TC was introduced in 1976.

Also introduced in 1976 was the 114, which is basically a 112 with a more powerful six cylinder IO-540. The 114 remained in production basically unchanged when production ceased in 1979, by which stage it had been named the Gran Turismo Commander. Meanwhile the improved 112B appeared in 1977, featuring an increased max takeoff weight and the extended wingtips introduced on the 112TC. By that stage the 112TC was designated the 112TC-A, later it became known as the Alpine Commander.

From 1992 the Commander Aircraft Company has been producing the improved 114B and 114TC, but these aircraft are described separately.

Photo: A Commander 114. (Bill Lines)

Rockwell Commander 500/560/680

Country of origin: United States of America

Type: Light utility/corporate transport

Powerplants: Aero Grand Commander 680FL – Two 285kW (380hp) Lycoming IGSO-540-B1A geared, supercharged and fuel injected flat six piston engines, driving three blade constant speed propellers. Rockwell 500S Shrike Commander – Two 215kW (290hp) Lycoming IO-540-E1B5 fuel injected flat sixes.

Performance: 680FL – Max cruising speed 393km/h (212kt), long range cruising speed 338km/h (183kt). Initial rate of climb 1285ft/min. Service ceiling 28,500ft. Max range 2315km (1250nm). 500S – Max speed 346km/h (187kt), max cruising speed 326km/h (176kt), long range cruise 298km/h (161kt). Initial rate of climb 1340ft/min. Service ceiling 19,400ft. Max range with reserves 1915km (1035nm).

Weights: 680FL – Empty 2360kg (5200lb), max takeoff 3855kg (8500lb). 500S – Empty 2102kg (4635lb), max TO 3060kg (6750lb).

Dimensions: 680FL – Wing span 14.95m (49ft 1in), length 12.58m (41ft 3in), height 4.42m (14ft 6in). Wing area 23.7m^2 (255sq ft). 500S – Same except length 11.22m (36ft 10in), height 4.56m (15ft 0in).

Capacity: Seating in standard length Commanders for five to seven, including one pilot. Stretched Grand Commander seats up to 11.

Production: Total includes 150 520s; 182 560As; 70 560Es; 254 680 Supers; 41 680Es and 13 720s.

History: The predecessor to this prolific series of twins was originally conceived by two Douglas employees who formed the Aero Design and Engineering Corporation in December 1944.

Their original design resulted in the Aero Commander Model L-3805, which flew for the first time on April 23 1948. From this aircraft was developed the first Aero Commander production model, the 520, which seated five to seven people and was powered by two 195kW (260hp) Lycoming GO-435s.

Approximately 150 Aero Commander 520s were built, subsequent development led to the more powerful 560 series (1954) with geared normally aspirated engines, and the 680 series (1955) with supercharged engines and the direct drive normally aspirated 500 series. Significant variants include the 560A which introduced the 25cm (10in) stretched fuselage that became the standard short fuselage length, the 560E which introduced the definitive wing span, the 720 Alti-Cruiser pressurised development of the 680 and the later pressurised 680PF.

The 560 and 680 were joined by the stretched 680FL Grand Commander from 1962, the 680FL also forming the basis for the Turbo Commanders, described separately. The longest living variant of the family, the 500 was introduced to production in 1958 and was originally intended as a low cost member of the Aero Commander family.

During 1967 North American Rockwell took over the Aero Commander line and from then on the Grand Commander became the Courser Commander and the 500 became the Shrike Commander (gaining its distinctive pointed nose at the same time). The Shrike Commander was also the last Commander to remain in production, manufacture ending in 1980.

The final piston powered model to appear was the Rockwell 685 Commander, which was a piston powered Turbo Commander.

Photo: A 680FL Grand Commander. (Bill Lines)

Rockwell Turbo Commander

Country of origin: United States of America

Type: Light utility/corporate transport & utility airliner

Powerplants: 690A – Two 520kW (700shp) Garrett AiResearch TPE331-5-251K turboprops, driving three blade constant speed propellers. Jetprop 1000 – Two 730kW (980shp) Garrett TPE331-10-501K flat rated to 610kW (820shp).

Performance: 690A – Max speed 528km/h (285kt), econ cruising speed 465km/h (251kt). Initial rate of climb 2850ft/min. Range with max payload and reserves 1370km (740nm). 1000 – Max speed 571km/h (308kt), economical cruising speed 474km/h (256kt). Initial rate of climb 2802ft/min. Max certificated altitude 35,000ft. Range with max payload and reserves 2430km (1311nm), with max fuel and reserves 3855km (2080nm).

Weights: 690A – Empty 2778kg (6126lb), loaded 4650kg (10,250lb). 1000 – Empty equipped 3307kg (7289lb), max TO 5080kg (11,200lb).

Dimensions: 690A – Wing span 14.22m (46ft 8in), length 13.52m (44ft 5in), height 4.56m (15ft 0in). Wing area 24.7m^2 (266sq ft). 1000 – Wing span 15.89m (52ft 2in), length 13.10m (43ft 0in), height 4.55m (15ft 0in). Wing area 26.0m^2 (279.4sq ft).

Capacity: Pilot and passenger or copilot on flightdeck. Main cabin seating for six to eight. Jetprop 1000 can seat 10 in main cabin.

Production: Approximate production of 1075 includes Gulfstream production of 122 Jetprop 840s, 42 Jetprop 900s, 84 Jetprop 980s and 108 Jetprop 1000s. Production ceased in 1985.

History: The turboprop powered developments of the Aero Commander family of light twins enjoyed a two decade long production run, and were built by three manufacturers before production ceased.

The Turboprop Commander was originally based on the 680FLP, and first flew on December 31 1964, but instead of piston engines power was supplied by 450kW (605shp) Garrett AiResearch TPE331 turboprops. This initial Turbo Commander model was designated the 680T and entered production in 1965.

Progressively improved developments of the basic Turbo Commander appeared, including the 680V, which introduced an increased maximum takeoff weight, and the 680W with improved engines. Following North American Rockwell's takeover of Aero Commander and the introduction of the further improved Model 681, the name Hawk Commander was adopted for a time, but it was dropped from 1971 with the release of the 681B.

By the time of the introduction of the 681B, Rockwell was already flight testing the upgraded Turbo Commander 690, which flew for the first time on March 3 1968 and was certificated in July 1971. Soon after the 690 though, Rockwell introduced the improved 690A.

In 1979 Rockwell flew the Jetprop Commander 840 and 980, developments of the 690 powered by 625kW (840shp) Garrett TPE331-5 and 730kW (980shp) TPE331-10 turboprops respectively. These went into production with Gulfstream, who had purchased Rockwell's GA activities in 1979. The Jetprop 1000 was similar in overall dimensions but introduced a revised interior that made better use of the available space and the 980's engines. The Jetprop 900 meanwhile coupled the revised interior with the 840's engines.

Photo: A Rockwell Turbo Commander 690. (Steve Allsopp)

Rockwell Sabreliner

Country of origin: United States of America

Type: Executive/corporate jet

Powerplants: 40 – Two 14.7kN (3300lb) Pratt & Whitney JT12A-8 turbojets. 75A – Two 20.2kN (4500lb) General Electric CF700-2D-2 turbofans.

Performance: 40 – Max cruising speed 810km/h (440kt), economical cruising speed 743km/h (400kt). Max rate of climb 4700ft/min. Service ceiling 45,000ft. Range with max fuel, four pax and reserves 3240km (1750nm). 75A – Max cruising speed 906km/h (490kt), economical cruising speed 772km/h (417kt). Service ceiling 45,000ft. Max range with max fuel, four pax and reserves 3174km (1713nm).

Weights: 40 – Empty equipped 5102kg (11,250lb), max takeoff 9150kg (20,172lb). 75A – Empty equipped 5990kg (13,200lb), max takeoff 10,435kg (23,000lb).

Dimensions: 40 – Wing span 13.61m (44ft 8in), length 14.30m (46ft 11in), height 4.88m (16ft 0in). Wing area 31.8m^2 (342.05sq ft). 75A – Wing span 13.61m (44ft 8in), length 14.38m (47ft 2in), height 5.26m (17ft 3in). Wing area 31.8m^2 (342.05sq ft).

Capacity: Flightcrew of two. Main cabin seats up to 10 in high density layout. Various other seating arrangements possible.

Production: Over 600 Sabreliners were built, including 200 T-39s. Most built for civil customers remain in service.

History: The Rockwell Sabreliner was originally designed to meet military requirements.

North American Aviation developed the Sabreliner to meet a US Air Force requirement for a utility jet aircraft capable of performing transport and combat readiness training missions under the program designation UTX. Development of the Sabreliner began in 1956 and a prototype (designated NA264) flew for the first time on September 16 1958. That year the US Air Force ordered the Sabreliner into production, purchasing two versions, the T-39A pilot proficiency and support transport and the T-39 radar trainer.

The first civil aircraft were equivalent to the T-39A, and were designated the NA265-40. Certificated in April 1963, the NA265-40 design was conventional and power was supplied by two Pratt & Whitney JT12 turbojets. The Series 40 followed from June 1966 and featured a higher cruising speed and greater internal cabin space. The Series 60 was stretched by 97cm (3ft 2in) and is identifiable by its five, rather than three, cabin windows per side. The Series 60A introduced aerodynamic changes over the 60. The Sabreliner 75 meanwhile is based on the 60 and 60A, but has a deeper fuselage with greater headroom.

Turbofan power was introduced to the Sabreliner family in 1973 (by which time North American had become part of Rockwell International) with the introduction of the General Electric CF700 turbofan powered 75A. Other changes introduced with the 75A were aerodynamic, plus improved cabin fittings, equipment and systems. The Series 65A meanwhile is similar to the 60A and 75 but is powered by Garrett AiResearch TFE731-3-1D turbofans. It was delivered from December 1979. Sabreliner production ceased in 1981.

Photo: The wing of the Sabreliner was based loosely on the F-86 Sabre's. Pictured is a US registered turbojet powered Sabreliner Series 40. (Gordon Reid)

Ruschmeyer R 90

Country of origin: Germany

Type: Four seat high performance light aircraft

Powerplant: R 90-230 RG – One 170kW (230hp) Textron Lycoming IO-540-C4D5 flat six piston engine (derated from 195kW/260hp), driving a four blade constant speed Mühlbauer composite propeller.

Performance: R 90-230 RG – Max speed 324km/h (175kt), max cruising speed 311km/h (168kt), economical cruising speed 267km/h (144kt). Initial rate of climb 1140ft/min. Service ceiling 16,000ft. Max range with reserves 1610km (870nm). Endurance 7.8hrs.

Weights: R 90-230 RG – Standard empty 898kg (1980lb), empty equipped 920kg (2030lb), max takeoff 1350kg (2976lb).

Dimensions: Wing span 9.50m (31ft 2in), length 7.93m (26ft 0in), height 2.73m (8ft 11in). Wing area 12.9m^2 (139.3sq ft).

Capacity: Typical seating for four.

Production: Approximately 130 built.

History: The R 90 is an all new four seater that should be the basis for a family of light aircraft.

The Ruschmeyer R90 is a new design based on the company's earlier MF-85, making use of a range of modern technologies and materials that doubtless would have been far more commonplace in GA aircraft had it not been for the crippling effects the USA's product liability laws had. The Ruschmeyer R 90 possesses one of the aerodynamically cleanest airframes in its class, something made possible by its glass fibre (with Rohacell core) construction. The advanced wing design features a 'rain tolerant' laminar flow aerofoil design, wet wing fuel tanks, up turned wingtips (for increased lateral stability, not drag reduction), small ailerons and inboard Fowler flaps.

For the initial R 90-230 RG production model, power is supplied by a fuel injected Textron Lycoming IO-540 flat six driving an advanced four blade composite construction propeller. A silencer on the engine, the four blade prop and the engine being derated to 170kW (230hp) from 195kW (260hp) combine to give very low interior and exterior noise levels. Even though the engine has been derated, because of the R 90's comparatively light structure its performance is better than more powerful competitors.

The R 90 series is based on Ruschmeyer's earlier Porsche powered MF-85 series, but the unavailability of the Porsche engines led to the development of the Textron Lycoming powered series. Initial production of the R 90 is of the high performance retractable undercarriage R 90-230 RG. This model of the R 90 first flew on August 8 1988, while German certification was awarded in June 1992.

Members of the expanded R 90 family include the fixed gear, 175kW (235hp) O-540-J powered R 90-230 FG, and the fixed undercarriage 135kW (180hp) IO-360 (flat rated to 150kW/100hp) powered R 90-180 FG. The R 90-250T RG powered by a 185kW (250hp) turbocharged engine (powerplant choice has yet to be made) and capable of 435km/h (235kt) cruising speed and the high performance five/six seat R 95 are under development. An Allison 250-B17 turboprop powered development, the R 90-420 AT, was flown, but production is not anticipated in the near term.

Photo: The R 90-230 RG in flight (Bob Grimstead)

Saab 340

Country of origin: Sweden

Type: Twin turboprop regional airliner

Powerplants: 340A – Two 1295kW (1735shp) General Electric CT7-5A2 turboprops, driving four blade constant speed Dowty or Hamilton Standard propellers. 340B – Two 1305kW (1750shp) CT7-9Bs.

Performance: 340A – Max cruising speed 515km/h (278kt), economical cruising speed 484km/h (260kt). Range with max payload 1455km (785nm), range with max fuel 3975km (2145nm). 340B – Max cruising speed 523km/h (282kt), long range cruising speed 467km/h (252kt). Range with 35 pax and reserves at max cruising speed 1490km (805nm), at long range cruising speed 1735km (935nm).

Weights: 340A – Operating empty 7810kg (17,215lb), max takeoff 12,370kg (27,275lb). 340B – Operating empty 8140kg (17,945lb), max takeoff 13,155kg (29,000lb).

Dimensions: Wing span 21.44m (70ft 4in), length 19.73m (64ft 9in), height 6.97m (22ft 11in). Wing area 41.8m^2 (450sq ft).

Capacity: Flightcrew of two. Main cabin seats up to 37, or typically 33 to 35 with a galley at three abreast and 76cm (30in) pitch. Combi seats 19 passengers and 1500kg (3310lb) of cargo. A small number of 340s are outfitted in VIP configurations.

Production: At late 1996 orders for over 440 Saab 340s were held, of which over 380 had been delivered. Production of the 340A ended in September 1989 after 159 had been built.

History: The Saab 340 began life in the early 1980s (program go-ahead was given in September 1980 with the aim of capturing 25 to 30% of its market) as the Saab-Fairchild SF340 following Saab's decision to diversify out of military aviation.

Before then, in 1979 Saab-Scania of Sweden and Fairchild in the USA reached an agreement to conduct joint feasibility and development studies on a 30 to 40 seat commuter. The resulting SF340 design was conventional in layout and construction and powered by two General Electric CT7s (a commercial development of the T700 which powers Sikorsky's S-70 series of military helicopters). Within the 65/35 Saab-Fairchild partnership Saab was responsible for the fuselage, fin and final assembly, while Fairchild was responsible for the wings, engine nacelles and empennage.

The first of three SF340 prototypes flew for the first time on January 25 1983, while the first production aircraft flew in early March 1984. US and European certification was awarded that June. From November 1 Saab assumed overall responsibility for the SF340 following Fairchild's decision to divest itself of its aircraft divisions. For a time Saab retained the SF340 designation, although this latter changed to 340A.

The first improved development of the Saab 340 is the 340B. More powerful engines improve hot and high performance, while other changes include a grater span tailplane, a higher max takeoff weight and better range. The first 340B delivery was in September 1989.

The latest development of the 340 is the 340B Plus, which introduces changes developed for the larger Saab 2000, including an improved cabin interior. The first 340B Plus was delivered in March 1994.

Photo: A Japan Air Commuter Saab 340. (Saab)

Saab 2000

Country of origin: Sweden

Type: High speed 50 seat regional airliner

Powerplants: Two 3075kW (4125shp) Allison AE 2100A turboprops, driving six blade constant speed Dowty propellers.

Performance: Max cruising speed 678km/h (366kt), long range cruising speed 556km/h (300kt). Initial rate of climb 2380ft/min. Service ceiling 31,000ft. Range with 50 passengers and reserves at max cruising speed 2325km (1255nm), at long range cruising speed 2640km (1425nm).

Weights: Operating empty 13,500kg (29,762lb), max takeoff 22,000kg (48,500lb).

Dimensions: Wing span 24.76m (81ft 3in), length 27.03m (88ft 8in), height 7.73m (25ft 4in). Wing area 55.7m^2 (600.0sq ft).

Capacity: Flightcrew of two. Normal passenger accommodation for 50 at three abreast and 81cm (32in) pitch. Max seating for 58 at three abreast and 76cm (30in) pitch, with repositioned galley and wardrobe.

Production: More than 42 Saab 2000s had been firmly ordered (plus 130 options) at the time of writing, of which approximately 35 had entered airline service by late 1996.

History: The Saab 2000 is a stretched development of the successful 340, Saab claiming it to be the fastest and quietest regional turboprop on the market.

With a cruise speed of over 665km/h (360kt), this claim is not surprising, and it seems Saab is close to meeting its design objective of combining near jet speeds, including near jet climb and descent speeds, with turboprop economy. Saab launched development of the 2000 in mid December 1988 with a launch order from Crossair for 25 (plus a further 25 on option) following definition and design studies that revealed a potentially lucrative market for a high speed regional turboprop.

The initial Saab 2000 development plan would have seen the 2000 in service in the second half of 1993, but delays pushed this back until the second half of 1994. The Saab 2000's first flight took place on March 26 1992, and certification from Europe's Joint Airworthiness Authorities and the US's FAA was granted in March and April 1994 respectively. Service entry with Crossair occurred a few months later.

While retaining the same cross section as the Saab 340, the 2000 is 7.30m (14ft) longer (seating 15 more passengers), while the same wing section is retained but the 2000's wing span is 15% longer than the 340's, and the engines are positioned further outboard. The 2000 is also the first civil application of the advanced Allison AE 2100 turboshaft (derived from the military T406 developed for the revolutionary V-22 Osprey tilt rotor), two of which drive slow turning six blade props. The powerful engines, advanced propellers and clean aerodynamic design all contribute to the Saab's good performance.

A number of European aerospace firms participate in the Saab 2000 manufacturing program including CASA who designs and builds the wing, Westland who manufactures the rear fuselage and Valmet of Finland who builds the tail.

Photo: The stretched fuselage and large engines for a 50 seat turboprop are clearly evident in this photo of a Air Marshall Islands 2000.

Schweizer/Hughes 300 (& 269)

Country of origin: United States of America

Type: Light utility helicopter

Powerplant: 300C – One 140kW (190hp) Textron Lycoming HIO-360-D1A fuel injected flat four derated from 170kW (225hp) driving a three blade main rotor and two blade tail rotor.

Performance: 300C – Max cruising speed 153km/h (82kt), max range cruising speed 124km/h (67kt). Initial rate of climb 750ft/min. Hovering ceiling in ground effect 5900ft. Service ceiling 10,200ft. Range with max fuel and no reserves 360km (195nm). Max endurance 3hrs.

Weights: 300C – Empty 474kg (1046lb), max takeoff 930kg (2050lb), or 975kg (2150lb) with an external sling load.

Dimensions: Main rotor diameter 8.18m (26ft 10in), length overall 9.40m (30ft 10in), fuselage length 6.80m (22ft 0in), height to top of rotor head 2.66m (8ft 9in). Main rotor disc area 52.5m^2 (565.5sq ft).

Capacity: Typical seating for three on a bench seat in 300 or two in 269. Many aircraft equipped for agricultural spraying and fitted with chemical hoppers and spray booms. Can lift a 475kg (1050lb) payload in an external sling load.

Production: Total 269/TH-58/300 production over 3300 aircraft, of which 2800 were built by Hughes before production transferred to Schweizer. Total includes military production.

History: With over 3000 built by two manufacturers over three decades, the Hughes/Schweizer 300 is the most successful three seat helicopter currently in production.

Development of this versatile utility helicopter dates back to the mid 1950s when Hughes flew the two seat Model 269 for the first time in October 1956. The basic design sparked US Army interest and five were ordered as the YHO-2HU for evaluation in the scout and observation roles. Deliveries of commercial equivalent Model 269A began in 1961.

The 269A program received a huge boost when Hughes won a US Army contract for a light helicopter primary trainer. Eventually a total of 792 were built as the TH-55A Osage and more than 60,000 US Army helicopter pilots learnt to fly in the type.

Hughes followed the two seat 269A with the slightly larger three seat 269B, which it marketed as the Hughes 300, which first flew in 1964. The 300 was followed from 1969 by the improved 300C, which introduced a more powerful 140kW (190hp) Lycoming HIO-360 engine and increased diameter main rotor, giving an increase in payload of 45%, plus overall performance improvements. The 300C (or 269C) flew in August 1969 and remains in production to this day, basically unchanged.

Since 1983 the 300C has been built by Schweizer in the USA. Schweizer built the 300C initially under licence for Hughes, and then acquired all rights to the helicopter in 1986. Under Schweizer's stewardship more than 250 minor improvements have been made to the 300C, but the basic design has been left unchanged. Schweizer also offers a version optimised for police work. Named the Sky Knight it is available with options such as a search light and infrared sensors.

The latest 300 model is the 300CB trainer powered by a HO-360-C1A and delivered from late 1995.

Photo: A Schweizer 300CB is designed to tackle the R22 head-on in the helicopter pilot trainer market. (Schweizer)

Schweizer 330

Country of origin: United States of America

Type: Light turbine powered utility helicopter

Powerplant: One 315kW (420shp) Allison 250-C20W turboprop, rated at 175kW (235shp) for takeoff and 165kW (220hp) max continuous operation, driving a three blade main rotor and two blade tail rotor.

Performance: Max cruising speed 200km/h (108kt), normal cruising speed 185km/h (100kt). Hovering ceiling in ground effect 14,100ft. Max range with no reserves 498km (269nm), endurance 4hr 12min.

Weights: Empty 508kg (1120lb), max takeoff 1000kg (2200lb).

Dimensions: Main rotor diameter 8.18m (26ft 10in), length overall 9.40m (30ft 10in), height overall 2.89m (9ft 6in). Main rotor disc area 52.5m^2 (565.5sq ft).

Capacity: Typical seating for three or four.

Production: Deliveries began in mid 1993.

History: The Schweizer 330 is the ultimate expression of the Hughes/Schweizer 300 series of two/three seat light piston engine helicopters that first flew in the mid 1950s.

The Schweizer company, a firm more known for its production of gliders over the last 50 years, acquired the production and manufacturing rights to the Hughes 300, which it had been building under licence since 1983, from McDonnell Douglas in November 1986. It was not long after that in 1987 Schweizer announced it was developing an improved turbine powered version.

The new model was dubbed the 330 and was aimed to fulfil a number of utility roles, including law enforcement, observation and patrol, aerial photography, utility transport and agricultural spraying, missions all ably filled by the earlier and smaller 300. Like the 300 though much of Schweizer's hopes with the 330 lay in fulfilling a vast need for pilot training. The company had hoped to meet the potentially massive US Army contract for a light turbine powered helicopter as its new basic pilot trainer, to replace the Hughes TH-58 Osage Model 269B (itself the predecessor of the 300). Unfortunately for Schweizer however this contract was awarded to Bell with its 206 JetRanger based TH-67 Creek. (Limited military sales success did come later when in early 1994 the Venezuelan Army ordered three TH-330 trainers).

The Schweizer 330 uses the dynamic components, rotors, controls and systems of the proven 300C, combined with an Allison 250-C20 turboshaft. The engine has been derated to just 165kW (220hp), giving the 330 excellent hot and high performance. For example the powerplant will reach its max rated power output right up to 18,000ft. Other changes compared with the 300C include what is essentially an all new fuselage, new vertical tail surfaces and new tail fairing.

The 330 first flew in the first half of 1988, being publicly demonstrated flying for the first time that June. Certification was awarded in September 1992 and first deliveries took place from mid 1993.

To enhance its appeal as a trainer the 330 is offered with a third set of flight controls, allowing the carriage of two pupils and an instructor on training flights.

Photo: The 330 retains the dynamic components, rotors and systems of its smaller brother, the 300.

Scottish Aviation Twin Pioneer

Country of origin: United Kingdom

Type: Utility transport

Powerplants: Series 3 – Two 475kW (640hp) Alvis Leonides 531 seven cylinder radial piston engines, driving three blade constant speed propellers.

Performance: Series 3 – Max cruising speed 257km/h (140kt), economical cruising speed 210km/h (114kt). Initial rate of climb 1370ft/min. Service ceiling 18,000ft. Max range at economical cruising speed 1287km (695nm), range with 1590kg (3500lb) payload 322km (175nm).

Weights: Series 3 – Empty 4630kg (10,200lb), max takeoff 6628kg (14,600lb).

Dimensions: Series 3 – Wing span 23.33m (76ft 6in), length 13.80m (45ft 3in), height 3.74m (12ft 3in). Wing area 62.3m^2 (670sq ft).

Capacity: Flightcrew of two. Main cabin seats 16 in passenger configuration, or 1540kg (3400lb) of freight. Has also been used as a platform for aerial photography.

Production: Total Twin Pioneer production of 91, including 32 CC.1s and seven CC.2s for the Royal Air Force and others for the Royal Malayan Air Force. Production ceased in 1964.

History: The Scottish Aviation Twin Pioneer utility transport saw limited commercial and military service, mainly in the UK and former colonies.

Despite its name, the Twin Pioneer is an all new aircraft compared with the Scottish Aviation Pioneer. The original Pioneer was a high wing single engined five seat light aircraft powered by an Alvis radial engine and built in small numbers for the Royal Air Force for liaison duties.

The Twin Pioneer is also powered by Alvis radials and features a high wing, but is much larger overall, capable of seating up to 16 passengers in the main cabin. Designed for both civil and military applications, the Twin Pioneer was also one of the few postwar aircraft to feature a high wing and tailwheel undercarriage, while its triple tail arrangement makes it easily recognisable.

The prototype Twin Pioneer flew for the first time on June 25 1955, and the first production examples were delivered from April 28 1956. By mid 1964, when production ceased, 94 of three different models had been built. Britain's Royal Air Force was the largest customer, taking delivery of 39 Twin Pioneers.

The RAF used its Twin Pioneers for a variety of transport and liaison roles, they could carry 13 troops, or 11 paratroops, or six stretchers and five sitting casualties or medical attendants. Another military operator was Malaysia (previously Malaya).

The initial Twin Pioneer production model was the Series 1, powered by two 410kW (550hp) Alvis Leonides 514/8 radials. The Series 2 was powered by Pratt & Whitney R-1340 radials. Final production was of the Series 3 (described above), powered by 475kW (640hp) Leonides 531/8 radials. In 1996 only a handful of Twin Pioneers remained in service, including two registered in Australia.

Photo: This Twin Pioneer is one of two flown by Sundown Airways, based out of Coolangtta on Australia's Gold Coast. (Keith Myers)

Seabird Seeker

Country of origin: Australia

Type: Two seat observation & utility light aircraft

Powerplant: SB7L-360A – One 125kW (168hp) Textron Lycoming O-360-B2C flat four piston engine, driving a two blade fixed pitch wooden pusher propeller.

Performance: SB7L-360A – Cruising speed at 75% power 208km/h (112kt). Initial rate of climb 944ft/min. Range with two crew and reserves at 75% power 730km (395nm), endurance at same conditions 3hr 33min. Range with two crew and reserves at patrolling speed 832km (450nm).

Weights: Basic empty (prototype, production aircraft expected to be less) 604kg (1332lb), max takeoff 897kg (1977lb).

Dimensions: Wing span 11.07m (36ft 4in), length 7.01m (23ft 0in), height overall prop turning 2.49m (8ft 2in). Wing area 13.1m^2 (141.0sq ft).

Capacity: Typical seating for two, side by side.

Production: Production of an initial batch of five began in late 1994.

History: Seabird's Seeker is one of just four Australian designed aircraft ever to be certificated to FAR Part 23 standards.

The innovative Seeker has been developed in response to a perceived need for a rugged, reliable and cost effective multirole surveillance platform capable of performing many traditional helicopter functions at far less cost. Intended roles include search and rescue, border patrol, aerial photography, powerline inspection, police work and news gathering.

The design aims explain the Seeker's unique configuration. The Seeker offers helicopter like forward vision, due to its braced high wing, rear pusher engine layout and forward cabin. A taildragger undercarriage arrangement was selected for rough field capability. The wing itself is laminar flow and is designed for a smooth ride in low level turbulence and to keep down flight loads imposed on the tail. A simple engine and systems and a rugged and conventional airframe construction are intended to keep operating costs similar or below those of similarly powered aircraft. Another design objective was excellent handling in all flight envelopes, but particularly at low speed, pilot reports confirm this has been achieved.

In keeping with its intended missions the Seeker is offered with several specialised options, including wing hardpoints, camera mounts, searchlight and loud hailer, and later FLIR. Floatplane and tricycle undercarriage developments are under consideration.

Design work on the Seeker began in the mid 1980s when in 1985 Seabird identified a worldwide niche market for such an aircraft. First flight of a Norton rotary powered prototype occurred on October 1 1989. Initially certification was awarded to cover the O-235 powered SB7L-235, in January 1994 it was extended to cover the definitive O-360 powered SB7L-360.

Production of an initial batch of five aircraft began in 1994, while discussions have been held to establish a Seeker production line outside Australia, possibly in Malaysia.

Photo: A Seabird Seeker development aircraft. The rear mounted engine allows unobstructed forward vision through a helicopter style nose. (Keith Myers)

Shorts Belfast

Country of origin: United Kingdom

Type: Heavy lift turboprop powered freighter

Powerplants: Four 4275kW (5730shp) Rolls-Royce Tyne RTy 12 turboprops driving four blade constant speed propellers.

Performance: Max cruising speed 566km/h (306kt), typical cruising speed 510km/h (275kt). Service ceiling 30,000ft. Range with max payload and reserves approximately 1575km (850nm), range with 10 tonne (22,000lb) payload 6200km (3350nm), range with max fuel and reserves 8530km (4605nm).

Weights: Operating empty 59,020kg (130,000lb), max takeoff 104,325kg (230,000lb). Max payload 34,000kg (75,000lb).

Dimensions: Wing span 48.41m (158ft 10in), length 41.58m (136ft 5in), height 14.33m (47ft 0in). Wing area 229.1m^2 (2466sq ft).

Capacity: Flightcrew of three or four comprising two pilots, a flight engineer and possibly a navigator. Can accommodate a wide variety of oversize and heavy cargoes such as heavy machinery, industrial equipment such as generators and small aircraft and helicopters.

Production: Only 10 Belfasts built specifically for the UK's Royal Air Force. Two remain in commercial service with Heavylift (none are in military service).

History: With a maximum takeoff weight of over 100 tonnes (220,500lb), Shorts' Belfast is one of the largest turboprop powered aircraft yet built, behind the massive 250 tonne (551,250lb) max takeoff An-22 (described separately) and Douglas' C-133 Cargomaster of the 1950s.

The Belfast was developed in response to a specific Royal Air Force requirement for a heavy lift freighter capable of carrying a wide range of military hardware, including artillery pieces, 200 plus troops, helicopters and guided missiles over relatively long ranges. Shorts had studied a number of large freighter designs during the late 1950s but what became the Belfast began life as the SC.5/10, design work on which began in February 1959.

Development of the SC.5/10 design resulted in a first flight of the Belfast on January 5 1964. Design features of this big aircraft included four Rolls-Royce Tyne turboprops mounted on a high wing, an 18 wheel undercarriage comprising two eight wheel main bogeys and two wheel nose undercarriage system and beaver tail rear loading doors and ramp. When the Belfast entered service with the RAF in January 1966 it was the largest aircraft to be operated by that service.

The Belfast's military career however was relatively short lived, and all 10 were retired in 1976. Heavylift (then TAC Heavylift) acquired five Belfasts for commercial service in 1977, and three have been in use since 1980. Marshall of Cambridge performed a number of modifications on the Belfast which allowed it to be certificated to civil standards on March 6 1980. Since then Heavylift's three Belfasts have given the company a unique heavylift capability to carry heavy and awkward sized loads. Two remained in use in 1996.

Photo: A Belfast in the colours of its sole civil operator, Heavylift. (Wally Civitico)

Shorts Skyvan & Skyliner

Country of origin: United Kingdom

Type: STOL utility transport and commuter airliner

Powerplants: Srs 3 – Two 535kW (715shp) Garrett TPE331-2-201A turboprops, driving three blade variable pitch Hartzell propellers.

Performance: Srs 3 – Max cruising speed 324km/h (175kt), normal cruising speed 311km/h (168kt), economical cruising speed 278km/h (150kt). Initial rate of climb 1640ft/min. Service ceiling 22,500ft. Range at long range cruising speed with reserves 1115km (600nm), range in typical freighter configuration with a 1815kg (4000lb) payload and reserves at economical cruising speed 300km (162nm).

Weights: Srs 3 – Basic operating 3331kg (7344lb) for Skyvan or 4055kg (8940lb) for Skyliner, max takeoff 5670kg (12,500lb).

Dimensions: Srs 3 – Wing span 19.79m (64ft 11in), length 12.21m (40ft 1in), or 12.60m (41ft 4in) with weather radar, height 4.60m (15ft 1in). Wing area 35.1m^2 (378sq ft).

Capacity: Flightcrew of one or two. Seating for up to 19 passengers at three abreast in Skyliner, or nine passengers in executive configuration.

Production: A total of 150 Skyvans and Skyliners built between the mid 1960s and 1987, almost all of which were Series 3s (including almost 60 military Series 3Ms).

History: The box like and rugged Shorts Skyvan and Skyliner date back to the Miles postwar Aerovan project.

Development of the Skyvan, or SC.7, began in 1959 when Shorts decided to design a small multirole transport with good STOL performance, with a squared sided fuselage to accommodate oversize loads. The new design incorporated the results of Miles research into high aspect ratio wings, with the Aerovan's wing design being adopted for the SC.7. The SC.7 first flew in Series 1 prototype form powered by two Continental 290kW (390hp) GTSIO-520 piston engines. First flight took place on January 17 1963.

Unlike the prototype, initial production aircraft were powered by 545kW (730shp) Turboméca Astazou XII turboprops. The original piston powered Series 1 prototype was the first Astazou powered Skyvan to fly (with 390kW/520shp Astazou IIs), in October 1963. The re-engined prototype was designated the Series 1A, while early Astazou powered production aircraft were designated Series 2.

Early on in the SC.7's production run however Shorts decided to switch the powerplant choice to 535kW (715shp) Garrett TPE331-201s, resulting in the definitive Series 3 (first flight December 15 1967). Many of the early build Series 2 Skyvans were also converted to Garrett power.

The basic Series 3 and the higher takeoff weight Series 3A aircraft perform a number of utility missions including passenger transport, ambulance, aerial survey and freight work, and are called Skyvans. The Skyliner airliner features an improved level of interior equipment and furnishing, while military Skyvans are designated Series 3M and 3M-200 with a higher max takeoff weight.

Photo: A Luxembourg registered Garrett TFE331 powered Series 3 Skyvan. (Paul Merritt)

Shorts 330

Country of origin: United Kingdom

Type: Regional airliner and utility freighter

Powerplants: 330-100 – Two 875kW (1173shp) Pratt & Whitney Canada PT6A-45 turboprops, driving five blade constant speed Hartzell propellers. 330-200 – Two 893kW (1198shp) PT6A-45Rs.

Performance: 330-100 – Max cruising speed 356km/h (192kt), long range cruising speed 296km/h (160kt). Initial rate of climb 1200ft/min. Range with 30 passengers and reserves 590km (320nm). 330-200 – Max cruising speed 352km/h (190kt), long range cruising speed 294km/h (159kt). Range with max payload 660km (473nm), range with max fuel and no reserves 1695km (915nm).

Weights: 330-100 – Empty equipped in airliner configuration 6577kg (14,500lb), max takeoff 10,160kg (22,400lb). 330-200 – Operating empty 6697kg (14,764lb), max takeoff 10,387kg (22,900lb).

Dimensions: Wing span 22.76m (74ft 8in), length 17.69m (58ft 1in), height 4.95m (16ft 3in). Wing area 42.1m^2 (453sq ft).

Capacity: Flightcrew of two. Typical passenger accommodation for 30 at three abreast and 76cm (30in) pitch in 10 rows of seats. In combi freight/passenger configuration the 330 houses freight in the forward fuselage and 18 passengers in the rear.

Production: Production of the 330 wound up in September 1992 after 136 had been built, including military C-23 Sherpas and 330UTs. Approximately 50 were in airline service at late 1996.

History: The Shorts 330, or 'Shed' as at least one regional airline has affectionately dubbed it, is an inexpensive and reliable 30 seat airliner, if somewhat slower than most of its pressurised competition.

The Shorts 330 is a stretched development of the modestly successful SC.7 Skyvan. Beginning life designated the SD3-30, the 330 retained the Skyvan's overall configuration, including the slab sided fuselage cross section, supercritical, braced, above fuselage mounted wing design (stretched by 2.97m/9ft 9in) and twin tails. Compared with the Skyvan though the fuselage is stretched by 3.78m (12ft 5in), allowing seating for over 10 more passengers. Improved performance over the fairly slow Skyvan is courtesy of the two Pratt & Whitney PT6A turboprops driving five blade props, pointed nose and retractable undercarriage. More than 60% greater fuel capacity boosts range significantly over the Skyvan.

An engineering prototype of the 330 flew for the first time on August 22 1974, while a production prototype flew on July 8 1975 and the first true production aircraft flew that December. The 330 entered airline service with Time Air of Canada in August 1976.

Initial Shorts 330s were powered by PT6A-45As and -45Bs and are known as 330-100s, while definitive 330s feature more powerful PT6A-45s. Known as 330-200s they also feature a number of detail improvements, while equipment previously available as options were made standard equipment.

Various freighter versions of the 330 have been developed, including the Sherpa with a rear loading ramp (in service with the US Air Force and Army as the C-23), and the military 330UT.

Photo: A 330 airliner in the colours of American Eagle. This aspect shows to good effect the Shorts' box like fuselage.

Shorts 360

Country of origin: United Kingdom

Type: 36 seat regional airliner

Powerplants: 360 – Two 990kW (1327shp) Pratt & Whitney Canada PT6A-65R turboprops, driving five blade constant speed Hartzell propellers. 360-300 – Two 1062kW (1424shp) PT6A-67Rs driving six blade props.

Performance: 360 – Max cruising speed 390km/h (210kt). Range at max cruising speed with 36 passengers 426km (230kt), range with max fuel 1055km (570nm). 360-300 – Typical cruising speed 400km/h (216kt). Max rate of climb 925ft/min. Range with 36 passengers and reserves at typical cruising speed 745km (402nm), with 31 passengers and reserves at 337km/h (182kt) cruising speed 1178km (636nm).

Weights: 360 – Operating empty 7350kg (16,600lb), max takeoff 11,657kg (25,700lb). 360-300 – Typical operating empty 7870kg (17,350lb), max takeoff 12,292kg (27,100lb).

Dimensions: Wing span 22.80m (74ft 10in), length 21.58m (70ft 10in), height 7.27m (23ft 10in). Wing area 42.2m^2 (454.0sq ft).

Capacity: Flightcrew of two. Typical passenger accommodation for 36 at three abreast and 76cm (30in) pitch in 12 seat rows. Optional seating for 39 in a high density configuration. Freighter 360-300F can house up to five standard LD3 containers or pallets.

Production: Production ceased in 1991 after approximately 165 had been delivered. Approximately 105 remained in airliner service in 1996.

History: The Shorts 360 is a stretched larger capacity and improved 36 seat derivative of the 30 seat Shorts 330.

The relative success of the rugged Shorts 330 prompted this Northern Ireland based manufacturer to study and subsequently develop a stretched derivative. Shorts announced it was developing the new airliner in mid 1980, and a prototype 360 flew for the first time almost a year later on June 1 1981. The first production 360 flew in August 1982 and certification was awarded on September 3 that year. The 360 entered service with Suburban Airlines in the US in November 1982.

The two Shorts airliners are very close in overall dimensions and size, but the later 360 is easily identified by its new conventional tail unit, mounted on a revised rear fuselage. The 360 meanwhile is 91cm (3ft) longer than the 330, with two more seat rows and six extra passengers to be carried, while the extra length also reduces drag. Power is supplied by two Pratt & Whitney PT6A-65s, and the 360's wing span is slightly greater. Otherwise the 330 and 360 are very similar, and the two types share a number of systems and components.

Shorts marketed a number of 360 developments, the first of which was the 360 Advanced whose main difference was the 1062kW (1424shp) PT6A-65ARs. The 360 Advanced was introduced in late 1985, but was soon followed by the further improved 360-300, which entered service in March 1987. The 360-300 introduced advanced six blade propellers, more powerful PT6A-67R engines giving a higher cruise speed and improved hot and high performance and other aerodynamic improvements. The 360-300 was also built in freighter 360-300F form.

Photo: The 360 is distinguished by its conventional tail and stretched fuselage, as evidenced in this photo of an Aer Lingus 360. (Shorts)

SIAI-Marchetti S.205 & S.208

Country of origin: Italy

Type: Four seat light aircraft

Powerplant: S.205-20 – One 150kW (200hp) Lycoming IO-360-A1B6D fuel injected flat four piston engine, driving a two blade constant speed propeller. S.208 – One 185kW (260hp) Lycoming 0-540-E4A5 flat six.

Performance: S.205-20 – Max speed 270km/h (146kt), max cruising speed 250km/h (136kt), normal cruising speed 243km/h (131kt). Initial rate of climb 826ft/min. Service ceiling 15,575ft. Range 1260km (680nm). S.208 – Max speed 320km/h (173kt), max cruising speed 300km/h (162kt). Initial rate of climb 985ft/min. Service ceiling 17,725ft/min. Range with tip tanks 1800km (970nm).

Weights: S.205-20 – Empty 760kg (1677lb), max takeoff 1300kg (2865lb). S.208 – Empty 827kg (1823lb), max TO 1500kg (3307lb).

Dimensions: S.205-20 – Wing span 10.86m (35ft 8in), length 8.00m (26ft 3in), height 2.89m (9ft 6in). Wing area 16.1m^2 (173sq ft). Same except span over tip tanks 11.23m (36ft 10in), length 8.09m (26ft 7in).

Capacity: Typical seating for four in S.205, up to five in S.208.

Production: Approximately 620 S.205s of all models were built, including 62 assembled by Waco in the USA. Approximately 120 S.208s built, including 40 for the Italian air force.

History: SIAI-Marchetti intended that this series of four seat light aircraft would provide it with a re-entry into the GA market.

When SIAI-Marchetti began work on the S.205, a modern four seat light aircraft design, the company intended to develop a series of aircraft with various powerplant and other options, such as retractable undercarriage and constant speed propellers. To this end the company was modestly successful, with several hundred S.205s and larger S.208s built, although most of these were for European customers.

The first of three S.205 prototypes flew for the first time during 1965. This initial aircraft was powered by a 135kW (180hp) Lycoming 0-360 and featured a fixed undercarriage and became the S.205-18/F (18 for 180hp, F for fixed undercarriage) in production. The first production S.205-18/F flew in February 1966 and deliveries commenced later that year. The model lineup was expanded to include the 150kW (200hp) fuel injected IO-360 powered and higher max takeoff weight S.205-20/F, and the retractable undercarriage S.205-18/R and S.205-20/R. The most powerful member of the S.205 family was the S.205-22/R. This aircraft was powered by a 165kW (220hp) Franklin 6A-350-C1 flat six and was also assembled in the USA by Waco as the S.220 Vela.

Production of the S.205 initially ceased in 1975, although it returned to production as the improved S.205AC from 1977 until 1980 against an order for 140 for the Italian Aero Club.

The S.208 is based on the S.205 but has a larger cabin with seating for five. First flown in 1968, it is powered by a 195kW (260hp) Lycoming 0-540 and has retractable undercarriage, a third cabin window per side, optional tip tanks and strengthened structure. Deliveries commenced in 1968, and 44 were built for the Italian air force. Production ceased in 1975 and then resumed in 1977 alongside the S.205AC until finally ceasing in 1980.

Photo: An Australian registered 205-18/F taxis at Sydney's Bankstown airport. (Lance Higgerson)

SIAI-Marchetti SF.260

Country of origin: Italy

Type: Two seat trainer and high performance light aircraft

Powerplant: SF.260A & C – One 195kW (260hp) Lycoming 0-540-E4A5 flat six piston engine, driving a two blade constant speed prop.

Performance: SF.260A – Max cruising speed 345km/h (186kt). Initial rate of climb 1770ft/min. Service ceiling 21,370ft. Range with max fuel 2050km (1107nm). SF.260C – Max speed 347km/h (187kt), max cruising speed 330km/h (178kt). Initial rate of climb 1790ft/min. Service ceiling 19,000ft. Max range 1490km (805nm).

Weights: SF.260A – Empty 700kg (1543lb), max takeoff (aerobatic) 1000kg (2405lb), max takeoff (utility) 1102kg (2430lb).

Dimensions: SF.260A – Wing span over tip tanks 8.40m (27ft 6in), length 7.02m (23ft 0in), height 2.60m (8ft 6in). Wing area 10.1m^2 (108.5sq ft). SF.260C – Wing span 8.35m (27ft 5in), length 7.10m (23ft 4in), height 2.41m (7ft 11in). Wing area 10.1m^2 (108.7sq ft).

Capacity: Typical seating for two, side by side, plus rear seat capable of seating one adult or two small children.

Production: Over 860 SF.260s have been built. Approximately 170 built for civil customers.

History: One of the most successful two seat military trainers in recent times, the nimble SIAI-Marchetti SF.260 has sold in modest numbers to civil operators worldwide.

The SF.260 was designed by famed Italian aircraft designer Stelio Frati (who was responsible for a number of renowned light aircraft designs) in the early 1960s. It was originally flown in 185kW (250hp) Lycoming 0-540 form by the Aviamilano company as the F.250. However SIAI-Marchetti has undertaken all production (initially under licence, it later assumed full responsibility for the program) as the 195kW (260hp) 0-540 powered SF.260. The second aircraft to fly was the first built by SIAI-Marchetti and the first powered by the more powerful version of the 0-540. This second prototype first flew in 1966.

Initial civil production was of the SF.260A, and a number were sold in the USA as the Waco Meteor. From 1974 production switched to the SF.260B which introduced improvements first developed for the military SF.260M, including a stronger undercarriage, a redesigned wing leading edge and a taller fin. The B was soon followed by the further improved SF.260C, which among other changes has an increased span wing.

While the SF.260 has been further developed into E and F forms these have been sold to military operators only. The 260kW (350shp) Allison 250-B17D turboprop powered SF.260TP meanwhile has been built since the early 1980s, but it too has been sold only to military customers. Nevertheless Italian civil certification was awarded in October 1993, opening the door for possible civil sales.

In civil use the SF.260 is now regarded as something of a classic thoroughbred as most are approaching two decades of service. Its relatively clean aerodynamic lines, retractable undercarriage and relatively powerful engine guarantee spirited performance. Early in its career many SF.260s were ordered by a number of airlines, including Sabena and Air France, for initial pilot training, while others have been used by aerobatic teams.

Photo: A demonstrator SF.260TP. (SIAI Marchetti)

Sikorsky S-55

Country of origin: United States of America

Type: Mid size utility helicopter

Powerplant: S-55C – One 520kW (700hp) Wright R-1340-3 nine cylinder radial piston engine, driving a three blade main rotor and two blade tail rotor. S-55T – One 625kW (840shp) Garrett AiResearch TSE331-3U-303 turboshaft derated to 485kW (650shp).

Performance: S-55C – Max speed 163km/h (88kt), cruising speed 137km/h (74kt). Initial rate of climb 700ft/min. Hovering ceiling in ground effect 2000ft. Service ceiling 10,500ft. Range 645km (350nm). S-55T – Max speed 183km/h (99kt), cruising speed 157km/h (85kt). Initial rate of climb 1200ft/min. Hovering ceiling in ground effect 10,000ft. Range 595km (320nm).

Weights: S-55C – Empty 2245kg (4950lb), max TO 3265kg (7200lb). S-55T – Empty equipped 2132kg (4700lb), max TO 3265kg (7200lb).

Dimensions: Main rotor diameter 16.16m (53ft 0in), fuselage length 12.87m (42ft 3in), height 4.06m (13ft 4in).

Capacity: Flightcrew of two. Typical seating in main cabin for eight to 12 passengers. Many aircraft configured in executive configurations, or to carry freight. Can also carry an external sling load.

Production: Total Sikorsky S-55 production of 1281 aircraft, most for military service with US forces, 44 built under licence in Japan and 400 as Westland Whirlwinds. Approximately 40 S-55T conversions.

History: Like many Sikorsky helicopters, the S-55 started out as a military helicopter for the US armed forces that was later adapted for civil commercial service.

Sikorsky developed the S-55 in response to a US military requirement for a large general purpose helicopter. The US Defense Department awarded Sikorsky a contract to develop such a helicopter in 1948, and the first prototype flew for the first time on November 10 1949. As the H-19 Chickasaw the S-55 saw widespread US military service, being one of the first helicopters to enter widespread use.

Civil certification for the commercial S-55 series was first awarded on March 25 1952. An unusual feature of this large helicopter was its nose mounted engine, the driveshaft to the main rotor passing over the main cabin and under the flightdeck.

The initial civil variant was the S-55, powered by a 450kW (600hp) Pratt & Whitney Wasp radial piston engine. Later civil variants of the S-55 include the S-55A which introduced the 520kW (700hp) Wright R-1340 radial piston engine, while the most developed version was the S-55C, with the P&W engine and repositioned tail boom of the S-55A.

Westland in the UK licence built 400 S-55s as the Whirlwind for mainly military but also for commercial use. Early Whirlwinds were similar to the S-55 save for their Alvis Leonides radial engine, later developments were powered by a 785kW (1050shp) Rolls-Royce Bristol Gnome H.1000 turboshaft. Licence manufacture of the S-55 was also undertaken in Japan and France.

In January 1971 Aviation Specialties was awarded a type certificate for its turboprop powered conversion of the S-55, dubbed the S-55T. Aviation Specialties formed the Helitec Corp to market and convert aircraft, and approximately 40 were fitted with a Garrett AiResearch TSE331 turboshaft.

Photo: An S-55B in agricultural configuration. (Dave Prossor)

Sikorsky S-58

Country of origin: United States of America

Type: Mid size utility helicopter

Powerplants: S-58 – One 1140kW (1525hp) Wright R-1820-84 radial piston engine, driving a four blade main rotor and four blade tail rotor. S-58T – One 1340kW (1800shp) Pratt & Whitney Canada PT6T-3 Twin Pac turboshaft (two PT6s linked through a combining transmission) or one 1400kW (1875shp) PT6T-6.

Performance: S-58 – Max speed 198km/h (107kt), cruising speed 158km/h (85kt). Initial rate of climb 1100ft/min. Hovering ceiling in ground effect 4900ft/min. Range 360km (195nm). S-58T (with PT6T-6s) – Max speed 222km/h (120kt), cruising speed 158km/h (85kt). Hovering ceiling out of ground effect 6500ft. Range 450km (243nm).

Weights: S-58 – Empty 3754kg (8725lb), max takeoff 6350kg (14,000lb). S-58T – Empty 3355kg (7400lb), max TO 5895kg (13,000lb).

Dimensions: S-58 – Main rotor diameter 17.07m (56ft 0in), fuselage length 14.25m (46ft 9in), height 4.36m (14ft 4in). Main rotor disc area 228.5m^2 (2460sq ft). S-58T – Same except for fuselage length 14.41m (47ft 3in).

Capacity: Flightcrew of two. Main cabin seating capacity for between 10 and 16 passengers or freight. Can also carry external sling loads.

Production: 1821 S-58s built mainly for military but also for civil use between 1954 and 1970.

History: The Sikorsky S-58 was one of the most successful piston powered mid size helicopters built, and continues to serve in small numbers in a range of commercial roles.

Sikorsky developed the S-58 in response to a US Navy requirement for an anti submarine warfare helicopter. What resulted was the S-58, which features a single Wright R-1820 radial piston engine mounted in the nose, one of the largest fuselages to be designed in a single piston powered helo and a raised flightdeck. As the XHSS-1 the S-58 flew for the first time on March 8 1954.

Large numbers of S-58s were subsequently built to serve with the US Navy in anti submarine warfare roles as the SH-34G and CH-34J Seabat, and later in utility roles as the CH-34 Seahorse. The US Army operated large numbers as the CH-34 Choctaw while many other allied countries operated the S-58 in various military roles. The UK for example licence built a turboprop development called the Wessex, some of which saw civil service.

Modest numbers of piston powered S-58s saw civil service, most were delivered to customers within the USA. The S-58 offered a very large fuselage and lifting capacity, but its piston engine made it expensive to operate.

In 1970 Sikorsky announced that it was developing a turboprop conversion package for the S-58. Turboprop powered S-58s are designated the S-58T and were initially powered by a 1340kW (1800shp) Pratt & Whitney PT6T-3, later aircraft a 1400kW (1875shp) PT6T-6. The first such S-58T conversion flew for the first time on August 19 1970. Sikorsky set up a production line to convert S-58s itself, offered kits for S-58 operators to perform the conversion themselves and purchased used S-58s, converted them to turbine power and offered them for resale. Small numbers remain in commercial service.

Photo: Today S-58s are becoming less and less common.

Sikorsky S-61L & S-61N

Country of origin: United States of America

Type: Heavy lift airliner & utility helo

Powerplants: S-61N Mk II – Two 1120kW (1500shp) General Electric CT58-140-1 or 140-2 turboshafts, driving a five blade main rotor and five blade tail rotor.

Performance: S-61N Mk II – Max cruising speed 240km/h (180kt), economical cruising speed 222km/h (120kt). Service ceiling 12,000ft. Range with max fuel and reserves 797km (430nm).

Weights: S-61N Mk II – Empty 5675kg (12,510lb), max takeoff 9300kg (20,500lb) or 9980kg (22,000lb) with an external load. S-61L Mk II – Empty 5,308kg (11,704lb).

Dimensions: Main rotor disc area 18.90m (62ft 0in), length overall 22.20m (72ft 10in), fuselage length 17.96m (58ft 11in), height 5.32m (17ft 6in). Main rotor disc area 280.5m^2 (3019.0sq ft).

Capacity: Flightcrew of two. Main cabin seating for up to 26 in early production aircraft and 30 in later production aircraft. Payloader can lift a 4990kg (11,000lb) payload externally in a sling load.

Production: By mid 1979 a total of 116 S-61Ns and S-61Ls had been delivered, when production had been completed.

History: Two of the most widely used airliner and oil rig support helicopters ever built, the Sikorsky S-61N and S-61L are based on SH-3/S-61A/B Sea King series originally developed in the late 1950s.

In September 1957 the US Navy awarded Sikorsky a development contract to produce an amphibious anti submarine warfare helicopter capable of detecting and attacking submarines. The prototype Sea King flew on March 11 1959, while production deliveries took place from September 1961. Power for initial production aircraft was supplied by two 930kW (1250shp) General Electric T58-GE-8B turboshafts.

Development of a civil version was undertaken almost concurrently, with the first commercial S-61L flying for the first time on November 2 1961. While based on the Sea King, the S-61L is 1.27m (4ft 3in) longer allowing it to carry a substantial payload of freight or passengers. Power for initial production S-61Ls was supplied by two 1005kW (1350shp) GE CT58-140 turboshafts, the civil equivalent of the T58.

Unlike the Sea King, the S-61L was intended for land operations only and features a modified landing gear without float stabilisers. The otherwise identical S-61N, which first flew on August 7 1962, retains the floats, making it suitable for overwater operations, particularly oil rig support. Both the S-61L and S-61N were subsequently updated to Mk II standard with improvements including more powerful CT58-110 engines giving better hot and high performance, vibration damping and other detail refinements.

A third civil development of the S-61 series to be offered was the Payloader, a stripped down machine optimised for aerial crane work. The Payloader features the fixed undercarriage of the S-61L, but with an empty weight almost 900kg (2000lb) less than the standard S-61N.

The S-61 Shortsky is a unique shortened (1.6m/50in) conversion of the S-61N and L, designed to increase single engine performance and external payload. The conversion first flew in February 1996 and is undertaken by Helipro in Washington State USA.

Photo: A British International Helicopters S-61N pictured at Shetland in Scotland. (Keith Gaskell)

Sikorsky S-62

Country of origin: United States of America

Type: Mid size utility helicopter

Powerplant: S-62A – One 785kW (1050shp) General Electric CT58-100-1 turboshaft, driving a three blade main rotor and two blade tail rotor. S-62C – One 930kW (1250shp) GE CT58-110-1.

Performance: S-62A – Max speed 175km/h (95kt), cruising speed 158km/h (85kt). Initial rate of climb 1300ft. Hovering ceiling out of ground effect 8000ft. Service ceiling 15,700ft. Typical range with reserves 410km (222nm). S-62C – Max speed 163km/h (88kt), max cruising speed 148km/h (80kt). Initial rate of climb 1140ft/min. Hovering ceiling in ground effect 17,800ft. Range with reserves 743km (400nm).

Weights: S-62A – Empty 2175kg (4789lb), max takeoff 3405kg (7500lb). S-62C – Empty equipped 2205kg (4860lb), max takeoff 3587kg (7900lb).

Dimensions: Main rotor diameter 16.17m (53ft 0in), fuselage length 13.60m (44ft 7in), height overall 4.32m (14ft 2in). Main rotor disc area 205m^2 (2206sq ft).

Capacity: Flightcrew of two. Main cabin seats 10 in typical passenger configuration. Alternatively can be configured for freight.

Production: Approximately 175 S-62s built, including 99 HH-52s for the US Coast Guard, 50 Sikorsky built S-62s for commercial operators and 25 under licence in Japan (including 18 for the Japanese military and three for Japanese commercial operators).

History: Although it resembles the much larger S-62/H-3 Sea King series, the single engine S-62 was in fact a much earlier design, based upon the piston powered S-55.

Although produced in only small numbers, the S-62 has the distinctions of being Sikorsky's first production design powered by a turboshaft (rather than piston) engine and Sikorsky's first amphibious helicopter.

The S-62 is based on one of Sikorsky's largest single piston engine designs, the S-55. The S-62 takes the S-55's dynamic systems, including the rotor blades, main and tail rotor heads, main, intermediate and tail gearboxes and components of other systems including hydraulics and flight controls coupled with a General Electric CT58 turboshaft and a new, larger fuselage. The new fuselage combined a hull and outrigger floats (housing retractable main undercarriage) giving it its amphibious capability and a larger more voluminous main cabin. The comparatively light weight of the turboshaft meanwhile meant that it could be mounted above the fuselage, rather than in the nose as on the S-55 and S-58.

The S-62 was produced in three versions. The prototype flew for the first time on May 14 1958, and the first of the initial production version, the S-62A was delivered to Los Angeles Helicopters in 1961. Only one of the developed S-62B flew, it differed from the S-62A in having the dynamic systems of the S-58 (described separately). The S-62C was a commercial development of the US Coast Guard's search and rescue HH-52A, with a more powerful engine.

Photo: Few S-62s remain in operation, although some examples survive thanks to the fast growing tourism industry. (Tony Arbon)

Sikorsky S-76

Country of origin: United States of America

Type: Mid size utility helicopter

Powerplants: S-76 Mk II – Two 485kW (650shp) takeoff rated Allison 250-C30S turboshafts, driving four blade main and tail rotors. S-76C – Two 539kW (723shp) takeoff rated Turboméca Arriel 1S1 turboshafts.

Performance: S-76 Mk II – Max cruising speed 286km/h (155kt), long range cruising speed 232km/h (125kt). Initial rate of climb 1350ft/min. Service ceiling 15,000ft. Range with 12 passengers, standard fuel and reserves 748km (404nm), with eight passengers, auxiliary fuel and reserves 1112km (600nm). S-76C – Max cruising speed 276km/h (149kt), long range cruising speed 248km/h (134kt). Max range with reserves 204km (380nm).

Weights: S-76 Mk II – Empty (standard equipment) 2540kg (5600lb), max takeoff 4672kg (10,300lb). S-76C – Empty (standard equipment) 2849kg (6282lb), max takeoff 5306kg (11,700lb).

Dimensions: Main rotor diameter 13.41m (44ft 0in), length overall 16.00m (52ft 6in), fuselage length 13.22m (43ft 4in), height overall 4.41m (14ft 6in). Main rotor disc area 141.3m^2 (1520.5sq ft).

Capacity: Flightcrew of two. Max seating for 12 or 13 passengers in oil rig support aircraft with a 79cm (31in) pitch. VIP configurations are offered in six or eight passenger seat form. EMS configured aircraft accommodate one or two stretchers and four medical attendants.

Production: Total S-76 production in late 1996 of approximately 445, comprising 283 S-76As, 76 S-76Bs, 17 S-76A+ and 29 S-76Cs, while more than 70 S-76As have been converted to S-76A+ standard. More than 380 S-76s are in service.

History: One of the few helicopters in its class designed from the ground up for commercial rather than military applications, the Sikorsky S-76 is employed on a number of civil roles.

Sikorsky developed the S-76 in part to diversify its product lineup away from military work, and in part to exploit the market potential of a modern mid size commercial helicopter. Sikorsky began development work on the S-76 (for a time named Spirit) in the mid 1970s and used technologies and knowledge gained from the military S-70 program. The resulting design was powered by two Allison 250-C30S turboshafts and was capable of seating 12, making it well suited for oil rig support work. The S-76's first flight took place on March 13 1977 and FAA certification was awarded in November 1978.

Since certification of the initial S-76A in 1978, Sikorsky has developed a number of improved models, differing mainly in the powerplant fitted. The first improved model is the S-76 Mark II (introduced in March 1982) with more powerful Allison engines and 40 detail refinements. The S-76B is powered by two Pratt & Whitney Canada PT6B-36s, while the S-76C is powered by two Turboméca Arriel 1S1 engines. The S-76A+ designation covers undelivered S-76As subsequently fitted and delivered with Arriel engines, and S-76As converted to Arriel power. The latest model is the S-76C+ with 18% more powerful Arriel 2S1 engines. Certification of the C+ was planned for the first half of 1996.

Photo: Filling a market niche challenged by no other make, the S-76 (here a Pratt & Whitney Canada PT6 powered S-76B) has to date sold over 400 examples. (Sikorsky)

Sikorsky S-92 Helibus

Country of origin: United States of America

Type: Medium to heavy lift airliner and utility helicopter

Powerplants: S-92C – Two 1305kW (1750shp) takeoff rated General Electric CT7-6D turboshafts, driving four blade main and tail rotors.

Performance: S-92C – Max cruising speed 287km/h (155kt), economical cruising speed 260km/h (140kt). Hovering ceiling in ground effect 9800ft, out of ground effect 5000ft. Range 945km (510nm).

Weights: S-92C – Empty 6743kg (14,866lb), max takeoff 10,930kg (24,100lb), max takeoff with sling load 12,020kg (26,500lb).

Dimensions: Main rotor diameter 17.71m (56ft 4in), length overall rotors turning 20.85m (68ft 5in), fuselage length 17.32m (56ft 10in), height overall 6.45m (21ft 2in). Main rotor disc area 231.6m^2 (2492.4sq ft).

Capacity: Flightcrew of two. Accommodation in main cabin for 19 passengers or up to three standard LD3 containers.

Production: Program launched mid 1995 with first deliveries planned for 2000. Sikorsky estimates a market for 5000 civil and military helicopters in S-92 class between 2000 and 2019. Unit cost approx $US12.5m.

History: The S-92 Helibus is a new medium/heavy lift helicopter using dynamic components from the military H-60/S-70 Hawk series.

Development of the S-92 was first announced in 1992 when Sikorsky unveiled a mockup of the new helicopter. In 1993 however Sikorsky postponed launching the S-92 due to the international helicopter market downturn and instead began searching for international risk sharing partners. By 1995 Sikorsky had formed its Team S-92 partners and formally launched the S-92 at that year's Paris Airshow.

Sikorsky will initially build five development S-92s. The first to fly will be a civil S-92C, with first flight scheduled for the second quarter of 1998. Two S-92Cs (named Helibus) and three military/international utility S-92IU development aircraft are planned. S-92C certification to FAR/JAR Pt 29 is scheduled for the first quarter of 2000, the S-92IU should get its ticket in the third quarter of that year.

The S-92 will combine the dynamic systems of the H-60/S-70 series with a larger cabin. Components based on those from the S-70 series include the rotor head, transmission and powerplants. Otherwise the S-92 will be all new with an all composite wide chord and drooped tip rotor blades (40% of the aircraft will be of composite construction). The main cabin is wider and longer than the H-60's and features a rear loading freight ramp, while the cockpit will feature four liquid crystal displays, with provision for a fifth.

Team S-92 members include risk sharing partners Mitsubishi Heavy Industries (7.5%, responsible for the main cabin), Gamesa of Spain (7% – cabin interior and transmission housing) and China's Jingdezhen Helicopter Group (2% – tail pylon and tailplane), while Taiwan Aerospace (6.5% – flightdeck) and Embraer (4% – sponsons and fuel system) are fixed price suppliers/partners. Russia's leading helicopter designer Mil is also a program participant.

The S-92 is similar in size to the S-61 and no doubt will form a useful replacement for the later helicopter. The S-92 is also in the same class as the popular Super Puma.

Photo: A mockup of the civil 19 seat S-92C Helibus. (Sikorsky)

Sino Swearingen SJ30

Country of origin: United States of America

Type: Entry level corporate jet

Powerplants: Two 8.45kN (1900lb) Williams Rolls FJ44 turbofans

Performance: Max cruising speed 825km/h (445kt), long range cruising speed 765km/h (413kt). Initial rate of climb 3920ft/min. Service ceiling 43,000ft. Range at 765km/h (413kt) cruising speed with reserves 3205km (1730nm).

Weights: Empty equipped 2817kg (6210lb), max takeoff 4720kg (10,400lb).

Dimensions: Wing span 11.07m (36ft 4in), length 12.98m (42ft 7in), height 4.24m (13ft 11in). Wing area 15.3m^2 (165.0sq ft).

Capacity: Typically pilot and passenger on flightdeck (or pilot and copilot). Main cabin seating for four in a club arrangement, or up to six in a high density arrangement.

Production: At late 1996 two prototypes had been built. First customer deliveries were then scheduled for 1998.

History: The promising Swearingen SJ30 is a six to eight place entry level business and corporate jet that has over the last few years threatened to enter production, but only now looks likely to begin rolling off the line.

The SJ30 concept was for an advanced technology and relatively high performance, yet low cost entry level corporate jet, and will compete against the quick selling and similarly sized and powered Cessna CitationJet and Raytheon Premier, plus corporate turboprops such as the King Air series. Originally Swearingen Engineering and Technology, under the leadership of Ed Swearingen (designer of the Metro and Merlin turboprops) was to design and develop the SJ30 for Gulfstream.

Gulfstream planned to market the aircraft as the SA-30 Gulfjet, however the company withdrew from the program on September 1 1989. The SJ30 program was set back somewhat, however the Jaffe Group took Gulfstream's place. At the time it was anticipated that the change in program partners, changes to the design and time to refinance the deal would set back scheduling by 18 to 20 months. As the Swearingen Jaffe SJ30, construction of a prototype began in San Antonio, Texas, however in 1990 the Jaffe Group also withdrew from the SJ30 program.

Development then progressed slowly until the 1994 announcement that Swearingen had begun forming a joint venture with Taiwanese investors (Sino Swearingen) to certificate and build the SJ30. Production is now due to take place at a specially designed factory to be built in Martinsburg West Virginia. Production deliveries are scheduled from 1998.

The first SJ30 prototype flew for the first time on February 13 1991, while the SJ30-2 prototype first flew in November 1996. Like the CitationJet the SJ30 is powered by two small Williams Rolls FJ44 turbofans (Williams Rolls is a partnership between cruise missile engine manufacturer Williams International and Rolls-Royce), and typically seats four in the main cabin. Unlike the CitationJet the SJ30 features a swept wing and a 825km/h (445kt) maximum cruising speed.

Photo: The sleek SJ30 is reminiscent of the smaller Foxjet concept of the seventies. (Swearingen)

Slingsby T67 Firefly

Country of origin: United Kingdom

Type: Two seat basic trainer

Powerplant: T67B – One 87kW (116hp) Textron Lycoming O-235-N2A flat four piston engine driving a two blade fixed pitch propeller. T67C – One 120kW (160hp) Textron Lycoming O-320-D2A flat four.

Performance: T67B – Max speed 213km/h (115kt), max cruising speed 204km/h (110kt). Initial rate of climb 660ft/min. Service ceiling 12,000ft. Range with reserves 835km (450nm). T67C – Max speed 235km/h (127kt), max cruising speed 215km/h (116kt). Initial rate of climb 900ft/min. Service ceiling 12,000ft. T67C3 – Range with max fuel and reserves at economical cruising speed 1025km (555nm).

Weights: T67B – Empty 610kg (1345lb), max takeoff 862kg (1900lb). T67C3 – Empty 685kg (1510lb), max takeoff 975kg (2150lb).

Dimensions: Wing span 10.59m (34ft 9in), length 7.32m (24ft 0in), height 2.36m (7ft 9in). Wing area 12.6m^2 (136sq ft).

Capacity: Typical seating for two, side by side.

Production: Almost 300 civil and military orders for T67s of all models built thus far, although most have been for military and quasi military customers.

History: Prior to purchasing the manufacturing and development rights for the French Fournier RF-6B two seat aerobatic basic trainer in 1981, Slingsby specialised in sailplane construction and composites materials, but now concentrates on its successful T67 Firefly.

The Firefly is a development of the Fournier RF-6B. The RF-6B first flew in March 1974, and Fournier built 45 RF-6B-100s powered by 75kW (100hp) Rolls-Royce Continental O-200 flat fours through to the early 1980s. In 1980 Fournier flew a more powerful development of the RF-6B, the 87kW (116hp) Lycoming O-235 powered RF-6B-120. It was this aircraft that formed the basis for Slingsby's T67 Firefly.

Slingsby initially built nine T67As, which were basically RF-6B-120s, before placing into production its own development of the type, the T67B. The T67B was the result of a fairly thorough redevelopment of the T67A. The main difference was that the T67B was made almost entirely from glassfibre reinforced plastics (GFRPs), Slingsby drawing on its very extensive experience in that field. The benefits of GFRP include better resistance to fatigue, less weight and less drag.

The definitive civil version of the Firefly is the T67C. The T67C is similar to the T67B except for its more powerful 120kW (160hp) Textron Lycoming O-320 engine. Variants of the T67C are the T67C1 with standard fuselage fuel tankage and one piece canopy, the T67C2 with a two piece canopy, and the T67C3 with wing tanks and three piece canopy. Many T67Cs have been sold to flying schools and academies (including KLM) while others are in military service.

The military Firefly is the T67M, which first flew in December 1982. Many are used for military initial pilot training and screening, 113 T67M260s (powered by a 195kW/260hp AEIO-540) have been ordered by the US Air Force as the T-3A Firefly, while some are used by civilian flight schools for airline and military training (the latter under government contract). T67Ms have aerobatic capable engines and two blade constant speed props, among other changes, compared with the T67C.

Photo: A T67M260 Firefly operated by Hunting Aircraft under contract for the UK's Joint Elementary Flying Training School. (Paul Merritt)

Socata GY-80 Horizon & ST10 Diplomate

Country of origin: France

Type: Four seat light aircraft

Powerplant: GY-80-160 – One 120kW (160hp) Lycoming O-320-D flat four piston engine, driving a two blade fixed pitch propeller. ST10 – One 150kW (200hp) Lycoming IO-360-C fuel injected flat four, driving a two blade fixed pitch or optional constant speed propeller.

Performance: GY-80-160 – Max speed 240km/h (130kt), cruising speed 234km/h (126kt). Initial rate of climb 690ft/min. Service ceiling 13,940ft. Range with max fuel 950km (515nm). ST10 – Max speed 280km/h (151kt), cruising speed 265km/h (143kt). Initial rate of climb 1005ft/min. Service ceiling 16,400ft. Range with four people on board 1385km (745nm).

Weights: GY-80-160 – Empty 620kg (1365lb), max takeoff 1100kg (2425lb). ST10 – Empty 723kg (1594lb), max takeoff 1220kg (2690lb).

Dimensions: GY-80-160 – Wing span 9.70m (31ft 10in), length 6.64m (21ft 10in), height 2.60m (8ft 6in). Wing area 13.0m^2 (139.9sq ft). ST10 – Same except length 7.26m (22ft 10in), height 2.88m (9ft 6in).

Capacity: Typical seating for four.

Production: Approximately 260 GY-80 Horizons of all models and 55 ST10 Diplomates were built. Production ceased in 1974.

History: Two of Europe's more obscure light aircraft, the Horizon and Diplomate are relatively high performance retractable undercarriage four seaters which were built in only modest numbers.

The initial GY-80 Horizon began life as a privately developed design penned by Yves Gardan, who had also been responsible for a number of other postwar light aircraft designs. Gardan built and flew a prototype as a private development, the prototype flying for the first time on July 21 1960. Two years later, Sud Aviation (now Aerospatiale) acquired the design and production rights for the GY-80, and placed the type into production. Sud Aviation built three pre production development aircraft before placing the GY-80 into production in late 1963.

A key aspect to the GY-80 was its simple design and method of construction. The GY-80 was of conventional construction, featuring retractable tricycle undercarriage, Frise slotted ailerons and Fowler flaps (the flaps, ailerons and horizontal tail pieces were interchangeable to reduce maintenance costs). The Horizon was built using car assembly techniques, with just 11 production jigs.

Three versions of the Horizon were built, differing only in powerplant and fuel tankage. These were the 110kW (150hp) Lycoming O-320-A powered GY-80-150, the 120kW (160hp) O-320-D powered GY-80-160, and the 135kW (180hp) Lycoming O-360-A powered GY-80-160. These were built firstly by Sud Aviation, and then by its newly established light aircraft division Socata from 1966.

Socata flew an improved development of the GY-80, initially called the Super Horizon 200, on November 7 1967. This new development featured a stretched cabin and a more powerful 150kW (200hp) fuel injected Lycoming IO-360-C. In production between 1969 and 1974, the Super Horizon was renamed Provence, and then the ST10 Diplomate, the latter becoming the type's definitive name.

Photo: A GY80-160D Horizon, note retractable undercarriage and relatively small cabin. (Jim Thorn)

Socata Rallye

Country of origin: France

Type: Series of two/four seat light aircraft

Powerplant: MS 880B – One 75kW (100hp) Continental O-220-A flat four piston engine, driving a two blade constant speed propeller. 235 GT – One 175kW (235hp) Lycoming O-540-B4B5 flat six driving a three blade constant speed propeller.

Performance: MS 880B – Max speed 195km/h (105kt), max cruising speed 174km/h (94kt). Initial rate of climb 540ft/min. Service ceiling 10,500ft. Max range 853km (460nm). 235 GT – Max speed 275km/h (150kt), max cruising speed 245km/h (132kt), normal cruising speed 231km/h (125kt). Initial rate of climb 980ft/min. Service ceiling 14,750ft/min. Max range with reserves 1090km (590nm).

Weights: MS 880B – Empty 450kg (990lb), max takeoff 770kg (1695lb). 235 GT – Empty 695kg (1530lb), max TO 1200kg (2645lb).

Dimensions: MS 880B – Wing span 9.61m (31ft 6in), length 6.97m (22ft 11in), height 2.69m (8ft 10in). Wing area 12.3m^2 (132sq ft). 235 GT – Wing span 9.74m (31ft 11in), length 7.25m (23ft 10in), height 3.67m (9ft 2in). Wing area 12.8m^2 (137.3sq ft).

Capacity: Seating for three adults or two adults and two children in MS 880B Rallye-Club/Rallye 100, Rallye 125 and the MS 886 Super Rallye/Rallye 150T. All other variants had seating for four adults.

Production: More than 3500 Rallyes built by Sud Aviation and Socata.

History: The prolific Rallye series of two/three/four seat light aircraft was the most successful aircraft of its type in Europe, and today remains in production in Poland as the Koliber (described separately).

Morane Saulnier originally designed the Rallye in response to a French government competition for a light aircraft in the late 1950s. Morane Saulnier's concept resulted in the Rallye, which flew for the first time on June 10 1959. This first MS 880A prototype was powered by a 67kW (90hp) Continental C90 flat four.

Sud Aviation and then Socata developed a wide range of Rallye models. The main two/three seat production version was the 75kW (100hp) Continental O-220 powered MS 880B Rallye-Club. Other Rallye-Clubs were the 78kW (105hp) Potez powered MS 881 and 85kW (115hp) Lycoming O-235 powered MS 883. A more powerful Rallye-Club development was the 110kW (145hp) Continental O-300 flat six powered Super Rallye (later to become the Rallye 150 S and 150 ST and later still the Garnament).

The first true four seater was the MS 890 Rallye Commodore, which differed from the Super Rallye in having a higher max takeoff weight and strengthened structure. Developments of the Commodore included the 110kW (150hp) Lycoming O-320 powered MS 892 Commodore 150 (later the Rallye 150 GT), the 135kW (180hp) O-360 powered MS 893 Commodore 180 (later the Rallye 180 GT and then the Gaillard) and the 165kW (220hp) powered MS 894 Rallye Minerva (later the Rallye 220 GT). Product improvements have led to the Rallye-Club based Rallye 100S with two seats and 100ST with three and then with a 82kW (110hp) engine the Rallye 100 ST Galopin; the Rallye 125; the glider towing 180 T Galerien; the 235 GT (later the Gabier); and the tail dragger Gaucho ag sprayer. French production ceased in 1983.

Photo: An example of the Continental O-220 powered MS 880B Rallye-Club. (Bill Lines)

Socata Tampico, Tobago & Trinidad

Country of origin: France

Type: Four/five seat light aircraft

Powerplant: TB 9 Tampico – One 120kW (160hp) Textron Lycoming O-360-A1AD flat four piston engine, driving a two blade fixed pitch Sensenich propeller. TB 21 Trinidad TC – One 185kW (250hp) Textron Lycoming TIO-540-AB1AD turbocharged and fuel injected flat six piston engine driving a two blade constant speed Hartzell prop.

Performance: TB 9 – Max speed 226km/h (122kt), max cruising speed 198km/h (107kt), economical cruising speed 194km/h (105kt). Initial rate of climb 750ft/min. Service ceiling 11,000ft. Max range 1030km (555nm). TB 21 – Max speed 370km/h (200kt), 75% power cruising speed 347km/h (187kt), economical cruising speed 315km/h (170kt). Rate of climb from sea level 1126ft/min. Service ceiling 25,000ft. Range with reserves at max cruising speed 1500km (810nm), at economical cruising speed 1780km (962nm).

Weights: TB 9 – Empty 647kg (1426lb), max takeoff 1060kg (2335lb). TB 21 – Empty 844kg (1860lb), max takeoff 1400kg (3086lb).

Dimensions: TB 9 – Wing span 9.76m (32ft 0in), length 7.70m (25ft 3in), height 3.02m (9ft 11in). Wing area 11.9m^2 (128.1sq ft). TB 21 – Same except length 7.71m (25ft 4in).

Capacity: Typical seating for four or five, with pilot and passenger on front bucket seats and two or three passengers on rear bench seat.

Production: Over 1500 of all models built thus far including over 300 Tampicos and Tampico Clubs, over 600 Tobagos and 600 Trinidads and Trinidad TCs.

History: Socata's stylish 'Caribbean' TB series of light singles is one of the most successful ranges currently in production, and spans from the basic fixed gear Tampico Club to the turbocharged 315km/h (170kt) cruise Trinidad TC.

Design work on the TB singles began in the mid 1970s, in part as a replacement for Socata's successful Rallye family. The first prototype, a TB 10 but powered by a 120kW (160hp) Lycoming O-320, flew for the first time on February 23 1977. Production began in 1979.

Three distinct versions of the TB series have been built. The TB 9 Tampico is powered by a four cylinder 120kW (160hp) Lycoming O-320. Until the late 1980s it was available with a fixed pitch propeller as the Tampico FP, or with a constant speed prop as the Tampico CS. Both the Tampico FP and CS had a more up market interior than the current TB 9 Tampico Club which has a two blade fixed pitch Sensenich propeller. The Tampico is marketed primarily as a trainer.

The TB 10 Tobago and TB 200 Tobago XL are similar to the Tampico but feature faired undercarriage, higher weights, a higher level of interior equipment, more powerful engines and constant speed props. The Tobago is powered by a 135kW (180hp) O-360, the Tobago XL a 150kW (200hp) fuel injected IO-360.

The top of the range models are the retractable undercarriage TB 20 Trinidad and TB 21 Trinidad TC. The Trinidad is powered by a 185kW (250hp) IO-540, the Trinidad TC a turbocharged TIO-540.

Photo: The top of the line, retractable gear, high performance turbocharged Trinidad TC. (Socata)

Socata Tangara & Gulfstream GA-7

Countries of origin: United States of America and France

Type: Four place light twin

Powerplants: GA-7 – Two 120kW (160hp) Lycoming O-320-D1D flat four piston engines, driving two blade constant speed propellers.

Performance: GA-7 – Max speed 311km/h (168kt), max cruising speed 296km/h (160kt), typical cruising speed 260km/h (140kt). Initial rate of climb 1150ft/min. Service ceiling 17,400ft. Max range with no reserves 2170km (1170nm).

Weights: GA-7 – Empty 1174kg (2588lb), max takeoff 1725kg (3800lb).

Dimensions: GA-7 – Wing span 11.24m (36ft 11in), length 9.09m (29ft 10in), height 3.16m (10ft 4in). Wing area 17.1m^2 (184sq ft).

Capacity: Standard seating for four.

Production: GA-7s were built in 1978 and 1979. Tangara production due to start in 1997.

History: The GA-7 Cougar light twin began life as a Grumman American design, saw limited production with Gulfstream in the late 1970s and is now due to enter production with France's Socata as the Tangara.

The prototype of the new twin took to the skies for the first time on December 20 1974, but over three years passed before the design entered production. By this time Grumman's light aircraft manufacturing division had been acquired by Gulfstream, who finally placed the GA-7 into production in 1978. The GA-7 design featured two 120kW (160hp) Lycoming O-320s, and the bonded honeycomb construction used on the AA-1 and AA-5. The initial GA-7 design featured a sliding cockpit canopy (again like that on the AA-1 and AA-5), and two cabin windows per side.

During the three years between first flight and production, numerous design changes were made including the adoption of a conventional cabin roof with cabin entry gained through a conventional door on the right hand side. The cabin itself was made larger and a third window was added to each side. The original prototype's single spar wing design was changed in production aircraft to be a twin spar design allowing an integral wet wing fuel tank, and the main undercarriage units retracted outwards, rather than inwards as on the prototype.

When the first production aircraft were delivered in February 1978 two basic variants were on offer, the standard GA-7 and the up spec GA-7 Cougar with a more comprehensive avionics fit and improved interior fittings. However sales of both aircraft were slow, in part because of the GA-7's relatively low combined power output of 240kW (320hp), whereas the competing Beechcraft Duchess and Piper Seminole were powered by two 135kW (180hp) powerplants.

Gulfstream proposed a turbocharged 120kW (160hp) model and a normally aspirated 135kW (180hp) version to overcome these problems, but neither was built as Gulfstream opted out of light aircraft production in 1979.

In 1995 Socata purchased the rights to the GA-7 and will place it back into production as the TB 320 Tangara. The Tangara will be powered by two 135kW (180hp) class engines and cruise at 165kt (306km/h). Socata is pitching it at the light twin trainer market.

Photo: A Gulfstream Cougar. (Bill Lines)

Socata TBM 700

Country of origin: France

Type: Single engine business turboprop

Powerplant: One 520kW (700shp) Pratt & Whitney Canada PT6A-64 turboprop, driving a four blade constant speed propeller.

Performance: Max cruising speed 555km/h (300kt), recommended cruising speed 540km/h (290kt), long range cruising speed 452km/h (244kt). Initial rate of climb 1875ft/min. Certificated service ceiling 30,000ft. Range with six passengers and reserves at max cruising speed 1768km (954nm), with four passengers, max fuel and reserves at max cruising speed 2465km (1330nm), with six passengers and reserves at long range cruising speed 2168km (1170nm), with four passengers, max fuel and reserves at long range cruising speed 3057km (1650nm).

Weights: Empty 1837kg (4050lb), max takeoff 2984kg (6579lb).

Dimensions: Wing span 12.56m (41ft 3in), length 10.43m (34ft 11in), height 4.19m (13ft 9in). Wing area 18.0m^2 (193.75sq ft).

Capacity: Two pilots or one pilot and one passenger on flightdeck. Main cabin seating for up to six, or typical accommodation for four in a club arrangement. The TBM 700 is also offered as a freighter.

Production: Approximately 120 ordered by late 1996, with more than 100 in service worldwide, including six for the French air force.

History: The sleek pressurised TBM 700 is a high performance single engine turboprop powered light business and corporate transport.

The TBM 700 is mainly optimised as a business transport in competition with established twin turboprops, mainly Beech's C90 King Air series. Unlike the similarly sized C90 King Airs though, the TBM 700's single engine layout is a major conceptual difference. With its single PT6 turboprop, rather than two on the King Air, the TBM 700 offers significantly lower operating costs yet comparable performance.

The TBM 700 was originally developed in partnership between Socata (Aerospatiale's General Aviation division) in France and Mooney in the USA, hence the TBM designation. The two companies formed TBM SA to build and market the TBM 700, with development responsibility for the project divided on a 70/30 basis between Socata and Mooney respectively.

The TBM 700 first flew on July 14 1988, and three prototypes were flown and participated in the flight test program that resulted in French certification being granted in January 1990. Shortly after the delivery of the first production aircraft in December 1990, Mooney withdrew from the program, leaving Socata with full responsibility for the aircraft.

The TBM 700 is of conventional design and construction, with a small amount of composite materials used in some areas. Flight controls, flaps and most of the empennage and fin are made from Nomex honeycomb and metal sheets. Leading edges and undercarriage doors meanwhile are made from a carbon and fibreglass composite.

Apart from the base aircraft the TBM 700 is offered as the TBM 700C freighter. Development of the stretched TBM 700S ceased in 1995.

Photo: TBM 700's sleek lines are evident in this photo. The TBM 700 is smaller than the similarly powered and configured Pilatus PC-12 and Cessna Caravan. (Socata)

Sukhoi Su-26, Su-29 & Su-31

Country of origin: Russia

Type: Aerobatic single and two seat light aircraft

Powerplants: Su-29M – One 270kW (360hp) Vedneyev/VOKBM nine cylinder radial piston engine, driving a constant speed three blade propeller (two blade prop optional). Su-31T – One 295kW (395hp) VOKBM M-14PF driving a three blade constant speed prop.

Performance: Su-29M – Max speed 310km/h (167kt), normal cruising speed 260km/h (140kt). Initial rate of climb 3540ft/min. Service ceiling 13,125ft. Ferry range 800km (430nm). Su-31T – Max speed 340km/h (185kt). Initial rate of climb 3540ft/min. Service ceiling 13,125ft. Range with internal fuel 290km (155nm), max ferry range up to 1200km (645nm).

Weights: Su-26M – Empty 705kg (1444lb), max TO 1000kg (2205lb). Su-31T – Empty equipped 670kg (1480lb), max TO 968kg (2134lb).

Dimensions: Su-26M – Wing span 7.80m (25ft 7in), length 6.85m (22ft 6in), height 2.78m (9ft 2in). Wing area 11.8m^2 (127.0sq ft). Su-31T – Same except length 6.90m (22ft 8in), height 2.76m (9ft 1in).

Capacity: Accommodation for pilot only in Su-26, Su-26M, Su-31T and Su-31U. Seating for two in tandem in Su-29.

Production: Total Su-26, Su-29 and Su-31 series production unclear, but includes approximately 40 Su-29s and 70 Su-26s.

History: Sukhoi's series of two and single seat aerobatic aircraft are regarded as the ultimate of their type, and have won a swag of medals and awards in international aerobatic competitions.

Sukhoi is perhaps better known as one of the two pre-eminent Russian high performance combat aircraft design bureaux, but it turned its attention to design and flying a single seat aircraft for unlimited aerobatics competitions in the early 1980s. The prototype of the single seat Su-26, the originator of the series, flew for the first time in June 1984, and remarkably competed in the World Aerobatic Championships held in Hungary only two months later.

Features introduced on the initial Su-26 that have remained with the series include the Vedneyev, now VOKBM, M-14 nine cylinder piston radial engine, which is highly regarded for its simplicity, power to weight ratio, fuel economy and low oil consumption. The airframe itself is extremely strong, capable of withstanding +11 and -9g, while the wing's aerofoil section is symmetrical and attached to the airframe at zero incidence and dihedral for similar positive and negative angle of attack flight characteristics.

Modifications to the Su-26 including a squared off vertical tail and less glass led to the Su-26M, which participated in the 1986 World Aerobatic Championships in the UK. The Su-26MX is an export version. The success of the Su-26 led Sukhoi to design a two seat development, the Su-29, with dual controls for training. The Su-29 flew for the first time during 1991. Differences to the Su-26 are mainly confined to the changes necessary for the second seat.

The ultimate development is the Su-31, which first flew in June 1992 as the Su-29T. The Su-31 is a single seater based on the Su-29, but with a more powerful engine. The basic version is the Su-31T, the Su-31U has retractable undercarriage. Production began in 1994.

Photo: A Lithuanian registered Su-31 single seater at rest. Note transparencies below the cockpit. (Paul Merritt)

Taylorcraft

Country of origin: United States of America

Type: Two seat light aircraft

Powerplant: BC-12D – One 50kW (65hp) Continental A65 flat four piston engine, driving a two blade fixed pitch propeller. F-21 – One 88kW (118hp) Avco Lycoming O-235-L2C flat four.

Performance: BC-12D – Max speed 177km/h (96kt), cruising speed 153km/h (83kt). Initial rate of climb 600ft/min. Service ceiling 17,000ft. Max range 805km (435nm). F-21 – Max cruising speed at 75% power 196km/h (106kt). Initial rate of climb 875ft/min. Service ceiling 18,000ft. Range with max fuel 645km (347nm).

Weights: BC-12D – Empty 304kg (670lb), max takeoff 522kg (1150lb). F-21 – Empty 450kg (990lb), max takeoff 680kg (1500lb).

Dimensions: BC-12D – Wing span 10.98m (36ft 0in), length 6.71m (22ft 0in), height 2.03m (6ft 8in). Wing area 17.1m^2 (183.5sq ft). F-21 – Wing span 10.98m (36ft 0in), length 6.78m (22ft 3in), height 1.98m (6ft 6in). Wing area 17.1m^2 (183.5sq ft).

Capacity: Seating for two side by side, except in the Model 15 Tourist, which seats four.

Production: Taylorcraft production includes 100 prewar Model As, 1800 military L-2s, more than 2800 postwar BC-12Ds, and more than 120 F-19 Sportsman.

History: The Taylor series of light aircraft has one of the most chequered production histories of any light aircraft.

The original Taylor Brother's Airplane Company was responsible for the Piper Cub design, William T Piper purchased the company and its designs in 1931 when it ran into financial difficulties. Gilbert Taylor stayed on as President with the company under Piper's ownership (the Taylor name was retained) until 1935 when he resigned to establish his own company, this time named Taylorcraft. Taylorcraft's first aircraft was very similar to the Piper Cub except that it sat two in tandem and was powered by a 30kW (40hp) Continental engine. Prewar it was built in A, B, D and D Tandem Trainer form, the last aircraft seating two in tandem.

The Tandem Trainer formed the basis for the wartime L-2, nicknamed Grasshopper, and more than 1600 were built during World War 2 for the US Army Air Force.

Postwar Taylorcraft resumed production of the prewar B-12 as the BC-12D. Almost 3000 BC-12Ds were built before the company encountered financial troubles and the firm was bought out by Gilbert Taylor again, in March 1947. The new Taylorcraft Inc then built the two seat Ace, Traveller, De Luxe and Sportsman; the four seat Tourist, Ranch Wagon, Topper agricultural aircraft and the float equipped Seabird and Zephyr.

Once more Taylorcraft ceased trading, and did not reform until 1968 when it was set up to support existing aircraft. In 1973 this company began building the Continental O-200 powered F-19 Sportsman 100, and from 1983 the Lycoming O-235 powered F-21, which were based on the prewar Model B, but production ceased in 1986. Then in January 1990 Taylorcraft flew the improved Textron Lycoming O-235-L2C powered F-22, small numbers of which were built before production ceased for the last time in October 1992.

Photo: The F-21B (pictured) was built between 1985 and '86. (Bill Lines)

Technoavia SM-92 Finist

Country of origin: Russia

Type: STOL utility transport

Powerplant: One 270kW (360hp) VOKBM M-14P geared and supercharged nine cylinder radial piston engine, driving a three blade variable pitch Mühlbauer MT propeller.

Performance: Max speed 290km/h (156kt), max cruising speed 230km/h (124kt), economical cruising speed 200km/h (108kt). Stalling speed with full flap 100km/h (50kt). Range with max fuel 1300km (700m). Endurance with max fuel 7hr 30min.

Weights: Empty equipped 1450kg (3200lb), max takeoff 2200kg (4850lb).

Dimensions: Wing span 14.60m (47ft 11in), length 9.13m (30ft 0in). Wing area 20.5m^2 (220.7sq ft)

Capacity: One pilot and one passenger on flightdeck. Seating for six passengers in main cabin arranged in pairs. Alternatively can accommodate six parachutists, or 600kg (1320lb) of freight.

Production: Production aircraft built at the Smolensk Aircraft Factory at the rate of four per month. Over 200 orders placed.

History: The Technoavia Finist is a big STOL piston powered utility transport in the best traditions of the venerable DHC-2 Beaver, and is one of the first Russian aircraft designed from the ground up to meet western (both FAA and JAA) certification requirements.

The Finist (a small Russian bird) is the first product of the newly established Technoavia Design Bureau. Technoavia was established in 1991 by Slava Kondratiev, a renowned Russian designer responsible for the world beating Sukhoi Su-26, Su-29 and Su-31 series of aerobatic aircraft. Kondratiev provided finance for the new company by purchasing the rights and placing into production the four seat Yak-18T light aircraft (described separately).

The Finist is one of a diverse range of designs from Russian studios aimed at meeting worldwide requirements for a utility transport, but unlike most of its contemporaries it has actually flown and is in production. The big yet elegant high wing aircraft features perhaps the best radial engine currently in production, the M-14P, which also powers the Sukhoi aerobatic aircraft. The design features a high aspect ratio (10.5) wing with Fowler flaps and Frise ailerons, a large main cabin door on the left side and faired steel main landing gear units. Skis and floats will be offered as options.

The prototype Finist only flew for the first time in mid 1994, while production deliveries began in January 1995. Technoavia is studying further developments of the basic aircraft. Foremost of these is a turbine powered variant, with power most likely being supplied by a Pratt & Whitney Canada PT6. The Finist's unit cost is just $US150,000.

Like the much older and out of production Beaver, the Finist is aimed at performing a wide variety of STOL utility missions, and with western certification behind it, it may become a realistic prospect for replacing the world's ageing fleet utility GA aircraft.

Photo: A viable successor to the venerable Beaver? Only time will tell but the Finist certainly looks better optimised for this role than most other designs. (Vance Ingham)

Transavia Airtruk & Skyfarmer

Country of origin: Australia

Type: Agricultural aircraft

Powerplant: PL12-U – One 225kW (300hp) Continental IO-520-D fuel injected flat six piston engine, driving a two blade constant speed McCauley propeller. T-300A – One 225kW (300hp) Textron Lycoming IO-540 fuel injected flat six, driving a three blade constant speed Hartzell prop.

Performance: PL12-U – Max cruising speed 188km/h (102kt). Initial rate of climb 800ft/min. Service ceiling 10,500ft. Range with max payload 1205km (650nm), with max fuel 1295km (700nm). T-300A – Max speed 196km/h (106kt), max cruising speed (75% power) 188km/h (102kt). Initial rate of climb 515ft/min. Service ceiling 12,500ft.

Weights: PL12-U – Empty 830kg (1830lb), max takeoff 1723kg (3800lb). T-300A – Typical empty 955kg (2100lb), max takeoff (ag category) 1925kg (4244lb).

Dimensions: PL12-U – Wing span 12.15m (39ft 11in), length 6.35m (20ft 10in), height 2.79m (9ft 2in). Wing area 23.5m^2 (252.7sq ft). T-300A – Wing span 11.98m (39ft 4in), length 6.35m (20ft 10in), height 2.79m (9ft 2in). Wing area (including lower stub wing) 24.5m^2 (264.0sq ft).

Capacity: Single pilot in all versions. PL12, T-300 and T-400 – Seats for two passengers and also fitted with a chemical hopper. PL12-U seats five with no hopper.

Production: Total PL12 and PL12-U production of 170, including 18 assembled in New Zealand. Production now completed.

History: The Airtruk and Skyfarmer owe their origins to New Zealand's first commercial aircraft, the Waitomo Airtruck.

The original Waitomo Airtruck was designed by Luigi Pellarini in the mid 1950s, and used a number of components from the North American T-6 Texan/Harvard series of piston engine advanced trainers. These included main undercarriage wheels, the front undercarriage assembly, fuel tanks and 410kW (550hp) Pratt & Whitney R-1340 radial piston engine. The Airtruck also featured a fairly tall and squat fuselage that accommodated a pilot, two passengers and a chemical hopper, tricycle undercarriage, a high mounted wing and boom mounted twin tails. The unusual twin tail configuration was adopted as it solved the problem of chemicals contaminating the rear fuselage, while it also allowed easier loading of the chemical hopper. The Airtruck first flew on August 2 1960.

The Airtruck was not built in New Zealand, and instead was further developed in Australia by Transavia as the PL12 Airtruk. The Airtruk differed from the Airtruck in having a flat six Continental engine and additional lower stub wings. It was delivered from December 1966.

The PL12-U utility version seats five and has the chemical tank deleted. It was delivered from 1971. The T-300 and T-300A Skyfarmers are improved developments of the PL12 with a Textron Lycoming IO-540 engine; the T-300 first flew in July 1971, the T-300A, which introduced aerodynamic improvements, first flew in 1981. The final development was the 300kW (400hp) flat eight IO-720 powered T-400, four were delivered to China. Production ceased in 1993.

Photo: A New Zealand registered T-300A Skyfarmer. (Peter Clark)

Tupolev Tu-134

Country of origin: Russia

Type: Short range airliner

Powerplants: Tu-134 – Two 64.9kN (14,490lb) Soloviev D-30 turbofans. Tu-134A – Two 66.2kN (14,990lb) Soloviev D-30 Series II turbofans.

Performance: Tu-134 – Max cruising speed 900km/h (485kt), economical cruising speed 750km/h (405kt). Normal operating ceiling 39,730ft. Range with 7000kg (15,420lb) payload and reserves 2400km (1295nm), with 3000kg (6600lb) payload 3500km (1890nm). Tu-134A – Max cruising speed 900km/h (485kt), economical cruising speed 750km/h (405kt). Range with 5000kg (11,025lb) payload and reserves 3020km (1630nm).

Weights: Tu-134 – Operating empty 27,500kg (60,627lb), max takeoff 44,500kg (98,105lb). Tu-134A – Operating empty 29,050kg (64,045lb), max takeoff 47,000kg (103,600lb).

Dimensions: Tu-134 – Wing span 29.00m (95ft 2in), length 34.35m (112ft 8in), height 9.02m (29ft 7in). Wing area 127.3m^2 (1370.3sq ft). Tu-134A – Same except length 37.05m (121ft 7in), height 9.14m (30ft 0in).

Capacity: Flightcrew of three, comprising two pilots and a navigator. Tu-134 seats 72 in a single class. Tu-134A seats up to 84 passengers in a single class at four abreast, or 12 first class and 54 economy class at four abreast in a two class arrangement. Tu-134B-3 can seat up to 96 in a single class.

Production: Production estimated at over 700, most for Aeroflot, but approximately 170 exported to various east European airlines and other Soviet client states. Over 420 were in service in 1996.

History: For many years the Tupolev Tu-134 was the standard short haul jet airliner in the Soviet Union and eastern Europe, being produced in greater numbers than many contemporary western aircraft.

The Tupolev design bureau was responsible for the Soviet Union's first jet powered airliner, the Tu-104 (which was based on the Tu-16 'Badger' bomber), and the Tu-104's smaller brother the Tu-124. Both of these short range jetliners had a number of performance and technology shortfalls however, and the Tu-134 was developed to address these. Initially the Tu-134 was based fairly closely on the Tu-124, and for a time was designated the Tu-124A. The decision was instead taken to change the aircraft's overall configuration to feature rear fuselage mounted engines and a T-tail and the designation was changed. Flight testing of the Tu-134 began during 1962, with six development aircraft being built. Production began in 1964 although it was not until September 1967 that Aeroflot launched full commercial services.

Initial production was of the standard fuselage length Tu-134. The stretched Tu-134A entered Aeroflot service in the second half of 1970. Seating up to 76 in a single class, the Tu-134A differed from the Tu-134 in having a 2.10m (6ft 11in) fuselage stretch, a reprofiled nose, more powerful D-30 engines and an APU. Other versions are the Tu-134B with a forward facing position for the third crew member between and behind the pilots, the Tu-134B-1 which has a revised interior to seat up to 90 passengers without a galley, and the Tu-134B-3 which can seat 96 with full galley and toilet facilities retained.

Photo: A Tu-134A of the Moldova government at London's Heathrow Airport. (Keith Gaskell)

Tupolev Tu-154

Country of origin: Russia

Type: Medium range airliner

Powerplants: Tu-154 – Three 93.9kN (20,950lb) Kuznetsov NK-8-2 turbofans. Tu-154M – Three 104kN (23,380lb) Aviadvigatel (Soloviev) D-30KU-154-II turbofans.

Performance: Tu-154 – Max cruising speed 975km/h (527kt), economical cruising speed 900km/h (486kt), long range cruising speed 850km/h (460kt). Range with max payload and reserves 3460km (1870nm), range with max fuel and 13,650kg (31,100lb) payload 5280km (2850nm). Tu-154M – Max cruising speed 950km/h (513kt). Range with max payload 3900km (2105nm), range with max fuel and 5450kg (12,015lb) payload 6600km (3563nm).

Weights: Tu-154 – Operating empty 43,500kg (95,900lb), max takeoff 90,000kg (198,415lb). Tu-154M – Basic operating empty 55,300kg (121,915lb), max takeoff 100,000kg (220,460lb).

Dimensions: Wing span 37.55m (123ft 3in), length 47.90m (157ft 2in), height 11.40m (37ft 5in). Wing area 201.5m^2 (2169sq ft).

Capacity: Flightcrew of three or four. Typical single class seating for 158 to 164 at six abreast, or 167 in a high density layout for Tu-154; Tu-154M seats a maximum of 180 at six abreast and 75cm (29.5in) seat pitch.

Production: Approximately 900 Tu-154s of all models have been built, including approximately 200 Tu-154Ms. An estimated 150 built for export to states outside the former Soviet Union. Approx 750 in service.

History: Currently the standard medium range airliner within the states of the former Soviet Union, and still in fairly widespread use in China and to a lesser extent in eastern Europe, the Tu-154 is Tupolev's sixth commercial airliner design.

The Tu-154 was developed to replace the turbojet powered Tupolev Tu-104, plus the An-10 and Il-18 turboprops. Design criteria in replacing these three relatively diverse aircraft included the ability to operate from gravel or packed earth airfields, be able to fly at high altitudes above most Soviet Union air traffic, and good field performance. In meeting these aims the initial Tu-154 design featured three Kuznetsov (now KKBM) NK-8 turbofans (as on the larger, longer range Il-62) which gave a relatively good thrust to weight ratio, double bogey main undercarriage units which retract into wing pods and a rear engine T-tail configuration.

The Tu-154's first flight occurred on October 4 1968, and the first production example was delivered to Aeroflot in early 1971, although regular commercial service did not begin until February 1972. Three Kuznetsov powered variants of the Tu-154 were built, the initial Tu-154, the improved Tu-154A with more powerful engines and a higher max takeoff weight, and the Tu-154B with a further increased max takeoff weight. Tu-154S is a freighter version of the Tu-154B.

Current production is of the Tu-154M, which first flew in 1982. The major change introduced on the M was the far more economical, quieter and reliable Soloviev (now Aviadvigatel) turbofans. Production of the Tu-154 is expected to be phased out as the Tu-204 comes on line, although Tupolev has proposed a further revised version, the Tu-154M2 with two PS-90A turbofans (as on the Tu-204).

Photo: A Tu-154M of Air Via. (Keith Gaskell)

Tupolev Tu-204, Tu-214, Tu-224 & Tu-234

Country of origin: Russia

Type: Medium range airliner

Powerplants: Tu-204 & -200 – Two 158.3kN (35,580lb) Aviadvigatel (Soloviev/Perm) PS-90A turbofans. Tu-204-220 – Two 191.7kN (43,100lb) Rolls-Royce RB211-535E4 or -535F5 turbofans.

Performance: Tu-204 – Cruising speed 810km/h to 850km/h (437 to 460kt). Range with max payload 2900km (1565nm). Tu-204-200 – Speeds same. Range with max payload 6330km (3415nm).

Weights: Tu-204 – Operating empty 58,300kg (128,530lb), max takeoff 94,600kg (208,550lb). Tu-204-200 & -220 – Operating empty 59,000kg (130,070lb), max takeoff 110,750kg (244,155lb).

Dimensions: Tu-204, -200 & -220 – Wing span 42.00m (137ft 10in), length 46.00m (150ft 11in), height 13.90m (45ft 7in). Wing area 182.4m^2 (99ft 0in).

Capacity: Flightcrew of two, Aeroflot aircraft will have a flight engineer. Standard fuselage versions seat up to 214 in a single class high density arrangement at six abreast and 81cm (32in). Three class arrangement for 190, comprising 12 first class at four abreast and 99cm (39in) pitch, 35 business class at six abreast and 96cm (38in) pitch and 143 economy class six abreast and 81cm (32in) pitch. Two class seating for 12 first and 184 economy, pitches as above. Tu-224/-234 seats 166 in a single class.

Production: Ten Tu-204s in service in 1996. Russian govt has ordered 15 for a state owned leasing company. Kato Group of Egypt has ordered 13 Tu-204-220s

History: The all new Tupolev Tu-204 medium range twin has been developed to meet a Russian requirement for around 700 replacement aircraft in this class, and in its Rolls-Royce powered Tu-204-220 form was the first Russian airliner to fly with western engines.

Tupolev began development of the Tu-204 at the behest of the Soviet Union state airline Aeroflot, who required a replacement for the medium range trijet Tu-154. Tupolev chose an all new twin engine configuration with a supercritical wing section, while engine designer Soloviev (now Aviadvigatel) specially developed the PS-90 turbofan. The first flight of a Tu-204 occurred on January 2 1989.

The Tu-204 is being offered in a number of models. The base model is the Tu-204, the first of which have entered service with a number of Russian airlines. The Tu-204-100, -200 and -200C meanwhile are similar to the base Tu-204 save for their higher max takeoff weights, more fuel and greater range. The Tu-204C is a pure freighter fitted with a forward main deck freight door, the Tu-214 is a combi.

Tupolev was keen to develop a westernised development of the Tu-204 to considerably broaden the type's market appeal. The Rolls-Royce RB211-535 powered Tu-204-120 and -220 are the end results of this enthusiasm, which first flew on August 14 1992. Marketed by Bravia (British Russian Aviation), it is offered with either Rockwell Collins (Tu-204-222) or Russian (-120/-220) avionics. The Kato Group of Eygpt is the launch customer.

Tupolev is also developing destretched developments, the 166 seat RR powered Tu-224 and PS-90 powered Tu-234. The Tu-234 prototype was publicly displayed at the 1995 Moscow Airshow

Photo: The Tu-214 combi. (Keith Gaskell)

Tupolev Tu-334

Country of origin: Russia

Type: Short to medium range airliner

Powerplants: Tu-334-100 – Two 73.6kN (16,535lb) ZMKB Progress D-436T1 turbofans. Tu-334-100D – Two 80.5kN (18,100lb) D-436T2s.

Performance: Tu-334-200 – Typical cruising speed range at 35,000ft 800 to 820km/h (430 to 442kt). Range with 102 passengers 2000km (1080nm). Tu-334-100D – Speeds same. Range with 102 passengers 4100km (2213nm).

Weights: Tu-334-100 – Empty 30,050kg (66,250lb), max takeoff 46,100kg (101,630lb). Tu-334-100D – Empty 34,375kg (75,785lb), max takeoff 54,420kg (119,975lb).

Dimensions: Tu-334-100 – Wing span 29.77m (97ft 8in), length overall 31.26m (102ft 7in), height overall 9.38m (30ft 9in). Wing area 83.2m^2 (895.8sq ft). Tu-334-100D – Same except for wing span 32.61m (107ft 0in). Wing area 100.0m^2 (1076.4sq ft).

Capacity: Flightcrew of two or three. Seats 102 in a single class arrangement at 78cm (31in) pitch six abreast, or alternatively 72 in a two class arrangement with 12 first class passengers at four abreast and 102cm (40in) pitch and 60 economy class passengers at 78cm (31in) pitch at six abreast.

Production: Production due to start in 1997/98 at Kiev and Taganrog. Provisional orders placed for 50 aircraft.

History: The advanced technology Tu-334 100 seat jet is being developed as a replacement for the ageing Tu-134.

Although development of a replacement for the Tu-134 has been underway since the late 1980s, it was not until August 1995 at the Moscow Airshow that the first prototype was displayed publicly. This first prototype had yet to fly at the time of writing, while second and third prototypes were under construction.

The Tu-334 is loosely based on the much larger Tu-204 twinjet as Tupolev used as many Tu-204 features in the new design as practical to reduce development time and costs. Examples of this include an identical cockpit and nose, and a shortened Tu-204 fuselage. In addition the Tu-334's wing is based on the Tu-204's, although the latter's is a significantly larger unit.

Apart from commonality with the Tu-204, other notable Tu-334 design features are the rear fuselage mounted Progress D-436 turbofans, T-tail and fly-by-wire flight controls.

The Tu-334 is being developed in three versions. The first is the basic Tu-334-100. The Tu-334-200 is a stretched, 35m (115ft) long 126 seater (in a single class). Apart from the fuselage stretch, changes will include more powerful D436T-2 or BMW Rolls-Royce BR715-55 turbofans, an increased span wing and four wheel main undercarriage units. The Tu-334-100D will be a longer range Tu-334-100, featuring the -100's standard length fuselage but with more powerful engines, increased fuel capacity, a higher max takeoff weight and the increased span wings of the Tu-334-200. In addition, Tupolev has also studied the Tu-334C, which would be a freighter.

The Tu-334 will enter service once Russian AP-23 certification is granted, possibly in late 1997.

Photo: The prototype Tu-334-100 on display at the Moscow Airshow in August 1995.

Vickers Viscount

Country of origin: United Kingdom

Type: Short range turboprop airliner

Powerplants: V.700 – Four 1220kW (1635ehp) Rolls-Royce Dart 506 turboprops, driving four blade constant speed propellers. V.810 – Four 1485kW (1990ehp) Dart 525s.

Performance: V.700 – Cruising speed 507km/h (274kt). Service ceiling 25,000ft. Range with max payload and no reserves 2815km (1520nm), range with max fuel and no reserves 2830km (1528nm). V.810 – Typical cruising speed 563km/h (304kt). Range with 64 passengers 2780km (1500nm), range with max fuel 2832km (1530nm).

Weights: V.700 – Operating empty 17,280kg (38,100lb), max takeoff 27,895kg (61,500lb). V.810 – Operating empty 19,959kg (43,200lb), max takeoff 32,866kg (72,500lb).

Dimensions: V.700 – Wing span 28.50m (93ft 9in), length 24.93m (81ft 9in), height 8.16m (26ft 9in). Wing area 89.5m^2 (963sq ft). V.800 – Same except for length 26.11m (85ft 8in).

Capacity: Flightcrew of two or three. V.700 – Typical layouts included 40 all premium class passengers, or between 47 to 63 economy class passengers at five abreast. V.800 – Single class seating for up to 69 passengers at five abreast and 86cm (34in) pitch.

Production: Total Viscount orders reached 438, plus development aircraft. Over 10 Viscounts remained in service in late 1996.

History: Vicker's Viscount is easily Britain's most successful turbine powered (jet or turboprop) airliner thus far and was the first turboprop airliner from any country to enter service.

The Viscount was one of the results of the UK's wartime Brabazon Committee, which was set up to encourage postwar commercial aviation in the UK. Discussions between the committee and Vickers designers in late 1944, who had already been working on an airliner development based on the Wellington bomber as the VC1 Viking, resulted in what was eventually to become the Viscount. By the end of 1945 Vickers had selected the Rolls-Royce Dart turboprop engine that was then under development to meet the committee's requirement for a 24 seat 1000 mile (1600km/865nm) range airliner.

In March 1946 the British government placed a contract with Vickers to build two prototypes of its design (called Viceroy), one powered by Darts, the other by Armstrong Siddeley Mamba turboprops. By the time of the Dart prototype's first flight on July 16 1948 the design had grown to seat 34. Airline indifference to the 34 seat Viscount and the availability of more powerful Dart variants however led Vickers to stretch the design to seat 40 at four abreast. This development was designated the Type 700, and flew for the first time on April 19 1950.

Airline interest in the Viscount 700 was much stronger, and after receiving certification on April 17 1953, it entered service with BEA the following day. The Viscount was the subject of numerous large orders including from North America, its smoothness, good operating economics, and pressurisation contributing to its success.

Capitalising on the 700's success Vickers developed the stretched 800 with seating for up to 69, while the final Viscount development was the 810 with more powerful engines and higher weights.

Photo: A Viscount 836 in British World colours. (Keith Gaskell)

Victa Airtourer

Country of origin: Australia

Type: Two seat light aircraft

Powerplant: 115 – One 85kW (115hp) Lycoming 0-235 flat four piston engine driving a two blade fixed pitch propeller. T4 – One 110kW (150hp) Lycoming 0-320.

Performance: 115 – Max speed 228km/h (123kt), max cruising speed 210km/h (113kt), long range cruising speed 177km/h (96kt). Initial rate of climb 900ft/min. Service ceiling 14,000ft. Max range with no reserves 1140km (617nm). T4 – Max speed 241km/h (130kt), max cruising speed 225km/h (122kt), long range cruising speed 198km/h (107kt). Initial rate of climb 1100ft/min. Service ceiling 15,500ft. Max range with no reserves 1005km (543nm).

Weights: 115 – Empty 490kg (1080lb), max takeoff 750kg (1650lb). T4 – Empty 528kg (1165lb), max takeoff 793kg (1750lb).

Dimensions: Wing span 7.92m (26ft 0in), length 6.55m (21ft 6in), height 2.13m (7ft 0in). Wing area 11.2m^2 (120sq ft).

Capacity: Seating for two, side by side.

Production: Totals include 170 Victa built 100s and 115s and New Zealand production of 94.

History: Australia's most successful light aircraft, the Airtourer was designed by Australian Dr Henry Millicer (chief aerodynamicist of Australia's Government Aircraft Factory) in response to the Light Aircraft Design competition sponsored by the Royal Aero Club in the UK.

Millicer's design won the competition, and the Ultra Light Aircraft Association of Australia formed the Air Tourer Group to build a 50kW (65hp) Continental powered wooden prototype of the design, which first flew on March 31 1959.

The wooden prototype aroused the interest of Victa (a company more known for its lawn mowers), who in 1960 decided to commercially design and produce the Airtourer series in Australia. Victa's first all metal prototype of the Airtourer was powered by a 75kW (100hp) Continental, and flew for the first time in December 1961. The first production Airtourer 100 flew in June 1962, and type approval was awarded the following month. The more powerful Airtourer 115 meanwhile flew for the first time in September 1962.

A total of 168 production Airtourers were built before Victa's inability to compete against very cheap mass produced imports which were swamping the Australian market and an absence of tariff protection forced the premature closure of production and the dropping of plans to build the four seat Aircruiser development (on which the Airtrainer is based, described separately). However New Zealand's AESL (Aero Engine Services Ltd) purchased design and production rights.

AESL (later NZAI, and now PAC) built the Airtourer 115, a more powerful 110kW (150hp) model Airtourer 150 and constant speed prop fitted Super 150. Later the 115 became the T2, the 150 the T4 and the Super 150 the T5. The T3 was powered by a 95kW (130hp) RR Continental 0-240, while the T6 was a militarised version based on the T5 built for New Zealand. NZAI production ceased in 1974, but Australian and New Zealand built Airtourers remain highly sought after in those countries as well as in Great Britain.

Photo: This civil registered Airtourer T6 wears Singapore air force colours. (Richard James)

VisionAire Vantage

Country of origin: United States of America

Type: Entry level corporate jet

Powerplants: One 12.9kN (2900lb) Pratt & Whitney Canada JT12D-5 turbofan.

Performance: Max cruising speed 648km/h (350kt), economical cruising speed 463km/h (250kt). Max initial rate of climb 4000ft/min. Service ceiling 41,000ft. Range at max cruising speed 1540km (830nm), at economical cruising speed 1780km (960nm).

Weights: Standard empty 1815kg (4000lb), max takeoff 3175kg (7000lb).

Dimensions: Wing span 14.49m (47ft 6in), length overall 12.50m (41ft), height 4.27m (14ft). Wing area 20.6m^2 (222sq ft).

Capacity: One pilot and passenger on flightdeck. Main cabin seats four in standard configuration in a club arrangement. Toilet and baggage compartment in rear of cabin.

Production: At the time of its first flight in November 1996 VisionAire claimed to hold 52 Vantage orders. Unit price at that time was $US1.65m. First deliveries due late 1998 or early 1999. Planned production rate of 115 per year by 2003.

History: The innovative Vantage is an all new single engine entry level corporate jet, designed to compete against the CitationJet and TBM700 turboprop.

Self flying businessman James O Rice Jr established VisionAire in St Louis in 1988 after deciding that there existed a significant market for a low cost entry level business jet. Design aims with the new jet include jet comfort and altitude, good short field performance, a large cabin and low acquisition and operating costs.

The Vantage was designed by VisionAire with the assistance of Scaled Composites (whose president is Burt Rutan), with the aircraft's definitive arrangement settled upon in 1993. In February 1996 VisionAire contracted Scaled Composites to design and build a proof of concept prototype, and this aircraft was rolled out from the latter's Mojave, California facility on November 8 1996.

This aircraft successfully flew for the first time on November 16 1996. Scaled Composites is contracted to test fly the proof of concept prototype until May 1997. This aircraft will be used to demonstrate performance and handling characteristics before a production configuration is settled upon. VisionAire aims to achieve certification for the Vantage by late 1998 or early 1999. Scaled Composites will build Vantage composite components in Colorado, while VisionAire will undertake final assembly in the Ames, Iowa area.

Design features of the Vantage include its single JT12D turbofan buried in the rear fuselage and fed by two air inlets on either side of the fuselage. The JT12D has been in operation since 1982 on the Beechjet 400 and Citation V, and VisionAire says the proven in service engine would have a shutdown rate per aircraft of once every 250 to 500 years if flown 500 hours per annum. Other notable features include the mid fuselage mounted forward swept wing of relatively large area and graphite composite airframe. It will be certificated to FAR Part 23.

Photo: The proof of concept Vantage prototype. The use of a single engine is designed to keep down acquisition and maintenance costs.

Weatherley 201, 620 & 620TP

Country of origin: United States of America

Type: Agricultural aircraft

Powerplants: 201C – One 335kW (450hp) Pratt & Whitney R-985 nine cylinder radial piston engine, driving a two blade constant speed Hartzell propeller. 620 – Same except for a three blade constant speed prop. 620TP – One 375kW (500shp) Pratt & Whitney Canada PT6A-11AG turboprop.

Performance: 201C – Typical cruising speed 170km/h (91kt). Initial rate of climb 960ft/min. 620 – Endurance 2hr 30min. 620TP – Endurance 2hr 0min.

Weights: 201C – Empty 1157kg (2550lb), max takeoff restricted category 2177kg (4800lb). 620 – Empty 1270kg (2800lb), max takeoff restricted category 2495kg (5500lb), design takeoff 1815kg (4000lb). 620TP – Empty 1135kg (2500lb), max takeoff restricted category 2450kg (5400lb), design takeoff 1815kg (4000lb).

Dimensions: 201C – Wing span 11.89m (39ft 0in), length 8.29m (27ft 3in), height 2.48m (8ft 2in). Wing area 23.3m^2 (251.5sq ft). 620 & 620TP – Wing span 12.50m (41ft 0in), or 14.33m (47ft 0in) with optional wingtip guide vanes.

Capacity: Single pilot only in all models. Hopper capacity in 201C is 1022 litres (270US gals/225Imp gal); hopper capacity in 620 is 1268 litres (335US gal/280Imp gal); hopper capacity in 620TP is 1287 litres (340US gal/283Imp gal).

Production: Weatherleys in production between 1967 and 1982. The three model types were built in relatively small numbers (including more than 100 Model 201s).

History: One of the more lesser known agricultural aircraft, the Weatherley series was built in relatively small numbers between the late 1960s and early 1980s.

The Weatherley 201 and its successors date back to 19 Weatherley WM-62C agricultural aircraft built between January 1961 and late 1965. The WM-62s were agricultural conversions of the basic Fairchild M-62 airframe, fitted with a chemical hopper, spray booms and either a Wright W670 or Pratt & Whitney R-985 radial engine.

Weatherley used its experience in designing and converting the WM-62s in developing its own agricultural aircraft design. The resulting Model 201 was a larger aircraft overall of conventional ag aircraft configuration, with a low wing, a Pratt & Whitney R-985 radial, integral chemical hopper and spray booms and an enclosed cockpit for the pilot. The initial production 201 was certificated in 1967, the improved 201C was granted its type certificate in 1975.

The Model 620 replaced the 201C in production from 1980. The 620 featured a longer span wing with optional wingtip vanes and a larger chemical hopper, but the same R-985 engine.

The Pratt & Whitney Canada PT6A-11AG turboprop powered 620TP joined the 620 in production in 1980, and featured a longer nose and a slightly larger chemical hopper. Production of the 620 and 620TP ceased in 1982.

Photo: A Weatherley 620B fitted with the wingtip vanes which were developed to increase the effective swath width, while reducing the amount of chemicals lost from the spraying swath. (Bill Lines)

Yakovlev Yak-18T

Country of origin: Russia

Type: Four seat light aircraft

Powerplant: One 265kW (355hp) Vedneyev/VOKBM M-14P nine cylinder piston radial engine, driving a two blade variable pitch propeller.

Performance: Max speed 295km/h (160kt), max cruising speed 250km/h (135kt), economical cruising speed 204km/h (110kt). Initial rate of climb 985ft/min. Service ceiling 18,000ft. Range with four people, max fuel and reserves 900km (485nm).

Weights: Max takeoff with two people on board 1500kg (3307lb), max takeoff with four people on board 1650kg (3637lb).

Dimensions: Wing span 11.16m (36ft 7in), length 8.39m (27ft 7in), height 2.80m (9ft 2in). Wing area 18.8m^2 (202.4sq ft).

Capacity: Typical seating for four in touring role, often used as a trainer with two on board.

Production: Estimated Yak-18T production of 200, with more than 150 still in service in Russia. Production initially ceased in 1989, but has been restarted against new orders including 20 for the Philippines Air Force.

History: One of the very few four seat aircraft to be built in the Soviet Union during the Cold War years, the rugged Yak-18T has its basis in the Yak-18 series of two seat trainers.

The Yak-18 first flew in 1946, and went on to be built in massive numbers, including more than 8000 for the Soviet air force, becoming that nation's standard military basic trainer for many decades. Most production was of the Yak-18A. Several single seat models were built, including the Yak-18P, Yak-18PM and Yak-18PS, these participating in world aerobatic competitions.

The Yak-18T was the last production model, and the most extensively modified. Compared with the single and two seat Yak-18 models, the Yak-18T introduced a much enlarged cabin with seating for four, tricycle undercarriage (single seat Yak-18PMs had tricycle undercarriage also), plus the 265kW (355hp) Vedneyev (now VOKBM) M-14 nine cylinder radial engine.

First flight occurred in mid 1967 and the Yak-18T was then subsequently placed in series production in Smolensk. The Yak-18T went on to become the standard basic trainer with Aeroflot flight schools, while small numbers also entered service with the Soviet air force as liaison and communications aircraft. After approximately 200 were built, mainly for Aeroflot, production ceased in the late 1980s. However in 1993 the type was placed back into production with the Smolensk Aircraft Factory, against a number of new contracts, including 20 for the Philippines air force. Several Yak-18Ts have also found their way into western ownership. Meanwhile Technoavia offers a developed Yak-18T as the SM-94.

Compared with western four seat light aircraft, the Yak-18T is much larger, heavier and less economic to operate with a far more powerful engine, although it was never intended for private pilot operation. Its strong construction and military background has given it an aerobatic capability, while its general handling characteristics are docile.

Photo: With a large airframe for a four seat tourer, the Yak-18T is also aerobatic and powered by a radial engine. (Bill Lines)

Yakovlev Yak-40

Country of origin: Russia

Type: Short range regional jet airliner

Powerplants: Yak-40 – Three 14.7kN (3300lb) Ivchenko AI-25 turbofans. Yak-40TL – Two 31.1kN (7000lb) Textron Lycoming LF 507-IN turbofans.

Performance: Yak-40 – Max cruising speed 550km/h (297kt), economical cruising speed 470km/h (355kt). Range with max payload of 32 passengers 1450km (780nm), range with max fuel 1800km (970nm). Yak-40TL – Cruising speed 550km/h (297kt). Range with normal payload and reserves 1250km (675nm), range with max fuel and reserves 1950km (1053nm).

Weights: Yak-40 – Empty 9400kg (20,725lb), max takeoff 16,000kg (35,275lb). Yak-40TL – Operating weight 10,885kg (23,950lb), max takeoff 16,575kg (36,540lb).

Dimensions: Wing span 25.00m (82ft 0in), length 20.36m (66ft 10in), height 6.50m (21ft 4in). Wing area 70.0m^2 (735.5sq ft).

Capacity: Flightcrew of two. Typical passenger seating arrangement for 27 at three abreast and 78cm (30in) pitch. Maximum seating for 32 in a high density four abreast configuration.

Production: Estimated total Yak-40 production is 1000, of which approximately 750 were for Aeroflot.

History: Yakovlev's first commercial jet aircraft, the Yak-40 is unique in that it is the only jet powered airliner in its class in service in large numbers anywhere in the world.

Design of the Yak-40 resulted from a mid 1960s Aeroflot requirement for a replacement for the thousands of Lisunov Li-2s (Soviet built DC-3s), Ilyushin Il-12s and Il-14s (described separately) then in service. Aeroflot attached great significance to the Yak-40 program, as the aircraft was intended to perform regional services that accounted for 50% of Aeroflot's passenger traffic.

The Yak-40 was designed under the leadership of A S Yakovlev (after whom the design bureau is named), and first mention of the program's existence was released on October 21 1966, when the first prototype made its maiden flight. The type entered production in 1967, and entered service with Aeroflot in September 1968.

Design features of the Yak-40 include its unique for its class trijet configuration, with three specially developed Ivchenko turbofans. The three jet engine configuration was chosen for its increased redundancy and short field and hot and high performance, which is very important in more remote areas of Russia. The unswept, high aspect ratio wing is also designed for good field performance. An APU and ventral airstairs also allow autonomous operation at remote airfields.

The Yak-40 remained basically unchanged during its production life, but a number of developments have been proposed. The Yak-40M was to be a 40 passenger stretched development, while for a time a US company, ICX Aviation, planned to build the type in the USA with western avionics and three Garrett TFE731 turbofans. The Yak-40TL twin engine conversion has also been offered. The main difference would be the replacement of the Yak-40's three engines with two Textron Lycoming LF 507s.

Photo: Three engines and a straight high lift wing allow the Yak-40 to operate from austere strips normally not available to jet operators.

Yakovlev Yak-42 & Yak-142

Country of origin: Russia

Type: Short range airliner

Powerplants: Three 63.7kN (14,330lb) ZMKB Progress (Lotarev) D-36 turbofans.

Performance: Yak-42 – Max cruising speed 810km/h (437kt), economical cruising speed 750km/h (405kt). Range with max payload and reserves 1380nm (745nm), with 120 passengers 2000km (1080nm), with 104 passengers 2300km (1240nm), with max fuel and 42 passengers 4100km (2215nm). Yak-42D – Range with 120 passengers 2200km (1185nm).

Weights: Yak-42 – Empty equipped with 104 seats 34,500kg (76,058lb), with 120 seats 34,515kg (76,092lb); max takeoff 57,000kg (125,660lb).

Dimensions: Wing span 34.88m (114ft 5in), length 36.38m (119ft 4in), height 9.83m (32ft 3in). Wing area 150.0m^2 (1615sq ft).

Capacity: Flightcrew of two pilots, with provision for a flight engineer. High density single class seating for 120 at six abreast and 75cm (30in) pitch. Two class seating for eight premium class passengers at four abreast and 96 economy class at six abreast.

Production: More than 270 built by late 1996, with most delivered to Aeroflot and its successors. Approximately 150 were in commercial service in 1996.

History: Yakovlev's second commercial airliner to enter production, the Yak-42 and developed Yak-142 also form the basis for the stretched and much developed Yak-242 twinjet currently in development.

The DC-9-30 and 737-200 class Yak-42 was developed as a replacement for Tupolev's Tu-134 twinjet and Antonov's An-24 turboprop, both of which are still in widespread use on Aeroflot's short range airline network. The Yak-42 is similar in configuration to the much smaller and earlier Yak-40, but is actually an all new design, developed in response to a different requirement. Nevertheless, the three engine configuration was selected for much the same reasons, redundancy and short field performance. A moderately swept wing was a compromise between the need for good field performance and high speed cruise capabilites. An integral airstair, APU and double main undercarriage are all incorporated into the Yak-42 design for austere airfield operations. The three Lotarev turbofans meanwhile were among the first true turbofans to be developed in the Soviet Union.

The first of three prototypes flew for the first time on March 7 1975. Development flying revealed the need for an increased sweep back on the wing, and this was in part responsible for the type's protracted gestation. The change of wing sweep back and suspected development hassles with the new three shaft turbofans meant a service entry of late 1980.

Most production has been of the standard Yak-42, while the Yak-42D is a longer range development with extra fuel. The Yak-42T is a freighter fitted with a main deck freight door, capacity is 12 tonnes in eight standard containers. The Yak-142 meanwhile is a development with an EFIS glass cockpit among other improvements. First displayed at the 1993 Paris Salon, it is now in production.

The Yak-242 is basically an all new design with the Yak-42's cross section, with two PS-90A turbofans and seating for up to 180.

Photo: A Yak-142 demonstrator. (Paul Merritt)

Zlin Trener & Akrobat

Country of origin: Czech Republic

Type: One and two seat aerobatic and training light aircraft

Powerplant: Z 226 – One 120kW (160hp) Walter Minor 6-III inverted inline six cylinder piston engine, driving a two blade fixed pitch propeller. Z 526F – One 135kW (180hp) Avia M 137 A inverted inline six, driving a two blade constant speed propeller.

Performance: Z 226 – Max speed 220km/h (120kt), normal cruising speed 195km/h (105kt). Initial rate of climb 950ft/min. Service ceiling 17,390ft. Range 485km (260nm). Z 526F – Max speed 244km/h (132kt), normal cruising speed 210km/h (113kt). Initial rate of climb 1180ft/min. Service ceiling 17,060ft. Range with standard fuel 475km (256nm), range with wingtip tanks 837km (452nm).

Weights: Z 226 – Empty 570kg (1257lb), max takeoff 820kg (1808lb). Z 526F – Empty 665kg (1465lb), max takeoff 975kg (2150lb).

Dimensions: Z 226 – Wing span 10.29m (33ft 9in), length 7.80m (25ft 7in, height 2.06m (6ft 9in). Wing area 14.9m^2 (160.4sq ft). Z 526F – Wing span 10.60m (34ft 9in), length 8.00m (26ft 3in), height 2.06m (6ft 9in). Wing area 15.5m^2 (166.3sq ft).

Capacity: Seating for two in tandem in Z 26, Z 126, Z 226, Z 326, Z 526 and Z 726. Pilot only in Z 226A, 326A, 526A, Z 526AF and Z 526AFS.

Production: More than 1400 of all variants built, many against military and government flying school orders.

History: The renowned Zlin series of two seat Trener trainers and single seat Akrobat aerobatic aircraft was a great success, snaring numerous world aerobatic championship titles during the 1960s.

The original Z 26 Trener was designed in response to a Czechoslovak government requirement for a two seat basic trainer for flying school and military use. The Z 26 was powered by a 78kW (105hp) Walter Minor 4-III inline four cylinder engine, featured wooden construction and a fixed taildragger undercarriage. The prototype flew for the first time in 1947. Production of the Z 26 reached 16 before it was replaced from 1953 by the metal construction Z 126.

Subsequent development over a three decade production run resulted in numerous further improved variants. In 1952 Zlin introduced the Z 226 Trener-6 which featured a more powerful 120kW (160hp) six cylinder Walter Minor 6-III engine. The Z 226 was also built in single seat Z 226A Akrobat form, the glider tug Z 226B and Z 226T trainer.

The similar Z 326 Trener-Master and single seat Z 326A Akrobat introduced retractable undercarriage, a feature that became standard on all subsequent models. Deliveries began in 1959. The Z 526 differed only in that the pilot flew the aircraft from the rear, rather than the front seat, with optional tip tanks and a constant speed prop. The Z 526F introduced in 1968 had a 135kW (180hp) Avia M137A engine, while the otherwise similar Z 526L differed in being powered by a 150kW (200hp) Lycoming AIO-360 flat four and was intended for export. Single seat Z 526s were the Z 526A, Z 526AS, and Z 526AFS. The Z 526 AFM was built between 1981 and 1984 and was powered by a 155kW (210hp) Avia M337 engine, had tip tanks and the Z 526AFS's lengthened fuselage.

Final development was the Z 726 series, the Z 726 Universal had reduced span wings, the Z 726K the 155kW (210hp) Avia M337 engine.

Photo: A Zlin Z 326 Trener-Master. (Bill Lines)

Zlin Z 42, Z 43, Z 142, Z 242 & Z 143

Country of origin: Czech Republic

Type: Two/four seat light aircraft

Powerplant: Z 43 & 142 – One 155kW (210hp) Avia M337 six cylinder inline inverted piston engine, driving a two blade propeller. Z 143 – One 175kW (235hp) Textron Lycoming O-540-J3A5 flat six driving a three blade variable pitch Mühlbauer prop.

Performance: Z 43 – Max speed 235km/h (127kt), cruising speed 210km/h (113kt). Initial rate of climb 690ft/min. Range with max fuel 1100km (595nm). Z 142 – Max cruising speed 190km/h (102kt). Initial rate of climb 865ft/min. Service ceiling 14,100ft. Max range 1050km (565nm). Z 143 – Max speed 265km/h (143kt), max cruising speed at 75% power 228km/h (123kt). Initial rate of climb 965ft/min. Service ceiling 18,700ft. Range at 65% power 1335km (720nm).

Weights: Z 43 – Empty 730kg (1609lb), max TO 1350kg (2976lb). Z 142 – Basic empty 730kg (1609lb), max TO 1090kg (2403lb). Z 143 – Empty equipped 830kg (1830lb), max TO 1350kg (2976lb).

Dimensions: Z 43 – Wing span 9.76m (32ft 0in), length 7.75m (25ft 5in), height 2.91m (9ft 7in). Wing area 14.5m^2 (156.1sq ft). Z 142 – Wing span 9.16m (30ft 0in), length 7.33m (24ft 1in), height 2.75m (9ft 0in). Z 143 – Wing span 10.14m (33ft 3in), length 7.58m (24ft 11in), height 2.91m (9ft 7in). Wing area 14.8m^2 (159.1sq ft).

Capacity: Seating for two in tandem in Z 42, Z 142 and Z 242, seating for four in Z 43 and Z 143.

Production: Total production includes more than 350 142s, 10 Z 242 Ls and prototype Z 143, including military orders.

History: This series of two seat trainers and four seat light aircraft was initially developed as a replacement for the successful Zlin Trener.

The initial Z 42 was developed during the mid 1960s and seats two side by side. It flew for the first time on October 17 1967. The improved Z 42M meanwhile introduced a constant speed propeller and the larger tail developed for the Z 43 four seater, and replaced the Z 42 in production in 1974.

Development of the two seat line continued with the further improved Z 142, which flew for the first time on December 29 1979. Changes introduced included a larger cockpit canopy and faired undercarriage. The Z 142 remains in production in Z 142C form. The latest two seater of this family to be developed is the 150kW (200hp) Textron Lycoming AEIO-360 flat four powered Z 242 L. Changes aside from the engine include a three blade constant speed prop and revised engine cowling profile.

Development of the four seat models, the Z 43 and Z 143, has followed that of the two seaters. The Z 43 appeared a year later than the Z 42, flying for the first time on December 10 1968. The Z 42 and Z 43 share the same basic airframe, but differ in that the Z 43 features a larger and wider cabin with seating for four, and a more powerful engine. The current Z 143 L flew for the first time on April 24 1992, and is similar in structure to the Z 242, but again differs in having a larger cabin with seating for four and a more powerful Textron Lycoming engine.

Like many Czech aircraft many of all variants have been sold in the west, with the Z 143 showing particular promise.

Photo: An Avia M337 powered Zlin Z 142. (Zlin)

THE 1997/98 WORLD AIRLINE GUIDE

The fleets of every airline operating as a minimum jet equipment, compiled by Gordon Reid.

ABAKAN AIR ENTERPRISE – BKN
Abakan Airport, Abakan 662608, Russia.
Tupolev Tu-154Mx2, Tu-154Bx4, Antonov An-24x4.
ABAKAN AVIA – ABG
Kantegir Hotel, Airport, Abakan 662608, Russia.
Ilyushin Il-76x2.
ACES COLOMBIA – VX/AES
Edif. del Cafe, Piso 34, AA6503, Medellin Colombia.
Boeing 727-200x5, 727-100x3, ATR 42x6, DHC-6-300x10.
ACTIVE AIR – AKV
Konakli Sokak no 10, Florya-Istanbul, Turkey.
Tupolev Tu-154Mx3.
ADC AIRLINES – ADK
PMB 6392, Ikeja, Nigeria.
Boeing 707-320Fx1, 727-200x2, MDC DC-9-30x1, BAC 111-400x1, 111-200x2, ATR 42x1.
ADJAL/ADJARIAN AIRLINES – ADJ
Batumi Airport, Batumi 384513, Georgia.
Yakovlev Yak-42Dx3, Tupolev Tu-134Ax2.
ADRIA AIRWAYS – JP/ADR
Kuzmiceva 7, SLO-61001 Ljubljana, Slovenia.
AI A320-200x3, MDC DC-9-30x2, Dash 7-100x2.
AECA/AEROSERVICIOS ECUATORIANOS – 2A/EAE
Apartado 4113, Guayaquil, Ecuador.
Boeing 707-320Fx4.
AER LINGUS – EI/EIN
PO Box 180, Dublin Airport, County Dublin, Ireland.
Boeing 747-100x1, 767-300x1, 737-400x6, 737-500x10, 737-200x2, AI A330-300x4.
AER LINGUS COMMUTER – EI/EIN
PO Box 180, Dublin Airport, County Dublin, Ireland.
BAe 146-300x4, Fokker 50x6.
AER TURAS – ATT
Corballis Park, Dublin Airport, County Dublin, Ireland.
MDC DC-8-63Fx2.
AERO ASIA INTERNATIONAL – E4/RSO
43-J, Block 6, Pechs, Karachi 75400, Pakistan.
Boeing 707-320Cx1, RomBAC 111-500x6.
AEROBRASIL CARGO
Rue Gen Paantaleao Telles 40, Sao Paulo, Brazil.
Boeing 707-320Fx3.
AERO CALIFORNIA – JR/SER
Apartado Postal 555, Hidalgo 316, La Paz, Mexico.
MDC DC-9-30x5, DC-9-10x11.
AEROCANCUN – RE/ACU
Edif. Oasis, Blvd Kukulcan 29, Cancun, Mexico.
AI A300-600x1, A310-300x1.
AEROCARIBE – QA/CBE
Int Airport, Zona Hangares, Merida 97291, Mexico.
MDC DC-9-10x3, Fairchild FH-227x5, F-27Jx3, F-27Fx1.
AERO CHILE
Maipu 170, Arica, Chile.
Boeing 737-200x1.
AERO CONTINENTE – N6/ACQ
Ave Francisco Masias 528, Of.901, Lima 27, Peru.
Boeing 727-100x3, 737-200x5, Fokker F28-1000 x1, Fairchild F-27Jx2.
AERO COSTA RICA – ML/AEK
San Pedro de Montes de OCA, San Jose, Costa Rica.
Boeing 737-200x2.
AEROEXO – SX/AJO
Humberto Lobo 660, Garza Garcia, Mexico.
Boeing 727-200x15, 727-100x2.
AEROFLOT RUSSIAN INT AIRLINES – SU/AFL
Sheremetyevo Airport, Moscow 103340, Russia.
Antonov An-124x2, MDC DC-10-30x1, Ilyushin Il-96-300x5, Il-86x20, Il-76x14, Il-62Mx27, Boeing 767-300x2, AI A310-300x10, Tupolev Tu-204x6, Tu-154Mx36, Tu-154Bx4, Tu-134Ax13.
AEROKUZNETSK – AKZ
Novokuznetsk Airport, Novokuznetsk 654051, Russia.
Tupolev Tu-154Mx3, Tu-154Bx6, Antonov An-26x5, An-24x6.
AEROLINEAS ARGENTINAS – AR/ARG
Bouchard 547, 1043 Buenos Aires, Argentina.
Boeing 747-200x6, 727-200x8, 737-200x11, AI A310-300x3, MDC MD-88x6, MD-83x1, Fokker F28-1000x3.
AEROLINEAS INTERNACIONALES – N2/LNT
Blvd Vicente Guerrero 46, Cuernavaca, Mexico.
Boeing 727-200x1, 727-100x2.
AERO LLOYD – YP/AEF
Lessingstr. 7-9, D-61440 Oberursel, Germany.
AI A321-200x2, A320-200x3, MDC MD-82x2, MD-83x15, MD-87x2.
On Order: A321-200x9, A320-200x2.
AEROMEXICO – AM/AMX
Paseo de la Reforma 445, 06500, Mexico.
Boeing 767-300x2, 757-200x6, MDC MD-82x10, MD-83x3, MD-87x2, MD-88x10, DC-9-30x18.
AEROMEXPRESS – QO/MPX
Avenue Texcoco s/n, Esq Tahel, 15620, Mexico.
Boeing 727-200Fx2.
AERO PERU – PL/PLI
Avenue Jose Pardo 601, Miraflores, Lima 18, Peru.
Boeing 757-200x2, 727-200x3, 727-100x3.
AEROPOSTAL – LAV
Torre Este, Parque Central, Caracas, Venezuala.
MDC MD-83x1, DC-9-50x6, DC-9-30x3.
AEROREPUBLICA COLOMBIA – P5/RPB
Carrera 10a, Santafe de Bogota, Colombia.
Boeing 727-100x2, MDC DC-9-30x7.
AERO SANTA – UJ/ASP
Apartado 1429, Lima 100, Peru.
Boeing 727-200x1, 737-200x2.
AEROSERVICE KAZAKHSTAN – AVZ
Algabasskaya 2a, Almaty 480028, Kazakhstan.
Tupolev Tu-154Bx2, Antonov An-26x1.
AEROSUCRE COLOMBIA – 6N/KRE
Avenida Eldorado, Santafe de Bogota, Colombia.
Boeing 727-200Fx1, 727-100Fx3, Aerospatiale Caravelle 10Bx2.
AERO SUR
Florida 939, 6 Piso, 1005 Buenos Aires, Argentina.
Boeing 727-200x2.
AEROSUR – 5L
Casilla Correo 3104, Santa Cruz de la Sierra, Bolivia.
Boeing 727-100x3, Yakovlev Yak 40x1, Fairchild Metrox2, LET 410UVPx3.
AEROTOUR DOMINICANO AIRLINES – 5N
Pl Merengue, Santo Domingo, Dominican Republic.
Boeing 727-200x1.
AEROVENCA – AVC
Aeropuerta Simon Bolivar, La Guaira, Venezuela.
Boeing 707-320Fx1.
AEROVIAS DAP
Casilla 406, Punta Arenas, Chile.
Boeing 727-100x1.
AEROVOLGA – VOG
Leningradskaya 75, Samara 443020, Russia.
Tupolev Tu-154Mx4, Yakovlev Yak-42Dx2.
AERO ZAMBIA – Z9/RZL
Private Bag E717, Lusaka, Zambia.
Boeing 737-200x2.
AFFFRETAIR – ZL/AFM
PO Box 655, Harare, Zimbabwe.
MDC DC-8-50Fx1.
AFRICAN AIRLINES INTERNATIONAL – AIK
PO Box 74772, Nairobi, Kenya.
Boeing 707-320x3.
AFRICAN CARGO SERVICES
PO Box 57683, Nairobi, Kenya.
Boeing 727-100Fx1.
AFRICAN INTERNATIONAL AIRWAYS – AIN
Brunel Ctr, Newton Rd, Crawley, West Sussex, UK.
MDC DC-8-50Fx3.
AIGLE AZUR – ZI/AAF
Aeroport de Paris-Pontoise, Cergy Pontoise, France
Boeing 737-200x1, Saab 340x1.
AIR AFRIQUE – RK/RKA
01 BP 3927, Abidjan 01, Ivory Coast.
MDC DC-10-30x2, AI A300-600x2, A300B4-200x3, A310-300x5, Boeing 707-320Fx2, 737-200x1, Antonov An-12x1.
AIR ALFA – H7/LFA
Yesilkoy Halkali Asfalti 9, Florya-Istanbul, Turkey.
AI A300B4-100x2, A300B4-200x3, Boeing 727-200x2.
AIR ALGERIE – AH/DAH
1 Place Maurice-Audin, Algiers, Algeria.
Boeing 767-300x3, 727-200x11, 737-200x15, AI A310-200x4, Lockheed L-100-30x2, Fokker F27-400x7.
AIR ARUBA – FQ/ARU
PO Box 1017, Oranjestad, Aruba.
MDC MD-88x2, MD-83x1, DC-9-30x1.
AIR ATLANTA ICELAND – CC/ABD
PO Box 80, IS-270 Mosfellsbaer, Iceland.
Boeing 747-200x1, 747-100x5, 737-300, 737-200 x1, 737-200Fx2, Lockheed L-1011x3.

This Air Littoral Canadair RJ wears Air France/Air Inter Express colours. (Keith Gaskell)

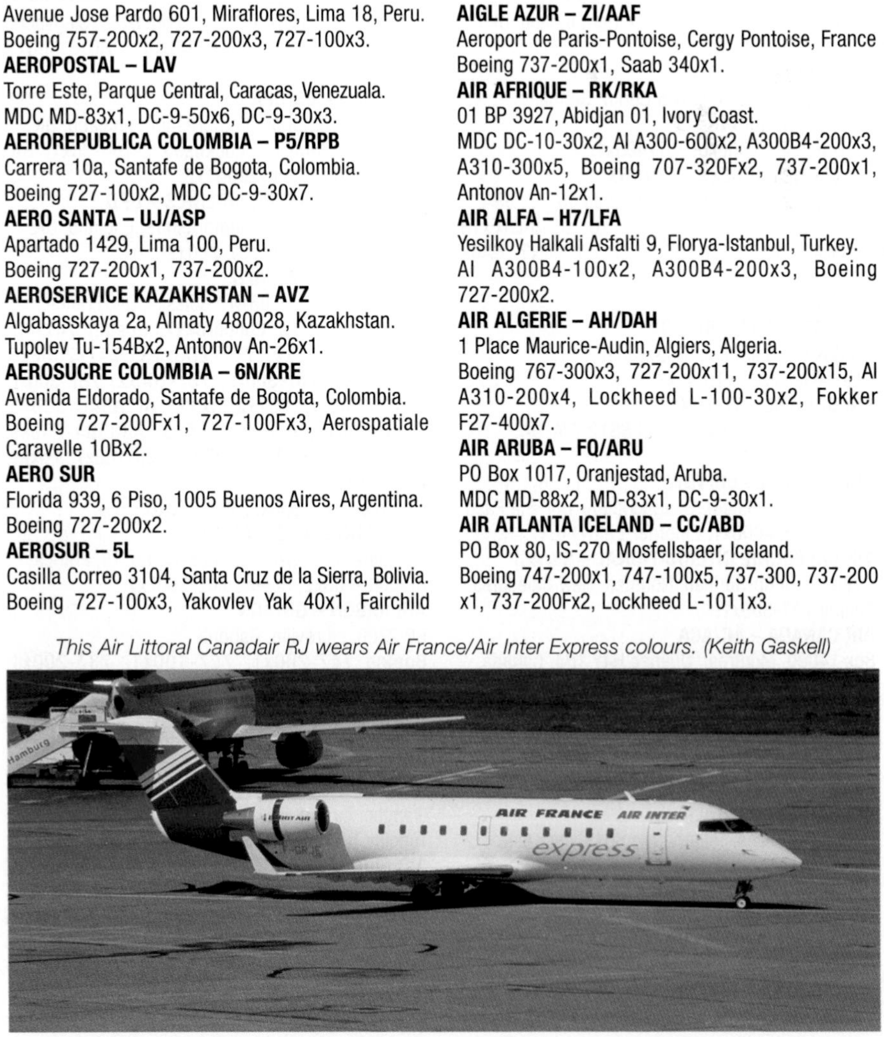

A CFM56 powered Air Jamaica A320. (Airbus)

AIR ATLANTIC – 9A/ATL
PO Box 248, Elmsdale, Nova Scotia, Canada.
BAe 146-200x3, Dash 8-100x3, Jetstream 41x5.
AIR ATLANTIC CARGO – ANI
179 High Street, Bromley, Kent BR1 1LB, UK.
Boeing 707-320Fx2.
AIR AUSTRAL – UU/REU
BP 611, F-97473 St Denis Cedex, Reunion.
Boeing 737-300x1, 737-500x1.
AIR BALTIC – BT/BTI
Riga Airport, Riga LV-1053, Latvia.
Avro RJ70x3, Saab 340x1.
AIRBC – ZX/ABL
5520 Miller Road, Richmond, BC V7B 1L9, Canada.
BAe 146-200x5, Dash 8-300x6, Dash 8-100x14, Jetstream 31x3.
AIR BELGIUM – AJ/ABB
Vilvoordelaan 192, B-1930 Zaventem, Belgium.
Boeing 757-200x1, 737-400x1, 737-300.
AIR BELFAST – 7L/AZX
Belfast Int Airport, Belfast, Northern Ireland, UK.
BAC 111-500x1.
AIR BERLIN – AB/BER
Flughafen-Tegel, D-13405 Berlin, Germany.
Boeing 737-400x10.
On Order: 737-800x6, 737-400x1.
AIRBORNE EXPRESS – GB/ABX
145 Hunter Drive, Wilmington, Ohio 45177, USA.
MDC DC-8-63Fx16, DC-8-62Fx6, DC-8-61Fx13, DC-9-40Fx19, DC-9-30Fx43, DC-9-10Fx2, NAMC YS-11x11.
On Order: Boeing 767-200Fx12.
AIR BOTSWANA – BP/BOT
PO Box 92, Gaborone, Botswana.
BAe 146-100x1, ATR 42x2.
AIR BRISTOL – 7L/AZX
PO Box 92, Patchway, Bristol BS12 7YA, UK.
BAC 111-500x2.
AIR BURKINA – VH/VBW
BP 1459, Ave Binger, Ouagadougou, Burkina Faso.
Fokker F28-4000x1, Embraer EMB-110x1.
AIR CALEDONIE INTERNATIONAL – SB/ACI
8 Rue Frederic-Surleau, Noumea, New Caledonia.
Boeing 737-300x1.
AIR CANADA – AC/ACA
Box 14000, Montreal, Quebec H4Y 1H4, Canada.
Boeing 747-400x3, 747-200x3, 747-100x3, 767-300x6, 767-200x23, Lockheed L-1011x4, AI A340-300x4, A320-200x34, MDC DC-9-30x35, Canadair RJ-100x24.
On Order: A340-300x4, A319-100x35.
AIR CARGO AUSTRALIA
1-7 Silicon Place, Tullamarine 3043, Australia.
Boeing 727-100Fx1.
AIR CESS – ACS
PO Box 37, B-8400 Ostend Airport, Belgium.
Boeing 707-320Fx2, Ilyushin Il-18Dx1, Antonov An-12x4, An-8x1, An-24x2.
AIR CHARTER – SF/ACF
4 Rue de la Couture, Rungis Cedex, France.
AI A300B4-200x2, A320-200x4, Boeing 737-500 x1, 737-200x2.
AIR CHINA – CA/CCA
Capital Int Airport, 100621 Beijing, China.
Boeing 747-400x8, 747-200x4, 747SPx4, 767-300x4, 767-200x6, 707-320x2, 737-300x19, BAe 146-100x4, Antonov An-12x2, Lockheed L-100-30x2, Yunshuji Y7x6.
On Order: 747-400x3, AI A340-300x3.
AIR CLUB INTERNATIONAL – HB/CLI
11905 Cargo Rd, Mirabel, Quebec, Canada.
AI A310-300x4.
AIR EUROPA – UX/AEA
Gran Via Asima 23, Palma de Mallorca, Spain.
Boeing 757-200x7, 737-400x5, 737-300x10.
On Order: 737-800x10.
AIR EUROPE – PE/AEL
Corso Sempione 15A, I-21013 Gallarate, Italy.
Boeing 767-300x4.
AIRFAST INDONESIA – AFE
Box 29, Jalan Kayu PO, Singapore 9180, Singapore.
Boeing 737-200x3, BAe 748x4, DHC-6-300x2, IPTN-212x1.
AIRFOYLE – GS/UPA
Luton Airport, Luton, Bedfordshire, England, UK.
Ilyushin Il-76MDx1, Lockheed L-100-30x1, BAe 146-300QTx7, 146-200QTx2.
AIRFOYLE CHARTER AIRLINES – UPD
Luton Airport, Luton, Bedfordshire, England, UK.
Boeing 737-300x1, 737-200x2.
AIR FRANCE – AF/AFR
45 rue de Paris, F-95747 Roissy-CDG, France.
Aerospatiale/BAe Concordex7, Boeing 747-400 x14, 747-300x2, 747-200x13, 747-200Fx9, 747-100x7, 767-300x5, 767-200x2, 737-300x6, 737-500x18, 737-200x19, AI A340-300x8, A340-200x3, A300B2-100x3, A300B4-200x9, A310-200x7, A320-200x23, A320-100x7, Fokker F27-500x10.
On Order: 767-300x7, 737-500x8.
AIR FRANCE ASIE – AF/AFR
1 Square Max Hymans, Paris-Cedex 15, France.
AI A340-200x2, Boeing 747-200Fx2.
AIR GABON – GN/AGN
BP 2206, Libreville, Gabon.
Boeing 747-200x1, 727-100x1, 737-200x1, Fokker F28-2000x2.
AIR GEORGIA – DA/GEO
Chavchavadze Av 49A, Tbilisi 380062, Georgia.
Tupolev Tu-154Bx1.
AIR GREAT WALL – G8/CGW
Jiangbei Airport, 631120 Chongqing, China.
Tupolev Tu-154Mx2, Boeing 737-200x3.
AIR GUINEE – GI/GIB
BP 12, Conakry, Guinea.
Boeing 737-200x1, Antonov An-26, An-24x2, Dash 7-100x1.
AIR HOLLAND – GG/AHR
PO Box 75116, Schipol Oost, Netherlands.
Boeing 757-200x3, 737-300x2.
AIR HONG KONG – LD/AHK
Tien Chu Ctr, Mok Cheong St, Kowloon, Hong Kong.
Boeing 747-200Fx4.
AIR-INDIA – AI/AIC
Air-India Bldg, Nariman Point, Mumbai, India.
Boeing 747-400x6, 747-300x2, 747-200x9, Lockheed L-1011-500x2, AI A300B4-200x3, A310-300x11.
AIR INTER EUROPE – IT/ITF
1 Ave Marechal Devaux, Paray Vieille Poste, France
AI A330-300x4, A300B4-200x5, A300B2-100x13, A300B2-300x1, A321-100x7, A320-200x23, A320-100x6, A319-100x5, Fokker 100x7.
On Order: A330-300x10, A320-200x1, A319-100x4.
AIR IVOIRE – VU/VUN
01 BP 1027, Abidjan 01, Ivory Coast.
Fokker 100x2, F28-1000x1, F27-600x1.
AIR JAMAICA – JM/AJM
72-76 Harbour Street, Kingston, Jamaica.
AI A300B4-200x3, A310-300x6, A320-200x4, Boeing 727-200x4.
AIR JET – YH/AIJ
BP 10297, F-95700 Roissy CDG, France.
BAe 146-200QCx3.
AIR KORYO – JS/KOR
Sunan District, Pyongyang, Democratic Korea.
Ilyushin Il-76MDx3, Il-62Mx4, Il-18x4, Tupolev Tu-154Bx4, Tu-134Bx2, Antonov An-24x8.
AIRLANKA – UL/ALK
York St, Colombo 1, Sri Lanka.
AI A340-300x3, A320-200x2, Lockheed L-1011-500x2, L-1011x2.
AIR LIBERTE – VD/LIB
3 Rue de Pont des Halles, Rungis Cedex, France.
MDC DC-10-30x4, MD-83x8, AI A300-600x2, A310-300x1, A310-200x2, Boeing 737-200x3.
AIRLINK – QF/QEA
Qantas Ctr, 203 Coward St, Mascot 2020, Australia.
BAe 146-300x2, 146-200x5, 146-100x5.
AIR LITHUANIA – TT/KLA
Veiveriu 132, 3010 Kaunas, Lithuania.
Tupolev Tu-134x1, Yakovlev Yak-40x6.
AIR LITTORAL – FU/LIT
417 rue Samuel Morse, Montpellier Cedex 2, France.
Fokker 100x2, Fokker 70x5, Canadair RJ-100x6, ATR 72x1, ATR 42x15, Embraer EMB-120x9.
On Order: ATR 42x5.
AIR MACAU – NX/AMU
PO Box 1910, Macau, Macau.
AI A321-100x2, A320-200x2.
AIR MADAGASCAR – MD/MDG
Ave de l'Independence, Antananarivo, Madagascar
Boeing 747-200x1, 737-300x1, 737-200x2, BAe 748x3, DHC-6-300x4.
AIR MALAWI – OM/AML
PO Box 84, Blantyre, Malawi.
Boeing 737-300x1, ATR 42x1, Dornier 228x1.
AIR MALDIVES – L6/AMI
PO Box 2049, Male 20-05, Maldives.
AI A300B4-200x1, Dornier 228x2.
AIR MALTA – KM/AMC
Luqa, Malta.
AI A320-200x3, Boeing 737-300x3, 737-200x2, Avro RJ70x4.
AIR MARSHALL ISLANDS – CW/MRS
PO Box 1319, Majuro, Marshall Islands 96960.
MDC DC-8-62x1, Saab 2000x1, Dornier 228-200x2.
AIR MAURITANIE – MR/MRT
BP 41, Nouakchott 174, Mauritania.
Fokker F28-4000x1, F28-3000x1.
AIR MAURITIUS – MK/MAU
5 President John Kennedy St, Port Louis, Mauritius.
AI A340-300x4, Boeing 767-200x2, ATR 42x2.
On Order: A340-300x2.

AIR MEMPHIS
2/1316 Elnozha Elgedida, Heliopolis, Egypt.
Boeing 707-320Fx1.

AIR MOLDOVA – 9U/MLD
Chisinau Airport, 277026 Chisinau, Moldova.
Tupolev Tu-154Bx7, Tu-134Ax11, Antonov An-26Bx4, An-24x7.

AIR NACOIA
Rua Com. Che Guevara 61-1e Ander, Luanda, Angola
Boeing 727-200x1, 727-100x1.

AIR NAMIBIA – SW/NMB
PO Box 731, Windhoek, Namibia.
Boeing 747SPx2, 737-200x1, Beech 1900Cx3.

AIR NAURU – ON/RON
Nauru International Airport, Nauru.
Boeing 737-400x1.

AIR NEW ZEALAND – NZ/ANZ
Private Bag 92007, Auckland 1020, New Zealand.
Boeing 747-400x5, 747-200x5, 767-300x7, 767-200x5, 737-200x12.
On Order: 747-400x1, 767-300x2, 737-???x6.

AIR NIPPON – EL/ANK
2-2-8 Higashi-Shinagawa, Tokyo 140, Japan.
Boeing 767-300x2, AI A320-200x4, Boeing 737-500 x7, 737-200x9, NAMC YS-11Ax18, DHC-6-300x2.

AIR NIUGINI – PX/ANG
PO Box 7186, Boroko, Papua New Guinea.
AI A310-300x2, Fokker F28-4000x3, F28-1000x5, Dash 7-100x2.

AIR NOVA – QK/ARN
Halifax Int Airport, Enfield, Nova Scotia, Canada.
BAe 146-200x5, Dash 8-100x13.

AIR ONE – AP/ADH
Via Sardegna 14, I-00187 Rome, Italy.
Boeing 737-300x2, 737-200x1.

AIR OSTRAVA – 8K/VTR
Ostrava Int Airport, Mosnov, Czech Republic.
Lockheed L-1011x1, Boeing 737-200x2, Saab 340x3, BAe Jetstream 31x2, Let 410UVPx2.

AIR PACIFIC – FJ/FJI
PO Box 9266, Nadi Airport, Fiji.
Boeing 747-200x1, 767-300x1, 737-300x1, 737-500x1.
On Order: 737-700x3.

AIR PHILIPPINES – GAP
Roxas Boulevard, Manila, Philippines.
Boeing 737-200x3.

AIR PROVENCE CHARTER
Rue de la Hayes, Roissy-CDG, France.
Boeing 737-300x2, Aerospatiale Caravelle 12x1.

AIR SERVICE UKRAINE – ASG
Ul. Klimenko 23, Kiev 252110, Ukraine.
Ilyushin Il-76x10.

AIR SEYCHELLES – HM/SEY
PO Box 386, Victoria, Mahe, Seychelles.
Boeing 767-200x1, 757-200x1, DHC-6-300x4.

AIR SICILIA – BM/SIC
Casella postale, I-90045 Cinisi, Italy.
Fokker F28-1000x1, ATR 42x1.

AIR SINAI – 4D/ASD
12 Kasr el Nil Street, Cairo, Egypt.
Boeing 737-200x1, Fokker F27-500x2.

AIR SLOVAKIA – SVK
PO Box 2, SK-820 01, Bratislava, Slovak Republic.
Boeing 727-200x1.

AIR SOUTH – WV/KKB
PO Box 11129, Columbus, South Carolina, USA.
Boeing 737-200x7.

AIRSTAN – JSC
Sultana 12, Kazan 420022, Russia.
Ilyushim Il-76x2, Antonov An-26x1, Yakovlev Yak-40x1.

AIR TANZANIA – TC/ATC
PO Box 543, Dar-es-Salaam, Tanzania.
Boeing 737-200x2, Fokker F27-600x3.

AIR TOULOUSE INTERNATIONAL – SH/TLE
BP 44, F-31702 Blagnac Cedex, France.
Boeing 737-200x5, Aerospatiale Caravelle 10Bx3, Embraer EMB-110x2.

AIRTOURS INTERNATIONAL – VZ/AIH
300 Princess Rd, Manchester, England, UK.
Boeing 767-300x2, 757-200x6, AI A320-200x10.
On Order: 767-300x1, 757-200x1

AIRTRAN – FL/MTE
6280 Hazeltine National Dr, Orlando, Florida, USA.
Boeing 737-200x11.

AIR TRANSAT – TS/TSC
Mirabel Int Airport, Mirabel, Quebec, Canada.
Lockheed L-1011x7, Boeing 757-200x4.

AIR TRANSPORT EUROPE – EAT
Airport Tatry, SK-058 98 Poprad, Slovak Republic.
Tupolev Tu-134Ax1.

AIR TRANSPORT INTERNATIONAL – 8C/ATN
3800 Rodney Parkway, Little Rock, Arkansas, USA.
MDC DC-8-71Fx10, DC-8-63Fx4, DC-8-62Fx7, DC-8-61Fx1.

AIR 21 – A7
5548 Air Terminal Drive, Fresno, California, USA.
Fokker F28-4000x3.

AIR 2000 – DP/AMM
London Road, Crawley, West Sussex, England, UK.
Boeing 757-200x14, AI A320-200x4.

AIR UK – UK/UKA
Stansted Airport, Stansted, Essex, England, UK.
Fokker 100x11, Fokker 50x9, F27-500x5, F27-100x1, BAe 146-300x11, 146-100x1.

AIR UK LEISURE – LEI
Stansted Airport, Stansted, Essex, England, UK.
AI A320-200x3.

AIR UKRAINE – 6U/UKR
Prospekt Peremogy 14, Kiev 252135, Ukraine.
Ilyushin Il-76x6, Il-62Mx8, Tupolev Tu-154Mx3, Tu-154Bx32, Tu-134Ax29, Yakovlev Yak-42x20, Yak-40x15, Boeing 737-200x1, Antonov An-72x1, An-32x2, An-30x9, An-26x9, An-24x47.

AIR UKRAINE CARGO – UKC
Pervomayskaya 12, Krivoy Rog 324099, Ukraine.
Ilyushin Il-76x4.

AIR VANUATU – NF/AVN
PO Box 148, Port Vila, Vanuatu.
Boeing 737-400x1, Embraer EMB-110x1.

AIRWORLD – RL/AWD
25 Elmfield Road, Bromley, Kent, England, UK.
AI A320-200x3.

AIR ZIMBABWE – UM/AZW
PO Box AP.1, Harare Airport, Harare, Zimbabwe.
Boeing 767-200x2, 707-320x2, 737-200x3, BAe 146-200x1, Fokker 50x2.

AIS AIRLINES – AIS
PO Box 11, Moscow 117133, Russia.
Tupolev Tu-154Bx1, Tu-134Ax2, Ilyushin Il-18x1.

AJT AIR INTERNATIONAL – E9/TRJ
Leningradski Prospekt, Moscow 125167, Russia.
Ilyushin Il-86x2.

ALAK AIRLINES – J4/LSV
Leningradski Prospekt, Moscow 125836, Russia.
Ilyushin Il-76x1, Tupolev Tu-154Mx3.

ALAS NACIONALES – ALW
Via Mirador 4, Puerto Plata, Dominican Republic.
Boeing 767-200x1.

ALASKA AIRLINES – AS/ASA
PO Box 68900, Seattle, Washington 98168, USA.
MDC MD-83x36, MD-82x10, Boeing 737-400x22, 737-200x10.
On Order: MD-83x2, 737-400x14.

ALBANIAN AIRLINES – LV/LBC
Rruga e Durresit 202, Tirana, Albania.
AI A320-200x1.

ALBATROSS AIRLINE – 8Z/ABK
Ataturk Havalimani, Yesilkoy-Istanbul, Turkey.
Boeing 737-200x2.

ALITALIA – AZ/AZA
Via Alessandro Marchetti 111, I-00148 Rome, Italy.
Boeing 747-200x8, 747-200Fx2, 767-300x5, MDC MD-11x8, MD-82x90, DC-9-30x13, AI A300B4-200 x11, A300B4-100x3, A321-100x16.
On Order: A321-100x24.

ALL CANADA EXPRESS – CNX
Burnham Thorpe Rd, Mississauga, Ontario, Canada.
Boeing 727-100Fx3, Convair 580x2.

This America West A320 models the Phoenix based airline's new corporate colours. The A320 has been Airbus' most successful product in North America, with sales to Air Canada, America West, Northwest, United Airlines and US Airways/USAir. (Airbus)

An American Trans Air 727-200 on approach to land at Orlando, Florida, in the USA. (Gary Gentle)

ALL LIESURE AIRLINES – ALT
London Road, Crawley, West Sussex, England, UK.
AI A320-200x1.

ALL NIPPON AIRWAYS – NH/ANA
2-5 Kasumigaseki, Chiyoda-ku, Tokyo 100, Japan.
Boeing 747-400x19, 747-200x6, 747SR-100x14, 777-200x6, 767-300x40, 767-200x25, AI A320-200x22.
On Order: 747-400x2, 777-300x10, 777-200x12, 767-300x2, A340-300x5, A321-100x10.

ALLEGRO AIR -GRO
San Nicolas de Las Garzas 66490, Mexico.
Boeing 727-200x3, MDC MD-83x2, DC-9-10x3.

ALLIANCE – Y2/AFJ
13 Kimathi Avenue, Kampala, Uganda.
Boeing 747SPx1.

ALM ANTILLEAN AIRLINES – LM/ALM
Aeropuerto Hato, Curacao, Netherlands Antilles.
MDC MD-82x3, Dash 8-300x2.

ALMAZY ROSSII SAKHA
Mirny Airport, Mirny 678170, Russia.
Ilyushin Il-76x4, Antonov An-26x4, An-24x10.

ALOHA AIRLINES – AQ/AAH
PO Box 30028, Honolulu, Hawaii 96820, USA.
Boeing 737-400x2, 737-300QCx2, 737-300x2, 737-200x16.

ALPI EAGLES – ELG
Via Gorizia 24, I-36016 Thiene, Italy.
Fokker 100x2.

AMERICA WEST AIRLINES – HP/AWE
4000 East Sky Harbor Blvd, Phoenix, Arizona, USA.
Boeing 757-200x14, 737-300x40, 737-200x20, 737-100x1, AI A320-200x32.
On Order: A320-200x28.

AMERICA WEST EXPRESS – HP/AWE
3237 East Bonanza Way, Phoenix, Arizona, USA.
Fokker 70x2.

AMERICAN AIRLINES – AA/AAL
Box 619616, DFW Int Airport, Texas 75261, USA.
MDC MD-11x18, DC-10-30x8, DC-10-10x39, MD-82x228, MD-83x33, Boeing 767-300x41, 767-200x30, 757-200x91, 727-200x81, 737-300 x7, AI A300-600x35, Fokker 100x75.

AMERICAN TRANS AIR – TZ/AMT
PO Box 51609, Indianapolis, Indiana 46251, USA.
Lockheed L-1011x17, Boeing 757-200x14, 727-200x24.
On Order: 757-200x2.

AMERICANA DE AVIACION – 8A
Avenue Larco 345, 3 Piso, Lima 18, Peru.
Boeing 727-200x1, 727-100x1, 737-200x2.

AMERIJET INTERNATIONAL – JH/AJT
498 SW 34th St, Fort Lauderdale, Florida, USA.
Boeing 727-200Fx11, 727-100Fx5.

AMURAVIA
Blagoveshchensk Airport, Blagoveshchensk, Russia
Tupolev Tu-154Mx2, Tu-154Bx1, Yakovlev Yak-40 x12, L 410UVPx2.

ANDES AIRLINES – EDA
Aeropuerto Simon Bolivar, Guayaquil, Ecuador.
MDC DC-8-50Fx1.

ANGOLA AIR CHARTER – C3/AGO
CP3010, Luanda, Angola
Boeing 707-300Fx4, 727-100Fx2, 737-200x1, Lockheed L-100-30x2.

ANSETT AUSTRALIA – AN/AAA
501 Swanston Street, Melbourne, 3000, Australia.
Boeing 747-300x3, 767-300x1, 767-200x9, 727-200 x5, 727-200Fx1, 737-300x22, AI A320-200x18, BAe 146-300x5, 146-200x7, 146-200QTx2, Fokker F28-4000x5.
On Order: A320-200x1.

ANSETT NEW ZEALAND – AN/AAA
PO Box 14-139, Christchurch Airport, New Zealand.
BAe 146-300x8, 146-200QCx1, Dash 8-100x4.

AOM FRENCH AIRLINES – IW/AOM
13/15 Rue du Pont des Halles, Rungis Cedex, France.
MDC DC-10-30x13, MD-83x10.

APOLLO AIRLINES – PJ/AOA
2 Vouligmenis Avenue, Hellinikon Athens, Greece.
AI A300B4-200x3.

ARAX AIRWAYS – Y5/RXR
Zvartnots Airport, 375042 Yerevan, Armenia.
Tupolev Tu-154Mx1.

ARCA COLOMBIA – ZU/AKC
Calle 19 No. 8-81, Santafe de Bogota, Colombia.
MDC DC-10-10Fx1, DC-8-50Fx3.

ARIANA AFGHAN AIRLINES – FG/AFG
PO Box 76, Ansari Watt, Kabul, Afghanistan.
Tupolev Tu-154Mx1, Boeing 727-200x3, 727-100 x2, Antonov An26x2, An-24x2, Yakovlev Yak-40x1.

ARKHANGELSK AIRLINES
Talagi Airport, Arkhangelesk 163053, Russia.
Tupolev Tu-154Bx5, Tu-134Ax15, Antonov An-26 x12, An-24x12.

ARKIA – IZ/AIZ
PO Box 39301, Dov Airport, Tel Aviv 61392, Israel.
Boeing 757-200x1, 737-200x3, Dash 7x10, DHC-6-300x1.

ARMENIAN AIRLINES – R3/RME
Zvartnots Airport, 375042 Yerevan, Armenia.
Ilyushin Il-86x2, Tupolev Tu-154Bx10, Tu-134Ax9, Yakovlev Yak-40x9.

ARROW AIR – JW/APW
PO Box 026062, Miami, Florida 33102, USA.
Lockheed L-1011Fx1, MDC DC-8-63Fx3, DC-8-62Fx3.

ASA AFRICAN SAFARI AIRWAYS – QSC
PO 158, CH-4030 Basel-Flughafen, Switzerland.
MDC DC-10-30x1.

ASERCA AIRLINES – R7/OCA
Avda Bolivar Norte, Of.8B, Valencia, Venezuala.
MDC DC-9-30x6.

ASIA SERVICE AIRLINES – Y3/ASQ
Ul. Kabanbay batyra 136, Almaty, Kazakstan.
Ilyushin Il-86x2.

ASIANA AIRLINES – OZ/AAR
PO Box 142, Seoul 100052, Republic of Korea.
Boeing 747-400x7, 747-400Fx2, 767-300x12, 767-300Fx1, 737-400x17, 737-500x6.
On Order: 747-400x1, 747-400Fx1, 767-300x5, 767-300Fx1, 737-400x5, AI A321-100x18.

ASTRAKHAN AIRLINES – ASZ
Narimanovo Airport, Astrakhan 414023, Russia.
Yakovlev Yak-42Dx2, Tupolev Tu-134Ax5, Antonov An-24x8.

ATLANT-SOYUZ AIRLINES – 3G/AYZ
Ul. Nikolskaya 10/2, Moscow 103012, Russia.
Ilyushin Il-86x1, Il-76x6, Il-62Mx2, Il-18x2, Tupolev Tu-154Mx1, Tu-154Bx1, Tu-134Ax1, Antonov An-12x2.

ATLANT-SV AIRCOMPANY – L4/ATG
Tsentrainy Airport, Simferopel 333902, Ukraine.
Ilyushin Il-76x34, Il-62x3.

ATC COLOMBIA – TCO
Carrera 22 No. 62-36, Santafe de Bogota, Colombia.
MDC DC-8-50Fx2.

ATLANT-SV AIRCOMPANY – L4/ATG
Central Airport, Simferopol 333902, Ukraine.
Ilyushin Il-76x40, Il-62x4.

ATLANTIC AIRWAYS – RC/FLI
Vagar Airport, FR-380 Soervagur, Faroe Islands.
BAe 146-200x1.

ATLANTIC SOUTHEAST AIRLINES – EV/ASE
100 Hartsfield Central Pkwy, Atlanta, Georgia USA.
BAe 146-200x5, ATR 72x12, Dash 7x2, Embraer EMB-120ERx64, EMB-110x10.

ATLAS AIR – 5Y/GTI
JFK Int Airport, Jamaica, New York 11430, USA.
Boeing 747-200Fx16, 747-200x1, 747-100Fx1.
On Order: 747-200Fx6.

ATRUVERA AIR TRANSPORT COMPANY – AUV
Ul.Basseinaya 33, St.Petersburg 196070, Russia.
Ilyushin Il-76x5.

ATS AIR TRANSPORT SERVICE – ATS
BP 13483, Kinshasa 1, Zaire.
Aerospatiale Caravelle 111x3.

AUSTRAL – AU/AUT
Ave L N Alem 1134, 1001 Buenos Aires, Argentina.
MDC MD-83x3, MD-81x2, DC-9-30x7.

AUSTRALIAN AIR EXPRESS – QF
PO Box 1324L, Melbourne, Victoria 3001, Australia.
Boeing 727-100Fx1, BAe 146-300QTx2, 146-100QTx1.

AUSTRIAN AIRLINES – OS/AUA
Postfach 50, A-1107 Wien, Austria.
AI A340-200x2, A310-300x4, A321-100x3, MDC MD-83x2, MD-82x6, MD-81x7, MD-87x5, Fokker 70x5, Fokker 50x3.
On Order: A340-300x2, A321-200x3, A320-200x7, Fokker 70x2.

AVATLANTIC – G6/KYC
Lee Wagner Blvd, Fort Lauderdale, Florida, USA.
Boeing 727-200x5, 727-100x2.

AVENSA – VE/AVE
Av Universidad, Caracas 101, Venezuala.
Boeing 727-200x5, 727-100x6, 737-300x1, 737-200x2, MDC DC-9-50x4, DC-9-30x1.

AVIACO – AO/AYC
Maudes 51, Edificio Minister, Madrid, Spain.
MDC MD-88x13, DC-9-30x20.

AVIACON ZITOTRANS – AZS
Oktyabrskaya pl 3, Ekaterinburg 620031, Russia.
Ilyushin Il-76x2, Tupolev Tu-154Mx1.

AVIACSA – 6A/CHP
Calle 30, Predio 130, Col Mexico, Merida, Mexico.
Boeing 727-200x8, 727-100x2.

AVIAENERGO – 7U/ERG
Alleya 1 oy Mayovki 15, Moskow 111395, Russia.
Ilyushin Il-76x2, Il-62Mx2, Tupolev Tu-154Mx3, Tu-134Bx1, Antonov An-74x1, Yakovlev Yak-40x1.

AVIAL AVIATION COMPANY – AK/RLC
Orlikov pereulok 1/11, Moscow 107139, Russia.
Ilyushin Il-76x2, Antonov An-12x2.

AVIANCA COLOMBIA – AV/AVA
Avenida Eldorado, Santafe de Bogota, Colombia.
Boeing 767-300x1, 767-200x2, 757-200x3, 727-200x3, MDC MD-83x11, Fokker 50x10.

AVIANOVA – RD/NOV
Via Carlo Veneziano 58, I-00148 Rome, Italy.
Fokker 70x10, ATR 72x4, ATR 42x10.
On Order: Fokker 70x5.
AVIATECA GUATEMALA – GU/GUG
Aeropuerto La Aurora, Guatemala City, Guatemala.
Boeing 737-200x5.
AVIATRANS CARGO AIRLINES – V8/VAS
66 Zemlianoi Val, Moscow 109004, Russia.
Ilyushin Il-76x7, Antonov An-12x8, An-32x3, An-26x6.
AVIOGENEX – JJ/AGX
Narodnih heroja 43, Novi Beograd, Yugoslavia.
Boeing 727-200x7.
AVIOIMPEX – M4/AXX
PO Box 544, 11 Oktomvri K14, Skopje, Macedonia.
MDC DC-9-30x1, Yakovlev Yak-42x1, Antonov An-12x1.
AVISTAR – KJA
PO Box 5532, Nicosia, Cyprus.
Boeing 707-320Fx1.
AZAMAT – ZD/AZB
Ul. Altysaryna 23a, Almaty 480000, Kazakhstan.
Tupolev Tu-154Mx1.
AZERBAIJAN AIRLINES – J2/AHY
Bini Airport, Baku 370109, Azerbaijan.
Boeing 707-320Fx2, 727-200x2, Tupolev Tu-154M x3, Tu-154Bx12, Tu-134Bx8, Yakovlev Yak-40x14, Antonov An-32x6, An-26x3.
AZZA TRANSPORT – AZZ
PO Box 11586, Khartoum, Sudan.
Boeing 707-320Fx2.
BAHAMASAIR – UP/BHS
PO Box N4881, Nassau, Bahamas.
Boeing 737-200x1, Dash 8-300x7, BAe 748x2, Shorts 360x1.
BAIKAL AIRLINES – X3/BKL
8 Shiryamova Street, Irkutsk 664009, Russia.
Ilyushin Il-76x7, Tupolev Tu-154Mx6, Tu-154Bx9, Boeing 757-200x1, Antonov An-12x6, An-26x7, An-24x9.
BALAIR CTA – BB/BBB
Case postale, CH-1215 Geneve 15, Switzerland.
AI A310-300x3.
BALKAN BULGARIAN AIRLINES – LZ/LAZ
Sofia Airport, 1540 Sofia, Bulgaria.
Boeing 767-200x2, 737-500x3, Tupolev Tu-154M x8, Tu-154Bx15, Tu-134x1, AI A320-200x3, Ilyushin Il-18x6, Antonov An-12x4, An-24x13.
BARNAUL AIR ENTERPRISE
Barnaul Airport, Barnaul 656030, Russia.
Ilyushin Il-76x3, Tupolev Tu-154Bx3, Antonov An-26x5, Yakovlev Yak-40x11, L 410UVPx8.
BASHKIRIAN AIRLINES – V9/BTC
Ufa Airport, Bashkortostan Republic, Russia.
Tupolev Tu-154Mx6, Tu-154Bx8, Tu-134Ax6, Antonov An-24x10.
BEL/BALTIC EXPRESS LINE – LTB
Gertrudes 5A, LV-1010, Riga, Latvia.
Tupolev Tu-154Mx1.
BELAIR BELARUSSIAN AIRLINES – BLI
Korotkevitsha 7, 220004 Minsk, Belarus.
Ilyushin Il-76x3, Tupolev Tu-134Ax2.
BELAVIA BELARUSSIAN AIRLINES – B2/BRU
4 Aerodromnaya Street, 220065 Minsk, Belarus.
Ilyushin Il-86x1, Tupolev Tu-154Mx6, Tu-154Bx17, Tu-134Ax18, Antonov An-26x7, An-24x16, Yakovlev Yak-40x8.
BELLVIEW AIRLINES – BX/BLV
PO Box 6571, Lagos, Nigeria.
MDC DC-9-30x2, Yakovlev Yak-40x1.
BEMOAIR PRAHA – BMI
Na prikope 12, Prague 1, Czech Republic.
Ilyushin Il-62Mx2, Boeing 727-200x1, L 410UVPx2.

Balkan Bulgarian Airlines flies 23 Tu-154 trijets. Note the triple bogey main undercarriage units. (Bruce Malcolm)

BHOJA AIRLINES – B4/BHO
Bhoja Terrace, Shahrah-E-Liaquat, Karachi, Pakistan.
Yakovlev Yak-42Dx2.
BIMAN BANGLADESH AIRLINES – BG/BBC
Biman Bhaban, Dhaka 1000, Bangladesh.
MDC DC-10-30x5, AI A310-300x2, Fokker F28-4000x2, BAe ATPx2.
BINTER CANARIAS – NT/IBB
Aeropuerto de Gran Canaria, E-35230, Telde, Spain.
MDC DC-9-30x4, ATR 72x6, CASA CN-235x4.
BIRGENAIR – KT/BHY
Cumhuriyet Caddesi 301, Harbiye-Istanbul, Turkey.
Boeing 767-200x1, 737-300x1.
BLUE AIRLINES – BUL
BP 1115, Kinshasa 1, Zaire.
Boeing 727-100x1, Lockheed L-188x2, Antonov An-26x1.
BLUE DART AVIATION
Mangala Bhavan, Vile Parle, Mumbai, India.
Boeing 737-200Fx2.
BOURAQ AIRLINES – BO/BOU
PO Box 2965, Jakarta 10720, Indonesia.
Boeing 737-200x8, BAe 748x14, IPTN 212x3.
BRAATHENS S.A.F.E. – BU/BRA
Postboks 55, N-1330 Oslo Lufthavn, Norway.
Boeing 737-400x7, 737-500x23, 737-200x2.
BRASAIR – BSI
Alameda dos Jurupis 1005, Sao Paulo, Brazil.
Boeing 707-320Fx2.
BRATSK AIR ENTERPRISE
Bratsk Airport, Bratsk 665711, Russia.
Tupolev Tu-154Mx4, Tu-154Bx1, Yakovlev Yak-40x11.
BRIT'AIR – DB/BZH
Aeroport, BP 156, F-29204 Morlaix Cedex, France.
Canadair RJ100x6, ATR 72x2, ATR 42x10, Saab 340x6.
On Order: RJ100x3.
BRITANNIA AIRWAYS – BY/BAL
Luton Int Airport, Luton, Bedfordshire, England, UK.
Boeing 767-300x3, 767-200x8, 757-200x20.
On Order: 767-300x1.
BRITISH AIRWAYS – BA/BAW
Heathrow Airport, Hounslow, Middlesex, UK.
Aerospatiale/BAe Concordex7, Boeing 747-400 x32, 747-200x16, 747-100x15, 777-200x6, 767-300 x24, 757-200x44, 737-400x35, 737-200x35, MDC DC-10-30x8, AI A320-200x5, A320-100x5, BAe ATPx14.
On Order: 747-400x20, 777-200x12, 757-200x3.
BRITISH ASIA AIRWAYS – BA
Heathrow Airport, Hounslow, Middlesex, UK.
Boeing 747-400x2.
BRITISH MEDITERRANEAN – KJ/LAJ
53 Mount Street, Mayfair, London W1Y 5RE, UK.
AI A320-200x1.
BRITISH MIDLAND – BD/BMA
Castle Donington, Derbyshire DE7 2SB, UK.
Boeing 737-400x6, 737-300x4, 737-500x14, MDC DC-9-30x3, Fokker 100x4, Fokker 70x6.
On Order: Fokker 70x1.
BRITISH WORLD AIRLINES – VF/BWL
Viscount House, Southend Airport, Essex, UK.
BAC 111-500x5, BAe 146-300x1, Vickers Viscount 800x8, ATR 72x2.
BSL AIRLINES – BSL
Vozdukhofflotsky Prospekt 33/2, Ukraine.
Ilyushin Il-78x10, Tupolev Tu-154Bx1.
BUFFALO AIRWAYS -BV/BVA
301 East 51st Street, Kansas City, Missouri, USA.
MDC DC-8-6F2x1, DC-8-61Fx2, DC-8-50Fx1, Canadair CL-44-0x1.
BURLINGTON AIR EXPRESS
1 Aircargo Parkway East, Swanton, Ohio, USA.
MDC DC-8-71Fx10, DC-8-63Fx4, Boeing 727-200Fx2, 727-100Fx2.
BUSINESS AIR – II/GNT
Dyce, Aberdeenshire AB2 0GL, Scotland, UK.
BAe 146-200x1, Saab 340x7.
BUSOL AIRCOMPANY – BUA
Ul. Leiptzigskaya 16, Kiev 252015, Ukraine.
Ilyushin Il-78x1, Il-76x5, Antonov An-12x2, An-26x2.
BWIA INTERNATIONAL – BW/BWA
Piarco Int Airport, Trinidad, West Indies.
Lockheed L-1011-500x5, AI A321-100x2, MDC MD-83x7.
BYKOVO AVIA – BKU
Ul. Sovetskaya 19, Bykovo 140150, Russia.
Yakovlev Yak-42x12, Antonov An-26x3, An-24x10.
C-AIR – CEE
PO 23416, Dubai, United Arab Emirates.
Ilyushin Il-76x1, Tupolev Tu-154Mx1.

Trinidad based BWIA International flies seven MD-80s. (Gary Gentle)

The 757 is the domestic workhorse of every major US airline – Continental (pictured), United, American, Trans World, Delta, US Airways/USAir, America West and Northwest. (Gary Gentle)

CALEDONIAN AIRWAYS – KG/CKT
Gatwick Airport, Crawley, West Sussex, UK.
MDC DC-10-30x2, Lockheed L-1011x5, AI A320-200x3.
CAMEROON AIRLINES – UY/UYC
BP 4092, Douala, Cameroon.
Boeing 747-200x1, 737-200x3, BAe 748x1.
CANADA 3000 AIRLINES – 2T/CMM
27 Fasken Drive, Toronto, Ontario, Canada.
Boeing 757-200x8, AI A320-200x5.
CANADIAN – CP/CDN
700-2nd Street SW, Calgary, Alberta, Canada.
Boeing 747-400x4, 767-300x11, 737-200x46, MDC DC-10-30x10, AI A320-200x17.
On Order: A320-200x5.
CANADIAN REGIONAL AIRLINES – KI/CDR
700-2nd Street SW, Calgary, Alberta, Canada.
Fokker F28-1000x17, Dash 8-300x14, Dash 8-100 x11, ATR 42-300x6, Shorts 360x2.
CANAIR – WW/CWW
Derry Road East, Mississauga, Ontario, Canada.
AI A320-200x1, Boeing 737-200x5, Convair 580x8, Shorts 330x1.
CAPE ATLANTIC AIR – CAO
Johannesburg International Airport, South Africa.
Boeing 727-100x2.
CAPITAL CARGO INTERNATIONAL AIRLINES
8963 Tradeport Drive, Orlando, Florida 32827, USA.
Boeing 727-200Fx1.
CAPITOL AIR EXPRESS – CEX
PO Box 559, Symrna, Tennessee 37167, USA.
Boeing 727-200x2.
CARGOLUX AIRLINES INTERNATIONAL – CV/CLX
Luxembourg Airport, GD Luxembourg.
Boeing 747-400Fx3, 747-200Fx4.
On Order: 747-400Fx1.
CARIB EXPRESS – IM/BCB
PO Box 934, Bridgetown, Barbados, West Indies.
BAe 146-100x2.
CARIBBEAN WINDS AIRLINES – WND
PO Box 2176, St John's, Antigua, West Indies.
Lockheed L-1011x2.
CARIBJET – CBJ
PO Box 1301, St John's, Antigua, West Indies.
Lockheed L-1011-500x3, AI A310-300x1.
CARNIVAL AIR LINES – KW/CAA
1815 Griffin Road, Dania, Florida 33004, USA.
AI A300B4-200x8, Boeing 727-200x6, 737-400x6, 737-200x3.
CASINO EXPRESS – XP/CXP
976 Mountain City Highway, Elko, Nevada, USA.
Boeing 737-200x2.
CASPIAN AIRLINES – CPN
Enghlab Avenue, Kaledge, Tehran, Iran.
Yakovlev Yak-42Dx3.
CATHAY PACIFIC – CX/CPA
9 Connaught Road, Central, Hong Kong.
Boeing 747-400x19, Boeing 747-400Fx2, Boeing 747-300x6, Boeing 747-200x6, 747-200Fx4, 777-200x4, AI A340-300x4, A340-200x4, A330-300x10.
On Order: 777-300x7, A340-300x5, A330-300x1.
CAYMAN AIRWAYS – KX/CAY
Georgetown, Grand Cayman, Cayman Islands.
Boeing 737-200x2.
CEBU PACIFIC AIR – 5J
Ortigas Avenue, Quezon City, Philippines.
MDC DC-9-30x4.
CHALLENGAIR – CHG
Avenue Louise 416, B-1050 Brussels, Belgium.
MDC DC-10-30x2.
CHALLENGE AIR CARGO – WE/CWC
PO Box 523979, Miami, Florida 33152, USA.
MDC DC-8-73Fx1, Boeing 707-300Fx1, 757-23APFx3.
CHAMPION AIR – MGM
5101 Vernon Ave South, Edina, Minnesota, USA.
MDC DC-8-62x1, Boeing 727-200x3, 727-100x3.
CHANNEL EXPRESS – LS/EXS
Bournemouth Int Airport, Christchurch, Dorset, UK.
AI A300F4-100Fx1, Lockheed L-188Fx5, Fokker F27-600x2, F27-500x3, Handley Page Heraldx8.
CHEBOKSARY AIR ENTERPRISE
Cheboksary Airport, Republic of Chuvakhia, Russia.
Tupolev Tu-134Ax5, Antonov An-24x6.
CHELYABINSK AIR ENTERPRISE – H6/CHB
Chelyabinsk Airport, Chelyabinsk 454043, Russia.
Tupolev Tu-154Bx6, Tu-134Ax3, Antonov 12x1, Yakovlev Yak-42Dx7, Yak-40x3.
CHERNOMORSKIE AIRLINES
Ul. Golubye Dachi 58/48, Sochi 354000, Russia.
Tupolev Tu-134Ax2.
CHINA AIRLINES – CI/CAL
131 Nanking East Road, Taipei 104, Taiwan.
Boeing 747-400x5, 747-200x3, 747-200Fx3, 747SPx3, 737-200x3, AI A300-600x6, A300B4-200x6, A320-200x2.
On Order: A300-600x2, 737-400x6, 737-800x6.
CHINA EASTERN AIRLINES – MU/CES
Hongqiao Int Airport, 200335 Shanghai, China.
MDC MD-11x5, MD-11Fx1, MD-90x3, MD-82x13, AI A340-300x3, A300-600x10, Fokker 100 x10, Yunshuji Y7x9, Y5x20, Antonov An-24Bx3.
On Order: A340-300x2, MD-90x6.
CHINA GENERAL AVIATION – GP/CTH
Wusu Airport, 030031, Taiyuan, China.
Yakovlev Yak-42Dx7.
CHINA NATIONAL AVIATION – F6/CAG
23 Qianmen Street East, 100006 Beijing, China.
Boeing 757-200x2, 737-300x6.
CHINA NORTHERN AIRLINES – CJ/CBF
3 Xiao He Yan Road, 110043 Shenyang, China.
AI A300-600x5, MDC MD-90x3, MD-82x26, Yunshuji Y7x11.
On Order: MD-90x8
CHINA NORTHWEST AIRLINES – WH/CNW
Laodang Nan Lu, 710082 Xian, China.
AI A300-600x5, A310-200x3, Tupolev Tu-154M x10, BAe146-300x7, 146-100x3, Yunshuji Y7x4.
On Order: A300-600x3.
CHINA SOUTHERN AIRLINES – CZ/CSN
Baiyun Int Airport, 510405 Guangzhou, China.
Boeing 777-200x2, 767-300x5, 757-200x20, 737-300x23, 737-500x12, Antonov An-24Bx5, Saab 340x4, Yunshuji Y7x5.
On Order: 777-200x4, AI A320-200x10.
CHINA SOUTHWEST AIRLINES – SZ/CXN
Shuangliu Airport, 610202 Chengdu, China.
Boeing 707-320Cx1, 757-200x13, 737-300x20, Tupolev Tu-154Mx5, Antonov An-24Bx1, Yunshuji Y7x3.
CHINA UNITED AIRLINES – HR/CUA
14A Fuxinglu Road, 100073 Beijing, China.
Ilyushin Il-76MDx3, Tupolev Tu-154Mx16, Boeing 737-300x6, Antonov An-26x8, An-24RVx9.
CHINA XINHUA AIRLINES – X2/CXH
1 Zuo an Donglu, Zuo'an Men Wai, Beijing, China.
Boeing 737-300x5.
CHINA XINJIANG AIRLINES – XO/CXJ
Diwobao Int Airport, 830016 Urumqi, China.
Ilyushin Il-86x3, Tupolev Tu-154Mx4, Boeing 737-300x4, Antonov An-24RVx3, DHC-6-300x2.
CHINA YUNNAN AIRLINES – 3Q/CYH
Wu Jiabao Airport, 650200 Kunming, China.
Boeing 767-300x2, 737-300x10
On Order: 767-300x1
CHITAAVIA – XW/CHF
Chita Airport, Chita 672018, Rusia.
Tupolev Tu-154Mx5, Tu-154Bx3, Antonov An-26x3, An-24x9.
CITYFLYER EXPRESS – FD/CFE
Gatwick Airport, West Sussex RH6 0PB, UK.
ATR 72x4, ATR 42x7.
On Order: Avro RJ100x2.
CITYJET – WX/BCY
Dublin Airport, County Dublin, Ireland.
BAe 146-200x2.
CLINTONDALE AVIATION
Business Center Westbridge, Moscow , Russia.
Tupolev Tu-134Ax1.
COMAIR – OH/COM
PO Box 75021, Cincinnati, Ohio 45275, USA.
Canadair RJ-100x45, Saab 340x16, Embraer EMB-120x40, EMB-110x2, Fairchild Metro IIIx8.
On Order: RJ-100x5.
COMAIR – MN/CAW
PO Box 7015, Bonaero Park 1622, South Africa.
Boeing 737-200x6, Fokker F27-200x4, ATR 42x2.
COMPAGNIE CORSE MEDITERRANEE – XK/CCM
BP 505, F-20186 Ajaccio Cedex, France.
Fokker 100x2, ATR 72x5.
CONDOR – DE/CFG
Postfach 1164, D-65440 Kelsterbach, Germany.
Boeing 747-400x1, 767-300x9, 757-200x18, 737-300x4, MDC DC-10-30x5.
On Order: 757-300x12.
CONSTELLATION INT AIRLINES – CQ/BFS
Brussels National Airport, Zaventem, Belgium.
Boeing 727-200x2.
CONTINENTAL AIRLINES – CO/COA
2929 Allen Parkway, Houston, Texas 77019, USA.
Boeing 747-200x3, 747-100x2, 757-200x17, 727-200x49, 737-300x65, 737-500x37, 737-200 x18, 737-100x12, MDC DC-10-30x15, DC-10-10 x6, MD-83x2, MD-82x60, MD-81x5, DC-9-30x31.
On Order: 777-200x5, 757-200x8, 737-800x30, 737-700x18.
CONTINENTAL AIRWAYS – PVV
Ul. Tallinskaya 32/1, Moscow 123458, Russia.
Ilyushin Il-86x2.

CONTINENTAL CARGO AIRLINES – CCL
PO Box 9945, Accra, Ghana.
Boeing 707-320Fx1, 727-200x1.
CONTINENTAL EXPRESS – CO/BTA
15333 JFK Boulevard, Houston, Texas 77032, USA.
ATR 72x3, ATR 42x46, Embraer EMB-120x32, Beech 1900Dx25.
On Order: EMB-145x25.
CONTINENTAL MICRONESIA – CS/CMI
862 South Marine Drive, Tamuning, Guam, USA.
Boeing 747-200x2, 727-200x12, 727-200Fx4, MDC DC-10-10x6.
COPA PANAMA – CM/CMP
Apartado Postal 1572, Republic of Panama.
Boeing 737-200x9.
CORSAIR – SS/CRL
24 Rue Saarinen, Rungis Silic Cedex, France.
Boeing 747-300x1, 747-200x2, 747-100x2, 747SP x1, 737-400x2, 737-200x1, MDC DC-10-30x1.
CROATIA AIRLINES – OU/CTN
Savska cesta 41, HR-41000, Zagreb, Croatia.
Boeing 737-200x5, ATR 42x3.
CRONUS AIRLINES – X5/CUS
500 Vouliagmenis Avenue, 56 Alimos, Greece.
Boeing 737-300x1.
CROSSAIR – LX/CRX
Postfach, CH-4002 Basel, Switzerland.
MDC MD-83x4, MD-82x4, Avro RJ100x12, RJ85x4, Saab 2000x21, 340x15.
CYPRUS AIRWAYS – CY/CYP
PO Box 1903, Nicosia, Cyprus.
AI A310-200x4, A320-200x5.
CSA CZECH AIRLINES – OK/CSA
Ruzyne Airport, Praha 6, Czech Republic.
AI A310-300x2, Tupolev Tu-154Mx4, Tu-134Ax3, Boeing 737-400x2, 737-500x5, ATR 72x4, ATR 42x2.
On Order: 737-500x10.
CUBANA – CU/CUB
Calle 23 No 64, Vedado, Havana 1040C, Cuba.
Ilyushin Il-76MDx2, Il-62Mx14, Tupolev Tu-154M x3, TU-154Bx4, Yakovlev Yak-42Dx4, Yak-40x8, Antonov An-26x19, An-24x8, Fokker F27-600x8.
DAALLO AIRLINES – D3/DAO
BP 1954, Djibouti, Djibouti.
Tupolev Tu-154Mx1, Antonov An-24x2, L 410UVPx3.
DACONA AIR – DCA
Bolshoi Savvinsky pereulok 9, Moscow, Russia.
Ilyushin Il-76x1, Yakovlev Yak-42Dx1.
DAS AIR CARGO – SE/DSR
Gatwick Road, Crawley, Sussex, England, UK.
MDC DC-10-30Fx1, Boeing 707-320Fx4.
DAT BELGIAN REGIONAL AIRLINES – DAT
Antwerp Airport, Bus 4, B-2100 Deurne, Belgium.
Avro RJ85x11, BAe 146-200x8, Fokker F28-4000 x3, F28-3000x1, F28-1000x4, Embraer EMB-120x9.
On Order: RJ85x12.
DEBONAIR AIRWAYS – 2G
London Luton Airport, Bedfordshire, England, UK.
BAe 146-200x2.
DELTA AIR LINES – DL/DAL
Hartsfield Atlanta Int Airport, Atlanta, Georgia, USA.
MDC MD-11x11, MD-88x125, MD-90x15, Lockheed L-1011-500x17, L-1011x38, Boeing 767-300x46, 767-200x15, 757-200x86, 727-200 x129, 737-300x13, 737-200x54.
On Order: MD-11x4, MD-90x16, 767-300x13, 757-200x4.
DEUTSCHE BA – DI/BAG
Post Bag 23 16 24, Munchen-Flughafen, Germany.
Boeing 737-300x9, Fokker 100x5, Saab 2000x5, 340x4.
DHL WORLDWIDE EXPRESS – ER/DHL
PO Box 75122, Cincinnati, Ohio 45275, USA.
MDC DC-8-73Fx7, Boeing 727-200Fx13, 727-100Fx11, Fairchild Expediterx10.

An EBA Eurobeglian Airlines 737-300 operating for Virgin Express. (Keith Gaskell)

DIAMOND SAKHA -D8/DSL
Ul. Lenina 6, Neryungri 678922, Russia.
AI A310-300x2.
DIGEX AERO CARGO
Aeroporto Int SP, Romota Central, Guarulhos, Brazil.
MDC DC-8-62Fx1, Boeing 727-100Fx1.
DINAR – D7/RDN
San Martin 320, Buenos Aires, Argentina.
Boeing 727-100x1, 737-200x2.
DNEPR-AIR – DJ/UDN
Dnepropetrovsk Airport, Dnepropetrovsk, Ukraine.
Yakovlev Yak-42x8, Yak-40x5, Antonov An-26x7.
DOBROLET AIRLINES – DOB
Sheremetyevo Airport, Moscow 103340, Russia.
Ilyushin Il-76x3.
DOMINICANA DE AVIACION – DO/DOA
Santo Domingo, Dominican Republic.
MDC DC-10-30x1, DC-6Ax1, Boeing 727-200x1.
DOMODEDOVO AIRLINES – E3/DMO
Domodedovo Airport, Moscow 103225, Russia.
Ilyushin Il-96x2, Il-76x4, Il-62x35, Il-18x3.
DONAVIA AIRLINES D9/DNV
Prospekt Sholokhova 272, Rostov-na-Donu, Russia.
Tupolev Tu-154Bx16, Tu-134Ax8, Antonov An-12 x5, Yakovlev Yak-40x11.
DONBASS AIR LINES – UDD
Donetsk Airport, Donetsk 340021, Ukraine.
Tupolev Tu-154Mx1, Antonov An-24x1, Yakovlev Yak-40x1.
DRAGONAIR – KA/HDA
979 Kings Road, Quarry Bay, Hong Kong.
AI A330-300x4, A320-200x7.
DRUK AIR – KB/DRK
PO Box 209, Thimphu, Bhutan.
BAe 146-100x2.
EAST WEST AIRLINES – 4S
18 New Kantwadi Road, Bandra, Mumbai, India.
Boeing 737-200x7, Fokker F27-500x3.
EASYJET AIRLINES – EZY
London Luton Airport, Bedfordshire, England, UK.
Boeing 737-300x1, 737-200x2.

EBA EUROBELGIAN AIRLINES – BQ/EBA
Building 116, B-1820 Melsbroek Airport, Belgium.
Boeing 737-400x3, 737-300x11.
On Order: 737-800x2, 737-400x2.
ECUATORIANA – EU/EEA
Colon y Reina Victoria, CP505, Quito, Ecuador.
MDC DC-10-30x1.
EDELWEISS AIR – EDW
Postfach, CH -8058 Zurich-Flughafen, Switzerland.
MDC MD-83x2.
EG&G
PO Box 93747, Las Vegas, Nevada 89193, USA.
Boeing 737-200x6.
EGYPT AIR – MS/MSR
Cairo International Airport, Heliopolis, Egypt.
Boeing 747-300x2, 767-300x2, 767-200x3, 707-320x1, 737-500x5, 737-200x2, AI A340-300 x1, A340-200x2, A300-600x9, A300B4-200x5, A320-200x7.
On Order: 777-200x3, A340-200x1, A321-100x4.
EL AL – LY/ELY
PO Box 41, Ben Gurion Int Airport 70100, Israel.
Boeing 747-400x3, 747-200x7, 747-200Fx2, 747-100Fx1, 767-200x4, 757-200x8, 737-200x2.
ELF AIR – E6/EFR
Zhukovsky Airport, Zhukovsky 140160, Russia.
Ilyushin Il-76x2, Il-18x1, Tupolev Tu-134x4, Antonov An-26x1, Yakovlev Yak-40x1.
ELK AIRWAYS – S8/ELK
26 Majaka Street, EE0014, Tallinn, Estonia.
Tupolev Tu-154Mx3, L 410UVPx2.
EMERY WORLDWIDE AIRLINES – EB/EWW
3350 West Bayshore, Palo Alto, California, USA.
MDC DC-8-73Fx8, DC-8-71Fx10, DC-8-63Fx10, DC-8-62Fx7, DC-8-50Fx2, DC-9-10Fx3, Boeing 727-200Fx15, 727-100Fx26.
EMIRATES – EK/UAE
PO Box 686, Dubai, United Arab Emirates.
AI A300-600x6, A310-300x10, Boeing 777-200x3.
On Order: 777-200x4, A330-200x16.

An Egypt Air A340-200. (Airbus)

ESTONIAN AIR – OV/ELL
Lennujaama 2, EE0011 Tallinn, Estonia.
Boeing 737-500x2, Tupolev Tu-134Ax5, Yakovlev Yak-40x4.
ESTRELLAS DEL AIRE – ETA
General Antonio Leon 56, Mexico City, Mexico.
MDC DC-9-10x1.
ETHIOPIAN AIRLINES – ET/ETH
PO Box 1755, Addis Ababa, Ethiopia.
Boeing 767-200x3, 707-300Fx1, 757-200x4, 757-200APFx1, 737-200x1, Lockheed L-100-30 x2, Fokker 50x5, DHC-5x1, DHC-6-300x5, ATR 42x2.
EURALAIR INTERNATIONAL – RN/EUL
Aeroport du Bourget, F-93350 Le Bourget, France.
AI A321-100x1, Boeing 737-500x3, 737-200x5, 737-200Fx1.
On Order: 777-200x2, AI A330-300x2, A321-100x1.
EUROCYPRIA AIRLINES – UI/ECA
PO Box 970, Larnaca, Cyprus.
AI A320-200x3.
EUROFLY – EEZ
Aeroporto, Citta de Torino, Caselle Torinese, Italy.
MDC MD-83x2, DC-9-50x2.
EUROPEAN AIR CHARTER – EAF
Bournemouth Int Airport, Christchurch, Dorset, UK.
Boeing 727-100x1, BAC 111-500x21.
EUROPEAN AIR TRANSPORT – QY/BCS
Brussels National Airport, Zaventem, Belgium.
Boeing 727-200Fx6, 727-100Fx6, Convair 580Fx9.
EUROWINGS – EW/EWG
Flughafenstrasse 100, Nurnberg, Germany.
BAe 146-300x2, 146-200x4, ATR 72x11, ATR 42x17.
On Order: AI A319-100x3.
EVA AIR – BR/EVA
376 Hsin-nan Road, Luchu, Taoyuan Hsien, Taiwan.
Boeing 747-400x12, 767-300x5, 767-200x4, MDC MD-11x3, MD-11Fx3.
On Order: MD-90x5.
EVERGREEN INTERNATIONAL AIRLINES – EZ/EIA
3850 Three Mile Lane, McMinnville, Oregon, USA.
Boeing 747-200Fx4, 747-100Fx8, MDC DC-8-62F x1, DC-9-30Fx6, DC-9-10Fx2.
EXCALIBUR AIRWAYS – EX/EXC
East Midlands Airport, Derby, England, UK.
MDC DC-10-30x2.
EXPRESS ONE INTERNATIONAL – EO/LHN
3890 West Northwest Highway, Dallas, Texas, USA.
Boeing 727-200Fx14, 727-100Fx6.
FALCON AVIATION – IH/FCN
Box 36, S-230 32 Malmo-Sturup, Sweden.
Boeing 737-300QCx3.
FAR EASTERN CARGO AIRLINES – FEW
Ul. Marsovaya 8, Khabarovsk 680011, Russia.
Ilyushin Il-62Mx2.
FAR EASTERN AIR TRANSPORT – EF/FEA
Tun Hwa N Road, FAT Building, Taipei, Taiwan.
Boeing 757-200x2, 737-200x2, MDC MD-83x1, MD-82x8.
FAST AIR CARRIER – UD/FST
Aeropuerto, Santiago de Chile, Chile.
MDC DC-8-71Fx5.
FAUCETT PERU – CF/CFP
Apartado 1429, Lima 100, Peru.
Lockheed L-1011x2, MDC DC-8-62Fx1, Boeing 727-200x2, 737-200x5, 737-100x1.
FEDERAL EXPRESS – FM/FDX
PO Box 727, Memphis, Tennessee 38194, USA.
Boeing 747-200Fx4, 727-200Fx95, 727-100Fx67, MDC MD-11Fx20, DC-10-30Fx22, DC-10-10Fx13, AI A300-600Fx25, A310-200Fx35, Fokker F27-600Fx8, F27-500Fx24, Cessna 208x253.
On Order: A300-600Fx11, A310-200Fx2.
FINE AIR – FB/FBF
PO Box 523726, Miami, Florida 33152, USA.
MDC DC-8-61Fx3, DC-8-50Fx9.
FINNAIR – AY/FIN
PL.15, FIN-01053 Finnair Vantaa, Finland.
MDC MD-11x4, DC-10-30x5, MD-83x8, MD-82 x10, MD-87x3, DC-9-50x12, AI A300B4-200x2, ATR 72x6, Saab 340x7.
On Order: Boeing 757-200x5.
FIRST AIR – 7F/FAB
Carp Airport, Carp, Ontario K0A 1L0, Canada.
Boeing 727-200x3, 727-100x3, BAe 748x8.
FLIGHTLINE – FLT
Southend Airport, Southend-on-Sea, Essex, UK.
BAe 146-300x1, 146-200x1, ATPx2, Embraer EMB-110x2.
FLORIDA WEST AIRLINES – RF/FWL
7500 NW 25th Street, Miami, Florida 33152, USA.
Boeing 707-320Fx2.
FLY – FLB
Ave Presidente Wilson 164, Rio de Janiero, Brazil.
Boeing 727-200x1.
FORMOSA AIRLINES
340 Tun Hwa North Road, Taipei 10592, Taiwan.
Fokker 100x2, Fokker 50x4, Dornier 328x2, 228x7, Saab 340x9.
On Order: Dornier 328x2.
FREEDOM AIR – FOM
698 New Market Lane, Auckland, New Zealand.
Boeing 737-300x1.
FRONTIER AIRLINES – F9/FFT
12015 East 46th Ave, Denver, Colorado, USA.
Boeing 737-300x2, 737-200x5.
FUERZA AEREA DEL PERU – FPR
Aeropuerto Jorge Chavez, Lima-Callao, Peru.
MDC DC-8-62x2, Boeing 707-320x1, Lockheed L-100-20x6, Fokker F28-1000x1, Antonov An-32x15.
FUTURA INTERNATIONAL AIRWAYS – FH/FUA
Gran Via Asima 17, Palma de Mallorca, Spain
Boeing 737-400x8.
GARUDA INDONESIA – GA/GIA
Medan Merdeka Selatan 13, Jakarta, Indonesia.
Boeing 747-400x5, 747-200x6, 737-400x7, 737-300x8, MDC MD-11x7, DC-10-30x6, A300-600x10, A300B4-200x9.

European Air Charter flies this sole 727-100 alongside a fleet of BAC One-Elevens. (Keith Gaskell)

On Order: AI A330-300x5, 747-400x4, 777-200x6, 737-500x6, 737-300x12, MD-11x2, A330-300x4.
GAS AIR – NGS
PMB 21231, Ikeja, Nigeria.
BAC 111-400x3.
GB AIRWAYS – GT/GBL
Gatwick Airport, West Sussex RH6 0PB, UK.
Boeing 737-400x3, 737-200x2.
GEORGIA AIR PRAGUE – PGU
Evropska 178, CZ-160 67, Prague, Czech Republic.
Ilyushin Il-62x3, Tupolev Tu-154Mx1.
GERMANIA – GMI
Flughafen Tegel, Gebaude 23, Berlin, Germany.
Boeing 737-300x12.
On Order: 737-700x12.
GHANA AIRWAYS – GH/GHA
PO Box 1636, Accra, Ghana.
MDC DC-10-30x1, DC-9-50x1, Fokker F28-4000 x1, F28-2000x1.
GM AIRLINES
Terminal Building, B-8400 Ostend, Belgium.
Boeing 707-320Fx1, 727-200x1.
GOMAIR – GMR
Aeroport Goma, Goma, Zaire.
Boeing 727-100x1.
GRAND AIR – 8L/GDI
Pasay City, Metro Manila, Philippines.
AI A300B4-200x1, A300B4-100x1, Boeing 737-200x1.
GREAT AMERICAN AIRWAYS – MV/GRA
PO Box 10165, Reno, Nevada 89510, USA.
MDC MD-87x3, MD-82x1, DC-9-10x3.
GREAT CHINA AIRLINES – IF
260 Pa-Teh Road, Section 2, Taipei, Taiwan.
Dash 8-300x12, Dash 8-100x2.
On Order: MD-90x1, Dash 8-400x12.
GULF AIR -GF/GFA
PO Box 138, Manama, Bahrain.
AI A340-300x6, A320-200x14, Lockheed L-1011 x5, Boeing 767-300x18.
On Order: A330-300x6.
GUYANA AIRWAYS – GY/GYA
PO Box 10223, Georgetown, Guyana.
Boeing 757-200x1, DHC-6-300x1.
HAINAN AIRLINES – H4/CHH
29 Haixiu Dadao, 570206 Haikou, China.
Boeing 737-400x3, 737-300x5, Fairchild Metrox6.
On Order: Metrox2.
HALISA AIR – WD/HBC
7270 NW 12th Street, Miami, Florida 33126, USA.
Boeing 737-200x1.
HAMBURG AIRLINES – HX/HAS
Flughafen, D-22335 Hamburg, Germany.
Bae 146-300x2, 146-200x2, Dash 8-300x2, Dash 8-100x3.
HAPAG-LLOYD – HF/HLF
Postfach 42 02 40, D-30662 Hannover, Germany.
AI A310-300x4, A310-200x4, Boeing 737-400x12, 737-500x5.
On Order: 737-800x16.
HARCO AIR SERVICES – HCO
42 Allen Avenue, Ikeja, Nigeria.
Boeing 727-200x2.
HAWAIIAN AIR – HA/HAL
PO Box 30008, Honolulu, Hawaii 96820, USA.
MDC DC-10-10x8, DC-9-50x13.
HEAVILIFT CARGO AIRLINES – NP/HLA
Stansted Airport, Stansted, Essex, England, UK.
Ilyushin Il-76TDx2, Shorts Belfastx2, Antonov An-12x1.
HELIOPOLIS AIRLINES
Heliopolis, Egypt.
MD-83x1.
On Order: MD-90x1.

HEMUS AIR – DU/HMS
Sofia Airport, 1540 Sofia, Bulgaria.
Tupolev Tu-134Ax2, Yakovlev Yak-40x11, L 410UVPx3.
HOLD-TRADE AIR
No 6A Sokoto Road, Kaduna, Nigeria.
BAC 111-200x3.
HOLIDAY AIR – HW/HLD
Besyol, Inonu Cad, Sefakoy-Istanbul, Turkey.
AI A300B4-100x1, A300B4-200x1, Boeing 727-200x1.
HORIZON AIR – QX/QXE
PO Box 48309, Seattle, Washington 98148, USA.
Fokker F28-1000x10, Dash 8-100x23, Dornier 328x20, Fairchild Metro IIIx28.
HOSEBA – HOS
Ul. Ternopolskaya 17, Kiev 252115, Ukraine.
Ilyushin Il-76x6.
HUNGARIAN-UKRAINIAN AIRLINES – HUK
Ferihegy Airport 1, H-1185 Budapest, Hungary.
Ilyushin Il-76TDx2.
HUNTING CARGO AIRLINES – AG/ABR
Dublin Airport, County Dublin, Ireland.
Boeing 727-200Fx10, Lockheed L-188Fx4.
IBERIA – IB/IBE
130 Calle Velazquez, E-28006 Madrid, Spain.
Boeing 747-200x7, 757-200x16, 727-200x28, AI A340-300x4, A300B4-100x8, A320-200x22, MDC DC-10-30x8, DC-8-62Fx2, DC-8-71Fx1, MD-87 x24, DC-9-30x15
On Order: A340-300x4.
IBIS AIR
PO Box 8, 1748 Lanseria, South Africa.
Boeing 727-100x2.
ICELANDAIR – FI/ICE
IS-101, Reykjavik, Iceland.
Boeing 757-200x4, 737-400x4, Fokker 50x4.
IGAP – IGP
Ivanovo Airport, Inanovo 153041, Russia.
Tupolev Tu-134Ax5, Antonov An24x6.
IMAIR – IK/ITX
115 Hasi Aslanov Street, Baku 370000, Azerbaijan.
Ilyushin Il-76x2, Tupolev Tu-154Mx2, Tu-154Bx1.
IMPERIAL AIR – 7I/IMP
Javier Prado 1380, Corpac San Isidro, Lima, Peru.
Boeing 727-100x1, Tupolev Tu-134Ax2, Antonov An-32x2.
INDEPENDENT AIR FREIGHTERS – IN/IPA
PO Box 560, Tullamarine, Victoria 3043, Australia.
MDC DC-9-30Fx2.
INDIAN AIRLINES – IC/IAC
Airlines House, Parliament Street, New Delhi, India.
AI A300B2-100x8, A300B4-200x2, A320-200x30, Boeing 737-200x15.
INTER AIR – D6/ILN
Johannesburg Int Airport 1627, South Africa.
Boeing 727-200x2.
INTER-CANADIAN – ICN
Stuart Graham Blvd North, Dorval, Quebec, Canada.
Fokker F28-1000x1, ATR 42-300x8.
INTERCONTINENTAL COLOMBIA – RS/ICT
Avenida Eldorado, Santafe de Bogota, Colombia.
MDC DC-9-10x16, Vickers Viscount 800x1.
INVERSIA – INV
Riga Airport, Riga LV-1053, Latvia.
Ilyushin Il-76x3, Antonov An-26x1.
IRAN AIR – IR/IRA
PO Box 13185-775, Tehran, Iran.
Boeing 747-200Fx1, 747-200x2, 747-100x1, 747SPx4, 707-320x3, 77-320Fx1, 727-200x5, 727-100x2, 737-200x3, AI A300-600x2, A300B2-200x5, Fokker 100x6.
IRAN AIR TOURS – IRB
191 Motahari Avenue, Tehran 15879, Iran.
Tupolev Tu-154Mx6.

One of eight Airbus A340-300s the Spanish flag carrier Iberia has ordered. (Airbus)

IRAN ASSEMAN AIRLINES – Y7/IRC
PO Box 13145-1476, Tehran, Iran.
Boeing 727-200x4, Fokker F28-4000x4, F28-1000 x2, ATR 72x4, ATR 42x1.
IRAQI AIRWAYS – IA/IAW
Saddam International Airport, Baghdad, Iraq.
Boeing 747-200x3, 747SPx1, 707-320x2, 727-200x6, 737-200x2.
IRON DRAGONFLY – F7/IDF
Ul. Dimitrova 11, Kazan, Republic Tatarstan, Russia.
Tupolev Tu-154Mx1.
ISTANBUL AIRLINES – IL/IST
Firuzkoy Yolu 26, 34850 Avcilar-Istanbul, Turkey.
Boeing 757-200x2, 727-200x7, 727-200Fx1, 737-400x6.
ITA ITAPEMIRIM CARGO – ITM
Pca Pio X, CEP-20040 Rio deJaneiro, Brazil.
Boeing 727-200Fx2, 727-100Fx4.
IZHAVIA – IZA
Izhevsk Airport, Republic of Udurmutia, Russia.
Tupolev Tu-134Ax4, Antonov An-26x3, An-24x4.
JAPAN AIR CHARTER – JZ/JAZ
18-16 Hamamatsu-Cho, Minato-ku, Tokyo, Japan.
Boeing 747-200x2, MDC DC-10-40x4.
JAPAN AIRLINES – JL/JAL
7F, 7-3 Marunouchi, Chiyoda-ku, Tokyo, Japan.
Boeing 747-400x32, 747-300x13, 747-200x20, 747-200Fx8, 747-100x7, 777-200x3, 767-300 x18, 767-200x3, 737-400x5, MDC MD-11x9, DC-10-40x13.
On Order: 747-400x18, 777-300x5, 777-200x7, MD-11x1.
JAPAN AIR SYSTEM – JD/JAS
5-1 Toranomon, 3-chome, Minato-ku, Tokyo, Japan.
MDC DC-10-30x2, MD-81x26, MD-87x8, DC-9-40 x6, Boeing 777-200x1, AI A300-600x17, A300B2-300x9, A300B4-200x8, NAMC YS-11x15.
On Order: MD-90x10, Boeing 777-200x6.
JAPAN ASIA AIRWAYS – EG/JAA
Minami-kan 7-1, Yurakucho, Tokyo 100, Japan.
Boeing 747-300x1, 747-200x2, 747-100x1, MDC DC-10-40x4.
JAPAN TRANSOCEAN AIR – NU/JTA
306-1 Kagamizu, Naha, Okinawa 901-01, Japan.
Boeing 737-400x4, 737-200x9, NAMC YS-11x5, DHC-6-300x4.
JAPAN UNIVERSAL SYSTEM TRANSPORT – JST
Haneda Airport, 2-chome, Ohta-ku, Tokyo, Japan.
Boeing 747-200Fx1.

JARO INTERNATIONAL – JT/MDJ
Str. Londra No 21, Sct.1, Bucuresti, Romania.
Boeing 707-320Cx2, 707-320Fx2, BAC 111-500x2.
JAT YUGOSLAV AIRLINES – JU/JAT
Ho Shi Minova 16, Novi Beograd, Yugoslavia.
MDC DC-10-30x1, DC-9-30x9, Boeing 727-200x8, 737-300x9, ATR 72x3.
JERSEY EUROPEAN AIRWAYS – JY/JEA
Exeter Airport, Exeter, Devon EX5 2BD, UK.
BAe 146-300x2, 146-200x4, 146-100x1, Fokker F27-500x8, Shorts 360x4.
JET AIRWAYS – 9W/JAI
Andheri-Kurla Road, Andheri, Mumbai,India.
Boeing 737-400x4, 737-300x4.
JETALL AIRWAYS – 8J/JTL
Tranmere Dr, Mississauga, Ontario, Canada.
Boeing 737-200x2, Convair 580x3, Fairchild Metrox9.
JET ASPEN – J9
715 West Main St, Aspen, Colorado 81611, USA.
BAe 146-200x2.
JET TRAIN – LF
Woodlawn Road, Aliquippa, Pennsylvania, USA.
MDC DC-9-30x2.
KABO AIR – KO/QNK
PO Box 3439, Kano, Nigeria.
Boeing 727-200x7, 727-100x1, BAC 111-400x3, 111-200x8.
KALININGRAD AIR ENTERPRISE – KLN
Khrabrova Airport, Kalinigrad 238315, Russia.
Tupolev Tu-154Mx2, Tu-134Ax10.
KALITTA AMERICAN INT AIRWAYS – CB/CKS
842 Willow Run Road, Ypsilanti, Michigan, USA.
Boeing 747-200Fx3, 747-100Fx3, 747-100x2, 727-200Fx13, 727-200x2, 727-100Fx3, 727-100 x2, Lockheed L-1011Fx5, MDC DC-8-63Fx7, DC-8-62Fx2, DC-8-62x2, DC-8-61Fx5, DC-8-50Fx11
KARAT – AKT
Prospekt Vernadskogo 125a, Moscow, Russia.
Yakovlev Yak-42x5.
KAZAKHSTAN AIRLINES – K4/KZA
Zholtoskan Street 59, Almaty 480004, Kazakhstan.
Boeing 747SPx1, Boeing 767-300x2, Ilyushin Il-86x7, Il-76x4, Tupolev Tu-154Mx4, Tu-154Bx23, Tu-134Ax11, Yakovlev Yak-42x6, Yak-40x30, Antonov An-26x10, An-30x9, An-24x33, An-72x1.
On Order: 767-300x2.

All three of Japan's major airlines – JAS (pictured), JAL and All Nippon have ordered the Boeing 777. Japan's aerospace industry has a major workshare of 777 production. (Boeing)

KELOWNA FLIGHTCRAFT AIR CHARTER – KFA
Kelowna Airport, British Columbia, Canada.
Boeing 727-200x1, 727-100x10, Convair 5800x2, 580x11.

KEMEROVO AIR ENTERPRISE
Kemerovo Airport, Kemerovo 650041, Russia.
Tupolev Tu-154Mx1, Tu-154Bx2, Antonov An-26x7, An-24x5.

KENYA AIRWAYS – KQ/KQA
PO Box 19002, Nairobi, Kenya.
AI A310-300x3, Boeing 737-200x2, Fokker 50x3.
On Order: 737-300x2.

KHABAROVSK AVIATION ENTERPRISE – H8
Khabarovsk Airport, Khabarovsk 680012, Russia.
Ilyushin Il-62Mx21, Tupolev Tu-154Bx22, Antonov An-26x10, An-24x16.

KHORS AIRCOMPANY – X6/KHO
Volinskaya 16, Kiev 252020, Ukraine.
Ilyushin Il-76x7, Antonov An-26x1, An-24x1, An-12x3.

KIBRIS TURKISH AIRLINES – YK/KYV
Bedreddin Demirel Ave, Yenisehir, Nicosia, Cyprus.
AI A310-200x1, Boeing 727-200x3.

KIROV AIR ENTERPRISE – KTA
Kirov Airport, Kirov 610009, Russia.
Tupolev Tu-134Ax3, Antonov An-24x5.

KISH AIR – KN/IRK
PO Box 19395-4639, Tehran 19697, Iran.
Tupolev Tu-154Mx4.

KITTY HAWK AIR CARGO – KR/KHA
PO Box 612787, DFW Int Airport, Texas, USA.
Boeing 727-200Fx7, MDC DC-9-10Fx5, Convair 600Fx13.

KIWI INTERNATIONAL AIRLINES – KP/KIA
US 1 & 9 South, Newark, New Jersey 07114, USA.
Boeing 727-200x15.

KLM CITYHOPPER – HN/KLC
Postbus 7700, Schipol-Oost, Netherlands.
Fokker 70x4, F28-4000x2, Fokker 50x10, Saab 340x11.

KLM ROYAL DUTCH AIRLINES – KL/KLM
Postbus 7700, Schipol-Oost, Netherlands.
Boeing 747-400x17, 747-300x3, 747-200x10, 767-300x8, 737-400x16, 737-300x15, MDC MD-11x9, AI A310-200x4, Fokker 100x6.
On Order: 747-400x3, 767-300x2, 737-300x2, MD-11x1.

KOGALYMAVIA – KGL
Kogalym Airport, Kogalym 626481, Russia.
Tupolev Tu-154Mx4, Tu-154Bx1.

KOMIAVIA
Ul. Pervomaiskaya 53, Republic of Komi, Russia.
Tupolev Tu-134Ax40, Antonov An-12x3, An-26x12, An-24x17, Yakovlev Yak-40x11.

KOREAN AIR – KE/KAL
Box 864, Seosomun-dong, Chung-gu, Seoul, Korea.
Boeing 747-400x21, 747-400Fx1, 747-300x3, 747-200x4, 747-200Fx11, 747SPx2, 727-200x3, MDC MD-11x3, MD-11Fx2, DC-10-30x3, MD-83 x3, MD-82x11, AI A300-600x21, A300B4-200Fx2, A300B4-100x8, Fokker 100x12.
On Order: 747-400x8, 747-400Fx3, 777-300x8, 777-200x4, A330-300x7, A330-200x2.

KOSMOS – KSM
Ul. Rejsovaja 12, Moscow 103027, Russia.
Ilyushin Il-76x1, Tupolev Tu-134Ax3, Antonov An-12x1, An-26x1.

KRAI AERO AIR COMPANY – K3/KIO
Vetoshny pereulok 13/15, Moscow 103012, Russia.
Tupolev Tu-154Mx2.

KRASNOYARSK AIRLINES – 7B/KJC
Yemelianova Airport, Krasnoyarsk 663020, Russia.
MDC DC-10-30x2, Ilyushin Il-86x4, Il-76x11, Il-62x7, Tupolev Tu-154Mx10, Tu-154Bx12, Yakovlev Yak-40x8, Antonov An-26x7.

KUBAN AIRLINES – KIL
Krasnodar Airport, Krasnodar 350026, Russia.
Yakovlev Yak-42x11, Antonov An-26x14, An-14x15.

KUWAIT AIRWAYS – KU/KAC
PO Box 394, Kuwait, State of Kuwait.
Boeing 747-400x1, 747-200x2, 707-320Fx2, 727-200, AI A340-300x4, A300-600x6, A310-300 x4, A320-200x3.
On Order: 777-200x2.

KYRGYZSTAN AIRLINES – K2/KGA
Manas Airport, Bishkek 720062, Kyrgyzstan.
Ilyushin Il-76x1, Tupolev Tu-154Mx2, Tu-154Bx12, Tu-134Ax6, Antonov An-26x1, Yakovlev Yak-40x11.

LAC CANARIAS – LCN
Avda Anaga 43, Santa Cruz de Tenerife, Spain.
MDC DC-9-40x2.

LAC COLOMBIA – LC/LIC
Carrera 56, Edificio LAC, Barranquilla, Colombia.
MDC DC-8-50Fx3.

LACSA – LR/LRC
Apartado 1531-1000, San Jose, Costa Rica.
AI A320-200x4, Boeing 737-200x6.

LADECO AIRLINES – UC/LCO
Alameda 107, Santiago de Chile, Chile.
AI A300B4-200x1, Boeing 757-200x2, 727-100x2, 737-300x1, 737-200x11.

L'AEROPOSTALE – ARP
BP 10454, F-95708 Roissy-CDG, France.
Boeing 727-200Fx2, 737-300QCx14, 737-200Cx4.

LAKER AIRWAYS – 7Z/LBH
1100 Lee Wagner Blvd, Ft Lauderdale, Florida, USA.
MDC DC-10-30x3.

LAM – TM/LAM
PO Box 2060, Maputo, Mozambique.
Boeing 767-200x1, 737-200x2, CASA 212x4.

LAN CHILE – LA/LAN
Estado 10, Casilla 147-D, Santiago de Chile, Chile.
Boeing 767-300x6, 737-200x8, BAe 146-200x2.

LANA AIRCOMPANY – RKS
Ul. Metrostroevskaya 11a, Liev 252054, Ukraine.
Ilyushin Il-76x3.

LAO AVIATION – QV/LAO
BP 119, 2 Rue Pang Kham, Vientiane, Laos.
Boeing 737-200x1, Xian Y7-100x5, Harbin Y12x6, Antonov An-24x3, ATR 72x1.

LAPA – MJ/LPR
Avenue Santa Fe 1970, Buenos Aires, Argentina.
Boeing 757-200x1, 737-200x6, Saab 340x2.

LAPSA/AIR PARAGUAY – PZ/LAP
Oliva 471, Asuncion, Paraguay.
AI A310-300x2, A320-200x3, Boeing 737-200x2.

LASER – LER
Torre Lara, Planta Baha, Caracas, Venezuela.
Boeing 727-200x1.

LAT CHARTER – LTC
Riga Airport, LV-1053 Riga, Latvia.
Tupolev Tu-134Bx4.

LATAVIO – PV/LTL
54 Brivibas Street, Riga LV-1050, Latvia.
Tupolev Tu-154Bx4, Tu-134Bx7, Antonov An-26x2, An-24x5.

LAUDA AIR – NG/LDA
Postfach 56, A-1300 Wien-Flughafen, Austria.
Boeing 767-300x5, 737-400x2, 737-300x2, Canadair RJ-100x7.
On Order: 777-200x4, 737-800x2.

LEISURE INTERNATIONAL AIRWAYS – ULE
Stansted Airport, Stansted, Essex, England, UK.
Boeing 767-300x2.
On Order: AI A321-200x4.

LIBERIA WORLD AIRLINES – LE/LWA
PO Box 24, Ostend Airport, Belgium.
MDC DC-8-50Fx2, Boeing 707-320x1, 707-320Fx1.

LIBYAN ARAB AIR CARGO – LCR
PO Box 2555, Tripoli, Libya.
Ilyushin Il-76x19, Lockheed L-100-20x2, L-100-30 x2, Antonov An-26x2.

LIBYAN ARAB AIRLINES – LN/LAA
PO Box 2555, Tripoli, Libya.
Boeing 707-320x3, 727-200x9, Fokker F28-4000 x3, F27-600x12, F27-500x2, F27-400x1.

LINA CONGO – GC/GCB
BP 2203, Brazzaville, Republic of Congo.
Boeing 737-200x1, Fokker F28-1000x1, F27-600 x2, DHC-6-300x1.

LINAIR-HUNGARIAN REGIONAL AIRLINES – LIN
Ecsedhaca Street 23, H-1171 Budapest, Hungary.
Yakovlev Yak-40x1.

LINEAS AEREAS SURAMERICANAS COLOMBIA
Aeropuerto Eldorado, Santafe de Bogota, Colombia.
Boeing 727-100Fx3, Aerospatiale Caravelle 10x3.

LIPETSK AIR ENTERPRISE
Lipetsk Airport, Lipetsk 398000, Russia.
Yakovlev Yak-42Dx2, Yak-40x10.

LITHUANIAN AIRLINES – TE/LIL
A Gustaicio 4, L-2038 Vilnius Airport, Lithuania.
Yakovlev Yak-42x11, Boeing 737-200x3, Tupolev Tu-134Ax5.

LLOYD AEREO BOLIVIANO – LB/LLB
Casilla Correo 132, Cochabamba, Bolivia.
AI A310-300x2, Boeing 707-300Fx1, 727-200x4, 727-100x3, Fokker F27-200x1.

LOT – POLSKIE LINIE LOTNICZE – LO/LOT
ul.17 Stycznia 39, PL-00-906 Warsaw, Poland.
Boeing 767-300x2, 767-200x2, 737-400x5, 737-500x6, Tupolev Tu-154Mx4, Tu-134Ax7, Antonov An-26x2, ATR 72x8.
On Order: 767-300x1, 737-400x2.

Martinair flies two GE CF6 powered 747-200s. (Keith Anderson)

LTE INTERNATIONAL AIRWAYS – XO/LTE
Calle del Ter 27, E-07009 Palma de Mallorca, Spain.
Boeing 757-200x3.
LTU INTERNATIONAL AIRWAYS – LT/LTU
Halle 8, Flughafen, D-40474 Dusseldorf, Germany.
MDC MD-11x4, AI A330-300x6.
On Order: AI A330-300x1.
LTU SUD INTERNATIONAL AIRWAYS – LTS
PO Box 231844, D-85327 Munchen, Germany.
Boeing 767-300x5, 757-200x10.
LUFTHANSA – LH/DLH
Von Gablenz Str. 2-6, D-50679 Koln, Germany.
Boeing 747-400x18, 747-200x8, 737-400x7, 737-300x46, 737-500x30, 737-200x23, AI A340-300x10, A340-200x6, A300-600x12, A310-300x12, A321-100x15, A320-200x33, A319-100x6.
On Order: 747-400x4, A300-600x2, A321-100x5, A319x14.
LUFTHANSA CARGO AIRLINES – LH/GEC
Postfach 1244, D-65441 Kelsterbach, Germany.
Boeing 747-200Fx11, 737-300Fx1, 737-200Fx2, MDC DC-8-73Fx5.
On Order: MD-11Fx5.
LUFTHANSA CARGO INDIA
5-6 Vasant Vihar, New Delhi 110057, India.
Boeing 727-200Fx5.
LUFTHANSA CITYLINE – CL/CLH
Postfach 1111, Am Holzweg 26, Kriftel, Germany.
Avro RJ85x15, Canadair RJ-100x30, Fokker 50x12.
On Order: RJ85x2
LUXAIR – LG/LGL
BP 2203, L-2987 Luxembourg, GD Luxembourg.
Boeing 737-400x2, 737-500x4, Fokker 50x4.
MACEDONIAN AIRLINES – IN/MAK
B. Partizanski Opodredi 17a, Skopje, Macedonia.
Yakovlev Yak-42x1.
MAERSK AIR – DM/DAN
Copenhagen Airport South, Dragoer, Denmark.
Boeing 737-300x15, 737-500x10, Fokker 50x8.
On Order: 737-700x6, 737-500x5.
MAERSK AIR – VB/MSK
2245-49 Coventry Rd, Sheldon, Birmingham, UK.
BAC 111-500x3, 111-400x4, BAe Jetstream 31x3.
MAGADAN AIRLINES – H5/MVL
7 Ulitsa Naberexhnaya, Magadan 685000, Russia.
Tupolev Tu-154Mx6, Tu-154Bx6.
MAGADANAEROGRUZ – MGG
Sokol Airport, Box 427, Magadan 685018, Russia.
Ilyushin Il-76x3, Antonov An-12x5.
MAHAN AIR – IRM
PO Box 76135-1663, Kerman, Iran.
Ilyushin Il-76TDx2, Tupolev Tu-154Mx2.
MAHFOOZ AVIATION – M2/MZS
PO Box 6664, Jeddah 21452, Saudi Arabia.
Boeing 707-300x2, 727-200x2.
MAKHACHKALA AIR ENTERPRISE
Makhachkala Airport, Dagestan, Russia.
Tupolev Tu-154Mx2, Antonov An-24x6.
MAKUNG AIRLINES – B7
No 305 Ho-Tung Road, Kaoshiung, Taiwan.
Boeing 757-200x1, BAe 146-300x5, 748x2.
On Order: MDC MD-90x5.
MALAYSIA AIRLINES – MH/MAS
Bangunan, Kuala Lumpur Malaysia.
Boeing 747-400x13, 747-300x1, 747-200Fx2, 737-400x40, 737-300Fx2, 737-500x9, MDC MD-11x3, MD-11Fx3, DC-10-30x4, AI A330-200 x12, Fokker 50x11, DHC-6-300x6.
On Order: 747-400x10, 777-300x4, 777-200x11, 737-400x2.
MALEV HUNGARIAN AIRLINES – MA/MAH
Rossevelt ter 2, H-1051 Budapest V, Hungary.
Boeing 767-200x2, 737-400x2, 737-300x4, 737-200x6, Tupolev Tu-154Bx9, Tu-134Ax6, Fokker 70x4.
MALMO AVIATION – 6E/SCW
Box 6, S-230 32 Malmo Sturup, Sweden.
BAe 146-200x9, 146-100x1.
MALS AIR COMPANY – MSL
PO Box 50, Lyubertsy 140000, Russia.
Tupolev Tu-154Mx1.
MANDALA AIRLINES – RI/MDL
Jalan Garuda 76, PO Box 3706, Jakarta, Indonesia.
Boeing 737-200x7.
MANDARIN AIRLINES – AE/MDA
134 Min Sheng East Rd, Section 3, Taipei, Taiwan.
Boeing 747-400x1, 747SPx1, MDC MD-11x4.
MANX AIRLINES – JE/MNX
Ronaldsway Airport, Ballasalla, Isle of Man, UK.
BAe 146-200x2, ATPx16, Jetstream 41x13, Jetstream 31x2.
MARTINAIR – MP/MPH
PO Box 7507, NL-1118 ZG Schipol, Netherlands.
Boeing 747-200x2, 747-200Fx1, 767-300x6, MDC MD-11CFx4, MD-11Fx1.
MERIDIANA – IG/ISS
Zona Industriale, I-07026 Olbia, Sardinia, Italy.
MDC MD-82x8, DC-9-50x6, BAe 146-200x4.
MERPATI – MZ/MNA
Kotak Pos 323, Jakarta 10720, Indonesia.
AI A310-300x2, Lockheed L-100-30x2, Boeing 737-200x3, Fokker 100x10, F28-4000x27, F28-3000x5, F27-500x13, BAe ATPx5, IPTN CN-235x23, IPTN 212x11, DHC-6-300x8.
On Order: Fokker 100x2, CN-235x7.
MESA AIRLINES – YV/ASH
1296 West Navajo St, Farmington, New Mexico, USA.
Embraer EMB-120x5, Beech 1900Dx20, Beech 1900C-1x9.
On Order:Canadair RJ-200x16, Beech 1900Dx5.
MEXICANA – MX/MXA
Xola 535, Piso 30, Mexico City 03100. Mexico.
Boeing 727-200x23, AI A320-200x14, Fokker 100x10.
On Order: AI A320-200x8.
MEXICARGO – GJ/MXC
640, Col. Pensador Mexicano, Mexico City, Mexico.
Boeing 727-200Fx1.
MIAMI AIR – GL/BSK
PO Box 660880, Miami, Florida 33266, USA.
Boeing 727-200x7.
MIAT MONGOLIAN AIRLINES – OM/MGL
Buyant-Ukhaa-34, Ulaanbaatar 210734, Mongolia.
Boeing 727-200x3, Antonov An-30x1, An-26x4, An-24x13, Harbin Y-12x5.
MIBA AVIATION
55 Blvd du Regent, B-1000 Brussels, Belgium.
Boeing 727-100Fx1.

One of eight Fokker 100s flown by Chicago based Midway Airlines. (Gary Gentle)

MIDAS AIRLINES – MIO
Apartado Correo 68817, Caracas 1060, Venezuela.
MDC DC-8-50Fx1.
MIDDLE EAST AIRLINES – ME/MEA
PO Box 206, Beirut, Lebanon.
Boeing 747-200x3, 707-320Cx8, AI A310-300x2, A310-200x2.
MIDWAY AIRLINES – JI/JEX
5713 South Cicero Avenue, Chicago, Illinois, USA.
AI A320-200x4, Fokker 100x12.
On Order: AI A320-200x4.
MIDWEST EXPRESS – YX/MEP
4915 Sth Howell Ave, Milwaukee, Wisconsin, USA.
MDC MD-88x2, DC-9-30x12, DC-9-10x8.
MILLON AIR – OX/OXO
PO Box 524057, Miami, Florida 33152, USA.
Lockheed L-1011Fx1, Boeing 707-320Fx5.
MK AIRLINES – 7G/MKA
Landhurst, Hartfield, East Sussex, England, UK.
MDC DC-8-50Fx5.
MISTRAL AIR – MSA
Aeroporto Ciampino Ovest, I-00040 Rome, Italy.
BAe 146-200QTx1.
MODILUFT – M9/MOD
98 Nehru Place, New Delhi 110019, India.
Boeing 737-400x3, 737-200x4.
MOLDAVIAN AIRLINES – 2M/MDV
Chisinau Airport, Chisinau 277026, Moldova.
Yakovlev Yak-42x2, Yak-40x2.
MONARCH AIRLINES – ZB/MON
Luton Airport, Luton, Bedfordshire, England, UK.
MDC DC-10-30x1, AI A300-600x4, A320-200x7, Boeing 757-200x8.
MORNINGSTAR AIR EXPRESS – MEI
11640-109 Street, Edmonton, Alberta, Canada.
Boeing 727-100Fx3, Fairchild Metrox1.
MOSCOW AIRWAYS – MAV
Sheremetyevo-1 Airport, Moscow 103340, Russia.
Ilyushin Il-76x1, Il-62Mx1, Antonov An-12, An-32x4.
MOSTRANSGAZ – OC/MTG
Komunarka, Gazoprovod 142770, Moscow.
Ilyushin Il-76x2, Antonov An-12x1, Yakovlev Yak-40x2.
MURMANSK AIRLINES – MNK
Murmansk Airport, Murmansk 184364, Russia.
Tupolev Tu-154Mx4.
MYANMA AIRWAYS – UB/UBA
104 Strand Road, Yangon, Myanmar.
Fokker F28-4000x2, F28-1000x1, F27-600x6, F27-400x1.
MYANMAR AIRWAYS INTERNATIONAL – UB/UBA
104 Strand Road, Yangon, Myanmar.
Boeing 737-400x2.

NATIONAL AIRLINES – N4/NCN
Ahumada 131, Santiago de Chile, Chile.
Boeing 737-200x4.
NATIONAL JET SYSTEMS – NC
James Schofield Dr, Adelaide Airport, Australia.
Avro RJ70x1, BAe 146-100x1, Dash 8-300x2, Dash 8-200x4, Dash 8-100x2, BAe Jetstream 41x1.
NATIONAL OVERSEAS AIRLINE – NOL
PO Box 2520, El Horria, Heliopolis, Egypt.
Boeing 707-320x1, 707-320Fx2, Yakovlev Yak-40x1.
NATIONS AIR – N5/NAE
2400 Herodian Way, Smyrna, Georgia 30080, USA.
Boeing 737-200x2.
NATIONWIDE AIR – NTW
PO Box 422, Lanseria 1748, South Africa.
BAC 111-500x6, 111-400x1.
NERYUNGRI SAKHA AIR ENTERPRISE
Chulman Airport, Republic Sakha-Yakutia, Russia.
Tupolev Tu-154Bx4, Yakovlev Yak-40x6.
NEW ACS – DF/NWC
PO Box 21236, Dar-es-Salaam, Tanzania.
Boeing 727-200x1.
NEW ACS – CHR
BP 5371, Kinshasa 10, Zaire.
Boeing 727-100x1.
NICA – 6Y/NIS
Apartado Postal 6018, Managua, Nicaragua.
Boeing 737-200x1, CASA 212x1.
NIGERIA AIRWAYS – WT/NGA
PMB 1024, Ikeja, Nigeria.
MDC DC-10-30x1, Boeing 707-320Cx1, 707-320F x1, 737-200x6, AI A310-200x4.
NIPPON CARGO AIRLINES – KZ/NCA
3-1 Toranomon, 4-chome, Minato-ku, Tokyo, Japan.
Boeing 747-200Fx6, 747-100Fx1.
NIZHNY NOVGOROD AIRLINES – NGL
Nizhny Novgorod Airport, Nizhny Novgorod, Russia.
Tupolev Tu-154Bx8, Tu-134Ax8, Antonov An-26x1, An-24x5.
NOMAN – U4/NOM
Corso Trieste 85, I-00198, Rome, Italy.
MDC DC-9-10x2.
NORDESTE – JH/NES
Avineda Dom Joao VI 259, Brotas, Salvador, Brazil.
Boeing 737-500x1, Fokker 50x2, Embraer EMB-120x2, EMB-110x4.
NORDIC EAST AIRWAYS – N7/ELN
Box 79, S-190 45 Stockholm-Arlanda, Sweden.
Lockheed L-1011x2, Boeing 737-400x1, 737-300x1.
NORTH AMERICAN AIRLINES – XG/NAO
JFK International Airport, New York 11430, USA.
Boeing 757-200x2, MDC MD-83x1.
NORTH-EAST AIRLINES – NEN
Murtala Muhammed Airport, Ikeja, Nigeria.
Boeing 727-100Fx1.
NORTHERN AIR CARGO – HU/NAC
3900 West Int Airport Rd, Anchorage, Alaska, USA.
Boeing 727-100Fx1, MDC DC-6Ax13.
NORTHERN AIR SANYA
Fenghuang Int Airport, 572000 Sanya, China.
MDC MD-82x3.
NORTHERN-EAST CARGO AIRLINES – MGD
Reki Magadanski 7, Magadan 685000, Russia.
Ilyushin Il-76x5, Antonov An-12x3.
NORTHWEST AIRLINES – NW/NWA
Minneapolis/St Paul Int Airport, Minnesota, USA.
Boeing 747-400x10, 747-200x20, 747-200Fx8, 747-100x3, 757-200x48, 727-200x45, MDC DC-10-30x12, DC-10-40x21, MD-82x8, DC-9-50 x35, DC-9-40x12, DC-9-30x116, DC-9-10x22, AI A320-200x50.
On Order: 747-400x6, 757-200x25, A330-300x16, A320-200x20.
NORTHWEST JETLINK – XJ/MES
7501 26th Ave South, Minneapolis, Minnesota, USA.
Dash 8-100x25, Saab 340x16, Fairchild Metrox23.
On Order: Avro RJ85x12, Saab 340x34.
NOUVELAIR TUNISIE – BJ/LBT
Case postale 66, Monastir-Aeroport Int, Tunisia.
MDC MD-83x3.
NWT AIR – NV/NWT
Yellowknife, Northwest Territories, Canada.
Boeing 737-200x3, Lockheed L-100-30x1.
OASIS INTERNATIONAL AIRLINES – OB/AAN
Calle Gobelas 17, La Florida, Madrid, Spain.
AI A310-300x1, MDC MD-83x3, MD-82x1.
OCCIDENTAL AIRLINES – OCT
Ostend Int Airport, B-8400, Belgium.
Boeing 707-320Fx1.
OKADA AIR – 9H/OKJ
17B Sapele Road, Benin City, Nigeria.
Boeing 747-100x1, 707-320Fx1, 727-200x3, BAC 111-500x3, 111-400x11, 111-300x3, 111-200x2.
OLYMPIC AIRWAYS – OA/OAL
96 Syngrou Avenue, GR-117 41 Athens, Greece.
Boeing 747-200x4, 727-200x9, 737-400x7, 737-200x11, AI A300-600x2, A300B4-200x2, A300B4-100x4.
OMAN AIR – WY/OMA
PO Box 58 CPO, Seeb International Airport, Oman.
AI A320-200x2, Fokker F27-500x5, DHC-6-300x1.
OMNI AIR EXPRESS – X9/OAE
PO Box 582527, Tulsa, Oklahoma 74158, USA.
Boeing 727-200Fx2, 727-100x1.
OMSKAVIA – OMS
Ul. Inzhenernaya 1, Omsk 644103, Russia.
Tupolev Tu-154Mx3, Tu-154Bx4, Antonov An-26x3, An-24x5.
ONUR AIR – 8Q/OHY
Senlik Mahellesi, 34810 Florya-Istanbul, Turkey.
AI A300B4-100x2, A321-100x3, A320-200x5.
On Order: MDC MD-88x5.
ORBI/GEORGIAN AIRWAYS – NQ/DVU
Tbilisi Airport, Tbilisi 380058, Georgia.
Tupolev Tu-154Bx8, Tu-134Ax5, Boeing 737-300 x1, Yakovlev Yak-40x10.
OREL AVIA – R6/UVL
Maly Poluyaroslavsky Pereulock 3/5, Moscow Russia.
Tupolev Tu-204Cx3, Yakovel Yak-42Dx4, Yak-40x1.
ORENBURG AIRLINES – R2/ORB
Central Airport, Orenburg 460049, Russia.
Tupolev Tu-154Mx1, Tu-154Bx4, Tu-134Ax6, Antonov An-24x5, Yakovlev Yak-40x3.
ORIENT EXPRESS AIR – OX
Baan Nai Fan, Chiang Mai, Thailand.
Boeing 727-200x4.
ORIENT AVIA – V6/ORT
2-aya Khutorskaya 29, Moscow 103287, Russia.
Ilyushin Il-86x1, Il-62Mx4, Tupolev Tu-134Ax2.
ORIENTAL AIRLINES – OAC
PO Box 75543, Victoria Island, Lagos, Nigeria.
BAC 111-500x5, 111-400x1.
PACIFIC AIR EXPRESS
Honiara, Solomon Islands.
Boeing 727-200Fx1.
PACIFIC AIRLINES – BL/PIC
Hong Ha St, Tan Binh Dist, Ho Chi Minh City, Vietnam.
Boeing 737-300x1, 737-200x2.
PACIFIC EAST ASIA CARGO – PEC
Manila Domestic Airport, Philippines.
Boeing 737-200Fx1, BAe 146-200QTx2.
PACIFIC INTERNATIONAL AIRLINES – P4/PFC
Apartado Postal 1592, Republic of Panama.
Boeing 727-100Fx2.
PACIFIC INTERNATIONAL AIRLINES – 9J/PSA
2285 East Elvira Rd, Tucson, Arizona 85706, USA.
Boeing 727-200x2.
PAKISTAN INTERNATIONAL AIRLINES – PK/PIA
Quaid-e-Azem Int Airport, Karachi 75200, Pakistan.
Boeing 747-200x8, 707-300Cx2, 737-300x7, AI A300B4-200x9, A310-300x6, Fokker F27-400x1, F27-200x12, DHC-6-300x2
PAL – LPA
Avenue Juarex 2107, Puebla 7200, Mexico.
Boeing 727-100x1.
PAN AIR – PA/PNR
Jose Silva 9, E-28043 Madrid, Spain.
BAe 146-300QTx1, 146-200QTx4, 146-100x2.
PAN AMERICAN WORLD AIRWAYS
9300 NW 36th Street, Miami, Florida 33178, USA.
AI A300B4-200x3.
PANAVIA PANAMA
Apt 6-4670, Panama City, Republic of Panama.
Boeing 727-100Fx1.
PEACE AIR TOGO – PCT
BP 10187, Lome, Togo.
Fokker 100x1, F28-1000x2.
PEGASUS AIRLINES – PGT
Istasyon Caddesi 24, Yesilyurt-Istanbul, Turkey.
Boeing 737-400x4.
PELITA – EP/PAS
Jalan Abdul Muis 52-56A, Jakarta, Indonesia.
Lockheed L-100-30x3, Fokker 70x2, F28-4000x4, Dash 7x5, IPTN 212x12.
On Order: Fokker 70x3.
PERM AIRLINES – PGP
Bolshoe Savino Airport, Perm 614078, Russia.
Tupolev Tu-154Bx3, Tu-134Ax5, Antonov An-26x3, An-24x3.
PHILIPPINE AIRLINES – PR/PAL
PO Box 954, Manila, Philippines.
Boeing 747-400x4, 747-200x11, 737-300x12, AI A340-200x2, A300B4-200x9, A300B4-100x2, Fokker 50x10.
On Order: 747-400x7, A340-300x4, A340-200x2, A330-300x8, A320-200x12.
PHOENIX AIRLINES – PHN
Aeroporto Int de Sao Paulo, Sao Paulo, Brazil.
Boeing 707-320Fx2.

Northwest flies GE powered McDonnell Douglas DC-10-30s (pictured) alongside Pratt powered DC-10-40s. (Keith Myers)

PLUNA – PU/PUA
Colonia 1013-1021, Montevideo, Uruguay.
MDC DC-10-30x1, Boeing 707-320x1, 737-200x4.
POLAR AIR CARGO – PO/PAC
100 Oceangate, Long Beach, California 90802, USA.
Boeing 747-100Fx12.
POLET – POT
Ul. Sofi Perovski 37A, Voronezh 394035, Russia.
Antonov An-124x4, An-12x2, Yakovlev Yak-42Dx1, Yak-40x1, Antonov An-26x1, An-24x1.
POLYNESIAN AIRLINES – PH/PAO
PO Box 599, Apia, Western Samoa.
Boeing 737-300x1, DHC-6-300x2, PBN BN-2Ax1.
PORTUGALIA – NI/PGA
Av Almirante Gago Coutinho 88, Lisbon, Portugal.
Fokker 100x6.
PREMIAIR – DK/VKG
Copenhagen Airport, DK-2791 Dragoer, Denmark.
MDC DC-10-10x6, AI A300B4-100x3, A320-200x6.
PREMIER AIRLINES – PN
PO Box 3017, Tullamarine, Victoria 3004, Australia.
Boeing 727-200Fx1.
PRESTIGE AIRWAYS – OI
9815 Godwin Dr, Manassas, Virginia 22111, USA.
Boeing 727-200x3.
PULKOVO AVIATION ENTERPRISE – PLK
Ul. Pilotov 18/4, St Petersburg 196210, Russia.
Ilyushin Il-86x9, Tupolev Tu-154Mx6, Tu-154Bx20, Tu-134Ax14, Antonov An-12x7.
QANTAS – QF/QFA
PO Box 489, Qantas Int Ctr, Sydney, Australia.
Boeing 747-400x18, 747-300x6, 747-200x5, 747SPx2, 767-300x17, 767-200x7, 737-400x22, 737-300x16, AI A300B4-200x4.
QATAR AIRWAYS – Q7/QTR
PO Box 22550, Doha, Qatar.
Boeing 747SPx3, 727-200x3.
REEVE ALEUTIAN AIRWAYS – RV/RVV
4700 West Int Airport Rd, Anchorage, Alaska, USA.
Boeing 727-100x2, Lockheed L-188x3, NAMC YS-11Ax2.
REGIONAL AIRLINES – VM/RGI
Aeroport Nantes Atlantique, Bouguenais, France.
Embraer EMB-145x1, Saab 2000x4, Saab 340x8, ATR 42x1, BAe Jetstream 31x9.
On Order: EMB-145x4.
RENAN – RAN
Chisinau Airport, 277026 Chisinau, Moldova.
Ilyushin Il-76x1, Antonov An-74x1, An-72x2.
RENNIES EXPRESS AIR SERVICE
PO Box 30056, Whitfield 1467, South Africa.
Boeing 727-100Fx1.
RENO AIR – QQ/ROA
PO Box 30059, Reno, Nevada 89520, USA.
MDC MD-90x2, MD-87x4, MD-83x14, MD-82x8.
RIAIR – GV/RIG
1 Melluzua Street, Riga LV-1067, Latvia.
Boeing 737-200x1.
RICH INTERNATIONAL AIRWAYS – JN/RIA
PO Box 522067, Miami, Florida 33152, USA.
Lockheed L-1011-500x2, L-1011x10, L-1011Fx1, MDC DC-8-63x1, DC-8-62x3.
RIO SUL – SL/RSL
Av Rio Branco 85-10 Andar, Rio de Janeiro, Brazil.
Boeing 737-500x7, Fokker 50x10, Embraer EMB-120x10.
ROMAVIA – VQ/RMV
B-dul Dimitrie Centemir, Bucuresti, Romania.
Boeing 707-320x1, Ilyushin Il-18Dx2, RomBAC 111-500x3.
ROMOCO CARGO
PO Box 9881, Hennopsmeer 0046, South Africa.
Ilyushin Il-76x1.
ROYAL AIR CAMBODGE – VJ
206A Norodom Street, Phnom Penh, Cambodia.
Boeing 737-400x2, ATR 72x3.
ROYAL AIR MAROC – AT/RAM
Aeroport Anfa, Casablanca, Morocco.
Boeing 747-400x1, 747-200x1, 757-200x2, 727-200x4, 737-400x7, 737-500x6, 737-200x6, ATR42-300x2.
On Order: 737-400x9.
ROYAL AVIATION – QN/ROY
6700 Cote de Liesse, Montreal, Quebec, Canada.
Lockheed L-1011x3, Boeing 727-200x7.
ROYAL BRUNEI AIRLINES – BI/RBA
Bandar Seri Begawan, Brunei Darussalam.
Boeing 767-300x9, 757-200x2, Fokker 50x2.
ROYAL JORDANIAN – RJ/RJA
PO Box 302, Amman, Jordan.
Lockheed L-1011-500x5, AI A310-300x4, A310-200x2, A320-200x3, Boeing 707-300Fx3, 727-200x2.
ROYAL NEPAL AIRLINES – RA/RNA
PO Box 401, Kathmandu, Nepal.
AI A310-300x1, Boeing 757-200x2, BAe 748x2, DHC-6-300x8.
ROYAL SWAZI NATIONAL AIRWAYS – ZC/RSN
PO Box 939, Manzini, Swaziland.
Fokker 100x1, F28-3000x1.
ROYAL TONGAN AIRLINES – WR/HRH
Private Bag 9, Nuku'alofa, Tonga.
Boeing 737-300x1, BAe 748x1, DHC-6-300x2.
RWANDAIR CARGO – RWC
BP 2885, Kigali, Rwanda.
Boeing 707-320Fx1.
RYAN INTERNATIONAL AIRLINES – HS/RYN
6810 West Kellogg, Wichita, Kansas 67209, USA.
Boeing 727-200Fx9, 727-100Fx28, 737-200x1, MDC DC-9-10Fx3.
RYANAIR – FR/RYR
Dublin Airport, County Dublin, Ireland.
Boeing 737-200x11.
SABENA – SN/SAB
Avenue E Mounier 2, B-1200 Brussels, Belgium.
Boeing 747-300x2, 737-400x3, 737-300x6, 737-500x6, 737-200x13, AI A340-300x2, A340-200x2, A310-300x1, A310-200x2, MDC DC-10-30x2, Dash 8-300x5.
SABRE AIRWAYS – TJ/SBE
County Oak Way, Crawley, West Sussex, UK.
Boeing 727-200x2, 737-200x2.
SAEAGA AIRLINES
Jalan Parliamen, Kuala Lumpur, Malaysia.
Canadair RJ-100x1, Dash 8-300x1, Dash 8-200x1.
SAETA – EH/SET
Av C J Arosemena KM 2.5, Guayaquil, Ecuador.
AI A310-300x2, A320-200x3, Boeing 727-200x1, 727-100x2, 737-300x1, 737-200x2.
SAFAIR – FA/SFR
PO Box 938, Kempton Park 1620, South Africa.
Boeing 707-320Fx1, 727-200x6, 727-100Fx1, Lockheed L-100-30x9.
SAHA AIRLINES
PO Box 13445-965, Tehran 13873, Iran.
Boeing 747-200Fx2, 747-100Fx2, 707-320x4, Fokker F27-600x2, F27-400x2.
SAHARA INDIA AIRLINES – S2
14 Kasturba Gandhi Marg, New Delhi, India.
Boeing 737-400x2, 737-200x1.
SAKHAAVIA – K7/IKT
Ul. Gagarina 10, Yakutsk, Sakha-Yakutia, Russia.
Ilyushin Il-76x4, Tupolev Tu-154Mx5, Tu-154Bx7, Antonov An-12x16, An-74x4, An-24x21, An-26x14, L 410UVPx25.
SAKHAVIATRANS – SVT
Airport, Yuzhno-Sakhalinsk 639015, Russia.
Ilyushin Il-76x1.
SAM COLOMBIA – MM/SAM
Apartado Aereo 1085, Medellin, Colombia.
Avro RJ100x9.
SAMARA AIRLINES – E5/BRZ
Kurumoch Airport, Samara 443064, Russia.
Ilyushin Il-76x3, Tupolev Tu-154Mx6, Tu-154Bx7, Tu-134Ax8, Antonov An-12x5.
SAN – WB/SAN
Av C J Arosemena KM 2.5, Guayaquil, Ecuador.
Boeing 727-100x1.
SARAVIA – SOV
Ul. Zhukovskogo 25, Saratov 410010, Russia.
Yakovlev Yak-42x11, Antonov An-24x5.
SASCO AIR LINES – SAC
PO Box 8260, Khartoum, Sudan.
Tupolev Tu-134Ax1.
SAT AIRCOMPANY – SHU
Airport, Yuzhno-Sakhalinsk 693015, Russia.
Boeing 737-200x1, Yakovlev Yak-40x1, Antonov An-26x3, An-24x7.
SATA AIR ACORES – SP/SAT
Av Infante D Henrique 55, Ponta Delgada, Portugal.
Boeing 737-300x1, BAe ATPx3, Dornier 228x1.
SAUDI ARABIAN AIRLINES – SV/SVA
PO Box 620, Jeddah 21231, Saudi Arabia.
Boeing 747-300x10, 747-200Fx2, 747-100x8, 747-SPx1, 737-200x19, Lockheed L-1011x17, AI A300-600x11, MDC DC-8-63Fx1.
On Order: 747-400x5, 777-200x23, MDC MD-11Fx4, MD-90x29.
SAYAKHAT – SAH
Bogenbay Batyra Street 124, Almaty, Kazakstan.
Ilyushin Il-76x6.
SCANDINAVIAN – SK/SAS
S-195 87, Stockholm-Bromma, Sweden.
Boeing 747-200Fx1, 767-300x14, 767-200x1, MDC MD-90x6, MD-81x39, MD-82x16, MD-83x4, MD-87x18, DC-9-40x24, DC-9-20x4, Fokker F28-4000x16, F28-1000x3.
On Order: 737-600x41, MD-90x2.

A Swissair MD-11 taxis at the airline's home base of Zurich. (Keith Gaskell)

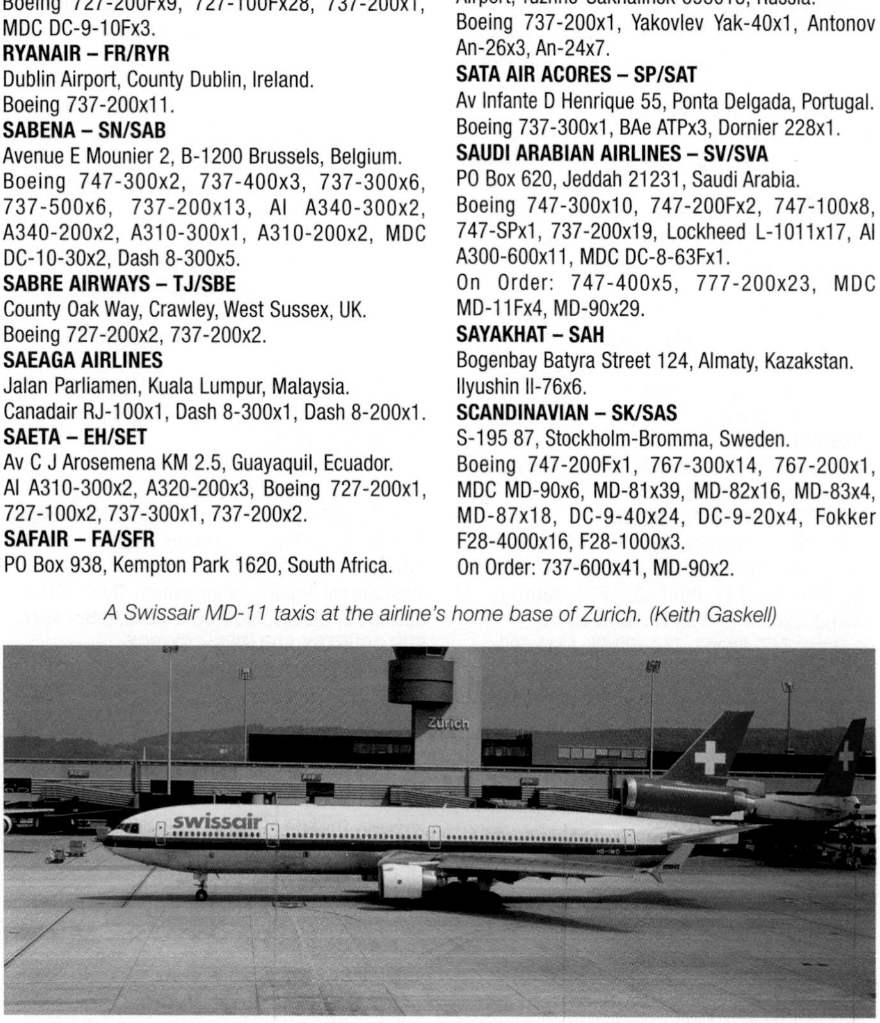

SCIBE-AIRLIFT ZAIRE – ZM/SBZ
BP 614, Kinshasa 1, Zaire.
Boeing 707-320Fx1, 727-100x2.
SEAGREEN AIR TRANSPORT – ESA
PO Box 392, St John's, Antigua, West Indies.
Boeing 707-320x3, 707-320Fx2, 727-100x1, 727-100Fx1.
SEMPATI AIR – SG/SSR
Halim Perdana Kusuma Airport, Jakarta, Indonesia.
AI A300B4-200x3, Boeing 737-200x7, Fokker 100x7, Fokker 70x10, F27-600x3, F27-200x2.
SERVIVENSA – VC/SVV
Av Universidad, Torre El Chorro, Caracas, Venezuala.
Boeing 727-200x4, 727-100x2, MDC DC-9-50x3, DC-9-30x8, DC-3x5.
SHABAIR – SS/SHB
Aeroport de la Luano, BP 1060, Lubumbashi, Zaire.
Boeing 707-320Fx1, Boeing 727-100x3, BAC 111-200x1.
SHANDONG AIRLINES – SC/CDG
Chaoshan Commercial Av, 250011 Jinan, China.
Boeing 737-300x3, Yunshuji Y7x1.
SHANGHAI AIRLINES – SF/CSH
Hongqiao Road, Hongqiao Airport, Shanghai, China.
Boeing 767-300x3, 757-200x9
On Order: 767-300x2.
SHAHEEN INTERNATIONAL – NL/SAI
Mereweather Road, Karachi 75350, Pakistan.
Boeing 737-200x2.
SHENZHEN AIRLINES – 4G/CSZ
Lingxiao Graden Airport, 518128 Shenzhen, China.
Boeing 737-300x5.
SHOROUK AIR – 7Q/SHK
El Shaheed Ismail Fahmy St, Heliopolis, Cairo, Egypt.
AI A320-200x2.
SIBERIA AIRLINES – S7/SBI
Tolmachevo Airport, Novosibirsk 633115, Russia.
Ilyushin Il-86x7, Tupolev Tu-154Mx7, Tu-154Bx6, Antonov An-32x1, An-26x4, An-24x4.
SICHUAN AIRLINES – 3U/CSC
Yihuan Road South, 610041 Chengdu, China.
Tupolev Tu-154Mx5, AI A320-200x3, Yunshuji Y7x5.
SIERRA PACIFIC AIRLINES – SI/SPA
North Business Park Drive, Tucson, Arizona, USA.
Boeing 737-200x1, Convair 580x7.
SILKAIR – MI/SLK
PO Box 501, Singapore, Republic of Singapore.
Boeing 737-300x5, Fokker 70x2.
SIMBA AIR CARGO – SMB
PO Box 59224, Nairobi, Kenya.
Boeing 707-320Fx1.
SIMBIRSK-AERO
Ulyanovsk Airport, Ulyanovsk 432040, Russia.
Yakovlev Yak-42x3, Yak-40x6.
SINGAPORE AIRLINES – SQ/SIA
PO Box 501, Singapore, Republic of Singapore.
Boeing 747-400x35, 747-400Fx6, 747-300x11, 747-200x4, 747-200Fx2, 737-300Fx1, AI A340-300x6, A310-300x17, A310-200x6.
On Order: 747-400x11, 777-200x28, A340-300x11.
SKYAIR CARGO – TAW
55-57 Park Royal Road, London NW10 7JH, UK.
Boeing 707-320Fx1.
SKYJET – SKJ
Boulevard Louis Schmidt 75, Brussels, Belguim.
MDC DC-10-30x1, DC-10-30Fx1.
SKYLINE NEPC – D2/DAM
77 Nehru Road, Mumbai 400099, India.
Boeing 737-200x4.
SKYSERVICE – SSV
9785 Ryan Avenue, Dorval, Quebec, Canada.
AI A320-200x3.
SKYWEST – OO/SKW
444 South River Rd, St George, Utah 84770, USA.
Canadair RJ-100x10, Embraer EMB-120x46, Fairchild Metrox19.
On Order: EMB-120x4.
SLOVTRANS AIR – SLV
Vazska 3580/28, Piestany, Slovak Republic.
Boeing 707-320x1.
SOBELAIR – S3/SLR
Av Frans Courtenslaan 131, Brussels, Belgium.
Boeing 767-300x2, 737-400x3, 737-300x1, 737-200x2.
SOLOMON AIRLINES – IE/SOL
PO Box 23, Honiara, Solomon Islands.
Boeing 737-300x1, DHC-6-300x2.
SONANGOL
CP 1316, Luanda, Angola.
Boeing 727-100x1, Fokker 50x1, F27-500x1.
SOUTH AFRICAN AIRWAYS – SA/SAA
PO Box 7778, Johannesburg 2000, South Africa.
Boeing 747-400x4, 747-300x4, 747-200x5, 747-200Fx1, 747SPx5, 767-200x1, 737-200x11, 737-200Fx2, AI A300B4-200x2, A300C4-200x1, A300B2-300x4, A320-200x7.
On Order: 747-400x1, 777-200x4.
SOUTHERN AIR TRANSPORT – SJ/SJM
PO Box 32-8988, Columbus, Ohio 43232, USA.
Boeing 747-200Fx4, MDC DC-8-73Fx3, DC-8-71Fx1, Lockheed L-100-30x15.
SOUTHERN AUSTRALIA AIRLINES – QF
PO Box 1080, Mildura, Victoria 3502, Australia.
BAe 146-200x2, Dash 8-100x3.
SOUTHWEST AIRLINES – WN/SWA
PO Box 36611, Dallas, Texas 75235, USA.
Boeing 737-300x168, 737-500x25, 737-200x50.
On Order: 737-700x63, 737-300x19.
SPAIR AIR TRANSPORTATION CO – S4/PAR
UL. Vishnevaya 69, Ekaterinburg 620000, Russia.
Ilyushin Il-76x3, Il-18x1, Tupolev 154Bx1, Antonov An-12x4.
SPANAIR – JK/SPP
PO Box 50086, E-07000 Palma de Mallorca, Spain.
Boeing 767-300x2, MDC MD-83x14, MD-82x1.
SPIRIT AIRLINES – NK/SWG
18121 East 8 Mile Rd, East Point, Michigan, USA.
MDC DC-9-30x9, DC-9-20x1.
STAR AIR – SRR
Copenhagen Airport South, Dragoer, Denmark.
Boeing 727-100Fx5, Fokker F27-500x1.
STAR EUROPE – 2R/SEU
10 Allee Bienvenue, Noisy-le-Grand, France.
Boeing 737-300x1.
STERLING EUROPEAN AIRLINES – NB/SNB
Copenhagen Airport, DK-2791 Dragoer, Denmark.
Boeing 727-200x6.
SUDAN AIRWAYS – SD/SUD
PO Box 253, Khartoum, Sudan.
AI A300-600x1, A310-300x2, A320-200x1, Boeing 707-320x3, 737-200x2, Fokker 50x2.
SUN AIR – BV/SSN
International Airport, Johannesburg, South Africa.
Boeing 727-200x1, MDC DC-9-30x5, BAe 748x1.
SUN COUNTRY AIRLINES – SY/SCX
2520 Pilot Knob Road, Minnesota 55120, USA.
MDC DC-10-30Fx3, DC-10-10x6, Boeing 727-200x10.
SUNEXPRESS – XQ/SXS
Fener Mahallesi, Sinanoglu Cad. Antalya, Turkey.
Boeing 737-400x2, 737-300x3.
SUN JET INTERNATIONAL – JX/SJI
11701 Belcher Road, Largo, Florida 34643, USA.
MDC MD-81x2, DC-9-50x2.
SUNWAY – IS/SWW
Cumhuriyet Caddesi, Elmadag-Istanbul, Turkey.
MDC MD-83x4.
SURINAM AIRWAYS – PY/SLM
PO Box 2029, Paramaribo, Suriname.
MDC MD-87x1, Dash 8-300x1, DHC-6-300x2.
SWISSAIR – SR/SWR
Postfach, CH-8058 Zurich-Flughafen, Switzerland.
Boeing 747-300x5, MDC MD-11x13, MD-81x13, MD-82x1, AI A310-300x5, A321-100x6, A320-200x13, A319-100x5, Fokker 100x6.
On Order: MD-11x3, A321-100x2, A320-200x5, A319-100x3.
SYRIANAIR – RB/SYR
PO Box 417, Damascus, Syria.
Boeing 747SPx2, 727-200x6, Ilyushin Il-76Mx4, Tupolev Tu-154Mx3, Tu-134Bx6, Antonov An-26x5, An-24x1, Yakovlev Yak-40x6.
TAAG ANGOLA AIRLINES – DT/DTA
CP3010, Luanda, Angola
Lockheed L-1011-500x1, Ilyushin Il-62Mx2, Boeing 707-300x1, 737-200x5, Fokker F27-600x3, F27-500x1, F27-400x1, F27-200x1.
TAB – BOL
Casilla Correo 12237, La Paz, Bolivia.
MDC DC-8-54Fx1, Lockheed L-100-20x1.
TACA INTERNATIONAL AIRLINES – TA/TAI
Edificio Caribe, 2 Piso, San Salvador, El Salvador.
Boeing 767-300x1, 767-200x1, 737-300x5, 737-200x6.
TACV CABO VERDE AIRLINES – VR/TCV
Caixa Postal 1, Ilha do Santiago, Cape Verde Islands.
Boeing 757-200x1, BAe 748x2, ATR 42x3, DHC-6-300x2.
TAESA – GD/TEJ
Aviacion Gen, Zona Hangares, Mexico City, Mexico.
MDC DC-10-30, DC-9-10x5, AI A300B4-200, Boeing 757-200x1, 727-100x6, 727-100Fx1, 737-300x4, 737-500x2, 737-200x2, ATR 42x1.
TAJIKISTAN AIRLINES – 7J/TJK
Titov Street 32/1, Dushanbe 734006, Tajikistan.
Tupolev Tu-154Mx3, Tu-154Bx11, Tu-134Ax9, Antonov An-26x2, An-24x5, Yakovlev Yak-40x20.
TAM – KK/TAM
Rua Monsenhor Antonio Pepe 94, Sao Paulo, Brazil.
Fokker 100x30, Fokker 50x10, F27-600x3, F27-500x4, EMB-110x4.
TAME – EQ/TAE
PO Box 17-07-8736, Quito, Ecuador.
Boeing 727-200x4, 727-100x3, Fokker F28-4000x1, BAe 748x2, DHC-6-300x3.
TAP AIR PORTUGAL – TP/TAP
Aeroporto de Lisboa, Lisboa Codex, Portugal.
AI A340-300x4, A310-300x5, A320-200x6, Lockheed L-1011-500x5, Boeing 737-300x10, 737-200x6.
On Order: A319-100x18.
TAMPA COLOMBIA – QT/TPA
Carrera 76 No. 34A-61, Medellin, Colombia.
MDC DC-8-71Fx2, Boeing 707-300Fx4.
TAROM – RO/ROT
Sos. Buchuresti-Ploiesti, Buchuresti, Romania.
Ilyushin Il-62Mx2, Il-18x4, AI A310-300x2, Boeing 707-320Cx2, 737-300x5, Tupolev Tu-154Bx6, RomBAC 111-500x6, BAC 111-500x6, 111-400x1, Antonov An-24x14.
TATARSTAN AIRLINES – KAZ
Kazan Airport, Tatarstan 420017, Russia.
Tupolev Tu-154Bx4, Yakovlev Yak-42x8, Yak-40x20, Antonov An-26x1, An-24x8.
TAT EUROPEAN AIRLINES – IJ/TAT
BP 0237, F-37002 Tours Cedex, France.
Boeing 737-300x2, 737-200x2, 737-200Cx3, Fokker 100x14, F28-4000x5, F28-2000x4, F28-1000x9, ATR 72x6, ATR 42x10, Fairchild FH-227x5, F-27Jx1.
TAYFUNAIR – Z4/TAY
Florya Caddesi 72/2, Florya-Istanbul, Turkey.
Boeing 727-200Fx1.

TEA CYPRUS – TEC
PO Box 1354, Limassol, Cyprus.
Boeing 737-200x1.
TEA SWITZERLAND – BH/TSW
Postfach, CH-4030 Basel-Flughafen, Switzerland.
Boeing 737-300x6.
On Order: 737-700x2, 737-300x1.
THAI AIRWAYS INTERNATIONAL – TG/THA
PO Box 1075 GPO, Bangkok 10900, Thailand.
Boeing 747-400x12, 747-300x2, 747-200x6, 777-200x4, 737-400x7, 737-200x3, MDC MD-11 x4, DC-10-30x3, AI A330-300x8, A300-600x16, A300B4-200x4, A300B4-100x3, A310-200x2, BAe 146-300x5, ATR 72x2, ATR 42x2.
On Order: 747-400x2, 777-200x4, 737-400x2, 737-500x2, A300-600x5, A330-300x12.
TITAN AIRWAYS – AWC
London Stansted Airport, Stansted, Essex, UK.
BAe 146-200QCx1, ATR 42x2, Shorts 360x2, 330x1.
TMA OF LEBANON – TL/TMA
Beirut International Airport, Beirut, Lebanon.
Boeing 707-320Fx6.
TOMSK AIR ENTERPRISE
Tomsk Airport, Tomsk 634011, Russia.
Tupolev Tu-154Mx1, Tu-154Bx3, Antonov An-26x5, An-24x5, L 410UVPx8.
TOP AIR – B6/TOP
Ataturk Havalimani, Yesilkoy-Islanbul, Turkey.
Boeing 727-200x3, Yakovlev Yak-42Dx1, Antonov An-24x2.
TOWER AIR – FF/TOW
JFK International Airport, Jamaica, New York, USA.
Boeing 747-200x10, 747-100x8, 747-100Fx2.
TRADEWINDS INT AIRLINES – WI/TDX
PO Box 35329, Greensboro, North Carolina, USA.
Lockheed L-1011Fx1, Canadair CL-44x5.
TRANSAERO AIRLINES – 4J/TSO
Sheremetyevo 1 Airport, Moscow 103340, Russia.
Ilyushin Il-86x1, Boeing 757-200x5, 737-200x5.
TRANSAERO-EXPRESS – TXE
Ul. Senezhskaya 1/9, Moscow 125413, Russia.
Tupolev Tu-134Ax1, Antonov An-26x1.
TRANSAERO-SAMARA AIRLINES – TSL
Smyshlyaevskoe shosse 1A, Samara, Russia.
Ilyushin Il-76x2, Yakovlev Yak-40x1.
TRANSAFRIK
CP 2839, Luanda, Angola.
Boeing 727-100x1, 727-100Fx4, Lockheed L-100-30x3.
TRANSAIR CARGO
14e Rue Limete, BP 7499, Kinshasa, Zaire.
Boeing 707-120Fx1, MDC DC-6Bx3, DC-4x1.
TRANS ARABIAN AIR TRANSPORT – TO/TRT
PO Box 1461, Khartoum, Sudan.
Boeing 707-320Fx3.
TRANSASIA AIRWAYS – GE/TNA
9F, 139 Cheng Chou Road, Taipei, Taiwan.
AI A321-100x4, A320-200x6, ATR 72x12, ATR 42x3
On Order: A321-100x2, A320-200x2.
TRANSAVIA AIRLINES – HV/TRA
PO Box 7777, Schipol Airport Centre, Netherlands.
Boeing 757-200x4, 737-300x14.
On Order: 737-800x8.
TRANS AVIA EXPORT CARGO AIRLINES – AL/TXC
44 Zakharov Street, Minsk 220034, Belarus.
Ilyushin Il-76x23.
TRANSBRASIL – TR/TBA
Rua General Pantaleao Telles 40, Sao Paulo, Brazil.
Boeing 767-300x3, 767-200x8, 737-400x5, 737-300x6.
TRANS-CHARTER AIRLINES – FZ/TCH
Leningradsky Prospekt 37, Moscow, Russia.
Antonov An-124x2, Ilyushin Il-76x3, Antonov An-32x2, Yakovlev Yak-40x1.
TRANS CONTINENTAL AIRLINES – TCN
842 Willow Run Airport, Ypsilanti, Michigan, USA.
MDC DC-8-62Fx1, DC-8-50Fx3.
TRANSLIFT AIRWAYS – T7/TLA
26 Upper Fitzwilliam Street, County Dublin, Ireland.
AI A300B4-200x2, A320-200x5.
TRANSMERIDIAN AIRLINES – T9/TRZ
2700 Post Oak Boulevard, Houston, Texas, USA.
AI A320-200x4.
TRANSMILE AIR SERVICES – TH/TSE
Box 20, Bukit Damansara, Kuala Lumpur, Malaysia.
Boeing 737-200Fx4.
TRANSWEDE AIRWAYS – TQ/TQA
Box 135, S-190 46 Stockholm-Arlanda, Sweden.
Fokker 100x5.
TRANSWEDE LEISURE – TWE
Box 135, S-190 46 Stockholm-Arlanda, Sweden.
Boeing 757-200x2, MDC MD-83x3, MD-87x2.
TRANS WORLD AIRLINES – TW/TWA
515 North 6th Street, St Louis, Missouri, USA.
Boeing 747-200x3, 747-100x9, 767-300x3, 767-200x12, 757-200x3, 727-200x40, 727-100 x8, Lockheed L-1011x14, MDC MD-83x21, MD-82x29, DC-9-50x12, DC-9-40x3, DC-9-30x36, DC-9-10x7.
On Order: 757-200x17, AI A330-300x10, MD-83x10.
TRIAX AIRLINES – TIX
Airport, Enugu, Nigeria.
Boeing 727-200x1, 727-100x2.
TRISTAR AIRLINES – T3/TRY
1050 East Flamingo Rd, Las Vegas, Nevada, USA.
BAe 146-200x3, 146-100x1.
TUNISAIR – TU/TAR
Boulevard 7 Novembre, Tunis, Tunisia.
AI A300B4-200x1, A320-200x8, Boeing 727-200 x7, 737-500x4, 737-200x4.
TURAN AIR – URN
R Rza kucasi 1/16, Baku 370000, Azerbaidjan.
Tupolev Tu-154Mx3.
TURKISH AIRLINES – TK/THY
Genel Yonetim Binsai, Yesilkoy-Istanbul, Turkey.
AI A340-300x4, A310-300x7, A310-200x8, Boeing 727-200x1, 727-200Fx3, 737-400x28, 737-500 x2, Avro RJ100x10, RJ70x4.
On Order: A340-300x1.
TURKMENISTAN AIR – T5/AKH
Airport, Ashkhabad 744008, Turkmenistan.
Ilyushin Il-76x8, Boeing 757-200x3, 737-300x3, Tupolev Tu-154Bx12, Yakovlev Yak-42Dx4, Antonov An-24x14.
TYROLEAN AIRWAYS – VO/TYR
Postfach 58, A-6026 Innsbruck, Austria.
Fokker 70x4, Canadair RJ-100x5, Dash 7x1, Dash 8-300x13, Dash 8-100x8.
TYUMEN AIRLINES – TYM
Roshchino Airport, Tyumen 625033, Russia.
Ilyushin Il-76x7, Tupolev Tu-154Bx16, Tu-134Ax16, Antonov An-12x8, An-26x6, An-24x10.
TYUMENAVIATRANS – P2/TMN
Plekhanovo Airport, Tyumen 625025, Russia.
Tupolev Tu-154Mx1, Tu-154Bx1, Antonov An-26 x12, An-24x10, Yakovlev Yak-40x19.
UGANDA AIRLINES – QU/UGA
PO Box 5740, Kampala, Uganda.
Boeing 737-500x1, 737-200x1, Fokker F27-600x1.
UKRAINE INTERNATIONAL AIRLINES – PS/AUI
14 Prospect Peremogy, Kiev 252135, Ukraine.
Boeing 737-300x1, 737-200x2.
U-LAND AIRLINES
163 Nanking East Road, Taipei 10572, Taiwan.
MDC MD-82x4.
UNITED AIRLINES – UA/UAL
PO Box 66100, Chicago, Illinois 60666, USA.
Boeing 747-400x26, 747-200x9, 747-100x18, 747SPx4, 777-200x16, 767-300x23, 767-200x19, 757-200x92, 727-200x75, 737-300x101, 737-500 x57, 737-200x69, MDC DC-10-10x44, AI A320-200x36.
On Order: 747-400x23, 777-200x20, 757-200x6, A320-200x14, A319-100x24.
UNITED EXPRESS/AIR WISCONSIN – AWI
W6390 Challenger Dr, Appleton, Wisconsin, USA.
BAe 146-300x5, 146-200x6, 146-100x2.
UNITED PARCEL SERVICE – 5X/UPS
1400 N Hurstbourne P'way, Louisville, Kentucky, USA.
Boeing 747-100Fx14, 767-300Fx15, 757-200APF x60, 727-200Fx8, 727-100QFx51, MDC DC-8-73F x28, DC-8-71Fx24, Fairchild Expediterx11.
On Order: 767-300Fx15, 757-200APFx15.
URAL – URW
Ul. Shaumyana 83, Ekaterinburg 620102, Russia.
Ilyushin Il-76x1, Antonov An-32x2, An-24x1.
URAL AIRLINES – U6/SVR
Ul. Sputnikov 6, Ekaterinburg 620025, Russia.
Ilyushin Il-86x4, Tupolev Tu-154Mx2, Tu-154Bx14, Antonov An-12x6, An-26x3, An-24x3.
URALINTERAVIA – U3/URA
Ul. Sputnikov 6, Ekaterinburg 620025, Russia.
Ilyushin Il-76x6.
US AIRWAYS – US/USA
2345 Crystal Drive, Arlington, Virginia 22227, USA.
Boeing 767-200x12, 757-200x34, 737-400x54, 737-300x101, 737-200x80, MDC MD-82x12, MD-81x19, DC-9-30x73, Fokker 100x40, F28-4000x19.
On Order: 757-200x7, AI A319/320/321x120.
USAIR SHUTTLE – TB/USS
La Guardia Airport, Flushing, New York 11371, USA.
Boeing 727-200x12, 727-100x1.
USA JET AIRLINES – U7/JUS
2064 D Street, Belleville, Michigan 48111, USA.
MDC DC-9-10Fx5, Dassault Falcon 20Fx16.

Despite an infusion of western equipment in recent years Vietnam Airlines continues to fly the Tu-134. (Peter Martinson)

One of five Xiamen Airlines 737-200s, on approach to Hong Kong. (Steve Allsopp)

UZBEKISTAN AIRWAYS – HY/UZB
Proletarskaya 41, Tashkent 700100, Uzbekistan.
Ilyushin Il-86x10, Il-76x15, Il-62x10, Boeing 767-300x2, 757-200x1, AI A310-300x2, Tupolev Tu-154Mx3, Tu-154Bx21, Yakovlev Yak-40x25, Antonov An-24x23.
VAK-ROSAT – VAK
Kurumoch Airport, Samara 443064, Russia.
Tupolev Tu-154Mx1, Yakovlev Yak-40x2.
VALUJET – J7/VJA
1800 Phoenix Boulevard, Atlanta, Georgia, USA.
MDC DC-9-30x30.
On Order: MD-95x50.
VANGUARD AIRLINES – NJ/VGD
Kansas City International Airport, Missouri, USA.
Boeing 737-300x3, 737-200x6.
VARIG – RG/VRG
Av Almirante Silvio de Noronha, Rio de Janiero, Brazil.
Boeing 747-300x5, 767-300x4, 767-200x6, 727-100Fx5, 737-300x25, 737-200x17, MDC MD-11x6, DC-10-30x8, DC-10-30Fx2.
On Order: 747-400x6, 737-300x11.
VASP – VP/VSP
Aeroporto de Congonhas, Sao Paulo, Brazil.
MDC MD-11x8, AI A300B2-200x3, Boeing 727-200x1, 737-300x2, 737-200x20, 737-200Fx2.
VENUS AIRLINES – V4/VER
Vougliamenis Yasinodou 2, Athens, Greece.
Boeing 757-200x2, 727-200x2, MDC MD-83x1.
VETERAN AIRLINES – VTN
Ul. Prechistenka 10/3, Moscow 119889, Russia.
Ilyushin Il-76x3.
VETERAN AIRLINES
Moskovskya 182a, Dzhankoy 334010, Ukraine.
Ilyushin Il-76x10.
VIA EST VITA – VL/VIM
54 G.M. Dimitros Boulevard, 1125 Sofia, Bulgaria.
Tupolev Tu-154Mx6.
VIASA – VA/VIA
Plaza Morelos, Los Caobos, Caracas, Venezuala.
MDC DC-10-30x6, Boeing 727-200x7.
VIETNAM AIRLINES – VN/HVN
Gialam Airport, Hanoi 1000, Vietnam.
Boeing 767-300x5, 767-200x1, AI A320-200x8, Tupolev Tu-134x13, Ilyushin Il-18x1, ATR 72x4, Yakovlev Yak-40x4.
On Order: A320-200x8.
VILOCITY – VKT
Novoprenensky pereulok 3, Moscow, Russia.
Ilyushin Il-76x1, Antonov An-12x1.
VIRGIN ATLANTIC AIRWAYS – VS/VIR
High Street, Crawley, West Sussex, England, UK.
Boeing 747-400x3, 747-200x5, 747-100x1, AI A340-300x4, A320-200x2.
On Order: A340-300x2.
VISCOUNT AIR SERVICE – VCT
1000 East Valencia, Tucson, Arizona 85706, USA.
Boeing 737-200x13.

VIVA AIR – FV/VIV
Camina de la Escollera 4, Palma de Mallorca, Spain.
Boeing 737-300x10.
VLADIVOSTOK AIR – XF/VLK
Ul. Portovaya 41, Artem 692811, Russia.
Ilyushin Il-76x3, Tupolev Tu-154Mx1, Yakovlev Yak-40x12.
VNUKOVO AIRLINES – V5/VKO
I-aya Reisovaya 12, Moscow 103027, Russia.
Ilyushin Il-86x22, Tupolev Tu-204x3, Tu-154Mx20, Tu-154Bx8.
VOLARE AIR TRANSPORT COMPANY – OP/VLR
Ul. 2-aya Peschanaya 6, Moscow 125252, Russia.
Ilyushin Il-76x2, Il-62x1, Il-18x1, Tupolev Tu-134A x1, Antonov An-12x1.
VOLGA AIRLINES – VLA
Volgograd Airport, Volgograd 400036, Russia.
Yakovlev Yak-42Dx10, Yak-40x8, Tupolev Tu-134Ax5.
VOLGA-DNEPR AIRLINES – VI/VDA
Ul. Karbisheva 14, Ulyanovsk 432062, Russia.
Antonov An-124x6, An-12x1, An-32x1, Ilyushin Il-76x4, Yakovlev Yak-40x1.
VORONEZHAVIA – VRN
Voronezh Airport, Voronezh 394025, Russia.
Yakovlev Yak-42x2, Tupolev Tu-134Ax13, Antonov An-24x10.
WALTAIR
3 Avenue Kalypso, B-1170, Brussels, Belgium.
Aerospatiale Caravelle 10Bx1.
WESTERN PACIFIC AIRLINES – W7/KMR
3 South Tejon St, Colorado Springs, Colorado, USA.
Boeing 737-300x13.
On Order: 737-300x6.
WETRAFA AIRLIFT
BP 1358 Limete, Kinshasa, Zaire.
Aerospatiale Caravelle x1.
WORLD AIRLINES
14a Ganton Street, London W1V 1LV, England, UK.
BAe 146-200x1.
WORLD AIRWAYS – WO/WOA
13873 Park Center Road, Herndon, Virginia, USA.
MDC MD-11x7, MD-11Fx2, DC-10-30x4.
WUHAN AIR LINES – WU/CWU
230-1 Hangkong Lu, 430030 Wuhan, China.
Boeing 737-300x3, Yunshuji Y7x4, Y5x2.
XIAMEN AIRLINES – MF/CXA
Gaoqi International Airport, 361009 Xiamen, China.
Boeing 757-200x5, 737-500x7, 737-200x5.
YEMENIA – IY/IYE
PO Box 1183, Sana'a, Republic of Yemen.
Ilyushin Il-76x2, AI A310-300x1, Boeing 707-320C x2, 727-200x5, 737-200x3, Lockheed L-100-20 x2, Dash 7x4, DHC-6-300x2.
On Order: A310-300x2.
YEREVAN AVIA – ERV
Zvartnots Airport, 375042 Yerevan, Armenia.
Ilyushin Il-76Mx2.
ZAIRE EXPRESS – EO/EZR
BP 12847, Kinshasa 1, Zaire.
Boeing 707-320Fx3, 737-200x1, 737-200Fx1, BAC 111-500x3.
ZANTOP INTERNATIONAL AIRWAYS – VK/ZAN
840 Willow Run Airport, Ypsilanti, Michigan, USA.
MDC DC-8-50Fx3, Lockheed L-188Fx17, Convair 640Fx10.
ZHONGYUAN AIRLINES – Z2/CYN
143 Minggonglu, 450000 Zhengzhou, China.
Boeing 737-300x3, Yunshuji Y7x3.
ZIMBABWE EXPRESS AIRLINES – Z7
PO Box 5130, Harare, Zimbabwe.
Boeing 727-100Fx1.
ZULIANA DE AVIACION – OD/ULA
PO Box 661570, Miami, Florida 33166, USA.
MDC DC-8-50Fx1, DC-9-30x5, Boeing 727-200x1.

INTERNATIONAL REGISTRATION PREFIXES

AP	PAKISTAN
A2	BOTSWANA
A3	TONGA
A40	OMAN
A5	BHUTAN
A6	UNITED ARAB EMIRATES
A7	QATAR
A9C	BAHRAIN
B	CHINA (Peoples Republic of)
B	CHINA (Taiwan)
C/CF	CANADA
CC	CHILE
CN	MOROCCO
CP	BOLIVIA
CS	PORTUGAL
CU	CUBA
CX	URUGUAY
C2	NAURU
C3	ANDORRA
C5	GAMBIA
C6	BAHAMAS
C9	MOZAMBIQUE
D	GERMANY
DQ	FIJI
D2	ANGOLA
D4	CAPE VERDE ISLANDS
D6	COMORO ISLANDS
EC	SPAIN
EI	EIRE
EK	ARMENIA
EL	LIBERIA
EP	IRAN
ER	MOLDOVA
ES	ESTONIA
ET	ETHIOPIA
EW	BELARUS
EX	KYRGYZSTAN
EY	TAJIKISTAN
EZ	TURKMENISTAN
E3	ERITREA
F	FRANCE
G	GREAT BRITAIN
H4	Solomon Islands
HA	HUNGARY
HB	SWITZERLAND & LIECHTENSTEIN
HC	ECUADOR
HH	HAITI
HI	DOMINICAN REPUBLIC
HK	COLOMBIA
HL	REPUBLIC OF KOREA
HP	PANAMA
HR	HONDURAS
HS	THAILAND
HV	THE VATICAN
HZ	SAUDI ARABIA
I	ITALY
JA	JAPAN
JY	JORDAN
J2	DJIBOUTI
J3	GRENADA
J5	GUINEA BISSAU
J6	ST LUCIA
J7	DOMINICA
J8	ST VINCENT & GRENADINES
LN	NORWAY
LV	ARGENTINA
LX	LUXEMBOURG
LY	LITHUANIA
LZ	BULGARIA
MT	MONGOLIA
N	USA
OB	PERU
OD	LEBANON
OE	AUSTRIA
OH	FINLAND
OK	CZECHIA
OM	SLOVAKIA
OO	BELGIUM
OY	DENMARK
P	KOREA (DPRK)
PH	NETHERLANDS
PJ	NETHERLANDS ANTILLES
PK	INDONESIA
PP/PT	BRAZIL
PZ	SURINAM
P2	PAPUA NEW GUINEA
P4	ARUBA
RA	RUSSIA
RDPL	LAOS
RP	PHILIPPINES
SE	SWEDEN
SP	POLAND
ST	SUDAN
SU	EGYPT
SX	GREECE
S2	BANGLADESH
S5	SLOVENIA
S7	SEYCHELLES
S9	SAO TOME
TC	TURKEY
TF	ICELAND
TG	GUATEMALA
TI	COSTA RICA
TJ	CAMEROON
TL	CENTRAL AFRICAN REPUBLIC
TN	CONGO BRAZZAVILLE
TR	GABON
TS	TUNISIA
TT	CHAD
TU	IVORY COAST
TY	BENIN
TZ	MALI
T2	TUVALU
T3	KIRIBATI
T7	SAN MARINO
UK	UZBEKISTAN
UN	KAZAKHSTAN
UR	UKRAINE
VH	AUSTRALIA
VN	VIETNAM
VP-F	FALKLAND ISLANDS
VP-LA	ANGUILLA
VP-LM	MONTSERRAT
VP-LV	BRITISH VIRGIN ISLANDS
VQ-T	TURKS & CAICOS ISLANDS
VR-B	BERMUDA
VR-C	CAYMAN ISLANDS
VR-G	GIBRALTAR
VR-H	HONG KONG
VT	INDIA
V2	ANTIGUA & BARBUDA
V3	BELIZE
V4	ST KITTS-NEVIS
V5	NAMIBIA
V7	MARSHALL ISLANDS
V8	BRUNEI
XA/XB/XC	MEXICO
XT	BURKINA FASO
XU	KAMPUCHEA
XY	MYANMAR
YA	AFGHANISTAN
YI	IRAQ
YJ	VANUATU
YK	SYRIA
YL	LATVIA
YN	NICARAGUA
YR	ROMANIA
YS	EL SALVADOR
YU	YUGOSLAVIA
YV	VENEZUELA
Z	ZIMBABWE
ZA	ALBANIA
ZK	NEW ZEALAND
ZP	PARAGUAY
Z3	MACEDONIA
3A	MONACO
3B	MAURITIUS
3C	EQUATORIAL GUINEA
3D	SWAZILAND
3X	GUINEA
4K	AZERBAIJAN
4L	GEORGIA
4R	SRI LANKA
4U	UNITED NATIONS
4X	ISRAEL
5A	LIBYA
5B	CYPRUS
5H	TANZANIA
5N	NIGERIA
5R	MADAGASCAR
5T	MAURITANIA
5U	NIGER
5V	TOGO
5W	WESTERN SAMOA
5X	UGANGA
5Y	KENYA
6O	SOMALIA
6V	SENEGAL
6Y	JAMAICA
7O	YEMEN
7P	LESOTHO
7Q	MALAWI
7T	ALGERIA
8P	BARBADOS
8Q	MALDIVES
8R	GUYANA
9A	CROATIA
9G	GHANA
9H	MALTA
9J	ZAMBIA
9K	KUWAIT
9L	SIERRA LEONE
9M	MALAYSIA
9N	NEPAL
9Q	ZAIRE
9U	BURUNDI
9V	SINGAPORE
9XR	RWANDA
9Y	TRINIDAD & TOBAGO

THE PHONETIC ALPHABET

A	Alpha	**N**	November
B	Bravo	**O**	Oscar
C	Charlie	**P**	Papa
D	Delta	**Q**	Quebec
E	Echo	**R**	Romeo
F	Foxtrot	**S**	Sierra
G	Golf	**T**	Tango
H	Hotel	**U**	Uniform
I	India	**V**	Victor
J	Juliet	**W**	Whiskey
K	Kilo	**X**	X-ray
L	Lima	**Y**	Yankee
M	Mike	**Z**	Zulu

INDEX